THE CONSTITUTION

OF

MEDIEVAL ENGLAND

FROM THE ENGLISH SETTLEMENT TO 1485

by

J. E. A. JOLLIFFE, M.A., F.R.Hist.S.
EMERITUS FELLOW OF KEBLE COLLEGE, OXFORD

FOURTH EDITION

The Norton Library
W · W · NORTON & COMPANY · INC ·
NEW YORK

FIRST PUBLISHED 1937
SECOND EDITION 1947
REPRINTED 1948
THIRD EDITION 1954
FOURTH EDITION 1961

ISBN 0 393 00417 1

PRINTED IN THE UNITED STATES OF AMERICA

2 3 4 5 6 7 8 9 0

CONTENTS

I

FROM THE ENGLISH SETTLEMENT TO THE REIGN OF ÆLFRED

II

FROM THE REIGN OF ÆLFRED TO THE NORMAN CONQUEST

III

FROM THE NORMAN CONQUEST TO THE REIGN OF HENRY III

IV

1272–1377

V

1377–1485

THE CONSTITUTIONAL HISTORY
OF MEDIEVAL ENGLAND

I

FROM THE ENGLISH SETTLEMENT TO THE
REIGN OF ÆLFRED

i

THE FOLK ORGANIZED BY KINDRED AND LORDSHIP

A CONSTITUTIONAL history of England may properly begin with *Introduc-* the English settlement. Whatever the degree of Romanization of *tory* the British Province, no trace of Latin influence upon the English peoples has been or is likely to be detected before the Gregorian mission introduced an ecclesiastical strand into the land law of the seventh century. There are some obvious survivals from the past in Northumbria and in the extreme west of the Midlands; but they are Celtic, and testify rather to the failure of Rome to change the essentials of life in the remoter parts of the island than to any permanent influence of Latin political or social forms. On the other hand, the customs of the various invading races, coming, as most of them did, from the most primitive north-western extensions of Germany, preserve in a very perfect form the principles of Germanic society. They share with all the northern peoples the essential ideas of the joint responsibility of kindreds before the law, the blood-feud and its compositions, and a primitive classification of society into the noble, the free, and the half-free, which is the outward manifestation of the predominance of the tie of blood and inheritance. This primitive phase of social organization gives its character to the centuries during which the English were building up the Heptarchy, and constitutes a defined epoch sharply distinguished from the age of feudalism which followed

I

it. It can only be understood in the terms which the Anglo-Saxons themselves used in codes and charters and in their courts, and by way of their own preconceptions as to the nature of their political and social system.

The nation

The most primitive idea as to the nation is that it is a kindred, enlarged past all rememberable degrees of relationship, but holding to a tradition of common ancestry, human or divine. Nations speak of themselves as Angel*cynn*,[1] Iutna*cynn*, and among many of the northern races a royal stock transmits the blood of the founder, bears his name, and embodies the legendary unity of the nation in the person of a king. So the oldest Danish dynasty are Ynglingas from the divine hero Yngvi, while in Britain the West Saxons call themselves Gewissae and trace the descent of the house of Cerdic from Gewiss.[2] Such groups, ideally kindred grown to nations, in practice political communities, are spoken of as late as the Alfredian chronicles and translations as *maegths*,[3] groups united by one blood and custom. This sense of common blood is carried deeply into the structure of the nation. The rank, status, and privilege of each man are his birthright. They are only valid if he can establish their inheritance from four generations and point to a full kindred extending through four degrees of descent. It is not until the requisite generations have inherited his freedom, and a free kin has been built upon an original act of emancipation, that his descendants will grow into their full right in the folk,[4] and what is true of the passage from slavery to freedom is said also to have been true of that from freedom to nobility. Only at the fourth generation does rank become heritable and carry with it its full privilege.[5]

The kindred

A full kindred is essential to the enjoyment of folkright for very practical reasons. Early law cannot and will not deal with the individual. The actions of every man involve his kinsmen, and they share his responsibility. The most striking instance of

[1] Anglo-Saxon Chronicle, 449A.
[2] Grimm, *Teutonic Mythology*, i. 354.
[3] Prologue to Wihtraed's Laws—cantwara *maegð*. Maegth = kindred.
[4] *Ibid.* 8. The man freed at the altar has no wergeld or inheritance.
[5] Norð Leoda Laga, 11. But it is doubtful whether the Anglo-Saxons recognized the possibility of transition from one to the other of their primitive birth-grades. The text cited is a late one and shows marked Celtic influence.

this is in the feud. In slaying or injuring another the offender not only brings upon himself the enmity of his victim's kin, but involves his own. By the act of the individual the families of both parties—to seven or nine degrees according to usage—are legally open to vengeance or committed to taking it, though they may, if they like, pay the heavy blood-price or _wergeld_ to "buy off the spear".[1] It is not until the reign of Eadmund that a man's kin can lawfully disclaim revenge and leave him to bear the feud alone.[2] The feud, moreover, is only the most striking and not the most important function of the blood-group, which is, in fact, fundamental to early English society. A man's whole citizenship depends upon his being backed by an adequate kindred. The law will not deal with individuals, will not admit them into its courts, or listen to their oaths, or accord them any sort of protection, unless they are vouched for by guarantors—_borh_ is the term used—who originally should be their blood-relations. If a man is to be treated as a member of the moot, with the legal rights of a freeman, there must be someone who will guarantee that he will behave lawfully, stand to justice if called upon, fulfil any judgment the court may put upon him, pay any damages which he may have incurred towards others.[3] Increasingly, as time goes on, lords will be required to take upon them this responsibility of borh towards their men ; but the natural and original warrantors of any man are his own kin,[4] his _maegburg_,[5] and only as a known resident with an adequate maegth can he be received as a responsible and lawful man who can sue and be sued, and whose oath is valid in law. The kindred is said to "domicile its members to folkright",[6] and the man who has no kin and can find no lord is outlaw, _caput gerit lupinum_.[7] Further, within the court itself, accepted and given legal standing there, he still cannot act alone. Stage by stage, in any cause he pleads, his own oath will not carry him; his kin must swear with him, twelve or more,[8] according to the cause, must offer themselves with him as oath-

---

[1] Ælfred, 27; I Cnut, 5, 2b. _Mid his magum, þae feh þe moton mid beran, oððe forebetan_: with his kin who must bear the feud with him or buy it off.

[2] II Eadmund, 1.   [3] Æthelbert, 23.

[4] II Æthelstan, 1. 3; 6. 1; III Æthelstan, 7. 2.   [5] Ine, 74. 1.

[6] II Æthelstan, 2.   [7] A twelfth century phrase.

[8] Ine, 21. 1; II Æthelstan, 11; VIII Æthelred, 23; Northumbrian Priest's Law, 51.

helpers, and thus, as by a combined act of the kin, a valid oath can be achieved. Thus, the individual as a person in law cannot act in isolation. His status is incomplete in itself, and his right is effective only as a member of the group with which he is joined by descent. As such it is known as his *maegth-law*,[1] and this, in turn, can be destroyed by outlawry, so that the outlaw's kin is loosed from all obligation.[2]

One form of the predominance of the blood-tie was lacking with the English and with almost all Teutonic peoples. By the period of their appearance in history they had abandoned the joint family holding of land which seems to have been common to all the primitive peoples of the North and which survived in Wales into the Middle Ages.[3] Even so, the practice of equal partition at each generation was common in many parts of England,[4] and shows the right of birth into the stock of descent still resisting the disintegrating forces of free economy and individual ownership. But, this apart, the Saxon freeman was involved in relationships natural or contracted, bound either by the ties of blood or by the conventionally idealized ties of lordship, which, as we shall see, were thought of as extensions of them. All that came of this heightened sense of kinship, the feud and its composition, surety-ship, compurgation, and the validity of legal standing and the power to offer oath—law-worthiness and oath-worthiness—is the mainspring of contemporary life, and makes up almost the whole equipment of ideas about law and social relations which the age needs or can conceive. It is natural, therefore, for the nation to be determined by race and descent, since it is the aggregate of the interrelated kindreds of its members, the common maegth of the Mercians or Kentings. So organized, society throws the weight of habit against the forces of free economy and individualism, and thinks less of land or other wealth as a criterion of rank or author-ity. Not until the exclusive reverence for descent has been sapped

[1] I Cnut, 5. 2d. The novice monk is said to "come out of his *maegthlage* when he enters his rule-law".

[2] III Eadgar, 7. 2.

[3] The right of pasture in a common waste used in many parts of Britain is another matter from the common right of property.

[4] Probably much more commonly than is yet realized. It was predominant in Kent as *gavelkind*, but it was also common in East Anglia and may be found in Dorset. The Lombards broke up their joint holdings by the practice of adfratellamentum-fictitious brotherhood.

by centuries of economic and political experience is the way clear
for the rudiments of feudalism and the territorial state.[1]

From the imagined community of descent a common inherit- *The law*
ance of law was deduced. Law was an attribute of the stock, and *and the*
every member of it was born into folkright, a complex of privi- *individual*
lege, status, and obligation coming to him with his father's blood
and his material inheritance of land and goods. Such a man was
said to be folk-free. There were slaves—*theows*—rightless men who
had sold themselves into slavery, or incurred it by their failure to
carry through the right expiation of some breach of custom, but
they had no place in kin [2] or community. Ideally, in the rule of
society held by the northern world as a whole, folkright endowed
the individual with all that was necessary for the completeness of
life—a sufficiency of land for rough parity among equals in rank,
and the status of his immediate ancestors, noble, free, or half-free.
An equal law gave him a sure process of defence in folkmoots,
where his landright and his person were defended by common
right and by judgment of his neighbours. His life was defended by
the blood-price or wergeld, by which his paternal and maternal
kindred would be appeased for his death; lesser prices, elaborately
graded according to the importance of the injured member, protected him limb by limb from maiming, and as the head of a
household he possessed over his house and dependants a peace of
which the King's Peace of later days was only one survival. The
fence about his house was a sacred mark in law; crimes done
within it bore a double and treble penalty, and with some nations
incurred the rarely inflicted judgment of death. Ideally, then, to be
born into the folk was to inherit full folkright, to take an equal
place in public assemblies, to possess a full right of inheritance, and
to come under the common burden of the folk, service in war and
suit and judgment in the courts. It is best to retain for this social
organization the name it gave itself—the *folc*; for democracy,
popular self-government, and so on, are phrases drawn from
entirely different political conditions. They are terms of politics

[1] This element in English history is best described in F. Seebohm, *Tribal
Custom in Anglo-Saxon Law*.   [2] II Eadward, 6.

and the early English peoples were primarily communities of law. How far these half-barbarous peoples observed their own principles is, of course, now past determining.

The grades of the folk   It may be that in some earlier phase of their history the German nations were societies of equals, neither noble nor half-free, free tribesmen of equal rank. Many savage races are. By the beginning of history they have developed a system of castes, most possessing a nobility, and many a caste of half-free cultivators. These castes do not anticipate feudal serfdom or the nobility of feudalism with its dominion by tenure. The two systems have scarcely anything in common. In no case is the oldest nobility of the North an outcome of tenure or property. Either it arises out of the primitive structure of the folk, as with the Bavarians, or, as among the Celts of Wales, nobility comes by office—the service of the king may be the sole source of nobility. Such lordship need not convey power over other freemen and has no necessary connection with land. It is a personal nobility by blood, office, or service. Quite literally, it enhances the value of its possessor, doubling, trebling, even raising sixfold the money value of the wergeld, of the compositions for bodily injuries, and of the price of the house-peace, making the noble's oath outweigh those of many commoners swearing together. But it is a privilege of the person simply. No more than the privilege of the common freeman is it, of itself, lordship of lands or men. The caste of freemen is, as it were, duplicated upon a higher standard of personal worth. The noble is said to be "dearer born"[1] than the freeman, and that is all.

To these two castes free and noble, many nations added a third identical in principle with the others. The *lazzi, liberti, leysings,* of certain German and Scandinavian peoples, the *taeogs* of Wales, lay below the other classes, enjoying point by point the same privilege, but at a lower price, half a freeman's wergeld, sometimes more than half, but throughout the scale at a lower value than the free. They were as a rule members of the community and shared its privileges and obligations: the Saxon *litus* sued and was judged in the public courts, and was represented in the annual assembly of the Marklo,[2] while the Lex Frisionum shows the Frisian *liti* accorded that right of making judicial oath which is the hall-mark of membership of the folk.[3] It is this which is the impassable line between

---

[1] Ine, 34. 1.   [2] Stubbs, *Constitutional History,* I, § 22.
[3] Lex Frisionum, iii. 4.

membership and non-membership of the community; the slave has no oath and no legal personality apart from his master. Thus in all civil right the *litus* stands with the free and even with the noble. The full member of the folk, folk-free, and an inheritor of law and estate, is, therefore, the type of the barbarian community, and, though above and below him lie the ranks of the noble and the half-free, their privilege is only the freeman's enhanced or diminished. Together these orders make up the folk, and their privilege and obligation is the sum of folkright. Here are rank, order, and degree, but not the lordship, vassalage, and customary servitude which come with feudal law.

Since blood-relationship was accepted as the bond of society, the *folc* was nominally equalitarian in its public life, equal, that is to say, within each of the birth-grades of which the folk was composed. *The Law and the Community* This found expression in the law, in the courts in which it was administered, in their composition and procedure, in the rights and duties of the individual. The oldest sections of the Germanic codes [1] are lists of the rights that all freemen have by birth into the *folc*, the landshare in the paternal *alod*,[2] the peace upon the land and the homestead, the blood-prices for death, for an eye, for a limb: all these, material and immaterial, were thought of as one undifferentiated birthright. The right of all free individuals of the race, and—upon the level of dearer birth—that of all nobles, was identical, a common racial inheritance. Handed down by tradition, or committed without conscious analysis to writing, it was the law of the Ripuarians, the Law of the Kentings, Mercnalage. The law-courts, therefore, deal with the adjustment of rights between individuals and kindreds. They do not, or at the beginning of our history they are only just beginning to conceive of the community as something more than the aggregate of its

[1] *E.g.* the primitive sections of the Ripuarian and Salian codes.
[2] Alod, *alodium*, is the term used by many continental nations for the original nucleus of the freeman's paternal inheritance, in some cases the *sors* or lot received at the settlement. It is not used in England until the eleventh century, when its meaning was extended to cover all land freely held, but the Saxon *eðel* may be equivalent. Alod is common enough as a term of legal science to be used in speaking of English institutions without any suggestion that the Saxons themselves employed it.

individuals and kindreds. A "breach of the peace" in itself means nothing,[1] for there is no general peace of the community, but only the thousands of islands of peace which surround the roof-tree of every householder, noble and simple, *eorl* and *ceorl*. The king's peace itself covers only his hall and his immediate presence. It is the dearest of peaces, but it protects no one but himself. For this reason, there is no punishment, or at least only for offences against nature. Acts of violence are civil wrongs done to the individual. They may still be wiped out by the feud, but commonly they will be compensated for by the *bot,* or payment of damages, appropriate to the injury done. Violence, therefore, will not appear as a crime, nor as an offence against king or state. Its effects are exhausted in the injury done to the offended party, and are fully atoned for if he and his kindred are satisfied by the *bot*.[2]

In all this there is little scope for interpretation since the law expresses the simple facts of life adequately and with the sanctity of race heritage; equally little for authority since the state is not a party to any cause. There are thus at first no royally made judges. Our oldest law, like that of the Germans and Celts, is one in which the appropriate maxim is on every man's lips as soon as the facts of any case have been determined. From this it follows that the court is a meeting of common men, neighbours, a folk-moot. Freed from questionings about law, since it has the acknowledged rules of folkright to apply, it expends its full force upon establishing the efficacy and integrity of its means of arriving at

The oath   right judgment. As the basis of its system it has established a conception of far-reaching importance, that of the " lawful man ", the man not only credible upon oath, but whose oath has in itself the decisive effect of proof. This conception is at once rational and religious. The lawful man is the man of standing in the community, of full and free kindred, of known residence and good repute. Such men, irrespective of wealth or influence, are "oath-

[1] The use of the word *fredum* for a fraction of the compensation for violence among the Franks used to be thought to prove an early notion of folk-peace or *landfried*. It is not found among the Saxons.

[2] The *wite* of Frisian and English law comes later to be used as a penalty, but in origin it may be a payment to the court for its work of umpirage, being derived from *witan*, to know or take cognizance of—or possibly a payment to the king's officer for arresting the culprit. Cf. p. 45 n. 1 *infra*.

worthy".[1] But in the act of swearing they achieve something more than credibility, and their oath as it is spoken takes a power over them and over their cause which is other than their own. It is in ritual form. Taking to witness at first the pagan and later the Christian divinities, and incorporating their names, it is at once an affirmation, an ordeal, and a doom.[2] For certain favoured classes and certain kinds of process the successful accomplishment of the oath is a final judgment; the priest swearing at the altar,[3] the king's thegn,[4] and the foreigner,[5] the man who has a royal charter for his land,[6] can put an end to any process against himself or his land-right by the swearing of a clean oath of defence.

The oath is, therefore, a vital sanction of Saxon public life. At the head of all his law Ælfred places this command: "I will that every man look well to his oath". The man who once foreswears himself is never again oathworthy and is refused Christian burial.[7] In ordinary processes the oath of one party may be countered by that of the other—in the event of a deadlock the solution is the ordeal of fire or water—and more than the single oath of principals is needed. The normal member of society, oathworthy and worthy of folkright though he may be, cannot of himself bring the oath into being in its full efficacy. He must be backed by associates, many or few according to the nature of the cause, who will swear to their belief in the honesty and truth of his oath: "by the Lord God, this oath that N. has sworn is clean and without guile".[8] Only with such support can a true oath, with its power to rebut accusations and establish right, be achieved. In the earliest law it is the kindred group which must come into court and swear with their kinsman,[9] and, no doubt, the whole system of compurgation

Oath-helping

---

1 I Edw. 3. Men who are notorious false swearers . . . shall never again be oathworthy, but only ordeal-worthy.

2 Leis Willelme, 21. 5: "According to English procedure a man's oath, once adjudged valid, cannot be set aside".

3 Wihtraed, 18. *Preost hine claensie sylfaes soþe*: a priest may clear himself with his unsupported oath.   4 *Ibid.* 20.   5 *Ibid.* 20.

6 *English Historical Review*, vol. l, p. 1.

7 II Æthelstan, 26. Let him never be oathworthy again.

8 Swerian, 6.

9 Ine, 21. 1. In the proportion of two-thirds of the paternal kin and one-third of the maternal kin as in payment of wergelds. II Æthelstan, 11. The requirement of an oath by the kindred in answer to such charges of violence as gave ground to the feud (the oldest branch of Teutonic law), lasted long after an oath by neighbours or friends had superseded it for other kinds of cause. In

finds its origin in the solidarity of the kin. Those who pay and receive the bot with their kinsman, the *maegburg*,[1] are the warrantors of his oathworthiness.

These practices and the theory which inspires them are the background of constitutional history. One of the decisive points of English history was that when the Christian church, having destroyed the authority of the old gods and with it the religious character of oath and ordeal and the validity of every process of law, took the law under its own sanction, lent the name of the Christian god to the formulae of oath, and devised a ceremony of ordeal with masses and the cleansing of the elements of iron and water. This was the bridge by which the pagan world carried its law unchanged into the Christian dispensation. Other changes came with time, more slowly, but everywhere the essentials remained. The neighbourhood replaced the family, but it took on the same duty of mutual warranty, and upon it fell the obligation of witness and oath. The folkmoot continued to be the centre of provincial life. Its elaborate procedure, moving from stage to stage by the oath of kinsmen, or neighbours in later times, setting and overseeing the mutual surety of its constituent townships to the peace, multiplying as time went on its devices of pledge, security, warranty, and witness, necessitated an open court free to all but the slave. Its assumption of the lawfulness of the common man, and its safeguards that he should be so, maintained a legally active community to serve it, and made its name of folkmoot a reality. The use of representation and the emergence of aristocratic leadership characterized its later phases; but its basis was popular, and, as feudalism began to take over this or that area from its jurisdiction, they passed into lordship with the forms and habits of action which the folkmoot had given them. From such courts came all those elements in the English polity which did not come from the Crown. They were the centres of our earliest political divisions, whether under such general names as the *provinciae* of Bede and the *maegths* of his ninth-century translator, or under the local forms of the *lathe* in Kent, the *rape* in Sussex, and the *scirs* of

The Folk-moot

the eleventh century even the priest was still required to rebut a charge of homicide by an oath of his kin. VIII Æthelred, 23. I Cnut, 5. 2b. "Let him swear himself clean with those relatives who would have to bear the feud with him."

[1] Ine, 74. 1.

the North and West. All English courts, shire and hundred, borough, wapentake, soke, and, in procedure at least, manor, were in origin and essence folkmoots, and the establishment of this organization of life on a personal basis, and its conversion in the tenth and eleventh centuries into a territorial community, are the contribution of the Anglo-Saxons to English history. With them, indeed, the essential qualities of English political life are established.

Such general principles govern all the English settlements, but *The Kent-* each of the political groups into which they fall has its own setting *ings* of the general theme. The earliest law of Kent, that of Æthelbert, shows a society of three ranks, eorls, ceorls, and *laets*, primitive folk-grades, rigid and determined by ancient racial rule. The nobility is *eorlcund*,[1] noble by blood and descent, and not by service of the king. It has a wergeld of three hundred gold shillings, three times that of the ceorls. Those who are not wholly free do not owe their inferiority to dependence on any lord, but to status. They form a caste, the laets, below, but only slightly below, the free ceorl in their blood-price, and, though no English record describes their custom, their possession of a substantial wergeld[2] makes it almost certain that they enjoyed the rights of the Saxon *liti*, attending folkmoots with the right of making oath there. Thus, the Kentings of the beginning of the seventh century were a perfect example of the folk in practice, since nobility and the semi-free status were merely special grades of a folk of which the common man was the type. These freemen themselves, the ceorls, had the personal peace or *mund* which is the common mark of Germanic freedom, and the eorl's *mundbyrd* or compensation for its violation, was, again, only three times the mundbyrd of the ceorl.[3] The principle of the kindred asserted itself strongly in the land-law. Every freeman of the stock was born into a full birthright of land which expressed itself in the equal partition of inheritance between all the sons at the father's death, and which

[1] Æthelbert, 13, 14, 75; Hlothaere and Eadric, 1.
[2] Æthelbert, 26. "If any one slays a laet, one of the highest class, he shall compound for him with eighty shillings." The right to a wergeld and the right of legal action in the moot go together. He who has them is called "worthy of folkright".
[3] *Ibid.* 13-16; Hlothaere and Eadric, 1.

preserved a universal peasant freehold into the Middle Ages.[1] In the seventh century and till modern times the kindred of a dead ceorl, and no lord, was guardian of his heirs and lands.[2] This was the custom of gavelkind, which Angevin judges called the Common Law of Kent, and throughout the county it took the place of villeinage.

The West Saxons   The codes of the late seventh century tell us little more of the basic rules of the folk, but in the laws of Ine (*circa* 690) they give us our first glimpse of the constitution of the West Saxons. Here, in contrast with Kent, we find three fully free classes, distinguished by wergelds of two hundred, six hundred, and twelve hundred silver shillings,[3] and the lowest class, the laets, is not mentioned. There has been no word of the Kentish laets since the beginning of the century, and it would be rash to assume that laets did not originally form a fourth class of the West Saxon community also, since we have no West Saxon code of the age of Æthelbert. With the Old Saxons of the Continent, the nearest to our island Saxon stock, the *liti* persisted as one of the principle grades of the nation. However that may be, the ceorl is presented as the lowest free rank of the West Saxon community, possessed of the normal marks of membership of the folk, a wergeld of two hundred shillings,[4] a legal personality which can be brought to judgment in the courts, and the right to make oath there[5] and offer ordeal.[6] Conversely, he is burdened with the duty of service in the *fyrd*, or national host, in war.[7] He has a mund or peace over his house, protected, like that of the Kenting, by a penalty for its breach,[8] and the breaking of his enclosure is an offence which, though vastly less costly, is of the same quality as the breaking of the defences of the king's *burh*.[9] Again, as with the Kenting, the inheritance of the Wessex ceorl and the wardship of his children lies with the kin,[10] and vouches for a heritable landright. Later the ceorls come under lordship, but, convenient as it would be to

---

[1] Cf. the *Consuetudines Kancie* printed in Lambarde's *Perambulation of Kent*.

[2] Hlothaere and Eadric, 6. The family of a serf, even that of a freedman, were in the lord's mund after his death, and the lord took the wergeld. *Consuetudines Kancie*: cf. Lambarde's *Perambulation of Kent*.

[3] Ine, 70.   [4] Ælfred, 25.   [5] Ine, 30.

[6] *Ibid.* 37.   [7] *Ibid.* 51.   [8] *Ibid.* 6. 3.

[9] Ælfred, 40. The burh is the boundary dyke surrounding some privileged mansion or settlement.

[10] Ine, 38. Clause 57 suggests the widow's dower of a third part of the inheritance.

derive them from the laets of old Saxony, their wergeld of a sixth part of the noble's is that of the Saxon freeman on both sides of the North Sea, and their treatment as the basic freemen of the folk forbids this simplification of history. As to the origin of the classes of the West Saxons whose wergelds stood at six hundred and twelve hundred shillings we know nothing. They seem to have derived their rank from birth, for, as contemporaries put it, they were "dearer born" than the ceorls,[1] and the phrase "eorl and ceorl", surviving as a comprehensive description of society, seems to set them upon the same footing as the Kentish eorlcund men. But their most common title, *twelfhynd* and *sixhynd*, tells us nothing, for it denotes the number of shillings in the wer. Of the other English races we know almost nothing, save that the Mercians divided their folk into blood-grades like those of the Saxons, while the Northumbrians knew no nobility but that of office.

Written law gives us a distorted picture of the seventh century. The main stream of custom was never put into writing. The whole land-law, the rules which governed kinship, and in general the accustomed ways of life, were the habit of the community, and passed from generation to generation by unwritten tradition. Thus it is that, while the codes reveal the solid and ancient structure by kin and descent implicitly and by oblique reference, they are directly concerned with what is new or exceptional. Consequently, the earlier Kentish codes were largely concerned with the incorporation of the foreign Christian clergy into the folk by means of analogy and legal fiction,[2] extending the king's mundbyrd to cover the peace of the Church,[3] and that of the folkmoot to protect the places of worship,[4] placing theft from a priest under the same penalty as theft from the king,[5] and making robbery from a common clerk equal to that from a ceorl.[6] Towards the end

---

[1] *Ibid.* 34. I.

[2] In later days this was described as the "setting of Holy Church to world-law", and was considered a great feat of legal wisdom. Griŏ, 24. So also in Cristne Saga, viii. II: "Christendom was taken into the law of Iceland".

[3] Ethelbert, I.   [4] *Loc. cit.*   [5] *Ibid.* I and 4.

[6] The expedient of grading the clergy according to the secular orders finally brought the priest to be classed as a thegn with the title of mass-thegn (Be Mirciscan Aŏe. 2).

of the seventh century the dooms became full of a similar problem, voluntarily accepted lordship, divorced in principle from the old nobility by blood, and abundantly illustrated in records of custom because the legists were labouring to bring it under rule and control by much the same methods that they had applied to the Church. While the old eorlcund rank was a passive privilege of blood and rank conferring authority of no kind over other men, *Lordship* this, the second phase of class distinction among the English, was lordship as we understand it in later times, the patronage of one man over another. It had its own terms; not the eorl, but in Kent the *dryhten* and in Wessex the *hlaford*, were the types of the magnates by lordship.

This conventional relation is created by the client taking his patron to *hlaford and to mundbora*, and in this phrase the full facts of lordship, both economic and legal, are expressed. The lord as hlaford [1] is the master of a plentiful household, from which he maintains those who seek him as his guests or dependants. As society becomes more wealthy the hlaford's benefits become less simple. The king or the noble becomes generous not so much in the mere elements of life as in gold and silver, gilded swords, and rings.[2] He is no longer only the *hlafweard* but the *goldweard*, the gold-giver,[3] the lord of gold.[4] Of this relation, half self-interest, half devotion, we hear much in law and poetry. At least by the seventh century, probably much earlier, there were many men, especially young men of ambition, who had left their kindred and attached themselves to the households of kings and nobles. Such men were called *gesiths*, companions of the prince, and we hear of young men of royal birth who were content to serve as gesiths to leaders of established fame,[5] and of young nobles bred up with king's sons to become their war-band.[6] This is the social and

---

1 Hlaford, i.e. hlafweard, bread-ward, or bread-giver.

2 Beowulf, l. 921: *Beahhorda weard.*

3 *Ibid.* l. 2652: *Goldgiefa.*

4 *Goldwine.*

5 J. M. Kemble, *Codex Diplomaticus*, 80: *Ego Æthelric subregulus atque comes* (gesith) *gloriosissimi principis Ethilbaldi*: I Æthelric, underking and gesith of the most glorious prince Æthelbald.

6 Earle and Plummer, *Two Saxon Chronicles*, i. 47. Military attendance upon the king and monastic vows seem to have been the only two careers for the young Northumbrian noble in the seventh century. Eddius, *Vita Wilfridi*, xxi.

economic aspect of primitive lordship, that maintenance of which
Ælfred speaks in his testament—"the men who now follow me
and whose vails I pay at Eastertide".[1] The client takes his patron "to
hlaford", "to mundbora"—protector and warrantor of legal
standing—"mund" is protection. The latter is the vital fact in law,
that which brings the institution of lordship within the rules of
folkright. The gesith or *gesithcundman*, the *geneat*, the cleric, and
the stranger, tend to receive similar treatment in law, and to find
their place in closely related clauses in the codes,[2] since they have all
left their kin and so divorced themselves from the normal safeguards,[3] or have impaired their standing with their kindred by
entering into artificial ties with a lord. In an age of war and
chivalry many of the gesiths were strangers, attracted by the
reputation of a foreign court for leadership or generosity.[4] To
such men the lord became the protector and warrantor in law,[5]
taking them into his mund or peace. By having found such a
warrantor the man recovers the legal standing which he can no
longer derive from a kindred. With his lord as mundbora he may
sue or be sued in the courts and offer oath and ordeal. Injuries
against him will be visited by the payment of the mundbyrd of
the lord whose protection has been violated. If he evades justice
his lord must make his offence good,[6] and he may assume the
legal personality of his man, and plead his cause if he is indicted
before king or ealdorman.[7] Thus he stands towards his gesith

[1] J. M. Kemble, *Codex Diplomaticus*, 314.   [2] Ine, 19-27.
[3] So the monk is said to "come out of his maegthlaw". VIII Æthelred, 25.
[4] Bede, *Historia Ecclesiastica*, iii. 14: *Undique ad eius* (Oswin of Northumbria)
ministerium de cunctis prope provinciis viri etiam nobilissimi concurrerunt: from all
the neighbouring nations the most noble men came to be his gesiths. Cf.
Beowulf, ll. 199-258.
[5] Beowulf, l. 1480. Beowulf begs that Hrothgar will take his place as
mundbora to his thegns after his death.
[6] Ine, 22; Ælfred, 21.
[7] Ine, 50: "If a gesithcund man acts as advocate for his household dependants
with (*Thingiath with*) the king or a king's ealdorman or with his lord. . . ."
This has been taken to imply private justice, of which there is no other trace
in this age. It seems, however, to be no more than the common German and
Scandinavian practice by which a man of influence or legal knowledge would
take the case of another less favourably placed upon his shoulders and argue it as
his own. Thus (W. de Gray Birch, *Cartularium Saxonicum*, 591) an anonymous
magnate writes to King Eadward telling him that Helmstan, being accused of
theft, came to him to seek his help as "fore-speaker" or advocate, and how the
writer agreed *and thingade him to Ælfrede cinge*. The reputation of Gunnar of Lith

instead of kindred, and can legalize his status in the same manner
as they. To the stranger and ecclesiastic the king is mundbora, and
the relation, akin to the tie of family,[1] honours lord and man alike.
"No kin is dearer to a man than his lord."[2]

*Lordship
and the
folk*

However ancient, even primitive, this kind of lordship may be,
in the codes of Ine and Wihtraed it is in process of being reconciled with the basic law. The folk, which is fundamentally a
pattern woven upon the threads of kindred, is being distorted by
individual power. But, while we recognize this, we must also
recognize that the folk's reaction was that of a vigorous body,
which could make its own terms with the future. Basically it had
been informed by loyalty of blood-relationship, it was now to incorporate the motive of loyalty between lord and man, but it did
so in its own fashion, by extending its own principles, not by
abandoning them.   There can, indeed, be no question of conscious conflict between the principle of kinship and the principle
of lordship. Both were relationships natural to a community where
economic life was non-competitive and action was governed by
personal associations and loyalties. As such, lordship was accepted
and even favoured and advanced by the impersonal reaction of
law and the conscious policy of the crown. The manner of this
was characteristic, though to us unfamiliar. It would, perhaps, be
rash to say that the tie of lord and man was regarded by way of
conscious fiction as analogous to blood-relationship, but it was
treated in practice as if it were, and the man was in effect taken
into his lord's *familia*. It was one of a group of relationships of
which the more intimate blend imperceptibly into physical kinship, and which tend to find similar treatment in law; foreign
residence,[3] hospitality,[4] vassalage, fosterage, the tie of the godson

End was founded upon such advocacies, in which the advocate really constitutes
himself a principal in the cause in his client's stead. So the reeve Abba asks
that successive abbots of St. Augustine's shall be to him and to his heirs *forespreoca and mundbora*, so that "they be in the abbot's *hlaforddome*" (*ibid.* 412,
A.D. 833). The case of the gesith who intercedes with his own lord for his man
may be that of one who secures his lord's aid as forespeaker in a public court.
The term has less precise applications in other contexts. The whole clause may
be compared with Ine. 76. 2.

    1 Eadward and Guthrum, 12. For the stranger and the cleric the king and
the bishop shall be *maeg and mundbora*. So Beowulf speaks of his gesiths as his
"brother thegns" (Beowulf, 1480).
    2 Anglo-Saxon Chronicle, 755A.
    3 Hlothaere and Eadric, 15; Ine, 20 and 21.
    4 Leges Edwardi Confessoris, 23. 1.

and his sponsors,[1] all are treated as in one degree or another parallel with the tie of kinship. The mund of lordship, originating in the peace of the house-father over his sons and men, spreads itself over that wider family of protected and commended dependants to whom the mundbora is not father but lord. *Mundbyrdnis* is, therefore, the term for lordship.

The process is the same which we have seen in the reception of the Church and clergy in Ethelbert's code, an incorporation of vassalage into the law of the folk, determined by the precedents of folkright and of the law of kindred, and extending to it many of the latter's incidents. The mund is transferred from the kindred to the lord, the lord replaces the kin as surety,[2] like the kin, he can swear against the slayer for his man's death,[3] the *mægbot*, amendment for loss of honour by insult to a kinsman, is reproduced in a *manbot* or lordship-price,[4] the *heriot*, or manly equipment of arms and horses, once the privilege of the eldest male of a dead man's kin, is now reserved for the lord.[5] Lord and man may wage the blood-feud for each other,[6] and for a kinless man the lord may take or pay the *wer*.[7]

Lordship and vassalage did not yet go to the root of social relations. They could not alter a man's grade in the folk by changing his birth-price. But they did convey valuable privileges, and these privileges were in the end to become the basis of a new grouping of society. Clientage might be no more than a temporary relation, honourable while it lasted, but making no permanent change in a man's status. In many cases, however, it was clearly a lifelong tie, and then its effects went deep. There is nothing in Wihtraed's laws or Ine's to prove that a caste of lords or a caste of vassals had yet come to be recognized. The gesith, apparently, *Lordship and new classes*

---

[1] Ine, 76; Lege Henrici Primi, 79.

[2] Ine, 22 and 50.   [3] *Ibid.* 21 and 21. 1.

[4] *Ibid.* 76: "Let the maegbot and the manbot be alike and increase in proportion to the wer". Cf. *ibid.* 70.

[5] *Harvard Essays in Anglo-Saxon Law*, p. 136. In later days the heriot of the West Saxon thegn was equated with the *halsfang*, or portion of the wer allotted to the immediate kin. Leges Henrici I, 14, 3.

[6] Alfred, 42. 5.

[7] Ine, 23. 1. The same is true of the foreigner, to whom the king is mundbora, and the monk. *Ibid.* 23. 2; Ælfred, 21.

remained twyhynd, sixhynd, or twelfhynd, according to his birth-right, in spite of his relation to the king.[1] But, beside the blood-price and its analogues, which continued to depend upon birth as long as the true traditions of the folk were in vigour, there are other money compensations defending the honour, prestige, and peace of individuals, and these are determined by official rank or proximity to the king. Such are the *bohrbryce* or amendment for breach of the protection extended to a dependant, the *burgbryce*, or compensation for violence done within the fortified enclosure of a notable, and the *oferhyrnes*, or that for disobedience or contempt of an order which he is qualified to give by virtue of his office or status. Such privileges are more elastic than the older bots, and increase with the status of the individual whatever his birth. Ealdor-men, bishops, gesiths, and thegns are entitled to such privilege in a rising scale according to their office and irrespective of their birth-price,[2] and they play an important part in the building of a new nobility by service, for the greater the lord the greater the man, whose service could enhance his privilege, though it could not alter his basic rank in the folk by kin and descent. The status of the individual is beginning to be affected by that of his mund-bora, though not yet in essentials. To be in the mund of a common man cannot improve the dependant's standing and may impair it. To be in that of a bishop or ealdorman or their like is a distinction. But to be in that of the king already confers privileges and marks of rank. The king's gesith has a higher burgbryce and a higher defence of his peace.[3] In its upper degrees, therefore, service is an active rival to blood as a determinant of social status.

The gesithcund class   In a rudimentary way it is also coming to be associated with land. By the end of the seventh century the king's benefactions to his *comites* were usually completed by cessions of estates, and such benefactions were clearly held to be in the public interest and to be essential to the gesith's function. The defence of the kingdom rested upon the fyrd in part, but also upon the many gesiths and

---

[1] Ine, 30: "The gesithman shall pay according to his wer"; *ibid.* 19: "The King's geneat if his wer is twelve hundred shillings. . . ."

[2] *Ibid.* 45. Cf. Leges Hen. I, 68. 3: *Omnis presbyter . . . in seculari dignitate thaini legem habeat, si tamen occidatur . . . secundum natale suum reddetur*: every priest enjoys a thegn's privilege in secular right . . . but if he is slain he is to be paid for according to his birth-price. Cf. Cnut, 6. 2a.

[3] Ine, 45.

men of noble rank who had been given land to equip them as military leaders. A career as a landed gesith for their sons was coming to be regarded by the nobility almost as a right, and such of the younger men as could get no hold upon the land at home were apt to carry their services abroad. The Northumbria of Bede's day was, indeed, losing its military strength because its kings preferred to use the available land to enrich the Church. Even the clergy who profited by it recognized the danger of this abuse.[1] Nothing was more likely to establish the gesithcundmen *The* as a permanent class than the association of their rank with land- *gesith and* holding, but the endowment of the gesiths did not come to them *the land* in full right of property. It would seem that in taking to the land they carried with them something of that relation of lord and man to which they owed their status. Their landright, as seen in the laws of Ine, is not unrestricted property. The gesithcund land-holder is privileged in contrast to his landless equal in status. His estate is normally between three and twenty hides in extent,[2] he has a moated burh, and a burhbryce only less than that of a king's thegn.[3] But the land and its cultivators are not given over to his discretion. Three-fifths of it must be kept in peasant occupation,[4] and the relation between this peasantry and the gesith must follow certain rules. From land, rent only may be exacted. The bodily labour which comes to be characteristic of the Midland *villanus* of later days can only be imposed if a homestead—and probably farming stock also—are provided by the gesith; that is to say, if there is an additional private bargain and a consequent advantage to the ceorl.[5] Again, if sentence of outlawry delivers the gesith to the feud, its executors must confine themselves to driving the outlaw himself from his capital messuage: they cannot touch his

[1] Bede, *Epistola ad Ecgbertum*. Bede complained of the cession of lands to monasteries instead of to gesiths. The point is almost certainly that grants to thegns would be by way of laen or temporary grant, those to the Church in perpetuity, and so permanently lost to the fisc. The same objection to grant other than by laen was felt in later days in the case of the Church.

[2] Ine, 64-66.

[3] *Ibid.* 45: "Burgbryce shall be paid for a king's thegn sixty shillings, for a gesithcund man who has land thirty-five shillings". (The landless gesith would obviously have no burh.)

[4] *Ibid.* 64-66: "He who has twenty hides shall show twelve hides in occupation" (*xii hida gesettes landes*).

[5] *Ibid.* 67.

dependent cultivators.[1] Similarly, if the gesith gives up his estate voluntarily, he must not impair its settlement. He may take his personal servants with him. The cultivators he must leave upon the land.[2] From these restrictions it is clear that the king's benefactions to his military followers were not gifts and did not constitute property nor confer heritable right. They bear some marks of the conditional grant or *laen* which was to play a great part throughout the history of Saxon land-law. They would, no doubt, like the laens, be granted for a term of years, for life, or for a short term of lives, and the fact that the gesiths as a class faded out of history from the eighth century onwards is amply explained by their failure to establish themselves in an hereditary grasp upon the soil.

Gesith and ceorl

But, though they had a comparatively short history themselves, the gesithcund land-holders left a permanent mark upon the peasantry. The major portion of the gesith's estate was *gesettland*, *i.e.* land peopled with cultivators. Presumably they with their land were under his mundbyrdnis, his lordship. There were several ways in which they may have entered into such dependence. The gesith's land was assessed in hides like the rest of the peopled land of England, and the hides and their fractions, the yardlands, were units of assessment for royal rents and public services such as were borne by the community at large. The first assumption must be that the greater number of the gesiths' dependants were ceorls of common standing who were required henceforth to pay to a lord what they had once paid to a king, the *gafol*,[3] or rent, and the *feorm*, or fixed renders of corn, meat, bread, and other provender. The profit of the gesiths may sometimes have consisted not in bringing landless men on to land of their own but in taking up the king's dues in rent and kind over ceorls on the king's land. Their service may have lain, for the most part, in arming and leading their dependants to the host. They could not strip the land of its

1 *Ibid.* 68. A similar principle guaranteed the return of laenland to its grantor when the holder suffered forfeiture for wrong done. A clause to secure this was inserted in some charters of laenland, for example, those of Bishop Oswald.

2 *Ibid.* 63.

3 Gafol was a royal rent of a penny or twopence upon the *sulung* (double hide) in Kent, and the twyhynd commoner of Wessex is called indifferently ceorl and *gafolgelda*. Ine, 6. 3, and Ælfred and Guthrum's Peace, 2: ðam ceorle ðe on gafollande sit. That the West Saxon kings granted away farm-rents to religious houses is proved by Ælfred, 2, and it is likely that the gesiths shared the same kind of grants.

men, and the latter's occupancy was secured to them in the event of their lord's outlawry. On the other hand, though the farming of the king's dues may have brought many ceorls under a shadow of lordship, there were others who took voluntarily to a lord. These entered into a contractual dependence. Two forms of contract existed in seventh-century Wessex by which the landless ceorl could obtain a holding and a lord. By one the land only was received in return for gafol, and by the other a homestead and, perhaps, farming stock with it, were included in the grant, and were paid for by peasant labour upon the lord's own fields.[1] In the example set by such indentured dependence we may see an outstanding factor in the decline of the common freeman of the Midlands towards the villeinage which bound his remote descendants under the Normans. Already in the code of Ine the class of ceorls was in process of fissure. There were gafolgeldas, those who now payed the ancient royal rents to a king's follower,[2] and *geburs*, who, in the language of the eleventh century as of the seventh, were propertyless contractors for land and stock. For them labour extended to three or even more days a week, with additional service in ploughing time and harvest,[3] and in them many types of villein find their prototypes. Such agrarian indentures did not at once debase the individuals who entered into them. Clearly, they did not impair the ceorls' standing in the folk for they retained their ceorl's wergeld,[4] their freemen's duty in the fyrd,[5] and their right of oath and ordeal.[6] If a proportion of them were transferred in the eleventh century to courts of franchise, not

---

[1] Ine, 67: "If a man take a yardland at an agreed gafol and plough it, and the lord later wishes to establish an obligation of labour as well as gafol, that man need not submit unless his lord has provided him with a homestead as well as the land".

[2] *Ibid.* 6. 3. The ceorlish class divided into gafolgeldas or geburs.

[3] Rectitudines Singularum Personarum (*circa* A.D. 1025), cap. 4: "Gebures riht. On some estates he must do two days of week-work of any work set him, and during Lent three days week-work, and from Candlemass to Easter three days, etc. And where such is the custom it is the gebur's right to be given two oxen, a cow, and six sheep to set him up on the land, and seven acres of his yardland ready sown." It can hardly be doubted that this gebur's right of the eleventh century is substantially that referred to in Ine 67; it is also typical of the villein right of middle England.

[4] Ælfred and Guthrum's Peace, 2.   [5] Ine, 51.

[6] Ælfred, 4. 2. Where the standard of the oath of the ceorl is set for certain causes.

private courts, they were courts which administered folkright by the universal procedure. Only as the sense of hereditary status died, and was replaced by the notion that personal freedom and the tenure of free land were part and parcel of each other, would freedom of person without free landright pass into quasi-servitude.

Growth of lordship   We happen to hear of these contractual relations in connection with the gesiths, but there is no reason to suppose that they were not being entered into between all grades of landed proprietors and those freemen who had no land or needed more. A slow change may have been going on at all levels. Though the lord who is a gesith takes the foremost place in the codes because his lordship has been imposed upon the peasantry by the king, the gesiths can have been only a minority of those who held lordship. There was already much "seeking to lordship" by lesser men. But we must not read into the mundbyrdnis and *hlafordscipe* of the eighth century more than a tithe of the *dominium* of the twelfth. The terms of lordship take new meanings as the centuries pass, and in the age of Ine and for some generations the thing itself has no roots in the soil. It is everywhere, but it is revocable, with less lasting effects and fewer implications in law than feudal lordship. Ideally, it can still be a natural relation, holding the affection and devotion which were to inspire feudal vassalage, and not perhaps yet altogether stultified by legal materialism. Such poetical or descriptive accounts as we have, the story of Cynewulf's thegns,[1] Beowulf, or the lament for Eadgar,[2] have the freshness of human feeling. At least lordship could be used to fortify all kinds of institutions without dishonour. The monastery sought a secular magnate as lord and the priest could call himself a mass-thegn. As yet its own traditions were in the making and it drew its law from that of the kindred, borrowing the various peaces, bots, and protections which surrounded the freeman's hearth and bound together his kin; in the seventh century it had not yet conquered the whole of life. There is no sound evidence that it gave a right of justice over those within its ambit,[3] it had only the most accidental relation to land, nor did it change the law of persons. The old system of courts, pleas, and procedure persists, together with the full public status of all members of the com-

---

[1] Anglo-Saxon Chronicle, 755E.   [2] *Ibid.* 975E.
[3] Cf. p. 64, *infra.*

munity. The folk community finds itself faced with an alien relation, emotionally like but a rival to the blood-tie, and it treats it on that analogy, absorbing it without any deep change in its theory or practice. The structure of society is altering, but the community interprets those changes according to its ancient law. It is always to alter itself thus by interpretation and slow change, keeping the spirit and letting the letter go. It is this power of absorption, displayed in the seventh, and again and again in later centuries, which brings the English state system through feudalism, enriched and elaborated, but essentially intact.

In the seventh century the distinction which we are used to *Society* drawing between public and private institutions was as yet not *and the* conceived of. "Constitutional principles" were merely special *state* manifestations, to us the most striking manifestations, of a general life-habit, arrived at for the most part unconsciously, but rising logically from the basis of the folk and the kindred. Thus, while it is convenient to isolate one aspect of early English life as the sphere of public action—assemblies, circumscriptions of government, officials, and so on—the division is really an anachronism. To contemporaries all these things were part of one folkright with the law of land and persons. Therefore, in so far as a theory of government existed in the three centuries after the settlement, it was the application upon a grand scale of those rules of personal association which we have just been considering. All that part of government which is not royal, was, indeed, in origin no more than the simple form of assembly necessary to secure impartial umpirage under an immutable law, and the minimum of officialdom necessary to enforce it. For the economist and the legal historian each of the Heptarchic nations has its distinctive customs, but their simple economy has a certain sameness in the factors of value which they will hand on to the West Saxon supremacy and to the later history of England. All proceed from the basic conception of the folk of lawful men as the inheritors and judges of their law. All deduce from that concept the law-worthiness and legal responsibility of all freemen, and give play to it either directly in folkmoots which all freemen attend, or indirectly through the vaguely conceived representative quality of notables, *sapientes*, *witan*. However it finds utterance, the law remains the domain of the community.

The king must not lay down the law unsupported, not because his folk are jealous, but because it is not in him so to do. Law is not in the king's mouth, but so surely in the voice of the nation that it matters little how it finds utterance. There is a deep conservatism in the procedure of the moots. Even the amendment of law is thought of as judgment, a speaking out of that element of law hitherto unrevealed, an act of judgment of the folk through its witan, and this, too, does not radically impair the equality of public life. Where every phase of judgment, oath, and ordeal reflects in word and gesture the principle from which it proceeds, the individuals who bear the moot's person are not jealously determined. The court speaks through them, *"dicit hundredum"*, *"teste tota scira"*, *"this is Angolcynnes witenes geraednes"*.[1] This legal popularism, elastic, practical, tolerant as to the composition of its assemblies, yet unyielding in its demand that lawful men shall pronounce right law, is the first and most far-reaching rule which united England inherited from the embryo states of the Heptarchy. It remained the prevailing current of life, strong, deep, for the most part invisible, but determining the range within which executive power could be exerted, and in the end forcing it into avowed conformity with itself.

Provinces of the folk   Almost automatically, then, the unwieldy masses of the nations fall into legal provinces not too large to make use of a single place of assembly, yet large enough to provide the knowledge and authority of a folkmoot. The ninth-century translator of Bede, when writing of the Midlands, called such subdivisions of the nation maegths, kindreds. We are suspicious of any suggestion of blood-relationship upon a provincial scale, but we have only to study the web of interrelationship which riddled the peasant tenure of any of the Kentish lathes in the Middle Ages, to see that it must have been very easy for such neighbourhoods to think of themselves as large and loosely related families. Allowing for a measure of sentiment and unreality in this, the basis of the provinces of the seventh-century kingdoms was in fact personal rather than territorial. In many parts of England they took their names from their communities, the "Men of the River Meon" (*Meonwara*), the "Men of the Chester" or "the Burh" (*Ceasterwara* of Rochester, and *Burhwara* of Canterbury), the "Settlers on the

[1] The hundred testifies. By the witness of the whole shire. This is the agreed edict of the witan of the English.

River Arrow" (*Arosetna*), the "Marshmen" (*Merscwara*), and the sense of this community forced a political framework into being to embody it. In this sense, also, as the nature of law and social relations would lead us to expect, the basis of public life was popular, and was not created by a scheme imposed from above.

Folkright made the common law-courts folkmoots, but the *Principle* function of judgment often fell to men of reputation who were *of witan* *seniores* or witan, as being wise in law. The popular principle in the moots was satisfied either when they embodied the folk directly or by delegation of function to those who were representative of the legal wisdom of the community,[1] and this made it possible for the judgments and political decisions of a nation to be made by a few of its wise men in council, the *witenagemot, consilium sapientum*.[2] The council of a great nation could not be a universal assembly, but the Kentings or Gewissae were thought to speak as fully through their *seniores* as in the open forum of their local moots. Although circumstances imposed a different composition upon the witenagemot, the scir-witan, and the hundred-witan, and required the former to act at times in what we have come to regard as matters of state, contemporaries had little inclination to draw such distinctions, or to invent constitutional rules on any ground of difference of function. Any alteration of custom would naturally affect the whole race, and so the central assembly was the authority for general codes, while the local moots were confined to judgment, but the witan of the English were not essentially different from those of the smallest folkmoot in the eyes of Saxon England. The lesser kingdoms used very full assemblies in their earlier days,[3] because it was practicable so to do, but as the kingdoms grew in size the witan came to be of greater distinction

[1] Anglo-Saxon Chronicle, 995F. The principle of the witan is exemplified by the choice by Archbishop Ælfric of "all the wisest men that he knew anywhere. . . . Such as most surely knew how all things stood in the land in their forefathers' days . . . and many ancient men told how the law was laid down soon after Augustine's day."

[2] Nom. sing., *wita*, a wise man; nom. plur., *witan*; gen. plur., *witena*; and so *witena gemot*, the assembly of wise men or notables.

[3] Æthelbert, 2: "If the King call his folk to him . . ."; Wihtraed, Prologue: "Every order of the Church and the loyal laity". So as late as Æthelstan the folk of the countryside intervene: "*tota populi generalitate ovanti*". (J. M. Kemble, *Codex Diplomaticus*, 364.)

and fewer. An original record of the Council of London of 811[1] professes to give the actual composition of a Mercian witenagemot. There were present King Coenwulf, the Queen, Sigered, king of Essex, the Archbishop, the bishops of Rochester, Worcester, and Selsey, three principes, four duces (these titles being apparently variants of the Mercian title of *heretoga*), Coenwald the king's nephew, and Cyneberht another relative, Æthelheah *pedes sessor*, two abbesses, and Cuthred the priest. Though smaller than many, this was by no means exceptional in its composition, but to the end the king and witan were at times afforced by a wider popular element, and they continued by their style to assert their claim to stand for the nation.[2] The witenagemot has no fixed composition. Wisdom, wealth, prestige make it inevitable that certain great men shall find a place there—"the most eminent of my people" is Ine's phrase—but there is no status of *wita, consiliarius*, no formal qualification or disqualification for attendance. The councils contain both clerical and lay notables,[3] "all orders of the Church" attend, ordinances both spiritual and secular are issued, and the king or the archbishop seems at any time after the seventh century to preside indifferently.

Witan and King As between two authorities, king and witan, each felt deeply if obscurely to bear the person of the race, there should be no conflict of powers. Where the first function of both is not to make law but to apply an unchanging custom, neither king nor witan has reason to assert a superiority over the other, and we cannot force upon these primitive assemblies the monarchy, aristocracy, or democracy of which it is so hard to rid our minds. For this reason our authorities show neither king nor witan superior in making dooms or decisions of policy, or in executive enactments. As the authority of the code of Wihtraed we have the prologue's dating "Wihtraed the most merciful king of the Kentings then ruling", but we are told almost immediately that the "magnates

[1] W. de Gray Birch, *Cartularium Saxonicum*, 335: *Concilium pergrande collectum habebatur in quo videlicet ipse rex Coenwulf . . . atque majores natu quorum nomina infra caraxantur*: A great council was held, in which (were) King Coenwulf himself . . . and the notables whose names are written below (in the test).

[2] Dunsaete, Prologue, Angelcynnes witan; V Æthelred, Inscr. Angolwitena.

[3] W. de Gray Birch, *Cartularium Saxonicum*, 386: "There was a synodical gemot at . . . Clovesho, and there were the said King Beornwulf, and his bishops and ealdormen, and all the witan of this people".

brought them in with the agreement of all". Ine's laws are conceived "with the counsel and wisdom . . . of all my ealdormen,
and the chief witan of my people". Ælfred claims that his dooms
are his own gathering from past law, but they have been shown to
his witan, and "they all liked them well to hold". At times the
form of the laws purports to record king and witan speaking with
one voice,[1] while at others our idea of their functions is reversed,
and it is the king who convenes and the witan who enact: "first
they decree as to holy orders", says the oldest text of Eadmund's
synod, and it is the notables, lay or clerical, who are thus made to
speak.[2]

The distinction between the grouped dooms of a code and the
single doom of an act of judgment is, of course, a modern one,
and in this too the king will have no distinctive power. At the
Clovesho synod or witenagemot of 825 a claim for right of pasture
was made by the bishop of Worcester against the reeve of Sutton,
and was judged by the Archbishop and "all the witan", although
the king was there.[3] Æthelstan of Sunbury had claim to an estate.
He came to King Eadgar, and "bade a doom of him": "then the
Mercian witan doomed him the land".[4] Again, Dunstan petitions
Eadgar on behalf of a widow whose husband Ecgferth has been
forfeit for theft, and who is in his mund; but the king has to
answer, "my witan has declared all Ecgferth's wealth forfeit".[5]
The king's interest may be overridden. A Mercian suit of the year
840 shows the bishop of Worcester successfully reclaiming land
which King Berhtwulf had taken from his church and given to
his personal followers. The bishop challenged his action at the
Easter witenagemot at Tamworth, and, in Berhtwulf's presence,
the witan judged that he had been unjustly dispoiled. Berhtwulf
returned the lands, and gave gifts to the church in reparation.[6]

1 Ælfred and Guthrum's Peace, 5: *And ealle we cwaedon.*

2 I Eadmund. London Synod, 1.

3 W. de Gray Birch, *Cartularium Saxonicum*, 386.

4 *Ibid.* 1063.

5 *Ibid.* 1063 and 1064.

6 J. M. Kemble, *Codex Diplomaticus*, 245: *Contigit autem quod Berhtwulf rex
Merciorum tolleret a nobis . . . terram nostram . . . rex praefatus suis propriis
hominibus condonavit, sicut se inimici homines docuerunt. Et ibi (ad Tomworthie)
ante regem suosque proceres fuerunt allecta (libertates et cartulae) et ibi Merciorum
optimates dejudicaverunt illi, ut male et injuste dispoliati essent*: it happened that
Berhtwulf, King of the Mercians, took away our land from us and made it

Individually, these tales may be no more than memories, but they vouch for a traditional belief as to the function of the Saxon king that carries conviction. It is uniformly held to and it is that of the feudal king after him. Land which lapses to the king through failure of heirs or forfeiture, or folkland which is granted to the king in the freer law of bookright, he must obtain by the judgment of his witan.¹ We must, however, be on our guard against giving a wrong interpretation of this. It is a practical application of the supremacy of law, and reflects no constitutional subordination of the king to the witan. Where his personal concern does not make his participation an obvious injustice, the king's is among the voices which pronounce judgment, and, if his character deserves it, it may be the leading one. Echoes of decisive sentences of Offa have come down to us,² and Ælfred clearly made himself the centre of English legal wisdom and its most trusted interpreter.³ The judgment which deposed Archbishop Wulfred from his see was made in a witenagemot at London, but was clearly prompted by the Mercian king Coenwulf.⁴ That of his milder successor Beornwulf, restoring him to his lands and honours, was equally clearly popular, and was made "with one mind and with common consent".⁵ Thus, circumstances and the play of personality thrust

over to his own men as certain enemies of ours had advised. But then at Tamworth our liberties and charters were adduced and the witan of the Mercians gave judgment to the king (that they had been wrongly taken away?). There is a break in the construction at this point.

¹ W. de Gray Birch, *Cartularium Saxonicum*, 390 (A.D. 825): *Optimorum meorum decreto adjudicante*: by the judgment of my notables. J. M. Kemble, *Codex Diplomaticus*, 1019.

² W. de Gray Birch, *Cartularium Saxonicum*, 293.

³ Asser, De Rebus Gestis, 106. Yet Ælfred placed himself upon the judgment of the witan as to whether his action under his father's will had been in conformity with folkright. J. M. Kemble, *Codex Diplomaticus*, 314.

⁴ *Ibid.* 220 (A.D. 825): *Rex Coenwulfus cum suis sapientibus ad regalem villam Lundoniae perveniens ad hoc eodemque concilio illum archiepiscopum . . . invitabat. Tunc in eodem concilio cum maxima districtione illo episcopo mandavit . . . disspoliatus debuisset fieri, omnique de patria ista esse profugus*: King Coenwulf came to the royal town of London with his witan and summoned the archbishop to the moot. Then in the said moot he ordained to the bishop by most strict judgment that he should be despoiled and outlawed from the whole realm.

⁵ *Loc. cit. Tunc vero omnis ille synodus ad aequitatem invenerunt huncque judicium unanimo consensu constituerunt*: then the whole synod deemed right and made this judgment by unanimous consent.

An instance of criminal judgment by the witan upon a great layman is that of the witan at Cirencester upon Ælfric Cild, Ealdorman of Mercia, for

to the fore now one element and now another. It is the indivisible law which speaks through king and witan, and for them the divided and often antagonistic functions and rights of more advanced political theory have no meaning.

The most characteristic function of the witenagemot, that from *Function which it took its name, was the giving of judgment, deeming of of the dooms[1] as *sapientes*, and it is of this function that we have most witan record. Of the same order of activity, according to the thought of the day, was the general scrutiny of the law and its working, the placing and keeping of men in their rank and due, and the safeguarding and amending of secular and spiritual custom. Of legislation, as we understand it, there was, of course, almost nothing. "To look to the needs of God's churches and the right keeping of monastic rule, and to take counsel for the stability of the secular state", is the account given of its own purpose by the Council of Clovesho of 825, and, as a means to that end, it set out to enquire "what men had been maintained in justice and equity, and who had been defrauded by violence and injustice, or dispoiled".[2] Evidence for such care is plentiful from the reign of Eadward the Elder to that of the Confessor, during which time the nation was building a new system of law and administration under the leadership of its kings. With nothing but the Ælfredian Chronicle to go upon, we can say little of it before the tenth century, and hardly more of the witan's part in affairs of state and executive government. What little is recorded shows the usual lack of precision as to the power that acts, for there is a prevailing confusion of the functions of the crown with those of the national council. We see Ecgfrith of Northumbria preparing to defend his people against Wulfhere *consilio senum*,[3] and the Mercian witan joining with their king to put themselves under Æthelwulf's leadership against the Danes in 853.[4] Oswiu consults his *sapientes* one by one as to the

treason in 985, *quando ad synodale concilium ad Cyrneceaster universi optimates simul in unum convenerunt et eundem Ælfricum maiestatis reum de hac patria profugum expulerunt* (J. M. Kemble, *Codex Diplomaticus*, 1312).

1 W. de Gray Birch, *Cartularium Saxonicum*, 115. The bishop of London describes a joint witenagemot of the kingdoms of Wessex and Essex, which met at Brentford in October, 705, as *reges ambarum partium, episcopi et abbates, judicesque reliqui*, i.e other doomsmen.

2 W. de Gray Birch, *Cartularium Saxonicum*, 384.

3 Eddius, *Vita Wilfridi*, xx. (Rolls Series.)

4 Anglo-Saxon Chronicle, 853A.

fitness of Wilfred for the Northumbrian see,[1] and Bede records a similar procedure when Northumbria receives Christianity.[2] *Hæc est voluntas regis et principum ejus.*[3] Under Offa the Lichfield archbishopric is created in the Synod of Chelsea,[4] but its first archbishop, Higbert, is recorded as chosen by the king.[5]

Succession and deposition of kings

To say without qualification that the witenagemot could elect and depose kings would be to ignore the changing value of terms. We have seen what power inherited place in the blood-grades of the folk had to determine status and right. The potentiality of kingship inhered in the highest kin of all, the *cynecynn*,[6] and was transmitted to all its members, together with the aetheling's wer,[7] and other marks of preëminence. From the cynecynn the choice of king must be made, for it only was royal. A ruler taken from a lesser stock was *dubius*,[8] *ungecynd*,[9] and, though the disorders of the eighth century produced some such monarchs, they were ill looked upon by responsible opinion.[10] But within the cynecynn —perhaps the kin within nine generations of descent—choice should in theory have been free, and seems often to have been so. Egbert, though of the "right kin that goeth unto Cerdic", was divided from the main line of descent from Coenred by five generations.

Within the covering principle of kinship, ability, family arrangement, and popularity produced a different solution at every vacancy of the throne. Ælfred was called to the crown over the heads of his elder brother's sons, and Asser tells us that, as the noblest of his family, he might have preceded his senior Æthelred,

---

[1] Eddius, *Vita Wilfridi*, xi.   [2] Bede, *Historia Ecclesiastica*, ii. 13.

[3] Eddius, *Vita Wilfridi*, lx.

[4] Anglo-Saxon Chronicle, 785A.

[5] *Loc. cit.*

[6] *Ibid.* 1067D: *Eadgar was Eadreding and swa forþ on þonne cynecynn. Ibid.* 449E, 547A.

[7] Ælfred translates Bede's *nobiles et regii viri*, in the account of the baptism of Eadwin's household, as *æðelingas þæs cynecynes. Historia Ecclesiastica*, ii. 14. According to the North People's Law (clause 1) the wer of the royal kin was uniform at 15,000 thrymsas, including the king himself.

[8] Bede, *Historia Ecclesiastica*, iv. 26. *Reges dubii vel extranei.*

[9] Anglo-Saxon Chronicle, 867E. The Northumbrians had deposed their king Osbryht and *ungecyndne cyning underfengon Ællan.*

[10] Asser, *De Rebus Gestis*, 27: *Tyrannus quidam, Aella nomine, non de regali prosapia progenitus, super regni apicem constituerant*: a certain tyrant, Ælla, not of the royal kin. . . .

had he been so minded, and reigned with general approval. Where there was no fixed rule of succession, the favour of the people must have kept its importance, and the witan's action in election, as in other matters, was then an act of the nation. Alcuin writes to the *nobiles et populus laudabilis, et regnum imperiale Cantuariorum* during the native Kentish régime which followed Offa's death and exhorts them *rectores vobis praeponite nobilitate claros*. The address is characteristic both in the width of its appeal to the Kentish nation as the basis of authority and in its lack of precision as to the allocation of constituent power. On the other hand, this same lack of rule must have given play to other than popular forces, to the exceptional power of individual claimants, or the policy of the throne's holder. The practice of naming a successor as *secundarius* during the reigning king's lifetime was not uncommon. Ecgfrith was king of the Mercians before Offa died, Æthelbald divided the kingdom with his father Æthelwulf, and Ælfred was *secundarius* under Æthelred. Æthelwulf's reign, indeed, is an example of how diverse considerations could affect the throne almost contemporaneously. Two years before his death the authority of the witan[1] carried through a partition of the kingdom between himself and his eldest son, but his will embodied a disposition of the crown between Æthelbald and Æthelbert, which was in fact carried into effect. Deposition was uncommon as long as the old national dynasties were able to produce suitable candidates, but we have an example in Sigebert, from whom "Cynewulf and the witan of the West Saxons took his realm for ill conduct",[2] and Æthelred, king of the Northumbrians, was deposed, thrown into prison, and restored at the end of the eighth century.[3] Instances both of election and deposition persist throughout the Saxon period,[4] but it is difficult to feel that they represent

[1] Asser, *De Rebus Gestis*, 12: *Omnium astipulatione nobilium*: with the assent of all the magnates.
[2] Anglo-Saxon Chronicle, 755A.
[3] Alcuin. Letter to Joseph. Haddan and Stubbs. *Councils*, iii. 495.
[4] Cf. the election of Eadred (J. M. Kemble, *Codex Diplomaticus*, 411), and of Eadward the Martyr (*Ibid.*, 1312), *omnes utriusque ordinis optimates . . . fratrem meum Eaduuarduum unanimiter elegerunt*: all the witan both spiritual and secular unanimously elected Edward my brother as king.

Anglo-Saxon Chronicle, 1016E: *Ealle þa witan þe on Lundene waron and se burhwaru gecuron Eadmund to cynge*: all the witan at London and the men of the borough chose Eadmund as king. *Ibid.* 1036, 1041.

a settled constitutional rule. Rather they are the result of social habit in the interplay of the principles of kinship within the royal house and of the folk principle throughout the whole community, finding their highest expression through the magnates in the witenagemot of the nation. These principles, though they cannot defeat the ambition of a Cnut or a Harold, suffice in the main to keep the throne within the cynecynn yet tolerably popular, but they are automatic responses to underlying social beliefs [1] rather than rules of the constitution.

Government, as we have described it so far, is in basis popular, either through the folk in council or through the "wise men". With no more than the rudimentary equipment of moots and some device of elective ealdormanry or moot presidency, great branches of the Northern races have made shift to maintain a stable government. The Icelandic settlements of the tenth century, and the Old Saxons, the Germanic stock nearest in custom to the West Saxons of Britain, had no non-popular executive until it was imposed upon the latter from without by Charlemagne. It is, perhaps, remarkable that all the large national units of the Anglo-Saxons maintained monarchies from the earliest times of their history, though several of them preserved the tradition that their founders were not kings, and only the house of Offa [2] claimed that its ancestors of the fourth century reigned in Germany. As a consequence of monarchy, from the earliest time of which we have any knowledge, lathe, scir, and rape were also the frames of *Provincial* an administration whose officers were the king's. He was the pro-*govern-* tector and executant, though not the fountain, of their law. They *ment* were heavily interlaced with the demesne lands and interests of the crown, and taxed to support it upon an assessment by townships and hamlets or ploughgangs in the North, and by hides or sulungs in the South. It is this phase of the provinces' functions which has found its way into record, and if we wish to describe them in detail we can only do so in so far as they are units in the king's fiscal and judicial administration. Even so, our knowledge is very

---

[1] In Kent there is some tendency for the crown to conform to the custom of gavelkind and to be departed between coheirs in each generation.
[2] Cf. H. M. Chadwick, *Origins of the English Nation*, chap. vi.

partial. We know something of the Anglo-Celtic administrations[1] of the North, and also of the lathe of the Jutish South-East, for they survived into the early Middle Ages, and we may suspect—without at present a shadow of proof—that East Anglia and Essex may have lain under a somewhat similar system. We know practically nothing as to Wessex or Mercia, but the few facts that we do know about those kingdoms suggest that their early administration developed along different lines from that of the others.

In Northumbria the Anglian king's state is roughly that of a North-Celtic prince, and the Northumbrian *scirs* of the twelfth century and the princely estates of medieval Wales are hardly to be distinguished. A central court—often adopted as the hundred court in the Middle Ages—serves the whole area, a capital township, *cinges tun*, or *urbs regis*, is the administrative seat of a reeve. A scattering of hamlets of *terra regis*, or demesne of some immunist, owner of liberty of court and administration, form, as it were, the agrarian nucleus of the scir; there is a common waste or shiremoor, and the folk of the countryside, holding by a custom called husbandry or bondage,[2] live in independent settlements or "bondage townships". Such hamlets contribute to general dues assessed on the scir, pasture rents like *cornage* and *neatgeld*, and the cattle rents of *vacca de metreth*, *cugeld*, or *beltancu*, of which the metreth is the *treth calan Mai* of Wales. They are under an obligation to provide house-room and provender for the king's servants going about their administrative duties. In Latin, these duties appear as *putura serjeantium*, or *forestariorum*, but the Welsh *cylch*[3] survives as far north and east as Staffordshire.[4] Besides this, there is the sending of labourers into the demesne harvest, keeping the hall and buildings of the demesne in repair, feeding, and training the lord's horses, hawks, and hounds, carting, errand-riding, and other various and variable services. These simple agrarian communities, which are the basis of the Anglian-Celtic folk, are politically quite unspecialized. To the modern mind it is impossible to decide where private life ends and public life begins. The demesne interest of the king or immunist generates no separate

North-umbria (margin note)

---

[1] J. E. A. Jolliffe, *Northumbrian Institutions, English Historical Review*, vol. xli. p. 1.
[2] Cf. the term boneddig for the free Welsh cultivator.
[3] Cf. Cylch hebbogyddion, or provisioning of foresters.
[4] Public Record Office. *Calendar of Inquisitions Post Mortem*, iii. 536.

officialdom. The reeve of the moots is also the bailiff of the king's lands. As he exacts the work of the men of the townships in his lord's harvest, or collects their renders of cattle, it is impossible to say whether he is more the steward or the tax-gatherer. The rudiments of taxation lie in these rustic dues of the homesteads and the fields. All the primitive crown can exact is that it shall live on the countryside, and that the men of the countryside shall come to the help of its great household of servants and officials with the work of their hands, and pass the king's officers freely fed and housed about their business. This is the king's revenue of the day, and exhausts the fiscal resources of the state. It is probably as contributing to such renders that the common folk of the North are spoken of in the eighth century as *tributarii*.

Monarchical influence is equally strong in the higher ranges of Northumbrian society. The governors of the subordinate national units within Northumbria are deputies of the crown—under-kings —and, as was usual in the Celtic kingdoms, nobility by office seems to have taken the place of the Germanic blood nobility. In Eddius and Bede it is the reeves who fill the foreground of Northern history. They are *heah-gerefan*, high reeves, and are the mainstay of the nobility, lying between the under-kings—whom the Saxon Chronicle calls ealdormen—on the one side, and the gesiths and king's thegns on the other. When Wilfred summoned the magnates of the North to the consecration of Ripon, it was in the persons of the two kings, Ecgfrith and Ælwin, and of "their abbots, reeves, and under-kings".[1] Bede, in arraigning the greed of the Northumbrian nobles, again, treats the reeves as the type of secular power: "there is scarce one of the reeves of that nation who in his term of office has not bought himself a house of religion . . . and, so far has the abuse been carried, that even the king's thegns and his domestics have been busy to imitate them".[2] Such men were clearly above the king's thegns, attended the witenagemot—one of them pronounced the witan's sentence upon Wilfred[3]—and attained to great wealth on the profits of

---

[1] Eddius, *Vita Wilfridi*, xvi.

[2] Bede, *Epistola ad Ecgbertum*, 13. So also the Anglo-Saxon Chronicle records (under ann. 779E) that the "high reeves of Northumbria" murdered ealdorman Beorn. The term seems here almost equivalent to magnates or *nobiles*.

[3] Eddius, *Vita Wilfridi*, lx.

their charge. It is not surprising, therefore, to find one of them described as *secundus a rege* and to hear that the conversion of the Lindiswaras turned upon that of Blaecca the reeve of Lincoln. Other than this officialdom, there seems, indeed, to have been no Northumbrian nobility. The Northern social ranks, unlike those of any other English people, are reckoned for wergeld according to official standing and not by the ancient blood-grades. The high-reeves of the North Peoples Law[1] have a wergeld of twice the value of the thegn's, and the latter derives his worth not from birth but from his thegnage. It is the Celtic social grading, as we see it in the Laws of Hoel Dda, strongly official in character and the antithesis of English usage.[2] Thus, Northumbria represents a growth of monarchical institutions more precocious than was usual with the Anglo-Saxons, and there is little doubt that the line of Ida took over the framework of a British kingship which was already highly developed. To this may be attributed the success of the Celtic missions in the North, while the absence of the normal tribal sanction in the crown may have had much to do with the instability of Northumbrian monarchy in the seventh and eighth centuries.

Small provinces are also found in the independent kingdom of *Kent* Kent, and, almost certainly, in Sussex and eastern Surrey. The social and administrative unit of the lathe can be carried back into the early eighth century of Kentish history.[3] The rape is obliquely but clearly referred to in a Surrey charter of 947,[4] and the Sussex rapes, though they do not appear *eo nomine* until the Confessor's reign, leave the mark of their general agrarian type in charters from the eighth century onwards. The remains of provincial organization surviving into the Middle Ages make their antiquity almost certain. This provincial organization is more clearly marked as we move eastwards towards its political centre in Kent, but it must have had a wider extension before the West Saxon conquest impaired the independence of the south-eastern kingdoms, and it has a strong hold upon the Jutish provinces of South Hampshire, the New Forest—Florence of Worcester's Ytene—and the

---

[1] Liebermann, *Gesetze der Angelsachsen*, p. 460.
[2] Bede, *Historia Ecclesiastica*, ii. 16.
[3] J. E. A. Jolliffe, *Pre-Feudal England: the Jutes*.
[4] W. de Gray Birch, *Cartularium Saxonicum*, 820.

Meonwara.[1] The structure of lathe and rape hardly differed from that of the northern scir in the essentials which concern the constitution. A central *villa regis*, a king's reeve, a court, a population of *tributarii*,[2] or gavelkinders, a provincial waste of forest, the wealds in Andred which were apportioned to each rape or lathe. The main difference is one of social habit, a stronger birthright bringing into being in Kent a peasant freehold with partition of inheritance between co-heirs. The dues of the crown differ in detail rather than in principle. The puture of the serjeants and foresters, which comes from the Celtic strain in the North, is absent in the South-East, and in Kent and part of east Sussex there is a money rent of gafol. Otherwise the occasional service on the demesne, and the work upon the king's hall and outbuildings, are much the same, as natural in the simple relation of a primitive kingship to the folk which maintains it in southern as in northern Britain. Scir, rape, lathe, are, indeed, natural outcomes of the phase of society they govern, and such variety as they display is the outcome of differences in private law and administrative history.

Wessex   It is remarkable that we know less of the early administration of Wessex, from which country the laws of Ine and Ælfred survive, together with some early charters, than we do of that of Northumbria, which has given us few public records from before the eleventh century. We know, in fact, almost nothing. The ealdorman had his *scir*, but there is nothing to show whether it was the large shire like the modern county of the South-West, or some smaller unit. The practice of Kent and Northumbria would lead us to expect that early Wessex should have been governed, not by the dual system of shire and hundred which was used by the English kingdom of the tenth century, but by a single system of provinces of manageable size, perhaps larger than the later hundred, and smaller than the county, which is inconveniently large for the meetings of a folkmoot. After the hundred was adopted in the tenth century many hundreds were annexed to royal townships, bore their name, and came under the jurisdiction of the reeve of the king's town, as were the scirs of Northumbria. Of sixty estates bequeathed by Ælfred in his will, twenty-nine have

[1] J. E. A. Jolliffe, *Pre-Feudal England*, p. 89.
[2] W. de Gray Birch, *Cartularium Saxonicum*, 50, 64, 144, 145, 198, 212, 262.

given their names to hundreds of later days.[1] In this one feature, therefore, we have a possible West Saxon parallel to the rape, and the lathe. The primitive unit of Wessex cannot have been the hundred, for that was a growth of the tenth century; on the other hand, many of the royal manors of Wessex were the capitals of large areas. In Cornwall the three medieval hundreds of Stratton, Lesnewth, and Trigg seem to have been formed from the older unit of Triggshire, or Triconscire, one of the *septem parvae scirae* into which ancient Cornwall was divided. Here even in name is the Celtic scir as it was in Northumbria. But where, in Wessex proper, "the pleas of Cicemantone and Sutlesberg hundreds belong to the farm of Malmesbury",[2] or "the soke of two hundreds lies in King's Somborne",[3] it may well be that the West Saxons of the tenth century, in the process of creating a uniform English administration, broke down a scir unit of their own to carve out hundreds within the boundaries of the scirs, but retaining the capital authority of the older *cynges tuns*. In so treating their own system they would have been doing no more than they had done in Kent and Cornwall.[4] This admitted, however, we should still be far from an identity of the Wessex scir with its Anglian-Celtic namesake, or with the lathe. There is an agrarian, social, and fiscal unity about these latter which is lacking in the greater part of Wessex. The hold of the king's vills of Wessex upon the hundreds is, as a rule, purely judicial and administrative, and before the reign of Ælfred there is no text to tell us that the reeves had a place in the folkmoots. There is no proof that the king's vills were the sites of courts, while, if the Saxon king drew his rents and services from them, as the Kentish king drew his gafol from the lathe, or as Celtic or English princes received the cornage and cattle rents of Northumbria and North Wales, or the *berbagium* of South Wales and Cornwall, we have yet to prove it. Nor is

[1] For what follows, Miss H. M. Cam's article, "Manerium cum Hundredo" (*English Historical Review*, xlvii.), from which facts and references have been taken, should be consulted.

[2] Domesday Book, i. 64b.

[3] *Ibid.* i. 39b.

[4] The most plausible instance of the survival of a primitive West Saxon scir is that of Wincelcumbscira (W. de Gray Birch, *Cartularium Saxonicum*, 309, A.D. 803), which Miss Cam considers may have included six or eight of the hundreds of Gloucestershire, with Winchcombe as capital (*Historical Essays in Honour of James Tait*, p. 18).

there, as a rule, that agrarian community of the whole province which is expressed in the wealds, or common woods, of the rapes and lathes, and the shire-moors[1] of the North. Such differences may well be accounted for by an original agrarian factor, such as the contrast between the close champion field of the Midlands village and the looser organization of the North, the East, and the West. If so the political system of the middle South may have had peculiarities which were not shared in by its Anglo-Celtic and Jutish neighbours, and which are not be explained away.

In fact, the earliest administration of Mercia seems to have been less monarchical than that of its neighbours. In early days it rests not upon the king's reeve but the ealdorman, and the ealdorman has the best claim of any Mercian title to an origin independent of the crown. *Heretoga*, the Mercian name for the office,[2] "leader of the host", carries us back to the time when there was no king as war-lord, and one may speculate on its relation to the *princeps* of Tacitus, or, with more reason, to those *satrapae* of the Old Saxons, who in Bede's day still cast lots for leadership on the outbreak of war.[3] An old document, known as the Tribal Hidage,[4] shows the Midlands divided into many units like the *provinciae* or maegths of Bede and his translator, and, as no king of Mercia is known before the seventh century, it may be that Penda's kingship was built upon a confederacy of such maegths and their "satraps".[5] Outside Mercia evidence is more dubious still. At least some of the lesser dynasties seem to have exchanged their royal for ducal rank, and so to have continued under their conquerors. Such was Ealdwulf, *rex*[6] or *dux* of the South Saxons. Here[7] "the relation of the ealdorman to the King has probably been created by commendation . . . and the hereditary descent of the office is only occasionally interfered with by royal nomina-

---

[1] Apparently the forest system of Wiltshire and south Somerset has points of similarity with that of the scir, but it is exceptional in Wessex.

[2] J. M. Kemble, *Codex Diplomaticus*, 557, etc. The word was still used in its literal sense as "leaders of the host", not ealdorman, in tenth-century Mercia, as in the Chronicles E and F, which have Mercian affinities, under 794, 993.

[3] Bede, *Historia Ecclesiastica*, v. 10.

[4] W. de Gray Birch, *Cartularium Saxonicum*, 297.

[5] Bede, *Historia Ecclesiastica*, iii. 24. Penda took thirty duces (Anglo-Saxon translation, *ealdormen and heretogena*) into battle at Winwaed.

[6] W. de Gray Birch, *Cartularium Saxonicum*, 197, 261.

[7] Stubbs, *Constitutional History*, i. 177.

tion". It is, of course, possible that the ealdormen of Wessex also may stand for some forgotten native rulers of the Sumorsaetas or Wilsaetas, but, on the whole, it is difficult to find reasons for believing that popular institutions were carried even so far among the West Saxons. We first meet with their ealdormen at a time when the crown was already head of an executive. Their position seems to have been that of royal governors and their full title "king's ealdormen".[1] The absence, in contrast with Northumbrian usage, of any distinctive ealdorman's wer, proves that they did not derive their status from any primitive standing by blood and descent, and their privileges are like those of the king's thegns, calculated to fortify their office, a higher mundbryce and burh-bryce,[2] which in Ine's law are said to be that of "any other eminent counsellor".[3] The burhbryce is lower than that of a bishop and only a little higher than that of a king's thegn.[4] They may forfeit their office for default of duty.[5] These are the marks of a *ministerium* rather than of an innate rank in the folk. The West Saxon ealdorman seems, however, to have been a public official above any king's reeve, his function centred upon a folkmoot rather than upon the *terra regis*, and he presided there upon occasion, having custody of prisoners,[6] enforcing the attendance of parties,[7] and guaranteeing the order of his court by his own mund.[8] He seems to have been responsible for the general government of the scir, for those domiciled within it could not leave his jurisdiction without his discharge.[9] It is probable, therefore, that we should be right in looking for more than one origin of the ealdormanry in different parts of England. That of Wessex is, perhaps, an officialdom nominated by the crown. Its status was markedly enhanced during the eighth and ninth centuries, for Ælfred's ealdormen have come to be of equal rank with bishops,[10] and their mundbyrd has been doubled.[11] But, outside Wessex, the Mercian heretogas, such as the ealdorman of the Gwrvas,[12] or of the Gaini,[13] may have begun as

[1] Ine, 50.   [2] *Ibid.* 45.   [3] *Ibid.* 6. 2.
[4] *Ibid.* 45.   [5] *Ibid.* 36. 1.   [6] *Ibid.* 36. 1.
[7] Ælfred, 42. 3.   [8] *Ibid.* 3. 38.   [9] *Ibid.* 37.
[10] *Ibid.* 15. In Ine's code, the ealdorman ranks below the bishop.
[11] *Ibid.* 3.
[12] Bede, *Historia Ecclesiastica*, iv. 19.
[13] W. de Gray Birch, *Cartularium Saxonicum*, 571. The charter is spurious, but the title is vouched for by Asser.

the heads of semi-independent maegths, and those of Sussex, Kent, and the Hwiccan as *sub-reguli*. Thus, the West Saxon ealdormen, who were upon the up-grade before the reign of Ælfred, joined with those representatives of the old royal stocks who were losing their royalty to form that class of great provincial governors of the tenth century of whom Æthelstan Half-King is the type.

Summary   It will be seen that many factors, racial custom derived from the common Germanic stock, contact with or borrowing from indigenous Celtic usages, the varied influences of social and economic change, have worked, with effects which we can only determine imperfectly, to preserve or weaken the distinctions between the several English settlements in Britain. Nearest, perhaps, to the equality of freedom which underlies, however remotely, all primitive life, are the Kentings in whom a free peasantry enjoys what is surely the most primitive of English customs, and where the reeves are confined to their fiscal and administrative functions and to the management of the *terra regis*. A somewhat similar system prevails in Northumbria, but the influence of monarchy is more strongly marked by the recognition of the high-reeves as a rank of the folk and the consequent obliteration of the primitive ranks of the noble and the free by blood. As to Wessex we may be more doubtful. The Wessex ceorl has become involved in a more definite economic dependence than have those of other nations. Lordship is perhaps more commonly associated with the possession if not the ownership of land. The village type of settlement of the Midlands is more favourable to the consolidation of lordship than are those of the hamlet and the small township. Even here we may doubt whether the freedom of the ealdormen from reeveship, domestic ministry of the king, may not be the mark of an older elective status. In all the Heptarchic states, not only in the earliest phase of their development, but in later centuries, when political and social change has widened the gulf between the king, the aristocracy and the common freeman, the structure of law and the theory from which its procedure arises preserve traditions of an originally free community. The ceorl retains his public standing whether in the fyrd or the moot, the process of the courts by oath and ordeal assumes the

essential equality of all, however much that equality may be obscured by the duties laid upon lords and their right to act through
and plead for their men. Less evidently, in politics, but still without possibility of misunderstanding, the general theory of the folk
informs those institutions which are less judicial and provincial
than general and of the nation. The theory of witan gives a representative value to the deliberations of national assemblies, which is
no less real because it is not created by election or formal commission. Monarchy itself is still an ideal personification of racial unity
and common descent. These survive as ideas rather than as explicit
maxims expressed in positive institutions, but they are, nevertheless, constantly operative. The governing preconceptions of any
age, feudalism, democracy, or, as here, the principles of the folk,
are seldom susceptible of precise definition or uniform in their
effects, but they set the limits within which institutions may
evolve, and they are a constant check upon rapid change. These
general habits of mind and action, arising in the last analysis from
their root in the folk united by kin and descent, and as late as the
ninth century essentially unimpaired, will be seen to extend their
influence into that most decisively formative period, the age of
Ælfred's successors. Much of the work of that great succession of
kings lay in the piecemeal amendment of law in the light of a
new and more practical view of social relations and in the creation
of a monarchy which could rise above racial loyalties, but the
process of their work was slow and in part unconscious, the past
was never broken with, and much, almost everything that was
of value in the freedom and integrity of racial institutions was
carried forward to the account of the English state.

ii

THE EARLY KINGSHIPS

Except in Northumbria, where it borrowed Celtic forms, and *Pagan*
in Kent, where Frankish precedents were available, the resources *kingship*
of English monarchy may be traced in process of evolution from
very simple beginnings. Ideas which form the background of
Anglo-Saxon thought about kingship may be found elsewhere in
the common German and Scandinavian tradition. The law does

not originally come from the king, he has no subjects as the modern state understands them, and few vassals such as he will come to have under feudalism, though he already holds the centre of the stage, having to the casual view much the same universality of relationship to the community and much the same ceremonial primacy, attracting the same semi-religious awe. His most essential quality to his people is something more subtle than executive power. In all ages and countries the king is representative. There are times when the nation must think as one, feel as one, and find issue for its common emotion in symbolic act. At such moments the king is the supreme individual of the race, incarnating its will in ritual act, giving to its ideal the coherence and endurance of personality. Just within the shadow at which the records of English history fail stands the sacrificial king. The three high feasts of English heathendom were Winter's Day (November 7), Mid-winter's Day (December 25), and Summer's Day (May 7). Under the Christian dispensation "thrice a year the king wore his crown. At Easter he wore it at Winchester, at Pentecost at Westminster, and at Midwinter at Gloucester", and there was feasting and entertainment of the king's faithful men—his *hyred* or great household.[1] These, in the pagan North, were the great ceremonial feasts when the king sacrificed for the people, on Winter's Day for a good year, at Midwinter for good crops, and on Summer's Day for victory in battle. That is the first and oldest function of the Germanic king. As the representative of the nation, the descendant of the gods, and their most acceptable votary, he "made the year".

The magical elements in kingship were slowly exorcized by Christianity, but the king remained the focus of emotions which were fundamentally pagan, and in his person the proper virtues of a barbaric folk were seen to be exemplified and ennobled. In this also the king was the type of his people, that he drew to a head the warlike prowess in which the race felt itself to live most keenly. Courage was less a quality of the individual king than a function of the crown, and its wealth was a trust for the endowment of war. The king was the gold-giver,[2] the treasurer of heroes,[3] the

---

[1] Anglo-Saxon Chronicle, 1086E.
[2] Beowulf, 1170. Goldwine gumena.
[3] *Ibid.* 1047. Hordweard hæleþa.

patron of warriors.[1] To this contrast between the pagan and Christian ideals of kingship we must attribute the violent fluctuations of conduct and fortune which came upon the first Christian kings. For the weak, the conflict was too great. Under an apostate king the gods were estranged, every man's virtue was affronted, and the very course of nature turned unkind. Some, like Redwald of East Anglia,[2] sacrificed after their conversion as before. Many gave up the struggle and became Christian monks, or vanished upon pilgrimage. Some were killed by their subjects, like that Sigebert of the East Saxons whom his kindred slew "because he forgave his enemies".[3] As conversion became real, this religious *Christian* and representative quality was Christianized, and remained a *kingship* principal justification of kingship. Alcuin, writing at the end of the eighth century, could still say, "in the king's righteousness is the common weal, victory in war, mildness of the seasons, abundance of crops, freedom from pestilence. It is for the king to atone with God for his whole people."[4] Christianity, indeed, brought with it a tradition of sympathy of church and crown, in which the latter also was a divinely given authority. Gregory put before Æthelbert the example of Constantine,[5] and Vitalian saw Oswy's kingship as the pledge of his people's conversion.[6] However imperfectly such theories were understood, they foreshadowed a new relation between king and folk, and one which might come to transcend the small patriotism of the races. On the whole, however, the first effect of Christianity was to impoverish the prestige of the barbarian thrones, and it was slow to confer upon them any countervailing lustre. Prayers *pro regibus ac ducibus* were introduced only by the Council of Clovesho of 747, and after protest against the clergy's indifference to secular welfare.[7] The bishops pursued a sectional ecclesiastical interest, and some-

---

[1] Beowulf, 1960. Wigendra hleo.

[2] Bede, *Historia Ecclesiastica*, ii. 15.　　　　　　　[3] *Ibid.* iii. 22.

[4] Alcuin, Letter to King Æthelred, A.D. 793: *Pro totius gentis prosperitate Deum deprecari debet*: it is for him to beseech God for the welfare of the whole people. The Swedes sacrificed their king, Olaf, to Odin when his own sacrifices had failed, blaming him for a succession of years of bad harvest: Ynglinga Saga, xlvii.

[5] Bede, *Historia Ecclesiastica*, i. 32.

[6] *Ibid.* iii. 29: *Dedi te in foedus populi etc.*: I have given thee as a pledge to the people.

[7] Haddan and Stubbs, *Councils*, iii. 375.

times tried to stand neutral in national quarrels.[1] Throughout the seventh century no English king ventured to style himself *rex Dei gratia* in public documents,[2] and Theodore, himself archbishop "by Divine favour", withheld that title from the kings to whom he wrote.[3] It cannot have been easy to accord, or, indeed, to accept. The claim of royalty rested so plainly upon divine and racial descent. Nine generations carried the royal kin to Woden or Saxneat, and Bishop Daniel recalls how the English clung to their divine genealogies in the face of reason, and how much of their sense of the antiquity and legitimacy of their state was bound up with them.[4] Alcuin attributed the chaos into which the kingly power had fallen in his day to their disrepute: "scarce one of the ancient royal kindreds survives, and by as much as their lineage is uncertain, by so much is their power enfeebled".[5]

Limited scope of kingship

To be king, then, meant, first and above all, to embody religion and racial pride, to lead the nation in war and bear its person in peace. To turn from the king as representative to the theory and practice of government, which came in later times to be his proper function, is to find him a vastly shrunken figure. Hardly more than a first estate of the folk, he reproduced upon a higher level the status of the noble. His family had special standing as the cynecynn, and he, at its head, had mund and wer at a higher value than the eorl. We cannot say that there were no powers of kingship, but they were few, and thrust upon him by necessity. Acts which we should accept as proper to the crown the seventh-century king did as if unconscious of their implication, and explained them as outcomes of his personal rank and privilege. Subjects, for their part, sought his protection not because of his

[1] So the Bishop of London writes to Archbishop Berctwald in 705 regretting the war between Essex and Wessex on the ground that "ecclesiastics who live under the two governments become involved willingly or unwillingly in their dissensions".

[2] Ine, in the prologue to his laws, is made to speak *Dei gratia*, but the text is of Ælfred's day. In genuine charters no West Saxon or Kentish king made the claim before Egbert, and in Mercia it did not become usual until the middle of the eighth century. [3] Eddius, *Vita Wilfridi*, xliii.

[4] Daniel's letter to Boniface, A.D. 719–722. Haddan and Stubbs, *Councils*, i. 304.

[5] Alcuin, letter to Eanbald: *tanto incertiores sunt originis, quanto minores sunt fortitudinis.*

royal authority, but because his mund was more dangerous to break, and his protection stronger than that of any noble. Essentially they were not different. The law was not the king's law, but the folk's—folkright. It was administered in district courts which were folkmoots, and where the judges were the men of the countryside. Neither the king nor his officers had the power of deeming dooms, judgment, nor were the acts of violence which we count as crimes and punish as offences against the state— against the king—then so regarded. To kill a man, or to wound him, were primarily acts of private wrong. If the killer suffered death, it was at the hands of his victim's kin, by feud and not in punishment. If he preferred to pay, it was by way of ransom, to wipe out the wrong done, and to appease his enemies. The king's part in law was to follow up the breach of folkright, to pursue outlawry, and to put down violence when it became too strong for the neighbourhoods and kindreds to resist. It was an extra-judicial authority. As with some other Germanic peoples, there was a money payment for the king to take, the wite, but it was insignificant beside the bot or composition for blood, and its origin was certainly not penal.[1] Neither in theory nor in practice did the king judge. The peace, again, was not the king's. During their sessions the courts lay under their own peace, *methel-frith* or *moot-frith*,[2] and this is as near as we get to any public peace in

---

[1] There seem to have been three ways of regarding these public payments which accompanied the bot. The Franks exacted a sum (five-sixteenths of the blood-price) *pro fredo*, "for the frith", and may possibly have regarded it as compensation for breach of a national peace. No such notion prevailed in England. The Old Saxons exacted a sum *pro wargida*, a payment to the freemen of the court for their services as judges, and a second sum, *pro destrictione*, if they had to take action to enforce the court's judgment. After the Frankish conquest, however, the latter payment lapsed to the king if the action took place before a royal *missus* (*Capitulare Saxonicum*, 4). With the Welsh also the king took a third of every blood-price "because it is for him to enforce judgment where a kindred is too weak" (Laws of Howel the Good, v. 20b, 14. A: Ed. Wade-Evans). With the Bavarians (Lex Baiuwariorum. Textus Primus. ii. 15), the *judex* took a ninth from every composition for his services. From one of these principles the English wite must be derived, and not from any theory of punishment. If the term comes from the root of "witan", to know, to be wise (in law), and, therefore, capable of giving judgment, it was originally a perquisite of the freemen as judges. The choice of origin lies between the wargida and the mulct *pro districtione* of the Old Saxons. In either case it had lapsed to the king by the period of record.

[2] Æthelbert, 6.

early England. The country was full of legal sanctuaries, but they were the preserves of individuals. The king's peace was like other men's. It lay upon his palace, it was over his household, he could extend it to his friends, servants, and messengers.[1] A man in the safe-conduct of the king is said to bear the king's *hand-grith*.[2] We shall find the king's mund extended by analogy and fiction in later days, but in this first age its use is almost wholly private, and confined to its avowed purpose. Even this personal peace is extinguished when the king enters a subject's house. The guest, king though he be, has come under his host's mund, and the relation of subject to sovereign is reversed.[3]

Functions of the crown

If we seek for any foreshadowing of what the crown will come to be, it must be in such rough essays in action as the titular head of a nation and its strongest member will do inevitably at any time or place. He is the nation's and the law's defender and has often been chosen as the most warlike of his kin. His household of gesiths is a natural rallying point. He is the spokesman of his people, though he speaks with and from among the notables, who embody the wisdom of the folk, and who are called the wise men, the *seniores*, the witan. Crises of war and peace, the reception of the Christian faith, the choice between the Scottish and Roman communions, may turn largely on his word. Force was sometimes too strong for local power, and then the king must intervene. It was a threat held *in terrorem*, hardly more than a corollary of the king's headship in war.[4] These may seem substantial functions. They were enough to make the throne the focus of history. But there was lacking almost everything of that power of later monarchy which rests upon law and lawful obedience. If the king acted it was to impose a sentence which was not his own. The life of the countryside in its villages and halls went on without the king. He did not make its law, he was only remotely its protector. What stability it had, came from its own specific gravity, the

[1] Pax (Liebermann, *Gesetze*, p. 390). Thus far shall be the king's grith from his burh-gate where he resides, in all four directions: three miles and three furlongs and three lineal acres and nine feet and nine inches and nine barley-corns.

[2] Eadweard and Guthrum, i.   [3] Æthelbert, 3.

[4] Ælfred, 42. 3. If he has sufficient force a man must bring one who has wronged him to court himself; if he has not, he may appeal to the ealdorman, and, if he will not act, to the king.

weight of innumerable immunities of ceorl and eorl guarded by peace which custom held inviolate. No tie bound the multitude of individuals to their king: rather, they were tied in the network of natural kinship and the loyalties and legal obligations of neighbourhood. Indeed, here lay such strength as the barbarian throne possessed, for upon it were projected the loyalties which made the common life stable. Bound in kindred, the folk saw in their king the purest and most jealously recorded ancestry of their race. Religious in every act of life, they had in him the eldest descendant of the gods. Warlike by instinct, they looked to him to exemplify and sustain the prowess of the nation. In its infancy as a principle of state, the throne yet answered to the religious and emotional needs of the community.

Such kingship could be strong, and the earliest dynasties seem *Growth of* to have maintained an unbroken succession. But its weakness was *theory and* that it rested on the past, upon paganism and the tribal com- *title of* munity. It was hard to extend these kingdoms which had their *kingship* roots in heathendom. The racial state was their natural scope, and rule over an alien kin could only be maintained by force.[1] The folkright of one nation was invalid with the others.[2] Æthelbert, Eadwin, and a few more, acquired a passing supremacy, and were called Bretwealdas, perhaps with some memory of Rome, but such power lasted only so long as they were victorious. The first monarchy to outgrow racialism to some degree arose in Mercia. Æthelbald in 716 succeeded to some sort of hegemony based upon the military strength of Penda and Wulfhere, and, in spite of defeats at the hands of Wessex, he and his successors maintained it, and gave it a fuller meaning. Æthelbald is not only the first king to incorporate the lordship of alien races into his title, claiming to be king "not only of the Mercians, but of those neighbouring peoples over whom God has set me",[3] but he is also the first to

[1] Cf. the story of the monks of Bardney, who refused to give burial to the body of Oswald of Northumbria "although they knew him to be a saint, because he, though of another nation by birth, had acquired the kingdom over them. So they pursued him even after his death with lasting hate" (Bede, *Historia Ecclesiastica*, iii. 11).

[2] Thus the oath, the crux of every legal suit, was invalid as between Welsh and English except by agreement. Ordinance Respecting the Dunsœtas, 2. 1.

[3] W. de Gray Birch, *Cartularium Saxonicum*, 181 (A.D. 755-757).

sign "by divine dispensation": he claims an *imperium divino suffragio fultus*, and once writes himself *rex Brittaniae*.[1] Æthelbald's was a new dynasty, not descended from Penda, and Bede, writing in 731, shows him established over all England south of the Humber except Kent, and of part of Wales. Such a leadership, almost a century old at his death, needed a fuller title than king of the Mercians. Intermittently Offa used the new titles, and added a further definition of what was coming to be a stable supremacy. He is the first to sink the identities of the southern English in a common *Regnum Anglorum*.[2] In the year 774, when, at Otford, he had subdued the Kentings, his charters adopt a form which must have been designed to exalt the Christian right of conquest over the right of native kings.[3] To the Pope and the Emperor he is preëminently *Rex Anglorum*, and to his own people *rex et decus Britanniae*.[4]

Offa   It is with Offa that the change in claim and title is first translated into a measure of fact. The Bretwealdarship was being outgrown. In the past the component peoples of that vague supremacy had kept their native dynasties and broken away when it suited them to do so. Offa was clearly driving towards a lasting kingdom of the English. The kings of the Hwiccas had already become *reguli* under Æthelbald.[5] Offa killed or dethroned those of the East Angles and Kentings, and absorbed their peoples into his own kingdom. The native dynasty of the South Saxons disappeared at this time also. Where he did not govern he interfered with government. The under-kings accepted the position of gesiths under him,[6] and he denied them the right of granting land by charter without his sanction,[7] while he himself used that right as a means to further Mercian influence and distributed the lands of Kent and the Mercians at his will. The halving of the see of Canterbury, and the

---

1 W. de Gray Birch, *Cartularium Saxonicum*, 155.
2 *Ibid.* 213 (A.D. 774) and 265 (A.D. 793).
3 *Ibid.* 213, 214 (A.D. 774): *In nomine Jhesu Christi . . . per quem reges regnunt et dividunt regna terrarum. Sicut dispensator universae terrae mihi distribuit . . . ego Offa Rex Anglorum dabo et concedo*: in the name of Christ Jesus . . . through Whom Kings rule and divide the nations of the world. As the Bestower of all lands has given to me . . . so I, Offa King of the Angles, give and grant.
4 J. M. Kemble, *Codex Diplomaticus*, 1020.
5 *Ibid.* 154: *Ic Aldred Wigracestres undercining*; cf. also Alcuin's letter to Offa.
6 This link had already been forged under Æthelbald. J. M. Kemble, *Codex Diplomaticus*, 80.   7 *Ibid.* 93, 97, 125.

establishment of a Mercian archbishopric of Lichfield, was not only an act of Mercian patriotism but a crippling blow to the Augustinian tradition upon which the sanctity of the heptarchic crowns had come to rest.[1] How great had been the power behind this breach with the old order the Pope's fear of dethronement through the influence of Offa[2] is witness, and in his successor's reign the prestige of Canterbury was so far impaired as to make a central see of London a conceivable alternative.[3]

The death of Offa stopped that normal development of a general English crown and title in which enlightened contemporaries had placed their faith.[4] Wessex had never lost her kingship, and Offa's successors sign as kings of the Mercians and Kentings, or maintain a Kentish kingdom for a Mercian prince until they lose their power at Ellendune. Thenceforward, they sign as kings of Mercia only, though Essex seems to have remained within their system. The conquests of Egbert were only effective south of the Thames, and, though he seems to have revived the *Regnum Anglorum* of Offa in his last years[5] after his nominal conquest of the North, his successors ruled only in the South, and, like the Mercians, made Kent an autonomous appanage of the Saxon house.[6] For the time being, indeed, the rise of Wessex hardened the political distinctions between the three principal states. What consolidation there was took place within the southern kingdom,[7] where the East Saxons, Kentings, South Saxons, and Surrey were thrown to- *Rise of West Saxon monarchy*

[1] The target which Offa was attacking appears in Alcuin's letter to the Kentings (A.D. 797): *vos vero principium salutis Anglorum, initium prosperitatis, portus intrantium, triumphi laus, sapientiæ origo, et a vobis Imperii potestas prius processit, et fidei catholicae origo exorta est*: for you are the source of the salvation of the Angles, the spring of their prosperity, a gateway for those who would enter, their boast, and the beginning of wisdom. From you their empire first came and the Catholic faith had birth.

[2] Haddan and Stubbs, *Councils and Ecclesiastical Documents*, iii. 440: letter of Adrian I to Charles.

[3] *Ibid*. iii. 521-525: letter of Cenwulf to Leo III.

[4] Cf. Alcuin's letter to Ecgfrith, Offa's destined successor, foretelling his reign *cunctis Anglorum populis prodesse in prosperitate*: to be for the prosperity of all the peoples of the Angles.

[5] J. M. Kemble, *Codex Diplomaticus*, 223.

[6] *Ibid*. 269.

[7] *Ibid*. 241: *Æthelwulf rex Occidentalium Saxonum, Centuriorum, nec non cunctibus (aus)trali populi*: Æthelwulf, king of the West Saxons, the Kentings, and of all the southern peoples. *Ibid*. 254: *Æðelwulf rex Australium populorum*: Æthelwulf, king of the southern peoples.

gether into a composite kingdom, which had a fleeting existence as the Eastrige,[1] served for a throne for the heir of Wessex until his succession, and may have done something to extinguish the sparks of Kentish and East Saxon nationalism. With the conquests of Ælfred's later years, we come to a revival of the English title, which, after various experiments, *Rex Saxonum, Rex Anglorum, Rex Anglorum et Saxonum*,[2] and the like, expands into the imperial roll of titles of his successors, kings of Britain.

Ælfred   The reign of Ælfred may be taken as a stage upon the path of kingship which now rose again after the eclipse of Mercia. It is the last reign of that tetrarchy which had grown out of the ruin of Offa's *Regnum Anglorum*, but its later years developed a power which was to carry Ælfred's successors to a general monarchy of Britain, and to a kingship new in kind. Perhaps no stronger than Offa's Bretwealdership, it had a greater grace and legitimacy. In the strength of Offa there was a relic of pagan violence.[3] He was a robber of monasteries, and popular belief canonized his victims.[4] In Ælfred the ideal of Christian kingship reached its fullness. Under him the most deeply felt attributes of the folk, their law and their descent, sought to justify themselves to the Christian world. Ælfred's laws are prefaced by the Mosaic law of Exodus, so that English custom, abandoning its barbarian tradition, may claim a place as a local variant of a law of Christendom. The genealogy of the royal kin,[5] though still advanced to prove the right of a king "whose fathers' kin goeth unto Cerdic", is Christianized. Woden, now no more than a royal ancestor, descends from Geat, "who some say was born in the Ark", and so, through the nine patriarchs, from Adam. The Ælfredian genealogies of the Chronicle and of Asser's Life are still apologies for the crown's right, and now borrow the ancestry of the Danish Scyldings to attract the loyalty of the Danes, but their pagan element is consciously rejected. They are the logical conclusion of the claim of English kings to rule "by Divine permission", and to stand in the

---

[1] Anglo-Saxon Chronicle, 836A.

[2] J. M. Kemble, *Codex Diplomaticus*, 324, 1069, etc. The charters of this reign are rarely of the first authority.

[3] Letter of Alcuin to Osbert: *pro confirmatione regni multum sanguinem effudit*: he shed much blood to fortify his kingdom.

[4] As it did Æthelbert of East Anglia, whom he had executed.

[5] Anglo-Saxon Chronicle, 855A.

succession of Old Testament kingship. Such changes in style and title, and in the historical origin which the crown imagined for itself, point to new claims made by the king upon the people. Kingship has found its place in the Christian hierarchy, a temporal vicariate of God, and imposes ties and loyalties stronger and more precise than those of paganism.

The feeling that the king was natural lord of all Englishmen *The king* was of slow growth in England, and before the Norman Conquest *as lord* not deeply held. Many had sought the king's mund, but great subjects might rival him in this. King Ecgfrith's quarrel with Wilfred was in part due to his jealousy of the bishop's following,[1] which was greater than his own. It is true that from the eighth century certain official relations have a colour of vassalage. Offa treated his under-kings as his *comites*. But this may have been by commendation, and the Ælfredian Chronicle is the first document which identifies the preëminence of the king with that of a lord over the men within his mund. Under the year 823 it is said that, for fear of the Mercians, the East Anglian king and his people sought King Egbert "to frith and to mundbora", and, whatever we may make of this cast backward over seventy years of tradition, the phrase was used of the king's power in Ælfred's own day, and in those of his successors.[2]

How far the lordship of the king over all the folk can be pressed is doubtful. The most generalized expression of a relation which depended upon interest and inclination as much as upon formal undertaking, it was, for that very reason, the least real, and might be forgotten in the special loyalty which bound the commended men to their lords. It was a natural term for the king's preëminence in an age which knew only the tie of blood and the tie of lordship, but where the hold-oath was widely sworn to the king it was by

[1] Eddius, *Vita Wilfridi*, xxiv.

[2] Asser, *De Rebus Gestis*, 80: *Reges Gwent . . . suapte eundem expetivere regem, ut dominum et defensionem ab eo pro inimicis suis haberent*: the kings of Gwent of their own free will sought the king as lord and mundbora against their enemies. So, Anglo-Saxon Chronicle, 774E. The Northumbrians dethrone Ælfred and take Æthelred, son of Moll, *to hlaforde*. Æthelred, who was more than ealdorman and less than king of Mercia, calls himself *Mircena hlaforde* (J. M. Kemble, *Codex Diplomaticus*, 339).

the massed assembly of the moots, and it might be a feeble counter to the personal contract between individual lord and man. Perhaps a half-century after Ælfred's death, words are ascribed to a king which show that the lordship of the crown had not yet created a community of unquestioning subjects: "think, ye who are my men, how unfitting it were if I should have the name of king and not the power: or what shall a man desire for his lord if not due authority?"[1]

Though the material strength of Offa's reign was regained by Ælfred, the functions of the crown were still few and unspecialized. The king summoned and dismissed the fyrd and such a king as Ælfred was the driving force of national defence. The *trinoda necessitas*—fyrd-service, burh- and bridge-building—though an ancient duty of all freemen, was at his disposal, and in and after his day a period of constant war exposed the local authorities to closer control in such matters than they had experienced before.[2]

Resources of the crown

But the activity even of an Ælfred was limited not only by habit but by lack of resources. There was as yet no taxation, and, unlike some other nations, Wessex may have left its kings entirely to the renders of royal estates and the profits of the courts.[3] Minor members of the royal family were ready to pool their lands and forgo their immediate inheritance in the interest of the ruling head of the house,[4] but, beyond narrow limits, the revenue was inexpansive, and yet Ælfred's use of it shows that it was more than sufficient for the range of function that he could conceive as natural to the crown. Yearly, half the king's revenue went to "God and the Church", and of this a quarter was given to the poor in alms, another quarter to his two foundations of Athelney and Shaftsbury, and the same as gifts to the king's school and to monasteries throughout his kingdom and abroad. The half kept

[1] Appendix to Ælfred and Guthrum's Peace (A.D. 940–956?).

[2] Asser, *De Rebus Gestis*, 91.

[3] Maitland's attempt (*Domesday Book and Beyond*, pp. 235-239) to prove that the West Saxon kings had a right of farm over their subjects' lands as well as their own turns mainly upon an interpretation of II Cnut, 69. 1 (wrongly quoted as II Cnut, 62), which seems unjustified. Such a right existed in Mercia. W. de Gray Birch, *Cartularium Saxonicum*, 366. Further enquiry may reveal it in Wessex, but it has not done so at present.

[4] Cf. Ælfred's own account of his and his brothers' resignation of their inheritance in favour of King Æthelbert (J. M. Kemble, *Codex Diplomaticus*, 314).

for secular purposes was divided equally between the pay and upkeep of his military attendants and thegns, the pay of native and foreign craftsmen, and gifts to foreign guests.[1] Charity, hospitality, the reconstruction of the various *cynges tuns*, and their rebuilding in more suitable sites, exhausted the practical ends of royal expenditure. Ælfred appears less as a king than as a great country gentleman, drawing his rents from his estates and spending them magnificently upon good works and a great household.

This is, perhaps, the most simple proof of the extent to which *The king* the latent potentialities of kingship remained unrealized at the end *and the* of the ninth century, and a like unconsciousness kept the crown *law* from intervening directly in law. The king is claiming to be mundbora to his folk. In so far as this is more than a phrase, it means that he will see that they are not denied the justice that is due to them, that folkright shall prevail over force and fraud. As mundbora the king will intervene when a plaintiff has been denied justice three times at home, and will deal with unjust reeves, and put down overmighty kindreds who deny right to their neighbours. On the basis of this mundbyrdnis the crown will intervene more and more during the next 150 years in the detailed working of law, will put an increasing number of offences under its personal ban and make them pleas of the king, and will lend its personal guarantee to the peace of the realm. But in the time of Ælfred these practical applications were not yet envisaged. Such legal authority as Ælfred has still comes from his private status even though in the earliest records the privilege to which it gave rise was tentatively applied to public ends by the use of the "king's wite". The highest wite for any offence which did not touch the king's person was sixty shillings (the "full wite" of Ine, 43), while any cause which did incurred the special king's wite of a hundred and twenty shillings.[2] This wite is variously explained. Originally his mundbryce,[3] incurred only by fighting in his presence or attacking persons in his special peace,[4] it defended no more than his private quality. Progress towards a fuller concept was made by the gradual realization of new

[1] Asser, *De Rebus Gestis*, 102.

[2] VIII Æthelred, 5. 1.

[3] Æthelbert, 3. The fifty-shilling king's mundbryce of Kent is the equivalent of the hundred-and-twenty-shilling wite of Wessex.

[4] Ine, 45.

matters in which the king's direct concern might be presumed, and where aggression might be said to violate his mund. The latter came to be extended over the church and churchmen. The bishop has the king's mundbryce,[1] fighting in a minster and false oath before a bishop come to bear the hundred-and-twenty-shilling wite.[2] The application of the mund to secular affairs may, perhaps, be seen in the burh-bryce for violence done within a king's burh,[3] in the fyrd-wite of a hundred and twenty shillings,[4] and—the furthest extension of the mund in Ine's reign —the same fine for gathering a host for unlawful purposes.[5] This principle was recognized in Ælfred's laws, but with little development. The greatest change was the increase from a hundred and twenty to three hundred Wessex shillings for the king's mundbryce.[6] But the king's protection was extended to no new field of law. There had been little progress. In one clause only do we see a new application of the king's responsibility for public order: fighting in the moot is construed as a violation of the king's mund.

Summary   A summary of the position of monarchy in the reign of Ælfred would show it balanced between two ages. It is thoroughly Christianized and can claim obedience as the temporal vicariate of God. It has extended beyond its racial home in Wessex, and there is no great likelihood of the revival of Mercia or the smaller kingdoms of the South. It is making some claim to a lordship over its subjects akin to that of a lord over his commended men. In law the king is thought of as mundbora of the nation, and, as such, charged to see that no man's rights are infringed and that the presiding officers of the moots know the law and interpret it justly. All this constitutes a great advance upon the limited, tribal, and half-pagan monarchy of the seventh century, and is a sufficient achievement for two hundred years, but it is rather the theory and potentiality of a new monarchy than its realization. Particularly is this so in law. The mundbora is the advocate of his men and will see that they are accorded their full legal right, but only in the last recourse.[7] There is as yet little notion of going beyond this to a special king's law to cover the more dangerous offences, and

[1] Wihtraed, 2.   [2] Ine, 13.   [3] *Ibid*. 45.
[4] *Ibid*. 51.   [5] *Ibid*. 14.   [6] Ælfred, 3.
[7] *Ibid*. 42. In the first instance the plaintiff is expected to besiege his adversary in his house and bring him to court. If his strength is insufficient he may appeal to the ealdorman to do so. If he fails him the king will act.

there are, perhaps, no true king's pleas. The mundbora will protect the individual's peace if it is infringed and he can get no redress, but there is no peace of the realm. The king cannot tax or legislate, he has no feudal right in the soil, no standing army. Under his mundbyrdnis the provinces live by their own custom in their own moots, members of the law of the West Saxons or Mercians far more truly than they are subjects of an English king. The creation of an English nation, of a crown and subjects, of a general peace, of a king's law, is a work of Ælfred's successors of which his own reign gives only the promise and which even they did not bring to completion.

II

FROM THE REIGN OF ÆLFRED TO THE NORMAN CONQUEST

i

THE FOLK ORGANIZED BY TERRITORIAL NEIGHBOURHOOD
AND LORDSHIP

Introductory WE may characterize the phase of English society seen in the codes of the seventh century as that in which the primitive organization of the folk is in process of invasion by the forces of lordship and Christianity, but has already shown that it will succeed in incorporating them both upon its own terms and will hand on its own essential principles unchanged. Of the two centuries from the reign of Ine to that of Ælfred little is known. The code of Offa has been lost, the church has declined from that power of orderly thinking which produced the Penitentials of Theodore and Bede, and we have only about fifty charters, genuine or in plausible copies. But from the time of Ælfred there begins a richer documentation, and almost every reign has left legal matter of importance. When we examine the first great document presented to us after the two centuries which alone deserve the name of the Dark Ages, we are conscious that the eclipse of learning has had a conservative effect. It is in the days of Ælfred's descendants that the great changes begin, for his own code repeats much of the code of Ine or supplements it with matter of the same archaic type.[1] There is no conscious remodelling of institutions such as was made by Charlemagne, and what change in private relations there has been has taken place unrecognized by, and here and there in avowed conflict with, public law. We know from other sources that society was in rapid evolution, and that Wessex was in the first

---

[1] Ælfred, Prologue: "I did not dare to set much of my own in writing . . . but what I found of Ine my kinsman, or of Offa the Mercian king's, or of Æthelbert's . . . of that I gathered such as seemed most just".

stages of advance towards vital change. There, and apparently in Mercia also, the position of the common freeman had been decisively worsened, for, while dependence had been sporadic under Ine, it had come to be the rule under Ælfred, and in social estimation the ceorl was now no more than equivalent with the Danish freedman.[1] His legal status was, however, still that of the free twyhynd ceorl of the past[2] and he retained his legal safeguards[3] and took an active part in the moots. Written law, and the law practised in the courts, still assumed the old dualism of eorl and ceorl, and continued to do so for another century. It would, indeed, be difficult to point to any section of the law in which, after a lapse of two centuries, the newer tendencies of Ine's reign were explicitly advanced by Ælfred, save for a sharpening of the sanctity of lordship and of the heinousness of conspiracy against it.[4] Public law still conformed to the original structure of the folk.

In spite of this legal conservatism in the Ælfredian laws, the country was upon the verge of one of the most profoundly revolutionary periods of its history, that in which the essentials of the territorial state were laid down and kingship first realized its trust of government and began to equip itself with powers to carry it out. Among these vital changes which were to occupy the years between 900 and 1066, the most profound of all, one whose effects are even now not exhausted, was the conversion of the older organization by kindreds into that matrix of the medieval and modern society, the territorial community.

The territorializing of all relations of life, beginning in the *Territorializing of legal process* sphere of private law and spreading outwards to all the institutions of state, is first to be traced in the procedure of the courts, and in the rights and obligations of the individual. The kindred did three things for its members. It made them oath-worthy and law-worthy: it made their oath valid by swearing a confirmatory oath: it acted as bohr or surety that they should stand to judgment. All

----

[1] Ælfred and Guthrum's Peace, 2.

[2] Ælfred, 39, 40, 44-77. The twyhynd man is still the typical freeman of the community.

[3] *Ibid.* 10, 11, 18. 1, 26, 29, 35, 39.

[4] The compassing of a lord's death is punished by death and forfeiture upon the analogy that homicide within the kin is unamendable.

three of these sanctions were needed in combination to achieve a legal standing for the individual and to constitute the multitude of individuals into a society. It is for this reason, because the legal virtue and status of each of its members was a creation of the solidarity of the kindred, that we say that English society was in the beginning based upon the tie of blood. But, with the lapse of time, mainly during the two centuries with which we have now to deal, each of these functions was transferred from the kindred of the individual to his neighbours, at first to those who in a general way lived near and knew him, and later to organized neighbourhoods, townships, titheings, and hundreds, which arose in response to the new stress laid upon the tie of vicinity and the need to give it territorial definition. This revolution of the tenth and eleventh centuries, silent and unconscious, was perhaps the most deeply formative change of life that the English people ever experienced, for upon the community which it brought into being arose the national state.

Terri-
torializing
of compur-
gation
Compurgation, arising in the oldest stratum of Teutonic law, that dealing with bodily wrongs such as led to the feud, was designed to force upon a kindred which was jointly responsible with its offending member the choice of telling the truth or affronting the gods, and so the principal's relations were made his oath-helpers with intention. But this is an archaic notion. In the laws of Ine there is already a hint of a more sceptical purpose, that of securing an oath which shall be independent of bias. A king's thegn is to be included among the oath-helpers of a man rebutting a charge of homicide.[1] The rise of other fields of law by the side of this primitive law of violence, creating new offences and calling for new expedients, strengthened this new demand, and the law of theft—at least in the elaborate form it took in the tenth century a new law—opened the way for new kinds of oath. Theft, a lonely and secret business, might take a man beyond the knowledge of his family;[2] it did not arouse the feud; and upon charges of theft the oath of the kindred, if it ever had been exacted, was then no longer enforced. It sufficed if the accused could induce men of his village to swear with him.[3] By the reign of Eadward the Elder a further step has been taken towards independent testimony. On a charge of theft a man may be forced to put himself

[1] Ine, 54.   [2] *Ibid.* 7. 1.   [3] I Eadward, 1. 4.

on the oath of compurgators nominated for him by the court from among his fellow villagers[1] or from within the administration in which he dwells.[2] No doubt by attraction, procedure in actions for property is moving in the same direction. By I Eadward, 1. 3 a man who defends his property may find his own oath-helpers if he can: in the next reign he must defend it by independent men chosen for him.[3] The crown also, with its absorbing preoccupation with the problem of the peace, uses this procedure in offences against the king's *grith*,[4] and for greater certainty a register of all lawful men is set up and from these the parties must choose their oath-helpers.[5] At last, accused of default from fyrd and borough service, a man clears himself by compurgation of his titheing.[6] The oath of defence of the Northumbrian thegn of the tenth century is an epitome of all the stages through which the practice of compurgation has passed.[7] He must clear himself with three groups of twelve, one of his own kindred, one chosen by himself from the open court, one chosen by the court for him. In this last stage of its evolution the oath of independent men must have given the same general safeguard of impartiality as the verdict of a jury, though it was still sworn to afforce the oath of the principal, and not to specific fact. In the eleventh century the notion of peerage, which is to play so great a part in the evolution of the jury, has already made its appearance. The landowner, the cleric, and the ceorl, will alike be required, perhaps will demand, to clear themselves by the oath of their equals, and the Norman will speak, in a parallel though distinct sense, of peers of a tenure.[8]

The kindred also ceases to be the sanction by which the mere *Terri-* capacity to enjoy the protection or share in the processes of the *torializing of war-* law is obtained. A full kindred once made a man oath-worthy and *ranty* law-worthy. The lord as mundbora was allowed to replace the deficiency of the kin, and in Æthelred's reign he was still guarantor

---

[1] The *gecorene að*, or oath chosen by the court.

[2] II Cnut, 22.   [3] II Æthelstan, 9.

[4] An oath of 36 compurgators, "and the reeve shall choose the oath". III Æthelred, 13.

[5] V Æthelstan, 1. 5.

[6] Consiliatio Cnuti, ĭi. 19. 2A: *Et si negat . . . ex propria sua decimatione secum juraturos assumet.*

[7] Northumbrian Priest's Law, 51.

[8] Domesday Book, i. 374A: *Willelmus de Perci advocat pares suos in testimonium quod . . . fuit ipse saisitus de Boditone.*

of his men's lawfulness.[1] But in the reign of Cnut that function also is found to have been placed upon the same territorial basis as compurgation. To "be worthy of his law and his wer", to have the right to make oath with legal effect, and receive compensation if successful, every freeman over twelve years of age must be "brought into hundred and into titheing", that is to say, he must be sworn a member of the titheing or township in which he lives;[2] the right of legal action and status has come to depend upon settlement. There has been much debate as to how far this responsibility of the titheing was carried. It appears first in the reign of Æthelstan as a voluntary association for legal help, but already territorialized.[3] By the reign of Henry I it has come to be responsible for the *frith-borh* or frankpledge, a mutual obligation of neighbours which bound the township to report to the hundred court all crime within its bounds, and to produce the criminal for judgment, in short, to act in that capacity of pledge or bohr in which lords had been allowed to act in the past, and for which men ·of doubtful reputation could once produce *festermen* or sworn sureties from among their neighbours.[4] It has been doubted whether the titheing was charged with the frankpledge before the Conquest, and there can be no certain answer. There was, no doubt, a period of transition during which all freemen derived their lawfulness from their titheing membership, yet had to provide a further guarantee of good behaviour by inducing a lord to stand pledge for them, or by arranging mutual surety privately with their neighbours. It is a question whether the transition was already completed by the reign of Cnut,[5] but the distinction is a very fine

---

[1] I Æthelred, 1. 2-4.
[2] II Cnut, 20.
[3] VI Æthelstan.
[4] Northumbrian Priest's Law, 2. 3.
[5] The problem turns upon a phrase of Cnut's ordinance (II Cnut, 20), which is and must remain ambiguous. Men are to be "brought into titheing and hundred", if they wish to be oath-worthy and law-worthy, but also in the following clause they are to be "brought into hundred and into bohr". Is it intended that, having made their legal standing valid by membership of a titheing, they are further to be placed in pledge by some lord or man of standing, or is the repetition no more than a pleonasm, bohr amplifying titheing and explaining its function? The Instituta Cnuti of the early twelfth century, translating this passage, assumes the latter, and thus betrays its opinion that the frankpledge was already the business of the titheings in the reign of Cnut. Lords of franchises of the thirteenth century occasionally claim that they hold the right of view of frankpledge *ex conquestu Angliae.* Cf. *Placita de Quo Warranto,* pp. 254, 721, etc.

one. The step from being guarantor of a man's legal standing to being responsible for the use he makes of it is easily taken: we know that lords had the option of forcing their men to find themselves sureties from among their fellows, and we must suppose that the hundred reeves might do the same. With the authorities, royal and private, imposing mutual surety upon a populace which was already organized by titheings, the titheing would soon become the normal form of frith-borh without any positive enactment. In making itself guarantor for the lawfulness of its members, the titheing had made it certain that it would become the vehicle of the frankpledge. The change from personal to territorial organization was already irrevocably made.

In all this we see the kindred organization of the past melting as law grows more elaborate and develops new needs and force and fraud come to be recognized as dangers to the community at large. The neighbourhood takes over the task of restraining them in hundred and titheing, in part at its own will and in part by national enactment. The principals in court actions now establish their oath not by the warranty of their kin, but by the impartial voice of the countryside. But the composition of the courts was affected only slowly by these changes. They remained folkmoots. The countrysides flocked into them as before, though now in their territorial grouping of the titheings where before they stood in their kindreds. The virtue and obligations of the individual juridically regarded, the *legalis homo*, were unchanged. The procedure moved through the same routine of oath and ordeal and exacted the same standard of integrity, though neighbourhood was now its basis. In short the English legal system had been individualized and territorialized, had taken the great step from the maegth to the community of the land, but had retained the vitality of its principles and continued to place the same political and judicial requirements upon its folk. In this sense, and it is the deepest sense of all, the community of medieval and modern England draws its tradition from a Saxon past.

But, though these essentials remained, there had been a subtle but radical change in the theory of legal administration, and this came in time to be reflected in the structure and practice of the

Effect upon the composition of moots

courts. As long as their sole duty was to set hostile kindreds at one, the impulse was towards full courts to which all freemen came. The kindreds with all their members were the natural components of the moots. But as these faded out of procedure the way was open to adjustments which might lessen the burden of attendance and make for efficiency. The courts were now dealing with individuals, and with titheings or townships which lent themselves to representation. Moreover, as we shall see later, though the old justice of tort between parties was still being judged, it had been supplemented by a new field of law which was not tied by the old rules. In this fresh matter the crown was asserting responsibility with an especial interest in the peace and in those kinds of theft which were in themselves violent or gave rise to disorder. In this the crown's interest was to secure intelligent and impartial witness, and its instinct was to deal not with masses but with selected individuals. Thus, though the theory and basis of the courts remained popular, their practice tended to become less so, and active participation was not so

Aristocracy in the moots

universal as it had been in the past. In time a legal artistocracy emerged and partially monopolized the active work of judgment and witness. Asser could still refer to the "judgment of eorl and ceorl" in the folkmoots, but by the Confessor's reign the latter's voice was of doubtful value.[1] We have seen how the courts of Æthelstan were constrained to confine the function of witness to a panel of "unlying men", and throughout the ensuing century the references to these legal worthies thicken. The *seniores*, the senior men of the court, the senior thegns,[2] are clearly coming to be relied upon for all processes of court where independence of word and judgment is needed. Æthelred, if I read the text rightly, takes an oath of twelve thegns to pledge a whole moot to just judgment.[3] Judgment by twelve judices seems to have been wide-

[1] William de Chernet claims this land . . . and adduces witness from among the wisest and most substantial (*de melioribus et antiquis*) men of the whole county and hundred. And Picot brings against them testimony from the villeins and obscure people and reeves (*de villanis et vili plebe et de prepositis*) who offer to make proof by oath or ordeal (*per sacramentum aut per dei judicium*): Domesday Book, i. 44B.

[2] III Æthelred, 3. 1.

[3] *Loc. cit.* Reading, 3. 1. with the previous clauses, this now seems to me the best explanation of the yldestan XII pegnas. It is, of course, true that the enactment is for a Danish administration where one might expect to find lawmen.

spread in Northumbria and in certain borough courts. The thegns of the county have by the time of the Conquest come to be synonymous with the county court in many Wessex shires.[1]

Later evidence, moreover, leads us to suspect that the number of suitors to the moots was in process of reduction not because of any shadow upon the free right of the countryside, but because a more complex law, and perhaps a denser population, was making necessary a kind of court less unwieldy than the old folkmoot. The shiremoot met twice a year in the tenth century,[2] the hundred every month.[3] By the twelfth century a readjustment has taken place, which, while it does not impair the standing of the common folk in the courts, yet relieves them of the burden of constant attendance. Twice a year courts are held to which the suit of all freemen is obligatory[4]—and in this sense those whom the law calls villeins are free—but they are courts of administration and not of judgment. In them the view of frankpledge is held, new members are sworn into titheing, the hundred hears any charge the sheriff's officers may have in hand from the king, and in later days swears fealty if ordered so to do. These biennial courts are called Lawdays of the Hundred, and attendance is said to be *per omnia capita*.[4] The London lawday appears as early as the reign of Henry I, and its name of Folkmoot points to its descent from the old full court of Saxon times. After the rise of the lawdays, judgment, on the contrary, no longer involves the common suit of the countryside. It is done not monthly, but in courts meeting, at intervals which have given their name to the jurisdiction, *De Tribus Septimanis in Tres Septimanas*, and to them the obligation of common suit is recognized, but exercised by representation only. The titheings appear by their headmen and four companions,[5] who present all causes within the jurisdiction of the court, and produce accused persons, and by this suit their constituents of the titheings are free, except such as are principals or witnesses in any suit. This is the basis of the legal system of the Middle Ages in shire and hundred, and though, as with the frankpledge itself, we may question whether the adjustment was made in Saxon or in

Narrowing of suit to shire and hundred

---

[1] J. M. Kemble, *Codex Diplomaticus*, 755, gives a good account of the leaders of the shiremoot of Hereford in Cnut's reign.

[2] III Edgar, 5. 1.   [3] I Edgar, 1.

[4] Leges Henrici Primi, 8.   [5] *Ibid.* 7. 7.

Norman times, the distinction is academic rather than historical. The institution of the titheing, not the refinement of its use, marks the territorializing of English country life.

Franchise jurisdiction

The Saxon king had no jurisdiction like that of the feudal lord to give his men. He could give his wites and withdraw his reeve, and nothing more. Even direct loss of legal administration, the passing of the men of the folkmoots into franchise courts, can be proved to have been in progress no earlier than the eleventh century and may fairly be conjectured of the tenth; before that it cannot be proved, nor is it, indeed, probable.

Clause 50 of Ine's code, which speaks of the gesith who "acts as intermediary for his man with—*þingað wið*—the king or a king's ealdorman or with his own lord", and, in so doing, loses his claim to the wite which will follow a condemnation, has been believed to refer to private jurisdiction. The lord in question, it has been thought, must have a court, since he is in a position to accord or withhold the profits of judgment. It is certain, however, that no unequivocal proof can be extracted from this provision.

Seventh-century evidence

The subject of the clause may be representing his dependant's innocence through his own lord, obtaining the latter's support in a court of king or ealdorman where all three, the gesith, his lord, and his man, are justiciable. The practice described—*þingan for his man*—is that of adopting the cause of a dependant as one's own and pleading it *in propria persona* in the courts,[1] of becoming his *forespreoca*, a general obligation of lordship throughout the Teutonic and Scandinavian North, and one which might easily be transferred from the gesith to a noble even better skilled and of greater influence to secure the small man's right than would be the gesith himself. On the other hand, the clause shows that the practice of according to a lord the profits of the justice done upon his men already prevails. The ground of this resignation of the wite to the lord is not entirely clear. In all probability it is done on the assumption that he produces his man for judgment, and so relieves the king and his reeves of that function by which the monarch earns the profits of justice, the function which is the justification of all money penalties in this age when the theory of crime does not yet exist. The gesith probably loses these wites because by his office he is, like the thegn of later days, under a

[1] Cf. p. 15 *supra*, note 7.

special obligation to the king to maintain order within his sphere of influence. He is the king's minister and representative. The wites are part of the privilege granted by charter from a very early date, and are especially freely conferred in the eighth century, where they appear as wites,[1] or *witerædden*[2]—the same term as is used in clause 50 of Ine—or in some less direct formula. There is, however, no single phrase or charter which explicitly grants jurisdiction as well as wites; on the contrary one latinization of the privilege describes it as the *vindicta popularium conciliorum*,[3] the "wites of the folkmoots", as though to leave no doubt that the immunist was empowered to collect the profits of judgment which took place in the courts of the community, but had neither need nor licence to hold his own. It is curious that the very charters which have been put forward as proving the existence of private courts at a slightly later date—in the ninth century—tell, with the exception of one formula of most dubious interpretation, against it. Upon Maitland's reading of these charters, and particularly *Weakness* upon that of two of them,[4] his argument for the existence of *of evi-* private justice in the eighth and ninth centuries largely rests, and *dence for* *it in the* in order to show its weakness we must commit ourselves to the *ninth* examination of an involved and difficult text. The charters in *century* question define the privilege of certain great churches as being that of clearing "the men of God's church", *i.e.* the commended men of the abbey, by the unsupported oath of the reeve or abbot, if they can conscientiously do so. The privilege is that defined in Wihtraed, 22-24, and so far the case is simple. But the charters go on to state what will happen if the reeve is uncertain of the man's innocence and will not venture upon the oath, and unfortunately do so in Latin which varies as between two texts,[4] and is too corrupt to admit of word-for-word translation: *sin autem ut recipiat alienam* (J. M. Kemble, *Codex Diplomaticus*, 236, ibid. 214 reading *aliam*) *justiciam huius vicissitudinis condicionem praefatum delictum cum simplo praetio componat. De illa autem tribulatione que witereden nominatur sit libera.* It would be natural to take the reading *alienam*, and—remembering that the act of exculpation by the sole oath of

[1] J. M. Kemble, *Codex Diplomaticus*, 206 (A.D. 814); *ibid.* 313: *And noht ut to wite.*

[2] *Ibid.* 1063: *Libera . . . a taxationibus quod dicimus wite redenne.*

[3] *Ibid.* 116.

[4] *Ibid.*,214 and 236. They are of doubtful authenticity.

an ecclesiastical person was regarded as a completed act of judgment, a self-doom—to construe the sentence as follows: "But if he accepts alien or independent judgment (*i.e.* in preference to the self judgment of the reeve), he must compound for the offence by damages (*singulare pretium*, *angyld*, to the plaintiff), but of the liability which is called *witereden* (the church) shall be free". The purpose of the clause seems, therefore, to be not to grant jurisdiction but to acknowledge the church's claim to the wite which the king may fairly grant since it is his own, and at the same time to secure that the plaintiff's damages (*simplex pretium*) shall not be drawn into the immunity also and lost to him.[1]

[1] Maitland's interpretation of these charters (*Domesday Book and Beyond*, p. 292) involves somewhat violent treatment of their texts, and the explanation of some of their terms in senses strange to the ninth century. His case really rests upon the formula used in J. M. Kemble, *Codex Diplomaticus*, 214 and 236, and specifically on the phrase *sin autem ut recipiat alienam* (*ibid.* 214 has *aliam*) *justiciam huius vicissitudinis condicionem praefatum delictum cum simplo praetio componat*. He explains it (very tentatively, "our best guess as to its meaning is this") as follows: If the reeve dare not make the sole oath, he may pay the damages claimed, and by performing this *condition* he may obtain a transfer (*vicissitudo*) of the cause and do what other justice remains to be done, *i.e.* he may exact the wite. "In guessing that *vicissitudo* points to a transfer of a suit, we have in mind the manner in which the Leges Henrici, 9, § 4, speak of the 'transition' of causes from court to court." The objections to this reading are very strong. In the first place, the reading *alienam justiciam* suits the case excellently. It is the external, alien judgment of the folkmoot where the defendant will be tried if his ecclesiastical lord and reeve dare not pronounce favourable judgment upon him by the sole oath. Maitland takes the weaker *aliam justiciam* of J. M. Kemble, *Codex Diplomaticus*, 214, and translates, "he may do what other justice remains to be done"; but there is no question of *other* justice; it is an alternative between the judgment by oath of the reeve or the judgment of the folkmoot, very aptly described as *aliena*.

Exception must again be taken to the reading of the words *vicissitudinis* and *condicionem*. The Latin of this hopelessly corrupt sentence is a debased example of charters in which *condicio* is used in the sense of "terms" or "obligations" of land-holding. Thus J. M. Kemble's *Codex Diplomaticus*, 199, has: *et ab universis etiam terrenis difficultatibus notis et ignotis condicionibus ac tributis . . . libera*, and *ibid.* 253 has: *ut regalium tributorum et principali dominatione, et in coacta operatione et poenalium conditionum*. *Vicissitudo* is probably no more than another of the exaggerated synonyms used for *onera*, of which *difficultas, obstaculum, gravitas, tribulatio, impedimentum, gravidinis, lesio*, and *molestia* are others. The *vicissitudinis condicio* of *ibid.* 214 and 236 is, indeed, a fairly evident synonym, slightly more rhetorical, for the *pœnalium conditiones* of its contemporary (*ibid.* 253).

Remembering the base and florid Latin of the day, and the law that underlies it, the following reading may be suggested as sounder, though less spectacular, than Maitland's: "Let him compound for his man's liabilities (*hujus vicissitudinis condicionem*) and for the aforesaid crime (*praefatum delictum*) by paying the angyld". This reading conforms to the legal terminology of the early ninth

Only Maitland's treatment of these clauses justifies their detailed examination, for they are dubiously authentic, of doubtful meaning, and are slight evidence to base a theory which would impose franchise of justice upon the ninth century. However, some charters of this age have their place in the general narrative of events, because, so far from proving the existence of franchise jurisdiction from the earliest times, they may be used to give us a date, and a comparatively late one, before which it is almost certain that such jurisdiction did not exist. These rare charters of the eighth and ninth centuries[1] contain clauses which, in addition to the ordinary promises of immunity from witeraeden and the like, tell us the conditions under which this immunity from wites is held. The immunist is to pay angyld, or *singulare pretium*, to the party against whom his vassal has done injury. Only on this condition, that the legitimate interest of the plaintiff shall be secured by the payment of the value of the property stolen from him, or the wergeld, or other bot, as the case may be, does the king promise that he will exact no wite, or, as more probably would happen, let it fall to the lord of the convicted man. It is evident that if the immunist possessed a court of his own, he would be able to exact his own wites there, and that these scrupulously worded and evidently coveted grants of the "wites of the folkmoots"[2] show that his men were, on the contrary, still justiciable by the public courts.

The charters which we have been discussing convey further privileges which tend to confirm this impression.[3] The grantee, in this case the abbot of Abingdon, may, if he believes in his man's

Privilege of self-oath

century in a way that Maitland's does not. It also places the immunity in an intelligible light, whereas Maitland has apparently failed to envisage fully the situation to which his suggestion might give rise, that the reeve, having refused to take the sole oath, and chosen the alternative of paying the angyld and claiming the case for his supposed court, might then on trial find the accused to be innocent. If we take the translation as suggested, we shall avoid fastening such an absurdity upon that very wideawake person the clerical immunist as the payment of damages against one of his men who was as yet untried. An immunity by which the king relieves the lord of the royal wites on condition that he indemnifies the injured party is a reasonable one and borne out by interpretation of the text of the charters in contemporary terms.

[1] J. M. Kemble, *Codex Diplomaticus*, 116, 117, 206, 214, 215, 216, 227, 236, 253, 262, 277, 313, 1068.

[2] *Ibid.* 116: *Vindicta popularium conciliorum.*

[3] *Ibid.* 214 and 236.

innocence, swear him clean of the charge by his unsupported oath, and by so swearing release him from all challenge by oath or ordeal. This privilege, which, as we have already had to consider, is not, as Maitland assumed it to be, the forerunner of the claiming of court of the Middle Ages,[1] by which the lord of an immunity could claim his men and their causes and have them transferred from the public courts to his own. That was a feudal usage, this is of the older world of the folkmoots, one more example of a rule of old standing, by which certain classes of persons to whose character or position the common process of oath-helping was unsuitable, were released from the obligation to find oath-helpers, and allowed to clear themselves by an unsupported or *self-oath*[2] taken at the altar, no doubt that of the church in which the ordeals of the folkmoot were sanctified. By the time of Wihtraed this privilege was shared by the king's thegn, the foreigner, priests, deacons, and the heads of monasteries,[3] and had been extended to cover the unfree servants of religious communities,[4] and kings' reeves and bishops' reeves as their deputies were able to swear away the guilt of their lords' servants by the same self-oath.[4] Now this process, so far from being a claiming of court, is a completed trial in the public court; the self-oath is itself the process and the judgment: in Icelandic law it would be said to be a *self-doom*. That the folkmoot was the place of trial is proved by the laws of Wihtraed. If the lord or his reeve will not venture on the oath, the accused is not remitted for trial to some private court, such as Maitland assumes to lie in the background, but is dealt with at once in the folkmoot and by the ordinary penalty of the unfree; his lord must deliver him to the lash.[4] The affinities of the Abingdon liberty are, therefore, not with immunity of court. They have their root in the age before feudalism in the archaic procedure of folk-justice.

Judicial powers by royal grant   Turning to the surer ground of later record, it seems that when judicial immunities arose they were not feudal in origin, that is to say, they could not be assumed in virtue of the mere fact of holding land or of having received the fealty of commended men and with it a claim upon their forfeitures. They were, as the lawyers of Edward I maintained, the effect of explicit royal grants. The later

---

[1] F. W. Maitland, *Domesday Book and Beyond*, p. 282.
[2] Wihtraed, 20. *Gest hine clænsie sylfes aþe on wifode.*
[3] *Ibid.* 17 18, 20.   [4] *Ibid.* 23.

Saxon kings were making such grants under two forms. By one, mainly, perhaps only, for the benefit of religious houses, they were granting the full administrative rights of the hundred. Hundreds so given were thenceforth governed by the reeves of bishop or abbot, and the hundred court became the court of an ecclesiastical immunity. The same pleas were tried there as before, the same suit was due, the same profits of jurisdiction were exacted, but now to the profit of the saint. How old such grants may be we cannot tell. Eadward the Confessor gave "the soke of the eight *Immunity* and a half hundreds of Thinghowe" to Saint Edmund,[1] and "the *of the* soke within Bichamdik" to Saint Benet of Ramsey,[2] and ordered *hundred* the shire of Norfolk to support the Abbot *ad justiciam* if necessary. Not long after the Conquest Ramsey was claiming hundred there over "all men that are moot-worthy, fyrd-worthy, and fold-worthy";[3] but records of such gifts are rare even in Eadward's reign. If we believed that there were no grants of this kind other than those for which genuine charters and writs have survived, we should find it hard to account for the very general possession of hundredal rights by the medieval churches and for the tradition which attributes to them a very great antiquity. We need not, indeed, accept the bishop of Salisbury's claim to the hundred of Ramsbury by grant of Offa, but such immunities as the three Worcester hundreds of Oswaldslaw coincide so clearly with the outline of the see of Worcester's lands in the tenth century that it is difficult to dissociate their origin from grants either of land and jurisdiction together, or of hundredal rights over land already held, and made in the tenth century as the church claimed. The Domesday hundreds of Kent are in their outline an epitome of the growth in landed estate of the archbishopric, the priory of Christchurch, and the abbey of Saint Augustine during the tenth and eleventh centuries. There seems no reason either in reliable tradition or record to carry back these ecclesiastical hundreds behind the reign of Eadgar [4]—the hundred itself was not much

[1] F. E. Harmer, *Anglo-Saxon Writs*, No. 9.   [2] *Ibid.* No. 60.

[3] *Ibid.* No. 61.

[4] J. M. Kemble, *Codex Diplomaticus*, 600. Eadgar's gift of a hundred hides at Taunton to Winchester, though it is silent as to jurisdiction, is a case in point, for the bishopric held the hundred court in the Confessor's reign. On the other hand, the Confessor's grant of Pershore to Westminster (F. E. Harmer, *Anglo-*

older—nor to extend the enjoyment of hundredal grants to the laity, but they have a large place in English life at the moment of the Conquest, and by the thirteenth century something like a quarter of the English hundreds must have come, some in fee, but more by lease in farm, into the hands of great feudatories.

Sake and soke

A second form of private justice, though still justice by royal grant, may be traced in record to Cnut. This is the grant of sake and soke, together with the special justice over thieves caught red-handed known as *infangentheof*, which may itself have been new in the tenth century. Cnut has convicted himself of conferring rights of justice upon his subjects, for his ordinances tell us that he will rarely give the highest of pleas to any subject, except to do him special honour.[1] Soke or *socn* means suit, among other things suit of court, but also suit in other matters. There is *fyrd-socn* and *ship-socn*, *fold-socn*, and so on, and the sense seems to be that of rendering any custom to the centre to which it is due. It is, no doubt, this soke of customs which we find at the beginning of the eleventh century.[2] Sake, on the other hand, is the Germanic *sache*, a cause or plea, and definitely confers jurisdiction when granted, and the right to hold a court.[3] What that jurisdiction was we are never told directly; perhaps all causes pertaining to wer and wite, which, in turn, should mean the old law of personal violence, such as gave rise to the feud, including theft, but often without the newer categories of justice, which were construed as touching the king and withheld as *cynges gerihta*. It was probably felt that such matters as were emendable by compensation between kindreds scarcely touched the common interest or the king's, and might be left to be settled within the lordship. Justice in actions for landed property, which the immunity of sake and soke un-doubtedly carried, would no doubt come under the same principle for it was a maxim of eleventh-century law that matters concerning the custom of any district should be judged by the peers of that custom and not by strangers. But though the social outlook of the day may have made such rights unobjectionable, there is

Saxon Writs, Nos. 99–101), at least as the monks saw it, seems to have treated jurisdiction as a separate privilege. [1] II Cnut, 12.

[2] *E.g.* in Wulfric's will. D. Whitelock, *Anglo-Saxon Wills*, xvii. A.D. 1002–1004.

[3] F. E. Harmer, *Anglo-Saxon Writs*, No. 28. *Ðæt he beo his saca ond socne wyrðe ond griðbryces ond hamsocne ond forstealles on infangenes þeofes ond flymena fyrmðde.*

no reason to suppose that they could be assumed as the prerogative of lordship or without royal license.

How soon the royal grants began we cannot say, though we have given reason to think that they are not older than the tenth century. Before the reign of the Confessor sake and soke was given by writ only, and not by charter, and our oldest writs are those of Cnut.[1] Nor can we be sure how completely a grant of soke freed the land and the men upon it from suit and other obligations of shire and hundred, and specifically from that obligation of frankpledge which, at some period or other of the eleventh century, was coming into being, and was closely associated with private justice. On the whole, Domesday suggests that a man under the soke of a lord was freed from suit to the hundred, and several of the Confessor's grants of sake and soke are accompanied by quittance *de hundredis et schiris*,[2] which must surely mean freedom from external suit. The commonest immunity of the medieval manor was that of holding a private view of frankpledge, and when the proctors of the crown examined the counties in the inquiries *De Quo Warranto* of the first three Edwards, there were many landholders who based their claim to the view upon their right of sake and soke,[3] or on such quittances from shire and hundred as were given by the Confessor.[4] Of the franchises of immunity from the view which riddled England in the Middle Ages, a great number are known to have been created by post-Conquest charters, and some arose by the neglect of the sheriff to exercise his right of view; but if frankpledge was already existing in the reigns of Cnut and the Confessor, we need not dismiss the possibility that it was a corollary of sake and soke, and part of a substantial growth of immunity, both judicial and administrative, in the last half-century of Saxon history.[5]

Thus aristocracy and franchise are increasingly the marks of

[1] The earliest being by Cnut to Archbishop Æthelnoth. F. E. Harmer, *Anglo-Saxon Writs*, No. 28. One possibly authentic writ of Æthelred survives.

[2] *Ibid.* No. 76.

[3] *Placita de Quo Warranto*, pp. 211, 244. The king's proctors denied this on occasion.   [4] *Ibid.* 290.

[5] As in Essex, where certain tenants "were so free that they could sell their land where they would, and the soke and sake with it" (Domesday Book, ii. 59A).

later Saxon history, and, while the common freeman is not dis-franchised, he is thrust into the background, required to act by representatives, and often subjected to the court of an immunity. He attends the folkmoots when the law needs him, or when he is specially concerned. Nevertheless, this growth of the aristocratic principle in the courts is compatible with conservatism in many spheres of the law, and apparently has little tendency to bring England into line with the movement towards feudalism which was developing in the empire of the Franks. More than any other side of English life, the growth of the English land system from Ælfred to the Conquest leaves the impression of a very remarkable blend of insularity and adaptability. In common with many of the Germanic codes the laws of the English contain no complete

Growth of statement of the custom of landright. It was known to all, needed
land-law no written record, and was spoken by verbal memory in the courts. What we know of it comes from charters which record only specialized forms of land-holding, and from the few records of sale and formulae of pleading which have survived, and from Domesday Book. Bearing in mind the nature of the feudal practice which is to be grafted upon England after the Con-quest, the distinctive fact of Saxon custom is that it is governed by the notion not of *dominium* but of property,[1] and almost entirely by the right of individuals. In some remote past the English may have shared with their German cousins a system of joint family holding of land, related groups maintaining an undivided birthright and cultivating the soil coöperatively. If so, the joint family must have lost its unity long before the migration. In Britain the only limit upon individual property is the rule of equal partition among heirs, which preserves the joint birthright of the stock of descent but expresses it in every generation by allotting an equal part of the inheritance to each of the heirs, with right to give, sell, and bequeath. Sometimes under the name of gavelkind, sometimes passing unnamed as local custom, this archaic rule was universal in Kent, common in East Anglia, and sporadic in part of the East Midlands, the West, Essex, and Sussex. The Borough English of the south-coast

1 More properly, a presumptive right in the possessor (F. Pollock and F. W. Maitland, *History of English Law*, i. 57), for which "property" is used in this section.

manors may have been a debased form of gavelkind,[1] but it is unlikely that gavelkind ever predominated in the purely Mercian and West Saxon settlement of the Midlands—it may well have reflected a difference of race—and there impartible descent may have been the rule from the earliest times. However that may be, landright everywhere seems to have shared the free right of alienation which prevailed in gavelkind if we may trust the few instances of gift in the spoken forms of ancient custom which have been recorded for us.[2] By the tenth century all Saxon landright seems to have been unbound by entail, except where a special deed of limitation had determined its descent, or where, as upon certain parts of the church lands, a customary prohibition against alienation was observed. Whether partible or impartible, all land held *Folk-land* by the ancient rules of inheritance was subject to action and defended in the folkmoots by the process of oath and ordeal, which was in itself part of landright. The property held in it, the right of inheritance, of gift and so forth, together with the forms of pleading appropriate to it, were that part of folkright which related to land. At least over a period of years at the end of the ninth and the beginning of the tenth centuries, land held in folkright seems to have been known as *folk-land*.[3]

This main stock of English land-law came, no doubt, from *Book-land* Germanic custom, and the greater part of the land was held in folkright, though, since *ex hypothesi* it passed by verbal transfer, we know little of it. But, imposed upon this Germanic foundation, was a foreign landright of Latin and clerical origin, which made land the subject of gift by *boc* or charter. At the time when charter grants were first made, perhaps in the age of Theodore, perhaps from the time of the conversion, the choice of written gift may in part have been dictated by the fact that it conveyed *perpetua et libera haereditas*, by which was meant—rather oddly— the right to give, sell, or devise, but this motive can only have

---

[1] It preserved the gavelkind rule of reserving the house and hearth to the eldest son, and in many cases enjoyed the security of *gavelate*, and gave the kin the prior right of purchase which is known as *retrait lignager*. J. E. A. Jolliffe, *Pre-Feudal England*, pp. 79 *et seq.*

[2] Cf. the Peterborough gifts and sales made in the hundred court with verbal guarantee (*festermen*) and witness, but without charter: W. de Gray Birch, *Cartularium Saxonicum*, 1128, 1130. They are of the late tenth century.

[3] Cf. F. W. Maitland, *Domesday Book and Beyond*, pp. 244-258.

been operative if, at that early period, rights of kindred and binding rules of descent hampered the free alienation of the paternal inheritance. In later days the charter usually gave rights of legal immunity, but in the early grants it is rare that more than simple landright should be conveyed. Certainly the most distinctive quality of book-land, chartered land, was that it was especially under the protection of the king, the witan, and the church, that the charter promised damnation to those who broke its terms, and that it could not be called in question in any lower court than the witenagemot.[1] Folkright in the folkmoots, bookright in the witenagemot before the king and the bishops, whose authority had instituted it, seems to have been the rule of law, and, when challenged, the holder by book had the supreme advantage that the production of his charter, backed by a competent oath, was sufficient to nullify all further question. The two forms of property, therefore, were distinguished from each other only by differences of authority, or of procedure, sanction, and venue, and holders by charter clung to their bookright century by century mainly because of the strong legal defence that it afforded them. In historical times the holder of folk-land seems to have been no less free to dispose of it, possessed of no less absolute property, than he who held book-land. We are brought, therefore, to conclude that in the tenth and eleventh centuries the Saxon land-holder was free both from customary rules such as may have prevailed in a remote past, and from the manifold restrictions upon tenant right and lord's right which were the essence of feudal *dominium*. The Saxon's right was, in short, not tenure but property.[2]

The free right of book-land and folk-land had, no doubt, its

[1] J. E. A. Jolliffe, "English Book-right", *English Historical Review*, vol. l.

[2] Norman scribes, faced with the contrast between the *feudum* and English book-land, imported for the latter the Continental term *alod*. This was used more loosely in the eleventh century, but had originally denoted the paternal inheritance of the freeman, the German *frei eigen* as opposed to *beneficium*, or even to land acquired by gift. In equating *alod* with book-land the Continentals were, no doubt, seizing upon the phrase *in aeternam haereditatem* in *bocs*. So, in the Norman translations known as the Instituta Cnuti, we have *Carta alodii ad aeternam haereditatem* (Instituta Cnuti, iii. 46), and *si liberalis homo, quem Angli thegen vocant, habet in alodio (id est bocland) suo ecclesiam* (I Cnut, 11). Cf. also II Cnut, 13. 1. In Domesday in the south-eastern counties, though not

advantages. It had, however, one serious drawback: gifts had to *Draw-* be made outright, and therefore without conditions. The lord who *backs of* wished to reward his man or retain a material pledge of his faith- *absolute* fulness could only do so by creating a right of property in the *property* donee as free as his own. This fact the formula of the charters reflects accurately by specifying that the land transferred has been given not on condition of future service but in reward for past service done. The *feudum*, the quintessential achievement of feudalism, provided a *via media* by which the giver could set up a dependent and heritable *dominium* in the donee, while himself retaining a parallel *dominium* in himself and his heirs. This bound the heirs of both parties to behave towards each other as lord and man in perpetuity, and at once rewarded the servant and secured the service and fealty of his descendants. The device of the fee the Saxons had not, nor by the date of the Norman Conquest is there any sign that they were on the way to acquiring it; nevertheless from very early times precisely the difficulty that the *feudum* was designed to solve was felt in England. If our estimate of the land-right of the gesiths of Ine is correct, they passed out of history because they had no property or inheritance in their lands, and their lords would not, or would but rarely, accord it them. Bede tells us how they tried to get book-land in perpetuity, posing as founders of monasteries, begging land from the king for that purpose, and if the abuse had not been checked the recurrent demands of generations of landless warriors exacting estates from the *terra regis* would have left the fisc bankrupt.

The case of that equally great landlord, the church, was even more difficult. Over a large portion of their lands, bishops, abbots, and monks had not the same right of free alienation as the layman. Every see had its permanent endowment *de episcopatu*, every monastery its lands *de abbatia, de victu*, or *de vestitu monachorum*, or the like,[1] and these were often ancient bequests, which by convention or rule could not be broken away from their sacred pur-

consistently, perhaps, *alodium* is used to denote the free English land-holding. It also occurs in certain charters conveying the dependence of thegns to the churches of Canterbury, *thegen* being Latinized *alodiarius*, no doubt as one who often held land in bookright.

[1] Domesday Book, i. 65B: *Haec sunt de victu monachorum . . . qui tenuerunt T.R.E. non poterant ab ecclesia separari. Ibid.* i. 135A: *Hoc manerium tenuerunt iii teigni . . . et vendere potuerunt. Hoc manerium non est de episcopatu.*

pose.[1] They formed the *firma* or consolidated fund of land for the up-keep of the necessary services of the community or see.[2] Moreover the great church estates were larger than most others, and might reach the dimensions of a province. They needed the services of laymen as administrators and protectors. Like others, they needed ready money, but they could not, as did the king and the magnates, reward the services of laymen by an outright gift of land. With perhaps the greatest need of all to render their resources liquid, they alone were restricted in their right to alienate. Consequently, we find them testing the resources of the law, seeking to render more elastic the rigid property of their lands, and producing a variety of experimental relations which keep the letter of inalienability, but approach, though they never realize, the device of the *feudum*.

The laen   The laen, or *praestitum*, the outstanding example of this, was arrived at at the latest very early in the ninth century,[3] when the see of Worcester, and, no doubt other religious houses, was making use of it. It was precisely what its name implies, a loan of land, usually for a term of three lives. Since it did not give property it could be granted on condition of service. At the end of the tenth century Bishop Oswald of Worcester was making loans of from one to five hides for three or five lives in return for an oath of general obedience,[4] and service of acting as bishop's messenger and travelling escort which he called *lex equitandi*, "riding custom", and which probably gave the name *radknight* to the recipients. These loans could not be construed as alienation, a strict check was kept on their terms of lives, and Oswald informed the king of their terms in a well-known letter,[5] so that Eadgar as patron of the church might know that no improper alienation was taking place. So, during the two hundred and fifty years through which we can trace it, the laen shows no sign of becoming hereditary: the

[1] Thus, Coenwulf of Mercia, in endowing Winchcombe, ordained that no grant for more than one life should be made from the monastery lands. J. M. Kemble, *Codex Diplomaticus*, 323.

[2] Domesday Book, i. 67B: *De eadem terra tenuit Aluric . . . unam hidam . . . ea conditione ut post mortem ejus rediret ad aecclesiam quia de dominica firma erat.*

[3] J. M. Kemble, *Codex Diplomaticus*, 279, 303, 315.

[4] *Ibid.* 1287: *Quamdiu ipsas terras tenent in mandatis pontificis humiliter . . . perseverare*: to observe the commands of the bishop with humility as long as they shall hold the said lands. This is not the hold-oath of a vassal, but an official's oath of obedience in his office.

[5] *Loc. cit.*

Domesday survey records the dependent estates of Worcester still carefully denoted as *praestita* not to be renewed without the bishop's leave.[1] One modification alone shows that it was a form of holding hardly secure enough to attract the type of men the churches desired, and this came to fill a useful niche in English land-law. Bishop Oswald himself made general the practice—he did not invent it—of giving greater stability to the laen by granting the recipient a book, while still preserving the reversion of the land to the see at the end of the allotted term of lives. To this end he issued charters converting *laen-land* into *book-land* for a period only,[2] borrowing the literal form of the diploma of gift, and creating a legal chimaera which, as he himself puts it, conveyed "eternal inheritance for three lives".[3] This did, in fact, produce a kind of holding which might carry a condition of service, lodged an effective right in the holder, gave him the paramount advantage of pleading by bookright, and yet secured ultimate reversion and avoided alienation. Thus, by a roundabout way, some of the advantages of the *feudum* were secured and the see was enabled to carry out something which had roughly the effect of an enfeoff-ment. The device was a clumsy one, but it had great success in the absence of a purer legal concept. The pretence of "eternal inherit-ance" being soon dropped,[4] other churches and even the king are found making gifts by book for a term of lives even up to the Conquest.[5] Such holdings, no doubt, underlie many of the un-explained restrictions upon those Domesday land-holders of King

Gifts for term of lives

[1] Domesday Book, i. 172B.

[2] F. W. Maitland, *Domesday Book and Beyond*, pp. 310-318, considered that the laen was the natural forerunner of the *feudum* and formed a link between a rudimentary English feudalism and that of the Normans. This was not so, for up to 1066 the laen showed no sign of becoming hereditary, did not necessarily create a lord and man relation (cf. note 5 *infra*), showed, in general, no sign of developing along the lines of the *feudum*.

[3] J. M. Kemble, *Codex Diplomaticus*, 617: *Oswald . . . bocath Eadrice his thegne . . . swa swa he aer haefde to lanlande*. Cf. also *ibid.* 651.

[4] *Ibid.* 586: *Perpetua largitus sum haereditate, et post vitae suae terminum duobus tantum heredibus immunem derelinquat*: I have granted in eternal inheritance and after his life he may leave it freely to two heirs only. This curious form persisted in the leases being made by Burton Abbey until well into the twelfth century.

[5] Domesday Book, i. 72A: *Toti emit eam T.R.E. de aecclesia Malmesburiensi ad etatem trium hominum, et infra hunc terminum poterat ire cum ea ad quem vellet dominum*: Tofi bought from the church of Malmesbury for a term of three lives in King Eadward's day. Within that term he could go with it to any lord he liked.

Eadward's day[1] who could not "go with their land",[2] though others were by the clear terms of the grant free to go. They are a striking proof of the incapacity of the English to develop the theory and practice of feudalism, since, advancing from the same point—the *praestitum*—which was the origin of the Frankish *feudum*, the English made scarcely any progress at all, and had to be contented with producing an illogical and contradictory blend of the laen and the alod, the conflicting elements of which were never properly reconciled, and certainly never acquired the clarity of feudal tenure.

Absence of feudalism in England

If, therefore, we are concerned with the technical form of law, we can say that England had not arrived at the *feudum* by 1066; if it be thought that this is a fact of antiquarian rather than historical interest, it must be answered that, because the English had not the fee, they also had not feudalism. There seem to have been three principal ways of land-holding in England of the eleventh century, by bookright, by folkright, and by laen.[3] Of these three ways of land-holding not one could create a permanent link between the component parts of any accumulation of property such as made the Norman honour indissoluble, nor bind the heirs of any lord and those of his vassal to each other through an indefinite future. In English law, unless there was specific limitation by will, no inheritance bound the inheritor,[4] whether in land or in lordship. Though Domesday speaks of the *Honour* of Bristric, the *Honour* of Wisgar, it is a misuse of terms, for the Norman honour had per-

---

[1] J. M. Kemble, *Codex Diplomaticus*, 1170, 1231.

[2] Domesday Book, i. 66B: *Tres hidas vendiderat abbas cuidam taino T.R.E. ad etatem trium hominum, . . . et postea debebat redire ad dominum*: the abbot sold three hides to a thegn for three lives in King Eadward's day . . . and after that term it ought to return to the original lord.

[3] *Ibid.* i. 257A: *Edricus tenuit de Episcopo et non poterat ab eo divertere quia de victu suo erat et ei prestiterat tantum in vita sua*: Eadric held it of the bishop and could not depart from him because it was *de victu suo* and he had loaned it to him for his life only.

[4] The generation of Ælfred tried to do something to remedy this defect by giving a right to entail book-land. Ælfred legislated with that intention (Ælfred, 41), and took advantage of the law in his will (J. M. Kemble, *Codex Diplomaticus*, 314), and his contemporary, Burhred of Mercia, adopted the same practice (*ibid.* 299), but the right was never reasserted in later reigns and seems to have fallen into desuetude.

manent existence, and the lands of any Saxon, however great, were no more than a casual grouping, inherited, bought, given by the king or others, commended to him by his followers at their own will and pleasure. Not only might they be dispersed within the owner's lifetime or by his testament, but they habitually were. The Englishman was, therefore, devoid of that dynastic sense which drove the feudatories of later days to project their ambitions into the future, scheming always to safeguard a dynastic estate and to augment it. The Saxon land-holder bestowed his lands at death not as a dynast, but so as to complete his own life, save his own soul, and satisfy his love for those whom he had known in his life-time. There was no leaning towards primogeniture in bequest, for there was no enduring unity, and no law which bound the future. Great accumulations of land and lordship rose and were dispersed within a lifetime, as was that of Wulfric, "thegn and dear to the heart of King Eadred", whose great estate of lands in Berkshire, Sussex, and Wiltshire were so broken after his death that they were in twenty-eight different hands in the days of the Confessor, or that of the Lady Æflaed, who willed her lands to the king and to nine different religious communities.

Because of this brittleness and impermanence in the higher strata of Saxon land-holding, no typically feudal policy develops, no leagues of nobles, no specifically feudal reaction against the crown. Throughout the whole Saxon period there is nothing that we can call a feudal rising. So the omission of four words —*in feodo et haereditate*—from the formulary of English land-law went far to determine the whole history of the later Saxon age.

The form taken by the English law of property was, therefore, the greatest factor in determining the evolution of social relations. It is directly reflected in the relation of lord and man. In the absence of dependent tenure, lordship was not feudal. There was, of course, no homage, that is to say, no oath or ceremony acknowledging dependent tenure and promising faith and service as from a given tenement and in virtue of it. A form described as "bowing"[1] to the lord, the *commendatio* of Domesday, was gone through and an oath

Lordship without feudalism

---

[1] *Mid þaem monnum ðe him to gebugon.* Anglo-Saxon Chronicle, 901A.
Ic wille ðat Ælfrich Modercope mot bugan to ðo tweyen abboten at seynt Eadmunde and at sancte Ætheldrede. F. E. Harmer, *Anglo-Saxon Writs*, No. 21.

was sworn to be in general faithful or *hold*, from which comes the common term *hold-oath* [1] for what was later called the oath of fealty. The characteristic phrase of the formula is the promise to "be hold and true to N., loving all that he loves and shunning all that he shuns". The hold-oath does not create the dependent tenure of feudal land. The advantage to the man was still, of course, the acquiring for himself and his property and dependents of the protection of the lord's *mund*,[2] and his maintenance in the courts. The lord could take his man's cause upon himself and plead it in the courts in his own person,[3] and there are many signs in the codes that lords were ready and able to save their men by force and guile from due process of law.[4] Such advantages were, of course, mutual. We are apt to think that a lord's one motive to increase his following must be economic, to establish a title to other men's lands, to get more rent and agrarian service. That is not so in the eleventh century. With many impalpable advantages of social prestige and security which we can no longer fully appreciate, man and lord could be of very solid use to each other at law. Maintenance, later the object of many denunciatory statutes, was still a motive force in legal procedure. The family had "maintained" its kinsmen by oath, warranty, and witness, and, as the family's obligation in such matters declined, the individual found himself still dependent upon the opinion of a court of neighbours. A trial which point by point judged by the public estimate of the parties, and required them to be backed by men

[1] Swerian, 1: *Ðus man shall swerigean hyldaðas.*

[2] D. Whitelock, *Anglo-Saxon Wills*, xvii. Wulfric (*circa* 1006) requests that Ælfhelm shall be mund to his daughter and to the land he leaves her.

Domesday Book, i. 32B: *Potuit ire quo voluit sed per defensionem sub abbatia se misit*: he could go where he would, but for his defence he put himself under the abbey. Leges Henrici Primi, 61. 17. D.B. i. 137B: *Postea ad Wigotum se vertit pro protectione*: afterwards he commended himself to Wigot for the mund. *Ibid.* i. 58A: *Potuit ire quo voluit sed pro sua defensione se commisit Hermanno Episcopo*: he could go where he would but commended himself to Bishop Herman for his defence. *Mundbyrdnis* is still the term for lordship in the late eleventh century, F. E. Harmer, *Anglo-Saxon Writs*, Nos. 99–101.

[3] For all capital causes a man might claim stay of process until his lord could appear on his behalf.

[4] Cf. Domesday Book, ii. 401B. Brungar was under the jurisdiction of the abbot of Ely, but was the man of Robert fitz Wymarc. Stolen horses were found in Brungar's possession, but Robert conferred with the abbot and no charge was made.

who were willing to swear to their right, put a premium upon good neighbourship, and still more upon good loi.. ..ip and faithful vassalage.[1] It was for this that in even later generations the greatest men of the realm bound their men to legal maintenance in the charters of their tenures.[2]

The incurable Gallicism of Domesday is such as at first sight to give the impression that conditional tenure existed in the days of King Eadward. The jurors were required to give an account of the state of vassalage and lordship. Whether the phrase was put into their mouths by their inquisitors or occurred to them spontaneously, they tell us that a vast number of Englishmen held *de* or *sub*[3] *Rege Edwardo*, and that an almost equal number held *of* bishops, earls, and lesser men whom we can often identify as king's thegns. In Norman legal speech the *tenet de* should denote tenure and point to a joint tenant's and lord's *dominium* in the soil,[4] and probably when used of the tenant of William's day it usually does so, but a very little examination of Eadward's men will show that, used of the vassals of his day, it stood for a less real and more personal tie, that of commendation by the hold-oath. We find that there are a vast number of men in the South-West and East[5] who hold *de Rege*,[6] or *de* or *sub* some lesser magnate, and yet are so free that they "can sell their land where they will", or "go with their land where they will", are *liberi homines*,[7] or "can become any man's

Dependent tenure not recorded in Domesday

[1] J. M. Kemble, *Codex Diplomaticus*, 328; II Cnut, 30. 1.

[2] *Cartularium Monasterii de Rameseia*, iii. 260: *Tali pacto, quod tam ipse, quam heres suus . . . totam terram Sancti Benedicti, pro posse suo, in omnibus defendat placitis, ubicunque opus fuerit*: on these terms, that he and his heir shall defend the whole land of St. Benet with all his power in every plea.

[3] To hold *sub* or *de* seem to be equivalent, the former being a variant expression in the East Midlands, Hertfordshire, Buckinghamshire, and East Anglia.

[4] *Cartularium Monasterii de Rameseia*, i. 141: *Et eadem terra est de feudo abbatis Ramesiae et Stephani Deseschalers, qui de abbate eam tenet* (T.R. Henry I).

[5] The tie of lordship is rarely recorded in Northumbria. It is likely that the West Saxon kings had little lordship there, for even in the South commendation to the king, not as monarch but as lord, was, of course, voluntary. Thus Swegen, though a subject, came to Eadward, and "promised that he would be his man" (Anglo-Saxon Chronicle, 1049C).

[6] Domesday Book, i. 144A: *Hoc manerium tenuerunt duo fratres, unus homo Ulfi et alter homo Eddevae. Potuerunt dare et vendere cui voluerint. Ibid*. i. 170A: *Clifton tenuit Seuuinus . . . de Rege Edwardo et poterat ire cum hac terra quo volebat*.

[7] This seems to be the meaning of *fuit liber homo* or *tenuit libere*, at least in the South and Midlands. *Ibid*. i. 248B: three men held Little Sandon, *duo eorum*

man",[1] according to the formula used in the county in question. They are commended, but can undo the act of commendation.[2] Occasionally the record is more explicit, and we can see how tenuous is the tie of lordship, and how easily loosed at the vassal's will: "Alric holds half a hide now. His father held it of King Eadward, but Alric himself has not sought the King."[3] The son has not felt the bond worth renewing and has let it drop, but he still holds the land. Another has taken the contrary course: "Tori's father held the land T.R.E. and could go where he would, but to get protection"—*pro sua defensione*—the old *to hlaford and to mundbora*—"he commended himself to Bishop Herman, and Tori has done the same to Bishop Osmund".[4] Sometimes we can see the owner exercising the right of alienation which such formulae imply: "Bolle held Windrush and could go with the land where he would, and he gave it to the abbey".[5]

Prevalence of free landright   Not to have the right to dispose of land is comparatively very uncommon. Buckinghamshire, for instance, is almost entirely under ecclesiastics and lay magnates, or under their *homines*, and, almost without exception, the latter can sell their lands where they will. Staffordshire, similarly, is monopolized by freemen who can sell their lands. In Cheshire they are largely preponderant, and in Sussex there are only a sprinkling of instances to the contrary. Moreover, familiarity with Domesday leads one to suppose that where it is silent we have to deal with some king's thegn or other notable whose freedom is too well known to need comment, often the general antecessor of the Norman tenant-in-chief. Usually we can assume that freedom to alienate was possessed unless there is

liberi fuerunt. Wicstui cum terra discedere non poterat. Domesday Book, i. 31A; Bromley: *Quattuor ex his hidis fuerunt liberorum hominum qui de Alnod secedere potuerunt.* There are exceptions, usually in East Anglia and near by, but there the notion of "freedom" is confused by that of freedom from certain customs such as foldsoke, and by the need of drawing a contrast with the prevalent holding in socage. Cf. *Ibid.* ii. 59B.

[1] *Ibid.* ii. 119A, Thetford: *Alii omnes poterant esse homines cujuslibet.*

[2] *Ibid.* ii. 47B: *Quidam liber homo erat commendatus Roberto . . . et poterat ire quo vellet.* It would seem that to contract a new vassalage a man would have to get his late lord's clearance of good-conduct (II Edward, 7), but III Æthelstan, 4 shows that the lord could not refuse it without convincing cause.

[3] *Ibid.* i. 50B. Sometimes the son had forgotten, or never known, to whom his father had been commended, so purely formal might its nature be in some instances.

[4] *Ibid.* i. 58A.   [5] *Ibid.* 165B.

explicit record to the contrary.[1] To be tied in landright to a lord was, therefore, an exception, though one shared by perhaps five per cent of the manorial land-holders of England, of whom Domesday records *non potuit vendere, non potuit recedere*, and the whole trend of the Survey suggests that these tied estates were not dependent tenures held in perpetuity after the manner of the *feudum*, but land not really in the ownership of the immediate occupier, being granted to him for a period or for life only,[2] as farm from clerk to layman, by some special contract, or, most commonly of all, by laen or gift for a fixed term of lives.[3] Such holdings are found, for the most part, about the demesnes of the church and the great units of *terra regis*, or great lay manors.

Thus, Old English land-law governs the custom of lordship, starving it of the soil of feudalism and confining it to a purely personal basis. That rigidity which provided no other alternative to the lord but the giving of land outright or the granting of temporary possession, prevents the assimilation of the tie of lord and man to that of *dominus* and *tenens*, and especially of that form of it in which a parallel *dominium* in the soil is held by both lord and tenant in a perpetuity of interdependence. In short, it bars the way to tenurial feudalism.

If we try to pierce below the stratum of the substantial land-holders we can say little with certainty. Beneath the uniformity of bookright there are many Englands, for each of the old kingdoms has maintained its ceorlish custom. It is virtually impossible to answer the old question as to the freedom or unfreedom of the eleventh-century peasant. There can be no one touchstone of freedom, such as the Angevin courts applied, to which Deira,

Lordship over ceorls

---

[1] No details of lordship are given in Yorkshire and Lincolnshire, but wills show the right of free alienation by gift or exchange. D. Whitelock, *Anglo-Saxon Wills*, p. 95.

[2] Domesday Book, i. 136B: *Hanc terram tenuit Godwinus de Ecclesia Sancti Petri. Non potuit vendere, sed post mortem ejus debebat ad ecclesiam redire.* Sometimes they were held by manorial servants. *Ibid.* i. 47A: *Wenesi tenuit de Rege Edwardo . . . sicut antecessor ejus tenuit qui fuit mediator caprorum. Non potuit se vertere ad alium dominum. Ibid.* ii. 41B: *Unam hidam quam tenuerunt ii servientes Wisgari. . . Nec poterant abire sine jussu domini sui.*

[3] *Ibid.* i. 257A: *Non potuit ab eo (Episcopo) divertere quia de victu suo erat et ei præstiterat tantum in vita sua.*

Bernicia, Mercia, East Anglia, Essex, Kent, and Wessex, will react alike. One thing only is clear, that the English peasantry moved across the line of the Conquest in every variety of dependence and independence, status, and relation to the state. Constitutional history can do no more than take note of this variety as the basis of its treatment of law and administration. Lordship over peasants settled upon the land of great men had by the tenth century some quality which made it different in kind from normal lordship, more real and enduring. In relation to the men upon his estate the lord was already the *land-rica*.[1] Both the name and the institution of the manor are lacking, but the law of the estate is coming to be thought of as something different from folkright.[2] Even by the reign of Ælfred, the ceorls of Wessex could be given no higher status than the Danish freedmen when a common standard between the ranks of the two peoples was sought,[3] and in the Midlands the manorial records of the Middle Ages reveal a considerable proportion of villages whose cultivators have no land-right apart from their lord, who cannot leave the estate, and whom the law reckons as unfree. The persistence with which such masses of landright preserved their unity, and were transferred from owner to owner unbroken, suggests that even in the Saxon age the Midland cultivators were involved in a lordship which could not be shaken off, and perhaps had forgotten that the possibility had ever existed.

Decline of the ceorl   We need not think that the Saxon lord enjoyed a feudal right over his peasants which in his own acres and for his commended men was not yet imagined. There were principles in English law which would in themselves suffice to keep the men of the townships immobile, though such principles had yet to be fused into a conscious rule of servile tenure. Precisely in that part of England, Mercia, and central Wessex, where villeinage was the rule in later days, the open fields, the interlocked tenements of the village, and the common ploughs, made the agricultural community almost indissoluble, and the greater number of such communities were under a single lord who was also its greatest proprietor. So early

---

1 IV Eadgar, 8. 1; VIII Æthelred, 8.

2 Gerefa, 1: *Se gerefa sceal aegðaer witan ge hlafordes landriht ge folces gerihtu*: a reeve must know both the custom of his lord's land and folkright.

3 Ælfred and Guthrum's Peace, 3.

as the seventh century we know that the ceorl who had no land, but settled upon a gesith's land as a gebur, was a common social type,[1] and a document of the eleventh century[2] shows the geburs as one of the two principal classes of the cultivators, still without landright of their own, and paying for a lord's loan of land and stock by labour. It would be rash to say that all those manors whose courts in the Middle Ages denied a heritable right to their villeins derived their custom from the geburs of Saxon England, but they were fewer than is commonly supposed, even in the servile Midlands, and the strength of peasant right of inheritance in such widely scattered lands as those of the churches of Winchester shows that the West Saxon ceorl had much of freedom to bequeath to his villein descendants. Continuity of lordship and commendation from generation to generation is likely to have been most common with the peasantry. It was perhaps almost universal in the Midlands, and might easily harden into an obligation where the lordship sought was that of the one man of standing, whose landright was the greatest in the community, and whose power was an ever-present reality. Fealty sworn generation by generation would easily become a necessity and a rule. A twofold origin, in grants made to landless men, and in commendation by ceorls who had landed right and inheritance but needed protection, may well be a sound analysis of the lordship of the land-rica over his peasantry, if we allow for that loss of the fine edge of definition which may come to unwritten right transmitted by memory and exercised in community under the shadow of social and material power.

The Domesday term *villanus*, which the surveyors scattered far *The vil-* and wide over the peasantry of England, seems to have borne *lanus of* little or no relation to its use in the courts of the thirteenth century. *Domesday* It is applied equally to the men of Kent, where villeinage was non-existent, to the bondagers of the North with their heritable Tenant Right, to many of the comparatively free peasantry of East Anglia and Essex, and to every variety of customary holding in Wessex and Mercia. It ignores the nature of the landright and of the service due from the holding. In so far as it was applied consistently, it seems to have been a simple borrowing of the Saxon term *tunesman*, and to have denoted a holder of land which could not be detached from the manor, and whose holder appeared before the law as a member of the township for which the manor answered, or of which it formed a part. As with the more considerable land-owners, so with the cultivators, the crown is primarily interested in determining the outlines of the estates, whether this or that man can or cannot "go with his land where he will", and we are again brought back to the condition of the *villanus* as bound to the soil on which he lives and to its lord. This, no doubt, was a limitation far more widely spread than heavy service of labour or precarious landright, and would justify in a large measure the Domesday extension of the villeins. There is no doubt that Saxon England had come to treat the cultivators of each estate as a unit for administration where such estates were compact areas. In part, this practice was, perhaps, due to the emergence of the township as the primary unit of administration in the tenth century, but, in addition, there are factors in the custom of lordship which may explain this restriction upon the mobility of the ceorl without appeal to any doctrine of servile tenure. Commendation was free to all and as free to be renounced as to be incurred, as far as the law went, but it had been hedged about with safeguards. From the time of Ælfred, it had had to be made publicly, and in a public court. A man wishing to seek new lordship must notify the authorities both of the shire to which he is going and of that which he is leaving.[1] Later law prescribed a clearance from the former lord, who must vouch for his man's past conduct, and declare him free from all legal charges and claims such as might be frustrated if he left secretly.[2] The crown, moreover, was using lordship as a compulsory guarantee of conduct. The lawless man, or the man who had no land and goods to serve as security, must be found a lord by his kin.[3] "To go where he would", always lawful for the lawful man, and easy for the commended man of property and clean record, might be a difficult matter for the man who had no land in his own right, whose stock had been lent him by his lord, and who was of too low a station to have that weight and responsibility which was required of the lawful man. Nor for a man whose

[1] The first administrative recognition of the private estate is, perhaps, that of Ælfred, requiring the cognizance of the ealdorman when a man leaves the *boldgetale* in which he has been serving. Ælfred, 37.

[2] II Eadward, 7.

[3] II Æthelstan, 2.

past and future were enclosed within the fields of a single lordship would it have seemed desirable or even possible. We may well believe successive peasant generations abode under the same mund until change became unthinkable, and yet doubt whether the law held them *adscripti glebae* or had found for the peasant a ground of dependent tenure which it had yet to arrive at for commended men of higher status. If we deny feudalism among the magnates, we should need convincing evidence to find it in the community of the village, and of such evidence there is no hint in charter, custumal, or law.

The terms upon which the Domesday *villanus*, the Saxon *tunesman*, lived with his lord hardly concern the constitution. In East Anglia the *villani* are not the principal stock of the peasantry. They are outnumbered by the *sokemen*, that is, by holders of small estates, who owe attendance to the hundred court, or to a lord who holds the immunity of sake and soke, and pay the miscellaneous customs which are due to the king from the hundred. These have an acknowledged landright, and for the most part commend themselves as they will. The North has more *villani* than sokemen, but the manorial records of the Middle Ages show us that they were *bondi* or *husbandmen*, who, in contrast to the Midlanders, enjoyed much freedom of right and lighter service. The Kentings had a free landright by custom of gavelkind: they could sue in the king's courts in the thirteenth century, and were lightly burdened, and, except for the absence of the right to sue by writ, a large proportion of the villages of Hampshire and Sussex had an almost equally free custom known as Borough English. The Midland counties and the middle South-West were the district of the most onerous villeinage, but even in the Midlands there was a proportion of comparatively free custom. This is the verdict of the charters, court-rolls, manorial surveys, final concords of the late twelfth and succeeding centuries, but it is contradicted by no evidence from the eleventh if the meaning of the Domesday *villanus* be rightly interpreted.

It has seemed best to reserve the thegns to the end of our survey *Thegnage* of the community because their status is to be explained neither by vassalage, nor birthright, nor property, nor tenure, and because attempts to treat them under one or more of those headings have led to confusion in the past, beginning from the moment when the Normans turned themselves to explain the society which they *The king's* conquered and never fully understood. The king's thegn has *thegns* already made his appearance once in Wihtraed's law, once in Ine's, and on a number of occasions in the Ecclesiastical History of Bede, where, as *minister*, he seems to be distinguished from the *comes* or gesith.[1] The mark of his status is a higher privilege than that of the latter,[2] and he is in some matters free from the common commitments of folkright. Royal patronage stands to him instead of kindred, for, like the priest, he can clear himself by his unsupported oath.[3] In origin, therefore, thegnage is an office, not a grade of the folk—the thegn may be either twelfhynd or twyhynd[4]—and it keeps this character until the rules of the folk fade out of memory. There is no indication that its holders were at first numerous. A couple of *ministri* attest Wulfred's charter of 674,[5] one thegn of Caedwalla of Wessex appears in 653,[6] and two attest a charter of Offa in 785.[7] If attestation of genuine charters is to be the test, it is not until the reign of Æthelwulf that the king's thegns begin to play an important part outside his immediate entourage,[8] and, though we must not place too much weight upon the practice of charter witness, it does indeed appear that the first great expansion of the thegnhood came with the military and political supremacy of Wessex.

The title of king's thegn may be applied to any official of high standing, but is especially used of the *ministri* below the rank of ealdorman and in constant and active service, and above all of those in immediate attendance on the king's person. We hear

[1] Bede, *Historia Ecclesiastica*, iii. 14. The Anglo-Saxon translator renders *miles* as *thegn* and *comes* as *gesith*. Cf. also W. de Gray Birch, *Cartularium Saxonicum*, 225, Cynewulf's grant: *Bican comiti meo et ministro*.

[2] Ine, 45: *Be burhbryce, Cyninges ðegnes lx scillinga: gesiðcundes monnes landhaebbendes xxxv scillinga*.

[3] Wihtraed, 20.

[4] III Æthelstan, Prologue: *Omnes Centescyre thaini, comites et villani*. F. E. Harmer, *Anglo-Saxon Writs*, No. 26, "all my thegns twyhynd and twelf hynd". Simeon of Durman. *De Gestis Regum*, ann. 884. The Norðleoda Laga, a Northumbrian text which betrays Celtic influence by allotting wergelds to each official rank, is the only pre-Norman code which gives the thegn a distinctive blood-price irrespective of birth (*loc. cit.* 5).

[5] W. de Gray Birch, *Cartularium Saxonicum*, 32.

[6] *Ibid.* 82.   [7] *Ibid.* 245.   [8] *Ibid.* 421 *et seq.*

of household officials, the *disc-thegn*,[1] perhaps the *pincerna* or butler, who might also be an ealdorman, of *hall-thegns*, of *bur-thegns*,[2] thegns of the king's bower or chamber, who survive as the servants of the Norman kings' *camera*, *horse-thegns*,[3] and *hrael-thegns*.[4] But, besides these holders of a working ministry about the court, there are other king's thegns of whom we can only say in general, as our texts say, that they are "very near to the king",[5] that they have "a special seat in the king's hall",[6] that they are in the king's *sundernot*, or personal service,[7] that he pays them a wage at Easter.[8] In later days the decisive act in recognizing a newly made baron was to allot him a seat at the tables of the king's hall, and authorize the livery of his own rations and those for the attendants custom allowed him in the palace. In all probability this would be the only tangible mark of the thegn's status also. As having this recognized provision about the king's person all the magnates, ealdormen, bishops, abbots, and the like were king's thegns,[9] as well as those who had no other standing but the king's ministry.

Beginning as a court officialdom—and although their title and office never became legally heritable[10]—the king's thegns were on the way to establishing themselves as a landed aristocracy by the middle of the ninth century. Principal links between the king and provincial administration, they were coming to have a foothold in the country as well as the court and to appear as county magnates. They were building estates of land upon the king's generosity, and their value in local government made the crown anxious to fortify their landed interest, limiting their court attendance to one month in three and leaving them free for the rest of the year to

The king's thegns and the land

---

[1] W. de Gray Birch, *Cartularium Saxonicum*, 912.

[2] J. M. Kemble, *Codex Diplomaticus*, 572.

[3] Anglo-Saxon Chronicle, 897A.

[4] W. de Gray Birch, *Cartularium Saxonicum*, 912.

[5] II Cnut, 71. 1.   [6] Geðincðo, 2.   [7] *Loc. cit.*

[8] J. M. Kemble, *Codex Diplomaticus*, 314.

[9] Anglo-Saxon Chronicle, 897A, gives the king's thegns who died in that year as the bishops of Dorchester and Rochester; the ealdormen of Kent, Essex, and Hampshire; Eadulf, a king's thegn of Sussex; Beornwulf, the wic-reeve of Winchester; and Ecgulf, the king's horse-thegn.

[10] They were renewed at the beginning of a new reign, and might be forfeited for misconduct. Cf. IV Eadgar, 2A: "All my thegns shall keep their (thegn)ship as in my father's day".

reside upon their estates.[1] Much land had been granted to individuals[2] as the reward of service and, unlike that of the gesiths of the past, it carried the free property of bookright. All these grants were, therefore, alienable at the discretion of the grantee and free of all conditions for the future.[3] There had been at least one distribution upon a national scale which can only be described as an endowment of the thegnage intended at once to secure their fidelity and to establish their material influence in the country. When Æthelwulf made his much debated decimation of his kingdom in favour of the churches he included in his benefaction his "thegns who are established throughout the said realm",[4] and,

---

[1] Asser, *De Rebus Gestis*, 101. *In tribus namque cohortibus praefati regis satellites prudentissime dividebantur, ita ut prima cohors uno mense in curto regio die noctuque administrans commoraretur, menseque finito, et adveniente alia cohorte, prima domum redibat.*

[2] W. de Gray Birch, *Cartularium Saxonicum*, 750 *et passim*.

[3] One royal charter only of this age, if it is correctly transcribed, represents an early attempt to fasten a condition of future service upon the recipient of book-land and his heirs—to make a holding of book-land dependent on thegn's service. W. de Gray Birch, *Cartularium Saxonicum*, 814: Edmund grants land at Weston to his thegn Æþelere, *eatenus ut vita comite tam fidus mente quam subditus operibus mihi placabile obsequium praebeat. Et post meum obitum cuicunque amicorum meorum amicorum voluero eadem fidelitate immobilis obediensque fiat. Sicque omnes posteriores praefatam terram possidentes in hoc decreto fideliter persistant sicuti decet ministro*: on condition that to the end of my life with faithful mind and bodily obedience he shall show me acceptable duty. And after my death he shall remain steadfast in the same faith and obedience to whomsoever of my friends I shall desire. And let all his successors who hold the same land hold faithfully to this provision as it behoves a thegn to do. (Notice how the king's reservation of the intention to bequeath the thegn's service after his death conforms to Saxon notions of the alienability of right, in contrast with the customary descent of the *feudum* through heirs. It is derived from the general notion of bookright.) A comparison of what is, in effect, a rough attempt to anticipate the principle of the *feudum* with a gift to a thegn in the common Saxon form will show how widely the former differs from Saxon notions. W. de Gray Birch, *Cartularium Saxonicum*, 1197: Eadgar grants to his faithful vassal Wulfoð three hides in Lesmannoc *liberaliter in æternam possessionem . . . ut illo predicto territorio voti compos vita perfruatur comite, et post obitum ejus cuicumque voluerit heredi derelinquat. Tam in minimis quam in magnis . . . immunem derelinquat. Prefatum siquidem rus omni servitio careat*: freely in eternal possession . . . so that he shall possess the said land during his life, and after his death leave it to any heir he will, free in great things and small. The aforesaid estate shall be immune from all service. The reservation of the *trinoda necessitas* which follows is, of course, that of a public obligation on all land.

[4] *Decimam partem terrarum per regnum non solum sanctis ecclesiis darem, verum eciam et ministris nostris in eodem constitutis (ibid.* 469). This is probably an original text, and is the centre of a group of charters of varying authenticity and intelligibility. By W. de Gray Birch, *Cartularium Saxonicum*, 486 (*Textus*

whatever the effect of his grants as regarded the church, the secular thegnage benefited by a series of charters conveying book-land. This endowment of 854 was typical of the second of three attempts to stabilize the king's dependants in the countrysides. The first ministry, of the gesithcund men, perhaps died away for lack of heritable right, the second, the king's thegnage, had property of which the king retained no power of regulating the descent, and so they dissipated their lands by bequest and gift, the third, the Norman enfeoffment, was to find in the *feudum* the key to the honour,[1] heritable in perpetuity, in general indivisible, and bound by perpetual service and fealty to the crown. If the thegn held other land not under bookright but under the common rules of folkright, as no doubt many did, that also was not held in any feudal tenure. It must, says a law passed within a half-century of the Conquest, be equitably distributed among his heirs.[2] Thus, while the *ministerium* of the king's thegns carried a duty of service less specific than that of feudal knight or baron, their landright was a thing apart from it, property not tenure.

There are already signs in the ninth century that with many thegns the provincial interest will outgrow that of court service, so that their attendance will come to be titular, or only exercized at the ceremonial courts of Christmas, Easter, and Michaelmas, or when the king, passing about his kingdom, resides and holds council in some provincial centre. In the attestations to charters we can trace some thegns in constant attendance in all parts of the realm, and some of these rise to be ealdormen and are clearly national figures.[3] But others seem to be provincial notables only, coming in from their country seats to Winchester or Canterbury.[4] Had Saxon government been less closely knit, the thegns might well have grown away from their ministerial origin, and survived as a landed nobility with nothing of ministry but the title. That

Functions of the king's thegns

Roffensis), the thegn Dunn receives land *pro decimatione agrorum quam Deo donante caeteris ministris meis facere decrevi*. Eadgar expresses the same motive (J. M. Kemble, *Codex Diplomaticus*, 536): *disposui ex opibus mihi a deo concessis meos fideles ministros cum consilio optimatum meorum ditare*: I have determined with the counsel of my magnates to endow my faithful thegns out of the wealth given me by God.

[1] Cf. p. 140, *infra*.   [2] II Cnut, 78.
[3] As did Eastmund under Æthelbert and Æthelred of Wessex. W. de Gray Birch, *Cartularium Saxonicum*, 506, 507, 516, 519.
[4] Like Lulla, Æthered, Wullaf, etc. *Ibid.* 449, 460, 467, 486, 501, 506, 519.

they did not do so was in part due to the fact that the king kept
in constant touch with the shires, and required of his thegns much
the same steady coöperation in the shire courts, of which they
formed the witan, as he did from the bishops, ealdormen, and
thegns about his person. The king's thegn was becoming the
knight of the shire of his day; he owed special obedience to the
king's ban,[1] and to the body of the shire-thegns the king's writs
were addressed.[2] The king maintained a tone of patronage to his
thegns, looked to them for a special standard of conduct, and
made use of their strength to afforce his reeves. In the eleventh
century he laid upon them the primary responsibility for judgment in shire and hundred,[3] Under like penalties with the king's
sheriffs and reeves, they were set to enforce the pacts of mutual
peace into which he persuaded the countrysides from time to
time,[4] to carry out the regulations against theft,[5] to force priests to
keep their rule,[6] to collect the dues of the church.[7] In such matters
the king's thegns and the king's reeves were on the same footing,
and were so treated in enactments.[8] Both came under similar
penalties for abusing their charge,[9] and where the reeve might lose
his office, the thegn might lose his thegnage.[10] These are particular
applications of the ministry which it was found necessary to
specify from time to time in royal ordinances. They were additional to duties in which the thegns were the executive hands of
the folkmoots. At least the leadership of the elaborate routine of
arrest, process serving, levying of distress, eviction for contempt
of judgment, pursuit of outlawry, and hue and cry, lay upon the
thegns who rode upon the court's errands and enforced its decrees[11]
with a growing sense of royal commission as the king's initiative
in law and order became more active. The tenth century was a
great age of the English crown, and the king's thegns were its

---

[1] *Rectitudines Singularum Personarum*, 1.

[2] F. E. Harmer, *Anglo-Saxon Writs*, No. 82. *Eadward kyng gret well . . . ealle
mine ðegnas on þam scyrum þar Sancte Peter into Westmynstre hafað land inne.* Cf.
also Nos. 11, 24, 29, etc.

[3] III Æthelred, 3. 1. *Ibid.* 13. 2.   [4] VI Æthelstan, 11.

[5] *Loc. cit.*   [6] IV Eadgar, 1. 8.

[7] Northumbrian Priests' Law, 57. 2.   [8] III Eadmund, 7. 2.

[9] The king's oferhyrnes or ban of 120/-. Cf. V Æthelstan, 1. 4 and VI. 11,
and III Eadmund, 7. 2.

[10] III Eadgar, 3. The judge who gives false judgment forfeits his thegnage.

[11] III Æthelred, 3. 1, 2; J. M. Kemble, *Codex Diplomaticus*, 755.

characteristic servants, a corps of provincial *ministeriales* more obedient, more at the mercy of the king, and more readily responsive to royal mandates than the Norman kings had in their barons. They were empowered to ride in the king's stead with his writ and summons,[1] and it is in this function that we see them intervening in the shire courts or local witenagemots of the tenth century with ordinances to proclaim, and commission to advise and coöperate in their execution.[2] Some of them were very great men indeed, and, though their commissions were not regularized as routine visitations, upon occasion they fulfilled something of the function of the Carolingian *missi*. Through them, as much as through reeves and ealdormen, the crown controlled the provinces.

Thegnage means no more than service, *ministerium*. From the ninth to the eleventh century it was the normal expedient for getting done any work of exploitation or administration which could not be conveniently left to the reeves, or for discharging such public duties as could be done by deputy. So, just as the king's thegns made themselves useful about his person or seconded the reeves of the shires and boroughs, so every great royal estate and every great private franchise had its thegns also. The thegns upon the king's estates are not king's thegns—though indirectly they are thegns of the king—for they take their orders from the reeve of the estate,[3] pay their rents into his farm,[4] attend his summons to court,[5] and go upon his errands. If they are amerced their fines go to the reeve, whereas those of the king's thegns go to the crown. Probably their heriots, which are small, go through the estate farm also. "They serve the reeve of the manor."[6] While no

The lesser thegns

[1] Geþyncðo, 3: *He þenode cynge and on his radstæfne rad: regi servisset et vice sua equitaret in missiatico regis.*

[2] VI Æthelstan, 10: "The witan at Thundersfield . . . to which Ælfheah Stybbe and Brihtnoth, son of Odda, came, bringing the king's word to the moot" (J. M. Kemble, *Codex Diplomaticus*, 755).

[3] Domesday Book, i. 269B. *Si cui jubebat in suum (prepositi) servitium ire et non ibat, iiii solidos emendebat*: if the reeve ordered any one of them to go on his errand and he did not go, he paid four shillings in amendment.

[4] As in the king's hundreds Inter Ripam et Mersam (Domesday Book, *loc. cit.*), and of Winnington in Cornwall (*ibid.* i. 120A). Cf. also *ibid.* I. 172A.

[5] *Ibid.* i. 269B: *Si . . . non ibat ad placitum ubi prepositus jubebat . . .*: if he did not go to the moot when the reeve ordered . . .

[6] *Ibid.* i. 86B: *Tres taini tenebant T.R.E. et serviebant preposito manerii*: three thegns held it T.R.E. and served the reeve of the manor.

one may have jurisdiction over a king's thegn except the king, the lesser thegns are transferred as a matter of course with the administration to which they belong.[1] It would be hopeless to try to reduce all these small *ministeriales* to a common standard. Subjection to local custom, absence of judicial privilege, obedience to reeves' authority, seem to have been their distinctive mark, and local custom varied endlessly. The habit of each group of such thegns was that of the administration to which they were attached. Nevertheless, there seems to have been some effort to legislate for them as a class. They were spoken of as *laess-thegns, mediocres taini, meduman thegene*,[2] meaning, perhaps, medial or mesne thegns, as standing at one degree removed from the cognizance and protection of the king. They were considered to have a uniform heriot of forty shillings,[3] and a man-bote of ten,[4] and, for those derelictions of duty for which the king's thegn paid the king's oferhyrnes of a hundred and twenty shillings, the medial thegns paid forty to the reeve.

The great units of *terra regis* are especially rich in these medial thegnages, above all in the north and west, where the great extent of the economic units made a class intermediate between the reeves and the peasantry almost necessary. There, as in the king's hundreds in Lancashire, they were liable for the ordinary dues of the countryside, worked on the king's buildings *sicut villani*, made the deer-hedge for the royal hunt, guarded the fisheries, and sent reapers into the king's fields for the harvest.[5] Small thegnages of this kind may be found upon many of the great clerical estates rendering their dues into the farms of the reeves of the immunity.[6] In some, as in those of Shaftsbury,[7] they owe services of ploughing and harvesting like the king's Lancashire thegns; in others there is no specified service, and one may suspect that, beyond a money rent, their principal use to their lords

[1] F. E. Harmer, *Anglo-Saxon Writs*, No. 108. *Eadgar cyning . . . bead ælcon his þegna þe enig land on þan lande* (Taunton) *hafde þat hi hit ofeodon be þeo biscopes gemedon.* King Edgar bade all his thegns who had land there to hold it at the bishop's will. Cf. also, less certainly authentic, *ibid.* No. 100.

[2] II Cnut, 71. 2.

[3] Domesday Book, i. 269B, 298B, and Hen. I, 1. 14.

[4] Domesday Book, i. 179A, and Leis Willelme, 7.

[5] Domesday Book, i. 269B.

[6] As at Worcester. *Ibid.* 172A.

[7] British Museum MSS. Cotton. Tiberius, 61.

was legal, maintenance in court, pursuance of legal process,[1] and responsible errand bearing. Very commonly, such thegns had no property, and therefore no inheritance in the estate their lords allowed them. Oswald's laens at Worcester were mostly made to the thegns of his church and for three lives only. The sons of the thegns between the Ribble and the Mersey were by custom allowed to take their fathers' lands, but there was no heritable property. In some cases a measure of independence was accorded by the commutation of the thegn's works and dues for a fixed farm, while certain of the great churches produced something which bore a remote simulacrum of knight service by setting apart a number of estates as *thegnland*,[2] keeping them inalienable,[3] but writing them off temporarily from the *firma ecclesiae*. That any heritable succession was allowed to establish itself in such lands before the Conquest is unlikely,[4] though after 1066 perpetuity was achieved by the introduction of *feudofirma* (heritable farm) at the Conquest.[5]

It will be seen that these various kinds of thegnage cannot really be classified. Besides the two outstanding types which we have described, there were thegns for every conceivable ministry, among them men serving Godwin, or Witgar, or Tostig with as much honour as the king's thegns served the king, and many whose service the Normans thought to be *sicut villani*. If we take the term thegn without qualification it is a parallel to the official or ministerial element in the royal and honorial barony and the grand and petty serjeanty of the Normans, but it has no element of feudal tenure. Instead of with the *feudum*, it is associated variously

Thegnage not feudal

---

[1] Geþyncðo, 3. The thegn may "make the foreoath for his lord and carry his cause to the end with full right", *i.e.* can act as his proctor in folkright.

[2] Domesday Book, i. 66B: *Unam hidam quae jure pertinet abbatiae de teinlande*: one hide which of right belongs to this abbey as thegnland. The Abingdon Chronicle is particularly rich in references to the thegnlands of the abbey.

[3] *Loc. cit.*: *Haec terra teinlande non potuit ab ecclesia separari*: this land, being thegnland, could not be taken away from the church.

[4] *Cartularium Monasterii de Rameseia*, i. 233 (1087–1096): *Si vero teinland tunc fuisse invenietur . . . si voluerit, eam abbas in dominio habeat*: if it is found to have been thegnland . . . let the abbot take it into demesne if he will.

[5] The elements from which the law of the thegn and his holding were being patched into a tenure of thegnage in the twelfth century are well seen in a charter recorded by Simeon of Durham (*Scriptores Tres*, lv.) granting Ellingham *in feodofirma theineslage*. Here we have the farm (a rent of £4), the fee giving perpetuity, and the "thegn's law" carrying heriot and service. It is a kind of rustic parody of the knight's fee.

with book-land, laen, bookright for terms of lives, farm. Nor can it be brought into any formal relation to the service of Norman knighthood. Based on no fee, it carried an infinitely variable service, and the one military obligation that can be posited of it at all times and places is the normal *trinoda necessitas*—fyrd, borough bot, and bridge bot—of folkright. This even the thegn's book-land owed. It is true that every thegn was in the special service of the king, or of some reeve or lord, and that it was an age of almost constant war, but Dr. Round's enquiries [1] have shown that his character was expressed in no such uniform incidents as that of the knight. The latter's place was in the feudal host; that of the thegn in time of war was in the fyrd [2] or as the personal guard of the king, though it might entail leadership and onerous duties during a campaign.

Thegnage and the social ranks

The variable functions of thegnage give it the widest distribution in every social degree, and it becomes perhaps the most outstanding fact in the society of the late Saxon age. It is not to be supposed that every landowner was a thegn, nor that every relation of lord and man carried with it the additional obligations of the thegn's service. Nevertheless, it was prevalent enough for official documents, at least in Wessex, to assume that the shires and boroughs whom they addressed were communities of thegns. Thegn and land-holder become in loose generalization interchangeable terms, and the old grades of the folk were coming to be forgotten. *Thegen and theoden* was now as natural a classification of society as *eorl and ceorl*. It is a curious phase of social growth of which one does not easily see the future, in which—without any real promise of coming feudalism—large sections of the community have become ministerialized, in which there is little

[1] Round, *Feudal England*.

[2] Some countrysides were allowed to compound for the levy *en masse* of the fyrd with one man from every five hides, the generality paying their expenses. It cannot be said categorically that no religious houses looked to their thegnlands to discharge this service, but there is no evidence that they did so. The Abingdon Charter, which purports to free all St. Mary's lands of service of war for a quota of twelve "vassals" (J. M. Kemble, *Codex Diplomaticus*, 214), is a most suspect document. The operative phrase *cum xij vassallis et cum tantis scutis exerceant* is of the twelfth century rather than the ninth. In general the five-hide quota system applies to the community at large and has nothing to do with the practice of Norman knight service by which a certain number of fees defended the whole honour and left the non-feudal lands immune.

tendency towards the growth of hereditary entail in landright. But thegnage, though it lacks the perpetuity of the feudal tie, is yet working powerfully to undermine those racial loyalties which were still the most serious rivals to English unity. In 1066 the Confessor's thegns were spread throughout Mercia and East Anglia as well as Wessex. If the laws of the Saxons, Danes, and Mercians were still distinct, a common law of thegnage and royal obedience already overspread them.

The tribal quality in institutions has been largely outgrown. *Growth* There is a common *Regnum Anglorum* as the basis of English *of a* supremacy over Celt and Dane,[1] and the king bears a kind of dual *territorial* *society* title as King of the English and King of Britain. The kingdom as a territorial power is vaguely foreshadowed in such recurrent phrases as *Rex regionis Angligenarum*,[2] *telluris Brittanicae*,[3] *Albionis*.[4] The old racial divisions are now thought of less as maegths than as provinces of law; a Danelaw, a West Seaxna Law, a Mircna Law, are recognized as principal components of the state, and, where the administrative ordinances once legislated for the *methel* or the *thing*, they now speak of the hundred and the shire. Clearly, the land has come to hold an equal place in imagination with the race. Ælfred's code is the last to use the old kindred grades as general categories of the folk, and to apply them to the common purposes of the law as a matter of course, and a treatise *Of Ranks and Laws*, of the middle eleventh century, writes their epitaph: "Time was in English law when status and privilege went by rank. Then were the wise given their due worship, each according to his degree, eorl and ceorl. . . ." In this text we may read what has been the common trend of English law since, perhaps, the reign of Æthelstan—the virtual abandonment of the old folk grades or their formal, hesitant, and often mistaken, use, and their supersession by newer classifications which have become more real in an age of wealth and lordship. "Rich and poor",[5] *landagenda and ceorl*,[6] *landrica and tunesman*,[7] *thegn and bonda*,[8] *thegn and theoden*,[9]

---

[1] J. M. Kemble, *Codex Diplomaticus*, 727. Cnut calls himself *Imperator regiminis Anglici in Insula.*   [2] *Ibid.* 641.   [3] *Ibid.* 534.
[4] *Ibid.* 537.   [5] IV Edgar, 2. 2.
[6] Northumbrian Priests' Law.   [7] North People's Law, 59.
[8] VII Æthelred, 3.   [9] Geþyncðo, 1.

replace the traditional twelfhynd and twyhynd, which linger only in the archaic formulae of writs. The spread of thegnage elevates the thegn as the principal element among the magnates almost to the position of the twelfhynd man. To the Norman latinizers of English texts the thegn is *plene nobilis*.[1] Where Celtic influence is strong, the Celtic usage of accommodating the wergeld to official and not to blood rank[2] has established itself. In Northumbria, the bishop, ealdorman, king's high reeve, priest, and thegn has each his appropriate wer.[3] There is also a tendency to grade the blood-price according to the amount of land.[4] It is not clear from the text whether this is held to be true of Englishman and Weahlishman alike, but, in any case, the custom seems to be characteristic of the Celtic fringes of the North and West, and is found as early as Ine's code in respect of the *Weahlcynn* of Wessex.[5] It is probable, indeed, that the whole system of wergelds displayed in the North People's Law is part of the Celtic legacy to that Anglo-Celtic people, the Northumbrians. No purely English text explicitly deserts the theory that the wer comes by blood, until commentaries upon English law begin to come from Norman scribes.[6] The tendency is rather for twelfhynd and twyhynd to be eliminated as classifications of society, and for more precise terms of social and economic meaning to take their place. The landhlaford, even if not a thegn, is coming to the fore in legal record, and for the first time the custom of private estates is being recognized—hlaford's law,[7] which the Normans will call the custom of the manor. In all this the eleventh century is seen as an age which has lost its hold upon its primitive social rules, and is seeking new ones, though as yet unsystematically, in a world where service and landed property are coming to a new importance in social relations which is as yet undefined.

Conclu-sion   This is a distinctive phase of society that has no close parallel, and one of which it is not easy to see the outcome. The common impression, that it lacked stability and the essentials for growth

[1] Quadripartitus; II Cnut, 31. IA.   [2] Cf. the Laws of Howel Dda.
[3] North People's Law, 3-5.   [4] *Ibid.* 7-12.
[5] Ine, 24. 2. Cf. also Dunsaete, 5.   [6] Leis Willelme, 8.
[7] Gerefa, 1. A competent reeve should know *hlafordes landriht* as well as *folces gerihtu*.

towards unity, probably does it less than justice. It is true that it had not that uniquely strong quality of feudalism which associated every relation, power, and duty with the material interest of tenure, but its lower ranks were held together by a common respect for law and legal process which was sanctified by religion. At no period, perhaps, was it more difficult to flout the conventions of lawful behaviour and to retain a standing in the community. The Norman régime inherited this strongly legalistic basis, and owed much of its strength to it, as did every reign until late in the fourteenth century. In the very general ministerializing of society—so general that it was a common assumption that the man of landed substance would be a king's thegn—the nation had a bond of discipline and stability which was comparatively new, but it also had the older lordship which was capable of building wide-spreading connections by fealty both for the king and the magnates, and which—perhaps because it was not materialized by association with land, and could be revoked without loss of estate—seems to have been free from the grosser abuses of feudalism. We know of no episode in Saxon history so dangerous to the state as some of feudal leagues of Norman and Angevin England, and the fate of Tostig and some episodes in the life of Godwin show that the tie of commendation could on occasion break when it was turned against the king. It is true that commendation and bookright built up no continuity of property and lordship, and that these were likely to be dispersed with every generation. At the moment of the Norman Conquest the shape of English life was governed no longer by the blood-relationship which had created it, and not yet by the nexus of tenure in which the Normans were to confine it, but in the main by personal and revocable agreements between lord and man. Yet the more mobile life of the eleventh century had inherited strength from the régime of the folk and was already deriving more from the growth of monarchy.

We cannot guess the future of this society had it been left to work out its own fate. On the eve of the Conquest its bent was not fully decided. It was territorialized, but not feudalized. It had lordship but not tenure; its nobles by blood had died out and its official notables had yet to be recognized as a nobility. If ever it had reached the phase of feudalism it would have done so but slowly in the absence of foreign intervention. It is possible that, since it had already made the transition from the tribal to the territorial state and developed a stable local administration, a strong succession of native kings might have guided it to become a kingdom of the Scandinavian type, but with greater stability, a more closely knit community, and a more complex government. If the successors of Harold had failed in leadership the kingdom of England could hardly have survived, and the Humber and the Thames might again have become national boundaries; normal ability in its kings would probably have kept the united kingdom one. Thus the groundwork of a nation state had been laid, perhaps more truly than in any Continental kingdom. It remained for the Normans to engraft into the community the endurance of the fees and honours, ultimately strengthening the fabric of society, though perhaps at some sacrifices of variety and energy, and to elaborate the court and household of the king into a judicial and fiscal machine which made a new epoch in the history of government. With that metamorphosis we enter upon a third and well-defined phase of English history.

ii

THE KINGDOM OF BRITAIN

Intro-
ductory

During its first four centuries English history is mainly determined from below. Economic forces and the initiative of the crown make head only very slowly against the innate conservatism of the community. In the century and a half between Ælfred and the Norman Conquest this is reversed. The crown comes to the fore and transforms its own status and powers, and the country begins to respond to its leadership. In this period are created a territorial community, the unified realm, a crown pre-eminent in the most important section of the law, a national peace, and the administrative frame of shires and hundreds as we know them in the Middle Ages. Not all these prerequisites of medieval government are achieved consciously, or recognized at once for what they are, but the revolution is there in fact, and, after due credit is given to the nation for its power of adaptability, it is mainly the work of a great succession of kings. The radical change which took place in the community is in the main a reorientation imposed from above. The chaos caused by the Danish wars gave the crown

its opportunity, for the nation could only survive at the cost of *Political*
reconstruction. By the time of Ælfred's death Mercia, East Anglia, *unification*
and Northumbria were extinct as native kingdoms, and there
were no rivals to the house of Wessex except the various governments of the Danes. An English victory must, therefore, mean a
single crown for all the Angles and Saxons, and, in all probability,
for the island of Britain. For that reason, together with the military
work of conquest, the first task of the dynasty was to find an
acceptable claim and title to the united realm. No tribal kingdom
of the Gewissae could long contain its diverse elements. At the
death of Ælfred only Wessex was directly in the hands of his son
Eadward. Mercia, under Æthelred and Æthelflaeda, preserved its
identity, and the Danish powers were bound to him only by
treaties of peace. In 912 Æthelred died, but the king contented
himself with adding to his kingdom only London and Oxford,
and "the land that belonged to them",[1] and thenceforward he
extended his power piecemeal by conquest in the border districts
of Essex (913), Bedford (918), and Northamptonshire (921).[2] In
the last years of his reign the cumulative effect of his victories
became apparent, and whole peoples began to "seek him to lord",
the Danes of Cambridge and East Anglia in 921, the North Welsh
in 922, while in the latter year the Lady of the Mercians died, and,
against some grudging by Mercian patriots, the lordship was
absorbed into the kingdom. In 924 Eadward reached his furthest
North, and, at Bakewell in Peakland, there "took him to father
and to lord" the Scottish king and all the Scots, Raegnald, who
may have been the head of the Danish power in York, Ealdred,
leader of the Northumbrian English, and the Welsh king of
Strathclyde. From this moment the British empire of the English
kings was in the letter complete.

We have no charters[3] from these years of Eadward's greatness— *Growth*
during his early years he attested himself *Rex Angol-Saxonum*[4] and *of the*
royal
Rex Anglorum,[5] as did his father—but Æthelstan at once assumes *title*
a status which is not in substance abandoned until the Norman
Conquest. In its fullest extension the title of Æthelstan and his

[1] Anglo-Saxon Chronicle, 912A.   [2] *Ibid. sub annis.*
[3] What follows does not rest on the genuineness of any given charter. These
royal styles and pretensions characterize a whole phase of English diplomatic.
[4] J. M. Kemble, *Codex Diplomaticus*, 333.   [5] *Ibid.* 337.

successors is Emperor of Albion or Britain, *Basileus Albionis monarchus*,[1] *totius Brittaniae Basileus*,[2] "King and Caesar of all Britain".[3] It is likely that these enhanced titles were put forward in part to discourage such imperial intervention as Charlemagne had been inclined to venture, but still more to cover the varying shades of authority and patronage which bound the English peoples to one king together with "all those races who dwell about them".[4] Though imperial in its independence and its power over conquered and allied nations, the realm of the English was still a racial one; a theory which should confine the royal right within the circle of the crown and make it a quality of the reigning monarch would have been unintelligible to the successors of Ælfred. The English peoples had come to realize their affinity, the West Saxon king now stood for all their various branches, and was *Basileus Anglicae Nationis*,[5] or *Rex Regionis Angligenarum*;[6] but the title was dual, as was the political fact it stood for. Over the *Imperium Britanniae* Angles the kingdom was still a racial right, but over the Britons and the "Pagans" it was the right of the Angles as a conquering and royal race—*Imperator regiminis Anglici in Insula*.[7] Thus, alternating with the sharp definition of the *regnum* or *imperium Britanniae*, are formulae which reveal its composite origin. *Rex*, or *Basileus Anglorum*, the king is *rector*,[8] *primicerius*,[9] *propugnator*[10] of the alien races. "King of the English and mundbora over many nations".[11] The crown of the tenth century is, perhaps, best described in King Eadred's own words upon his accession: "it came to pass on the death of King Eadmund, who most royally governed the realms of the Anglo-Saxons, the Northumbrians, the Heathen, and the Britons, that in the same year I, Eadred, his uterine brother was called by the choice of the witan, and by apostolic authority received catholic consecration as king and ruler of the fourfold realm".[12] Over the diversity of peoples is set the imperial crown

---

1 J. M. Kemble, *Codex Diplomaticus*, 461.   2 *Ibid.* 357.

3 *Cyning and casere totius Britanniae. Ibid.* 433.

4 *Ibid.* 372: *Basileus . . . Anglorum cunctarumque gentium in circuitu persistentium.*

5 *Ibid.* 622, 636, 638, 640.   6 *Ibid.* 641, 743.

7 *Ibid.* 435: *Basileos Anglorum, huiusque insulae barbarorum. Ibid.* 424.

8 *Ibid.* 426.   9 *Ibid.* 434, 441, 442.   10 *Ibid.* 426.

11 *Ibid.* 378, 385, 377: *Rex Anglorum et curagulus multarum gentium.*

12 *Ibid.* 411: *Regna quadripertiti regiminis.*

with its trebly reiterated sanction of birth, election, and apostolic consecration.

The *populus Anglorum* is still the first constituent of the king- *Imperial* ship, but as time goes on the crown seeks to incorporate all its *Councils* provinces in its constitution. As in the past, the king's authority and the witan's, like the obverse and reverse faces of a coin, together give currency to national acts, and the king's power is personified in the composition of his assemblies. The normal governing force of the tenth century is the witenagemot of the real English of the South and Midlands, the bishops of the southern province, the five or six ealdormen who survive south of Trent, and lesser thegns and churchmen whom we may guess to have been southerners also. Such councils reflect the older, more common, and more real title of the king as *Rex Anglorum*. Beginning, however, with Eadward's Bakewell council of 924, the full extension of the empire is at times exemplified in a witenagemot which can fairly be called imperial. One such Æthelstan held in the autumn of 931 at Luton,[1] and another at Pentecost, 934, at Winchester.[2] To them, in addition to the English witan of the South, came Welsh kings—among them the great law-giver Howel Dda—the archbishop of York and the Northumbrian bishops, the northerners Ealdred and Uhtred, with Osuulf, later high-reeve of Bamborough, and many *duces* who by their names must have been the Danish eorls of Yorkshire and the Five Boroughs, Guthrum, and Haward, Gunner, Hadd, Scule, Inhwaer, and Halfdene. Eadmund held an assembly of this kind in 942.[3] Eadred's accession council of 946 was an especially magnificent example.[4] Six kings were with Eadgar at Chester in 973, and legend has chosen this occasion as the culminating glory of the Saxon monarchy.[5]

These great witenagemots are special and occasional demonstrations of the *Imperium Britanniae*. The attendance of the northern archbishop at more ordinary meetings, which becomes common from the last years of Eadmund,[6] is, perhaps, a better test of its reality, but in any case we could hardly expect a rapid absorption

---

[1] J. M. Kemble, *Codex Diplomaticus*, 353.   [2] *Ibid.* 364.
[3] *Ibid.* 392.   [4] *Ibid.* 411.   [5] Anglo-Saxon Chronicle, 972B.
[6] Eadmund is the first king to legislate with the counsel of both archbishops. I Eadmund, Prologue.

of the other kingdoms into Wessex. It is, on the contrary, a very gradual process. The basic folkright of each of the nations was still *The union* indefeasible. Æthelstan seems at times to be unconscious that his *of the* law-making can extend beyond Wessex.[1] Eadgar recognizes the *laws* variant laws: "I will that secular law shall stand in each folk as can best be established".[2] The autonomy of the Danes is especially affirmed: "I will that secular law shall stand with the Danes by as good custom as they may be able to choose",[3] and Eadgar expressly limits most of the new laws of his witan's making to the English. The imperial witenagemots of the early tenth century were, therefore, clearly ceremonial and not legislative, and not till Eadgar's reign do we find the first edicts common to all the nations. His elaborate scheme of precautions against theft and the disposal of stolen goods is imposed upon the whole Island: "the following edict shall be common to every folk, Angles, Danes, and Britons in every quarter of my realm".[4] By this enactment the Danish administrative units make their first appearance in English law, and the wapentake is appropriated to the carrying out of an English king's orders, as in Wessex and Mercia the hundred. As yet this is an exception, and Eadgar expressly promises that it shall be so: "my witan and I have chosen what the penalty shall be, let the Danes choose according to their law".[5] But the slow fusion has begun. It is possible that, at least as far as new enactments were concerned, Mercia and Wessex were now treated as a common English law.[6] Æthelred, though recognizing the Danelah as distinct, legislates for it with far more confidence than Eadgar. The ordinances of Wantage constitute a complete enactment of procedure and police regulations for the Five Boroughs, their courts, and officials. They are not all new, but by naming the reeves of the Danelah as king's reeves,[7] and by ordering that the right of Christ and the special right of the king should be protected under Danish procedure as under English,[8] Æthelred was establishing the status of an English crown in an alien folk. If Eadward and his successors were lords and mundboras of the Danes, Æthelred was their king.

---

[1] II Æthelstan, 14. 2.   [2] IV Eadgar, 2
[3] *Ibid.* 2. 1.   [4] *Ibid.* 2. 2.   [5] *Ibid.* 14, 13. 1.
[6] Mercian law was theoretically distinct in the early twelfth century.
[7] III Æthelred, 1. 1.   [8] V Æthelred, 31.

The final absorption of the Danelah into the English monarchy, *The King* inevitable though it was, came almost suddenly with the accession *of Eng-* of a Danish king. Cnut bound both Dane and Saxon by the law *land* of Eadgar.[1] Natural king of the Danes and king by election and conquest of the English, he spoke to his realm as one nation,[2] which, for him, a foreigner, with no native right, appeared as a territorial rather than a racial power. Alone among his contemporaries, he took his title from the English land,[3] ordered his edicts to be observed "over all England",[4] and, in the spirit of Æthelred, but more explicitly, warned every man, Dane or Englishman, that, if he defied the law of God or the king's royal right, he would be driven from the realm.[5] One, and not the least important element in this royal right of which he speaks, we may see in the full enumeration of all the special powers of the king, the *cynescipe*, in the form which custom gave them in the Danelah, the king's pleas, the *trinoda necessitas*, the special wites of the king, and the heriots of the thegns. This, at least, was a law binding "over all England". The foundation was Æthelred's work, but the strong reign of Cnut established that balance of royal preëminence and local folkright by which, in the words of the Norman legist, "the law of England is threefold, of Wessex, Mercia, and the Danelah . . . and above it we acknowledge the royal right of the king's majesty as most fearfully to be obeyed".[6] It was no empty phrase that Cnut used when he abandoned the vaguer claim to a British *Imperium*, and called his kingdom England.[7]

There remained, of course, an ingrained provincialism which *Lordship* even Glanvill recognized. The exalted titles which came into *and the* fashion in the tenth century were, in fact, deceptive. They reflected *king*

[1] Anglo-Saxon Chronicle, 1018D. *Dene and Engle wurdon sammæle æt Oxanaforda to Eadgares Lage.*

[2] *Rationabili consideratione decrevit, quatinus sicut uno rege, ita et una lege universum Angliae regnum regeretur* (Consiliatio Cnuti (1110–1130), Proem, 2).

[3] Cnut, 1027, Proem: *Canutus, rex totius Angliae*; I Cnut, Proem: *Cnut cyning, ealles Englalandes cyningc.*

[4] II Cnut, Prologue.   [5] Cnut, 1020. 9–10.

[6] Leges Henrici Primi, 6. 2: *Preter hoc tremendum regie maiestatis imperium titulamus.*

[7] In his few charters Cnut used the title *Rex Anglorum*, but charter formulae were traditional.

the geographical extension of the monarchy rather than its effective core. That was still the *Regnum Anglorum*, and the English kings' power could grow only with the advance of purely English notions. The general hardening of the sense of political obligation is, of course, the product of many factors and is hardly susceptible of analysis. That the kingship of the Confessor was more full and more deeply felt than that of Ælfred, is true, but it is not the subject of contemporary record. Again, it will not be supposed that lordship will have the same formative effect in Saxon England as in a feudal kingdom. Since its emotional force was a loan from that of the kindred, and since it had not succeeded in associating itself with the tenure of land, it is unlikely that lordship was a stronger bond in the eleventh century than it had been in the seventh, and, indeed, the period before the Conquest is one in which authority is watching its effects closely, and passing laws to control its abuse. Nevertheless, the tie of lord and man was felt to be one of the natural relations and therefore beneficial to the state. Ælfred's condemnation of treachery was reiterated,[1] and it was one of the ties which the crown sought to turn to its own advantage in an age of conquest. As in the common social life, so in politics, the chief value of lordship is to establish a tie of sentiment and obedience where there is no tie of blood. Kings who were not native, *gecyndne*, might be received as hlaford and mundbora. A taking of Eadward to lord was, as we have seen, the form in which eorl Thurkill accepted English rule in 918, and in 921 Thurferth and the men of Northampton "sought him to lord and to mundbora", while in the lyrical passages of the Chronicle, which preserve traditional epithets and old ways of thought, the distinction between the right of Ælfred's house in Mercia and in their native Wessex is still maintained: "Eadgar, ruler of all the Angles, darling of the West Saxons, mundbora of the Mercians".[2]

The oath of loyalty   From the period of Eadward the Elder the swearing of fealty to the king became part of English political practice, and was handed on to the Norman kings as their most effective counter to the act of homage between vassals and sub-vassals. There is no proof that the oath was put to the generality in their local moots, but—of instances which have come down to us—it was taken from the witan by Eadward, Eadmund, and Æthelred, and such an oath

[1] II Æthelstan, 4.   [2] Anglo-Saxon Chronicle, 975E.

by the witan was representative of the nation. The oath sworn was
the common hold-oath. Eadward's witan at Exeter followed its
terms with the conventional formula "to love all that the king
loves and to shun all that he shuns",[1] the witan at Colyton swore
"faith to King Eadmund as a man ought to bear faith to his lord",[2]
and, on Æthelred's restoration, that of 1014 enacted that all should
"be hold to one royal lord".[3] Cnut, with that note of authority
that is in all his utterances, promised at the beginning of his settled
reign, to "be good lord to all his people". Until the feudalization
of lordship, however, it remained a revocable and dubious tie,
countered by innumerable private, and, no doubt, more effective
agreements of fealty between subjects. The king himself constantly
accepted the special commendation of individuals, and thereby
proved that effective kingship needed specific agreements to bring
it into being. In 1051 the Confessor did not dare to allow Godwin
into his presence until he had induced the former's thegns to
transfer their fealty to himself,[4] and it is this immediate, commended
vassalage that we find in the submission of the Cambridge Danes
in 921, when they took the king one by one—*synderlice*—to lord,
and strengthened their act with oaths.[5] If such a fealty as that of
921 had become the rule, the crown might have acquired from it
some of the security which it afterwards sought from liege vassalage, but we do not know that the experiment was repeated on a
national scale, and the king continued to form his own personal
connection of commended men like any other magnate. Kingship
was not to be radically strengthened by such devices, although
the general sworn fealty of the magnates was, at any given time,
an enhancement of royal power.

And yet the strength of the crown was advancing rapidly be- *The King*
tween 900 and 1066. The king, once no more than the avenger of *and the*
the law in the last recourse, was becoming its arbiter, partly by pla- *Law*
cing one legal safeguard after another under his special protection,
partly by turning his personally given peace to legal and political
ends, partly by taking over from the moots the coercive force of
outlawry. In the past, outlawry had been reserved for exceptional *Outlawry*

[1] II Eadward, 1. 1.   [2] III Eadmund, 1.   [3] VIII Æthelred, 44. 1.
          [5] Anglo-Saxon Chronicle, 1051E.   [6] *Ibid.* 921A.

offences which were regarded as heinous—killing within the kin, or the betrayal of a lord by his man. By the tenth century it had come to be a common process of coercive procedure, and a penalty for many offences of violence. The thief,[1] the lord who connived at his vassal's theft,[2] the man of such bad repute that he could get no lord,[3] were all outlaw. Even civil offences, such as refusal to attend the hue and cry, were outlaw's work if habitual.[4] The pressure upon the outlaw became irresistible when the sentence came to hold good everywhere. At Wantage the witan of Æthelred ordained that outlawry in one district should hold good in all,[5] and the condemned man was to be outlaw *wið eal folc*.[6] Outlawry had been the *ultima ratio* of the folkmoots; given into the hands of the king it invested him with the final sanction of the law, and under Cnut the sole right of extending the peace to outlaws and bringing them back into the peace was secured to the king,[7] and the process put under his mund and the defence of his mundbryce. Æthelred, twenty years before this, had been compelled to go through the clumsy form of binding the magnates severally by oath not to harbour Leofsige of Essex after he had killed one of the king's officers,[8] but, twenty years later again, the Confessor was able to use outlawry with effect against Swegen and Godwin.[9] Not only legally, in imposing the peace, but politically, against great offenders, the crown had gained a decisive weapon. This change in procedure is characteristic of the advance of the crown and of the methods by which it was being brought about. In Cnut's appropriation of the process of outlawing and inlawing we see the private privilege of the king, his grith and mund, becoming the normal mode of restoring the lawless man into peace and folkright. A like use of the king's mund to safeguard the passage from un-law to law is found in an addition to the law of homicide under Eadmund, whereby, the promise to forgo the feud having been made, and surety to pay the wergeld given, the "king's mund is raised", and if either party breaks the peace he incurs the king's mundbryce.

The king's mund

Less effective in government, but of increasing importance in

---

1 I Æthelred, 1. 9A.   2 *Ibid.* 1. 13.   3 II Æthelstan, 2. 1.
4 I Eadgar, 3.   5 III Æthelred, 10.   6 I Æthelred, 1. 9A.
7 II Cnut, 13.   8 J. M. Kemble, *Codex Diplomaticus*, 1289.
9 Anglo-Saxon Chronicle, 1048E.

law, is the converse side of the king's authority, the right to ban.
The king's wite of a hundred and twenty shillings has been exacted
for attacks upon his own dignity and privilege from the time of
Ine. A specialized use of it comes into being in the tenth century,
and is swiftly extended. Wherever the king has enjoined or prohibited a certain course by his express orders, failure to obey
makes the offender liable to pay the king's wite on the ground of
oferhyrnes, or disobedience. This use begins in the reign of Eadward *The king's*
the Elder—since the seventh century the Frankish kings have *oferhyrnes*
enjoyed the ban—and is responsible for an unparalleled growth of
the king's official responsibility for the enforcement of law and
order. No very clear system guided the stigmatizing of certain
offences as oferhyrnes. Rather, the authorities seem to have imposed
the wite arbitrarily, wherever they felt the need of an exceptional
safeguard, and principally as an incentive to the king's reeves and
thegns to carry out the new peace edicts. Reeves who take bribes
to pervert justice,[1] or who fail to enforce the rights of the church,[2]
are liable to it. The whole machinery of the edict of Grateley, and
so the newest and most effective regulations against theft and
disorder, is put under its sanction.[3] It is in general used to secure
enforced obedience not only from the officials but also from the
justiciables of the courts. By Eadward's first ordinance, buying
and selling outside a licensed borough,[4] and repeated refusals to
comply with an adverse judgment in land-suits[5] are marked as
oferhyrnes. Æthelstan adds the withholding of suit from the public
moots,[6] and failure to ride upon the orders of the court to put
defaulters under distraint,[7] and Cnut extends the oferhyrnes to the
neglect of hue and cry.[8] This use of the king's ban reflects a new
phase in the crown's relation to justice in which the balance of
moots begins to swing from popular to royal authority. The
crown is no longer only mundbora—a remote providence under
which the moots work in independence—it has come to intervene,
to improve procedure by edict, to watch over its working, and
to punish those who hinder or rebel against it. Where once the
moots, and sometimes the parties themselves, were left to execute
the judgments they secured, these were now enforced by the

[1] V Æthelstan, 1. 3. [2] I Æthelstan, 5. [3] II Æthelstan.
[4] I Eadward, 1. 1. [5] *Ibid.* 2. 1. [6] II Æthelstan, 20.
[7] *Ibid.* 20. 2. [8] II Cnut, 29. 1.

king's ban.[1] Æthelstan's imposition of the oferhyrnes fine for corrupt judgment is a final and striking proof of the distance the crown has travelled towards a sense of responsibility for justice.

The king's pleas From this enhanced sense of responsibility it is but a step to the conclusion that the offences covered by the king's mund, the king's oferhyrnes, and the king's wite, form a homogeneous body of law, and one which, in some special sense, is the business of the king. The Leges Henrici Primi[2] bring together all such pleas under the rubric *jura quae rex super omnes homines habet*, and refer to them in a later section[3] as *propria placita regis*. They are some forty in number, and, in addition to six which are said to be the *placita gladii*, pleas of the sword of the Norman Duke,[4] they include such ancient occasions of the oferhyrnes as refusing to coöperate in the *frith*,[5] failing to perform the *trinoda necessitas*, and unrighteous judgment,[6] the breaches of the king's mund under the headings of *hamsocn* or violent entry into dwellings,[7] harbouring of outlaws,[8] and bohrbryce,[9] together with those offences which could only be expiated by death unless the king extended to them his mercy, violation of the king's handgrith or peace personally given,[10] fighting in the king's hall,[11] treason,[12] incendiarism.[13] A phrase of Cnut's law[14] records as the "rights which the king has over all men in Wessex", mundbryce, hamsocn, *forsteall*, and *fyrdwite* (these he will grant only to such subjects as he wishes specially to honour), but they are, as we have seen, only a few of the more important of those royal pleas that have been coming into the king's hand, beginning with Ine and accumulating rapidly under the successors of Ælfred, and which are, perhaps, first specified as a coherent body of law in those "kingship rights in every shire and borough" claimed by Eadgar.[15]

Procedure of the king's pleas Besides the fact that initiative in these causes lay specially with the king, and that his officers were specially bound to pursue

[1] II Eadward, 1. 3. No man shall withhold from another his right. For the third offence he shall pay 120/- to the king.

[2] Leges Henrici Primi, 10. [3] *Ibid.* 52.

[4] But all these, except *murdrum*, seem to be synonyms of Saxon pleas.

[5] *Commoda pacis ac securitatis institucione retenta*: apparently a Latin paraphrase of II Æthelstan, 25.

[6] From III Eadgar, 3. [7] II Eadmund, 6.

[8] II Cnut, 13. [9] Ælfred, 3. [10] III Æthelred, 1.

[11] Ine, 6. [12] Ælfred, 4. [13] II Æthelstan, 6. 2.

[14] II Cnut, 12. [15] IV Eadgar, 2A.

them, they were pleas of the crown in the sense that the wites due from them went not into the reeves' farms, but direct to the king,[1] and—a decisive criterion for the eleventh century—in being sued under a special royal procedure, which denied the accused those safeguards and delays in which Saxon folkright abounded. He could attend no other summons until the king was satisfied,[2] on the first summons he must give pledge to the king's officer to stand to right, he must attend on the day of summons to plead without respite or essoin,[3] or, in default, be condemned in absence; he might not claim remand until his lord could come to assist him; if he refused pledge he incurred the oferhyrnes, and might be imprisoned until he found it.[4] The sum of these truncations of common folkright make up a royal procedure distinct in kind, uniform in contrast to the various provincial laws, and of a severity which reflects the weakness of popular law in a lawless age, and the readiness of contemporaries to accept a new interpretation of the status of the crown in order to counteract it. To say that this field of law, perhaps the most important of all, had come under the king's prerogative would be to speak intelligibly, but at the cost of anachronism. The Norman lawyers, who spoke of the king's rents as *dominica firma*, and of the king's thegns as *taini dominici*, called the growing body of the king's causes *dominica placita regis*[5]—they were personally his as were his demesne lands and the thegns of his household; they were *les plais ki afierent a la curune la rei*.[6] But they were merely glossing a Saxon crown-right in Norman terms. The Saxon kings, with no reasoned doctrine of *dominium* to guide them, yet saw these pleas as a coherent juris-diction appertinent to the crown and separate from folkright—part of the *cynescipe*. Before the Conquest, in the Confessor's charter to Ramsey, the concept is as fully realized as it was to be for a generation after it: "all the pleas that belong to my crown", *ealle tha gyltas tha belimpeth to mine kinehelme, omnes forisfacturae quae pertinent ad regiam coronam meam*.[7] The pleas of the crown, in substance, were already in being.

[1] Leges Henrici Primi, 10. 4; Domesday Book, i. 252A: *Has iii forisfacturas habebat in dominio rex Edwardus . . . extra firmas.*

[2] *Ibid.* 43. I am assuming that the legist is here reflecting Saxon usage.

[3] Essoin = the acceptance of surety for attendance at court on some future date.   [4] Leges Henrici Primi, 52.   [5] *Ibid.* 10. 4.

[6] Leis Willelme, 2.   [7] J. Earle, *Land Charters*, p. 344.

The king's reeves and the moots   All this growth of royal process gave the king a new relation to the law, and the king's reeves a new standing in the moots. Asser shows Ælfred taking the lead in a renaissance of law,[1] judging ealdormen and reeves by their honesty and knowledge of custom, and revealing a clear sense of authority over their office. They hold, the king tells them, a *ministerium* from God and himself. The illiterate and dishonest the king can and will degrade. Ælfred, then, appears as the active head of the executive not only in general but in legal administration; provincial moots no longer function in isolation, for a national discipline unites them under the crown. Moreover, the reeves and ealdormen, who are so clearly recognized as the king's officers, are themselves widening

The reeve as judex   the scope of their position in the courts. A commonplace of English legal history[2] is the gulf that separates the suitors as doomsmen from the presiding officer, sheriff, reeve, in Norman times justiciar. The doomsmen give judgment, the reeve demands it from them, and executes the judgment made. Thus the archaic principle that law is folkright is underlined and the way barred to a king's judiciary. But, in the crucial century and a half from Ælfred's reign, that bar was in some measure weakened. Possibly Frankish influence, certainly the authority of Isidore of Seville,[3] was accustoming English legists to apply the term *judex* not only to the witan of the moots but also to their presiding officer, and the natural evolution of the *gerefa's* function was in practice associating him more closely with the moot. Ælfred placed upon his reeves and ealdormen the duty of knowing the written law and imposing it upon the courts,[4] and regarded an illiterate reeve as an anachronism. In the new, written dooms the reeve was "wise" in a way in which the provincial suitors were not, and, since it was he who called for the judgment of the doomsmen at each point of the trial, he must have had the qualities if not the function of a doomsman himself.[5] Understandably enough, therefore, Ælfred called

1 *De Rebus Gestis*, cap. 106.

2 F. Pollock and F. W. Maitland, *History of English Law*, i. 548.

3 Cf. especially the text *Judex*, which is largely a borrowing from Isidore. The first use of *judex* for reeve seems to be Mercian of the year 844. W. de Gray Birch, *Cartularium Saxonicum*, 443.

4 Asser, *De Rebus Gestis*, 106.

5 I Eadward, Prologue: "King Eadward bids all reeves that they deem right dooms according to their knowledge as it stands in the doombook"; Cnut. 1020. 11.

the reeve's office a *ministerium sapientum*, "an office of the moot", and throughout the tenth and eleventh centuries the king's officers were commonly given the name of *judex*. There is a remote Saxon anticipation in these *judices* of the Norman sheriff as justiciar of his county, and they mark an essential phase of transition in the judicial development of the country. The royal delegate was now established beside the popular element even in the provincial courts of law. Thus the old popular judgment is associated with a controlling and directing executive. If the folkmoots stand for the rule of law and for individual right, the kings of the tenth century display a new care for the general peace, and a sense that rights, and the just assessment of right between parties, are not the only concern of law, and need stronger safeguards than the old folk-right provided. With Eadward begins a series of enactments, proceeding from king and witan, and comparable with the Frankish capitularies, having for their aim the suppression of disorder, the building up of a peace of the realm, the refinement of legal procedure and its enforcement by penalty. The archaic reliance upon self-help as the sanction of individual and public right is partially eliminated, and if this is done by national edicts, it can be put into effect only because a completed system of administration gives the king access to every court, and enables him partially to command their obedience. Through the confusion of provincial forms, much of the outlines of which we have lost, this great principle has been working towards its completion, that the order, and the executive power of the assemblies rest with royal officials and are a national whole, and that a great part of the national law is the province of the king.

Linking the growth of the supremacy of the crown in law and the reforms in political administration, of which we still have to speak, is the evolution of the legal doctrine of the peace. From Ælfred to Æthelred English statesmen were obsessed by this problem, internal peace against theft and disorder and external peace against the Danes, and the legal history of the period is largely that of an intense effort to bring about a common peace in a nation where every minister and church, every local assembly, *The king and the peace* every great landowner and official, had his several peace, but where there was no peace of the realm. In this effort every witena-gemote becomes a peace conference and every edict an edict of peace, and in the end they achieved a peace which, if it was not universal and perpetual, sufficed for crucial needs and occasions. The Leges Edwardi Confessoris record that the king's peace lies upon the seasons of Christmas, Easter, and Pentecost, over the four main highways, and over the navigable rivers,[1] but in practice the king's grith is applied variously, as occasion demands, to great matters and small. It may cover the individual with the king's special protection, as Eadward gave Swegen grith for safe-conduct in 1046, in spite of his outlawry,[2] or it may be used more widely to check disorder, as when in 1051 the same king, caught between the factions of Godwin and Leofric, stopped an appeal to arms by placing them both and their supporters "under God's grith and his own friendship".[3] It is not surprising that first among the com-mands of the Wantage edict "for bettering the peace" it stands that "the king's grith shall be established as firmly as ever it was in his father's day", and that breach of that given by his own hand shall be inexpiable.

Frith *and* grith   The distinction drawn between the *grith*, or personal peace of individuals, and the *frith*, or peace set between nations—or, as in the Empire, the land-friede, or peace of a whole community—is no doubt a sound one, but in the tenth century, much to the benefit of the realm, the distinction was becoming obscured.[4] The friths between the English and the successive Danish and Nor-wegian armadas are the sum of individual gages of peace, the leading men of either race speaking for themselves by oath and pledge, and thereby binding those under them.[5] The grith of Ælfred, Eadward, or Æthelred is the core of the English frith, as that of Guthrum, Olaf, or Justin is of that of the Northmen, but the peaces of the great East Anglian and Mercian ealdormen are

[1] Leges Edwardi Confessoris, 12.

[2] Anglo-Saxon Chronicle, 1046E.

[3] *Ibid.* 1051E.

[4] Cf. the use of frith and grith in Anglo-Saxon Chronicle, 1002E, 1004E, and in VI Æthelred, 42.

[5] Ælfred and Guthrum's Frith, Proem. This is the frith that King Ælfred and King Guthrum and all the witan of the English race, and all the folk among the East Angles, have agreed upon, strengthening it with oaths for themselves and their subordinates.

constituents of it also, with those of many lesser men, which on occasion may be used to set up local friths while the main bodies of the nations are still at war. So the Western magnates, Ælfric for Hampshire, Æthelweard for the South-western counties, and Archbishop Sigeric, made frith with Olaf Tryggvason;[1] so also Ulfkytel and the East Anglian witan used their own griths to come to terms with Swegen in 1004.[2] Thus afforced by the griths of his magnates, who, in their turn, speak for their countrysides, the king's grith is not far from being the pledged frith of a nation. In this sense, all those, both Norse and English, who are within the frith set between Æthelred and Olaf are "King Æthelred's *frith-men*".[3] All others are outlaw, and, for the term of the treaty, to be law-worthy in the king's realm is to be in the king's frith.

The characteristics which distinguish these early experiments in the peace from its later and perfected form in English law are its partial and occasional application, and the underlying theory that the king's is only one, though the greatest, of a number of griths placed for the occasion at the disposal of the state. Much of the enforcement of law even in the tenth century was still left to self-help, licensed violence, while the Danish wars had so thrown the country into disorder that whole provinces lightly changed their allegiance. Royal efforts to beat down disorder thus reflect something of the tradition of civil warfare, and their aim was steadily directed towards the establishment of a frith. Eadward, at Exeter, with his counsellors, "seeks how our frith may be made better", and "receives oath and pledge from all the nation" that they will hold to it.[4] Æthelstan, again, at Grateley, complains "that our frith is ill kept," and "takes oaths, pledges, and sureties" from the witan there.[5] Thus the internal order of the realm rests upon much the same sworn and pledged frith, centring upon the king's personal peace or grith, but strengthened by those of the magnates, as was set up during brief intervals of peace between the Danish fleets and the English. It is now applied as the domestic frith of the nation, and comes to be the principal object of the great reforming councils of the tenth century and is embodied in their edicts.

The national frith

---

[1] II Æthelred, 1.   [2] Anglo-Saxon Chronicle, 1004E.
[3] II Æthelred, 3. 1. So, in 921, the men of Huntingdon "sought King Eadward's frith". Anglo-Saxon Chronicle, 921A.
[4] II Eadward, Proem.   [5] V Æthelstan, Prologue.

Grateley, indeed, and its sequels at Exeter, Faversham, and Thundersfield, is the inspiration of a great combined effort of king and people to put the realm under a standing frith, every magnate and reeve at those councils taking oath that "he will hold all that frith that King Æthelstan and his witan set at Grateley",[1] and the reeves exacting pledges from the communities they govern that they too will hold it. In London the response to this was the founding of a formal frith-guild, in which eorl and ceorl were bound into a common obedience to the decrees against robbery and violence, and to joint action to pursue them to justice.[2] In all this we are very near to an effective peace of the realm. It is true that its basis is as yet uncertain. The frith founded at Grateley is the sum of multitudinous griths sworn and pledged in provincial moots and royal councils, and it might well have hardened into a peace of the folk such as the German *landfriede*. On the other hand, the king's share is already predominant, his own grith the greatest peace involved, and its enforcement by the reeves ordered under penalty of the special wite for contempt of the king's authority, the king's wite.[3] By the reign of Æthelstan the king is claiming to impose his will upon the communities as to what actions or persons shall be recognised as within the peace. Upon the whole is set, as the most impressive authority, the sanction or the king's mund.[4] The king demands, and, on the whole, secures, that his people shall "frith all that he will frith",[5] and, as the administration grows ever stronger and more specialized, it becomes increasingly probable that it will be upon the king's peace that the order of the realm will in the end come to rest. Cnut promises that he "will make full frith through the power that God has given me".[6]

The hundred

An entirely new set of institutions arose to make this concern for the frith effective and to give it permanency, those that centred upon the hundred. There can be little doubt that the hundreds were first formed as private associations or frith-guilds and were

---

[1] VI Æthelstan, 10.   [2] *Ibid. passim.*   [3] II Æthelstan, 25.
[4] *Ibid.* 25. 2.
[5] *Ibid.* 20. 3: "It shall be proclaimed in the moots that men shall frith all that the king wills to be frithed".   [6] Cnut, 1020. 3.

part of the response of the countrysides to the edict of Grateley, with those of Exeter, Faversham, and Thundersfield. The *societas hundredi* is a common phrase of Anglo-Norman law, and the voluntary origin of the hundred is marked by the fact that it is protected against disobedience to its authority, judgments, and rules, not by a crown wite, but by the oferhyrnes of its principal members, the thegn's oferhyrnes of five mancuses, or thirty shillings.[1] Unlike the usage of all other courts, conviction in the hundred carries with it the normal wite and bote, and "thirty shillings to the hundred" in addition,[2] and, finally, the hundred shares in the chattels of condemned thieves,[3] a right never in Saxon law accorded to doomsmen proper, and, it might be thought, *pessimi exempli* had the men of the hundred been in origin judges of a court. In fact the function of the hundred is not at first one of judgment, rather a special application of the universal privilege of self-help against theft, by which, as the Grateley frith decreed, thieves must be hunted down by the hue and cry and slain.[4] This organized self-help under royal patronage, so characteristic of the age, we may see in the frith-guild of the *Judicia Civitatis Lundoniae*, explicitly formed to put in action the Grateley decrees,[5] charged with the duty of suppressing theft, defended by the oferhyrnes of its members,[6] enjoying a share of the chattels of felons,[7] and placed on a semi-public footing, in that it could command the service of the king's reeves.[8] Though the guild of the *Judicia* has not yet the right of oath and ordeal and cannot, therefore, technically embody a court, Æthelstan has already given it the substance of judgment. Its extra-judicial enquiries into the guilt of thieves are to have the authority of the ordeal.[9]

The voluntary hundred

[1] Leges Henrici Primi, 35; Liebermann, *Sachglossar*, p. 461.

[2] III Eadmund, 2; II Cnut, 15. 2; Leis Willeme, 42. 1.

[3] I Eadgar, 2. 1. VI Æthelstan, 1. 1.

[4] II Æthelstan, 1. As late as the reign of Eadward the Elder the responsibility of following up stolen cattle lay with the loser.

[5] VI Æthelstan, Proem: "To make more effective the dooms which were set at Grateley, Exeter, and Thundersfield".

[6] *Ibid.* 7: "Let him not abandon the enquiry on pain of our oferhyrnes".

[7] *Ibid.* 1. 1.

[8] *Ibid.* 8. 4.

[9] *Ibid.* 9: "Thieves who are not manifestly guilty on the spot, but found so by subsequent enquiry (by the guild), may be redeemed by their lords or kinsmen as though they had been condemned by ordeal". The process of "enquiry"

Here we have a frith-guild anticipating the hundred in many essentials, as the hundred, when established, retains many of the significant characters of the frith-guild. The name of the hundred is there, for the guildsmen are bound by groups, or titheings, of ten, into a combined *hynden*, or hundred under a *hyndenman*,[1] and, though the intention is to form a personal association, it is quasi-territorial from the first, for allowance has to be made for titheings of greater or less population.[2] It has an inchoate right of judgment, since its inquests have the effect of trial, though conducted without the traditional forms. The hundred is adopted and made obligatory on the whole country by Eadmund as an association of eorl and ceorl in thief-taking, and retains its oferhyrnes,[3] but it is Eadgar's fuller code that confers the formal status of a court of judgment in folkright with oath and ordeal, and which, for the first time, shows the adoption of the private organization into the machine of government. In words which would have been inapplicable if the hundred had been a pre-existing jurisdiction already exercising the ancient law and procedure, he provides that "in the hundred, as in other moots, we will that every case be conducted by the rules of folkright",[4] fixes the meeting of the court every four weeks[5] —this was the interval at which the hyndens of the London frith-guild held their meetings[6]—orders that judgment shall be given within a fixed term, and the parties mulcted with the thirty shilling *bot* to the hundred if they do not appear,[7]

The hundred as a national obligation

is here *geaxian*, not by formal judicial procedure and doom, but in a quite general sense. Cf. Ælfred, Introduction, 49. 3: *We geascodon = audivimus*, "we have learned". Ine, 39. If a man flee from his lord and is discovered (*hine mon geaxie*). In the tenth century *geaxian* is used of the official but non-judicial investigations of the reeve. IV Edgar, 10 (enquiry into the truth of warranty of sale).

[1] VI Æthelstan, 3.

[2] Liebermann considered that these titheings were preëxisting territorial units, but if such had existed Grateley would have mentioned them. The members of the *hyndens* were neighbours of standing, with slaves and commended men, a fact which at once gave the titheing the quality of a territorial neighbourhood. The phase during which the original grouping by ten men was being abandoned is recalled in Consiliatio Cnuti, ii. 19. 2D: *Alicubi (dicitur) vero decimatio (titheing), quia ad minus debent inesse.*

[3] III Eadmund, 2.

[4] I Eadgar, 7. This clause proves conclusively that hundredal *process of judgment* was new in Eadgar's reign.

[5] *Ibid.* 1.   [6] VI Æthelstan, 8. 1.

[7] According to Liebermann the oferhyrnes was not the thirty-shilling bot, but the fine of thirty pence found in VI Æthelstan, 3, and also in I Eadgar, 3. This

and, finally, defines the duty of the hundred, like other courts, to proceed by oath and ordeal.[1] Besides these clauses, which convert the powers of informal inquest—*geaxian*—conferred by Æthelstan into a true power of judgment—*deman*—recognize the guild meetings as courts, and confine them to the strict rule of oath and ordeal, Eadgar's Ordinance of the Hundred is largely a fortification of the objects and functions of the voluntary hundred of the *Judicia*,[2] which, in turn, has been inspired by the national decrees of Grateley. Thus, the series of peace enactments from Æthelstan to Eadgar should be regarded as a whole, theft and its suppression, both equally violent, being the most notorious of contemporary threats to the frith. Reign by reign the edicts grow stricter, more elaborate, and of more general application, till they gain their full embodiment in the hundred. It is Æthelstan who licenses the hundred guild as an allowable interpretation of the intentions of the witan at Grateley. It is Eadmund who adopts the guild and makes it of universal obligation. It is Eadgar who recognizes that the inquests of the guildsmen are in substance trials, and forces upon them regular periods of meeting and the oath and ordeal of folkright. In so doing he[3] takes the final step and adds a new circle of judicature and administration to English government. It need not be suggested that the London frith-guild is the sole root of all this. It may have drawn upon similar associations in other districts whose provisions we have lost, though it is true that a report of the measures taken by the county of Kent on the same occasion that produced the *Judicia* of London[4] takes much more conservative measures to meet the king's demands. But guild

is impossible, since the latter is a variable fine, and divided between the hundred and the criminal's lord. Moreover, the thegn's oferhyrnes was thirty shillings, not pence.   [1] I Eadgar, 9.

[2] In substance, I Eadgar, 2, 3, 4, and 5, are taken from the *Judicia*.

[3] I suggested in *Essays in Honour of James Tait* (p. 164) that a lost edict of Eadmund, in which, according to Eadgar, he ordered "the doing to the thief his right", might be the origin of the hundredal jurisdiction as it is found in Kent. I now believe that this refers to the sanction of the right of extra-legal enquiry (*geaxian*) conferred by VI Æthelstan, 9, and the making of it generally applicable by Eadmund. The substitution of a folkright trial for this informal process seems to be the main purpose of I Eadgar, the "Ordinance of the Hundred".

[4] III Æthelstan: "The decree of the bishops and other witan of Kent . . . (2) as to our peace, which all the people wish to be observed as your witan at Grateley decreed".

influence, almost certainly guild origin, left its mark on the hundred in name, in the element of guild profit from money penalties, and, possibly, in some parts of England, in the elective nature of the bailiffry.[1] The primary purpose of both the frith-guild and the hundred is to organize the primitive and undisciplined "riding after thieves" which is an original right and duty of the Saxon countryside. The duty and power of trial is historically an after-thought. Some such disciplining of the practice of extra-judicial remedy was essential to the effectuation of the Grateley frith, for, not only did it provide that the community as a whole should take up the defence of individuals, but it secured the country from the dangers of a lynch law which was lawful yet unregulated, and as great a source of feuds, disorders, and injustice as theft itself. The principles common to the London frith-guild and the hundred substituted community action for individual self-help, and enabled the crown to deal with an organized territorial unit instead of a formless crowd of individuals. In assuming a joint responsibility for order and for the suppression of the most prevalent form of crime, the hundred was offering itself to the crown as, for many important matters, a juridical whole in a new sense. It was this legal unity, the guild quality, almost a legal personality, of the hundred, voluntarily assumed at first and subsequently enforced, that made the hundreds susceptible to the constant imposition of new obligations and to that system of amercements upon which much of the authority of the Norman kings ultimately rested.

Spread of the hundred beyond Wessex

While its initial function in the tenth century reform is the repression of the typical disorder of the epoch and the administrative embodiment of the peace, the hundred came to play its part in a general reconstruction of government. The reconquest under Ælfred and his sons placed the crown in possession not of a government of England but of the ruins of at least eight national constitutions. Besides reconstituting her own shire system, whatever it was, Wessex was faced with the task of bringing into a common administrative scheme the trithings and wapentakes which the Danes had set up or taken over in the North, the Celtic scirs, the lathes, the rapes, and whatever local units of Essex, East Anglia, and Mercia have passed out of history. In the hundred she possessed

[1] As in the Eastrey and Wingham hundreds of Kent, and the Rotherbridge hundred of Sussex. *Victoria County History of Sussex*, ii. 172.

an institution which was readily exportable. It conformed to the
contemporary fear of theft and violence, and it was voluntary in
origin—lynch law legalized. As a popular special judicature it
could be added to the existing moots, or set up beside them,
without fear of a conflict of laws and loyalties. The *hundraed
saetene*, right to initiate the hundred, *constitutio hundredi*,[1] was therefore freely conferred or imposed upon communities and influential
subjects, and during the second and third quarters of the tenth
century must have been carried far and wide throughout the
country. It became, indeed, the one administration common to all
the peoples confederate under the *Regnum Anglorum*. Not only
Wessex but all the countries sometime of the Heptarchy save Bernicia have been invaded by the hundredal system by the time of
Domesday. Thus, in Kent the surface of the lathes is overwritten
with some sixty hundreds, some of them reckonable in acres, one
conterminous with the lathe of Milton. It is the lathe courts, as at
Milton and Wye, that entertain the old justice and the pleas of the
crown, and, when they have decayed, the latter go to the county.
The hundreds, not only in Kent, but in many parts of south England, tend to be *ad latronem judicandum*, that is,[2] they have only that
specifically hundredal function which runs back in the cognizance
of theft, through the edicts of Cnut, Eadmund, and Aethelstan, to
the edict of Grateley and its London offshoot. Yet, as a special *The
hundred
and older
jurisdic-
tions* jurisdiction supplementary to older jurisdictions the hundred has
often come to be blended and confused with them, and so its
spread has produced that bewildering appearance of diversity of
size and jurisdiction which has baffled historians. Added to the
lathe court of Milton, the hundred conformed to the boundaries
of the lathe, which was, therefore, called both lathe and hundred
in Domesday. Milton *curia* continued to exercise both its old
criminal jurisdiction and that of the hundred, and finally in the
thirteenth century came to be classed as a hundred court. In East

[1] III Cnut, 58.
[2] *E.g.* Kingston Hundred (Surrey), *pro latronibus judicandis et praeceptis Regis
exequendis* (*Placita de Quo Warranto*, p. 741). The private hundreds of Hampshire claim only gallows, which is a synonym for infangentheof. *Ibid.* 764, 767,
769. Cf. also Berkshire, *ibid.* 81, 152; Gloucestershire, *ibid.* 256, and Devon, *ibid.*
167, 171. In general, compare *Essays in Honour of James Tait*, pp. 155 *et seq.*
Certain other pleas, usually that of *sanguinis effusio*, were attracted here and
there into the cognizance of the hundred, but it is not common. Cf. Elham
Hundred and Axtan Hundred (Kent), *Placita de Quo Warranto*, pp. 324 and 345.

Sussex, on the contrary, the same amalgamation produced the opposite effect; the rape absorbed the hundreds, and did their work in its three-weekly lathe court.[1] In Lancashire the administrative divisions preserved the names of both hundred and scir, and we find hundreds of Blackburnshire or West Derbyshire, which were also called wapentakes; three administrative epochs were compounded in these names. In the middle north, on the contrary, the wapentakes—whether Danish or Anglian[2]—tended to survive, and, with the hundreds as their administrative subordinates, remained courts of criminal pleas into the Middle Ages. Thus the hundred, even when remaining in the hand of the crown, was patient of almost every conceivable combination with the older circles, and the position is complicated even further by the number of private immunities. Theft and the peace went together, and suretyship for their men was freely laid upon the shoulders of lords. It was, perhaps, as much this as any sense of due privilege, which led to the widespread attribution of hundredal power to private immunists during the eleventh and twelfth centuries, whether in fee or farm.[3] We have no valid reason for carrying hundredal immunity behind the eleventh century, nor for believing that it had gained its full momentum before the Conquest, but the *hundraed saetene* of both crown and immunist acted everywhere as a corrosive against the ancient provincial scheme of the Heptarchy, and had much to do with its replacement by an English system of courts and administrative districts. We cannot, therefore, claim that this change of the hundred from the thief-taking of the Judicia to the court of all purposes of the first Norman reigns can be clearly understood. The final picture is of a judicial system upon

---

[1] Cf. H. M. Cam, *Essays in Honour of James Tait*, p. 24.

[2] The wapentake is usually said to be Danish in origin. There is no evidence that any Scandinavian unit of government bore that name, but *vapnatak*, "the resumption of arms", is the term for the closing of the session of the Icelandic Althing. The distribution of the wapentakes in England has not been scientifically studied. In medieval records it is used in the country between the Trent and the Tees; but learned clerks were apt to apply it arbitrarily elsewhere.

[3] The lapse of the hundredal administration into private hands probably began with the greater ecclesiastics. III Cnut, 58 (Instituta, 1103–1120): *Episcopi . . . in multis tamen locis secundum iusticiam in sua propria terra et in suis villis debent habere constitutionem hundredi, quod Angli dicunt hundraedsetene*: bishops ought in many districts rightfully to have the setting up of the hundred in their own lands and townships.

two levels, the hundred accroaching to itself all pleas in first instance, except those of bookland, and the shire holding pleas in default of judgment in the hundred and coercing those who were too strong to obey it. But the process by which this alignment was brought into being is, and will in all probability always remain, obscure.

The Danish invasions had wiped out the structure of Mercia: its *The* many ealdormanries vanished, and were replaced by the single *ealdor-* great ealdormanry, lordship, or sub-kingdom, of Æthelred and the *manries* Lady Æthelflaeda, and a great change came upon England south of the Thames also. Ælfred's ealdormen of the several Wessex shires seem to have held their charges to the end of their lives, but, as they died, their ealdormanries were not renewed. Instead, a division was made which conformed in general with the old national frontiers. Mercia remained a whole, though a second ealdormanry, centred upon Hereford, appears for a time. East Anglia and Essex—probably including Hertfordshire and Middlesex—were each left as separate provinces, and Wessex was divided under two ealdormen, sometimes called of Devon and Hampshire, and in one charter, those of the Western Provinces and of Winchester.[1] Whether Kent and Sussex lay in the Winchester province, and where the line was drawn between that province and the Western ealdormanry is not known.[2] This redistribution must have transformed the problem of English government in its lowest stratum, and, with it, the nature of ealdormanry. An ealdorman who governed all Mercia was in an entirely different position from those who once governed a single county, and, for this reason, if for no other, the tenth-century crown was faced with the need to find a new method of direct administration for the vastly enlarged area of the West Saxon supremacy. This method they had developed securely before the end of the Saxon *The* era, its components being the modern county with its sheriff, and *sheriff* the hundred; but the process of the reconstitution of the shire was too gradual to be allotted to any one reign, nor, at present, can we

---

[1] J. M. Kemble, *Codex Diplomaticus*, 698. *Æthelweard Occidentalium Provinciarum Dux: Ælfric Wentanensium Provinciarum Dux.*

[2] An ealdorman of Sussex appears once in Æthelred's reign.

do more than conjecture the main outline of its growth. The sheriff, *eo nomine*, does not make his appearance until the reign of Cnut, but from that of Æthelred we hear of a *scirman*, one Wulfsige the Priest, holding that position in Kent, and apparently discharging the sheriff's office,[1] and under Eadgar[2] a regulation ordering its court to meet twice yearly gives us our first mention of the modern county. In this edict, indeed, the units of shire, hundred, and borough appear for the first time together, and Eadgar's reign must, therefore, be taken as the time at which English administration reached its formal completion.

The boroughs From the time when the Danish invasions wrecked the ancient provinces of middle and eastern England to that when the modern system emerged under Eadgar, there was, however, an interlude in civil government, during which courts and reeves retired into the fortified centres. From Ælfred's day to Eadgar's the king's reeve rules not the shire but the borough, and the borough itself is the primary unit of government.[3] A few English towns, notably Cantérbury, were known as boroughs before the reign of Ælfred, but their multiplication seems to have been caused by the great Danish war of 870–920. They were the burhs, or towns "timbered" or fortified by a containing wall in the process of defending Wessex and reconquering Mercia. The first hint that they have become the primary units of organization for defence is the annal of 894[4] in the Anglo-Saxon Chronicle. Here, for the time being at least, we see the king's officers in garrison throughout a range of burhs covering most of England that was in English hands, and, as the English passed to the offensive, the building of boroughs became the routine method of securing recovered territory: "in this year Æthelflaed timbered Tamworth and Stafford burh, and in the same year, at Martinmas, King Eadward had the north burh at Hertford timbered between Maran, Beane, and Lea".[5] Taken by themselves, these facts stand for no more than a revolution in the art of war, but, as later in Saxony, strategical considerations came to bear upon the administrative system, and changed it

---

[1] J. M. Kemble, *Codex Diplomaticus*, 1288 and 929.
[2] III Eadgar, 5. 1. In succeeding charters of Cnut's reign (J. M. Kemble, *Codex Diplomaticus*, 731, 732), Æthelwine appears as shireman and later as sheriff.
[3] II Æthelstan, 20. 1.
[4] Anglo-Saxon Chronicle, 894A.
[5] *Ibid.* 913D.

vitally. Wessex before the reign of Ælfred was governed certainly
by the ealdormen and moots of the provincial units south of the
Thames, and possibly also by subordinate units of which the
various king's towns were the capitals. For a period after Ælfred
the traditional circles of government seem to have been in abeyance, and Mercia and Wessex alike were controlled from boroughs,
the only courts below the witenagemots of the ealdormanries
being borough courts, and the only officials under the ealdormen
borough reeves. This phase may not have lasted long. The shire
moot was meeting again by the time of Eadgar, and it was, perhaps, a war measure by which the civil power took refuge within
the borough walls. But Æthelstan's laws assume that all courts
will be borough courts,[1] and that borough reeves are in control of
the royal estates,[2] while the author of the *Judex*, speaking in general
of the justiciables of any moot, takes it that they will be those of a
borough.[3]

A document known as the Burghal Hidage, and assigned with
some probability to the years 911–919,[4] gives, evidently with some
corruption, a record of the districts subject to the various boroughs
of Wessex, and of several districts of Mercia.[5] For Wessex these
areas are irregular, and break up the ninth-century shires, but some
of the boroughs are known to have been *villae regales*,[6] royal
townships, and in Sussex the burghal area seems to have had some
relation to the rape.[7] It is not improbable, therefore, that the
period of burghal government may have marked a time when
many of the royal towns became indefensible and when the moots
were withdrawn into such of them as had been timbered, and whose
position was particularly strong,[8] the reeves following them, but
retaining the stewardship of the royal estates whose *curiae* were
abandoned. If so, burghal administration, drawing upon past
institutions, preserved something, though not all, of their outlines.

---

[1] II Æthelstan, 20. 1.   [2] I Æthelstan, Prologue.
[3] *Ibid.* 9. 1. As the text dates from after 980, this may already have been an
archaism.
[4] H. M. Chadwick, *Anglo-Saxon Institutions*, p. 207.
[5] W. de Gray Birch, *Cartularium Saxonicum*, 1335.
[6] Southampton, Wilton, Winchester, Exeter, Bath.
[7] The burghal areas of Sussex are Heorepebura (Hooe Rape Burh?), Hastings,
Lewes, Burpham, Chichester.
[8] Thus, in Dorset, Dorchester was ignored, and Wareham taken as a burghal
site.

The number of centres of government being thus reduced—there *The high-* were four survivals in Hampshire, Porchester, Southampton, *reeves* Winchester, and Twynham—and the supervision of the ealdormen being relaxed by the reduction in their number, the borough reeves must have risen in importance. In Oxford, Worcester, and Warwick, the only boroughs in their shires, they must have been sheriffs in all but name, and it is, perhaps, in these circumstances that a new title, that of high-reeve, comes into the official language of southern England. Eadmund, in his edict of Colyton,[1] speaks, apparently of the borough reeves, as *summi prepositi*, while the Chronicle reports two *heah-gerefan* as being killed in the Danish raid on Hampshire in 1001,[2] and of another, Æfic, as being murdered by the ealdorman of Essex in the following year.[3]

The shire Against this predominance of the borough and the high-reeve, we have to place the fact that the shire had already revived by Eadgar's reign, and was holding a court twice yearly in addition to that held three times a year for the borough, and that the importance of the shire was marked by the attendance of the ealdorman and bishop at its court.[4] The phase during which the shire reasserted its supremacy cannot, therefore, be described with any certainty. It is only clear that it did in fact succeed in shaking itself clear from the rivalry of the borough, and that, as a result, the sheriff was established as the principal local officer of the crown. The appearance of Wulfsige the shireman in the reign of Æthelred gives us, perhaps, the latest date for the completion of the process. Thus, the burghal phase of administration is no more than an interlude, but one which helped to break up the circumscriptions of the Heptarchy, and to clear the ground for the English shire and hundred. In the counties of the South the larger divisions of Wessex, Hampshire, Dorset, and the other small ealdormanries of the ninth century reasserted themselves to determine the shire boundaries of the tenth. Essex, Kent, Sussex, Surrey, and the two East Anglian folks are primitive divisions of even greater age. But in Mercia the borough had the last word. The counties of the east Midlands may have begun in the burghal areas of the Five Boroughs of the Danes. Those in the west take their names from the Eadwardian boroughs built in the re-conquest, and the central

---

[1] III Eadmund, 5.
[2] Anglo-Saxon Chronicle, 1001A.
[3] *Ibid.* 1002B.
[4] III Eadgar, 5. 1.

location of their capitals and the rounded assessments in hides, 1200, 2400, and the like, which "lie into" them, are strong arguments for their creation as an act of deliberate statesmanship.[1] Indeed, though older units had not all been obliterated, by the time of Eadgar all England south of the Humber was set out to plan, the variety of the minor kingdoms, West Saxon scir, Mercian ealdormanry, and petty kingdom, drawn into one common structure of government, the moots losing their sense of provincial identity in a new common status as shire-thegns of an English king.

Returning to the main theme of kingship, and to its new status *The king's* as a political monarchy of Britain, it is difficult to determine how *fisc* far this revolution in the crown had called into being a specialized central ministry, or was supported by any organized system of finance. The tenth and eleventh centuries were not an age of record. The sole source of revenue for Wessex, until the introduction of the feudal aids after the Conquest, was the produce of the royal lands and the wites of the courts. Danegeld, which was paid seven times between 996 and 1118, was the only direct tax upon the land of the whole country, and can hardly be counted as revenue. According to Asser,[2] a distinction between the lands of the crown and the personal lands of the king had already been *Royal* established by the reign of Æthelwulf, who, in his testament, *land* commended the *pecunia regni* to his two elder sons, who were to reign simultaneously over Wessex and the Eastrey, and bequeathed his *propria haereditas* to his younger children and to remoter connections. Æthelred II, in one of his charters,[3] amply confirms this. On the death of his father Eadgar, he tells us, the witan chose his elder brother Eadward as king, and conferred upon himself the lands of the ethelings, the *terrae ad regios pertinentes filios*. On the death of Eadward, Æthelred received both the lands of the ethelings and also the *regales terrae*. These he distinguishes from his *propria haereditas* which he can alienate at will. Substantial crown lands, for whose conservation the witan felt themselves respon-

---

1 F. W. Maitland, *Domesday Book and Beyond*, pp. 502 *et seq.*
2 *De Rebus Gestis*, 16.
3 J. M. Kemble, *Codex Diplomaticus*, 1312.

sible, seem, therefore, to have been established as early as the ninth century, and it is, no doubt, the remnant of the crown demesnes which appears in the Domesday of East Anglia as *terra de regno*,[1] and in Devonshire as *dominicatus regis ad regnum pertinens*. The distinction was one which could not survive under a doctrine of feudal tenure, and lapsed with the Conquest, but, since all grants by charter were unconditional as far as the giver was concerned, it must have been a necessary restriction if the Saxon crown were not to be stripped of all its resources.

The king's farm   As seen in Domesday, the profits of these lands are consolidated into farms, or fixed renders from the shires, which the sheriff must produce annually, irrespective of the actual yield of the year, making profit or loss according to fortune. This practice of fixing a yearly quota was of such old standing in exploiting the property of individuals and religious communities, that there can be little doubt that the general principle had long governed royal as well as private finance. From as early as 836 we have the record of a fixed farm from the land of Challock in Kent,[2] and a schedule of provender "from ten hides to foster" is usually taken to be Ine's regulation of the farm to be paid to him from his land. The *regiae census*, of Ælfred may, perhaps, be taken to be the king's farm, *cyniges feorm*, that he sometimes granted to monasteries,[3] and with Æthelstan, who orders the maintenance of one poor person from every two of his farms,[4] the system is clearly established. The normal method of organizing individual estates under this system seems to have been to lay upon them the farm of one or more days,[5] presumably a sufficiency of provender to maintain their owners' household during that time. Domesday shows the principal royal manors of Wessex thus burdened by a farm or provision for one night—*firma unius noctis*—and, since the same practice was in use in the monastic estates of Winchester as early as A.D. 931,[6] it must have been one of old standing. The Chronicle calls such estates *feorm hams*.[7]

[1] Domesday Book, 1. 183: *Istud castellum est de regno Angliae. Non subjacet alicui hundret.* "Kingship lands" would probably be the old English equivalent.
[2] J. M. Kemble, *Codex Diplomaticus*, 235.
[3] Ælfred, 2.   [4] Æthelstan, Alms. 1.
[5] The abbey of Ramsey arranged its manors in groups to render the farm of two weeks.   [6] J. M. Kemble, *Codex Diplomaticus*, 353.
[7] Anglo-Saxon Chronicle, 1087B.

How far the *feorm* was available in money is another matter. Perhaps in very early times the king circled the country, living upon his own estates, and even as late as 1006 Æthelred wintered in Shropshire upon the local king's farm.[1] It used to be held, on the authority of the *Dialogus de Scaccario*, that the *firma comitatus* continued to be paid in kind until the reign of Henry I, but this can no longer be believed.[2] Even Ælfred could clearly turn his *regiae census* into coin if he did not receive them as such; his household received wages at Easter, and he could send money to distant monasteries. Asser's account, indeed, takes a budgetary form as for a money revenue, and the provision that, where offences involve disobedience to two ealdormen, the wite shall be paid to the king half in one scir and half in the other,[3] strongly suggests a scir-farm whose reeve could not afford to allow its profits to reach the king through other channels. With Æthelstan the presumption of an organized farm becomes certainty. When, after a period of ignorance, we see the farm in the Confessor's reign, it is already the *firma comitatus* in its Domesday form, accounted for—and, presumably, for the most part, rendered—in coin by the sheriff to a treasury.

The king's *gold-horde* is spoken of in the earliest days of kingship. It is said that Eadred lodged records and his inherited wealth in Dunstan's abbey,[4] and this is the first hint of the treasure as an institution of state. A charter of Cnut's reign is recorded as being deposited "in the king's *haligdom*",[5] and a similar reference under the Confessor is Latinized *in thesaurum regis*.[6] Florence of Worcester, writing, of course, a century later, records that Harold Harefoot seized the treasure which Cnut had left to his queen Emma, and that it was at Winchester.[7] Two of the Confessor's chamberlains, Aluric and Henry,[8] called in Norman times *thesau-*

The king's treasure

---

[1] Anglo-Saxon Chronicle, 1006E.

[2] Round, *Commune of London*.   [3] Ælfred, 37. 1.

[4] *Memorials of St. Dunstan* (Rolls Series), 29.

[5] J. M. Kemble, *Codex Diplomaticus*, 1327.

[6] *Ibid.* 932.

[7] *Gazarum opumque, quas rex Cnutus Alfgivae reliquerat reginae.* This is to some extent confirmed by Anglo-Saxon Chronicle, 1035C and D. The previous citations are taken from L. M. Larson's *King's Household*.

[8] Domesday Book, i. 49A, 49B, and 151A. Aluric's lands were given to William's chamberlains, Humfrid and Alberic. It is possible that the tenure of Wenesi Camerarius Regis Eadwardi near Neatham in Hants should be added. *Ibid.* i. 47A.

rarius, already held land near Winchester before the Conquest. It is possible to suppose from this that the treasure was now a permanent institution and usually lodged at the capital of Wessex. A solid establishment of the treasure from at least the reign of Cnut is, indeed, necessary to explain the degree to which its financial methods were advanced by that of the Confessor. From before the Conquest we have clear proof of a consolidated sheriff's farm, for the Domesday entries for the Confessor's day proceed on that assumption. This the treasury was expert enough to supervise, making deductions on account of lands withdrawn from the sheriff's charge, and possessing the essentials of later treasury technique in accounting—almost certainly by tallies—and in securing a standard purity in coin of the sheriff's render. The assaying of coins for their content of silver by weighing them against a standard measure (*ad pensum*), and for its purity by melting and removing the dross from a sample of the metal (*moneta alba* or *blanca*), were in practice in the late Saxon period.[1]

Financial officials The administration of this routine seems to have lain until well into the Norman period in the hands of the king's domestic attendants. Of such officials we know very little. It is possible that there was no title of chief horderer, or treasurer, even under the Confessor,[2] but officers of the treasury there must have been. A late authority [3] asserts that the keeping of Eadward's records in his treasury was entrusted to Hugelinus, who appears in charters as *cubicularius* and *burthegn*,[4] and in Domesday as Hugo Camerarius.[5] The continuity of the office in the days of the Norman kings makes it certain that Hugo, or Hugelin, and the two other known *camerarii*[6] of Eadward were the principal financial ministers of the crown. The title is of purely domestic origin. Burthegn, officer of the king's bower or chamber, is its English form, but it was one of importance from at least the reign of Eadgar. Both he[7] and the

[1] Domesday Book, i. 2B, 132B, 143A, 163A, 190A.

[2] "Henry the Treasurer" was in possession of his tenement both before and after the Conquest but it is not clear that he was a treasurer in both reigns.

[3] *Cartularium Monasterii de Rameseia*, p. 170 (Larson, *op. cit.*).

[4] J. M. Kemble, *Codex Diplomaticus*, 904.

[5] Domesday Book, i. 208A.

[6] *Ibid*. i. 151A, Aluric; *ibid*. i. 47A, 151A, Wenesi.

[7] Titstan, Winstan, and Æthelsie. J. M. Kemble, *Codex Diplomaticus*, 489, 503, 572, 1247 (Larson, *op. cit.*).

Confessor seem to have had three such ministers in office simultaneously, and, except for the reference in the Ramsey Chronicle, we have no reason to believe that any one of these was more prominent than the others, or that the office of treasurer was led up to by one of chief chamberlain. The keeping, accounting, and expense of the treasure must, in short, have been part of the routine of the king's chamber, or bower. It is, however, unnecessary to put too much weight upon the questions of origin and title alone. The office was, no doubt, a growing one, and, while that of Eadgar's chamberlains cannot have been purely fiscal, the absence of a principal chamberlain or treasurer under the Confessor must not obscure our sense of the skill and experience needed for a conduct of the treasure largely identical in practice with that of the first generation after the Conquest.[1] Saxon custom, as opposed to that of the Franks, was against the growth of single officers for each office of state. Ælfred had divided each ministry among three ministers, charging them with a monthly term of office, and even in the Confessor's reign such ministries as those of the *stallers* and burthegns were held by several persons simultaneously. The absence of a single treasurer is not, therefore, a sign of imperfectly specialized routine. It is true, on the other hand, that the fissure between the *thesaurus* and *camera* is only beginning in the reign of Henry I. The evolution of fiscal administration seems to be steady and broken by no sudden change of principle, but its specialized growth is of the twelfth century.

A similar problem is that of the secretarial work of government. *The king's* Primitive kings and ealdormen were not, as a rule, literate,[2] but *writers* from the days of Theodore the charters were composed and put into writing, and the difficult distinctions of Saxon law were Latinized. There is some indication of a royal or conciliar secretary at the height of the Mercian supremacy in the early ninth century. Under Coenwulf one or more simple priests are found attesting *The pedis-secus*

[1] "The existence of such a system indicates a relatively advanced machinery at the Treasury" (R. L. Poole, *Exchequer in the Twelfth Century*, p. 31).

[2] Cf. V. H. Galbraith, Raleigh Lecture on History, 1935: "The Literacy of the Medieval English Kings", *Proceedings of the British Academy*, vol. xxi.

charters over a period of years, making their cross at the foot of those of the magnates ecclesiastical and lay,[1] or as the last of the spiritual order, and before the laymen.[2] It is these men who are given the much debated title of *pedissecus* or *pedesessor*[3]—follower of the footsteps, or sitter at the feet, presumably of the king. The presence of a single priest in a subordinate position in the council, but attendant upon the king, and probably literate, can hardly be explained by any other position than that of secretary, and the forgotten names of Cuthred, Bola, Æthelheah, and their colleagues may deserve a niche in history, the first as the scribe of the great London council of 811,[4] the second as that of Clovesho in 824,[5] and the remote forerunners of the English chancellors.[6] The practice of adding the test of the *pedissecus*, with his title, to the charter, seems to have been peculiar to Mercia of the early ninth century, but Eadred at his accession council at Kingston gave land to Wulfric *pedisequus*,[7] and in 955 to the *pedisequs* Uhtred Child,[8] while a charter of 968 purports to be witnessed by *duces, disciferi, pedissequi, et ministri* ;[9] but two of these charters come from a single codex, and no more can be said than that they give some support to the belief that the *pedisseci* persisted under the Ælfredian dynasty. We need not, of course, believe that their office was purely secretarial. The burthegns, from whose ranks the chamberlains of the treasury arose, began, no doubt, as general keepers of the king's chamber, and the *pedisseci*, if they were indeed the forerunners of the later secretariate, may well have come from the body of the king's priests and attendants upon the royal chapel. The latter are an important element in Ælfred's court, and, though they appear less frequently as charter witnesses in the next century, Eadred in his testament left a substantial bequest

---

1 W. de Gray Birch, *Cartularium Saxonicum*, 322, 335, 341, 373, 378.

2 *Ibid.* 357.

3 *Ibid.* 341, *Æthelheah ped. seq.*; 364, *Cudred pedisequus*; 378, 384, *Bola Pedissecus.* Preserving what tradition we do not know, the Crowland archivist seized upon these attendant priests as the composers of their versions of charters: *ego Turstanus presbyter domini mei regis Withlaphii, hoc cirographum manu mea scripsi, Ibid.* 325.

4 *Ibid.* 335.   5 *Ibid.* 378.

6 The Merovingian kings had their *referendarii* or *cancellarii* by the eighth century, so an English parallel is more than probable.

7 *Ibid.* 815.   8 *Ibid.* 911.

9 *Ibid.* 1211.

to his mass-priests, mentioning them next after the officers of the household.

That the ecclesiastics of the court were charged with the writing *The chan-* of its letters and charters we can hardly doubt, but of a chancellor *cellors* *eo nomine* there is no evidence until the reign of the Confessor, when Regenbald appears in a reputable English charter as Regenbold *cancheler*,[1] and in several Domesday entries as chancellor of William. That his qualification was that of king's priest we see from the Conqueror's mode of address to him, and his importance may be gauged from his wealth in lands and from the sixteen churches which he was able to bequeath at his death.[2] From the fact that the Confessor had a seal,[3] and from the later history of the chancery, it is fair to assume that Regenbald kept the king's seal, and saw to the drawing up of charters,[4] and of the writs which ordered the local authorities to give effect to them, and which, perhaps, were beginning to take their place. The title, and with it the enjoyment by one of the clerical ministers of a permanent charge, cannot be carried behind the reign of the Confessor, and, though Florence of Worcester gives Regenbald a forerunner in Leofric, bishop of Exeter, his authority is not decisive on such a point. The function cannot, however, but have some earlier history. Ælfric speaks familiarly in the Homilies of the king's writ and seal, and its use seems to be a certainty under Æthelred II,[5] from whose time may come the first writ which approaches the common form later used by Eadward's chancellor. Domesday suggests that such writs, under the king's seal and presented to the hundred court, had become a common reinforcement to the witness of the hundred in the establishment of a title to land before the Conquest,[6] and, if that is so, not only the chancellor of the

[1] J. M. Kemble, *Codex Diplomaticus*, 891.

[2] Round, *Feudal England*, p. 421.

[3] The latest discussion as to sealing in the courts of the late Saxon kings is to be found in F. E. Harmer's *Anglo-Saxon Writs*.

[4] Professor Tout (*Chapters in Administrative History*, i. 130) was of the opinion that the fact that the Norman chancellors witnessed charters proved them to have been "somewhat aloof from the clerical work of drafting".

[5] F. E. Harmer, *Anglo-Saxon Writs*, pp. 235 *et seq.*

[6] Domesday Book, i. 50A: *De ista hida . . . dicit hundredum quod T.R.E. quieta et soluta fuit, et inde habet Aluui sigillum regis Edwardi. Ibid.* i. 50A, i. 197A, i. 208A.

Confessor, but the untitled clerks who preceded him, must have needed the method and consistency in practice which only the traditions of an established writing office could give.

The king's household Perhaps because of Ælfred's triple division of the ministries,[1] the secular household of the king developed upon lines very different from those followed by the great palatine offices of the Franks. There was no mayoralty of the palace, no one chief butler, steward, marshal, or constable, in fact no great officers who exceeded the scope of their palace ministry or appeared as officers of state. We have occasional references to the butlers (*pincernae, byrele*) and to the *disc-thegns*, or *dapiferi*, attendants upon the king's table, but there are always several of equal status, and they have no more than domestic importance and do not equal the ealdormen in rank. Eadred's will,[2] the best source in this matter, leaves eighty *mancuses* to each "disc-thegn, hraelthegn, and biriele" actually in service at his death, which is a little more than he left to each of his mass-priests. Eadgar had, apparently, three burthegns, the Confessor three stallers,[3] so that the triplication of officers begun by Ælfred seems to have persisted. One office seems to have been added under Scandinavian influence, that of the stallers, who first appear in a charter of the year 1032.[4] In later Norse history the staller was the king's spokesman on official occasions, and might represent him as justiciar, but in England, where, as with the other offices, there were always several stallers functioning together, they must have had less influence individually. Possibly misunderstanding the title, which seems to come from the high-seat or stall in the king's house, the Normans were inclined to treat the stallers as marshals or constables—Bondig the Staller appears once in Domesday as *constabularius*[5]—but the Saxon court already had its marshals, the horse-thegns,[6] and they were of little account in a state where cavalry was of no repute. We shall probably be right, therefore, in assuming that the staller was a steward of the king's hall with domestic rather than military or political significance.

It is difficult to say whether the crown gained or lost by the

---

1 Cf. p. 131, *supra*.
2 W. de Gray Birch, *Cartularium Saxonicum*, 912.
3 Larson, *op. cit.* p. 151.
4 J. M. Kemble, *Codex Diplomaticus*, 1327.
5 Domesday Book, i. 151A.
6 Wulfric and Ecgulf under Ælfred. Anglo-Saxon Chronicle, 897A.

purely domestic nature of its court. Any weakness from this cause *Resources* was in part obscured by the greatness of the successors of Ælfred, *of the* but the violence of the reaction against such royal favourites as *crown for govern-* Æthelsige[1] shows that it left the throne dangerously isolated during *ment* a minority. A mayoralty of the palace might have regularized the position of Godwin, and, by satisfying the ambition of Harold, have averted the dynastic quarrel of which the Conqueror took advantage. In general, however, there is little reason to think that the crown lacked hands to do its work. If there was as yet no bureaucracy, the whole order of the secular thegns and ecclesiastics was at its disposal. The minute subdivision of the country into hundreds for the peace multiplied the reeves and brought the king's discipline to every village. To keep in touch with the provinces, the king had legation and writ. The magnate bearing the king's *writ and insegl*[2] was a familiar figure in the courts and to the provincial witan,[3] initiating process, promulgating national edicts, and advising as to their putting into action. The judicial function of the eyre was lacking, with all its schedule of agenda and its periodicity, but the crown itself, and with it the witan, was itinerant. Eadgar toured his whole kingdom in winter and spring to oversee justice,[4] and we find the Confessor hearing cases in the west country and proroguing them to the great Christmas court.[5] The holding of witenagemots in the principal provincial centres was a recognized means of securing the coöperation of the country-sides in new schemes for order. Such a series of *gemots* were those at Grateley, Exeter, Faversham, and Thundersfield which enacted and enforced the peace edicts. To fill the intervals between these royal iters there were the five or six great ealdormen, who, with certain disloyal exceptions, multiplied the power of the king and carried out his orders without standing between him and the shires. Except perhaps for the North, the king's writs went out to

1 J. M. Kemble, *Codex Diplomaticus*, 700.

2 Domesday Book, i. 50A, 197A, 208B, etc., J. M. Kemble, *Codex Diplomaticus*, 693.

3 VI Æthelstan, 10: "The witan at Thundersfield gave their pledges (to the peace) . . . when Ælfheah Stybb and Brihtnoth, son of Odda came to them at the word of the king"; III Æthelstan, 1: The Kentish witan have taken counsel as to the peace *auxilio sapientum eorum quos ad nos misisti*: by the advice of those witan whom you sent to us.

4 Florence of Worcester, *sub anno* 975.

5 Domesday Book, i. 252B: *inducians donec ad curiam instantis natalis domini.*

eorl and bishop but also to the sheriff and the king's shire-thegns. The king and the witan could appoint and depose ealdormen, and their official status seems to have been emphasized by the enjoyment of state lands *de comitatu*. Cnut turned the great ealdormanries to the account of his government in his four eorldoms, and it is probably from his reign the eorl's share of a third of the borough and county wites must be dated. If we except the treason of Ælfric and Eadric in Æthelred's reign, and the misgovernment of Tostig and his deposition by the Northumbrians, there is not much evidence that the eorldoms were failing to fulfil their purpose. If they were dangerous to unity it was certainly not from any feudal quality, which they altogether lacked, but from the possibility that racial feeling might revive and gather round any long succession of ealdormen of the same stock. This seems to have happened in Northumbria, but not elsewhere.

Summary   In contrast with the earliest phase of English kingship, that of the tenth and eleventh centuries appears as a time of rapid growth of royal power, of the invention of new ties between king and people, of the merging of the ancient racial monarchies in a new kingdom of Britain. It is the time of the reconciliation of laws under a common kingly right, of the appearance of the frame of provincial government in outlines which were to be final, in short, of the rudiments of a territorial and political kingdom. Taking our standpoint in the twelfth century, we should be conscious of a strong contrast with the feudal and bureaucratic stability of the Angevin crown. There is the cardinal difference that the rule of the house of Ælfred was based less upon the land than upon the folk. The obligatory, lasting bond of homage, riveted into the land by the material interest of tenure, was absent. The hold of the Saxon king upon his subjects was still compounded of strands of feeling and habit, the sense of racial unity finding its focus in the cyne-cynn, the personal, contracted loyalty of his commended men and of their men under them, the claim of Christian kingship. Crown and people were beginning to be interlocked in the hard structure of a royal pre-eminence in law and in a royal administration. The Saxon king was still weak where, in comparison, his Angevin successor was to be strong, but found reserves of impalpable strength where no foreign dynasty could. In many of its essentials the old English throne was like the constitutional monarchy of to-day. It had few positive powers, but it had access to reserves of loyalty and affection not to be explained by the legal rights of the crown, or even by an unbiassed estimate of the individual who bore it. Rightly carried, the crown could gather the nation to great exertions and sustain them over long periods of years. The conquest of the Danelah—ably conducted or not, we can hardly judge—was an extraordinary feat of endurance, in which Wessex was kept to a continued strain of war throughout a generation. The rallying of a disordered and demoralized nation to peace in the half-century succeeding the reconquest was an even more remarkable effort, in which Æthelstan, Eadmund, Eadred, and Eadgar point by point relied upon the response of their people to insistent leadership. Without the inspiration of the king, and, equally, without the loyal following of the subjects, nothing could have been accomplished, for all the reforming councils from Grateley onwards drew their authority from voluntary agreement. What coercive rights the crown finally acquired, it came by during the struggle to construct peace and order, and as an outcome of it.

The very effort to throw off the virus of the Viking attacks had brought the elements of stable life into being. Possessed of a uniform and intensive legal and administrative system in the shire and the hundred, of a monopoly of the higher criminal pleas and an agreed national peace, the late Saxon kings were vastly stronger than any dynasty which had gone before them. It might be just to recast the established judgment upon the England of 1066, and to say that the strength of its crown lay in an effective administration, a secure if partial control of the law, and a powerful ministerialized nobility in which it was not markedly weaker than the Norman monarchy, while its weakness lay in the fact that unity between the divergent elements of which the new realm of England was composed was only partially achieved. Here much turned upon the personality of the monarch. Only a strong king could keep the provincial nationalism of Northumbria, and the less intense nationalism of Mercia, in abeyance, and the dangers which were obscured by the exceptional abilities of the kings who ruled the country from 870 to 975 asserted themselves under Æthelred

II, and again to some extent under the Confessor. For this racial disunity the most certain and rapid remedy of that age was feudalism, and the spread of the Norman feudal lordships across the country, binding the looser constituents of English life into a new unity of material interest, marks a radical break in history.

III

FROM THE NORMAN CONQUEST TO THE REIGN
OF HENRY III

i

THE FEUDAL RÉGIME

"Feudalism in both tenure and government was, so far as it existed in England, brought full-grown from France."[1] The introduction of the *feudum*, bringing with it the recognition of a perpetual right of one party in the lands of another, created a revolution in the upper layers of social life in England, and set new principles at work in its constitutional and political history. Two things made this wholesale change practicable, the conversion of English legal and administrative procedure from kindred to territorial organization in the preceding hundred and fifty years, and the old-established use of lordship and vassalage, which, though not territorial, made a workable bridge to feudalism. It is difficult to say precisely how the destruction of the ancient alodial right of Englishmen and its replacement by feudal tenure was justified. Heir though he was of the Confessor, the Conqueror is said to have asserted the king's lordship over every acre of land in England, by however many degrees of tenure it was separated from the throne.[2] But besides this, which is difficult of proof, there was the sentence vouched for by the *Dialogus de Scaccario* that all who resisted the

The theory of the Conquest

[1] Stubbs, *Constitutional History of England*, i. 273 n.
[2] F. Pollock and F. W. Maitland, *History of English Law*, i. 69. "The great generalization which governs the whole scheme of Domesday Book." Anglo-Saxon Chronicle, 1066E. Archbishop Ældred and the Ætheling's party "bought their lands" of the king. A century later Richard de Luci claimed, "*de conquisitione apud Bellum facta feodati sumus*": we were enfeoffed as of the conquest made at Battle. M. M. Bigelow, *Placita Anglo-Normannica*, p. 221. *Placita de Quo Warranto*, 4. *Manifestum est quod in conquestu Anglie quelibet jurisdictio ad Coronam Regiam fuit annexa*: it is patent that by the conquest of England every jurisdiction was annexed to the royal crown.

Conquest thereby forfeited their landright, though such forfeiture was harder measure than was usually meted out to rebels under Norman feudal law. Upon the theory of forfeiture the battle of Hastings and the succeeding risings in the North, West, and East were almost, though not entirely, sufficient to absolve William from putting forward any other principle.[1] In practice each considerable estate seems to have been allotted to a Norman as its Saxon owner incurred confiscation, the former entering into the latter's general right; those who were allotted no such "antecessor" would be expected to justify their possession of any manor by royal writ and seal.[2]

Introduction of the feudum

On the whole, the evidence is not sufficient to prove that, even in 1086, the surveyors saw absolutely clearly the nature of the contrast between the landrights of the Saxon and the Norman (any attempt to prove that they used *tenuit sub* to denote commendation, and *tenet de* of tenure in Norman fee, breaks down at once),[3] but the whole tenor of Domesday is best explained by the assumption of the universal overlordship of the king and of the rules of the fee. Not only is the term *feudum* frequently used in Domesday for the grouped manors which have come into the hands of the principal Normans,[4] while it is so rarely applied to Saxon landholding as to seem to be used in error,[5] but the earliest-known Norman writ professes to grant *in feudo*, and in this presents an

[1] Anglo-Saxon Chronicle, 1067E. On his return from Normandy William "gave away the lands of all whom he came against".

[2] A test case seems to be that of Tederley (Domesday Book, i. 50A). Three freemen held it before Hastings. Two of them were killed there and Alwin Ret got possession. The men of the hundred say "*quod nunquam viderunt sigillum vel legatum regis qui saississet Aluuinum Ret . . . de isto manerio et nisi rex testificetur nichil habet ibi*": they have never seen the seal or any messenger of the king to seize Alwin of this manor, and, unless the king will warrant him, he can have nothing there. The Confessor's writ is commonly pleaded when the right oı the crown is affected, as when grants are made from the royal demesne (*ibid.* ii. 409B), king's farm (*ibid.* i. 60B and i. 197A), royal soke (*ibid.* i. 208B), king's forfeitures (*ibid.* ii. 195A), quittance from geld (*ibid.* i. 154B), rights in boroughs (*ibid.* i. 208A). There are a few exceptions.

[3] Cf. p. 81, *supra*.

[4] *Feudum Lisois* (Domesday Book, i. 212B); *feudum quem emit Willelmus episcopus* (*ibid.* i. 134A); *Rogeri Comitis* (*ibid.* i. 62B).

[5] *Ibid.* i. 19A and i. 23A. Certain other cases such as the *feuda* or *honores* of Eadnoth, Brictric, Asgar, Phin Dacus, and Wisgar, are those of Englishmen who survived the Conquest a while and so may have held in fee from William.

abrupt contrast with any writ of the Confessor.[1] The handling of lordship and landright within each of the Norman honours testifies *The fee or* to the change which has taken place. A simple and quite normal *honour of* instance of this is the Domesday fee of Geoffrey de Mandeville, *ville* which reveals the structure of an honour over a range of differing custom from Surrey to East Anglia. Primarily, Geoffrey was the successor of Asgar the Staller, and the jurors challenged the right to his four Surrey manors *quia ad terram Asgari non pertinent*. They had never seen the king's writ for them, and he held them *injuste, sine dono regis et sine waranto*.[2] He should, another entry implies, enjoy only *quod posset deratiocinari ad feudum suum*,[3] principally the *feudum* or *honor*[4] of Asgar, who was his chief antecessor. That was the English view. What was finally reckoned in this *feudum* is, however, a striking proof of the change that feudalism had wrought in a generation. The chief weight of Geoffrey's inheritance from Asgar lay, indeed, in the latter's own property, something round two hundred and fifty hides in the Midlands,[5] but, though one entry expresses the opinion that the fee of Asgar should be interpreted as including no more than his personal estate of land, at most the lands of those men who could not leave his lordship,[6] the whole of the Mandeville fee in Cambridgeshire, most of it in Hertfordshire, and part of the lands in Buckinghamshire and Middlesex, is made up of lands held under the Confessor by freemen who had property in their land, and the right to sell,[7] or otherwise dispose of it, and who had entered only into the voluntary and revocable tie of commendation with Asgar. In all, about seventy hides were added in this way, and some forty freemen and sokemen, in purely personal vassalage to Asgar, found themselves involved, on his fall and the transference of his succession to

---

[1] Cf. the writ printed by Professor D. C. Douglas, *English Historical Review*, xlii. p. 247, conferring lands to Peter the king's knight, "*feodo libere*". *In dominio* is, however, more common under the Conqueror and Rufus than *in feudo*; cf. *Chronicon Monasterii de Abingdon*, ii. 8.

[2] Domesday Book, i. 36A.   [3] *Ibid.* ii. 61A.   [4] *Ibid.* ii. 412B.

[5] In Berks, Oxford, Cambridge, Herts, Northants, Warwick, Essex, Suffolk, and Middlesex.

[6] Domesday Book, ii. 57B: *Non fuit de feudo Ansgari sed tantum fuit homo suus.* This distinction is much more accurately maintained in the Domesday record of the *honor Ordulfi* in Devonshire. *Ibid.* i. 105, iv. 190, 201, 468.

[7] One had exercised this right and sold to the bishop of London, but the latter had not succeeded in getting the land from Geoffrey.

Geoffrey, in the feudal structure of the Honour of Mandeville, to which their lands—held by themselves henceforth as dependent tenants, or taken from them by forfeiture or violence—were now annexed in perpetuity.

Eadric of Laxfield's mund-byrdnes   Beside this very moderate instance of what the doctrine of the fee could do to alter the map of land-holding, we may set the extreme case of an east-country honour in a district where the free landright of small men was the rule. The power—the mundbyrdnis, contemporaries would have called it—of Eadric of Laxfield in Suffolk, with some minor additions from those of Halden and others, passed to William Malet at the Conquest and in 1076 to his heir Robert.[1] There was, of course, a proportion of demesne land which had been the personal property of Eadric, but, besides this, fourteen hundred *liberi homines*, commended for the most part to the latter, were caught into this new complex of Norman right, and confined permanently within Robert's fee. This is the application of feudal tenure to a whole countryside which had formerly lived under the loose bond of commendation, and it is worth reflecting on the history of Eadric's men during the years about 1066 and on the effect of the Conquest enfeoffment upon such complexes of right and indirectly upon the history of the nation. Eadric's power was an extreme instance of the brittleness of Saxon lordship.   Its base in landed property was very narrow, for it rested mainly upon a wide connection of commended men. At some period before the Conquest Eadric was outlawed,[2] and the impermanence of his estate was at once revealed. The commended men scattered; some took lordship with the king, some with Harold, or Godric,[3] and nothing was left but the comparatively insignificant core of Eadric's real property, then in the king's hand. Again before the Conquest, he was inlawed, and presumably restored to favour, and Eadward granted his men leave to seek him again as lord,[4] and the majority, though not all, seem to have done so. In this phase of its history the connection passed to William Malet, who, at the Conquest, was seized[5] of Eadric's lands and men alike. William's seizin did not in most cases

[1] Domesday Book, ii. 304A *et seq.*
[2] *Ibid.* 310B.   [3] *Ibid.* 310B, 313A, 317B.
[4] *Ibid.* 310B: *Dedit etiam brevem et sigillum ut quicunque de suis liberis commendatis hominibus ad eum vellent redire suo concessu rediret.*
[5] *Ibid.* 317 *et alibi.*

drive the commended men from their lands, for they were mostly men of no importance, but it involved them in a new *dominium* of a tenant-*in-capite*, which pervaded the whole, made it henceforth indivisible,[1] a fee and an honour,[2] and introduced between the *dominus superior* and the immediate tenants of the soil a group of Normans whose names, Glanville, Gulaffre, and so on, proclaim them the ancestors of the tenants in knight service of Henry II's day.[3] The connection in the Confessor's reign was personal, revocable, dependent upon the mere right of patronage in Eadric, and by the one fact of his fall scattered into its elements, and, had it not been for the change from Saxon to Norman law, the same scattering would have been repeated within a few years, on the death of William Malet. But the one act of William's seizen made *The* it a whole and heritable, and did what six hundred years of Saxon *honour* custom had failed to do, stamping an indelible unity upon Eadric's *of Eye* countryside. Robert Malet after him succeeded to a legal unit, the honour of Eye, which, surviving forfeiture to Henry I, transferred unbroken to Stephen of Blois, returning to the crown at his death, used as a bait to draw Boulogne into war on the side of the young Henry in 1173, granted to the Duke of Louvain by Richard I, passing then to Richard of Almain and the house of Lancaster, became a permanent factor in English history.

Beyond setting up the perpetual complementary rights of lord and man,[4] the doctrine of the fee made no general change in the custom of the land. Any description of durable profit could be held in fee, an office, as of bailiff or forester, a rent,[5] land, and, consequently, we find the principles of feudal custom applied to the full gamut of Saxon rights, which are taken over wholesale into Norman tenure. Domesday records meticulously every item of custom from the Confessor's reign that can be profitable as valid in William's, but it shows that almost nothing has been added— apart from illicit encroachments—upon any new principle, for to

[1] Since baronies were indivisible except between coheiresses.

[2] *Dominus meus Willelmus rex Angliae . . . honorem mihi dedit* (charter of Robert Malet to Eye Priory, F. M. Stenton, *English Feudalism*, p. 56, and *Monasticon Anglicanum*, iii. 405).

[3] *Red Book of Exchequer*, p. 411.

[4] *Eadem terra est de feudo abbatis . . . et Stephani qui de abbate eam tenet: Cartularium Monasterii de Rameseia*, i. 141.

[5] *Ibid.* i. 153: *Concessimus . . . ut duo miliaria anguillarum habeat in feuodum et hereditatem:* two thousand eels in fee and inheritance.

hold in fee does not in itself give the right to any category of public jurisdiction with which the Saxons were familiar, nor to those rents in money, kind, or labour which were known as *consuetudines*. This is especially marked in the Malet fee in Suffolk,[1] and others like it. The commended men, of whom it is largely made up, had come in to Eadric of Laxfield still bound by and bringing with them their ancient public obligations. Almost all of them were under the soke, not of Eadric, but of their hundreds, or of the ecclesiastical lords of East Anglia. Accordingly, Malet seldom had the sake and soke, except in his demesne manors,[2] and often had not the customs. The fine confusion of a predominantly free Saxon countryside was carried into the Norman honour. In most of the demesne manors Malet probably had the customs and the soke, a few of the men outside the demesne are said to be his sokemen, the vast majority of Eadric's commended men were of the soke of the abbots of Ely or Bury St. Edmunds, the rest mostly in that of the king or of the king and earl jointly, and as it was in Eadric's day, so it remained in William's. The new honour of Eye had not the soke over a great proportion of its lordship.

The small-holders   Just as the creation of a fee did not destroy the external commitments of its members, so, equally, it left their internal rights intact in substance. An honour and its component manors might contain freemen, sokemen, and villeins. Of these the freemen who passed from the lordship of Asgar or Eadric into the feudal lordship of Mandeville or Malet, did not cease to be *liberi homines*. They retained their right to sell their land, and their right of inheritance. They had lost only their right to seek a new lord with their land, for, if they sold their holdings, their successors must enter into the lordship and hold of the manor and the fee in which the land lay. In law—in fact, no doubt, there was often irregularity and oppression—no iota of their custom could be changed, no rent added and no new custom imposed.[3] The sokemen, those freemen the suit of many of whom had been cut away from the

---

[1] Domesday Book, ii. 304 *et seq*.

[2] His grant to his foundation of Eye of sake and soke in certain lands, and all rights and liberties which the Conqueror gave him, can mean no more than granting soke where he had it. *Monasticon Anglicanum*, iii. 405; and F. M. Stenton, *English Feudalism*, p. 56.

[3] Leis Willelme, 29. No exaction beyond their due rent shall be made from the cultivators.

hundred court and thrown under a lord by a royal grant of sake and soke, retained their right in the soil as it had stood under the Confessor, though henceforth it was blended with the feudal right of a lord. The villeins, if their right was descended from that of the geburs who took land by contract, could hardly be touched by the change to feudal lordship, since the landright already lay with their lords. If Norman theory touched them at all, it would be to sanction and stabilize an existing propertyless and dependent security. "No lord may eject his cultivators from their land as long as they can do their due service."[1] "*Nativi* who leave the estate where they were born" are to be arrested and sent back.[2] In law, even in fact, Norman lordship made little difference to the economic and social structure of England in its lower ranks.

With the exception of that feudal justice of which we shall speak later, the same conservatism prevailed in jurisdiction. It has been held[3] that the baron was essentially the same as the king's thegn, and that both had a distinctive and identical right of justice in Normandy justice over thieves taken within the honour and *causes citeines*, and in England sake and soke and infangentheof. If we are to accept this theory we must be careful upon what grounds we do so. The qualification of baronial status becomes of the greatest importance in the later history of parliament. The baron's right was in part derived from and associated with a territorial barony, indivisible and heritable. In this territorial sense king's thegnage did not exist, but was an immaterial thing, a *ministerium*. Again, though a parallel development of the law of theft in both countries had given the barons a *justice de leur larruns*[4] in Normandy which is hardly to be distinguished from infangentheof, the *causes citeines*, if they are rightly explained as "civil causes", are not the English sake and soke. Such niceties of distinction might well be obscured in the disorder of the Conquest, but, setting them aside, it is clear that there was no common right of jurisdiction in the thegnage. Some king's thegns had their soke and some had not. Jurisdiction was, in fact, granted freely to men of importance both

[margin: Jurisdiction: king's thegnage and barony]

[1] Leis Willelme, 29. 1. According to Liebermann the Leis Willelme dates from between A.D. 1090 and 1135.

[2] *Ibid.* 30. 1.

[3] R. R. Reid, "Barony and Thanage", *English Historical Review*, xxxv. p. 161.

[4] Tres Ancien Coutumier, 41.

before and after the Conquest,[1] but in Domesday it is determined by no criterion of rank, and in the *Quo Warranto* it is claimed not by right of barony but by special grant or by prescription proved from manor to manor.[2] Indeed, it is in the manor, and not in the honour or the barony, that the right of sake and soke and infangentheof inheres. It is a franchise of certain individuals, part of the special right of a Saxon antecessor, or created by special grant after the Conquest,[3] and in the main its distribution is perpetuated, not obliterated, by the coming of feudalism. Private hundredal justice is comparatively rare, and there is never any doubt that it lies at the king's discretion.[4] But, though it does not seem possible to establish an identity of king's thegn and baron on the ground of jurisdiction, or indeed to determine any fixed jurisdiction or administrative immunity for either, the two titles are persistently associated in early Norman texts. The baron of the Leis Willelme is clearly intended to parallel the "king's thegn who is nighest to him" of Cnut's Law[5] in the clause fixing reliefs, and, like that of the king's thegn, the baron's person is justiciable only by the king. There seems to be between the two ranks a rough identity of personal quality, and this is derived from their "immediacy" to the crown; "the king's thegn who is nighest to him", *barones dominici mei*.[6] Moreover, there is at least something of the ministerial function of thegnage in the king's barons. They are the king's leading judges in the counties[7] and we find them used freely as justiciars when the royal justice becomes itinerant. If the identity were not

[1] Domesday Book, i. 1B. The Kentish Domesday gives us our one exhaustive list of the holders of sake and soke in any administration, and though many of the king's thegns of West Kent have justice over their men and lands, others (Alnod Cild, who was certainly, and Godric Carlesone, Turgis, and Norman who were almost certainly king's thegns) have none.

[2] The Leges Henrici Primi (20) attributes sake and soke to bishops and earls, but in the next clause speaks indirectly of baronial lands in which the king has soke. In the pleadings in *Quo Warranto* William de Say explicitly disclaims rights of jurisdiction throughout his barony in Kent. *Loc. cit.*, 315.

[3] *Placita de Quo Warranto*, 123: *quo ad . . . infangenethef . . . illa libertas est mere regalia quod nulli licet in regno hujusmodi libertatem habere sine speciali facto domini Regis*: as for infangentheof, that liberty is fully royal, so that no one in the realm can have such franchise without the special act of the lord king.

[4] *Ibid.* p. 179. *Nullo liceat hundredum habere nisi specialiter de dono domini Regis*: no one may have the hundred except exceptionally by the gift of the lord king.   [5] Leis Willelme, 20. 1: II Cnut, 71. 1.

[6] Hen. I. Ordinance of Shires and Hundreds.

[7] Leges Hen. I. 29. : *Regis judices sint barones comitatus.*

expressly made by contemporaries we should still conclude that the general place of the king's thegn in the royal system of Confessor was taken by the baron of the Conqueror. Baron, like thegn, is an ambiguous term. There is an honorial baronage, barons of the king's tenants-in-chief, and in a general sense, as thegn need mean no more than minister, so *baro* may mean no more than *homo*. All the king's tenants-in-chief are in that sense his barons. Yet, just as truly as king's thegnage existed, there are barons *par excellence*—in later days they will be called *majores barones*—and in the absence of any more definite criterion, since some criterion we must believe existed, we may take it that they were those who, like the king's thegns, had constant access to his person and court, a place in his hall and at his table, at least at the three great feasts of the year, and during that period livery along with the household for such attendants as custom allowed, in short, that they were there with an established place in the great *hyred* or *curia*.[1] The creation of the abbey of Battle brought a new spiritual barony into being, and the sole clause of the charter[2] bearing upon the secular status of the abbot allots his place and living in the *curia*. It may be that we see in this curial, dominical status the vital fact in the creation of a baron. In a feudal state which associated tenure closely with office the heritable honour *per baroniam*, which chiefly distinguishes barony from thegnage, is a necessary outcome of the changed state of land-law. Barony, we might say, is king's thegnage feudalized, and for that reason destined to play a very different part in the life of the nation.

Apart from the greater justice, there is the justice of the manor court, and we may legitimately doubt whence this has come. It is *Manorial justice*

[1] There is some evidence that certain of the king's ministries carried barony with them, for in the reign of Henry III Hugh de Ver held much of his land "*per baroniam essendi camerarius regis*", and this is in itself indicative of the personal and ministerial quality of baronage. Public Record Office. *Inquisitions Post Mortem*, Henry III, 31 (1). The Chamberlain's barony is a composite one, including some of the manors which Aubrey de Ver held in 1086. Since Geoffrey de Coutances' manor of Kensington is incorporated in it, his barony can hardly be of the Conqueror's reign. The de Ver chamberlainship was created by charter of 1133. J. H. Round, *Geoffrey de Mandeville*, p. 390.

[2] H. W. C. Davis, *Regesta Regum*, no. 60 (1070–1071). The abbot is authorized to come to court at Easter, Whitsuntide, and Christmas, and to have the court-livery of victuals and lights for himself and two attendants. This is the "seat in the king's hall" of Cnut's thegns. The Abbot of Battle owed no knight service but was summoned personally to the host and to Parliament.

certain that the Norman lord could hold a court for his men from the mere fact of being a lord,[1] and, indeed, every lord of a manor seems to have done so, and to have claimed that it was of common right,[2] and needed no royal grant such as was necessary for the enjoyment of sake and soke. A memorandum, apparently of the early fourteenth century,[3] tells us what that jurisdiction was—debt under forty shillings, contracts and conventions made within the power of the lord, cattle wounding *et hujusmodi*, damage to crops by animals, assault not leading to bloodshed, trespass or damaging of timber where the king's peace was not involved, and actions about land by writ of right up to the stage of their removal to the king's court for the grand assize. Action upon the writ of right is held because all causes arising out of the land-tenure of free-holders were in principle tried in such courts, while their removal to the king's court was mainly subsequent to the reforms of Henry II. *A fortiori*, the customary tenures must have been justici-able there also. Both might follow from the feudal doctrine that lordship of itself carries jurisdiction, and, as there is no evidence to carry it behind the Conquest, we may well believe it to have been Norman. As to the trespasses and petty assaults, it is to be noted that they are such as Saxon folkright seems to have left out of account. In the codes they are either ignored, or else explicitly left to the individual to find his own redress.[4] It is possible, therefore, that, while the hundred was set up to put the outstanding and more dangerous field of self-help against theft under the check of a jurisdiction, the townships may have acted informally for less important disputes between neighbours, and this is the opinion which was held in the first half of the twelfth century. The Leges Edwardi Confessoris describe such matters[5] as township or titheing causes, despatched *inter villas et inter vicinos* by the titheing men, who refer more important causes to the hundred. They were, it is

---

[1] Leges Henrici Primi, 55. 1.

[2] *Placita de Quo Warranto*, p. 313. *Habere liberam curiam de tenentibus . . . non est libertas nec regale*: to have free court of tenants is neither a franchise nor a royal right.

[3] British Museum MSS. Arundel, 310, f. 86A.

[4] There is no penalty in folkright for assault *sine effusione sanguinis*. Tres-passing cattle might be killed on the spot if they did damage. Ine, 42. 1. There is a composition for felling timber in Ine 44, but in no later law.

[5] *Videlicet de pascuis, de pratis, de messibus, de decertationibus inter vicinos et de multis hujusmodi*. Leges Edwardi Confessoris, 28. 1.

implied, a petty arbitration of Saxon date, but post-dating the creation of the hundred, licensed by the witan when it was found that the hundred and frankpledge did not suffice to prevent all cause of dissension. There is reason, then, to think that the jurisdiction of the manor is adequately accounted for by a combination of Norman custom together with such small matters of dispute as had come under the law's notice only at the end of the Saxon epoch, and had been allowed to fall to the comparatively new units of the townships. Thus feudal justice as such was confined within very narrow limits, and where the higher justice came into the hands of subjects it was by grant of the king. Short of unpardonable laxness by the crown, there was no danger of a general liquidation of the judicial system among the feudatories.

The administrative framework of Eadward's day was equally *Adminis-* resistant and continued to serve the Conqueror. Feudal tenure *tration* gave of itself no freedom from hundred or titheing, no exemption from suit of hundred and shire. Unless by royal grant, no fee was immune from the entry of the crown's bailiffs to serve the king's writs, or make arrest, or take pledge, or follow up stray cattle. Feudal land as such was not privileged. Its tenants performed suit, followed the hue and cry, made presentment of Englishry, were viewed in their frankpledges, kept watch and ward upon the roads or the sea-coast. Conversely, if individually or by communities they made default, their duty was brought home to them by personal or common amercement with the rest of their shire or hundred. In respect of all this the land and tenantry were said to be "geldable",[1] or to be "in scot[2] and lot" with the shire, and, though there were countless exemptions, the greatest barons were forced to admit that part of their lands were geldable, and the

[1] The geldable is that portion of the shire not in any immunity, but fully under the king's administration. Cf. *Placita de Quo Warranto*, p. 224. Custom varies, but the obligations of the geldable in Lincolnshire are a fair example: *solebant esse geldabiles, dare auxilium vicecomitis, murdrum, commune amerciamentum, et facere unicum adventum ad wappentachum . . . et dare visum franci plegii*: they used to be geldable, giving sheriff's aid, murdrum, common amercement, making one suit to the wapentake with view to frankpledge. *Ibid.* p. 408. So at Winchcombe in Gloucestershire: *esse geldabiles et facere sectam ad hundredum domini Regis et facere vigilias et dare theloneum et amerciari inter alios de villa*: geldable, and making suit to the hundred of the lord king with watch and ward, paying toll, and being liable to amercement with the rest of the township. *Ibid.* 250.

[2] The Confessor's phrase *scotfreo fram heregelde aud fram eghwilc oðer gafol* (F. E. Harmer, *Anglo-Saxon Writs*, No. 15) is as near as a Saxon king gets to this.

crown continued to assert that immunity from the administrative duties of the geldable was not of the common right of feudalism,[1] and that the right to them constituted *regalia, mere domini Regi spectantes*. Within the franchises the provincial routine of law and administration was perpetuated by franchisal bailiffs,[2] and from the reign of Henry II these officials became subject to recurrent enquiries as to their conduct. Thus the English countryside absorbed feudalism into its communities. Royal power reached downward to involve the common men of the titheings, shires, hundreds, and boroughs through threads of authority which were purely Saxon, and in this the Conqueror is most clearly seen to be the heir of the Confessor. These, as much as the high matters of justice for which the name *cynerihta* was reserved, convey the real continuity of the English and Norman crowns.

Continuity of Norman with Saxon England

In the light of this summary we may hazard some very general conclusions as to what the introduction of feudalism did and did not do in England. Feudal tenure had no immediate revolutionary effect upon the mass of the people, in so far as the essentials of their material life, their security of holding, and their personal status were concerned. Outside the honours, the landed rights of all free men had their defence in shire and hundred as before. Not even an earl's right carried the jurisdiction of shire or hundred without special grant. Earls and barons had an immunity as such, but it was of their own persons only. They claimed to be tried by their peers, and though much of their land might be subject to common amercement, they themselves were not.[3] For at least a further generation hundred and shire functioned as before.[4] There was no sudden radical change of system, nor, as has sometimes been suggested, revival, for since the reign of Æthelred no decline in

---

[1] *Placita de Quo Warranto*, p. 245: *Private persone . . . non habuerunt potestatem aliquem feoffare de hujusmodi (sci. libertatibus de visu franciplegii et weif) cum sint mere ad Coronam domini Regis spectantes*: private persons could not enfeoff others of this kind of franchise, etc.

[2] *Ibid.* 677: *Tenere duas magnas curias in eodem manerio et in curia illa placitare omnia placita que vicecomes placitat in turno suo*: to hold two great courts in the said manor, and in them to implead all pleas that the sheriff impleads in his tourn.

[3] Barons ought to be amerced before the king's council. Letters Close, 3 Hen. III, p. 383.

[4] William I, Latin Articles, 8. 1: *Requiratur hundred et comitatus sicut antecessores nostri statuerunt.*

the English system had taken place. The essentially popular basis of justice was untouched. As in the sheriff's courts, so in the courts of those magnates who held private jurisdiction of the hundred, or sake and soke, the custom of the countryside prevailed, and even down to the manorial courts, the lord's reeve was no more than incorporating officer of the court, and villeins, as judges of the manor custom, determined each other's right. Judgment by suitors was as proper to feudalism as to the system which it superseded, and the two systems were not far apart. Almost all the kindred procedure had been eliminated from the old English local moots before the Conquest, and for it had been substituted judgment and oath-helping by neighbours, preferably neighbours of the same order and standing as the litigants; this preference for an equivalence of the standing of judges and parties conformed strictly to Norman prejudice and lent itself readily to feudal expression. Judgment by neighbours, for choice of equal rank, developed into judgment by tenants of the same administration or liberty, preferably equals in tenure. The *judicium vicinorum*, almost imperceptibly modified, passed into the *judicium parium* which was the ideal, if not the rule, of Norman justice.[1] We shall, in fact, misunderstand the course of history if we fail to realize the flow of the broad stream of English custom across the line of the Norman Conquest and into the Middle Ages. That custom, and the community it has formed, remain the basis of the English state, and, as time goes on, the crown is content more and more to go down into the county courts and hundreds to find lawful men to activate its procedure in common law and administration. The drawing together in a common task of government of a crown which claims an English descent and a nation which has not abandoned its immemorial custom is one of the two outstanding facts of the Middle Ages. In this we see the English nation coming to the lordship of feudalism and yet preserving the essentials of community. But this is only one, though, perhaps, the more powerful of the two impulses which determined the rise of the English polity. The Norman Conquest brought into England a crown which was in two minds between its royal Saxon and its Norman

---

[1] Leges Henrici Primi, 31. 7: *Unusquisque per pares suos iudicandus est et eiusdem provincie*: every man is to be judged by his peers and those of the same administration.

ducal right, but which in the end did its work through its feudal power of jurisdiction. Royal lordship proved to be more effective than the Saxon cyneryhta. Still, for two centuries and more, England had rulers who, according to their individual temperaments, behaved now as king and now as lord. The cleavage between the two societies and the two races was not, of course, absolute. The gradation from the highest feudal tenure to the lowest servitude was by imperceptible stages. But in broad outline it is the fissure within the nation set up in 1066 which gives to the central institutions of medieval English government their characteristic trend. For from feudal discontents, arising from specifically feudal burdens, and from the ambitions of a few feudatories, came first rebellion, and as rebellion failed, a more considered resistance to the crown which broadened into a common interest with the nation.

Feudal theory

The material detail of feudalism, its incidents, and the struggle between the crown seeking to turn them into an elastic source of revenue and of the feudatories refusing to exceed their customary liabilities may, for the moment, be deferred. They are the absorbing consideration of a later age. But some description of the ideas which inspired the feudal order and led to the more notable actions of its leaders is necessary, for it is against a background of feudalism that the kings fought their way to an overmastering crown, and not the least part of their struggle was to resolve within their own minds the implications of their dual status as lord and king. The units of feudal society are fees, baronies, and earldoms, the two last impartible in law. The term honour was applied in general to any of them which achieved a degree of structural unity, and, though the doctrines of tenure came to pervade all relations of life, it was in the honour that feudal values were brought to a focus and most clearly expressed. The Mandeville barony, of which something has been said already, shows the honour well enough in its average form. Except in the North and upon the Welsh Marches, it is rare for the lands of any one lordship to lie contiguous to each other. The scattering of manors in several counties, each with its own customary court and officials, is the common rule, and the honour appears, therefore, rather as a

The honour

confederation of social-economic units than as a compact whole, the superstructure of central obedience and common administration and jurisdiction which reconciles this disunity being an outcome of Norman lordship and concerned solely with the strictly feudal elements, tenures in free fee, tenures in knight-service.

The binding tie of this knightly and baronial feudalism is the *Homage* swearing of homage.[1] It is distinguished from the oath of fealty and the English hold-oath by its greater precision, by identifying the tie of lord and man with that of tenure. Being made for a certain tenement, and constituting a contract by which that tenement is held, it has a material guarantee in law. The hold-oath was a solemn promise, the breach of which incurred moral reprobation; the breaking of homage gave rise to an action at law, and made the tenant liable to lose his tenement. Homage was a solemn act, bringing into being the most deeply felt relation of the feudal world, and it bound the heirs of both lord and tenant in perpetuity.[2] Its action was symbolical of fidelity and reverence on the part of the man, who knelt bare-headed, and of dominance and protection on the lord's part, as he received his vassal's hands between his own.[3] The material purport of the ritual was a contract; upon the vassal's side to "become your man for the tenement I hold of you, and bear faith to you of life and members and earthly honour against all other men, saving the faith I hold to our Lord King"; upon that of the lord to maintain his tenant in his tenement, rights, and custom, to warrant his tenure in law, and to defend him against all other men. "Homage is a bond of law by which one is holden and bound to warrant, defend, and acquit the tenant in his seisin against all men, in return for a fixed service named and expressed in the gift, and whereby the tenant is bound to keep faith with his lord and to perform the due service: and such is the relation of homage that the lord owes as much to the tenant as the tenant to the lord, save only reverence."

It is necessary to dwell upon this act and its implications because *Homage a contract*

---

[1] F. Pollock and F. W. Maitland, *History of English Law*, i. 296-307.

[2] The lord can be compelled to take the homage of his dead tenant's heir or show cause *quare non fecerit*. Glanvill, *Tractatus de Legibus*, ix. 4.

[3] *English Historical Review*, xlii. 247. A writ of William I records, *Petrum . . . militem Sancti Aedmundi et Baldewini abbatis manibus iunctis fore feodalem hominem. Black Book of St. Augustine's* (British Academy), ii. 462: *Domini sui quorum homo manibus suis fuerit.*

it is the strongest sanction of the unity of the honour,[1] and because in it feudal England, in common with the feudal world, brings to the surface much which underlies its theory of society, but in England, at least, seldom gets explicit acknowledgment. It is, in fact, the clearest formularization of the feudal contract—a concept, which, though it is never openly embodied in a general feudal code, yet haunts the background of English politics for at least two centuries, and from time to time finds outlet in action. In virtue of the contract of homage and of the tenure which it set up, the lord could exact from his tenants in fee and inheritance service which was fixed by agreement at the creation of the tenure [2] or had *Feudal* become customary. A substantial proportion of the tenements *service* granted by lay and spiritual lords would be given to be held *per servitium militare* with the original intention of meeting the *servitium debitum* or service of knights demanded by the Conqueror from the tenant-in-chief, and, at least by the reign of Henry II, these would have come to owe a number of incidents which are substantially the same throughout England; relief, or fine for entering upon the tenure; wardship and marriage, by which the tutelage of heirs under age and of their estates lay with the lord together with a veto upon marriage to anyone in the lord's disfavour; aid, or an agreed subsidy usually demanded when the lord's eldest son was knighted, or his eldest daughter was married, or to ransom his body from captivity; and scutage, recoverable from the sub-tenants when the king had levied it upon the tenant-in-capite. In a more general way, feudal lordship reproduced or perpetuated many of the privileges and restraints of Saxon lordship, the power of advocacy by the lord,[3] and the right of the man to plead the lord's cause for him at law, the prohibition of joining in judgment upon one's lord, even in a plea of the crown,[4] and the general obligation of lord and man to maintain each other against all others in litigation and to provide good counsel for the furtherance of any purpose either may have at heart. Such coöperation, recalling the legal value of the Saxon mund, was still a principal motive

[1] So much so that "the homage" can be used as a synonym for "the honour", *Cartularium Monasterii de Rameseia*, i. 155.

[2] Glanvill, *Tractatus de Legibus*, ix. 2: *Fiunt autem homagia . . . de servitiis de redditibus certis assignatis in denariis vel in aliis rebus.*

[3] Only a lord could replace the kin in bringing accusation of homicide. Glanvill, *Tractatus de Legibus*, xiv. 3.   [4] *Leges Henrici Primi*, 30 and 32. 2.

in the relation of lord and vassal, and explicitly specified in some charters as a condition of tenure.[1]

The law which provides the ceremony of homage for the form- *Diffidation* ing of the contract between lord and man has an equivalent form for its ending, the *diffidatio*. The condition of vassalage is fidelity and service upon the one hand and warranty and protection upon the other. The tie cannot lightly be broken, but either lord or man, by failing to perform his share of the contract and refusing redress after legal complaint, gives to the other the right to defy him in ritual form, to put him out of his faith, and to coerce him with all the means in his power. The conditions under which a vassal may consider himself free of his homage are carefully delimited. They are the taking away of the fee or right for which homage is due, or the deserting of the vassal in mortal necessity.[2] The diffidation must be made in due form and after a year's delay, during which the tenant must require redress from his lord, informally by the intercession of his peers, of his neighbours, and familiars, and legally of any independent jurisdiction to which he may have access.[3]

---

[1] *Black Book of St. Augustine's* (British Academy), ii. 462: *Eo tenore quod Hamo Dapifer, si opus fuerit, ecclesiae et michi vel successoribus meis de placitis in comitatu sive in curia regis contra aliquem baronem consulat, adiuvet et succurat, exceptis dominis suis quorum homo manibus suis fuerit*: on the condition that Hamo Dapifer shall give counsel and maintenance to this church, to me and my successors, in pleas in the shire-moot or in the king's court if need arise, except against those lords of whom he shall have become the man. *Chronicon Monasterii de Abingdona*, ii. 133. *In curia etiam regis si abbate placitum aliquod forte habendum contigerit, ipsius abbatis parti idem aderit, nisi contra regem*: and if the abbot shall have any plea in the king's court he shall adhere to the part of the said abbot, save only against the king. *Cartularium Monasterii de Rameseia*, i. 153: *Quia vero predictus Robertus vir nobilis erat et sapiens . . . retinuimus hominium suum ad servitium ecclesiae*: and because the said Robert was a man of worth and wisdom we retained his homage for the service of the church.

[2] Bracton, *Note Book*, i. 78. Leges Henrici, 43. 8.

[3] *Ibid.* 43. 9. The ground of the loosing of homage is well put for Richard Marshal by Matthew Paris (*sub anno* 1233): *Proditio non egi contra Regem, quia sine judicio parium meorum et injuste ab officio Mariscalciae me spoliavit . . . cum semper paratus essem in curia sua juri parere, et stare judicio parium meorum. Unde homo suus non fui, sed ab ipsius homagio non per me, sed per ipsum licenter absolvebar*: I have done no treason against the king, for he has disseized me of my office of the Marshalsea unlawfully and without judgment of peers . . . whereas I have ever been ready to appear in his court to fulfil the law and to stand to the judgment of my peers. So I was not his man (when I took arms against him), but stood absolved from his homage rightfully, and not by my own doing but by his. Cf. Wendover, iii. 65.

Limitations on feudal right

Feudalism is, therefore, contractual, but there are effectual limitations upon its tendency to disintegrate, especially so in England, where feudal custom is a newcomer and has to adjust itself within a law of violence which is still in full force. In contrast with Normandy, war between subjects has been illegal for centuries, and the right of lord and man to fight each other's battles is narrowly confined by old-standing restrictions upon violence.[1] Again, feudal justice has safeguards for both lord and man arising out of its own constitution, which guarantee the right of judgment in open court. No man can forfeit his heirs' right except for felony,[2] or betrayal of his lord,[3] or persistent default of service, and in the event of denial of justice by the lord, such as the rules of diffidation have in mind, the vassal has a right of action in the king's court,[4] to which he would be required to have resort rather than to self-help. He must, in short, appeal to the king,[5] and is, indeed, required to do so. Conversely, the king accepts the honour jurisdiction as part of the public order, will afforce his baron's courts for them if they are too feeble to act alone,[6] and will compel the tenants to take their legal action therein.[7] By such

[1] Leges Henrici Primi, 82. 3.   [2] *Ibid.* 88. 14.

[3] This is broadly interpreted, and may include advocacy of another's legal plea against one's own lord. *Ibid.* 43. 3. A good instance of the grounds upon which the king may exact forfeiture of lands is that of Grimbald of Bayeux (H. W. C. Davis, *Regesta Regum*, 76): *Pro reatu infidelitatis suae et crimine insidiarum suarum quibus adversus me perjuraverat*: for his infidelity and for the crime of conspiracy with which he forswore himself towards me. So, in 1172, *Adam de Port calumniatus est de morte et proditione regis*, and was outlawed and his fee declared forfeit: Adam de Port was accused of conspiring the death and betrayal of the king. Benedict, i. 35.

[4] The lord is said to lose his court if he denies justice to a litigant, that is to say, the plea is removed to the court of the king. Leges Henrici Primi, 57. 5.

[5] *Ibid.* 59. 19. The transference of the plea must be effected by a formal denunciation of the lord's default, *curiam domini sacramento falsificare*, an oath being taken upon the Gospel. M. M. Bigelow, *Placita Anglo-Normannica*, 212. Glanvill, *Tractatus de Legibus*, xii.

[6] Letters Patent, 6 John, p. 51: *Nolumus quod judicia curie Pagani de Rupeforti de Hathfeld remaneant per defectum hominum . . . immo precipimus quod judicia curie illius procedant et fiant per milites de comitatu de quibus Vicecomiti Essexie precepimus quod illos illuc venire faciat*: we are unwilling that judgments shall go unmade in Pain de Rochford's court of Hatfield for default of suitors and therefore we command that the judgments of his said court shall proceed and be made by those knights of the county whom we have ordered the sheriff of Essex to make to attend there.

[7] So Henry I orders that if Goscelin has any claim in the lands of St. Mary of Abingdon *eat in curiam Abbatis, et ipse Abbas sit ei ad rectum: et defendo ipsi*

safeguards every door to violence is closed, while the doctrine of mutual responsibility of lord to man is approved and reinforced. There is, therefore, no inevitable antagonism between the crown *Rule of* and the legalized feudalism of the twelfth century, and such ex- *Law* pressions as "feudal anarchy" are peculiarly inapt to describe the normal mind of feudalism, which maintained, on the contrary, an all-pervading respect for law, a respect so strong that it asserted its sanctity above that of any of the authorities which were empowered to carry it out. The rule of law was the most clearly realized political principle of the feudal age, governing the conduct of lord and vassal alike,[1] and the right of diffidation, the right to denounce the contract of homage, was valid precisely and only when the supreme judicial authority failed in its trust of affording fair trial of right; for equally fundamental was the principle that, as the lord was bound to offer fair judgment, so the vassal was bound to place himself upon it. The feudal subject might rebel not when he felt himself to be wronged, nor when he had suffered material loss from the action of the state or of individuals, but when in pursuing the proper channels of law he was refused judgment, a judgment which when lawfully pronounced, whatever its verdict, he must accept.[2] It will be seen by this that the English feudatory was under two degrees of obligation, derived from successive layers of history. As a member of the English community, either by birth or in right of his Saxon antecessor, he was born into a birthright of English law, which he could neither evade nor annul. This was subject to no contract, and constituted an unbreakable tie, one the breaking of which was inconceivable. No English magnate of the feudal age ever formed the ambition of breaking loose from the community of English law, and turning his fee into an independent state. But, with the authority to which the protection and

---

Abbati quod non respondeat inde Goscelino in alio loco: let him enter the abbot's court, and let the abbot there do him right; and I forbid the abbot to answer Goscelin in any other place in this plea. *Chronicon Monasterii de Abingdon,* ii. 93.

[1] The dealings of the lord with his vassal must be *justa secundum considerationem curiae suae et consuetudinem rationabilem.* Glanvill, *Tractatus de Legibus,* ix. 8.

[2] Both aspects of this principle are shown in Langton's justification of a subject's refusal to support his prince in a disseisin not preceded by legal judgment. "If the king attacks a castle unjustly are his people bound to support him? If without judgment, no. If after judgment, yes: *cum populus non habet discutere de sententia.*" F. M. Powicke, "Stephen Langton", p. 95. Note 1.

enforcement of the law was entrusted his relation was conditional, or so it seemed to an aristocracy which had become steeped in Frankish feudalism. Because the *feudum*, bestowed by a lord and earned by the service of a vassal, had come to be the universal land-right of Normandy and therefore predominant in England, the holders of English fees thought of themselves as first and foremost vassals, whose duty towards the king was created by enfeoffment and was therefore subject to the conditions and limitations of feudal tenure and by the terms of homage revocable. In so far as they could see beyond the individual relation, the king appeared to them as the guardian of the national custom, whose claim to obedience, either by divine or secular right, was nullified if he failed to fulfil his trust. The maxim that the power of a king who acts as a tyrant is illegitimate, which almost exhausts contemporary theorizing about monarchy, and to us seems to be an ineffectual truism, was thus in the twelfth and thirteenth centuries the corner-stone of legal security.

Feudal revolt

Feudal action, therefore, as long as it is guided by principle—and it is rarely that the individual can divest himself of the preconceptions of his age—is primarily legal: but, when refused legal redress, the aggrieved party is entirely within his rights in declaring his obligation of vassalage at an end, making war upon his king, and coercing him by every means in his power to do him right. From its very nature, we cannot go to crown records for this strand of theory, but it governs the treatment of historical events in chronicles and popular literature. One of the few surviving romances of English chivalry, the legend of Fulk fitz Warin,[1] gives an excellent example of the behaviour that was thought proper from an injured vassal to his king. Maurice fitz Roger of Powys had ejected Fulk's father, Warin, from his fief of Blancheville, and Fulk, as his heir, had claimed justice and been denied it by King John. Fulk defies him in these terms: "Lord King, you are my liege lord, and I was bound to you by fealty as long as I was in your service and held lands of you: and it was for you to maintain me in right, and you failed me in right and common law. Never was there good king who denied his free tenants right in his court.

---

[1] The historical Fulk fitz Warin was lord of Whittington, and was one of barons excommunicated by Innocent in January, 1216 for his opposition to John (Rymer, *Foedera*, i. 139). The romance is of the early fourteenth century.

For this I render you back your homage." This is not history but
romance, popular sentiment, and it shows what was acceptable
among the French-speaking gentry for whom the tale was written,
for Fulk was the idealized hero of the revolt against John. Coming
nearer to history, for he was a clerk in Henry's employ, we have
Jordan Fantosme's account of the reasoning of William the Lion
before he entered the war of 1173 against the elder Henry.[1] He is
represented as regretting, on the ground of right, his promise to
join the son in rebellion: "to the old king, equally, he owes homage
and service, true allegiance. It is not right that he should make war
on his lands without first demanding his inheritance" (Northumbria, to which Henry II denied his claim). "If he refuse, then
he may, at his will, renounce his homage without blame." In
the same category of war made by individuals in legal form and
without sense of illegality, to secure their right, we may place the
action of the sons of Robert de Beauchamp in 1138 when they
fortified Bedford against Stephen: "not that they meant to deny
their due obedience or service to their lord, but because they had
heard that the king had given the daughter of Simon de Beauchamp
to Hugh le Poer with her father's honour, and they feared to lose
their whole inheritance".[2]

We should probably find this grievance of default of justice,
with its consequence of legal diffidation, at the back of most feudal
"revolts". They are hardly rebellions as we understand it, and
certainly not treason. The term *gwerra* used for them could bear
the sense of right sought by legitimate force, almost of wager of
battle. That of 1173 was led by men whom Henry II had "dis-
inherited",[3] that of 1191 was mainly caused by the Chancellor's
resumption of Richard's sales of honours to finance the Crusade,[4] *The*
and the terms of peace required that the former should "disseize no *barons*
one without judgment of the king's court". In the long discon- *and the*
tents against John, the charge of selling and withholding justice *crown*
was fundamental to the opposition case. Indeed, with so many
warnings that the sanctity of law did not in itself guarantee the
rights of individuals, the voluntary nature of vassalage was from

[1] Fantosme, p. 227.   [2] Orderic, III. xiii. 17.
[3] Ralf de Diceto, 371. The disinheritance was, no doubt, in part of royal
castles which had been held long enough to breed a sense of prescription.
[4] Richard of Devizes, §§11-32.

time to time made an excuse for exacting a specific contract at the moment of homage, and even for anticipating its withdrawal in given circumstances. Robert of Gloucester did homage to Stephen in 1136 *sub conditione quadam*,[1] as did the bishops,[2] and withdrew it in 1138 "according to the customary form", and in 1199 the earls of Derby, Chester, Warwick, and others sold their fealty to John on the condition *ut redderet unicuique jus suum*, which *jus* we may take to be such definite objects as the share of the Peverel lands which had been pursued by the earls of Derby since 1153, and the Chester claims in South Lancashire.[3] The safeguard of the Great Charter of 1215 rested, indeed, upon a wholesale application of this principle, for the homage of twenty-five of the greatest barons was sworn on condition of the charter's observance and revocable on its breach. Thus, on the part of those barons who stand as types of the feudal order, there is a deep sense of their feudal status. Let the king touch their individual *jus*—and the ramification of claims and counterclaims was too intricate to admit of legal settlement without cavil—and they are ready with the cry of default of right and the weapon of withdrawal of homage. Almost always, it would seem, the quasi-legal conventions are preserved, and the form of diffidation gone through. Robert of Gloucester, as against Stephen in 1138,[4] on a personal issue, and the barons of the Charter before Runneymede,[5] in a general cause, equally present their defiance and so hold to convention in making war on their king, and Henry III himself against Richard Marshall in 1233 and before Lewes in 1264, feels bound to use the ceremony of diffidation against the rebels before he takes the field:[6] *vos tamquam nostrorum ... inimicos diffidamus*. The feudal standing of monarch and subject as parties to a revocable compact appears in this defiance of his subjects by a king, as it does in the letter of the charter barons to John denouncing him as perjured *et baronibus rebellis*.[7]

Divided loyalties

It is hard to determine how far this feudal diplomacy was backed

[1] Malmsbury, 707: *Scilicet quamdiu ille dignitatem integre custodiret et sibi pacta servaret.*

[2] *Quamdiu ille libertatem ecclesiae et vigorem disciplinae conservaret.*

[3] Derby actually got his demands in 1199 (*Rotuli de Oblatis*, 3). Chester had to wait for his until a later crisis at the end of the reign. *Placita de Quo Warranto*, 387.

[4] *Historia Novella*, i. §18.

[5] Coventry, 219.

[6] Rishanger, p. 28.

[7] Wendover, ii. 117.

by feudal power. The most considerable warlike efforts of individual barons seem to have been made with foreign mercenaries.
Ralf Guader intended to hire a Danish force, Robert of Gloucester
won the battle of Lincoln with Welsh mercenaries, and in 1173
Leicester, Mowbray, and Norfolk fought with armies of hired
Flemings. The amercements in the Pipe Roll of 1175 and 1176
reveal almost no trace of any English following.[1] Indeed, the cross-
currents of obligation in which the English vassals were involved
made it hard for king or baron's strength to gather head. Homage
might be done to several lords for different tenements, and those
lords might be at variance. If the tenant were drawn into advocacy
of one lord against the other at law, or had to take up arms, he
should by feudal custom forfeit the tenement held of the lord he
had deserted. The lord, also, though he exacted the strict letter of
service from the man whose homage he shared with his enemy,
might still lose the full and willing support of his vassal. Many
devices were put forward to solve this kind of dilemma. The lord
could at least insist that the resources of the fees held of himself
should not be used against him.[2] Many vassals, however, felt that
they had discharged their obligation if they rendered their strict
servitium debitum to their lord, and might use the rest of their
resources as they liked, even to the point of throwing them on the
side of his enemies. The count of Flanders had a standing agreement with England to limit his service to the king of France in
this way, and the same evasion was apt to be made in England.[3] In
1141 many barons came in person to Stephen's host at Lincoln
with their customary quota, but sent the rest of their men to join
the Angevins against him,[4] while in 1215, after their knights had
gone over to the opposition, certain of the magnates felt bound to
continue with the king *tanquam domino adhaerentes*.[5] Some attempt
was made to clear up this ambiguity by introducing the conception
of ligeance,[6] liege homage, and liege fealty, which set up a prior *Liege*
claim upon the service and fidelity of the liege vassal, and it was *homage*
further accepted that a man's liege lord should be he of whom he

[1] There was some disturbance in York, and round the Mowbray's stronghold
of Thirsk.   [2] Leges Henrici Primi, 59. 12A.
[3] Cf. the treaty between the earls of Chester and Leicester (1147–1151).
Stubbs, *Select Charters*, p. 140.
[4] Orderic, III. xiii. 21.   [5] Coventry, 220.
[6] From *ledic*, "direct or unrestricted", as opposed to *simplex homagium*.

held his principal fee, *cujus residens est*.[1] The effect of this, of course, would be to strengthen the hold of the king upon the barons, who held their *capita honorum* from him, but also that of the barons over the tenants of the fees held in mesne tenure from them. On the whole, it would tend to arrest the dissipation of feudal loyalty and so solidify the sense of unity in the honours, and it had little bearing upon the main problem of the eleventh and twelfth centuries, the reconciling of the king's claim to general obedience with the special obligations of tenure. Besides the ambiguities inherent in the feudal system itself, there is the fact that by Norman, but still more by English tradition, the royal person was something more than lordship.

Fealty to the king

Whatever had been his rights in Normandy, the Conqueror inherited a claim to, or at least an expectation of general fealty, which the English kings since Eadward the Elder had received from the nation through the mouths of the witan. This had been thought of as a taking of the king to *cynehlaford*, and it had apparently been sworn in the form of the ordinary hold-oath of man to lord. Under the Norman kings this fealty to the king was renewed in every reign, at the celebrated meeting at Salisbury in 1086,[2] to

---

[1] Leges Henrici Primi, 55. 2. Some charters require that the homager shall remain resident, and thus not impair his ligeance. *Cartularium Monasterii de Rameseia*, i. 144.

[2] The oath of 1086 has been a source of debate, and historians have given it a kind of fundamental importance as "The Oath of Salisbury". It does not seem, in fact, to differ essentially from the swearing of fealty in the next year to Rufus, in 1100 to Henry, or from the hold-oaths sworn to Eadward the Elder, Eadmund, or Æthelred. The combination of respect and hesitation with which it has been approached arises from the fact that, though explicitly stated to have been exacted from sub-tenants as well as from tenants-*in-capite*, it has been taken for an act of homage. The English term used when homage is intended is usually *manraed*, though this is a distortion of its original meaning, and in 1086 the Anglo-Saxon Chronicle—of which Florence of Worcester's account can hardly be more than a paraphrase—is clear that the oath sworn was the hold-oath: "they all bowed to him, and became his men, and swore hold-oaths to him". But behind any question of contemporary terms lies the simple fact that an oath of homage from mesne-tenants to the king was at that time impossible in law. The same tenement could not bear a double or multiple homage to a series of superior lords, since homage carried liabilities of relief, wardship, marriage, escheat, and other personal services which could not be shared. By the time of Glanvill's tractate (*Tractatus de Legibus*, ix. 2), a restricted form of homage had been devised, which excluded liability for the feudal incidents while carrying an equal sense of general submission, and this was taken to the king and to the king only, and created no conflict of services when he exacted it from the vassals of his barons. *Fiunt*

Rufus in 1087, when "all the men of England bowed to him and swore oaths",[1] to Henry in 1100, when "all the men of this nation bowed to him and swore him oaths and became his men".[1] Stephen, more Norman and less statesmanlike than his predecessors, seems to have pretermitted the rite, but it was renewed by Henry II, and more effectively, since it was sworn to by all classes in their hundred moots, and thenceforth it became a part of the normal routine of government.

The Saxon hold-oath and Anglo-Norman fealty were, however, in practice less effective than the full tenurial bond, and may be said to have maintained a conflict of principles within the state rather than to have nullified the effects of homage. Feudal sentiment enforced duty to an immediate lord: monarchical and national tradition placed the peace of the realm and sworn fealty to the crown above it. It cannot be said that the conflict was effectively laid to rest in any reign until that of Edward I. It is true that common law closely restricted the limits within which a man

Conflict of royal and feudal principles

autem homagia de terris et tenementis liberis tantummodo de servitiis de redditibus certis assignatis in denariis vel in aliis rebus. Pro solo vero dominio fieri non debent homagia alicui excepto principe. This may well have been the *ligeantia* exacted from his barons' knights by Henry II in 1166, the homage twice sworn to the young king and to Henry of Anjou himself in 1153,—it would serve its purpose of constituting an immediate or prospective recognition of right in him who received it, without setting up a conflict of immediate obligations *de servitiis*, which was precisely what Henry fitz Roy made the pretext of his revolt—but there is no mention of it in the Leges Henrici Primi, and certainly no reason to suppose it had been invented by the reign of the Conqueror. Fealty was a much less tangible tie than homage, if only from the fact that, while homage was protected by an action at law, and its breach would lead to the loss of the tenement from which it was due, a breach of fealty, unless aggravated by criminal acts, was no more than a moral offence. It was proper for the king to take fealty of the whole nation as far as they could be approached effectively, and by the time of the Conquest it was usual for the king so to do. It was an oath which might be sworn to without difficulty by all subjects "whosesoever men they were": but it could not have the rigid legal effect of homage, and was, no doubt, apt to cover many degrees of feeling towards the king, and to admit of all sorts of subordinate commitments which were not felt necessarily to conflict with the general allegiance of the subject. Probably, the difficulties of the Conquest made it advisable to postpone the ceremony until the end of the reign, while Rufus and Henry carried it through on their accessions. The knowledge of the English tenantry gained from the Domesday survey may also have helped to make it possible. A sense of its having marked the culmination of the reign may have led the Chronicler to give it a somewhat misleading emphasis compared with that allowed to earlier and later instances of equal constitutional importance.

[1] Anglo-Saxon Chronicle, *sub annis*.

could support his lord without committing felony, and that the oath of homage and charters of enfeoffment included the phrase *salva debita fide Domini Regis*, or the like, but in practice, as we have seen, feudal motives prevailed in many crises of history, and feudal convention was followed. It is, indeed, far from clear that the strongest kings were consistent in holding aloof from feudal motives. Rebellions were made as legally justified war against the king, and were so accepted by him. That of 1215, the rising of the Marshal in 1233, end, not with punishment, but with a peace; *hominium et fidelitatem de novo facientes*. The treaty ending the war of 1173-4, when the barons were at Henry's mercy, shows a nice discrimination, by which what we should hold to be the crime of rebellion and treason is condoned, and the common law offences committed in the course of it are left open to prosecution.[1] Here the exact letter of English feudalism as set out in the Leges Henrici Primi seems to have been observed—the right to urge the cause of a lord, in this case the young king, to whom homage had been done, but with no privilege to commit felony. No forfeitures follow this revolt, and, indeed, that rebellion as such is treason is not a doctrine of public law until the fourteenth century.[2] The great forfeitures of the twelfth century, those of Robert of Bellême,[3] William Peverel, and Henry de Essex, were for felonies in the strict feudal sense, betrayal of a lord, poisoning, desertion of a lord on the field of battle. If the chroniclers are to be believed, the strongest of kings were capable of strange lapses into feudal sentiment. The civil war may explain such concessions of hereditary jurisdiction as the Empress Matilda made to Aubrey de Vere or Geoffrey de Mandeville, *convenciones* in treaty form guaranteed by the count of Anjou and the king of France,[4] but Henry I needed to be convinced of his right to disinherit Robert

---

[1] Foedera, i. 30: *Omnes illi qui recesserant ab eo post filium . . . ad pacem ejus (Regis patris) revertantur; . . . ita quod de . . . morte vel perditione alicujus membri respondeant secundum judicium et consuetudinem terrae*: all those who seceded from him with his son may return to his peace, answering for death or maiming by judgment and the custom of the land. Even after Evesham the Dictum de Kenilworth admitted the rebels to peace—*non fiat exhæredatio sed redemptio*. Stubbs, *Select Charters*, p. 407 (citations throughout are from the Ninth Edition).

[2] In 1386 Gloucester took legal advice as to whether a right of diffidation still existed. *Rotuli Parliamentorum*, iii. 379.

[3] Orderic, III. xi. 3. *Crimen proditoris confessus.*

[4] J. H. Round, *Geoffrey de Mandeville*, p. 176.

de Bellême,[1] and accorded the earl's captured garrison of Bridgnorth freedom and the honours of war *quia fidem principi suo servabant ut decuit*.[2]

Feudal aims, therefore, seem to have been limited by the very doubtful hold which any feudatory outside the Welsh March had upon his lesser tenantry, by the restrictions of common law and the law of felony, and by the essentially legalistic outlook engendered by feudalism itself. But the Norman barons and their *The community of the honour* knight tenants and greater freeholders formed to a limited degree a community within the community, governed as to part of their actions by ideals of tenure and chivalry, and often taking action against the king on purely feudal grounds. The executive machinery of a great lordship was not unlike that of the kingdom,[3] which was itself still rudimentary and domestic. No lay honour seems to have developed a regular chancery, but at least one private exchequer, that of the earl of Gloucester at Bristol, is known, and the greatest men, like Stephen when still count of Mortain and lord of Furness, Eye, and much else in England, address their writs to their justiciars, though it may be suspected *Organization of the honour* that the title often stood for no specialized office.[4] The *dapifer* or seneschal occurs frequently, holding courts in his lord's absence, receiving fealty and giving seizin,[5] and, in the greater immunities, occupying the bench together with the visiting justices of the crown. The dispenser appears as directing issues for expenses and alms. Constables, originally commanders of the knights of the household, act in the twelfth century more commonly as castellans of individual castles, and rarely, as at Richmond and Chester— where the lords of Mold, themselves powerful barons at Widnes and elsewhere, held the hereditary constableship of the earldom—

[1] Orderic, III. x. 16.

[2] *Ibid.* III. xi. 3. Cf. with this the lenient treatment accorded to the vassals of Simon de Montfort after Evesham. They were fined only a tenth of the proportion of their revenue that the principals had to pay to make their peace. Dictum de Kenilworth, 29; Stubbs, *Select Charters*, p. 407.

[3] F. M. Stenton, *English Feudalism*, pp. 65-82.

[4] Cf. Waleran of Meulan's writ to his justices of Sturminster, who can hardly have been more than manorial reeves. *Ibid.* p. 67.

[5] *Chronicon Monasterii de Abingdon*, ii. 59: *Investituram, id est saisitionem, accepit per manum Picoti, dapiferi Albrici* (de Ver).

do they remain, even in title, military chiefs of the whole honour. In general, there is less rigidity, and probably less effective special. ization of function in baronial than in royal administration, but the impression given is still of a system amply sufficient to the full exploitation of the estates, and to their coördination as military, and, to a lesser degree, social units.

Social unity is, indeed, for the most part confined to the feudal gentry whose mesne tenure is the binding force of the honour. The free tenants of the fees of a great lordship were involved in a common obligation to the *dominus superior*, and as time went on

Honorial courts

their tenure and service tended to take some measure of local uniformity, and to be thought of as the custom of the honour.[1] The knights could be spoken of as *pares* of the honour,[2] as mutually associated in one law, and so a new institution came into being, the latest juridical institution to be created by the spontaneous vigour of private right, and the last to emerge before the crown assumed and retained the initiative in all judicial and administrative change. As with the hundred, so with the honour, the test of its vitality is that it had the strength to embody its community in a court. Above the manor courts or soke courts, which any considerable barony would, as a rule, include, with no point of contact with them, confined to the suit of tenants in fee and interpreting feudal custom throughout the honour, rose a *curia domini, curia baronum, curia militum, magna curia*. It can hardly be doubted that the power to hold such courts is a product of the rules of the *feudum*. The estates of the Saxon thegns, quickly acquired and lightly dispersed, gave neither time nor motive for them to arise. The Norman magnates and their tenants in fee must look forward to a permanent association between their heirs. There must be a *modus vivendi* for all time. Such courts are clearly defined by the reign of Henry I. They excite no criticism and are of accepted standing. They owe their validity purely to the honorial

---

[1] Chester, an exceptional case, of course, produced a comprehensive code of feudal custom in the Magna Carta of the earldom. Cf. J. Tait, *Chartulary of Chester Abbey.*

[2] *Cartularium Monasterii de Rameseia*, i. 154: *Per servitium duorum militum in omnibus servitiis quae facient compares sui de eodem feuodo*: by service of two knights in all services which are done by their peers of the same fee.

right of their lords. They are not confused with the *halimotes* of the manors, nor with the jurisdiction of soke which came from the English,[1] but are privileges in the common right of Norman feudalism, lord's right from the very fact of lordship. This right is so explicitly set forth by the Henrician jurisconsult who sought to coördinate feudal custom with Saxon law, that we may be sure that he saw it to be part of a new, though settled, order. The right to exact suit as from man to lord is explained, and with it the basic right to endow the suitors with the quality of doomsmen,[2] and so to bring a court into being, and they are of common right for all who hold in fee. It is, however, to be noted that they are already forced to conform to an established territorial scheme, they are already honorial. A lord may summon men to his court from the furthest manors of the honour, but not from beyond it,[3] however far his lordship may extend, and in time it will come to be contended that even that right is not valid unless suit is specified in the charter of enfeoffment. The judicial fact of the honour determines the suit, not the personal fact of lordship and tenure, and this, no doubt, is the prime factor making against the absorption of one honour by another and the growth of feudal sub-states within the nation. Within fifty years of the Conquest, therefore, the honours had become substantive parts of the English legal and social system, had defined their legal boundaries, determined the obligations of their members, and embodied their jurisdiction in permanent courts, but, at the same time, had reached their furthest extension.

Except when the honour included some pre-existing public administration—as in Holderness, where the lord appointed a sheriff, and the honorial suit was done to the wapentake—the honorial court could have had very little relation to the customary tenants, sokemen, and small freeholders, that is, to the bulk of the population. We can see this in such an honour as that of Boulogne, which had manors in Essex, Kent, Surrey, and Suffolk, whose knightly tenants did suit every month to the honour court of Witham in Essex, and to a six-monthly court at St. Martin-le-Grand, while the manorial tenants were confined to their manor

[1] Leges Henrici Primi, 9. 4; 56. 4; 57. 8.

[2] *Ibid.* 32. 3: *Si dominus placitet contra hominem suum, potest in consilio suo habitos judices informare, si opus sit*: if a lord brings a plea against one of his men, he may constitute judges in his own council if need be.

[3] *Ibid.* 55. 1A.

courts, and were in some cases involved in forinsec[1] jurisdictions.[2] An attempt to extend the honorial suit beyond the free tenants might be resisted, as when the men of Thanet asserted that their duty was only to their halimotes, and refused to attend St. Augustine's court at Canterbury even upon personal summons. Remarkably enough, the Kentish peasantry and the king's chancery were at one in asserting the reality of the older outlines of landright and jurisdiction as against the feudal honour. For many common purposes of administration and judicature the crown would not recognize honour or barony. The right to neither could be sued for *eo nomine* by writ. Thus, when in 12 Edward I[3] the crown "challenged the barony of Dalston with its appertinences as his right against the bishop of Carlisle," the bishop was able to reply that the writ was not good in form, *debet enim dominus Rex petere per maneria, vel per messuagia, vel in aliquo certo loco,*[4] and his objection was acknowledged and the object of the writ amended to *manerium de Dalston . . . cum omnibus membris suis, tam in dominicis quam serviciis, redditibus et villenagiis, et cum advocacione ecclesie et tota soka et omnibus pertinenciis suis,* the specification of the barony as the object of the suit dropping out. Throughout the Edwardian enquiry *de quo warranto* the crown refuses to recognize any general honorial or baronial immunity[5] from royal courts or administration as apart from what is proved as the privilege of the component manors or justified by a general royal charter.

The court and the honorial community   The interest of honorial justice, therefore, lies in the history of the feudal aristocracy, the barons, and their free tenants, and has only an indirect reaction upon the nation. Responding to the Norman instinct for judgment of like by like, the honour court provided a forum where the knights sued for their tenures, where

---

[1] *I.e.* foreign to the honour, belonging to some exterior court public or private.

[2] As with Boughton Alulf in Kent, whose holder in knight service did suit to Witham, while his tenants in gavelkind attended the abbot of Battle's court of Wye. So also, the Lincolnshire townships of the honour of Eye do their suit to the wapentake of Sedgebrook in that county. Public Record Office. *Calendar of Inquisitions Post Mortem,* iii. 604.

[3] *Placita de Quo Warranto,* p. 112.

[4] "Manor by manor and messuage by messuage, or as incident to some place named."

[5] So Ralf de Beauchamp's claim of view in Eton on the ground *quod capud baronie sue est* is rejected by the king's proctor. *Placita de Quo Warranto,* p. 3.

feudal custom could develop and clarify its rules, and where feudal policy and interests were furthered. Like the *curia Regis*, it was at once a court of justice and a council in which the lord sought the advice of his men.[1] "The baronial courts of the Norman age did justice between their peers, advised their lords in the crises which continually arose in the history of every great fee, and thereby evolved in course of time a coherent scheme of rights and duties out of the tangle of personal relationships produced by the sudden introduction of feudal tenure into England".[2] The period during which this influence was at its height was hardly more than a century. With the creation of the assizes under Henry II a form of trial better than ordeal by battle was offered by the royal courts, the barons were rarely empowered to administer it, and their courts quickly fell out of favour. They remained, however, the pivots upon which social and political feudalism turned. Much of the domestic history of feudalism was enacted in the lords' courts, and with their witness and warranty. Robert de Bagpuize wishes to add to the lands of his younger brother, John. He grants him a knight's fee in Bentley and Barton with the witness of William Ferrers of Derby, of the earl's brother and uncles, of his steward, and of certain knight tenants of the honour. John then becomes his brother's man *in curia domini mei Comitis Willelmi de Ferrers*.[3] William fitz Richard makes a clean partition of inheritance with his brother Gervase. It is done by resigning the estate, a knight's fee, into the hand of Geoffrey Ridel, the lord, whose court then makes recognition of the surrender, upon which Geoffrey gives seizin to Gervase and receives his homage.[4] The security of family settlements might often rest upon this recognition by the lord's court.[5] Again, the incidents of knight service call at times for

---

[1] The honorial court as council is well illustrated in the case of Abingdon (M. M. Bigelow, *Placita Anglo-Normannica*, p. 168). The abbot receiving what he believes to be an unjust order from King Stephen to return certain lands to Turstin Basset, *adunata . . . curia sua, diem statuit quo, habita deliberatione, excogitaret quid super hoc responderet*: summoned his court and appointed a day when he might take counsel what answer he should make in this affair. For another instance in the honour of Battle, *ibid.* pp. 115 and 178.

[2] F. M. Stenton, *English Feudalism*, p. 44.

[3] I. H. Jeayes, *Derbyshire Charters*, 239.   [4] *Ibid.* 1078.

[5] Thus the abbot and chamberlain of Ramsey bring "before the barons of the church of Ramsey" an agreement they have come to in the chapter, and the barons *recordati sunt et concesserunt. Cartularium Monasterii de Rameseia*, i. 142.

adjustments and concessions, and these also may be made before the lord or his seneschal. So Richard de Curzon, who has had to pay the customary aids to the earl Ferrers, and has been helped to do so by Thomas Curzon of Kedleston, in return excuses Thomas the same aids to himself, and does so with the witness of Ralf fitz Nicholas, the earl's seneschal.[1]

Wardship and marriage
Another side of feudal obligation, which worked to give the honour a common interest, and to produce a uniform honorial type, was the lord's right of wardship and marriage. The tutelage of heirs under age and of their lands brought every family into intimate personal relationship from time to time with its overlord, in whose household the heir would be bred up, and with whose patronage and good-will marriages were made. At its best, this could inject a kind of paternalism into the feudal bond,[2] and the interweaving of lordship and family ties within the honour could make it a very close community. The knight tenants, in the larger honours barons of their lords, formed his council (judgment and counsel being, indeed, inseparable functions), and, as the domestic fortunes of the tenants were again and again conducted under his guidance, so they lent their counsel and consent to the lord's actions,[3] which thus became, as it were, public acts of the honour, as those of the king and his *curia* were public acts of the realm.[4]

The year 1066 was the beginning of innumerable adjustments due to the passage of the community from organization first by kindreds and then by neighbourhood to a feudal grouping, but they are too intricate to be presented as an intelligible whole. The reception of Norman feudalism, with the rise of the honours, and their impact upon politics and the constitution, has, on the contrary, effects which are plain to see. *Ex conquestu* there sprang into

[1] I. H. Jeayes, *Derbyshire Charters*, 1500.

[2] So Henry I gives the daughter of Geoffrey Ridel in marriage *requisicione et consilio . . . parentum suorum*: by the request and counsel of her relatives. Here we have the two interests blended in the petitioners, that of the family implied in the request, and that of the lord who is counselled that he may justly and in his own interest make the marriage. Stenton, *English Feudalism*, p. 259.

[3] *Chronicon Monasterii de Abingdon*, ii. 20. Hugh of Chester says: *locutus sum ✳. . . cum meis baronibus, et inveni in meo consilio quod concedam eam (terram) Deo*: I have taken counsel with my barons, and have been convinced in my council that I ought to give the land to God.

[4] *Ibid.* ii. 136. The abbot grants *consensu omnium monachorum et auctoritate militum*: by the consent of all the monks, and by the authority of the knights.

being a hundred or more feudal dynasties, of which at least the greater were responsible for a dual effect upon the life of the nation. The reigning tenant by barony had his place in the *consilium regis*, which was the highest court of the realm, while for the same lord the *caput honoris* was the centre of a provincial policy which aimed at the extension of family lands by marriage, by legal finesse, and, in some extreme instances, by selling the support of a great landed interest to the crown. The first, the influence of the barons, individually or together, in the king's council, was a constant factor, effective even under the strongest Norman kings: but until the last decade of the twelfth century, when custom and common law began to be threatened, it was applied equably and produced its effects without challenge. The duty of the vassal in the lord's *curia* was to give him favourable counsel. A basic identity of interest was assumed, and the right or duty to oppose the lord's will arose only in extremity to save him from his own folly.[1] From its very nature the great council of the Norman kings was unfitted for the functions of a parliament, and the nature or authority of counsel, the place in government of the king's personal will, the relation of both to the supremacy of the law, were matters which were beginning to exercise a handful of lawyers and churchmen only. It would take a hundred years from the Conquest to digest them into political creeds.

Thus the strength and ambition of the Norman feudatories at first found an outlet in domestic diplomacy. The interests of the greater honours were pressed individually, and from generation to generation determined the attitude of their lords to their neighbours and to the crown. The great lords of the Welsh March were possessed of regal powers[2] within their lordships, and had their enmities and alliances with English barons and foreign powers, and, until the crushing defeat of eight of the leading families in 1174, or, perhaps, even until Evesham, there seemed to be no necessary limit to the ambitions even of the purely English magnates. Between 1073 and 1098 the Montgomerys, already possessed

External diplomacy of the honours

---

[1] Becket's words to Henry II—*eo quod dominus, debeo et offero vobis consilium*— might have been taken for, and probably was, a calculated impertinence but it was good custom. Letters of St. Thomas (ed. Giles), no. 179.

[2] Cf. Hugh de Louther's comment upon the Mortimers' powers at Cleobury: *predicte libertates faciunt quandam coronam integram per quam quis est rex. Placita de Quo Warranto*, p. 675.

of Shrewsbury and South Lancashire, conquered all middle Wales, imposed their overlordship on Cardigan, and founded a third Montgomery lordship in Pembroke. When Robert of Bellême rose in 1102 it was in alliance with the princes of Powys, the king of Dublin, and the Norse king of Man. If the earls of Chester had realized at any one time all their claims by inheritance, conquest, and royal grant, they would have held, besides Chester, North Wales to Anglesey, Cumberland, South Lancashire, Staffordshire, the honours of Bligh, Peverel, and Eye, the sokes of Torksey, Oswardbeck, Mansfield, Rutland, and Stanley, the towns and castles of Stafford, Derby, and Nottingham.[1] These are extreme instances, but within such great fields of forfeited or unrealized ambitions, which were never really abandoned, there was motive for generations of intrigue, of which the crown was inevitably the focus. Confused with these *jura* of inherited and acquired lands, indeed, in this age of feudalized administration, never distinguished from them, were devolved rights of government, justiciarships, shrievalties, custodies of castles, granted in any moment of the crown's weakness, and in every degree of fee and inheritance, farm, grant for terms of years, or during pleasure. These, in earlier times a pretext for rebellion,[2] became in the thirteenth century the least reputable part of the political pretension of the magnates, so that the need for good government was identical in their minds with the government of the provinces by baronial sheriffs and the lodging of the principal castles in the hands of English nobles. Between 1135 and 1232 such claims were pressed against the crown not only by the earls of Chester, but by the great line of feudatories, Leicester, Derby, Aumâle, and Norfolk, which lay across the north Midlands, and whose lands, almost marching with each other, became the fixed centre of baronial opposition in the Middle Ages. The Marchers, on the contrary, possessed by custom of almost royal rights in their honours, and threatened by the rise of Gwynedd, remained, upon the whole, loyal. They saved the crown in 1174, in 1216, and in 1265, though, no less than the disloyalty of those who were beyond the danger of the border,

---

[1] Rymer's *Foedera*, i. 16.
[2] For example, the young Henry bribed the earl of Norfolk in 1173 with the promise of the constableship of Norwich castle in fee and inheritance. Benedict, i. 45.

their loyalty was determined by honorial interests.

There were few of the great families that did not at one time or another seek to get from the crown by force, individually or by sectional leagues, what they could not get by law, but feudal grievances and the wars they occasioned widened as time went on, fastened upon causes which were common to the whole order, and were urged more peacefully. There is no one time at which we can say that the old local ambitions are extinguished, or that the barons have taken to legitimate courses as an opposition in council, but, as the crown grows stronger, single adventures have less and less prospect of succeeding, and the spirit of opposition becomes a struggle to limit feudal obligations, against the rise of too powerful ministries, and even, under John, to defend the basic rights of person and property. The families who made the last league for purely selfish aims in 1173 are foremost in what was in some measure a war for common right in 1215.

In a very real sense, then, the conciliar elements of our constitution, and the temper in which it worked to keep the crown responsible to the law and to perpetuate the elementary rights of the subject, owed much to feudalism. The king's *curia* of feudatories acquired in the thirteenth century the methods and outlook of a political assembly, though it was that of a very narrow-minded one, and though the specialized quality of feudal counsel was only changed to the free spirit of parliamentary counsel by a painful process of evolution. The material strength which made sustained opposition possible was the indefeasible feudal right in the soil of the honours. The habit of opposition grew imperceptibly out of feudal ambitions and broadened until it was a general cause, and the right, in the last recourse, to oppose the crown with war was no more than the right of diffidation derived from the contractual element in homage. No doubt other systems of right and other ways of thinking might have thrown up habits and conventions of constitutional action not unlike those of the thirteenth-century baronage, but as a matter of history it is from the act of homage that these are in practice deduced. *Constitutional element in feudalism*

History, therefore, cannot afford to ignore the habit of thought bred in the private life of the honours, and, far more than the tenets of the schoolmen, with which it often conflicts, it is the governing thought behind political action. It will be centuries

The Honour of England

from the introduction of tenure and homage before the leaders of English politics will entirely rid themselves of the notion that the *regnum Angliae* is no more than the greatest of the honours, and from this half-conscious prejudice come most of the extreme actions in the cause either of king or barons. The limits of the range of English medieval politics are the belief of the king and his servants that the crown is a tenure of the honour of England,[1] and its lands and profits his demesne, and, against this, the belief of the feudatories that, as barons of that same honour of the realm, they are the *communitas regni*, the repositories of its law, its natural judges, and coadjutors with the king in his task of government—counsellors in the *commune consilium regni*, and at need masters of the king. However unwilling the magnates may be to do the practical work of governing, they recur again and again in opposition to the simple type of the honour as their ideal of the state. Against the *curiales* of Henry I, against Longchamps, Henry III, and Edward II, the basis of baronial politics, even under the sophistication of the fourteenth century, is the return in one recasting or another to the unity of the feudal *curia*, to government by the king with and through his peers. The justiciars of the king should be his barons, his great officers, if not barons, at least such as they can trust and appointed in concert with them, his primary council the *curia* of his tenants in chief, the whole held steady, as in the Charters, by the recognition of a fundamental law, of which their tenure and franchise is a part. This was an ineffectual barrier to oppose to the inevitable pressure of the state towards subdivision of ministry, skilled officialdom, and impersonality of government—upon every occasion when a feudal party secured control it came to disaster—but, variously embodied according to the circumstances of the time, it was the governing concept of medieval opposition and the forerunner of constitutionalism in parliament.

ii

FEUDAL MONARCHY AND BUREAUCRACY, 1066–1189

One essential of the strength of William's kingdom, as of that of all the kings who came after him, was that it was territorial. That

[1] *Barones mei honoris*, Henry I. Ordinance of Shire and Hundred.

is to say, that he could address his writ to the presiding official of *The* any administration with the effect of binding the court and all the *Norman* persons who lived within that administration; that he could place *crown* all such persons under common amercement for default of administrative duty or false judgment. These rights of territorial kingship he owed partly to his predecessors from the year 900. One bond which held the realm together was still the English expedient of the peace[1] and the English oath of fidelity.[2] To this, feudalism added something which English kingship had not known, the jurisdiction inherent in feudal lordship, by which it was within the lord's right to hold court for all the pleas of land of his men—the men *i.e.* who held of him direct, his tenants in capite—and the complementary right to make justiciars to hold pleas, to maintain the authority of his courts, to compel attendance at them and to enforce their decrees. In this right the folkmoots of the shire and hundred became with a new meaning courts of his lordship;[3] sheriff and bailiff merged into his general justicial power as *minores justiciarii regis*. There was, perhaps, no conscious innovation. Cnut legislated mainly to confirm what his predecessors had devised. Most of the enactments bearing the Conqueror's name are conservative in intention.[4] His recorded "institutes"[5] secure that Normans shall enjoy their own custom of pleading when challenged by the English, and shall not be called upon to offer the difficult formulaic Saxon oaths.[6] The Ten Articles, which were compiled after 1100, and the Leis Willelme, which may be as early as 1090, are mostly excerpted from the law of Ælfred and from Cnut's second code, and what is new to us is yet small matter of English custom. In substance, William's intention was to grant the law of the Confessor to the English and to make the

[1] The Charter of Henry I makes the first explicit claim that the king sets the peace of the realm—*pacem firmam in toto regno meo pono*—but it is only a shade more categorical than Cnut's promise that he will "make full frith everywhere". Cnut, 1020. 3.

[2] William's Ten Articles, 1 and 2. Anglo-Saxon Chronicle, 1085E. "There came to him . . . all the landholding men of any worth over all England, whosesoever men they were . . . and swore him hold-oaths".

[3] *Concedo et precipio ut amodo comitatus mei et hundreta . . . sedeant sicut sederunt in tempore regis Eadwardi.* Henry I, Ordinance for his Shires and Hundreds.

[4] *Ut omnes habeant et teneant legem Eadwardi Regis in terris et in omnibus rebus*: William I, Latin Articles, 7. All men shall have and maintain the law of King Edward in lands and in all things.   [5] William. Lad.   [6] *Loc. cit.*

Normans immune from it only where it might bear upon them unfairly. Contemporaries were, indeed, hardly conscious that the régime had changed with the ruler,[1] and habitually confused the incidents of Norman custom with their nearest English analogies.[2] Yet the change was from a king holding a few pleas and folk-moots largely self-determining to a king holding a universal juris-diction throughout his lordship, and, in the end, that would move many landmarks and open the way to a king's law.

The Norman curia

The Conqueror was elected by customary acclamation, and swore the traditional oath to the Church and the Law.[3] The crown-wearings continued at the three annual feasts,[4] and were held at Gloucester, Winchester, and Westminster. The Chronicler of Peterborough, writing in English, calls them *hyreds*,[5] households, and says that some of them at least were accompanied by a witena-gemot. Later chroniclers speak of them as *curiae* or *concilia*. They were, unlike their Saxon predecessors, meetings of tenants who had done homage to the king, but we cannot believe that this restricted William's practical right to summon whom he would, or gave any prerogative of attendance against his will. He could call the men who held immediately of him within his honour to counsel with him. The duty to attend was at times enforced by penalties.[6] The chronicler tells us that "all the great men of England, archbishops, bishops, abbots, earls, thegns, and knights", were with the king at his crown-wearings, so that, though it is probable that the baron, like the king's thegn before him, had a ministerial quality which gave him a place in the king's hall by custom,[7] and placed him under a special obligation in council and in war, at court, and in the provinces, the *curiae* were by no means confined to prelates, earls, and tenants *per baroniam*. Pleas were judged at these assemblies, as in the Confessor's reign, and deci-

[1] This is very noticeable in the references to the Norman *curiae* in the Anglo-Saxon Chronicle. So, Geoffrey Baynard's appeal of William of Eu for treason was tried in the witenagemot held at Salisbury immediately after Epiphany 1096. Odo of Champagne was also convicted there on the king's oath and suffered forfeiture. Anglo-Saxon Chronicle, 1096E.

[2] Cf. Leis Willelme, 20.   [3] Florence of Worcester, 1066.

[4] Anglo-Saxon Chronicle, 1086E.

[5] While Domesday calls Eadward's hyreds *curiae*.

[6] Anglo-Saxon Chronicle, 1095E. Robert Mowbray was put out of the king's peace for refusing to attend the Easter court.

[7] H. W. C. Davis, *Regesta Regum*, no. 60.

sions made on all questions too serious to pass as executive routine, but a comparison between the authority of the king and the magnates within the council would have little more meaning in Norman than in Saxon times, though the temper of the Conqueror and his sons was such as to dominate any constitution. If we believe—it is, of course, possible to do so—that the Anglo-Norman *curia*, almost exclusively Norman in blood, and bound to the king by feudal tenure, had little sense of English tradition, still the feudal *consilium* is the Teutonic moot passed through the tincture of feudalism. It retained the basic assumptions of the latter as to the nature of law and judgment.

It is still true of the *curia* as it was of the witenagemot, that the king cannot give a valid sentence without the *judicium sapientum*;[1] he calls for their judgment.[2] It is also true that their joint authority inspires every act of state. The term 'folkright' dies at the Conquest, but the *consuetudo Angliae* which takes its place is equally authoritative and all-sufficient as a body of principles for public and private action.[3] Reforms through administrative edicts—true legislation is in the future—are still thought of as the fuller expression of a law which is essentially immutable, and so, by extension, judgments, and as such are made by the king in and with the highest court of the realm: *communi concilio et consilio . . . omnium principum regni mei emendendas iudicavi.*[4] The revenues of the crown as well as of subjects, except in so far as they are gifts *ex mera gratia* from man to lord, are so stabilized by custom that they cannot well be modified without a judgment. The Treasury and the Exchequer are courts of fiscal causes from the beginning. Even war, as between the king and his overlord of France, is so conditioned by the overruling conventions of European feudal law as to seem a judgment of the

Law and judgment

[1] H. W. C. Davis, *Regesta Regum*, 118. An instance of 1175 shows how rigidly Henry II interpreted this limitation. The abbot of Battle brought to him a charter which had perished with time and asked for its renewal: *non hoc, inquit rex, nisi ex judicio curiae meae facturus sum*: I must not do this, said the king, without judgment of my court. M. M. Bigelow, *Placita Anglo-Normannica*, p. 221.

[2] Loc. cit. *Inquit Ricardus de Luci . . . 'quoniam judicium nostrum . . . exigitis . . . [sic] adjudicamus'*: since you have demanded judgment from us we pronounce judgment.

[3] Cf. the suit for the Bigod inheritance. *Ibid.* 230 (1177). *Dominus rex . . . praecepit eis Lundonias venire, ut ibidem consilio comitum et baronum suorum eis secundum rectum et patriae consuetudinem satisfaceret.*

[4] William I, *Episcopal Laws*, 1.

curia of the English vassals—*judicium super eum ire*—and coercive action against a subject by the mere authority of the king—*ire super eum sine judicio*—is the act of a tyrant. It is true that the Norman reigns see a partial withdrawal of the magnates from the routine of justice, and the beginning of the transference of their function to professional judges of no tenurial standing, but there is no sign of this in the first generation of the Conquest, and—long after they have ceased to try the demesne pleas of the crown, and the pleas of parties other than those of their own order—the magnates habitually join in those acts of state, which it would be truer to the mind of the age to call judgments of state, but which are the rudiments of legislation. The king, then, must in theory act with his council, and, indeed, in so far as his outlook is that of feudalism at its best, he will wish to do so, and will think that his power is best served, and his dignity highest, when his whole honour is gathered about him in his great court of magnates.[1] There is, thus, much in the underlying truth of the Conquest régime to explain the English belief in the continuity of government and the legists' appraisement of Norman institutions in English terms.[2] Whether that sense of standing for the nation that the witan had held in the tenth century and the magnates were to regain in the thirteenth, was entirely replaced by the sense of individual standing and vassalage, no evidence remains fine enough to determine.

The Norman curia

We must not, then, look for rapid change in the administrative framework of the community. But the spirit in which institutions were worked was feudal, and, inspired by the Norman tenurial relation of lord and man, conformed to the Norman feudatories' conception of the kingdom as the greatest of feudal honours. In the course of a generation that will give the sheriffs a new jurisdiction. At first government was aristocratic rather than specialized or

[1] Counsel is an obligation upon the baron: *Letters of St. Thomas* (ed. Giles), no. 179. Becket to Henry: *eo quod dominus, debeo et offero vobis consilium meum.*

[2] It is curious to notice the strength of the English contingent at the Whitsun *hyred* of 1068. Of the witnesses of a grant to Wells (H. W. C. Davis, *Regesta Regum*, 23), six out of nine bishops, all four abbots, two out of five earls are English, and, among about twenty other notables, are some of the Confessor's greatest thegns, Ælfgeard Thorne, Bundi the Staller, Robert fitz Wimarc, Azor, Brixi, and Brihtric, with other lesser Englishmen.

official. There were baronial sheriffs and the barons were the main-stay of the king's capital *curia*. A professional council of justice was not of the Conqueror's reign. Only the king's *hyred* was perman-ent, for it was his household. The crown-wearings, though they were households, *curiae*, were baronial also, for under the paternal-ism of feudal crowns the magnates were *dominici barones regis*.[1] Already the whole *curia* did not withdraw when the councils dis-persed, nor was William without baronial attendance in the inter-vals between the great festivals. There are few writs which are not witnessed by at least some of those who were nearest to him, Montgomery, Warenne, Clare, his brothers, or some of the bishops. There were curial officers who were barons, and so in constant attendance, the *dapifers*, William fitz Osbern, and later Eudes and Hamo, the constables who were heads of the knights, riding servants, huntsmen, and foresters, and their deputy, the marshal. But, beside them, were literate ministers, the chancellor, *cubicularii* or chamberlains, and the chaplains. There were thus already the elements of a curial government which were always about the king.

Within the household there were already signs of departmental-ism. The chamber, as under the Confessor, ministered to the king's person, the chancellor, perhaps, already had his clerks and super-vised the writs, the chapel had its staff of king's priests and chaplains. It is probable that any act of moment received the con-sideration of the familiar barons and the more dignified officials, the stewards or *dapifers* certainly, and perhaps the *pincernae*—butlers. The constables and the chancellor stood upon a lower plane, but their prestige was rising. The directive force of goveri-ment was, however, still baronial rather than official. It was through such barons as were resident in the household, a small body of great men, with such ministers as could not be dispensed with, that the king habitually acted between the great councils. In this sense, though in this only, there was a "lesser *curia*". It was no defined body, its only essential member was the king, and it might vary from day to day. If in the Conqueror's day any one officer was required regularly to witness the king's precepts, it was the *dapifer*, as in the honours, and even his witness was not essential.

The lesser curia

[1] Hen. I, *Comitatus et Hundreda*, 3.

When William was in Normandy a similar group remained in control in England, and its principal members, often Lanfranc, Odo, or Geoffrey, acting alone, signified to the other barons the commands received from the king. No one claimed a sole title as Justiciar. They informed their peers what William required "of us his barons".[1] If the ideal of *curia* in its fullness was the great assembly of the vassals at the crown-wearing and its common expression in practice the counsel of a few of the greatest of them, there was no sense of contrast between the two. Both were thought of as *curia regis*, both were *rex cum consilio baronum*. In this the history of the *curia* is that of the witenagemot reset in terms of baronial tenure. Justice seems to have been little more centralized under the Conqueror than under the Confessor. It was seldom that a plea was summoned out of the counties. If it was it was to a court of barons. The title *iustitiarius*, later confined to judges with special royal commissions, stood for the king's deputed jurisdiction over his feudatories as lord, but it was still unspecialized in application, and continued to be so until the reign of Stephen. The *justitiarii regis* were not yet a defined ministry, still less a special judicature. There was no chief justiciar. Pleas of the crown continued to come before the sheriffs, and, though occasional courts were held in the provinces by magnates under special commission, these also were not yet a settled institution.

The enfeoffment   This is a confused and little-known reign. There is the skill to exploit the advantages of both the kingdom and the duchy, with the notion of the king's lordship running through all. The Conquest was carried through with confident empiricism. In the South and Midlands, where the Normans were secure, the grouping of the lordships upon the day that Eadward was quick and dead was allowed to determine the permanent lines of English landlordship. Upon the frontiers, where the Conquest still had enemies, the Norman palatine system was applied in its pure form. The lords of the five baronies which defend the Channel in Sussex are the palatines of the southern border of Normandy, Eu, Mor-

---

[1] Lanfranc to Earl Roger: *Dominus noster . . . salutat vos et nos omnes sicut fideles suos . . . et mandat ut quantum possumus curam habeamus de castellis suis*: our lord greets you and us his faithful men . . . and bids us take as good care of his castles as we may.

tain, Warenne, Braiose, and Montgomery. The great earldoms were not done away with, but left to stand the test of time, though one may doubt whether Eadwine and Morcar, half guests, half hostages, would have been allowed to resume their full power. The earldom of the East Angles was retained for Ralf Guader, and William persisted in keeping that of Northumbria intact until two English earls had failed him and Commines had been murdered with all his knights. The enfeoffment was like the settlement of an army upon the land. Whatever the relation of the Norman successor to the land and its folk, to the king he remained a unit of the feudal host, and his tenure in peace was allotted him as an earnest of future service in war. The units of the host lay upon the land in the tens and multiples and fractions of tens with which it was organized for the field, a full constabulary of ten knights from the barony of moderate size, from many fewer, from a handful of great men, more. The extent of land held had only the very roughest relation to the *servitium debitum*,[1] for it was the result of no assessment, and was to all appearances made in the first years of the Conquest before the land was fully conquered or the Domesday survey thought of.[2] Some estimate of the standing of the recipient in the host was, perhaps, the determining factor of his obligation, and some rough approximation in office or rank to that of a Saxon antecessor the sole considerations in the choice made of his fees.

The county and hundredal systems were treated in the same spirit. Inevitably, they remained the mainstay of law and order, but, since a completely English officialdom was impossible,[3] and the Conquest could provide no sufficient body of *ministeriales*, the barons were sheriffs in the counties of their chief power, and some retained the shrievalty in their own hands throughout their lives, and even handed it to the second generation, or nominated dependants. Both these expedients, the palatinate and the baronial shrievalty, were dangerous. During William's reign or soon after it, much of his work had to be undone: the palatines rebelled one by one and their honours were destroyed, and under Henry I a

Administration

---

[1] Thus, the abbot of Abingdon owed sixty knights, the abbot of Ramsey four.

[2] Cf. J. H. Round, *Feudal England*.

[3] Many Englishmen were retained as sheriffs.

shrievalty of royal ministers replaced the barons. They were, no doubt, necessary during the phase of consolidation, and in that phase least dangerous. As long as Gospatric and the Confessor's kindred troubled Northumbrian loyalty from their lodgment among the Scots, an English rising might be feared, and the Normans served themselves best by obedience to the king. Nevertheless, the greatness of the Conqueror was not that of the legislator or of the founder of new systems of state, but a greatness of character so strong and equable as to approach genius. So formidable was his will that he could afford to rule by deputy, to declare his English kingship and assume that he would be obeyed as English kings had been, granting great latitude of tenurial and administrative power to a handful of feudatories, requiring that they should exercise it in his interest and not their own. "Among the rest there must not be forgotten the good peace he made in this land. He was a stern man and terrible, so that none dared to thwart his will. Earls who went against him he put in fetters, and bishops he deposed from their bishoprics, and abbots from their abbacies, and at the last he spared not his own brother." [1]

The Norman crown

Yet, though its founder was no innovator, the future of the Norman crown was to lie along new lines. The native English kings had summoned the goodwill of the nation to make peace and order an institution. This was no longer enough, for the coming of feudalism set loose forces which would gather will and direction of their own if they were confronted by nothing more lasting than the common will to peace. That had been born of the reaction from the miseries of the Danish wars, and rested on sworn coöperation and the leadership of a succession of great kings, whose personal landed estate would hardly have sufficed to maintain the throne in a feudal age. Such landed power the new royal house was better suited to supply. It is not fanciful to see in the half-feudal dynasty of the Norman kings an intensified interest in what may be called the demesne concerns of the crown. The *cyneryhta*, the *jura regalia*, had been developed by the Saxon kings to place part of the law under the direct protection of the monarch

[1] Anglo-Saxon Chronicle, 1086E.

in a special way, as part of his equipment for the maintenance of law and order. Feudalism associated power, office, and material wealth from the crown downwards, in the comprehensive notion of *dominium*. And the outcome of that was jurisdiction. Both as wealth and power, the crown of England was honorial and its lands and rights were demesne of the king. As late as 1264 the gravamen against Henry III was that he treated the realm as the same unfettered demesne as an earl's honour. Thus, while the Ælfredian kings expended their energy upon the strengthening of provincial life, the hundred, the peace, and the new punitive element in the law, and achieved substantial success, the Norman kings, enjoying *dominium*, turned inwards to the resources of the crown itself. The springs of Norman monarchy are jurisdiction and the *terra regis*. Its genius goes to the fostering of this permanent fund of wealth, and of the trade in justice which had no visible limits if it were pressed actively and efficiently. To further this there came into being a domestic bureaucracy which, without at once departing radically from the traditional routine of government, so minuted, exacted, and augmented the *jura regalia* that they became the object of a new art of government and of a yet closer relation of the crown to the community.

The Conqueror set himself from the beginning to increase the *The fisc* revenue and estates of the crown. After the Conquest he kept as *terra regis* lands which brought in roughly double the revenue of the Confessor, some £11,000 yearly, as against the £30,000 of rents which were allotted to the hundred and seventy baronies.[1] He used the old machinery of exaction and account. Beyond a possible increase in their number, the record of the chamberlains' holdings in Domesday[2] suggests no difference in the composition of the chamber and treasure; the Chronicle for 1087 gives us our first clear mention of a treasure-house at Winchester, but it is doubtful evidence for the date; the Survey reflects no radical change in the fiscal system such as any break in the routine of the chamber might cause. The only visible alteration in policy, made

[1] W. J. Corbett, *Cambridge Medieval History*, v. 507.
[2] Humfrid and Alberic, chamberlains of William, succeeded Aluric, a chamberlain of Eadward in his lands. Domesday Book, i. 49A, 49B, 151A. The mention of Henry the Treasurer may stand for the regular association of one of the chamberlains with the treasure. Whether this dates from Eadward's reign we do not know.

in a number of districts, but quite without system,[1] is the insistence on blanched money—coin assayed by melting and refining—or payment *ad pondus*, by weighing a sample of coin against a fixed standard, as against the cruder payment *ad numerum*, which was the commoner practice under the Confessor, though the more accurate processes were known and practised, especially upon Eadward's demesne. This may reflect a more businesslike policy in the chamber—payment *ad pondus* might add 30 per cent to the value of the farm[2]—but it is so local and unsystematic[3] that it is more likely to be the result of intelligent exploitation by the sheriffs. The heavy increases in the nominal rates of the farms, equally unsystematic,[4] are also, in all likelihood, due to shrieval initiative. The Chronicle puts the blame for the racking of the royal estates upon the king,[5] but there is little sign of any attempt to devise a common policy for the realm, or to attack the inconsistencies in the management of the king's estates. Conservatism, a very free hand for local authorities, and sporadic severity of exactions, seem to have taken the place of policy in William's exploitation of his demesne.

The Chamber and the treasure

The Chamber must have continued, as under the Confessor, to be the authority by which the king's cash was carried with him and spent. It remained intimately domestic, but, though there is only a single indication of this in the Pipe Roll of Henry I, it retained

[1] This occurs in Surrey, Wiltshire, probably Hampshire, Buckinghamshire, Cambridgeshire, Northamptonshire, and Sussex. In Oxfordshire and Huntingdonshire payment was still *ad numerum* in 1086. Parts of the west, especially Herefordshire and Devon, already payed in blanched money T.R.E.

[2] Domesday Book, i. 16A. For the technical reasons leading to this change see *Dialogus de Scaccario*, i. 7, though the change is wrongly attributed to Henry I.

[3] The chaos which existed in the fiscal scheme of a great royal manor may be seen at Dartford. T.R.E. its farm value was £60. The French reeve who farmed it in 1086 said that it was really worth £90. The English jurors said that it ought still to be at £60. The actual farmer in fact paid £82 : 13 : 2 in coin assayed by three different methods. Domesday Book, i. 12B.

[4] The royal manors of Leicestershire had their farms roughly doubled between 1066 and 1086, while those of Cambridgeshire were left at the old amounts but were put under the stricter form of assay. At Havering in Essex the value T.R.E. was £40, but the sheriff was taking £90 in 1086. *Ibid.* ii. 3A.

[5] "The king farmed his land as dearly as he might. If a second came and bid more, and a third, he let him who bid most have it, and cared nothing with what sin the reeves must exact it of poor men." (Anglo-Saxon Chronicle, 1086E.) The large sums paid by farmers *de gersuma*, *i.e.* as premiums, were, no doubt, an additional burden on the land.

enough of its fiscal habit to be expanded into a household exchequer by Henry II, receiving many payments directly, and making payments for wages and expenses. The treasure, which at some period of the eleventh century had come to lie at Winchester, began to attract the regular attendance of one or more of the officers of the Chamber, and slowly to gain an identity of its own. In Rufus' reign, and again in that of Henry I, an occasional turn of phrase speaks of one or other of the chamberlains as *cubicularius et thesaurarius*. One Herbert is the bearer of this double charge under Rufus and Henry I, and under Henry Geoffrey de Clinton gives himself the same ambiguous title, now *camerarius* and now *thesaurarius*. In 1129–30 he accounts *pro ministerio thesauri Wintonie*.[1] Still, however, the fiscal arrangements seem to be completely fluid. For a term previous to Clinton's, William Pont de l'Arche accounts to the commission of audit of the treasure,[2] his office being a *ministerium camere curie*.[3] The treasure is a material fact. It has a normal location at Winchester, some form of account has to be made there, and it comes to require the constant service of a minister, and his ministry may lead to his being spoken of currently as *thesaurarius*. Courts may be held there for the settlement of fiscal causes. But seventy years after the Conquest there is no exclusive or permanent office of treasurer, and the qualification for custody of the treasure is still office in the king's Chamber.[4] Nor can we feel certain that the custodian at any given time was immune from intervention, coöperation, or supersession by one or other of his fellow chamberlains of the *camera*. For the first recognition of a treasurer as equal with and distinct from the *Magister Camerarius* we must wait until after the reign of Henry I,[5] and, in its purely domestic nature as a phase of the ministry of the king's private chamber, held by lay, and therefore illiterate, servants, the Treasury of the Norman kings has its affinities with the past rather than with the future.

[1] Pipe Roll, 31 Henry I, p. 105: *Idem Gaufridus reddit compotum de ccc et x marcis argenti pro ministerio thesauri Wintonie*: the same Geoffrey renders account for three hundred and ten marks of silver for the ministry of the Winchester treasure. It is possible that he was acting as subordinate to Robert Mauduit. *Ibid.* p. 37.   [2] *Ibid.* p. 130.

[3] He had apparently bought it with the heiress of Robert Mauduit. *Ibid.* p. 37.

[4] *Chronicon Monasterii de Abingdon*, ii. 116. Herbert, sitting *in curia apud Wintoniam in thesauro*, is entitled *Herbertus Camerarius*.

[5] *Red Book of the Exchequer*, pp. 807 *et seq*.

The Exchequer   Upon this small and comparatively unspecialized staff of clerks was imposed a task which increased in elaboration as time went on. But, though the rule of progress was uncalculated, almost automatic, evolution, the twelfth century was already making a beginning of science in law and government. At some time near its outset conscious planning of a new kind seems to have been brought to bear upon the working of the king's fisc, and to have added to the Treasury an entirely new office of receipt and account, the Exchequer. For the period of its institution we are dependent upon charters to which dates can only be affixed within wide terms of years. In these the term *scaccarium* itself[1] appears in some year not later than 1118, the *curia* is found in the Exchequer in a charter from between 1108 and 1127, and in others from between 1110 and 1127 Henry speaks of record *in rotulis meis*, and in all probability refers by this to the Great Roll of the Pipe, or central record of the Exchequer.[2] From the fiscal year 1129–30 a complete roll of the Exchequer survives. The general character of the Exchequer is that of a commission of receipt of revenue, and of audit of accounts, which is also a court in which disputes arising during the audit may be settled. In the reign of Henry II it meets at Westminster, and summonses the sheriffs of every shire, together with many others who have separate charges, to present their revenue account for the year, together with that of all arrears and of any deductions to which they may be entitled on the ground of expenses, previous payments, or diminution of profits due to exemptions granted by the king. That such an account had been made for some generations, more lately in the Treasury, before whatever session of chamberlains or *cubicularii* and magnates were deputed to receive it, is a conclusion we can hardly avoid. What is new in the Exchequer, and stamps it as one of the achievements of an inventive age, is its centralizing of various branches of fiscal administration, the completeness of its arrangements to secure adequate knowledge and authority for its action, and its new method of calculating its accounts.

The staffing of the Exchequer points to its being a composite

[1] T. F. Tout, *Chapters in Administrative History*, i. 93.

[2] A custumal of Ringwood of 39 Edw. III (Public Record Office. Rentals and Surveys. General Series. Portfolio 14, 54) professes to quote from *pipa Domini Regis apud Westmonasterium . . . in anno viij° regis Henrici Primi*, i.e. 1107–8. A charter printed in D. C. Douglas, *Feudal-Documents from the Abbey of Bury St. Edmunds*, p. 67, suggests that there was no exchequer in 1104–6.

body put together *ad hoc* from the personnel of the Treasury, the *The* Chamber, and the wider circle of the *curia*. Each of these sets of *Exchequer* officers brought its particular aptitude and authority to the audit. *centralizes* The treasurer, as soon as one existed, with two chamberlains who *accounts* shared his acts and responsibility, received only the sheriff's *of all* *compotus* of the *firma comitatus*, that is, the revenue which we *branches of* must believe to have been accounted for in earlier times to the *the curia* Treasury. He, or rather his scribe, wrote this, with all other items, upon the principal roll of the Exchequer, which, from its shape, was called the Roll of the Pipe. For all items, except the record of the sums actually paid *in thesauro*,[1] his roll was subject to the correction of the chancellor. For payments *in thesauro*, that is, for the coin of which his office of the treasury was the storehouse, his authority was absolute. This division in the authority of the roll points again to the composite origin of the Exchequer, and to the historical evolution of the work of the Treasury officials *ad scaccarium* from their function in the Winchester Treasury. The officialdom of the *curia*, with the chancellor and his clerk, seems to have been superimposed upon this Treasury machinery in part as a check—the chancellor's clerk checks and copies the roll of the treasurer—in part for its special function of drafting, for the chancellor has charge of all writs issued from the Exchequer. But it also has its separate field of knowledge arising from the chancellor's custody of escheats.[2] All outstanding revenue owed by the sheriff in arrears of his farm is noted and exacted from him by the chancellor's clerk.[3] The chancellor, in fact, is the accounting officer for all the king's casual revenue, as being in a general sense his secretary, while the treasurer accounts for the ancient crown revenue of the *firma comitatus*. Similarly, the constable, who in the household was charged with the supervision of the king's domestic ministers, especially those of the military household and the officials of the hunt and the forests, attends, or sends his deputy to the Exchequer,

---

[1] *Dialogus de Scaccario*, I. v. B: *De omni scriptura rotuli cancellarius eque tenetur ut thesaurarius, excepto dumtaxat de hoc quod scribitur "in thesauro receptum"*: the chancellor is equally accountable with the treasurer for the writing of the whole roll, except for what is entered as "received into the Treasury". It was thought by some that the treasurer was only responsible for that part of the roll which recorded payments *in thesauro. Ibid.* I. iii. B.

[2] That is, estates falling in to the crown by failure of heirs, etc.

[3] *Dialogus de Scaccario*, I. vi. C.

in general to confirm the witness of the chancellor to all transactions, but in particular to compute and pay the liveries of officials of his own ministry.[1] His representation of the *curia* is further emphasized by the fact that his clerk brings with him the record of all writs issued in the course of his function and presents them in the Exchequer.[2] Having regard, therefore, to the diverse elements of administration which compose the Exchequer, it would be fair to assume that one of the chief motives for its creation was the desire to centralize and bring under a common authority the various offices which had been growing haphazard and without decisive common control.[3] Such a scheme would have suggested itself above all to that masterful and ubiquitous man of King Henry's affairs, Roger of Salisbury, who impressed the next generation as having been, what in fact he was not, justiciar, chancellor, and treasurer at once. The constable with his domestic pay-roll, the chancellor with his irregular revenue from amercements, escheats, and so forth, the Treasury with its old-established hold upon the *firma comitatus*, are brought to a common place and system of audit, and their accounts digested upon a common roll. The foundation of the Exchequer was, in fact, the essential preliminary to a consolidated royal revenue, and to a national control of expense.

Exchequer court

No Norman system of audit is possible without a court, still less the vast audit of England. In every rent and due, in every individual's obligations, in every reeve's powers, there lurks the potentiality of dispute. Where no two manors' customs are identical, where shires are fields of divergent law, there must be an arbitrating authority between the subject who pays and the official who exacts.[4] The Exchequer, therefore, is a court, and perhaps it is in this form that it would must readily present itself to contemporaries—*Curia Regis ad scaccarium*.[5] Of that court all

---

[1] *Dialogus de Scaccario*, I. v. F.: *Stipendarii regis . . . sive sint residentes in castris regis sive non.* [2] *Ibid.* I. vi. D.

[3] To secure such control magnates were detached from the *curia* to the Exchequer, and the *Dialogus* dwells upon the inferior status of the Treasury officials to that of the non-official element.

[4] *Ibid.* I. iv. C.

[5] M. M. Bigelow, *Placita Anglo-Normannica*, p. 174. At the beginning of Henry II's reign the abbot of Battle had to complain that the sheriff had received certain dues from his land unjustly, *quo cognito, abbas unum ex monachis suis cum cartis . . . libertatum suarum ad scaccarium transmisit . . . Monachus vero eo perveniens coram*

the primary officers were deemed members, and, presumably, could act through their deputies. But the crown explicitly recognized the judicial nature of the audit by adding from time to time magnates who had no *ex officio* standing in the Exchequer, but who had knowledge of special value, or prestige.[1] The treasurer and chamberlains, at least, were too near their petty ministerial origin to be freed from curial supervision.[2] The king himself sat there at times, either to intervene in a plea of special moment, or to dispatch some cause in the convenient surroundings of the fisc with its records and special experience. Well into the thirteenth century he might entertain a cause in his council and upon its revealing financial implications remove himself, the cause and the counsellors into the Exchequer, and there conclude it. More normally he will detach barons to act for him, but king or baron there must be if the authority of *curia regis* is to inhere in any commission of the early feudal age. Magnates who are commissioned to the Exchequer are the future Barons of the Exchequer, for that function hardens into a defined legal office of the crown.[3] At the time of which we are writing, they must have been a variable body, barons in the Exchequer, but in no permanent sense of it.[4] By the reign of Henry II the justiciar comes to sit there, and certain persons other than the Exchequer's permanent officers are present at every session, the bishop of Winchester, and Master Thomas Brown, lately head of the Sicilian *dogana*, but now in

Roberto comite Legacestriae et Ricardo de Luci . . . et coram aliis baronibus scaccarii . . . restitutionem ablatorum expetit: when this was found out the abbot sent one of his monks to the Exchequer with the charters of his liberties. The monk presented himself before Robert, earl of Leicester and Richard de Luci and the other barons of the Exchequer, and demanded restitution. The court had the money restored, the tallies broken, and the record expunged from the roll *"unanimi judicio"*. *Ibid.* p. 235. The Justiciar pronounces the judgment of the Exchequer on the liberties of Abingdon.

1 *Dialogus de Scaccario,* I. iv. B: *Quidam ex officio, quidam ex sola iussione principis resident.*

2 The Discipulus asks, *numquid a thesauraris compotus suscipitur cum illic multo sint qui ratione potestatis maioris videantur?:* why should the Treasurer receive the account when there are many others of higher station there?

3 The earliest official use of the title seems to occur in a writ of *Nigellus Eliensis episcopus et baro de Scaccario (circa* 1156). M. M. Bigelow, *Placita Anglo-Normannica,* p. 188. The distinction between the executive origin of the treasurer and chamberlains and that of the barons of the Exchequer in audit and judgment, is presented in the practice of directing writs of *liberate* to the former, writs of *computate* and *perdono* to the latter. *Dialogus de Scaccario,* I. vi. A.

4 *Barones esse dicimus eo quod suis locis barones sedere solebant. Fleta,* ii. 26.

exile and in English service. He keeps a roll "of the king's secrets", which may have been the origin of the roll of the King's Remembrancer.

System of account   In this accumulation of authority, and even more in the expert system of account, the Norman age has found something new in government. The processes in the Lower Exchequer of receipt, of which we have said nothing, weighing, counting, blanching, storing, and issue on *liberate*, may not have been greatly in advance of Old English usage. The Upper Exchequer, that Exchequer of account which we have been describing, has at the centre of its practice a method of computation and of displaying its results vividly, which is so new and so characteristic of the early twelfth century that it has been thought to be the discovery which itself inspired the creation of the Exchequer. It is, in fact, that from which the Exchequer takes its name. The *scaccarium* is the squared cloth, divided into columns for tens of thousands, thousands, hundreds of pounds, pounds, shillings, and pence, upon which counters were placed to demonstrate to the illiterate sheriff the sum of his account, and to compute it after the manner of the abacus. By this "game of the abacus" a more ready reckoning than in the past was possible, and the Pipe Roll upon which it was entered opened a new conspectus of provincial life to the crown, which was for the first time provided with the guidance of statistics. Authority, knowledge, the growth of ordered routine, all in some measure achieved within the Norman reigns by the concentration of the divergent ministerial functions within it, combine to make the Exchequer the pivot of the Norman and still more of the Angevin state. It marks, indeed, an epoch in the art of government.

The king and justice   The function of the Saxon king was not a jurisdiction; rather, he ordered the defaulting moot to act. He had no inherent right, in the feudal term, *justiciare*, and the moots, as a whole, enforced their own authority, kept their own order, carried out their own distraints and arrests,[1] had their own oferhiernes.[2] None of the Saxon *cyneryhta* were abandoned by the Conqueror, but with time they gradually lost their force; the power of the Norman

[1] II Æthelstan, 20, 1 and 4. II Cnut, 10, 25, and 25a.
[2] II Cnut, 15, 2.

kings in law flowed mainly from a concept of jurisdiction as
inherent in all lordship which they inherited from the Frankish
West. This jurisdiction was an outcome of *dominium*. In Maitland's words,[1] "jurisdiction is a proprietary right, intertwined with
the laws of property and of personal status, implicated with the
land law", and such a function the Saxon kings, in their world of
folkright and alod, could scarcely achieve. The right of jurisdiction implies the right to appoint justiciars, and we are soon aware
of the spread of the king's justiciarate across the legal maze of
Anglo-Norman England. The network of authority, *justiciandi,
jus faciendi*, comes to be unbroken, from the justiciarships of the
king's great *familiares* to the sheriffs,[2] the bailiffs of the hundreds.[3]
Jurisdiction, jurisdiction of lordship, jurisdiction of kingship, is a
part of Norman landright, running *ex conquestu Angliae*. It makes
valid all the bailiffries of England.[4] Through it the Norman and
Angevin sheriffs exercise their dual function of holding pleas and
making distraints.[5] The Anglo-Norman law-books are slow to
find terms for this. Even Glanvill has not the word "jurisdictio",
and the early legists exhaust themselves in such synonyms as "jus",
"censura", "districtio", "observancia", to supply its place. Most of
all they use that overworked word "justitia", with a dozen slants
and nuances, to mean the moral quality of justice, the power of
justice, an occasion of judgment, an act of judgment, and the
persons who apply it.

A wrong turn may therefore be given to the legal history of this
period by a false kind of emphasis upon such trials as that at
Penenden and its like. The Conqueror has *justitia*, jurisdiction,
but it is his successors who find a permanent embodiment for it in
persons and offices. Geoffrey of Coutances, and those who acted
upon similar occasions, had no permanent title and office of
justiciar. Those who are known to have been left in charge of the
realm when William was in Normandy had no title of chief

[1] Pollock and Maitland, *History of English Law*, i. 527.
[2] Leges Henrici Primi, 29. 1b.
[3] *Loc. cit.*
[4] *Justiciarius dicitur ballivus patrie qui, institutus a principe vel duce, justiciandi
et jus faciendi subjecto sibi populo obtinet potestatem. Summa de Legibus Norman-
nie*, iv.
[5] Glanvill, *De Legibus*, xii. 9.

justiciar.[1] The notion of a developed justiciarship introduced by the Conqueror has also led to the belief that the eyres were borrowed directly from the *missi* of the Emperor. No such anticipation of the Angevin justiciarship seems to be warranted by the evidence, and, indeed, the *Constitutio Domus Regis* of Stephen's reign has still no place for Magnus Justiciarius. In the Conqueror's reign, and for long after it, *justicia, justiciarius*, was a universal term for those who presided at any court, if only for a single great plea—*quibus mei imposuit hanc justitiam*. The sheriff,[2] the bailiff or doomsmen of a hundred,[3] honour,[4] borough,[5] or manor,[6] all, as summoning and directing the courts in which they sat, were *justiciarii*. The writ which initiated the trial at Penenden[7] went out, naturally, to Lanfranc, Geoffrey, Roger, count of Eu, Richard fitz Gilbert, Hugh de Montfort, and all the *proceres regni Angliae*—*quibus hanc justitiam imposui*—and, though when the day came it was Geoffrey who was *in loco regis*, he was doing no more than his fellow barons had it in their quality to do by royal precept. All, if not *justiciarii*, were judges, since *regis judices sint barones comitatus*,[8] and between the *multi barones coram quibus* Odo and the abbot of Evesham sued each other in 1077,[9] between Lanfranc, Geoffrey, and Count Robert trying the liberties of Ely *ex precepto regis*, and Lanfranc, Eudo Dapifer, William des Arches, and Ralf de Curbespine trying the right of Saint Augustine in Newington as part of their routine as *barones comitatus*, there can have been little difference—to be

[1] H. W. C. Davis, *Regesta Regum*, 78-83. The editor describes certain of these writs as by "Lanfranc (as Justiciar of England)", but no reason can be assigned for his doing so.

[2] *Cartularium Monasterii de Rameseia*, i. 149; *Chronicon Monasterii de Abingdon*, ii. 43; H. W. C. Davis, *Regesta Regum*, 59; M. M. Bigelow, *Placita Anglo-Normannica*, p. 165.

[3] *Chronicon Monasterii de Abingdon*, ii. 118. *Justiciarii hundredi*.

[4] Howden, i. 225. Becket is made to speak of *justitiarii curiae meae*.

[5] M. M. Bigelow, *Placita Anglo-Normannica*, p. 165. *Justiciariis et ministris de Rouecestra*.

[6] F. W. Stenton, *English Feudalism*, p. 67. Waleran de Meulan addresses his "justices of Sturminster".

[7] M. M. Bigelow, *Placita Anglo-Normannica*, p. 4.

[8] *Leges Henrici Primi*, 29.

[9] M. M. Bigelow, p. 20. William's letters seem to assume that Lanfranc, Robert of Eu, Haimo the sheriff, Haimo Dapifer or Richard fitz Gilbert will normally be directing justice in the county of Kent—at least such cases as affect

precise, the difference of the reception or not of a writ *ad hoc*. Normally, the king moves the *proceres* to hold his pleas by writ. He does not yet create fixed jurisdictions or judicial offices.

It is true that the practice of commissioning one or more barons to try a single plea *ex precepto regis, loco regis*, was, as far as records go, common in the first two Norman reigns and also that the commission was likeliest to fall upon one of a few men, Lanfranc, Odo, Geoffrey, Robert of Mortain, Hugh de Montfort, Richard fitz Gilbert, being those most commonly chosen. But this seems not to have conferred upon them in their day that permanent title of justiciar which was attached to these magnates by Heming, Orderic, Malmsbury, and other later writers. The first officials whose title to be justiciar and little else the eleventh century would have recognized are found not in the circle of the baronage but in the shire and in the king's *curia*, for, from Rufus' reign, the sheriff had usually[1] been stripped of all but the pettiest pleas of the crown, and had beside him a *justicia comitatus*,[2] whose office was a normal part of shire administration until the accession of Henry II. Passelewe was one of these justices—for Norfolk—about the year 1100, Henry I granted the Londoners the right to choose their own resident justice and keeper of king's pleas, while Stephen and the Empress competed to buy the loyalty of Mandeville or Miles of Gloucester with the justiciarships of their counties in fee.

Meaning of justiciar

At the same time as these professional but stationary justices of the county came into being, the earliest itinerant commissions were going out. If we can believe our authority,[3] Devon and Cornwall were thus visited in 1096 by the bishop of Winchester, the king's chaplain, William Capra, and Hardin fitz Belnold *ad investiganda regalia placita*. It will be noticed that the types of royal justice by commission were multiplying, the precept to one or more barons to try a single plea or group of pleas urged by one

the royal demesne—even while the king is in England. This is much like the function of the Saxon shire-thegn.

[1] Not always, for the reversal to trial of pleas of the crown by the sheriff was still a recognized abuse in 1215.

[2] The two offices were at times reunited in one man, *e.g.* Hugh de Buckland *Berchescire vicecomes, et publicarum justiciarius compellationum*: *Chronicon Monasterii de Abingdon*, ii. 43 (1087-1100).

[3] M. M. Bigelow, *Placita Anglo-Normannica*, 69.

plaintiff, the itinerant commission to investigate all outstanding pleas of one type—as, for instance, pleas of the crown—or the resident justiciar. With this went an equal variety of venue, though the court summoned is usually one of the customary jurisdictions of the past, the shire-court, the moot of several shires, or, on occasion, the entry of a king's delegate into the court of an honour at the request of the immunist.[1] Slight as the evidence is, it seems that the reign of Rufus began a definite change in the king's exercise of these various forms of judicial initiative, which was being gradually withdrawn from the baronage into the household of the king. The commission of 1096 was made by a bishop and a king's chaplain, and the only recorded commission on a private plea, that between Pagan Peverel and the abbot of Ramsey,[2] was held by "H. Camerarius", almost certainly Herbert the Chamberlain. It is therefore possible to accept the somewhat late authority of the Peterborough Chronicle that Ralf Flambard "was the driving force of all the king's moots throughout England",[3] and to divine a little of what nature these moots were.

Both the developments which we have been considering, the shire justiciars and the occasional commissions, have elements of the later itinerant justice, though neither possesses them all. The shire justices are professional in habit—some are drawn from the shrievalty and the exchequer[4]—they try the whole range of the royal pleas, but they are resident, not itinerant. In the reign of Henry I an occasional commission seems to have been issued which combined the qualities of the two types of justice, and which was near to, though not identical with, the itinerant justice of his grandson. Their nature is revealed only by the single instance in the Pipe Roll of 31 Henry I, the session of Geoffrey de Clinton and his colleagues which was known as the Pleas of Blythe. This superseded the justiciars of the counties for the nonce, for it dealt with at least three shires, Derby and Nottingham, and Yorkshire, possibly including Westmorland and the extreme North as outliers of the Yorkshire sheriffdom;[5] it evidently dealt with the

---

[1] *Cartularium Monasterii de Rameseia*, i. 239.　　[2] *Ibid. loc. cit.*

[3] *Ealle his gemot ofer eall Engleland draf*: Anglo-Saxon Chronicle, 1099E.

[4] *Chronicon Monasterii de Abingdon*, ii. 43.

[5] E.g. from Notts-Derby, *placitum de quo implacitatus fuit apud Blidam.* Pipe Roll, 31 Hen. I, p. 10. Yorkshire-Northumberland, *de xxxv marcis argenti de placitis de Blida. Ibid.*, p. 25.

general pleas of the country, for the profits were substantial, but it was not itinerant through the counties like the later eyres. Geoffrey settled himself at the royal manor of Blythe and there summoned the North to him, nor did he summon the counties by hundreds and vills as did Henry II's justices, but had before him the shire courts in their ancient constitutions.[1] The session was therefore judicial and not, as it came to be later, largely inquisitional. Of such a kind, transitional from the new to the old, may have been that "strong moot" which Ralf Basset held at Hundehoge in 1124 and "hanged there in a little while four and forty men",[2] and Clinton himself had been trying pleas in the South-Eastern counties, and, apparently upon two occasions in the Middle West.

It is noteworthy that the chronicler, now almost contemporary, calls the Hundehoge pleas a witenagemot.[3] In this, an English writer sees the present in the light of the past. For him, the ancient English judgment, the witenagemot, even one summoned by the king's writ, obscures the royal jurisdiction by which it is called. Thus seen, such courts descend from the witan who decided the rights of Rochester under Æthelred and William. More truly, in trying, as they apparently do, not a single plea or a group of pleas, but all the royal pleas of the shires summoned, they are in the line of the *justiciarii comitatus*. At much the same time as the pleas of Clinton, Walter l'Espec and Eustace fitz John, both Northumbrian barons, were moving about Yorkshire, Northumberland, and Westmorland, and the vacant bishopric of Durham, apparently conducting an enquiry into the state of the king's lands, seeing to the refortification of castles, and the restocking of the king's manors,[4] but also holding pleas. No more than the pleas of Blyth can these be taken as identical with the later eyre justice, but they have with it the similarity that they combine the care of the *terra regis* with justice, and so have something of the eyre's omni-competence. To become the itinerant commissions of Henry II they need to combine these jurisdictions and to take the further step of carrying their court through the several counties of their

---

[1] The *judicatores comitatus*, Pipe Roll, 29–30 Hen. I, p. 27.

[2] Anglo-Saxon Chronicle, 1124E.

[3] *Ibid. Thaes ilces geares . . . held Raulf Basset and thes kinges thaeines gewitenamot.*

[4] *In restauratione maneriorum Regis per Walterum Espec et Eustacium filium Johannis:* Pipe Roll, 31 Hen. I, pp. 24, 33.

commission, instead of summoning the shires to them as did the
pleas of Blyth.

The chief
justiciar No chief justiciar, *secundus a rege* and head of the judicial body *ex
officio*, had arisen in Henry I's reign out of this variety of commissions. It is, however, likely that a specialized group was beginning
to detach itself from the multitude of officials who did justice,
resident or itinerant, up and down England, and that, in distinction from those who did justice in a shire or a hundred, they were
coming to be called *justitiarii regis totius Angliae*, *capitales justitiarii*,
justices of the king's capital *curia*, whose commission is valid
throughout the realm.[1] No more than this is, perhaps, meant in
a writ of Henry I promising Holy Trinity, Aldgate, that its men
shall not plead *nisi coram me vel capitali justitiarii meo*.[2] The justice
the canons were most likely to fear was that of the sheriff or justiciar
of London; Henry puts them under his capital judiciary. It is,
again, likely that within the group of the *capitales justiciarii* the
preëminence of one or more outstanding personalities was recognized, together with the king's especial reliance upon his initiative.
Ranulf Flambard, the Chronicler says, was the driving force of
Rufus' "moots throughout England".[3] Only such a gradual narrowing of the authority and title of *capitalis justitiarius* upon first a few
and then a single justiciar will explain the confidence with which the
historians of the middle twelfth century attribute preëminence to
Roger of Salisbury[4] at a time when at least Richard[5] and Ralf[6]
Basset were also *capitales justiciarii*, and when Henry while in
Normandy was ordering "his justiciars" to defer to Anselm.[7] All
agree that Roger was the virtual head of the kingdom, yet neither
chronicler nor record can give us the technical formula of writ or
commission which would convince us that his authority was one
of recognized sole Justiciar of England. In the one writ preserved

---

[1] So of Ralf Basset, *Chronicon Monasterii de Abingdon*, ii. 170, *in omni Angliae
regno justitiae habens dignitatem*. Thus in Glanvill we have *capitales barones regis*
for barons holding immediately of the king (*Tractatus de Legibus*, ix. 6), and
capitalis curia regis for the court *de banco* or *coram rege* as opposed to the eyre
(*ibid.* ix. 11).

[2] Rymer, *Foedera*, i. 12.   [3] Anglo-Saxon Chronicle, 1099E.

[4] William of Malmsbury, *Historia Novella* II. Epistolae Herberti Losingae,
p. 51.

[5] Henry of Huntingdon, *De Contemptu Mundi* (*Anglia Sacra*, ii. 701); Orderic,
xiii. 26.   [6] *Chronicon Monasterii de Abingdon*, ii. 170.

[7] Stubbs, *Constitutional History*, i. 378.

from his government during Henry's absence he styles himself, by a title often use of the seneschal, *procurator regni Angliae*.[1]

The same process of specialization was carried through in local administration. Henry I's edict ordering the trial in the county of pleas between tenants of different honours[2] made it no longer a court only in default of justice in the hundred but a jurisdiction in first instance. Now, if ever, it called for the direct grasp of the king's hand. The heirs of Baldwin of Exeter, Hamo Dapifer, Robert of Stafford, Hugh de Port, and Hugh de Grantmesnil, were all holding in the second generation sheriffdoms granted by the Conqueror. The move to extricate local administration from the feudal monopoly had been begun on a small scale under Rufus. The county justiciars were beginning to relieve the sheriffs from the greater pleas, and at least two sheriffs were in office before 1100 who were landless and owed their position solely to the crown. These were Osbert the Priest in Lincolnshire, and Hugh of Buckland, who held several midland shires together. The position was not greatly altered by Henry's accession, though Leicestershire and Shropshire were forfeited by the risings of 1102, but after Tinchebrai in 1106 the pace of reform quickened. By 1110 Surrey, Cambridge, Huntingdon, Leicester, Warwick, and Northants were held by men of no more than knightly rank, while the future chamberlain of the treasury, William Pont de l'Arche, held Wiltshire and Hampshire. Hugh of Buckland held at that time eight shires together. The distribution of the counties already shows a clear correspondence with the process of elaboration and definition which was being pursued in Henry's *curia*. The new sheriffs appeared to the clerics and nobles who suffered under them as men of no standing, unscrupulously subservient to the king's greed for money. Actually, many of them were drawn from that small body of the king's ministers who had served a clerical or financial apprenticeship and were imbued with the skill and zeal of office which were bringing the Exchequer into being. Such certainly were William Pont de l'Arche and Aubrey the Chamberlain in the first half of the reign, and Ralf Basset and Geoffrey de Clinton in the second, all men with experience in the *camera*, while to them we must add those who rose through the

The curial sheriffs

---

[1] D. M. Stenton, *English Historical Review*, xxxix.
[2] Edict for the Shire and Hundred (1109–1111), 3.

minor reeveships of the crown, men such as Serlo de Burg, whose first substantial charge was the custody of the see of York from 1114 to 1119 *sede vacante*. Better accounting at the Exchequer audit, the authority of the Exchequer court and its accumulation of precedent, were carrying the influence of the *curia* into the counties. Sheriffs were being appointed no longer to appease local interests but to reflect Exchequer policy. On occasion they were being fined for corruption or incapacity, and one, Restold of Oxfordshire, was dismissed. It is possible, of course, to exaggerate both the independence of the baronial sheriff and the degree of control that the crown could exercise even over its own nominees. Local government was never free of abuses in the Middle Ages. But, as long as the custody of the royal castles, the initiation of the pleas of the crown, the order of the county through the frank-pledge and the pursuit of felons, and even the incorporation of its courts and the execution of writs, lay with a hierarchy of bailiffs of which the sheriff was the head, the king's power could only reach the provinces through an obedient shrievalty, and a great feudatory who was also sheriff over a long term of years might enjoy something approaching palatine status.

The inquest   In procedure, as in most other matters, the Normans were alternately conservative and experimental. From their Frankish contacts they brought, as an incident of jurisdiction, what is perhaps the most vital weapon of medieval administration, the sworn inquest, but they used it occasionally and without much system. The Saxons had rid their form of trial of that element of unreason and bias which was inherent in the solidarity of the kin for oath-helping. They used witness and compurgation by independent voices of the neighbourhood. But they could not arrive at a sworn verdict without going through a complete form of trial between parties, and the oath-helper, swearing to the general credibility of his principal's oath, could not be interrogated as to questions of fact. Nor, apparently, could the king or his ministers put the subject upon oath *ex officio* in order to obtain such facts as were necessary in the course of administration or to establish his customary rights. The member of the community was, in short, still irresponsible to anything but the routine of folkright, and in this, as in so many other matters, is not to be called a subject. The Frankish kings, on the other hand, perhaps drawing upon Roman procedure, had succeeded in extracting the oath from its place in the form of trial, and had converted it from a privilege to an obligation, and the Conqueror was able to put specific questions as to fact and law, and to demand a sworn answer from the men of the county and hundred, or to nominate groups of individuals who were likely to have special knowledge to declare it upon oath. Possibly the Norman kings made more use of "recognition", as this method of ascertainment was called, than records survive to prove—the outstanding example is the Domesday inquest, when the whole nation answered by sworn inquests of hundreds and vills to innumerable questions of ownership, possession, extent, value, and custom which were the aftermath of the Conquest— but examples of its application to ordinary justice are not common, and for the most part proof of right was still committed to the old practice of challenge between parties, trial, oath, and witness. Mainly from the somewhat doubtful source of the Liber Eliensis, we have instances of recognition even in William's reign. To establish what lands the church of Ely held at the Conquest "Englishmen who know how the lands of the said church lay on the day that King Eadward died" were elected *et ibidem jurando testentur*,[1] or later the bounds between the king's manor of Torksey and the neighbouring manor of Stow were sworn to by the "lawful men of Lincolnshire"—*facite recognoscere per probos homines de comitatu*.[2] Yet, were it not for the one wholesale instance of Domesday, the number of cases and the authority on which they rest would hardly be sufficient to persuade us that inquest was more than a power unrealized or held in reserve in William's day, or even Henry's. The Leges Henrici Primi, so generous in detail of the older forms of trial, omit inquest altogether from their survey of Norman justice.

Important as Henry I's revolution is in the history of administration, it is almost more so in revealing the mind of the Norman monarchy as to its own function in the state. The demesne interest of the crown, its interest as the greatest of all lords of estate, had come progressively to the fore as its avowed preoccupation during

Centralizing trend of royal policy

[1] Such questions were later the matter of the possessory assizes. M. M. Bigelow, *Placita Anglo-Normannica*, p. 25.

[2] *Ibid.* 139. So, in Rufus' reign, the shire of Northampton is convened to "recognize" whether land at Isham is thegnland or farm. *Cartularium Monasterii de Rameseia*, i. 233.

three successive reigns. Rufus allowed Flambard to do his exaction for him; Henry I openly devoted himself to enriching the crown by shrewd and businesslike government, working through men who were too insignificant to share the king's responsibility, and who at times were revolted by the work they had to do.[1] This was not the rôle either of an English king or of a feudal overlord as they had been understood in the past. It carried Henry away from that close coöperation with the feudatories which the Conqueror and probably Rufus had maintained, and which was the traditional basis of the régime. It is true that a section of the baronage put itself out of court by rebellion, and that a few, notably Robert of Mellent, worked amicably with Henry to the end, and it is probable that he would have ventured no major act of state without the form of baronial counsel. But, for all that, a gap had opened between the crown and its vassals, and it is most unlikely that feudal England could have been driven much further along the course that Henry had set. It was one which Henry II followed with far greater caution, and which caused civil war under John and Henry III. Though the king exacted his farms, and fines, and amercements remorselessly, sold his justice and withdrew his ministries from the hands of the magnates, so that the crown of England was contracted to the scope of a particular interest, its feudal quality was not and could not be shaken. Indeed, it might be said that in displaying the *terra regis* and the *jura regalia* as the greatest and most jealously cultivated *dominium*, Henry was stimulating the least desirable elements in feudalism. At its best a feudal realm achieved stability by the collaboration of the king and the feudatories, and government was the expression of a common mind. Neither the governing theory of feudal relations nor any feudal state which then existed could have borne the strain of a crown which abandoned the pretence of good lordship and governed to the last iota of its right. Upon this rock successive English reigns foundered. The king who so governed realized the type of the tyrant as tyrants were estimated in the twelfth century, and could not take the further, as yet inconceivable, step of legiti-

[1] Cf. the admission of one of Henry's justices: *Induimus animos tyrannorum: et hanc rabiem nobis induxere divitiae*: lured by the madness of riches we have become tyrants. Leges Henrici Primi, 6. 5B. Cf. F. M. Stenton, *English Feudalism* p. 218.

mizing a despotism. Far from destroying feudal right, Henry's reign is that in which the law of English tenure is formulated. The so-called Leges Henrici Primi, our most purely feudal code, were compiled by a justice of the king's *curia* in Henry's reign, and they mark the high-water mark of feudal right in England. In organizing its *curia*, crystallizing its rights at their highest value and developing new ministries, the crown was followed, though at a distance, by the magnates. In Henry's reign and in Stephen's the great honours achieved their maximum unity, and their lords began to exploit their economic resources. An extreme consequence of this feudal growth might be the adoption of an interpretation of feudal monarchy which made it nothing but lordship. Such a theory was latent in England until Henry's ruthlessness brought it to the surface, and then, when the conflicting claims of Stephen and Matilda gave it its opportunity, it asserted and forced Stephen to accept the crown on an avowedly contractual basis.

If the history of the twelfth century is to be that of one process only—the growth of monarchy and centralized administration— the reign of Stephen is empty of interest. Stephen succeeded as the choice of the great Conquest baronage, who had realized to what end Henry I's reign was leading them, who resented the loss of shrievalties and castellanships, and feared a continuance of the rule of the *novi homines* under a crown weakened by a female succession. It is said that the barons' first choice was Stephen's elder brother Theobald, but they rallied immediately to the king, and his first court at Reading was attended by such of the really great men as could reach it—Bigod, Say, three of the Clares, and Robert de Ferrars—and his Lenten court at London was "among the most splendid ever held in England for the numbers and the rank of those who attended".[1] On the other hand, with certain exceptions, Henry's servants, some of whom were already established as barons of secondary rank, held aloof,[2] or received Stephen with reservations. Thus from the beginning the future civil war was foreshadowed by a cleavage of loyalties, in which Henry's sons

Reaction under Stephen

[1] Henry of Huntingdon, *Historiae*, Lib. viii.
[2] Keeping to their castles and refusing homage because of their oath to Matilda, and because they feared the barons. *Gesta Stephani*, 15.

and servants temporized with the barons' king, and waited for the moment when they should be able to bring back the throne to the direct line and restore their own supremacy. The war which broke out in 1138, and continued intermittently for fifteen years, roughly conformed to this cleavage between the old and new nobilities—it was a division of society which was to persist for another half-century. Robert of Gloucester could count upon the steady loyalty of men like Payn fitz John, Eustace fitz John, Miles of Hereford, Geoffrey Talbot, and William fitz Alan, while, though there were men of violence like Mandeville who kept no loyalty, and though exceptional quarrels, such as made Stephen break with the earl of Chester in 1141, might shake their allegiance, the king was followed by the great feudatories with as much consistency as any claim was likely to evoke in the early twelfth century. The social division carried with it a territorial one also, since Henry had enfeoffed his son Robert in Gloucester and entrenched his *curiales* strongly in the March of Wales, and the war soon settled into a deadlock based upon rival governments of the east and west.[1]

Assertion of feudal theory

With power thus balanced, the North exposed to the invasion of David the Scotch king, and Stephen and the Empress outbidding each other as embodiments of feudal lordship, the reign yields no precedents for strong kingship. It has, indeed, been doubted whether the administrative machine continued to work beyond the immediate range of London, whether the Exchequer continued to sit, or the courts to meet with any regularity. On the whole, the scanty evidence points to a weakened action of government within the spheres of the two parties, and to its partial cessation in areas where neither could maintain a stable power.[2] The interest of the reign, however, lies not there, but in the assertion of what may be called the alternative political theory of the day, that which had played a great part under the Conqueror, had been forced into the background by Henry I, and which now imposed itself more freely than at any time in English history. Stephen's accession charter strikes a far lower note than had that of Henry. Where

1 In 1138 Robert of Gloucester had a strong hold upon Kent, where he held Dover and Canterbury and was supported by Walkelin Maminot, but this was soon lost. Orderic, III. xiii. 17. The garrison of Wallingford came to be the easternmost point of the Angevin power.

2 J. H. Round, *Geoffrey de Mandeville*; G. L. Turner, *Transactions of the Royal Historical Society*, New Series, xii.

the latter speaks only of hereditary right—*post obitum patris sui Dei gratia rex Anglorum*, Stephen's appeals to election—*Dei gratia assensu cleri et populi electus*. Since the direct line was broken and Stephen's right plainly elective, not too much need be made of this, but the principal friends of Matilda enforced its meaning by a pretension which is drastic as from English vassals to their king. Robert of Gloucester appealed to the contractual clauses in the formula of homage, making his submission to Stephen "on conditions, that is to say for as long as the king should maintain him in his honour, and keep his pledges entered into",[1] and in this he was followed by the prelates, who thus exploited the feudal relation to bind the new king to the "liberties of the church".[2] It is this element of contract and convention as between king and vassal which gives the reign its special interest, and saves it from the character of anarchy. In 1138 Gloucester's conditional allegiance had its sequel in a formal diffidation, "revoking his homage and withdrawing his friendship and fealty in the ancient customary forms";[3] in this Gloucester was followed by the barons of Matilda's party, and as the kingly power is relaxed the relations of both Stephen and Matilda with their supporters seem more and more to be determined by the tacit recognition of a contract. The charters by which both sovereigns bid for support take on many of the forms of private agreements between equal parties,[4] and they are required to grant away all and more than William I had allowed to the magnates or Henry I had reclaimed from them. The sheriffdoms revert to the great barons, those who are best worth placating, and now they are granted not during pleasure but in fee and inheritance. With the sheriff's administering powers go the judicial authority which has lately been created in the *justicia comitatus*. Between such hereditary viscounties and the palatine earldoms there is, indeed, hardly more than a difference of name. The most striking of these immunities was that of Geoffrey de Mandeville who received the shrievalties of London, Essex, Middlesex, and

---

[1] William of Malmsbury, *Gesta Regum*, 707: *Homagium regi fecit sub conditione quadam, scilicet quamdiu ille dignitatem suam integre custodiret et sibi pacta servaret.*

[2] *Loc. cit. quamdiu ille libertatem ecclesiae et vigorem disciplinae conservaret.*

[3] William of Malmsbury, *Historia Novella*, i. 18: *Regi more majorum amicitiam et fidem interdixit, homagio etiam abdicato.*

[4] J. H. Round, *Geoffrey de Mandeville*, p. 11: *Ego ut dominus et Rex convencionavi ei sicut Baroni et Justiciario meo.*

Hertfordshire in fee and inheritance, but this is only the most extreme of several instances, of which Miles of Gloucester's shrievalty of Hereford, and the creation of fifteen earls, not endowed with territorial earldoms but still enriched by grants of revenue and lands from the fisc, which seriously weakened the crown, are others.[1] This was the position which faced Henry II when he succeeded to the throne. Not only was the local government largely feudalized, but the king's castles had been allowed to lapse into the hands of the King of Scotland, William de Warenne, the earl of Chester, the earl of Norfolk, and others, the royal demesne had been freely alienated, and both Stephen and Henry had been forced to recognize an immense power in the earl of Chester, which stretched from one side of the north Midlands to the other. It was fortunate for Henry that the two Midland powers of Chester and Peverel destroyed each other by William Peverel's murder of earl Ralf in 1153 and that these two great honours fell into the hands of the crown. The work of Henry I was in fact to be done again, and with far greater thoroughness and with a new wisdom in political practice which would enlist instead of alienating the mass of the nation.

Angevin kingship   In the obscurity of the reign of Stephen England shared only partially in the swift intellectual movement of the times, and the men who took control after the peace seem by contrast in advance of their predecessors by more than a normal generation. Henry, Becket, Richard de Lucy, Glanvill, Richard fitz Neal, each in his own way, was more than a man of affairs, and was prepared to develop the routine of administration in the light of principles which he desired to see realized in law and government. This power of systematic design, at least in degree, new, reached far into the background of thought.[2] It was the time of the first treatises upon the state, and in the light of the new science of politics the twelfth-century crown first realized how far it had come from the restricted kingship of the eleventh, and found justification for a new scope and meaning in monarchy. Past

[1] *Omnia pene ad fiscum pertinentia minus caute distribuerat.* Robert de Monte, *sub anno* 1155.

[2] Cf. F. M. Powicke, *Stephen Langton*, p. 91.

theorizing about the crown had assumed that the king's function was limited to a narrow range, and his right scarcely more than *primus inter pares*. The compiler of the Leges Henrici Primi ranked the king's law as the most exalted, but recognized the popular laws of Wessex, Mercia, and the Danelah as of equal and independent validity.[1] Hugh of Fleury[2] made the crown his subject, but was concerned primarily with defining the boundary between the *regnum* and the *sacerdotium*. To neither of these writers was sovereignty itself a conscious problem, nor had they any inkling that it might come to be the impulse of every act of state, and the prime question of politics. But the men of Henry II's generation knew that there was coming to be a new power for which there was as yet no name, unrealized, and therefore bound by no limits, and this they sought to understand and to justify. There must be a divine virtue in princes, says John of Salisbury, since all men submit to them, and offer their necks to the axe.[3] The mystery of tyrannous kings must be accepted as a judgment upon their peoples. Like Attila, they are the scourge of God. He who resists power resists God. It is not to be wrongly used, being a trust for the execution of justice, and the evil king is responsible to Heaven. Nevertheless, acting in the spirit of their office, kings are not to be questioned; their will has the force of law, and is, in fact, the sole guarantee of justice and public good. All this will come to be the commonplace of medieval thought about kingship, and treads so nicely the line between responsibility and irresponsibility that it can be used to justify almost any political creed. But such writing is an historical event because it abandons the old unspeculative acceptance of official acts as conforming to or offending custom, and therefore good or bad *per se*. It is the first recognition of power and will in the state, forces not to be confined within the customary right of the king, already outgrowing his traditional functions, and to be estimated only in terms of a more sophisticated political experience than that of Norman England. When English kingship comes to be thought of in terms of the Digest, Cicero, and Vegetius Renatus, the subject matter is the crown rather than

[1] Leges Henrici Primi, 6. 2: *Legis etiam Anglice trina est particio . . . preter tremendum regie maiestatis . . . imperium.*

[2] Baluze, *Miscellanea*, ii. 184. The exordium to the *Dialogus de Scaccario* follows Hugh very closely.

[3] John of Salisbury, *Policraticus*, iv. 1.

the king, and the concept of a crown which is the embodiment of the community is not far from explicit utterance in John of Salisbury's *princeps est potestas publica*[1]: *publicae ergo utilitatis minister et aequitatis servus est princeps: princeps personam publicam gerit.*[2]

Growth of definition in feudal obligations It is true that Roman formulae fit the English twelfth century badly, but there was beginning in every sphere a process of analysis and consequent definition of what before was ill-defined. The king's government began to move according to general rules, its offices and routine were stereotyped, law was coming to be treated as a science—and there the result was something of a revolution—and the custom of feudalism, which had had only a general uniformity, came, though less effectively, under review. In this last sphere the realization of the crown that vagueness might be manipulated to its own profit, and the slower realization of the feudal order that its obligations were being increased and its right delimited thereby, led up to the tension and conflict of the Charter. In the course of this clarification and intensifying of its practice the crown made contact with the community at the expense of localism, conservatism, and the immunity of the honours. Henry II himself was a feudalist in politics, but his was a feudalism rigidly confined by rule, in which obligations to the supreme lord were multiplied and strictly enforced. In this spirit, he saw that the oaths of homage and ligeance were exacted and repeated[3] from the feudal order. No longer was the taking of liege homage from the knights of the king's barons an exception[4]—it was taken in a new form *de dominio solo* and generally imposed upon the honours in 1166—and fealty taken in the hundred courts was made the common link between the king and the countrysides.[5] Fealty and homage so reiterated, and becoming matters of routine, were, perhaps, intended to extract more from the feudal oaths than they traditionally carried, and they were in fact being brought home to those who took them with a new literalness. An administrative order to a great man was apt in Henry's reign to be enforced by

[1] John of Salisbury, *Policraticus*, iv. 1.   [2] *Ibid.* iv. 2.

[3] The duty of exacting homages which had not been performed was enjoined on the justices in 1170 and 1176.

[4] *Red Book of the Exchequer*, vol. i., and J. H. Round, *Feudal England*, p. 236.

[5] Assize of Northampton, 6: *Justitiae capiant domini regis fidelitates . . . ab omnibus, scilicet comitibus, baronibus, militibus, et libere tenentibus, et etiam rusticis, qui in regno manere voluerint.*

a reminder that the recipient had sworn oaths to the king, and that he expected not only a vassal's service in extremities, but specific obedience to his writs.[1] *Ligeantia* is hardening towards allegiance—obedience of the subject—though without offence to the letter of feudalism, and John, with his habitual distrust of the feudal tie, will propound this altered fealty as the basis of a commune of England, binding all men against the foreign and domestic enemies of the crown.[2] By that time he was not alone in seeing it as the political form of the future.[3]

The drawing of the community into responsibility to the crown is seen in Henry II's new process of law. It is an exercise of the Norman king's practice of redressing disseizin, but now done after inquest and not by a mere equitable re-seizin without trial.[4] Since the Conquest the crown had, and from time to time used, a means of arriving at facts more precise and quicker than trial and judgment, the inquest of sworn recognition. The simplest and most far-reaching of legal revolutions was achieved by eliciting the crucial point of fact in a series of different types of action, making the issue of the trial turn upon that one point, and submitting it to a sworn inquest of neighbours. Of the possible actions concerning land some were seen to turn upon a claim that the defendant had obtained possession wrongfully from the plaintiff —*novel disseizin* [5]—others on whether the plaintiff's ancestor had died in possession—*mort d'ancestre* [6]—while, if the right of property which underlay the fact of possession were challenged, that too could be tried by inquest—*magna assisa*.[7] In ecclesiastical matters, the possession of patronage might be determined by enquiring

The inquest

---

[1] M. M. Bigelow, *Placita Anglo-Normannica*, p. 241. The justiciar enjoins Archbishop Baldwin to withhold legal action against Christ Church *per fidem quam ei (regi) debes et per sacramentum quod ei fecisti*. In 1166 the return of the *servitia debita* of the knights was enjoined on the barons *per fidem et ligantiam quam (mihi debetis)*: Stubbs, *Select Charters*, p. 173. The commonalty are required to equip themselves and hold their arms *ad fidem domini regis et regni*: Assize of Arms. Letters Patent, 4 John, p. 72, prohibits the clergy from demanding new taxes from the laity *in fide qua nobis tenemini (ibid.* 76), prohibits the Irish lieges *in fide qua nobis tenemini* from answering any but the king or the justiciar's writ.

[2] Gervase of Canterbury, ii. 96.

[3] Cf. the London *pseudo-leges* of William I (*c.* 1210), *Statuimus ut omnes liberi homines regni nostri sint fratres conjurati ad monarchiam nostram et ad regnum nostrum*.

[4] *Chronicon Monasterii de Abingdon*, ii. p. 166; *Chronicon Monasterii Gloucestria*, i. p. 242; *Cartularium Monasterii de Rameseia*, i. p. 234.

[5] Assize of Northampton. Stubbs, *Select Charters*, p. 152.   [6] *Ibid.* p. 151.

[7] Glanvill, *Tractatus de Legibus*, ii. x.

The Assizes who made the presentment upon the last vacancy—*darrein present-ment*[1]—and a whole class of litigation could be avoided by enquiry whether disputed land were held in frankalmoign or lay fee—assize *utrum*—and should be justiciable in the spiritual or secular court. Where Henry I would eject a disseizor by his mere will, Henry II would do so by form of assize.[2] For each of such actions a single writ would suffice, and might be issued in common form as sued for. In addition, Henry enacted that no action for free tenement should be entertained without king's writ. The effect of this procedure was to deprive the defendant of the delays of the old process of judgment and also to prevent his possession being troubled by the threat of force inherent in challenge to ordeal by battle, and, although assize was not made obligatory *Growth of* but was at the discretion of the defendant, its advantages were *king's law* sufficient to bring about its general adoption within perhaps a generation. So the king's law grew at the expense of the law of the honours and of trial before the sheriffs, for the assize could be taken only before a king's justiciar, and every defendant who put himself upon it came out of the court of his lord and took his trial before that of the king. The courts of the itinerant justices who took the assizes began to be called *curia regis* equally with those held *coram rege*, and the king's processes administered under the assizes came to make up the great body of the law. Initiated by uniform writs which ran through every county and franchise, it had issue in uniform procedure, and was everywhere matter of common jurisdiction. Superseding the variant customs of the Danelah, Mercia, and Wessex, and the customs of the honours, this king's law became recognized as the Common Law of England.

The inquest in adminis- tration In extending the *recognitio*, even permissively, to every disputed case of property and possession, Henry was revolutionizing the procedure of civil law, but he was not acting without precedent. His predecessors had used the inquest to ascertain facts which were essential to determining landed right, though they had used it only occasionally—in the Conqueror's reign almost solely in order to get an English verdict on the position in the Confessor's day, in later reigns more generally, but still not often. In the

---

[1] Glanvill, *Tractatus de Legibus*, xiii. 21.

[2] Up to 1166 he was still using forceable re-seizin. Cf. *Chronicon Monasterii de Abingdon*, ii. p. 223; *Historia Monasterii Sancti Augustini*, p. 409; Douglas, *Feudal Documents of the Abbey of Bury St. Edmunds*, p. 94.

administrative use of the inquest, however, Henry seems to have been entirely an innovator, and in making it the almost invariable means of securing the knowledge necessary to action he was creating something new in the practice of the state—government which could establish its rights and assess its revenues by information which was authentic because local and sworn to by oath. It was an essential, perhaps the one essential equipment of bureaucratic monarchy.

As recognition became part of the routine of the counties it established the habit of response and obedience to the crown. The earliest enactment of inquest as the basis of administrative action is that of criminal presentment by the Assize of Clarendon[1] in 1166. The hundreds by the oath of twelve men, and the townships by four, are required to make presentment of all felons.[2] This is an administrative expedient, but it also has judicial effect—it is the forerunner of our grand jury—since the sworn accusation by neighbours deprives the accused of the right to make a rebutting oath, and drives him without preliminary to the test of ordeal.[3] Even if cleared by the ordeal, the accused must abjure the realm or be outlaw, unless he is of hitherto unblemished repute.[4] The verdict of the *jurati* is, therefore, for practical purposes equivalent to a judgment, and, though the principle that notorious ill-fame deprives the accused of the right of defence by oath is of Saxon origin,[5] this is the first wholesale attack upon the cumbrous machinery of the old English trial as the Normans perpetuated it, and, except for its stronghold in the larger boroughs, the older criminal justice was soon swept away.[6] Upon the administrative side presentment reinforces the responsibility of the countrysides for their own immunity from disorder and theft, and its perfected form in the *Edictum Regium* of 1195 provides for a regular delation of felons to knights assigned *ad hoc*, who have been taken to be the first forerunners of the justices of the peace.[7]

It is possible that the settled years of government were begun by

Criminal present-ment

---

[1] Stubbs, *Select Charters*, p. 170.

[2] Assize of Clarendon, 1.   [3] *Ibid*. 2.   [4] *Ibid*. 14.

[5] There is here an interesting dovetailing of Saxon and Frankish procedure.

[6] Some resistance from those who stood by the old safeguards of Saxon or Norman trial is shown by the many fines for refusing to swear to the king's assize which were exacted by the eyre of 1166.

[7] Howden, iii. 300.

Inquest of sheriffs a general inquest as to secular services in 1163.[1] A few years later we find recognition applied to almost the whole field of administration.[2] The inquest of 1170 is known as the Inquest of Sheriffs, but its verdict was to be given equally upon the administration of bishops and barons in their own estates, upon that of the bailiffs holding royal custodies, of the foresters, and of the holders of any itinerant office. It was, in fact, a general inquest upon grievances throughout the country both under royal and baronial officials, and into any leakage of revenue, as from the *aide pur fille marier*, the chattels of felons, or amercements, and finally as to the state of the royal manors, and is as remarkable in its scope as the Domesday survey itself. The immediate occasion of this inquest may have been dissatisfaction with the officialdom of the day—many of the sheriffs were displaced after it—but its historical importance is as

Royal commission and local verdict the beginning of a new practice of administration, the regular association of a commission from the *curia* with the independent verdict of the hundreds and vills upon the conduct of provincial officials and their handling of the sources of revenue. In 1170 the inquest was taken before a commission of barons itinerant. Later their place was taken by a routine of *justitiarii itinerantes*, and the

The eyre first list of the articles of enquiry of the general eyre which has survived, that of 1194,[3] has much in common with those of 1170. The Inquest of Sheriffs, in fact, set the precedent for a recurrent inquest by the shires and hundreds upon the king's affairs, and in some measure upon their own.[4] Inquest was also applied to a widening range of subjects for which special juries were empanelled. Glanvill tells us of juries to delate encroachments—purprestures—upon the king's rights,[5] to decide the degree to which criminals might be amerced without ruin—*salvo contenemento*[6]—and to decide disputed bounds,[7] while in 1185 verdicts upon heirs under age within the king's lordship were entered upon the *Rotuli de Dominabus*. Towards the end of the reign two great constructive

---

1 Ralf de Diceto, 311.
2 Inquest of Sheriffs. Stubbs, *Select Charters*, p. 175.
3 *Ibid.* p. 252. A link between the enquiry into the king's demesne in 1170 and the regular practice of such enquiry in the eyres is afforded by the undated articles which Benedict and Howden associated with the Assize of Northampton. Howden, ii. 89.
4 Cf. clause 25 of the Articles of 1194.
5 Glanvill, *Tractatus de Legibus*, ix. 11.   6 *Loc. cit.*   7 *Ibid.* ix. 13.

innovations, the Assize of Arms and the assessment of the Saladin Tithe, were both prepared by inquest, and in Richard's reign the precedent of the latter is consolidated by the assessment by inquest of the carucage tax of 1198. The crown will in future rely upon countryside verdicts for the statistics upon which its increasingly ambitious and complex finance and administration is to rest. After 1194, at least, the juries will commonly be elected,[1] and not least important for the future is the fact that in the revived contact of the monarchy with the community the villein's oath will be accepted equally with that of the free.[2] Thus, the division between free and unfree tenure, which had gained recognition in law, failed to effect a lodgment in the constitution. Much of the development of the English state turns upon this point of administrative practice.

As the monarchy increased its demands upon the counties, it became necessary to strengthen and regularize their supervision from Westminster, which was now to some extent a capital of government.[3] The unspecialized shrievalty and the compromise *The judiciary* of the shire justiciary were outgrown.[4] With the experience gathered in Henry I's reign to draw upon, an itinerant judiciary was certain to be adopted, and Henry gave his whole genius to devising a system and to experimenting with men of various temper and qualifications to exercise it.[5] As with procedure, so with the machine which directed it, the king's work was done by trial and experience, and revealed its final form only towards the

[1] The Articles of the eyre of 1194 (Stubbs, *Select Charters*, p. 252) order the election in each county of four knights, who are to elect two knights from each hundred, who in their turn are to choose ten knights or freemen to form with them the grand jury of the hundred. The procedure may, of course, be older than 1194.

[2] By the Assize of Northampton the presenting jury must be knights or freemen, as again in 1194. The four men of the vill would, of course, sometimes be villeins, as might the *quatuor vel sex viri legitimi*, who were to swear to assessments under the Saladin Tithe. The jurors of the assizes, as dealing with free tenements, were naturally freemen. Villeins swore to the Inquest of Sheriffs—though Benedict (p. 5) considered the result unsatisfactory—and to the carucage assessment of 1198.

[3] The Exchequer began to sit there regularly from 1156. T. F. Tout, *Chapters in Administrative History*, i. 102.

[4] Sheriffs were prohibited from holding pleas of the crown in their own shires in 1194, and by Magna Carta from hearing them at all.

[5] Ralf de Diceto, 434: *Abbates modo, comites modo, capitaneos modo, domesticos modo, familiarissimos modo, causis audiendis et examinandis praeposuit.*

close of his reign. The Assize of Clarendon of 1166 is in the form of instructions to justiciars who are to combine a fiscal review of the counties with a drastic purge of their crimes by presentment. The eyre which it instructed was carried through in the same year by Richard de Lucy and Geoffrey de Mandeville, and may be distinguished from the later itinerant judiciary, which made use of more justices, and included men of lesser rank. The eyres, indeed, take during the first half of the reign the form of special commissions to which the hearing of general pleas is secondary, and, while the eyre of 1166 inaugurated the presentment of criminals under the new Assize of Clarendon, that of 1167 was concerned with forests, that of 1168 was sent out to collect the *aide pur fille marier*, while the commissions of 1170 were to take recognition of the sheriff's delicts, and that of 1173 was for the collection of a tallage. Most of these commissions also held pleas, but they are clearly characteristic of the formative period in the greater emphasis on their fiscal than on their judicial function and in the variety of experiments which lead up to the perfected system. The eyre of 1166 was made by two justiciars who reviewed eighteen counties unsupported, those of 1168 and 1173, as befitted their primary purpose, were made by barons of the Exchequer, the Inquest of Sheriffs was carried through by large groups of commissioners, acting each over perhaps half a dozen counties, and, for obvious reasons, contained an element of the non-official baronage.

Itinerant commissions

It is in 1176 that we are first conscious that experiment is over and the time come for the parcelling of the kingdom into areas for regular judicial visitation. Six groups, of three justices each, perambulated the country, and dealt with almost all the business which came to be that of the eyre, criminal pleas, the assizes, and every kind of plea initiated under the king's writ, provided that it did not concern a tenement of more than a half knight's fee, together with the normal enquiry into the royal demesne, escheats, and other profitable rights of the crown. Three years later experience dictated a recasting, though not a revocation of the scheme of 1176. The eyres were reduced from six to four, each with five justices, and, because the justices of 1176 were found to be oppressive, a bishop was associated with each of the three southern commissions, and Ranulf Glanvill, about to succeed de Lucy as chief justiciar, with that of the North. The two experiments of 1176 and 1179 mark the final achievement of Henry's work in this sphere, and the beginning of an annual eyre as the principal weapon of provincial administration and justice. In 1194 the further precaution was taken of removing from the sheriffs even the keeping of the pleas of the crown, their reception, record, and the production of parties before the justices, and of entrusting them to three knights and a clerk elected in every county. The instructions of that year exemplify eyre jurisdiction in its completed form. Inspired by Hubert Walter, they set out the pleas of the crown by name as the principal business of the session, the grand assize for property of an annual value of less than five pounds, the affairs of the Jews, the state of the king's wardships, escheats, farms, and churches, while with this judicial and inquisitorial work goes the collection of tallage of boroughs and demesne townships of the crown. In this form the eyre typifies the final coördination of central bureaucracy with the communities of the counties as the administrative system of Henry's choice, and the permanent system of the Angevin state.

As in the provincial judiciary, so in the central *curia* and its staff, *The* an ordered scheme emerges from Henry II's reign and fulfils the *central* undeveloped precedents of his grandfather. Henry never allowed *curia* the routine action of any office to establish a bar between himself and the free exercise of his own judicial function. Difficult or momentous cases were regularly reserved for the king's consideration, and even when he was abroad he allowed his subjects free access to himself, and from time to time issued writs to the appropriate officials over the justiciar's head.[1] The latter deferred matters beyond his own judgment to the king over seas.[2] Nor, it would seem, did Henry abandon the principle that the commission of his justices was a special form of the authority of the king *in consilio sapientum.* Much judgment was done with the counsel of his barons, and the principal assizes of the reign were evolved in such baronial *curiae.* And yet it is during Henry's reign that the great *The chief* offices of state assume unmistakable identity and establish their *justiciar* full dignity. If the preëminence of Roger of Salisbury was rather personal than of office, and was felt equally in the justiciary, the Chancery, and the Treasury, the beginning of Henry's reign pro-

[1] M. M. Bigelow, *Placita Anglo-Normannica*, 233.　　　[2] *Ibid.* 242.

duces a Chancery with an increasing clerical staff, a Chief Justiciarship of the title of which there can be no doubt, and a Treasurer
with settled and defined duties. The essential function of the chief
justiciar's office is identical with that of his subordinate colleagues
—the function of judgment—and it is a reminder of his emergence
from the rank and file of the judiciary that there are two chief
justiciars holding office together during Henry's early years.[1] But it
has become a permanent distinction,[2] and we can see that the chief
justiciar habitually acts as the leader in every court, and is often
entrusted with any routine powers that the king is disposed to
delegate when he is not in England, though he may find himself
disavowed in the most serious matters, as did Richard de Lucy
when he suspended the forest regulations during the revolt of
1173.[3] When the king refers a petitioner to his *curia* it is
the justiciar whom the suitor approaches.[4] Richard de Lucy is
constantly found taking a decisive lead in discussions between the
judges,[5] and, when they have agreed, the justiciar announces their
judgment,[6] as Robert of Leicester pronounced judgment upon
Becket. A plea for justice from a great vassal will now as a rule
receive from him its immediate answer.[7] At times the king, though
present, will retire from the court and leave the justiciar to preside.[8]
When he is abroad he will sometimes address the earl of Leicester
or Richard de Lucy by name, ordering them to set the county
court or some appropriate official to action.[9] Intermittently during
the king's absence the chief justiciar will issue writs under his own
name, which are qualified as *brevia de ultra mare*.[10] The fact that he
is the chief justiciar in every court gives him the presidency of the
Exchequer, and there Glanvill pronounces the judgment of the
curia in scaccario after consultation with the bishops and justices
who sit with him.[11] Besides leading in the courts, the chief justiciar
will have occasional duties of legal administration of a dignified
kind to perform, as when the earl of Leicester accompanies

[1] Richard de Lucy and the earl of Leicester.

[2] Richard de Lucy held from 1154 to 1179, Ralf Glanvill finished out the
reign.   [3] Howden, ii. 79.

[4] M. M. Bigelow, *Placita Anglo-Normannica*, 221.

[5] *Loc. cit.*   [6] *Ibid.* 214.   [7] *Ibid.* 239.

[8] *Ibid.* 199.   [9] *Ibid.* 204.   [10] *Ibid.* 210, 241.

[11] *Ibid.* 235. It is perhaps as from the Exchequer that the justiciar sanctions
expenditure on castellation and other royal works. Pipe Roll, Hen. II, ann. 13.
(Lancs). *Ibid.* ann. 14. (Lancs).

Reginald of Cornwall to verify Becket's plea of illness as a reason for disobeying the king's summons to trial.[1] In short his office is to do *vice rege* all that the king does in his *curia* in demanding, advising, and pronouncing judgment, and to give the necessary effect to the court's verdict, either by himself approaching great persons who cannot be handled by subalterns, by issuing writs to executive officials, or by ordering their preparation by the chancellor. In the king's absence this may become, in fact at least, a vicegerency.

The process of specialization which produced the chief justiciarship and the eyre also brought the jurisdiction of the central *curia* to definition. This had remained, at least in theory, as a function of the council of magnates, stiffened by curialists learned in law, and under the personal presidency of the king, and in theory, indeed, this remained its ultimate authority whatever adjustments of routine and personnel were adopted;[2] but it is clear that, at least by 1154, the king had been delegating his powers on occa- *The court* sion.[3] A precedent had, of course, existed from at least the Con- *of 1178* quest in the commissions detached to try some one important plea, and latterly the itinerant judiciary had familiarized the country with the idea that king's justice could be done other than *coram rege*. With this went the assumption that the king's commission to a justiciar gave him the judicial power of the king *in consilio magnatum*, and made him the peer in judgment of the king's barons, and without this assumption the benches of the law could never have come into being. In virtue of this fiction delegation was regularized in 1178, and a commission of five justices was appointed to try the pleas of the kingdom, such as involved difficulties being reserved for the king and his council. Henceforth, as the charter tests show, Henry travelled with the Justiciar and two other lay justices,[4] and from this court, which tried a mixed justice of common and crown pleas, the later benches were derived.

[1] M. M. Bigelow, *Placita Anglo-Normannica*, 215.

[2] Causes beyond the competence of the five justices of 1178 were to be presented *auditui regis, et sicut ei, et sapientioribus regni placeret, terminaretur*: to the audience of the king, to be determined by his pleasure and that of the wise men of the realm. Benedict, i. 208.

[3] Thus, in 1175 the abbot of Battle is referred by Henry to the *curia* under Richard de Lucy. M. M. Bigelow, 221.

[4] Usually, Robert de Witefeld, William de Bendings, or Michael Belet. Delisle, *Recueil des Actes de Henri II*, ii. pp. 122, 141, 210, 248, 307, etc.

At some period after 1178 a division took place between king's bench pleas and the *placita communia*, and the Great Charter accepted a court of Common Pleas as an established fact and fixed its session at Westminster, where all subjects might have fixed and easy access to justice.

Thus, during Henry's reign, the law, the courts, and the officials reach a condition which at least foreshadows their final state. There is as yet little feeling that the crown is bound by its own routine,[1] and, though the Exchequer's jurisdiction is made necessary by financial disputes, while that of the King's Bench—though not yet clearly defined—safeguards the rights of the crown, and Common Bench those of private parties, it will be long before the king or the justiciar will feel bound to refer every plea to its appropriate court. Much justice, also, is still done, and will continue to be done, in unspecialized great councils. But, in spite of this, law is diverging into separate streams, which find their channels in the several courts, and the general shape of the system will not be altered. That it was recognized and accepted as a system, and one directed to the public good, we may be sure from the general approval given it by the rebellious baronage in the Charter.

It is common to speak of household government or personal government in this period. I doubt if either term is apt. The king's will pervaded every part of the state, so that "personal government" tells us nothing new, and most of the household offices hardly rose above the hall, the kitchen, and the dispense. A much truer picture is given if we think of the executive as a growing corps of skilful clerks and forceful laymen distributed over the shrievalties, the castles, the custodies of escheats, the various commissions such as the keeperships of the wines, the ships and the ports, the mint, the exchange, the stanneries, and so forth, all of them constantly responsive to the royal precept, known to the king, responsible to the king alone. If we need a general name, we might call this familiar government, for again and again the de-

---

[1] John will plead the *lex scaccarii* as a justification of his action against Braiose. *Liber Niger Scaccarii*, i. 378.

scription of *familiares*, familiar clerk, *dilectus et familiaris*, is given to these royal agents. They are the *iniquissimi consiliarii* of the hostile chronicles, the king's *familiaris* of all ranks, and through them the reign is governed. It is not yet a metropolitan government and the counties, the castleries, and the custodies are kept in tune and obedience by the constant itineration of the king.

As coördinating authorities under which these men mostly act, we should probably single out the Seneschalcy and the Chamber. The Seneschal's was the office for the provisioning of the king's hall and household and his eyres, and seems, under the Angevins, to have replaced the Constableship as the head of the *Familia Militaris*. Castellanships, in many cases shrievalties, commands in war and diplomatic missions fell regularly to the senior Knights of the Household. They were the backbone of the secular, unlettered half of government. Upon the clerical, financial side the one office of weight was the Chamber, but the importance of that was such as to make it a major factor in administration.

Absence of record may cover some development already made *The* in the Chamber of Henry I. The Pipe Rolls of Henry II and the *executive* Chancery Rolls of John bear witness to it on every page. A separation between the Chamberlains of the Exchequer and the Chamber was made in 1158, in which year Warin fitz Gerold ceased to function there, and the Chamber was thenceforth left free to develop as an office in its own right. Successively, the characteristic officials of an Angevin *officium* made their appearance, a household chamberlain, Richard Ruffus in 1166, a Clerk of the Chamber in the early 'seventies. The Ushership of the Chamber must have been a much older office, but the first usher to appear in record is Walter de Camera who attests charters from about 1182. It is already a lesser treasury, following the king, and receiving and spending for his daily work of government. Under Henry and John it was vital as the personal treasure, receiving money from the Treasury,[1] from escheated honours such as Rayleigh and Boulogne, from various offices,[2] from sheriffs,[3] custodians,[4] or the

---

[1] Letters Close, John, pp. 28, 74, 75.
[2] *Ibid.* 22, 39, 74.   [3] *Ibid.* 19, 25, 34.
[4] *Ibid.* 34, 72, 108. During the vacancy of the bishopric of Exeter in 1207 it was in the custody of king's clerks and its revenues were paid into the Chamber. *Ibid.* 76. Formerly it would have been in custody of the chancellor *sede vacante.*

The Chamber

king's debtors,[1] who were ordered to pay direct into the Chamber, the Exchequer writing them quit on the king's writ of *computate*. In turn, it might, if convenient, make livery of cash for every exceptional or urgent service, for the king's personal needs, the wages of mercenaries,[2] pensions,[3] garrison or repair of castles, equipping of vessels, or for innumerable other needs.[4] As the immediate source of finance for the executive, it was itinerant with the king, and it followed him abroad in 1206 and 1214, drawing as much as twelve thousand marks at a time[5] to constitute his war-chest.[6] Often using the small seal,[7] and staffed by his confidential clerks, it was the organ of his personal diplomacy—the charters by which he bound reluctant barons to special subservience were stored in the Chamber[8] and Chamber clerks were often charged with the invidious business of the baronial hostages[9]—and by providing messengers between the various offices and officials it was the motive force of government. Constantly these move about the country, bearing letters to sheriffs, justiciars, and custodians of every kind, and moneys by which the king's orders may be carried out. Reflecting the government of the realm in miniature, and forming the web of com-

---

[1] Letters Close, John, pp. 29, 36, 66.

[2] *Ibid.* 21.

[3] Letters Patent, 8 John, p. 5.

[4] J. E. A. Jolliffe, *Angevin Kingship*, pp. 226 *et seq.* and *English Historical Review*, Vol. LXVIII.

[5] Letters Close, 8 John, p. 75.

[6] At Porchester in 1205, when the king believed himself to be on the point of sailing for France, it became the immediate treasury of receipt, receiving 900 marks by the hands of London citizens, 350 marks from Hugh Nevill from the forests, and 300 marks from the Treasury of Ireland, *Ibid.* 7 John, pp. 35, 36. At the end of the reign payments are beginning to be made into the inner chamber of the Wardrobe, which was soon to supersede the Chamber. Letters Close, 15 John, p. 145, J. E. A. Jolliffe, *Angevin Kingship*, p. 275.

[7] This practice began, according to Professor Tout (*Chapters in Administrative History*, i. 158), "at least from 1208". The letters issued from Poitou in 1206 *per parvum sigillum quia magnum non erat praesens* (Letters Patent, 8 John, p. 66), must have formed a precedent. It is in 1208 that we first find an admission that the small seal is coming to be appropriate to the Chamber: *has litteras fecimus signari parvo sigillo nostro, quia hec debita volumus reddi in cameram nostram, quas fecissemus signari majori sigillo nostro si ea ad scaccarium nostrum reddi vellemus*: we have had these writs sealed with our small seal because the debts they refer to are to be rendered into our chamber, etc., etc. (Letters Close, 9 John, p. 115).

[8] Letters Patent, 8 John, p. 66.

[9] *Loc. cit.*

munication on which it is borne, the Chamber causes the whole system to feel and respond to the king's will.

As an outward manifestation of the growing expertness of the *Growth of* age, rolls come into being for one branch of the administration *record* after another. The Exchequer had recorded its business from the beginning. To that, perhaps, it owed that continuity of tradition in which it spoke of the *lex scaccarii*. From 1195 it, or rather the Treasury, was preserving record of the fines or agreed settlements made between party and party, and it came to be a repository of much court record. Chancery rolls in general date from the reign of John, and it has been conjectured that the need for more consistent record may have arisen when Longchamps, driven from the judiciary and the Exchequer by the revolution of November 1191, retained the chancellorship, and carried out what duties he was allowed to perform without access to the Treasury. The roll of the king's letters patent [1]—open in charter form with pendant seal—or close [2]—folded and sealed—the *Rotuli de Oblatis* of fines offered to the king for privileges or favour,[3] and the Charter Roll,[4] all mark at once the increasing subdivision of business, and the mounting volume of information by which the Angevin offices governed reign by reign more intensely and surely.

The task of the Angevin monarchy was not alone to rule by *Crown* ever-improving devices of government, but to remain in harmony *and* with the prevailing social forms and to turn them to its service. *community* It has already been said that Henry accepted the implications of feudalism to the full. And yet, paradoxically, his reign saw such a narrowing of the scope of feudalism and its liberties that the whole outlook of the landed aristocracy was permanently modified, and their ambitions diverted into quasi-constitutional channels. At the beginning, the flow of military power, which had swelled unchecked under Stephen, was arrested. The destruction of the adulterine castles and the withdrawal of the royal castles from baronial custody was apparently completed by about 1160. In 1166 the baronial knighthood was bound by oath to the king. Not only the *servitium debitum* or customary obligation, but any additional knights whom policy had led the lord to enfeoff—the

<hr>

[1] From September 1201.   [2] From June 1204.
[3] From 1199.   [4] From 1199.

novum feoffamentum—and those kept at salary in his household were forced to do liege homage. Thus, faith to the king was made the primary sacramental duty of all the military tenants of every baron. The rebels who rose in 1173 had no sufficient following of familiar knights, and fought their campaign with hired Flemings.

Clarification of the law of tenure

It is easy to exaggerate the degree to which the rules and incidents of feudalism were already determined in the Norman reigns. The reign of Henry II saw a clarification of feudal custom such as was characteristic of him. Twice general inquests were made into the conduct of feudal liberties, and, on the whole, the power and profits of the king as supreme lord were markedly increased. A preliminary question might have been whether the obligations of knight service lay upon all the fees held under the barons, or only upon those of the *servitium debitum* of the Conquest enfeoffment.[1] By 1166 Henry had decided this crux in favour of the crown. All fees, *de antiquo feoffamento* and *de novo*, came under contribution to the aide *pur fille marier* and the scutage of 1168,[2] and all were subject to a new homage *de solo dominio*. Thus, at the outset, Henry destroyed the threat of a new, uncovenanted feudalism, such as arose in the fifteenth century, and which might have grown in the twelfth from the swelling of the military households of the barons by enfeoffments free from royal oath and service, or by the retaining of landless knights.

The assessment to knight service

The incidents of knight service: aid

So far Henry went in bringing obligation to rule. But, while the assessment could be settled at a stroke, the number and nature of the incidents of service could not, nor was a degree of uncertainty unfavourable to the crown. Definition, when it came, was at the demand of the feudatories. Glanvill doubted whether a lord might not exact an aid for the general purposes of war,[3] and if this had become an established right, the coming struggle over scutage might have been avoided, and the quarter of century of war from 1192 to 1217, which wrecked the Angevin system of finance, might have been paid for without a clash with the baronage. But Glanvill

---

[1] J. H. Round, *Feudal England*, p. 285. The clerical tenants preserved the distinction between the old and new assessments and continued to protest against the latter.

[2] Before 1166 scutage was taken from the fees of the *servitium debitum* only. *Ibid.* p. 273.

[3] Private charters exist in which the lord claims aid for the redeeming of his honour, which is almost the general aid of Glanvill. Glanvill admits, however, that current usage is against such aids: *obtinet autem quod non.* Glanvill, *Tractatus de Legibus*, ix. 8.

did not venture to put forward such aids as the clear right of the crown or of any lord, and, by a definition which did at least full justice to the feudatories, the occasions of aid came in this reign to be accepted as those four—upon the lord's accession, for the knighting of his eldest son, the marriage of his eldest daughter, and for the ransom of his body[1]—which were to be sanctioned by the Great Charter; Henry II, in fact, took only one aid during his reign, that for the Saxon marriage of Matilda. Nevertheless, *auxilium* was a term of dubious application. It was extended to aids from freemen, towns, and royal demesnes, and others not of the feudal order, and its sanction, whether by the authority of the lord or by the mere grace of the tenant, was then not fully determined.

Equally doubtful were the rules of service in the host. It does *Service in* not seem that they were questioned in Henry's reign, and he was *the host* able on occasion to extend the traditional forty days to service of a full year,[2] or to add an additional levy of serjeants for an extended period, as he did for the Welsh war,[3] but subsequent reigns saw the duty of serving beyond the seas, the nature of the contingents, and their time of service, all become political issues. Where there was such doubt as to the service itself it was certain that its commutation into scutage would be open to manipulation by the king. The solid basis of the composition known as scutage seems to have been the buying-off of a traditional forty days of *servitium debitum* at the accepted rate of eightpence a day, the pay *Scutage* and maintenance of a single knight. The standard rate of scutage was thus two marks, and at that rate it was exacted in 1159. It is therefore unlikely that any formal institution of scutage as a new tax is to be looked for. Domesday shows us that even the fyrd service of the Confessor was susceptible of a similar composition, and scutage from individuals, especially from the ecclesiastical honours, is recorded in the reign of Henry I,[4] though we know of no occasion when even a great part of the baronage bought off their service. But the imposition was seldom allowed to rest at

[1] Glanvill, *Tractatus de Legibus*, ix. 8.

[2] Benedict, i. 138. This was in 1177, when the rebels of 1174 were still in need of conciliating the king.

[3] J. H. Round, *Feudal England*, p. 282.   [4] *Ibid.* p. 268.

that. From 1166 it was exacted not only from the *servitium debitum*, but from all fees, and it was apt to be supplemented by levies from lands not held in barony or knight service, or to be coupled with additional military exactions from the barons. Thus, in 1159, a far larger sum was raised in the form of gifts—*dona*—from the ecclesiastical tenants than was derived from the scutage of their *servitium debitum*,[1] while in 1165 many of the greater tenants, both spiritual and lay, paid several times their scutage liability in contributions to the special levy of serjeants.[2] The impression left by Henry's treatment of scutage is one of adroit manipulation, by which the basis of the contributions to his wars was kept an open question, and considerable sums raised without any manifest breach of principle. Scutages were taken seven times during the reign, never at more than the two marks which were a fair composition for the forty days' service, often at a pound or a single mark. There is better evidence to show their exaction from the lands in the king's hand than from those of the feudatories, and little to show that the alternative of payment was forced upon barons who preferred to serve. The question of consent, soon to become a burning one, was thus never forced to an issue, and was, perhaps, hardly within the competence of the twelfth century, with its automatic response to custom, to raise.

Personal relations of feudalism

But the uncertainties of feudalism went deeper than this. Besides his essentially public obligations, the tenant was involved in a dependence which survived from his tenure's origin in a voluntary seeking of lordship, and which had been devised for a lord and not a sovereign. Into this relation remote forerunners had entered in the confidence of good lordship, but in the twelfth century it already put the goodwill of king and subject to an impossibly high test. In every fee there were recurrent crises which placed the holders at the king's mercy. Every tenant-in-chief under age was in the king's wardship. If he were of sufficient importance, he might be required to live at court and receive his upbringing there, or the king might place him under the tutelage of a sheriff, or sell his wardship to the highest bidder. Until he came of age the profits of his estates went to his guardian, upon whom he depended for a maintenance suitable to his rank. The fate of the women of the feudal families was even more completely in the king's hands.

[1] J. H. Round, *Feudal England*, p. 279.   [2] *Ibid.* p. 282.

As the guardian of the heiress or widow of a dead vassal their marriage was at his discretion, nor could a feudatory marry his daughters during his own lifetime without the king's leave. Such invidious rights placed immense influence in any lord's hands, and especially were they a most dangerous privilege for monarchy. Its control of wardship and marriage might be a powerful weapon of feudal diplomacy by bringing the great honours within the circle of the royal family or marrying their heirs to the king's *Wardship* friends, and, though his grandson was a greater exponent of this *and marriage* policy, Henry II used it to secure the earldom of Gloucester and the marriage of its heiress for John. But there was a corresponding danger in the intimacy of the relation of wardship. The king, as overlord, was the virtual head of every magnate's family, and the position was one which could not be filled acceptably unless he in some degree realized the conventional ideal of lordship. Both William des Longchamps and John owed some of their personal unpopularity to their indifference to decency in this relation.

The gap between the death of a tenant and the seizin of his heir *Relief* was an especially dangerous time, for the inheritance was in the king's hand. The new tenure should in theory be established by the payment of a relief. The knight's relief, according to the Leis Willelme and to Glanvill, was a hundred shillings, but Henry I's charter promised only that it should be reasonable and just, and the baron's relief was at the king's mercy. In fact the king took what he would or could. Henry I's single Pipe Roll is full of entries of payments *pro concessu terrae patris sui* and the like, and many of them were high.[1] There are few such reliefs in Henry II's rolls, presumably because they were not accounted for at the Exchequer audit, but, in the separate roll *De Oblatis*, which appears in John's reign, they rise to far higher amounts.

In spite of much individual hardship, there seems to have been little tendency for private grievances to gather head in concerted unrest under the old king after 1174. Still less is there any sign of constitutional resistance. In this again, however, as in some other matters, the reign of Henry II is one of those profoundly formative periods the effects of which are not seen till after a lapse

[1] Pipe Roll 31, Hen. I (Oxford), John de St. John, 160 marks. *Ibid.* (Notts), Ralf Halselin, 200 marks. *Ibid.* (Hants), Herbert, son of Herbert the Chamberlain, 353 marks.

of time. In retrospect, one may fairly attribute to it the creation of the Common Law and its courts, of a sense in the provincial communities, willing or unwilling, of solidarity with the government, and, both in response and reaction to these, the preparing of a reasoned temper of opposition among the barons, who had reacted to earlier and more brutal assertions of royal power blindly and by rebellion. No one of these developments reached finality in the king's lifetime, but the changed mood of the baronage grew so quickly to a crisis under his sons that its origin within his reign should be explained in so far as it can be. To the feudatories the government of Henry brought at one and the same time a new and welcome security of right in their tenures, and an increasing knowledge that they were at the mercy of the crown's interpretation of the obligations that arose from them. That land actions should need the sanction of a royal writ, that no seizin should be disturbed without reasonable process, nor withheld without cause shown— both before the neutral court of the king—gave to landright a solidity which it had not had before.[1] Harshly as he could act, we know of occasions [2] when Henry might have procured judgments which would have brought him considerable accessions of power, and when, by his own voice, he decided against his own interest. The barons rightly felt that such security was cheap at some loss of jurisdiction, and no challenge to the constructive side of Henry's revolution in justice ever found a place among their grievances. Nor was it easy to accept the king's law, and at the same time to reject the courts and officials that directed it, though from time to time the barons were inclined to question whether the justices could be regarded as their natural judges and to claim that judgment should be resumed by the full *curia* of the magnates when one of their own order was arraigned.

Baronial attitude to reforms

The danger of the reforms

But, in spite of much that was agreeable to the barons, the reforms of Henry II created constitutional opposition in its medieval form. By crushing the revolt of 1173-4 he had shown the feudatories that they could gain nothing by extreme indi-

---

[1] In 1208 the Irish feudatories were assured, as of a valuable safeguard, *nec aliquis vobis aliquid auferat nec vos possit dissaisire de liberis tenementis vestris per alicujus breve nisi per nostrum vel Justiciarii nostri.* Letters Patent, 9 John, p. 76.

[2] Benedict, i. p. 133. In one of these the beneficiary was the earl of Leicester, who two years before had been in rebellion, and who put himself in the king's mercy, fearing to plead against him.

vidualism, and, by bringing every legal action under writ, and permissively under assize, he had diverted their interest from sheriffs' courts and honorial courts to his own, whether itinerant or *de banco*. Criticism would henceforth be directed upon a central judicature, and legal process now drew its chief authority from the crown. Henry's legal revolution had made good justice available, but he sold it for what it would fetch; since pleas of land could not now begin without a writ, he could set his own price. Richard de Morvill paid two hundred marks for a writ of right to bring action for his wife's land in the sixteenth year,[1] and it is not surprising to find him in revolt in the twentieth. The instance, indeed, is an extreme one, and, on the whole, Henry's prices were lower than John's, and, perhaps, than those of his grandfather, but his enemies were able to call him *dilator et venditor justitiae*. Indeed, the *Selling of* demands of all feudal kings kept no proportion that we should *justice* recognize. The sums paid for the king's peace in 1175 after rebellion were comparatively low beside the price of offences which we should think far less. Hamo de Masci bought his peace for three hundred marks.[2] Richard fitz Roger, for marrying his daughter without the king's leave, had all his land sequestrated, and redeemed it for a hundred pounds, though it was only seven-tenths of a knight's fee and some carucates of thegnage.[3]

Upon the criminal side of law, moreover, there remained an *Arbitrary* element of uncertainty as to penalty. The fixed compositions, wer *element in* and wite, of Saxon law had come to be succeeded by a system, or *procedure* lack of system, by which the convicted party was "in the king's mercy", as might happen to communities as well as individuals, and, though it was becoming usual to decide the fine which the king might impose *in misericordia* by an oath of neighbours and to restrict it to a sum which did not cripple the culprit, arbitrary and excessive amercement was not unknown. It seems, moreover, established that Henry II was not above setting aside the due course of law, and resorting on occasion to arbitrary imprisonment, to which the penalty *pro despectu brevi regis* easily lent itself. As against this ill-defined prerogative in criminal law, there was already established the notion that the crown was bound by its own procedure. It is probable that Henry's thirty-five years were sufficient

[1] Pipe Roll, 16 Hen. II (Lancs).
[2] *Ibid.* 22 Hen. II (Staffs).   [3] *Ibid.* 26 Hen. II (Lancs).

to accustom the barons to a common law which was conterminous with the nation and brought it under a common guarantee of right, and in this they were no more than abreast of an age which was turning to legal antiquarianism to satisfy a new sense of the value and unity of the English legal heritage.[1] Richard on his accession felt it right to release all those who had been imprisoned in his father's reign without legal process, and, in so doing, admitted that no subject ought to suffer in his civil rights except *per commune rettum*.[2] The succeeding reigns were to show that the barons accepted such process without reserve, and were ready to pose as its legitimate defenders if the king, as principal trustee, made default. It is true, as has already been said, that the great councils were inadequate as a means of bringing pressure upon the crown, and that opposition was fitful and took in extremity the feudal form of diffidation and war, but the lawyer's aphorism, *quod aequitatis servus est princeps*, was dangerously near to being given a political interpretation[3] and becoming a principle of political opposition. There is much in the risings of 1191 and 1215 which foreshadows the more purely political activity of the later thirteenth century.

Prospect of later opposition By the end of the twelfth century, therefore, it can no longer be taken for granted that the feudal order will be indifferent to law and order. This change in outlook was in itself a major revolution in the constitutional situation, but its effects were hastened and made inevitable by the ambiguous standing of the magnates' special custom, that of knight service and baronage. Henry's government had been conservative in taxation with the one exception of the Saladin Tithe, and had supported itself by feudal services which were not intolerably burdensome. There was almost no incident of military tenure, relief, wardship, marriage, scutage, aid, or bodily service which was free from ambiguities. Yet the belief of the barons, as of all other free men, was that their obligations were fixed by custom, and beyond the power of their lord to vary. On the whole, Henry II, though he introduced variations into its incidents which had no warrant in the past, seems to

[1] As in the London texts of the Laws of Cnut, the Confessor, and the Conqueror.

[2] Howden, iii. 4. That is, by common presentment.

[3] Giraldus, *De Principis Instructione*, viii. 33: *Terrena justitia . . . per quam humana societas et cohabitatio confoederantur.*

have satisfied his tenants that he was remaining within the general scope of custom, that he was not making the vagueness of their services an excuse for increasing them beyond measure, nor turning customary dues into an elastic source of revenue. Here, again, the Angevin dynasty might be on the edge of a drastic clarification. It only needed a period of unbroken war, a burden for which the customary services of feudalism were never devised, to make the need for a steady and greatly increased revenue imperative. When that happened there would be a strong temptation for the crown to find its money in the only quarter where it had a traditional right to ask for it, from its vassals, by exploiting the element of indefiniteness in feudal service. The reign of Henry had prepared the way for opposition as much by its reforms in the field of law as by its conservatism in finance. Careless or unjust administration, coupled with an attempt to turn customs into unlimited, arbitrary taxation, would almost certainly precipitate a reaction.

iii

ANGEVIN MONARCHY IN CRISIS. 1189–1216

From 1066 to 1189 there had been a steady growth in the power of the crown and in its resources of administration. But that power in the English polity which resided in the council of the notables, or in its local assemblies, had, no doubt, survived without much real diminution. With the accession of Richard we come to a new phase of its evolution, in which the community begins to realize the potentialities of bureaucracy for oppression, while the baronage remembers that it is an integral part of the government, and begins to reclaim in action what it has never lost in principle. In part this is due to the fact that officials are multiplying and government is becoming more intense, in part to the fact that the loss of Normandy freed a proportion of the barons from continental interests, but most of all to a change in the tenure of the crown. Only one king between 1066 and 1189 was weak, and none was wholly tyrannous, while from 1189 to 1272 the throne was occupied first by a Crusader, then by an incalculable egotist, then by a minor and a monarch of obstinate but weak will dominated by foreign politicians. Under such kings the baronage, which had partly shed its particularist ambitions, and was coming to think of itself as leader of the community, entered increasingly into the foreground of history. The reign of Richard continued the routine of his father, and, though it produced certain elaborations of Henry's methods of local government which have rightly aroused the attention of historians, its essential interest is in the abandonment of the Henrician bureaucracy to justify itself to the country under vicegerents in the absence of the crusading king. From December 1189 to October 1191 England was in the hands of the Norman William des Longchamps—a man of no standing save such as his abilities had gained him in the service of Geoffrey of York and as chancellor to Duke Richard—who combined the offices of justiciar, chancellor, and legate, and thus concentrated in himself the responsibility of both church and state. Than this no better test of the solidity of Henry's governmental system could have been devised.

Accession of Richard I   The strength of the feudal relation as it had been left by Henry enabled Richard's lordship to be assumed from the moment of his father's death. Queen Eleanor went at once upon a provincial progress, receiving the homages of all freemen to Richard as *Dominus Angliae*. The coronation itself, which followed two months after Henry's death, confirmed the dignity of the crown by its unusual pomp and by its conformity with English precedent. Ceremony apart, the situation was overshadowed by the need to devise what must in effect be a continuance of the régime without the ruler. The past seventy years had seen the daily government of the country withdrawn from the baronial counsellors by imperceptible stages, and entrusted to *familiares*, of whom only a minority were barons, but whose actions might still, upon a favourable interpretation, be thought of as those of ministers of the king in an honorial state. Richard's original scheme for government during his absence continued this tradition. A committee of the judiciary was appointed with the bishop of Durham and William de Mandeville, earl of Essex and Aumale, as principal justiciars. The former, being newly earl of Northumberland, was probably chosen for his power over the North, while Mandeville was one of the greatest earls and a trusted statesman of Henry II. With them were associated *ad regimen regni* four of the justices of the late reign. Geoffrey fitz Peter, William Briwere, Robert de Wihtefeld,

Government in Richard's absence

and Roger fitz Rainfrai. William des Longchamps was made chancellor of England. The commission of government thus represented both the professionals and magnates of the *curia*, and perpetuated their close relation with each other, and Richard sought to make its task easier by placating the most influential of the magnates by wholesale grants of local authority. Of Henry's ministers, Hubert Walter was made bishop of Salisbury, Richard fitz Neal, the treasurer, bishop of London, Godfrey fitz Lucy, bishop of Winchester. William Marshal was given the honour of Pembroke. Hugh, bishop of Coventry, was allowed to buy three sheriffdoms, the bishop of Winchester that of Hampshire.[1] Of Henry's sons, Geoffrey was assured of the archbishopric of York and forced to take orders and to swear to absent himself until Richard returned, while to John, the most dangerous factor of all, were given the earldom of Gloucester, the counties of Cornwall, Devon, Somerset, Dorset, and Derby, and the castles of Marlborough, Lancaster, Ludgershall, the Peak, and Bolsover. On the whole, this commission of government retained its hold upon the country to an extraordinary degree during the four and a half years of the king's absence, and might have been entirely successful had it not been for the death of William de Mandeville and the supersession of the bishop of Durham by the chancellor, William des Longchamps, who from December 1189 combined the offices of justiciar,[2] chancellor, and legate.[3] The consequence of his rise to power was to destroy the balance of forces which Richard had planned, and to throw into the background the judiciary and with it the baronage, since Longchamps habitually used his title of chancellor[4] and governed mainly through his influence in the Exchequer.

Longchamps' career is an illuminating example of the power which had come to be latent in the offices, and which the par- *Longchamps' predominance*

[1] An equal motive for these grants was, of course, the great sums for which they were bought. They were made to ecclesiastics and courtiers and, if the cession to John be regarded as upon a different footing, their extent and unwisdom has been exaggerated.

[2] Whether he should be given the title of chief justiciar is doubtful. Richard's commission from Bayonne (June 6, 1190) does not give it. Diceto, ii. 83.

[3] The combination of supreme spiritual and temporal power came to be feared, and was afterwards objected against the appointment of Hubert Walter. Diceto, ii. 128.

[4] *Epistolae Cantuariensis*, 367–370.

ticular distribution of office in 1189 brought to the surface. Under Henry II the routine of administration had been stereotyped, and the officials responsible would no longer act unless they had the authority of writ from the appropriate minister authenticated by the king's seal.[1] In Henry's reign the seals were already two, duplicate seals of majesty, one resident in the Treasury, and the other, *sigillum deambulatorium*, itinerant with the king. It is possible that there was also a third, small seal for less formal business.[2] Most of the routine of government turned upon the two greater seals, and both were in the custody of the chancellor,[3] who supervised the form of all writs personally or through his deputies, and by sealing them gave them currency and effect. When the king was in England, or was represented by a strong justiciar, the sealing function of the chancellor was, no doubt, automatic, though *The Seals* it has been suggested that Henry II's preference for employing a vice-chancellor or *custos* was based on experience of the obstinacy of chancellors. Then the writs of the Exchequer—*liberate, computate,* and *perdono*—would nominally be ordered by the chief justiciar, the legal writs would be matters of routine, and letters ordering less specialized action would proceed from the initiative of the king and *curia* in the form of letters close and patent. But immediately on the departure of Richard and the death of William de Mandeville, Hugh of Durham being left sole justiciar, the strength of a recalcitrant chancellor became apparent. Hugh's authority was rejected by the barons of the Exchequer.[4] Whether this was brought about by the chancellor refusing to seal writs at his order, or by the treasurer refusing to initiate them, we do not know, but it must have been due to Longchamps' influence in the Exchequer, and its effect was to deprive Hugh of all financial resources. For this reason, if for no other, his justiciarship was inoperative from the outset, and Longchamps secured his supersession from Richard without difficulty.

It is significant that when installed in power Longchamps habitually emphasized his title as chancellor—the more so if he

---

[1] *Dialogus de Scaccario*, i. 15.

[2] For much of what follows see T. F. Tout, *Chapters in Administrative History*, vol. i.

[3] The seal of the Exchequer, that in *thesauro*, was in the treasurer's charge, but was kept in a bag sealed by the chancellor.

[4] Devizes, §15: *A baronibus scaccarii non receptus.*

had the status of Chief Justiciar—governing *per breve cancellarii*. The reason for this must be that he had merely replaced Hugh of Durham, and had not rid himself of the four justiciars associated *ad regimen regni*, for whose authority in the general business of the kingdom Richard had left a small seal, *regia maiestate signatum*, taking the deambulatory seal with him.[1] In the autumn of 1191, when it was safe to do so, these justiciars testified that Longchamps had habitually ignored them in all matters of importance, and it is to be supposed that it was to make this independence effective that he refused to use the king's seal, and as a rule authenticated his acts of government with his own private seal. The chancellor's writ, therefore, appears during this interlude of masterless government, as expressing the personal will of the chancellor, who, controlling the Exchequer through the great seal *in thesauro*, and the *Bureaucracy* rest of the administration with his signet, evades every constitu- *without* tional check upon his power, and is truly, as William of Newburgh *the King* says, *Caesar et plus quam Caesare*.[2] Thus, the effect of check and balance, which highly developed administrative offices are bound to exercise upon each other, was nullified, and the united power of the Angevin bureaucracy flowed through the chancellor's single will. Supreme in the Exchequer, he was able to maintain a mercenary army of knights and sergeants by drafts upon the farms of the counties[3] and upon the Treasury,[4] to garrison the castles in his own, and, as he maintained, in the king's interest, and to move about the country in safety. His personal retinue was of a thousand men-at-arms, and the sheriffs were empowered to establish their own mercenary guards *pro pace servanda*.[5] More limited, but formidable when freed from royal supervision, was his power in Chancery. The see of Canterbury was in the chancellor's custody *sede vacante*. He used his authority to inhibit Walter of Coutances' intervention in the imminent election,[6] and to scheme for his own succession, which would have made him impregnable. As chancellor, the escheats were in his special charge,[7] and the crown ward-

---

1 T. F. Tout, *Chapters in Administrative History*, i. 148 and note.

2 William of Newburgh, p. 331.

3 Pipe Roll, 3 Rich. I (Kent).

4 *Ibid.* (Tower of London). Henry de Cornhill accounts for £1200 *de thesauro per breve cancellarii . . . ad faciendum liberationes militum.*

5 *Ibid.* (Staffs). W. Newburgh, 334, calls them *armatae inmanum barbarorum catervae.*   6 Diceto, ii. 93.   7 *Ibid.* ii. 91.

ships placed in his hands the heirs of a number of the great honours. Beyond all this was that general power over the *negotia regni* which he should have exercised in concert with the justices his subordinate colleagues, but which he in fact exercised by his sole discretion and by his personal writ.

Baronial opposition The form taken by reaction against such an exaggeration of the bureaucracy cannot but be of historical importance. How far the country had travelled from the mood of 1173 is proved by the closeness with which all parties to that reaction adhered to the spirit of Henry's government. The first occasion of opposition was, it is true, such a grievance as might have been urged twenty years earlier. Gerard de Camville's castellanry of Lincoln was reclaimed by the chancellor for the king. He did homage to John to gain his protection, and the two raised the cry that it was against custom that such custodies should be taken from men of standing in the realm and given to obscure foreigners.[1] But, though John's opposition began with an echo of feudal ambitions and concealed a plot to oust Arthur from his claim to the succession, and though it came near to an armed clash with the king's officers at Lincoln, Tickhill, and Nottingham, it gathered no feudal support, and was almost immediately brought under the control of more responsible forces. Assessors, among whom the earls Warenne, Albini, and Clare represented the chancellor, met at Winchester on April 25, 1191, and imposed a settlement, favourable to John, but preserving the form of royal supremacy, since his castles were to be surrendered, though only as a prelude to their return to his castellans. Soon after this Walter de Coutances, archbishop of Rouen, reached England with letters from the king, though he did not for some time produce them. They were designed to adjust the balance of the government, if necessary; one was addressed to Longchamps and the other justices of the commission, authorized Walter to associate himself with them, and ordered them to do nothing without his advice, while an alternative commission to William Marshal and his colleagues authorized them to act without the chancellor if he should appear unfaithful.[2] By the middle of May, therefore, there was in England, though as yet unknown to any but its bearer, a commission alternative to that of Longchamps, which might become available

[1] Devizes, §38.   [2] Diceto, ii. 90, 91.

to legitimize any opposition which should justify itself in Walter's judgment. It was in these circumstances that, taking advantage of the truce and of the failure of the archbishop to produce Richard's letters, the chancellor again moved against Camville in the summer. It is noteworthy that he thought it possible to call out a third of the feudal levy to support him, and that an arbitration similar to the last, with the justiciars and the earls still upon his side, produced for him a better settlement than the last. The final crisis came when the justices were dispersed about the country upon eyre, and it was, perhaps, the first in which moderate men could have felt Longchamps to be entirely in the wrong. Archbishop Geoffrey, still bound, according to Longchamps, by his oath not to enter England, freed from it, according to his own account, by the king, landed at Dover, and, on the chancellor's instructions, was arrested. Probably without the latter's connivance, he was somewhat roughly handled, and kept for eight days a prisoner in Dover Castle. Parallels, not entirely justified, with the martyrdom of Becket were imagined,[1] and during those eight days the whole country united against Longchamps, making, as Giraldus says, the archbishop's cause their own.[2]

The most striking feature of this movement is that it was, within the range of ideas of the day, constitutional, that is to say that it produced no free-lance outbreaks for sectional ends, that its first appeal was to the justiciars,[3] that it drew together the spiritual and temporal baronage to a common cause, and brought them to a succession of meetings at Marlborough, Reading, and London whose claim was that, although ready to use force, they were the feudatories in legitimate council. From the moment of John's general summons issued from Marlborough[4] the crisis was, indeed, a rivalry between the chancellor and his opponents to set the stamp of constitutional legality upon their own standing, and to brand that of the other party with rebellion. The justiciars and

[1] *Epistolae Cantuarienses*, 370.
[2] Giraldus, *Vita Galfridi*, 397.
[3] *Ibid.* 396: *Primo . . . Willelmum Marescallum . . . deinde Willelmum Briware . . . et Galfridum filium Petri . . . Rothomagensem quoque Archiepiscopum Walterum . . . et Episcopum Wintoniensem.*
[4] This convoked the notables *sicut diligitis honorem Dei, et ecclesiae, et domini regis, et regni, et meum . . . tractaturi de quibus magnis et arduis negotiis domini regis et regni*: the question of authority is evaded, but the summons is upon the king's business. Diceto, ii. 98.

the barons summoned Longchamps to appear before them to receive the *judicium regni*.[1] He, in his turn, cited the magnates for treason, the bishops by their regalia and the barons by their baronies, and ordered them to desert John as conspiring to the crown.[2] Upon this the magnates advanced through Oxford to Reading, and there, hearing for the first time the text of the king's letters associating the archbishop of Rouen with the government [3] and the statement of the justiciars that they had been deprived of their due authority, prepared to meet Longchamps as a constituted government under the royal authority of Walter de Coutances and those who were now his colleagues.

Constitutional basis of the opposition

All this, inevitable in view of Richard's absence and John's ambitions, is interesting mainly as anticipating the later movement of the Charter, with which it has in common the nature of the provocation which caused it, its considered and moderate aims, and its regular course of action. Above all, it is clear that, in spite of the rapid growth of officialdom and *ex officio* action, the baronage, lay and spiritual, have maintained their sense of being an integral part of the régime—*judices* if not—without special commission—*justiciarii regis*, and counsellors. It is this that they assert against a chancellor who is only one of five justiciars, whose authority is the king's letter ordering the obedience and counsel of his lieges, but who has consistently avoided that counsel and governed alone.[4] Not only the special grievance of Gerard de Camvill and his patron John, but the general grievances, true or false, of unjust levies and abusive treatment of the royal wards in his care as chancellor, aroused individual resentment and might have been pressed with individual violence. Instead, John's treasonous aims were subdued to the common purpose, and the opposition moved through increasingly constitutional stages till it embodied the new government under the king's commission. To the baronage archbishop Walter appealed as to the legitimate force by which the king's letters might be put into effect when the executive had got out of control, *ut in cancellarium unanimimiter insurgerent,*

[1] Giraldus, *De Vita Galfridi*, 397.   [2] *Loc. cit.*

[3] *Diceto*, 400. Benedict (ii. 213) says the commission was not produced till the last moment in London, but this hardly seems possible.

[4] Howden, iii. 143. Giraldus, *Vita Galfridi*, 400. *Alii justiciarii, quos ei socios et coadjutores a principio rex adjunxerat, publice proclamarunt, quia nihil omnino eorum consiliis actum est.*

et eum tanquam inutilem regi et regno a potestate dejicerent, aliumque magis accomodum communi consilio instituerent.[1]

The chancellor was, indeed, deposed from the supreme power *Reconsententia diffinitiva, communi censura omnium*, and, from the moment of his elimination, abruptly the government reverted to its due monarchical style. The arrogant authority of the chancellor's writs, *Willelmus Dei gratia Eliensis episcopus, apostolicæ sedis legatus, et domini regis cancellarius*, with the convenient *teste meipso* avoiding the conciliation of witnesses, gave place again to the fiction of the king's presence, *Ricardus Dei gratia rex*, and the test of the new justiciar.[2] The wheels of the constitution settled back into their wonted coördination. Archbishop Walter is put in Longchamps' place; not absolutely—he is to act by the will and assent of his associate justiciars, and by the counsel of the barons of the Exchequer,[3] who are changed for supporters of the *coup d'état*.[4] The seal, to Longchamps' exasperation, is borne for the new ministry by his old subordinate, Benedict of Sansetun.[5] Government is of set intent brought again under the king's seal,[6] and in this we may see how clearly the opposition had analysed the disruption of Henry's machine, and the evils of an irresponsible executive. The St. Paul's council of October 8[7] takes on something of the pretensions of a constituent assembly, and, having recreated a régime,[8] invests John with the empty title of *summus rector totius regni*, and grants the Londoners their commune. Until Richard's return

[marginal note: Reconstruction of the Government]

---

[1] Giraldus, *Vita Galfridi*, 400. To rise against the chancellor with one accord and depose him as useless to the king and kingdom, and to appoint a more suitable person by common consent.

[2] *Epistolae Cantuarienses*, 377, Oct. 10, 1191.

[3] Howden, iii. 141.

[4] Devizes, §50.

[5] Howden, iii. 154.

[6] *Epistolae Cantuarienses*, 378 (John and Walter to Christ Church): *Propter praeteritas quas audisti contentiones communi deliberatione fidelium domini regis statutum est, ut sub sigillo domini regis de negotio regis mandata regia fiant communiter et discurrant*: because of the late dissensions of which you have heard, it is decreed by common deliberation of the king's lieges, that the king's writs upon his affairs shall run under the seal of the lord king.

[7] Howden, iii. 141.

[8] *Justiciarius supremus post comitem, justiciarii errantes, custodes scaccarii, castrorum constabularii, omnes novi de novo instituuntur*: a justiciar ranking first after earl John, justices in eyre, Exchequer officials, castellans, all new men with fresh commissions. Devizes, 50.

frequent councils[1] secure that the regent judiciary, already brought into harmony with the Chancery and Exchequer, shall not again lose touch with the magnates, and in executive routine and in every crisis of those troubled years we find the justiciars acting in common[2] in the interest of the crown.

Nature of the crisis of 1191

Taken in its essentials, apart from the personal factors of John's treason and Richard's ambiguous policy, the episode of 1189–91 reveals the dangers of Angevin administration when the departments were not kept under rigid control, and the attitude of the barons towards it. To put that attitude into words is, no doubt, to give it a precision which it did not yet possess. The conventions of feudalism in private relations were already defined; the action of a council of tenants-in-chief in a constitutional crisis was not. In 1191, therefore, step by step, the profounder issues of constitutional right were evaded because not clearly seen. There is confusion, which, indeed, corresponds to reality, between the rights and functions of the king's born counsellors, the barons, and those of his commissioned officers, the justiciars; the lines between counsel, judgment, and constitutional action are altogether blurred. The baronial attitude is one of acceptance of the principles of Angevin government, but of acceptance upon the implied understanding that the executive of judiciary and finance is in essence a contracted expression of government by *rex in consilio sapientum*, that its action must follow accepted channels, secure that warrant of the seals which guarantees its coördination under the crown, and be kept in general conformity with the views of the wider and vaguer *curia* of the magnates. These are indefinite principles drawn from the accepted relation of lord and vassal rather than from experience of politics, but, in the light of them, the barons retained their sense of being the natural counsellors of the king, and were capable in emergency of laying hands upon the parts of the executive and moulding it to their convictions. 1191 was in the nature of a *coup d'essai*. Within a generation they were to find a greater cause and a more formidable antagonist, but this

[1] As in 1192 at Windsor, Oxford, London, and Winchester to counter John's disposition to visit France. Devizes, §75.

[2] Howden, iii. 187, 204, 205, 207, 210, 212, 225. So, in November 1191, John, Walter, *et alii justitiarii nostri* intervene in the Canterbury election *communi familiarum et fidelium nostrorum consilio. Epistolae Cantuarienses,* 371.

view of the constitution was to guide them for the next century.

The crisis of 1191 marks the entry of the baronage into the political field, not as individual parties to tenurial contracts but as critics of and participators in government, and is, in a sense, a *King and* prelude to the greater effort of 1215, but it has the exceptional *baronage* qualities of a crisis and of an absent crown. With that revolution before us it becomes profitable to enquire how far the magnates claimed, or were accorded, a share in government not in crises but in the common course of affairs, for what acts of state the *consilium et consensus baronum* was required.

The old tradition was government with counsel, as that of the Saxons had been government by *sapientes*. There is as yet no notion of treating the *consilium* as a body whose function it is to oppose, nor any demand for a defined council of fixed membership. If anything, the barons are losing influence between 1154 and 1189. The great feasts which they attend have lost their business function. The king conforms with ceremony and then passes on to work through the year in a series of councils whose composition is determined by the place where they are held and the business to be done.[1] Henry kept the *Baronial* Christmas court of 1176 at Nottingham, and then moved at once *counsel* to Northampton—the road centre of the north Midlands—and held a great council with the bishops, earls, and barons of the kingdom. Flemish ambassadors were received and dismissed with proposals for an alliance. William of Albini was made earl of Sussex and given his father's lands. The honours of the earls of Chester and Leicester were restored to them, their rebellion being now purged. One great judgment was delivered, that between the earl of Leicester and William de Cahaignes, and the canons of Waltham resigned their house into the king's hand. This was clearly government *cum consilio magnatum* at its fullest. But in February the king was at Winchester, with what attendance we are not told, though evidently with no great assembly, and there ordered a levy of the feudal host, not for the customary forty days, but for a full year at the barons' charges, and this we are told he did at the prompting of his household, *per consilia familiarum*

[1] The following is the account of Benedict of Peterborough.

suorum.[1] On May 2, at Geddington, a king's house on the North Road, Henry summoned the archbishop of York and three bishops and many earls and barons to meet him *ad tractandum de pace et stabilitate regni.* On the 8th he was at Windsor, and met a much fuller council, "almost all" the bishops, earls, barons, and knights: in fact, the feudal levy that he had ordered in February. Again there was much debate as to the peace and security of the realm, and by the counsel of the bishops, earls, and barons, the castellans were removed throughout England and knights of the king's household placed in their stead, the earl of Chester's castles were given back to him, and he was commissioned to reduce Ireland to order in anticipation of Prince John's visit. Later in May a conference with the Welsh was held at Oxford, their princes did homage, and John was made king of Ireland in the presence of the magnates of the new realm, and certain honours were allotted to the service of Waterford, Wexford, and Dublin.

In all this there is clearly no rule, save that the king acts with counsel, and probably with as much compliant counsel as he can get. The principle is nothing more defined than common sense making the best of time, place, and persons in using the baron's duty of counsel. There is no jealousy as to attendance or exclusion,[2] and, unless we may find it in the making of an exceptional feudal levy "by the advice of the king's familiars", no attempt to evade discussion. Equally there is no attempt to prescribe a quorum without which initiative is invalid. Indeed, the line between the *familiares* and the wider circle of magnates is not yet one of class or office if we exclude the now established practice of judgment through a high court of justiciars not all of baronial rank. The group of barons who act with Henry throughout their lives— William de Mandeville, the earl of Arundel, Richard de Humez, and a few more—are *familiares*, but emphatically of the great baronage. Officials like Richard fitz Neal, or Richard de Lucy, are men of hardly lesser rank, and after 1177 the chancellor was the king's son. The king, indeed, has come to be the one fixed centre of government, and *consilium—magnum* or otherwise—does not call

---

[1] The collection of the Saladin Tithe in 1188 was determined *consilio fidelium (regis)*, which seems to point to a similar group of *familiares.*

[2] The king forbade access to the court to the rebels of 1177 until they had purged their offence, but this is an evident exception.

for the definite article. Counsel seeks no stable embodiment, but is spoken through the mouths of *sapientes, familiares, magnates regni*, who come and go as the king's affairs or their own move them. Such varied counsel is accepted as a fulfilment of the principle that the king's councillors are his barons, for, on the whole, the magnates trust and accept the régime.[1]

It is certain that however far back in English or Norman history we go we shall find that the function of judgment was inherent in assemblies of notables. So much is basic in the public life of the northern world, and, while the reign of law was supreme and legislation as such unknown, this one function embodied public life at its fullest in the *curia*. This was true of honour and kingdom alike. But by the twelfth century it was no longer enough. Innovations in custom were becoming too numerous to pass uncriticized, and refinements in the procedure of courts were in sum altering their whole basis. Acts of state could no longer be explained solely *Assize* as judgments or recognitions of custom. With the reign of Henry II a new device, the assize, comes into politics. It is something set by agreement—*assisa statuta, assisam statuere* are common amplifications—and it marks the first realization that custom can be changed by the will of those who live under it or govern by it. With the assize we are at the headspring of English legislation, which, strangely, descends not from the national code-making of the eleventh century, but from the agreements of feudal tenants and their lords. The assize may be used for a number of cognate purposes, but it keeps within a narrow range. It may settle and declare points of custom which are open, it may bring inequalities of custom to a common rule among peers of any honour or administration, or, more fruitfully, it may make innovations in procedure or service such as are felt to lie within the spirit, but not the letter, of existing custom. The same principle of agreed and established, assized clarification or innovation may be found in the *redditus assisae, opera assisa*, of most manors, in the standards set for the staple trades, such as the assizes of Cloth, Bread, and Ale, or in the assizes of the Forest or of Arms, which bind all freemen of

---

1 The undifferentiated standing of officials and magnates in counsel is expressed in a favourite phrase of Richard's *communi familiarum et fidelium nostrorum consilio* (Epistolae Cantuarienses, 379 [1191]), *a plerisque magnatibus et familiaribus nostris suaderetur* (Diceto, ii. 128 [1195]).

the realm. The distinguishing marks of the assize, by which in combination it is distinguished from the *judicia* or recognitions of the past, are that it is admittedly new enactment, that it requires the consent of the lord or prince,[1] and that it must apply throughout the area of administration for which it is promulgated.[2] In this it is *communis assisa*, and is not the effect of individual submission but of common assent,[3] though such assent may be expressed without the formality and conclusiveness of the decisions of assemblies in later days. Such assizes, essentially legislative, will, if they are applied often enough and to matters of sufficient importance, bring the problems of will and authority, counsel and the initiative of the prince into an entirely new light.[4]

We must not exaggerate the importance of assizes at the beginning of the thirteenth century. They were the first link in the chain of legislation, and this link was from the beginning partly held by subjects, so that legislation began with the principle of assent; but they were the first link only. The legal assizes of Henry II were, of course, of the greatest value for the future, and to some extent their importance was realized at the time. During an episode of legal revolution the acquiescence of the magnates was vital. Henry had promised "that all my men shall enjoy their liberties and free customs" undisturbed,[5] and not without "long and deep counsel" could he have disquieted, as the proprietary and possessory assizes did, that ancient custom which accorded to all freemen

Limited scope of assize

---

[1] Letters Patent, 8 John, p. 72: *Est inauditum tempore antecessorum nostrorum et nostris quod assisa nova statuatur in terra alicuius sine assensu principis terre illius*: it has been unknown in our time or our ancestors' that a new assize should be set up in any land without the prince's assent.

[2] Glanvill, *Tractatus de Legibus*, ix. 10, distinguishes between what is *per assisam generalem determinatum* and *consuetudo singulorum comitatuum*.

[3] Assize of Clarendon, 1: *Facta a rege Henrico . . . de assensu Archiepiscoporum, episcoporum, abbatum, comitum, baronum, totius Angliae*. The Grand Assize was made *de consilio procerum*: Glanvill, *Tractatus de Legibus*, ii. 7. The assize of the Forest, *per consilium et assensum (magnatum) totius Angliae*: Stubbs, *Select Charters*, p. 186.

[4] It is possible that Glanvill saw some relevance to this in his paraphrase of the Institutes: *Leges Anglicanas licet non scriptas, leges appellari non videtur absurdum . . . eas scilicet quas super dubiis in concilio definiendis, procerum quidem consilio et principis accedente auctoritate constat esse promulgatas*: English laws may be called laws without absurdity, although they are unwritten ones, since they are promulgated . . . by the authority of the prince and the counsel of the notables. Prologue, Glanvill, *Tractatus de Legibus*.

[5] Coronation Charter; Stubbs, *Select Charters*, p. 158.

a defence of their life and lands by oath and ordeal. As it was, many feared and resisted the change.[1] But normally assize was rare, and consisted of minor standardizations of the material incidents of custom. There seem to have been four recorded assizes during John's early years, all *communi consilio baronum, per commune consilium regni*, and the like. The most important, perhaps, was the assize of money in 1205,[2] the least so the fixing of the price of lampreys *per consilium baronum nostrorum*.[3] The importance here is one of theory, and for the future. It is hardly likely to precipitate a constitutional struggle or to count among the major pretensions of the charter. Yet it is all that stands for legislation in this age and its nature is apparently already realized.

Royal finance is equally limited by its feudal preconceptions. *Authority* Only upon rare occasions did the aids conflict with custom. *of the* When, therefore, Howden and Coggeshall tell us that the aid for *aids and* the acknowledged occasion of Richard's ransom was authorized *services* at once by request of the king and by statute or edict of the justiciars,[4] contemporaries must have been much less conscious of the contradiction than are we ourselves. A king's ransom was a recognized occasion of aid; for the amount he must observe custom, and since custom will ultimately be determined by his court,[5] he is to some degree at the mercy of his vassals. Thus it is that the fact or fiction—it could be either in any given instance— that the aid is an act of grace, recurs uncriticized in royal and baronial correspondence,[6] while, at the same time, the earlier instances of resistance are individual and based upon some peculiarity in the tenure of the objector. It is the same with the duty of corporal service. When it is resisted it is usually by individuals who plead some special right—the refusal of 1205 to serve beyond

[1] Pipe Rolls, 13 Henry II, *passim*. Fines of those who refused to swear to the king's assize. Cf. also *Dialogus de Scaccario*, II. x. F.

[2] Letters Patent, 6 John, p. 54.

[3] *Ibid.* 8 John, p. 68.

[4] Howden, iii. 210; Coggeshall, 101.

[5] Glanvill, *Tractatus de Legibus*, ix. 8: *Iuste secundum considerationem curiae suae et consuetudinem rationabilem.*

[6] *Humiliter postulavit ut universi . . . tale auxilium facerent ei ad redimendum eum, unde ipse sciret eis grates.* Howden, iii. 208.

the sea was professedly in the king's own interest—or by groups who claim some difference of tenure in common. St. Hugh in 1198 pleaded that the see of Lincoln was exempt from service abroad, and in 1213 the *Northanhimbrenses* claimed the same, though they held by lay barony—"their charters" confined their service to England [1]—no doubt recalling that, in the case of some at least, their Saxon antecessors' service was that of *endemot* or defence between the Rere Cross of Stainmore and the Scotch border.[2] Such resistance was hardly a "landmark in constitutional history".[3] Rather, it revealed the absence of any sense of the nation or of any beyond a feudal responsibility, and it was probably coming to be realized as hopeless even in the reign of John. In 1205 the *assensus* of magnates was held sufficient to bind the knights of England to combine to produce a tenth of their number for an indefinite term of service and to impose forfeiture on those who defaulted.[4] The king himself determined the period of service [5] and soon was visiting individual defaults by disseizin without trial.[6]

Consent to exceptional aids On the other hand, it would seem that already in John's reign the feudal conscience was awake to the distinction between customary aids on the lord's accession and on the three non-recurrent occasions, and exceptional aids for other purposes, such as Glanvill thought to be doubtfully due, and that for such it was beginning to apply principles which were later of vital importance to the constitution. The latter were held to be of mere grace,[7] and latitude was allowed to the king as to their nature and incidence,

---

[1] Coggeshall, p. 167: *Asserentes non in hoc ei obnoxios esse secundum munia terrarum suarum.*

[2] Thus Patrick of Dunbar owed service of defence (*inborh* and *outborh*) in the march between England and Scotland for the barony of Beanly. Public Record Office. *Inquisitions Post-Mortem.* Edward I. ii. 741. The cornage tenures of Cumberland serve "in exercitu Scocie", *Testa de Nevill*, i. 350, and do not pay scutage under Henry II. Others pay. Pipe Roll, 18 Henry II.

[3] Stubbs, *Constitutional History*, i. 548 (of St. Hugh in 1198).

[4] Letters Patent, 6 John, p. 55.

[5] Letters Close, 6 John, p. 54: *standum nobiscum ad minus per duas quadragesimas*: to remain with us for at least two periods of forty days.

[6] *Ibid.* 14 John, p. 117.

[7] Glanvill, *Tractatus de Legibus*, ix. 8. Cf. John's appeal to the barons of Meath and Leinster for an aid: *precamur eciam quatinus pro amore nostro auxilium . . . faciatis ad civitatem nostram Dublin firmandam, tantum inde facientes quod justis petitionibus vestris nos libentius exaudire debeamus*: we pray you, as you love us . . . accord us an aid. Letters Patent, 8 John, p. 69.

so that a very fruitful license to experiment and innovate was permitted. Both king and subject might find it convenient to go beyond the traditional fixed levy upon the knight's fee. We may see these principles at work in the treatment of the aid of February 1207. No expedition to France could be pleaded as an excuse for a scutage, and seven scutages had already been taken since John's accession. He now asked for a proportion of revenue from the churches, which was refused, and the burden fell upon secular lands. At Oxford an aid of twelve pence in the mark of revenue, commonly referred to as a thirteenth, was granted *per commune consilium et assensum concilii.*[1] In addition, the king appealed to the clergy of Canterbury, citing the generosity of the council; but, being put off by promises of consideration which were not fulfilled, wrote a second letter asking that each individual should state upon a roll the amount that he personally was prepared to give. The difference in basis between these two levies is clear. The clergy could not be brought to the point of grant. The king, therefore, was at their mercy—since the aid was secular and for the general purpose of defence—and he bargained with them as individuals, though the interdict and the outlawry of the clergy were scarcely two months old. Of the obligatory nature of the secular aid, however, though it was for general defence, fell upon all who held lay fees, and was in an unaccustomed form, and so failed in every test of custom, there was never any doubt since it had received "common assent". Those who evaded it were to lose their lands or be reduced to slavery, the Northern religious houses, which had allowed their neighbours to hide their chattels with them to avoid assessment, were brusquely ordered to return them to their owners,[2] and the constable of Richmond,[3] who had made default, found his castle of Richmond sequestrated, and in eight days made his submission.[4] Aid granted by the order concerned, although not one of the three sanctioned by custom, is already valid and binding. Aid not so granted is dependent upon the mere grace of individuals.[5] How long this has been true we

[1] Letters Patent, 8 John, p. 72   [2] *Ibid.* p. 71.
[3] *Ibid.* p. 73.   [4] *Ibid.* p. 73.
[5] As, presumably, with the Londoners' aid of 1205, of which John received into the Camera 900 marks *de promisso quod nobis fecerunt ad auxilium nostre transfretacionis.* Letters Close, 7 John, p. 35. Mesne tenants were less fortunate and the king constantly granted his tenants-in-chief writs for aids for such various

cannot say, but it is possible that we may see the power of the *consilium* to bind the generality hardening during the first decade of John's reign. In 1199 the Cistercian abbots objected that they were bound not to make aid to secular powers *nisi communi consilio et assensu generalis capituli*,[1] while the canons of York pleaded the "liberties of their church". John did not feel able to put any of the penalties of 1207 in force against the abbots in 1199, and contented himself with putting them out of his protection, and turning their beasts out of his forest pastures. In 1207, on the other hand, Geoffrey of York resisted the aid, apparently as affecting the secular tenants of his church, and, with no more mercy than was shown to the constable of Richmond, his see was sequestrated, and he went into exile. In eight years practice, or theory, or both, have hardened, and the right of both king and magnates has moved towards definition.

Scutage   Scutage, unlike aid, seems to have been upon a prerogative basis, and there is no evidence of baronial consent. At least in his later years, John's practice was to proclaim a campaign, designate certain barons to follow him *per preceptum regis*,[2] perhaps even to allot others to garrison and council at home,[3] to issue writs granting their scutage to those who were crossing with him, and then to order the Exchequer to collect from the remaining fees at the prescribed rate and without further parley. *Scutagium statuimus*[4] is the phrase which governs the enactment, and, short of insisting on serving personally at many times the cost of the scutage, forcibly preventing the king from leaving England, or proving that he had never intended to do so, there was little customary ground for resistance. Indeed, this was not the end of the king's exactions on

purposes as the payment of their reliefs, or their debts, to equip them for his own service, and the like. The Charter reduced the aids of mesne tenants to the three customary aids of the realm, though this was not strictly observed.

    1 Coggeshall, p. 102.

    2 Hugh Peverel was excused scutage in 1214 as he was in Poitou *per preceptum regis*. Letters Close, 16 John, p. 167.

    3 Letters Patent, 16 John, p. 118. Barons urged to come to France *exceptis illis qui de consilio venerabilium patrum nostrorum domini Petri Wintoniensis Episcopi Justiciarii, etc. . . . in Anglia moram sunt facturi.*

    4 Letters Close, 16 John, p. 166: *Statuimus tres marcas capi de scutagio ad opus nostrum de singulis feodis. Ideo vobis mandamus quod scutagia illa . . . capi faciatis . . . preterquam de feodis militum . . . pro quibus litteras nostras de scutagio suo habendo warantum suscepitis.*

the score of scutage. John used even more summary methods at times, ordering his sheriffs to collect the levy direct from the sub-tenants over the heads of their lords,[1] and even permitting a magnate in favour to impose a scutage upon his tenants when there was none ordered from the realm.[2] Thus, the normal limita-tion of the sub-tenants' liability to the occasion *quando scutagium regis currit per patriam* was nullified, and a dangerous door was opened to indirect taxation of the lower grades of feudal tenure.

The executive, the most powerful force in the state, was *The barons* growing beyond the range of criticism and control. It had arisen *and war* within the sphere of the king's household, and was as personal to him as the household of any lord. Only in war, when the king's officers were in part his barons, could the voice of the council be effective, as when the king's galleys were allotted their stations *communi consilio baronum* in 1205,[3] or when the barons destroyed the king's hopes of an invasion of France in that year. Even here the constraint was military rather than constitutional, for the king was ready to turn from the barons to his bachelors, the squires and knights of his military household, and to lead a mercenary host out of England. Indeed, as John drew away from feudal towards mercenary war, the influence of English chivalry declined. The two most impressive and typical military achievements of the reign, the organization of sea-borne transport and supply under William de Wrotham, master of the king's ships and archdeacon of Taunton, and the defence of the West Country castles in 1216, turn entirely upon the trained capacity of officials and the loyalty of portsmen and mercenaries and are royal enterprises far beyond the scope and control of feudal magnates The administration as a whole could be and was given a quasi-military character which favoured John's tendency to treat it as an extension of his military household. Longchamps had shown how the shrievalty could be militarized, and in the second half of his reign John made free

---

[1] Letters Close, 8 John, p. 46: *Mandatum est Vicecomiti Kancie quod non distringet Johannem de Augi ad reddendum scutagium de tenemento quod tenet de feodo comitis Arundel . . . quia idem comes inde domino Regi respondebit.*

[2] *Ibid.* 14 John, p. 127. In 1212 he authorized William of Salisbury to take a scutage of three marks from his lands in seventeen counties. There was no national scutage in that year. Entries in the Fine Rolls suggest that John was allowing scutages to be taken in order to enable magnates to pay their fines to him. *Rotuli de Oblatis,* 16 John, 531.

[3] Letters Patent, 6 John, p. 52.

use of his foreign captains as sheriffs,[1] and, while the order of the realm rested ultimately upon the strength of the castles, their personal control by the king was so jealously guarded that at crucial moments, as in 1212, the custodians would not accept the authority of letters patent for their surrender, but demanded their delivery by a known intimate of the king.[2]

It is evident, therefore, that the reigns of Henry II, Richard I, and John are a period when many aspects of society, the state, and government are undergoing a process of analysis and clarification, with the result that the underlying principles of medieval politics are emerging into conscious appraisal. It is becoming

The final crisis probable indeed that certain of them will conflict with others. The feudatory sees the state as an honour upon a large scale. He knows that if its law is to be changed it must be by common assent of the tenants-in-chief, and that equally its contributions to the king are fixed by custom and cannot be increased arbitrarily or changed as to their nature. He knows that every judgment should be by the court of vassals, and he is only slowly realizing that the executive cannot be adequately discharged by a few great officials of baronial rank—stewards, constables, and the like. Even the sheriffs have at times been barons. But against all this the king has been governing through familiars and ministeriales. The Chamber, the Seneschalcy, the Chancery, and the Exchequer are its characteristic servants. Even judgment is being done on a large scale by justiciars, fewer and fewer of whom are of clear baronial standing. The principle of consent to non-customary taxation is not to be denied—but what is custom? The quarrels of the future, the very real constitutional differences of the thirteenth century come into view as soon as the skill of an analytical age has had time to exercise itself upon the raw mass of custom. The coming age, because it is one of perfected and rationalized law and administration will, for that very reason, be one of constitutional strife.

1 1208; Gerard d'Athies, Gloucester and Hereford: Philip Marc, Notts and Derby.

2 Letters Patent, 14 John, p. 94: *Quia credimus vos nolle castrum illud (Tickhill) liberare sola litterarum nostrarum auctoritate, mittimus ad vos dilectum et fidelem nostrum Magistrum Ricardum de Marisco. Ibid.* 16 John, p. 116. This came to be a normal safeguard under Henry III.

Nevertheless we must expect the constitutional principles of the opposition to John still to be, for the most part, those deducible from the rules of tenure and to reflect a very rudimentary political experience. The Articles of the barons and the Great Charter stood mainly for two things, the reassertion of the Henrician rule of law generally, but especially as it affected the great feudatories, and the clarification of the uncertainties of feudal custom, with some attempt to reintroduce the conventional standards of lordship into the relation of the king to those who were his subjects but also his vassals. Both of these ends would have been secured in a more experienced age by setting a permanent control upon the actions of the crown and its officials. The barons of 1215 sought the same end by the only means they knew and attempted a recognition of certain essential points of the law; we know now that no code of custom, however full, can of itself provide against every possibility of misinterpretation and abuse. The real problem was one of administration and of the character of the king, for no king could govern the Anglo-Norman baronage who did not himself exemplify the virtues of good lordship. Alone of his brothers, John was temperamentally *mauvais sire*, for chivalry and feudal convention, both in their strength and weakness, were antipathetic to him. He despised the military and administrative incompetence of the knightly order and its lack of conclusive purpose. He knew his barons to be treacherous subjects and contemptible enemies, and found loyalty, courage, and the skill of the new age in mercenaries and civilian clerks. But he underrated the cumulative force of a moral code which was higher than his own, and decisively nearer to that ideal of right Christian government which was held by all thinking men of his day. How *John and* far he was a tyrant to common men is doubtful. At least he knew *the people* where Angevin government pressed them, and in 1212, when he had discovered the treachery of his barons, and was confiscating their castles, he bid high for the support of the counties and boroughs, restoring the forest custom of his father,[1] and limiting the prises of his galley captains upon the ports.[2] In 1213,[3] and again

---

[1] Coventry, 214. Annals of Dunstable, *ann.* 1211. A writ of May 1212 ordering knights who are not verderers to meet Brian de Insula in every county north of Trent suggests that this concession was planned before the baronial treason. Letters Close, 14 John, p. 129.   [2] Coventry, 207.

[3] Letters Patent, 14 John, p. 97. Inquisitions on oppressions by the sheriffs of

in 1215, under the prompting of Nicholas of Tusculum, he entered upon an enquiry as to the sheriff's exactions, though the second inquest was interrupted by the barons' rising. The best known of his local officials were men who had served the nation well under Richard.[1] With his subjects, other than of the knightly order, he was accounted peace-loving and charitable.[2] London owed him gratitude for his share in creating her commune, and throughout his reign he sold municipal liberties freely. In return, reading the king's heart rightly or wrongly, the country did not follow the barons against him. London was surprised into admitting the barons' army and could not shake it off,[3] but the ports stood by him with persistent loyalty,[4] York stood a siege for him in 1216,[5] and beyond the range of the rebels' arms the land lay quiet.[6]

Yet we cannot doubt that John was a bad king for his age. Nature and experience turned his familiarity with the great feudatories into dislike and suspicion. When it was inexpedient to retaliate, as with William Marshal in 1205, he left the offender in no doubt as to the bitterness of his resentment. When, as against the Braioses, he was free to act, his revenge went beyond all reason. As the reign went on his temper hardened into contemptuous rejection of all the normal sanctions of vassalage, and to a suspension of many of the safeguards of common right.

Lincolnshire and Yorkshire. In 1212 he had allowed the knights of at least one shrievalty (Somerset-Dorset) *habere vicecomites ex seipsis*. Letters Close, 14 John, p. 131. Cornwall was entirely disafforested. *Ibid.* 16 John, p. 197.

[1] W. A. Morris, *Medieval Sheriff*, p. 163.

[2] Coventry, 207: *Viduis dicitur propitius extitisse, et pacis provisioni, quantum ad temporalia attinet, satis sedulus extitisse*: he is said to have been merciful to widows, and to have exerted himself constantly to maintain the peace in secular matters.

[3] Coventry, 220. Wendover, 116.

[4] Coggeshall, 181. The Cinque Ports submitted to Louis in collusion with John. Annals of Dunstable, 46. Seaford provides an interesting example of a borough which adhered to John against the orders of its rebel lord Gilbert de l'Aigle: *eidem Gileberto nec alicui alii inimico nostro aliquid unquam facere voluisti quod ad dispendium corone nostre redundaret*: you have never willingly helped the said Gilbert or any other enemy of ours against the interests of our crown. Letters Patent, 18 John, p. 196 (John's letter of thanks to the town).

[5] The mayor was rewarded with a grant of rebels' lands in 1215. Letters Close, 17 John, p. 260.

[6] There were riots in Northampton, and a baronial force at Exeter was dispersed. Coventry, p. 220; Annals of Dunstable, 48.

Judging from the Close, Patent, and Fine Rolls, John preserved the system of his father and brother without any glaring abuses during the first half of his reign, and remained upon terms with his barons which allowed of their meeting in council.[1] In 1205 came *John and the feudatories* the refusal of service beyond the sea by the magnates of the host, and in July Hubert Walter's restraint was removed by death. The year 1207 saw the quarrel with Rome, and 1208 the interdict and the sequestration of the church lands. For four years from 1208 the Chancery Rolls are lacking, but the sparse records of the chronicles suggest a growth of tension. The Christmas reunion of chivalry had been held by John for one day only in 1204.[2] By 1209 the barons attended reluctantly from fear of the king.[3] When we have the light of the Rolls again we find John upon the point of discovering the treason of 1212, and it is not too much to say that in this second phase of his reign he has changed from a king in the hard Angevin tradition to one who, at least to his nobles, is a tyrant.

No doubt the change was gradual. Already before 1208 the bad *Baronial hostages* precedent had been set of taking the heirs and friends of the barons as hostages, and so betraying the king's mistrust for the loyalty sworn in homage. It would seem to have begun, perhaps pardonably, with the taking of hostages from the Irish barons. In 1212, at least for the northerners, it had become almost a normal incident of tenure.[4] They were not always badly treated. The sons of Richard de Umfraville came in charge of their tutor, and were set to serve the queen's table,[5] but the pressure which could be brought to bear through them is shown by John's words to earl David in August 1212: "you have given us your son as hostage . . . therefore we order you to yield us your castle at Fotheringhay".[6] As John cut away his vassals' duty from its legiti- *Disseizin* mate basis and put it upon one of fear, he was also undermining their common law right. It is impossible to tell how many of John's

---

[1] Thus, in the spring of 1207 there were councils at London and Oxford, and an aid was granted.

[2] Wendover, ii. 9.   [3] *Ibid.* iii. 231.

[4] In 1212–13 we know of hostages held from Vaux, Lucy of Egremont, earl David, Muschamp, Umfraville, Merlay, Mowbray, Bruce, Clifford, Lindsay, Avenel, Comyn, Patrick of Dunbar. It is fair to say that he was only using a primitive right of the Norman dukes.

[5] Letters Close, 14 John, p. 122.   [6] Letters Patent, 14 John, p. 94.

orders to take lands into his hand were disseizins without judgment—possibly all that are minuted *per preceptum Regis*, and they are many—but of some instances we can be certain. In May 1212 the king ordered Ralf Berners to be disseized of his lands and his nephew given seizen if he did not cross to Poitou,[1] and in the same year the custos of Warkworth is warned that if he does not at once produce the pledge which his lord, earl Ferrars, has promised the king, the earl will be disseized of certain lands he holds in fee-farm.[2] Here John is using disseizin as an act of administrative routine, a kind of stronger distraint, and that he had come to adopt it as a principle we can infer from his admission in June 1215, "we are to restore to our barons all those lands, castles, and rights of which we have disseized any of them unjustly and without judgment".[3]

Charters of fealty

From 1212 an increasing number of the barons passed under a system which joined both these devices of terrorism, the exaction of hostages and the denial of legal defence, into a yoke which was inescapable. The pledge of hostages began to be supplemented or exchanged for a special charter from vassal to king, which renewed the obligation of fidelity, renounced all treasonous correspondence, and agreed that by the mere fact of such treason the lands, and in some the life, of the tenant should be *ipso facto* at the mercy of the crown. Apparently such charters developed out of John's agreements with foreign auxiliaries who were not bound to him as "natural lord"—the first of the kind seems to be that which gave a lodgment in English feudalism to Savary de Mauleon in 1206[4]—but after 1212 they become increasingly common as between the king and his native vassals. On August 24 of that year, within a week of John's discovery of the plot to seize him in the host, Richard de Umfraville yielded him a charter[5] promising his

---

[1] Letters Close, 14 John, p. 117. So Richard fitz Henry was disseized for not joining the army in 1213, and was only to be restored on compliance. *Ibid.* 15 John, p. 148.   [2] *Ibid.* 14 John, p. 119.

[3] The bulk of the lands referred to were probably seized after the barons had made their diffidation (*ibid.* 16 John, p. 200), but as early as 1213 the king found it necessary to command an inquisition whether Geoffrey de Lucy has been disseized of Newington *per voluntatem nostram vel per judicium curie nostre* (ibid. 15 John, p. 136). Other instances are Fine Rolls, 15 John, p. 471. Another not uncommon device of John's was to sell a writ for an inquisition to one party, and a second quashing the effect of the inquest to the other. Fine Rolls, p. 23.

[4] Letters Patent, 8 John, p. 66.   [5] Letters Close, 14 John, p. 122.

four sons as hostages with the cession of Prudhoe castle, and agreeing that if he should be discovered to have had part in the recent
treason, his sons, his lands, and his castle should be at the crown's
mercy, and that "we may do with his body as with that of a
traitor". The substance of this charter was suggested by suspicion
of treason, but John was quick to see its possibilities in the general
field of vassalage. In September 1213, John, constable of Chester,
could only secure his inheritance by binding himself by a similar
charter by which, though it acknowledged the special loyalty of
his father and himself,[1] he agreed *quod si unquam a servicio domini
regis recesserit et ad inimicos domini Regis divertit omnes terre sue et
tenementa sua domino Regi incurrantur*.[2] When, in the spring of 1216
many barons came to make submission, they found that they
could only do so by placing their lands and liberties outside the
law by such a *carta de fidelitate Regi*.[3] The king's plans for the
future state of his barons may be seen by the terms upon which
Gilbert fitz Reinfred,[4] one of the oldest servants of his own and his
brother's reign, but taken in arms in Rochester castle, purchased
his peace. He paid 12,000 marks, gave up Kendal and Merhull
castles with twelve hostages from the principal families of north
Lancashire, recanted his oath to the charter and to all the king's
enemies, swore to serve John faithfully all his life, and to submit
to perpetual disherison if he broke any part of his agreement. It is
fair to say that the charters of fealty were first prompted by a
legitimate fear of treason, and that record of them is most common
in the last year of the reign, when they became general. But a
clause of the charter[5] demands the giving back of all such charters
delivered to the king, and they must have been numerous by
1215. Had John reëstablished his power, there can be little doubt
that they would have superseded the legitimate feudal tie with its
patiently evolved safeguards of law. Their essence was that they
disclaimed the right of legal defence in advance, and made the

---

[1] *Pro bono et fideli servicio predicti patris ipsius . . . et servicio ejusdem Johannis
quod bonum et fidele dominus Rex spectat habere.* Fine Rolls, 15 John, p. 494.

[2] *Ibid.* p. 495: that if he ever went back from the service of the lord king, and
joined his enemies all his lands and tenements should be forfeit to the lord king.

[3] *Secundum tenorem aliarum cartarum quas alii qui ad pacem domini Regis venerunt
fecerunt.* Fine Rolls, 17 John, p. 575.

[4] W. Farrer, *Lancashire Pipe Rolls*, p. 257.

[5] Magna Carta, 49: *Omnes . . . cartas statim reddemus que liberate fuerunt nobis
ab Anglicis in securitatem pacis vel fidelis servicii.*

king's mercy the normal state of vassalage. They made homage meaningless, put tenure upon the ground of private agreement, and were, in effect, the forced acceptance by great individuals of that disherison without trial as the sanction of the king's precepts that John was making the rule in dealings with his feudal subjects as a whole.

The approach to the Charter

It was with this overwhelming threat to common right, and especially with certain great instances of its operation in their minds, that the barons approached the crisis of the charter. The natural point of departure for opposition in 1215 was, indeed, a legal one. In 1191 it could be maintained that the status of the chancellor was irregular, and there was a premature concentration upon the powers of the justiciary and the use of the seals, which was really beyond the natural capacity of the age. Not for sixty years would these issues be incorporated into an attack upon the crown as such. In 1215 the executive was that of the king without doubt, and its legitimacy was therefore beyond challenge. Only his use of it could be attacked, and that, with the ideas of that generation, could only be approached by the one channel in which he was responsible for his actions. The king was custodian of the law. Law must be restated and reaffirmed. There could be no disposition to criticize the basis or authority of administration; only to bring it back to its subservience to custom. It is said that at St. Paul's in the summer of 1213 Langton encouraged the barons to believe that they might recover their lost rights—*jura*—and that this was the mainspring of the revolt. The primary meaning of such terms would be concrete, relating to individual claims by inheritance or to defined points of customary right. The magnates had bargained with John upon his succession, exacting a promise *quod redderet unicuique illorum jus suum,*[1] such *jura*, no doubt, as the Ferrars claim to a share in the Peverel lands, which the earl did indeed receive in 1199.[2] The course of the charter negotiations shows that such rights were in the forefront of the barons' minds, and the first of all their demands, propounded five weeks before the general programme of the barons' Articles, and a

[1] Howden, *sub anno* 1199.
[2] The hundreds of Hecham, Blisworth, and Newbottle. Fine Rolls, 1 John, p. 3. The *comites Angliae* made the same claim before they would cross the sea in 1201.

condition to entering into treaty at all, was for the restoration of
the course of law. "We have conceded to the barons who are
against us that we will not take nor disseize them nor their men":
nisi per legem regni nostri vel per judicium parium suorum in curia Restora-
nostra.[1] Upon that same day, May 10, the parties to two of the *tion of*
great causes of the day, the Braiose bishop of Hereford and *judgment*
Geoffrey de Mandeville, ventured to test the king's sincerity in the *of court*
restoration of legal process, and brought their causes into court.
Geoffrey's case shows how plainly the special charters of the king
stood for the opposition in the forefront of his denial of the
common course of justice. A year earlier he had been granted the
marriage of the heiress of Gloucester with her honour, for which
a fine of 20,000 marks was imposed by way both of marriage
purchase and relief. By charter he had agreed to complete his
payment in sums of five thousand marks at successive terms
within the year, and to surrender all his lands to the king if he
failed at any one term.[2] In brief, much like his peers, who were
forced to warrant their loyalty by putting themselves in the king's
mercy, he had risked the tenurial right of all his lands, and debarred
himself from legal action upon his bargain. Assured now of the
judgment of his peers, he wished "to have the judgment of our
court as to the debt which is being exacted from him for having the
Countess Isabella to wife".[3] With him all those who had been deprived of their lands by the king's mere precept, and those who had
offered up their right by charter, would, by John's surrender of May
10, be restored to the primary right of their tenure—judgment.

In May the magnates were still concerned to restore a safe legal *The*
basis for themselves, for without it they could not have remained *barons'*
within range of the king's power. The privilege of May 10 is *right in*
therefore for the king's barons in the king's court. The legal pro- *judgment*
gramme of the Articles of the barons and the Great Charter[4]
broadens to the full scope of the law, covers the right of all those
who have a tenure in fee or socage, and makes provision for im-
provements in Henry II's procedural changes in the light of a

---

[1] Letters Patent, 16 John, p. 141: except by the law of our realm or by judgment of their peers in our court.
[2] Fine Rolls, 15 John, p. 521.   [3] Patent Rolls, 16 John, p. 141.
[4] The authenticity of the so-called Unknown Charter and its origin remain
matters of pure speculation, and it seems unsafe to use it in argument. Cf. W. S.
McKechnie, *Magna Carta*, pp. 171–5, and Appendix.

generation of experience. It is, in fact a restoration of Henry's law with such adjustment as time has suggested. The primary legal clause, from which all the others take their tone, reflects the fact that a process older than the assizes of Henry still holds part of the field, and that—perhaps especially for their own order—the magnates wish it retained. The king promises that no free man shall be imprisoned, disseized, or outlawed *nisi per legale judicium parium suorum vel per legem terrae.*[1] By one of the two forms, either assize or *judicium*, every man must be accorded fair trial of right. By 1215 most causes will, indeed, be decided *per legem terrae* but without judgment in the archaic sense of the term which still prevailed.[2] For every freeman there remained, however, the choice of the older English medial doom in civil causes and the Norman judgment after suit and witness, and the barons believe, and in part establish, that as barons they are immune from presentment for crime, and may seek judgment of court for that also. In May they had expressed this immunity as a right to judgment *in curia regis*: in June they found a more accurate and comprehensive term, the *judicium parium*, which, though it failed to become a decisive factor in English common law, was part of the feudal theory of justice. For the freeman not of baronial rank the judgment of peers would be fulfilled by judgment in his county, for the baron it meant trial by his own order in the king's presence, or at least in that of his chief justiciar, and they must have had in mind that deceptive correctness with which John had evaded trial of Eustace de Vesci and Robert fitz Walter before their peers in 1212.[3]

Safeguards of common law

Except for this touch of conservatism, the demand of the Charter is for the regular application of the common law as it then

[1] Magna Carta, 39.

[2] If the subject has been presented by his neighbours on a criminal charge under the Assize of Clarendon, or has applied for a writ of assize, there will, of course, be no *judicium parium*, for he will go at once to the ordeal, or stand or fall by the inquest. *Judicium parium* and *lex terrae* are therefore contrasted with each other. These processes, though not yet old, are assizes, and therefore part of the *consuetudo patriae, lex terrae.*

[3] Robert fitz Walter was cited for treason in four successive courts of his county of Essex, and outlawed by a Saxon enactment whose antiquity must have commended itself to the most austere defender of custom among the barons. But it was custom applied by the commonalty of a county under the eye of Geoffrey fitz Peter. Letters Close, 15 John, p. 165. Howden says that the same procedure was adopted in the case of Eustace de Vesci. The Devil was quoting scripture, as John often liked to do.

stood, and the Charter's legal clauses stand in natural succession to the great assizes of Henry. Experience must have taught the need of dividing the pleas of the crown, with their restricted right of delay and essoin, from the common pleas between subject and subject, and the Charter demands that *communia placita* shall no longer follow the king, but shall be tried in some fixed place.[1] It is the first clear recognition of a Common Bench. The assizes are to be taken four times a year by justiciars in every county,[2] and in this the whole Henrician system of writs and processes as Glanvill described them is seen to be accepted. Of all Henry's work, only the writ called *Praecipe*, which placed the justiciars in immediate jurisdiction of any cause to which it was applied, was singled out for condemnation: it deprived the plaintiff equally with the defendant of his choice of jurisdiction, and was a direct invasion of the judicial immunity of his lord. Thereby, "a free man might lose his court",[3] and the defendant his choice between judgment and assize.

The clauses dealing with the administrative safeguards of justice *Administrative safeguards of justice* are in advance of anything which has gone before them. They include a curious attempt to reconcile the old judicial quality of the *seniores* of the shire communities with the new commissioned justice; the itinerant justiciars are to have four knights elected by the county courts as associates in taking the assizes.[4] Here, too, we may detect the contemporary reverence for peerage. Glanvill's rule that amercements should be assized by the oath of neighbours and should not exceed the capacity of the payer is reiterated,[5] no king's officer is to have the right of putting men to the ordeal without adequate witness,[6] the writ *de odio et atia*, protecting the subject from malicious prosecution, is to be free to all,[7] and to no man "will the king sell,[8] or deny, or delay justice."[9] The process

---

[1] Magna Carta, 17.   [2] *Ibid.* 19.   [3] *Ibid.* 34.
[4] *Ibid.* 18.   [5] *Ibid.* 20.   [6] *Ibid.* 38.   [7] *Ibid.* 36.
[8] A reasonable and uniform charge for writs was never abandoned, but the monarchy had been used to selling inquests at prices which corresponded, if with anything, with the wealth of the suitor and the value of the land sued for. Thus in 1213 Alan of Galloway fined 340 marks for an inquest as to his mother's lands. Fine Rolls, 15 John, p. 467. A simple instance of the sale of justice is that of William de Braiose who buys a trial *coram rege* and will pay 700 marks if he wins and £100 if he loses (*ibid.* 1 John, p. 46). In the year 1200 William de Mowbray fined 2000 marks *ut dominus rex faciat eum deduci juste et secundum consuetudinem Anglie in loquela quae est inter ipsum et Willelmum de Stutevilla* (*ibid.* p. 102).   [9] Magna Carta, 40.

of stripping the sheriffs of their power of justice is completed, and none of the resident provincial officials are henceforth to hold the pleas of the crown. Taken together, these provisions well represent that phase of English jurisprudence when the practice of popular justice was giving place to judgment by special commission, and go as far towards securing that the new judiciary shall be an independent one as was then possible.

Feudal obligations defined

Most of this legal matter may be regarded as the vindication of preëxisting common right. The second great work of the charter is to bring to an end the indefiniteness of feudalism. For the first time the custom of English feudal tenure ceases to be a fluctuating, variously interpreted convention between lord and man, and takes its place as a defined component of English common law. We have seen how the feudalism of Henry lacked that fixity which might have safeguarded it from exploitation by John. The latter was no innovator in this, but his exactions were ceaseless and heavy, falling especially upon the open points of relief, wardship, marriage, aid, and scutage, and to prove them it should be sufficient to point to the rolls. They contain such outstanding cases as John of Chester's seven thousand mark fine for taking up his barony,[1] or William de Braiose's five thousand marks for his Irish lands—which ended by ruining him[2]—and they bear constant witness to the sale of wardships at prices which could hardly be recovered by fair means during a minority,[3] to fines exacted before their dower was accorded to widows,[4] for leave to remain unmarried[5] or marry where they will,[6] for the marriage of heirs and heiresses.[7] The charter seeks to fix what can be fixed at a reasonable level, enormously lower than the average exaction of the crown, and to protect women and minors in those relations with the king which were unavoidable in feudalism and capable of abuse, but which could not be reduced to figures. Relief is to be divorced

---

[1] *Fine Rolls*, 15 John, p. 483. Thurstan Banaster fined 500 marks for Makerfield (*ibid.* 15 John, p. 488). Its farm stood at about £23 when it was in the king's hand (W. Farrer, *Lancashire Pipe Rolls*, p. 246). This would be about fifteen years' purchase, and the last holder, Warin Banaster, had already been fined 400 marks in 1204 (Fine Rolls, 6 John, p. 207).

[2] *Ibid.* 6 John, p. 232.   [3] *Ibid.* 7 John, p. 316.
[4] *Ibid.* 6 John, p. 232.   [5] *Ibid.* 2 John, p. 82.
[6] *Ibid.* 2 John, pp. 91, 96.   [7] *Ibid.* 1 John, pp. 8, 24, 45, 57.

from the value of the inheritance and fixed at what the barons believed to have been its "ancient" rate, an earl for his barony, and a baron for his, a hundred pounds, a knight for a full knight's fee a hundred shillings, and from fractions of fees less.[1] No more than reasonable profit, without waste of men and chattels, is to be taken from estates under wardship,[2] and the estate is to be returned to the heir in full order when he comes of age.[3] Heirs are to be married within their own rank—*absque disparagatione*[4]—and after due notice to the kin. Widows shall not be compelled to remarry against their will[5] and shall receive their inheritance, marriage portion, and dower without fine.[6]

The greater levies, being general to the whole feudal order, could be determined by assize, and were capable of more precise definition. No scutage or aid, except the three customary aids, and those at a reasonable rate, were to be taken *nisi per commune concilium regni*,[7] the authority of such councils being the inherent function of tenants-in-chief of making provision or assize in the court of their lord. Such assizes were of original feudal right, and, according to the assumptions of feudal statesmen, were treated as equivalent to those of the community at large. The amount of the aid or scutage was to be decided by assize *secundum consilium illorum qui presentes fuerint*,[8] and in order to obtain this common voice the king would summon his tenants in chief, the greater barons directly by writ, and the lesser barons through the sheriff. The assembly would thus be the *curia* of the king's immediate tenants and nothing more. The *regnum* is regarded as the circle of the immediate vassals: indeed, though the charter recurs several times to the term "community", that community's contact with the crown is always thought of as being maintained indirectly through the medium of tenure. That such a council could hardly meet is, perhaps, of little importance, and was, indeed, recognized at the time, but, in addition, its sessions were limited to those occasions, which it was hoped would be rare, when an exceptional levy was demanded, and its function was purely that of assizing the aid.[9] *Commune consilium regni*, thus defined and applied, meant,

Aids and scutages

Commune consilium

---

[1] Magna Carta, 2.   [2] *Ibid.* 4.   [3] *Ibid.* 5.
[4] *Ibid.* 6.   [5] *Ibid.* 8.   [6] *Ibid.* 7.
[7] *Ibid.* 12.   [8] *Ibid.* 14.

[9] *Ibid.* 14: *de auxilio assidendo.*

therefore, far less than the terms suggest, and, since such counsel lay in the full tradition of feudal assemblies, the Charter's greatest innovation may be thought to lie in the insistence on formal summons and the right of attendance. In the light of the barons' tendency themselves to assume the status of a national representative it is not surprising that in 1216 the whole clause was dropped, for, while it called for attendance far beyond the circle of the barons, it held nothing of direct value for the shires and boroughs. The financial check had a more important future. It was, no doubt, implicit in the feudal relation, but here it was set out for the first time explicitly, and, because of the wide interpretation which the word "aid" had been given during the past twenty years, it was one capable of covering other forms of taxation than those based on the fees. The subsidies upon revenue and other chattels which were to finance the crown during the following period were in origin varieties of the aid. The tallages of London were reckoned as *auxilia*, and safeguarded by the same clause as the aids of the barons, though the privilege was soon let slip.

The defensores
Of constitutional plan the Charter contained little. Its final clause is a provision which has been thought to aim at a kind of executive council, and which seems to have had something of the effect of such a council in the August of 1215, but the intention of which was in fact very different. The barons are to elect twenty-five of their number "to observe, hold, and make to be observed the peace and liberties which we have conceded to them". If those liberties are broken and the king refuses amends, the Twenty-Five are to rouse the *communa regni* against him, and make war against his lands, castles, and possessions, saving his person and those of the queen and the princes. Of this body it may be said outright that they in no way anticipate the conciliar committees of the succeeding reigns. Their function is the diffidation followed by the lawful rebellion of feudalism, their status is that of *fidejussores* such as swore to most treaties in the twelfth century, twelve or more barons of the kings of France or England, or the count of Flanders, pledging themselves to renounce their liegeance and make war upon their natural lord if he breaks the treaty to which he and they have set their hands.[1] A device essentially the same had been used

[1] Cf. the Treaty of 1201 between John and Philip. Howden, iv. 175. So also the Treaty of Falaise.

by John in the charters which he exacted from the barons *de fidelitate*,[1] and it had been the normal guarantee of conventions between English parties for three generations.[2] There was thus no conciliar scheme of control, it was some years too early for that; but there was this advance, that, for the first time, the crown was forced to sacrifice its servants to administrative expediency. John is to remove from office all the adherents of Gerard d'Athies and certain other foreigners[3] and to confine his choice of justiciars, constables, sheriffs, and bailiffs to such as know the law and are willing to observe it.[4] There had never before been any tendency to turn the tables on the king and claim to determine the custody of his castles,[5] but from this time onwards the control of castles and counties becomes a recurrent issue of politics, and in the reign of Henry III every change in the political balance will be reflected in a change of constables and sheriffs.

The Great Charter offers little to reward the historian in search of "constitutional precedents"; perhaps the assizing of the aids and the design for *commune consilium* might be accepted as such. It was, indeed, essentially what the king called it, "a peace between us and our barons"; we cannot detect any very deep stirring of the nation, and if John had lived another twenty years it might almost have come to be forgotten. The political events which surrounded it and every clause of its articles bear a feudal colour, though it is that of Henry's tamed and legalized feudalism.[6] The rising was not treason—indeed the barons asserted that the king had rebelled against them[7]—it was preceded by diffidation,[8] carried through in legitimate warfare,[9] closed with a peace, "so

General effect of the charter

[1] Rotuli de oblatis, 15 John, p. 494. Twenty knights of the constable of Chester swear *si predictus Johannes a servicio Domini Regis recesserit . . . ipsi cum omnibus tenementis suis ad Dominum Regem se divertent.*

[2] Cf. the charter of Treaty between Stephen and Henry of Anjou. Rymer, *Foedera*, i. 3.   [3] Magna Carta, 50.   [4] *Ibid.* 45.

[5] In August 1215 castellans were being appointed *de communi consilio* (Letters Patent, 17 John, p. 181). The barons were also seizing the shrievalties (Coventry, 224).

[6] Those clauses touching the villein and the merchant may be explained by the profit these classes brought to the land-owner. The king and other great persons had their own merchants, *mercator meus*, under their personal protection.   [7] *Perjurus et baronibus rebellis.* Wendover, ii. 117.

[8] *Regem diffiduciantes . . . et hominia sua reddentes.* Coventry, p. 219.

[9] *Guerra mota inter Dominum Regem Johannem . . . et barones Anglie* is the normal formula of the rolls.

that we have taken again our barons' homages".[1] The text itself is a medley of recognition, assize, and feudal *conventio*. Its ultimate sanction is the implied feudal contract and its immediate safeguards the *fidejussores* of feudal treaties and the *diffidatio*. Yet, taken together, the events of 1215-16, the Great Charter, and the death of John, constitute one of the crucial episodes of English history.

The legal changes of Henry II have come to stand to us for a great reform, a common law, and a general safeguard of right. So the great lawyer intended each assize individually to be. But collectively they might have turned into something different. When it became true that no claim for free tenement could be initiated without the king's writ—and this was established when Glanvill's book was written—a profound revolution had been completed. Since the beginning of her history—though decreasingly so during the Norman reigns—the law of England had been put into motion by the self-directed machinery of moot jurisdictions which were in effect autonomous legal republics. The oath of a plaintiff of sound lawful standing was of itself sufficient to throw open to him the court of shire or hundred, to bring his antagonist into court, and to command judgment of his cause. No change could affect the fibre of life more deeply than one which destroyed this open access to law and denied the courts to those from whom the king's writ was withheld. Henceforth the civil rights of any Englishman were at the discretion of a power other than that of himself and his neighbours. Henry II was, in fact, probably the first king of whom even an unjustified accusation of denying or delaying justice could have had any real meaning.

The sanctity of law

Between 1154 and 1216 the system by which the king accorded judgment as a royal boon and not a right was itself upon trial. This was the first great test of the responsibility of the crown, for such a power could be exercised with various effect. If the belief that almost all men of learning held—that the king was trustee for the law which must itself determine his actions—were to become fact, then the king's will must be an impersonal force, activating procedure automatically, having issue, often by deputy, in impartial judgment. The personal will of the king must become a fiction, while the authority of the crown through its writs remained the

[1] Letters Patent, 17 John, p. 143: *Firma pax facta est per Dei gratiam inter nos et barones nostros . . . ita quod eorum homagia eodem die ibidem cepimus.*

most formidable guarantee of legality. The rising tide of early thirteenth-century thought, with its desire to bring political expediency to the test of moral law,[1] was against *vis et voluntas* and in favour of the triumph of reasoned order in jurisprudence, but it was exposed to an assault by men of action who put reason of state before individual right, and would make the king the master and not the servant of law. This was the threat to which English law was at least occasionally exposed under Henry II, and which materialized as a sporadic attack upon the great units of property under John. In his last year many of the strongest feudatories were at his mercy, and, had his reign continued, the whole basis of common law might have been subverted. Exacted by magnates, the liberties of 1215 were appropriated by a commonalty of free men. In 1219, when the judgment and assize of the county of Lincoln in favour of Gilbert de Gant had been traversed by the Marshal's writ, the full county court appealed to the *libertas concessa et jurata*, and made a great baron's cause that of the community of the realm—*cum eo et pro eo acclamante, immo pro se ipsis, et pro communi totius regni.*[2]

To the enlightened, therefore, the "liberties of free men" were those of the community at large. To say in retrospect that they and the community they protected were alike of the feudal order is almost meaningless. If by the accusation of feudal interest the individualist spirit of 1173 is meant, that had been dead for forty years as an effective force, though echoes of it recur for a couple of centuries; if the ordered, writ-controlled feudalism of Henry II, it was precisely a reassertion of feudalism that was needed, for his reign had made tenurial right part of a common law of the realm. The two seem in that day identical. There is and can be no claim to speak for the magnates alone. Relations are too closely interwoven, the man of great tenure in one county is too often the small tenant of another, to make anything short of a general defence of the law of free tenures possible. In a society in which the greatest earl was at once lord of hundreds, subject in royal and private hundreds, tenant by barony, knight service, serjeanty, socage, fee-farm, and term of years, the concept of the *liber homo*, standing for all tenures—other than the precarious right

The freeman of the Charter

[1] F. M. Powicke, *Stephen Langton*, p. 90, and J. E. A. Jolliffe, *Angevin Kingship*, cap. III.
[2] *Royal Letters of Henry III* (ed. Shirley), i. 20.

of villeinage—can be nothing short of the type of the community.
Without any sense of incongruity, therefore, the magnates use the
terms of political community which are at this very time making
their way into common speech. They speak of *communa totius
Angliae, commune consilium regni*. But their understanding of
politics is still not that of the state but of the fee. For them the
regnum is primarily the *dominium* of the king over his immediate
tenants. The mesne tenures remain in the background, taking their
place through the derived right of the tenures *in capite*. Upon the
fringes of the feudal order are persons and tenures—burgesses and
sokemen of varying degrees of independence—whose place in the
communa they would find it difficult either to define or deny.
Villeins, who have no land in fee, or landless freemen, are beyond
their view, which is essentially one of a community of tenures. It
is a political idea which needs to be clarified and translated into
the terms of the state; yet, imperfectly detached from notions of
tenure as it is, this baronial conception of *communitas*, and the sense
of their own quality as its natural representatives, inspires the
baronage to act as a national opposition in the thirteenth century,
and is an important phase in the growth of constitutional theory.
For the first time, though imperfectly, it is asserted in the Great
Charter.

The communa of the Charter

To the edge of such community the country had been brought by
sixty years of Angevin rule. The federalism of the past, federalism
of races and laws under the Saxons, of feudal honours under the
Normans, was now reconciled under the growing predominance
of the crown. Law was one in essentials throughout the kingdom,
and the dependence of judgment upon the king's writ had turned
folkright into king's law. A legal community of the realm was
now a realized fact, and a political community could not be far in
the future. The national fibre had, moreover, been strong enough
to impose its virtue upon the government. Thirteenth-century
administration derived most of its efficacy from inquest, and therefore rested upon the integrity and independence of the legal
communities of the shires. In this it inherited the spirit of the
English past. Under John, working through the magnates, this
spirit had set final limits beyond which the crown might not
depart from tradition, and it may be thought that what was best
in both régimes had survived—the strength of Saxon provincial

communities and the administrative efficiency of the foreign crown. Because this balance of the two traditions had been achieved, and would not be substantially changed in the future, the death of John closed a stage in English history. For the future, the struggle for civil right being won, the concern of the nation is to be the imposition of political control upon the crown, and the battle shifts from the ground of law to that of the constitution.

iv

CROWN AND UNIVERSITAS. 1216–1272

The death of John on October 19, 1216, destroyed his tyranny *The new* at the moment when it seemed to be becoming secure, and the *reign* balance reverted to that baronial interpretation of the régime which had prevailed in the movement against Longchamps and, more crudely, in that of the Charter. As was usual in these recurrent reversals, the form of the executive was not challenged, and the majority of John's officials were retained. William Marshal replaced or afforced Hubert de Burgh as justiciar in the crisis of the king's death,[1] but resigned almost immediately. Hubert, Richard Marsh the chancellor, the chamberlain Geoffrey Nevill, continued in office, as did the justiciar of Ireland, and many of the sheriffs. The government was, in fact, John's, but with a policy which differed from that of the opposition only in being more deliberate. The minority of the king drove the magnates to the partial precedent of 1191, and on or before November 20[2] the marshal was bearing the title *Rector Regis et Regni.* Unlike the Supreme Rectorship of John, his office was a real one. There was no regent judiciary to dispute his power, and until his death in 1219 writs ran under his private seal and over the witness *Teste Comite.*[3]

A great council at Bristol from November 13 to 20 founded the new reign. There homage was sworn, the king was crowned, the Charters reiterated, and the Marshal assumed the rectorship. The caution of the guiding magnates, and perhaps the policy of

[1] Letters Close, 1 Henry III, p. 293 (Nov. 13): *Teste Comite Willelmo Marescallo Justiciario Anglie apud Bristollium.*   [2] *Loc. cit.*

[3] *Quia nondum habuimus sigillum has litteras sigillo dilecti et fidelis Comitis Willelmi Marescalli rectoris nostri et regni nostri fecimus sigillari. Ibid.* p. 293. The influence of the legates was constant and at certain times crucial, but since they acted by Apostolic authority their action was not directly constitutional.

the legate, took care that the right of Henry should in no way be tarnished by the recent challenge to his father's. An affirmation of the Charter was essential from every point of view, but it was to be detached from the events of 1215, and to appear as a spontaneous act of the new reign and its counsellors. "Our late Lord and Father being happily passed from the light of our day, and his soul gathered to the elect . . . we have heard how indignation arose between the said lord our Father and certain of the nobles of our realm, whether with good cause or none we know not . . . wherefore, according to every man his right . . . and abating in our realm all evil customs . . . we will to restore the good days of our *The* forefathers."[1] The new charter of liberties issued from Bristol *Charter* three weeks after the king's death, immediately after the corona- *reissued* tion, and as a response to the homage of the lieges. It was substantially the same as that of 1215. Clauses Twelve and Fourteen of the former, calling for the assent of *commune consilium* to aids and scutages, and defining common counsel as the assembly of all tenants-in-chief, were omitted as *gravia et dubitabilia*, and with them the clause which limited the aids of mesne tenants to the three customary occasions.[2] Half the baronage was in homage to Louis of France, and likely to remain so, and the counsellors of the minority could not make supply contingent upon the remote possibility of a *commune consilium regni* as defined in 1215. Perhaps the provision of the reissue of 1217, that scutage should be taken as it was in the time of King Henry II, expressed the general intention to get the consent of the *curia* without attempting to define its composition.

Nature A minority was, indeed, calculated to prolong the Henrician *of the* transition phase of government by a developed executive in ill- *régime* determined relation to an acknowledged tenurial right of counsel, and in November 1216 the barons were well placed to hold their own. Lands and custodies were left as they were held before the war, and, though it was agreed that no binding alienations of royal lands should be made until Henry's majority,[3] many great men were

---

[1] Stubbs, *Select Charters*, p. 333.

[2] The magnates were, in fact, authorized to take aids from their tenants for very varied purposes. Letters Close, 1 Hen. III, pp. 319, 330.

[3] *Ibid.* 4 Hen. III, p. 437: *communi omnium magnatum nostrorum consilio provisum esset ne quid sigillo nostro firmum fieret usque ad etatem nostram.*

bought with grants of castles or counties in ward.[1] Territorially
the magnates were stronger than at any time since 1154,[2] and the
government dealt more loosely with nobles and officials than was
the habit of the Angevin kings.[3] William Marshall, and, in the early
years of his predominance, Hubert de Burgh, ruled with a
varying group of officials and barons, sometimes small, sometimes
large, occasionally swelling to *commune consilium*, and apparently
determined only by the nature of the business in hand. There was
no defined *concilium regis*, but the function of counsel inherent in
baronage was called upon as it was needed.[4] The witness to letters
and writs gives us our only hint as to the composition of counsel,
and they record only such names as were needed to warrant the
chancellor in affixing the great seal. But over long periods we find
letters close and patent going out *teste Comite coram Episcopis
Londoniense et Wintoniense*, or *teste Huberto coram Episcopis Bath-
oniense et Sarisberiense*,[5] and we may infer that small groups of
magnates, working with the necessary clerical and official advice,
were the *consilium regis* by which daily administration was being
done. A summons to the prince of Connaught in 1226 was
witnessed by two bishops, the justiciar, the earl of Gloucester,
Richard of Argentien, Hugh Mortimer, the steward Geoffrey de
Crowcombe, five *curiales* of no special note, the archbishop of
Dublin, Roger Waspail the seneschal of Ulster, and three Irish
tenants, Geoffrey de Costentin, Nicholas of Verdun, and Walter
de Riddleford.[6] By this test Henry's minority councils were in
the common course much like those of John; but aids, scutages,

[1] Aumâle received Rockingham and Sauvey in December 1216 (Letters
Patent, 1 Hen. III, p. 13), and Salisbury Sherborne castle and the county of
Somerset in March 1217 (*ibid.* p. 38). In certain cases, as with Ferrars, Walter
de Lacy, Brian de Insula, and Reginald de Braiose, the castles were to be retained
until the end of the king's fourteenth year.

[2] The fact that William Marshall the younger held Marlborough and
Ludgershall was a strong motive for giving him the king's sister as wife.
Royal Letters of Henry III (ed. Shirley), i. 244. Fawkes was accused of making
a large fortune from his counties. *Ibid.* i. 313.

[3] *Ibid.* vol. i. pp. 19, 47, 71, 73.

[4] So Lechlade was granted to Fawkes de Breauté *per ipsum Marescallum et
consilium domini Eboraci Archiepiscopi et Episcoporum Wintonensis, Dunholmensis,
Willemi Briwere.* Letters Close, 2 Hen. III, p. 371. Llewellyn was accorded a
day of trial *de consilio venerabilium patrum Cantuariensis Archiepiscopi, Episcopi
Herefordensis, Huberti de Burgo Justicarii nostri et baronum nostrorum Marchie.*
Ibid. 4 Hen. III, p. 434.

[5] During the years 1224-5-6.

[6] Letters Patent, 10 Hen. III, p. 48.

hidages, carucages—imperfectly distinguished from aids—were faithfully requested from the *commune consilium*, in spite of the dropping from the Charter of the obligation to do so.[1] In 1230, when both the king and the justiciar left the country, the regency of the chancellor and Segrave, the sealing of the various classes of writs, and the custody of the seals, were determined *de communi consilio*.[2] Here, as at Bristol in 1216, the refounding or recasting of the government was matter for the whole body of the feudatories.

Coöpera-tion of crown and baronage

The minority is the last series of years during which the crown and the baronage act together uncritically upon the old feudal assumptions, largely unconscious of divergent interests. Many factors made it possible for them to do so, the prestige of the Marshal, the Apostolic overlordship transcending local rights and ambitions, the childhood of the king. On the whole, the clauses of the Charter in which the magnates had thought specially for them-selves were adhered to. The custody of many of the royal castles was in their hands and gave them a kind of inviolability,[3] reliefs were kept rigidly to the low sums determined in 1215,[4] there was no conspicuous abuse of wardship and marriage, and, though the barons were usually content to submit their causes to assize, they would on occasion demand judgment of their peers.[5] But, as Henry grows towards manhood, signs of strain begin to appear, and it is seen that the thirteenth century will have to deal with con-

---

[1] Letters Close, 4 Hen. III, p. 437: *concesserunt nobis sui gratia communiter omnes magnates et fideles totius regni nostri donum.*

[2] Letters Patent, 14 Hen. III, p. 339: *de communi consilio comitum et baronum et omnium fidelium nostrorum qui nobiscum aderant apud Portesmue ante transfretationem nostram.*

[3] Fawkes de Breauté, who held six of them, said that if the English barons wanted to try his strength, "he would give them such a war as all England could not hold".

[4] Letters Close, 4 Hen. III, p. 438. The earl of Warwick, £100. For a list of knight's reliefs at 100s. the fee cf. Letters Patent, 2 Hen. III, p. 173.

[5] Letters Patent, 10 Hen. III, p. 82. The young king is made to grant that *dominus rex . . . faciet habere dicto Comiti Marescallo judicium parium suorum de . . . jure et saisina* as to his right in Caerleon. The right of amercement by peers is preserved in the instructions to justices. Letters Close, 3 Hen. III, p. 383. Barons to be amerced *coram consilio nostro*. Refusal of judgment by his peers was one pretext for Richard Marshal's revolt in 1233. Cf. Matthew Paris, *Chronica Majora, sub anno.*

stitutional problems altogether different from those of the past. *Narrowing of the basis of the government*
Like other "national" governments, that of Henry's minority
owed much of its strength to a few individuals who were thought
to be strong and of wide sympathies, and to its adoption of a
middle course in politics. As time went on, it began to lose its
inclusive character. In the summer of 1217 it had rejected the
demand that the earl of Chester should be associated with the
marshal as rector[1]; in May 1219 the marshal died, and Pierre des
Roches, linked in the unofficial mind with John's rule, was given
the guardianship of the king; in 1221 Langton induced Honorius
to recall Pandulf from his legation. So it happened that at the very
time when the government was announcing the end of the
troubled years and celebrating it by the second coronation of the
king in May 1220, the circle of its supporters was becoming
dangerously narrowed and division was beginning among its
leaders.

Nevertheless, this was the moment chosen to initiate a new *Hubert de Burgh gains in power*
policy which came to appear more and more that of the justiciar,
and which ended in opening again that gulf between the more
independent of the baronage and the crown which the compromise of 1216 had closed. The minority satisfied the extremists
because their hold upon the custodies made them secure in the
provinces. In the autumn of 1219 William of Aumâle incurred
excommunication for defying the edict against the holding of
tournaments, and subsequently refused to surrender the castles of
Rockingham and Sauvey.[2] Perhaps as a consequence of this, the
coronation was made the justification for an attempted resumption.
The Pope wrote ordering ecclesiastical and other magnates to
return the royal castles to the king,[3] and on August 9, 1220, there
appeared the writ for the first general enquiry *quo warranto* in
English history. All those who held royal demesne were ordered
to prove their warrant for doing so at the Michaelmas Exchequer.[4]
The adventure was not carried through. The reduction of Aumâle
cost the country a scutage and a campaign, and there is no sign

[1] *Royal Letters of Henry III* (ed. Shirley), i. 532. Later the Pope considered the
failure to secure the full coöperation of Ranulf Blundevill as a danger to the
régime. Cf. *Ibid.* i. 225.
[2] *Letters Close*, 4 Hen. III, p. 434.
[3] *Royal Letters of Henry III* (ed. Shirley), i. 535.
[4] *Letters Close*, 4 Hen. III, p. 437.

that the *quo warranto* returns were acted upon, or, in fact, made. But the episode was significant. Hubert was turning against the less responsible feudatories, and henceforth his government could no longer claim to be that to which they had acceded in 1216. The policy of resumption was pursued, but cautiously. In November 1221 Corfe was recovered from Peter de Mauley,[1] and Bolsover and the Peak from earl Ferrars[2] in the summer of 1222. The earl left the council in anger, and the earl of Chester, hitherto one of the crown's principal supporters, protested to the verge of rebellion, but once more unity was outwardly maintained. It was broken finally when in 1223 the Pope declared Henry of age and Hubert carried through a wholesale resumption at the expense of Fawkes de Breauté and the earl of Chester.[3]

Move against the feudatories   It is evident that Hubert's action was made possible by divisions which had been growing for some time within the ranks of the magnates. Fawkes attributed his disgrace to the treachery of the English barons[4] and as early as 1221 he had attracted the enmity of the Courtneys and the younger William Briwere in the West, and knew that the king's uncle Salisbury was behind their hostility.[5] At that time he was so sure of Hubert's friendship that he begged him not to judge them too hastily out of favour to himself. But a year later he had quarrelled with the young earl Marshal,[6] and the earl was already betrothed to the king's sister. In 1224 Shrewsbury[7] and Pembroke[8] urged the case against him in concert.[9] Thus, the crisis of 1223 presented itself to contemporaries not as a turn away

---

[1] Letters Patent, 6 Hen. III, p. 321.

[2] *Ibid.* 6 Hen. III, p. 335. Ferrar's custodies of Bolsover and the Peak terminated with the completion of the king's fourteenth year according to an agreement of 1216. *Ibid.* 1 Hen. III, p. 1.

[3] As to Chester, the motive for depriving him of his hold on the north-west Midlands was probably his intervention to defend Llewellyn from the royal expedition of 1223.

[4] *Royal Letters of Henry III* (ed. Shirley), vol. i. pp. 221-222.

[5] *Ibid.* vol. i. p. 172.   [6] *Ibid.* vol. i. p. 175.

[7] *Ibid.* vol. i. p. 221.   [8] *Ibid.* vol. i p. 222.

[9] Fawkes submitted, as did Chester and others, to the deprivation of his castles and sheriffdoms in January 1224, but was involved in a number of private actions for redress, some of them fomented by Salisbury and Pembroke, and was finally ruined by his brother's violence against Henry of Braybrook, one of the justices who had presided in his cause. He was proclaimed *inimicus manifestus regis* on July 11, and soon after left the kingdom.

from the baronage, but as the ruin of a faction.[1] Though Chester
and Llewellyn[2] favoured Fawkes and resisted the redistribution of
power—civil war was only narrowly avoided at the Christmas
council of Northampton[3]—a substantial body of nobles stood by
Hubert and made his action possible. Nevertheless, in historical
perspective, the proclamation of Henry's majority, accompanied
by acts which bear every mark of a conscious shifting of the
centre of power,[4] may be taken as the beginning of a new phase
of monarchical government. The redistribution of the custodies
was so managed as to restore the provincial authority which had
passed from the bureaucracy in 1216. The earl of Chester lost
the castles of Shrewsbury, Bridgnorth, and Lancaster, with the
custody of the counties of Stafford, Shropshire, and Lancaster;
Fawkes surrendered eight castles and the county of Oxford;
Engelard de Cigogné, Windsor and Odiham; Pierre des Roches,
Winchester, Porchester, and the county of Hampshire. In all, about
thirty castles changed hands,[5] and were entrusted for the most
part to the king's servants and knights, men who drew their
liveries from the Chamber, and most of whom had seen service
under John and been moderately endowed from the forfeitures
of 1215.[6] John's experiment of entrusting the counties as custodies
at will, and not at farm, was also revived, so that the sheriffs

*Resump-
tion of
castles*

---

1 It is noteworthy that the earl of Salisbury had confirmed to him the
custodies granted him by John, and was allowed to dispose of them in his will
(Letters Patent, 10 Hen. III, p. 12), and that William Marshal was made justiciar
of Ireland (*ibid.* 8 Hen. III, p. 437). In Rome it was feared that the barons as a
whole would be moved to rebellion. *Royal Letters of Henry III* (ed. Shirley),
i. 240.

2 Cf. Llewellyn's bold and dignified explanation of his defence of Fawkes
(*ibid.* i. 229), and the Earl of Chester's (*ibid.* i. 233).

3 *Ibid.* vol. i. p. 225. A fragmentary safe-conduct suggests that Gloucester,
Aumâle, the constable of Chester, Brian de Insula, Robert de Vipont, and
Engelard de Cigogné were involved (Letters Patent, 8 Hen. III, p. 481),
and this is roughly the list given by Matthew Paris (*Chronica Majora, sub
anno* 1224).

4 Matthew Paris (Stubbs, *Select Charters*, 322), says that the Pope's letter
empowered Henry to govern thenceforth *cum suorum domesticorum consilio* and
that the barons protested.

5 Letters Patent, 8 Hen. III, pp. 417-420, 427, 429.

6 Hugh Despenser (Letters Close, 2 Hen. III, p. 345; *ibid.* 6 Hen. III, p. 494);
John Russell (*ibid.* 17 John, p. 232; *ibid.* 2 Hen. III, p. 345); William de Einesford,
Senescallus Regis (*ibid.* 7 John, p. 43); Stephen Segrave (*ibid.* 2 Hen. III, p. 365);
Robert Lupus (*ibid.* 9 John, p. 108; *ibid.* 9 Hen. III, p. 500); William de Rughe-
don (*ibid.* 9 Hen. III, p. 508); Waleran Teutonicus (*ibid.* 16 John p. 218; *ibid.*

henceforth returned every detail of their revenue, and the Exchequer might hold them to an itemized account.

Clerical element in Hubert's government

There was a strong clerical element in this government of Hubert. The bishops took a leading part in the recovery of the custodies,[1] and the suffragans of Canterbury came of their own free will to the siege of Bedford, and granted a special carucage from their demesne lands.[2] From its inception, that is from the winter of 1223, to the beginning of 1226, the bishops of Bath and Salisbury—sometimes joined by the bishop of London and the inescapable William Briwere—are the usual witnesses to the justiciar's executive acts. The basis of the government is also narrower. The phrase *per consilium regis, coram consilio regis* is markedly rarer than in the early years of the reign. In consequence the household executive, which had been so powerful under John, and of which we hear little at the beginning of the minority,

The Wardrobe

wakes to a new activity. The Wardrobe had begun to replace the Chamber in the last years of John; in the first years of Henry the Seneschal replaced both Chamber and Wardrobe as receiver for the Household;[3] but a Roll of the Wardrobe is again mentioned in 1217, and after about 1219 the Chancery Rolls show it drawing upon the Exchequer for the king's personal expenses. The crisis of 1223–4 is reflected by the dismissal of its principal clerk, Peter des Rievaulx, son of the discredited bishop of Winchester, and almost immediately the office is thrust into the foreground as a principal department of state. Much more markedly than under John, the Wardrobe of the years 1224–7 becomes the receiving and spending department for a considerable proportion of the revenue. Under the new clerks, Walter de Brackley and Walter de Kirkham, the Wardrobe receipts spring from the £2000 of 1223 to £9000, £8800, and £6700 in the eighth, ninth, and tenth years, so that they almost equal those of the Chamber of John.

9 Hen. III, p. 511); Walter de Fauconberg (*ibid.* 7 Hen. III, p. 561). T. F. Tout, *Chapters in Administrative History*, i. 203 *n.* Richard of Argentien, *Senescallus Regis*; Tout, *op. cit.* i. 203 *n.*; Ralf fitz Nicholas, *Senescallus Regis*. Letters Patent, 11 Hen. III, p. 162.

[1] About half were resigned into the hands of one or other of the bishops.

[2] Letters Patent, 8 Hen. III, p. 464.

[3] Or his deputy Robert de Bareville. Letters Close, 3 Henry III, pp. 384, 386, 401 ; 5 Henry III, pp. 444, 457, 458.

It is not difficult to see that this rise was due to a revival of John's *The* fiscal policy at the expense of the Exchequer. Under Peter, the *Wardrobe* Wardrobe had drawn upon the Treasury, which retained a virtual *and finance* monopoly of receipts, or had received minor sums directly from sheriffs and debtors. Under Kirkham and Brackley the whole render of certain taxes was diverted. The bishops paid the clerical carucage of August 1224 into the Wardrobe,[1] Fawkes' great fine of seven hundred marks was taken over by its clerks from the Temple,[2] and the chattels forfeited by his fellow-sufferers were received there without passing through the treasurer's hands. During the same period items of revenue which had been received in the Exchequer were transferred immediately en bloc to the Wardrobe, as was the tallage of the Jews of 1225.[3] In addition, the principal tax of that year, the Fifteenth granted in February, was cut out entirely from the purview of the Exchequer, received by a special commissioner at Winchester,[4] and committed to the bishops of Bath and Salisbury, Hubert's confidants, by whom it was delivered to the Temple, the Wardrobe, or the Treasury, or transmitted direct to the army in Gascony through the hands of Walter de Kirkham or others as occasion demanded.[5] Until the beginning of 1227, when it seems to have been exhausted, the crown was assured of a revenue[6] independent of the Treasury. A Treasurer of the Chamber or Wardrobe appears,[7] with functions like those of the Clerk of the Chamber of John.

The effect of all this may not have struck contemporaries. It was what, in one degree or another, had been the Angevin monarchy's financial practice almost from the year of Henry II's accession. Hubert continued to conform to the general lines of the settlement of 1216, and bought the aids of 1225 by a final recasting and reissue of the Charter, though it may be significant that it was issued *spontanea et bona voluntate regis*. Nevertheless, by eliminating Fawkes and restricting earl Ranulf's hostile influence to his

[1] Letters Patent, 8 Hen. III, p. 473 *et seq.*

[2] *Ibid.* p. 467.   [3] *Ibid.* 9 Hen. III, p. 513.

[4] William de Castellis, who sat from June 17 to July 20 and from September 29 to November 21, 1225. *Ibid.* p. 541, and 10 Hen. III, p. 6.

[5] Letters Patent, 9 and 10 Hen. III, *passim.*

[6] The fifteenth is said to have raised a sum of 87,000 marks: Stubbs, *Constitutional History*, ii. 38.

[7] T. F. Tout, *Chapters in Administrative History*, i. 196.

own earldoms, the justiciar had enabled bureaucracy to resume that course of development which had been interrupted by John's *débâcle*, and this time it was no longer crippled by being linked with an attack upon civil liberties. What Hubert restored Henry inherited, and his personal rule is an exaggerated outcome of the justiciar's last eight years of government.

Unpopularity of Hubert

Hubert's fall in July 1232 may be ascribed to many reasons. The Angevin system was essentially monarchical, and intolerable when it lacked the grace of divine and seigneurial right. William des Longchamps, Hubert de Burgh, and Simon de Montfort were all hated because they carried an authority which was essential to them, but which the nobles would bear, if at all, only from a king; and of necessity they strengthened their material power in a way which made the older feudatories more jealous still. As earl of Kent, lord of much of South Wales, holding profitable wardships and custodies, brother by marriage of the Scotch king, Hubert was growing as far beyond the ancient nobility in territorial power as he was below them in birth. Since the Angevin régime lacked the theory of a conventional crown,[1] these grand vizierates were bound to appear intermittently, and were always disastrous to their holders. Inevitably, Hubert had made many enemies, among them the greatest of all, Ranulf Blundevill, *semper mihi molestus*, and, towards the end, the young king, whose initiation into knighthood he turned to lasting discredit. Indeed, the bungling of the French war of 1230, the defeats in Wales, and the confusion in the finances, go far to justify Henry's desire for emancipation when at the age of twenty-five he had been twice crowned and twice proclaimed of age.

Rise of Pierre des Roches

The seizure of power by Pierre des Roches in the spring of 1232 had, therefore, some practical excuse. It produced a measure of financial reform[2] and satisfied the desire of all parties for the humiliation of the great justiciar. Peter, however, though he was perhaps the one man who had the standing and adroitness to unseat the government, fell short of some quality which was

---

[1] The notion of an impersonal crown as a legal entity distinct from its wearer does not appear until the fourteenth century.

[2] M. H. Mills, *Transactions of the Royal Historical Society*, 4th series, x.

needed to govern the England of 1232. Deliberately, he displayed his belief that the baronage had not changed,[1] denounced compromise, turned the *coup d'état* against the magnates who had favoured it, and reverted to the methods of John to cow them into submission. The first sign of unrest called forth government reaction in the full spirit of the almost forgotten tyranny, and, after sixteen years of security of law, pledge by hostages[2] and the hated charters of special fealty[3] were revived, and mercenaries were brought in from Poitou and Brittany. Peter had clearly learned nothing of English politics since 1216. The barons of 1232 were, however, no longer weak nor divided. Refusing to obey successive summonses to council, they demanded the dismissal of the Poitevins, and were joined by the clergy under Edmund Rich. The marshal, earl Richard of Pembroke, who had retired from the court and been proclaimed traitor, found general support, and the magnates raised the old cry of right of trial by peers. By April 1234 his success against Henry in the field brought the king to admit that he had been wrongly counselled and to dismiss the Poitevin ministers. The episode of the return of Pierre des Roches to power and his defeat brings together elements both of the past and of the future. The bishop, himself one of the most notable financiers and soldiers of the last generation, had played his part in a violent and unscrupulous age, and the appearance of better times did not convince him. He assumed that sixteen years had *His re-* made no essential change, and that the barons would take advan- *actionary* tage of any show of weakness, and could best be kept in hand by *policy* suspending their civil rights at the first sign of disobedience. He began, in short, at the point at which he had last laid down power. Outwardly, therefore, his short ministry is of the past, and is the last echo of John's tyranny and the last threat to common right. It was met by a violent burst of opposition, in which church and

1 Matthew Paris, *Historia Minor*, ii. 354: *Quod adhuc reliquias odii et guerrae, quas olim Angli contra regem Johannem . . . suscitabant, merito debet habere suspectas*: the remnant of the former war and hatred which they had stirred up against King John in the past ought still to be guarded against.

2 The barons of the March gave hostages at the Worcester council of 1233. Letters Close, 17 Hen. III, p. 312.

3 From William Mauduit, John of Evreux, Matthew de Meung, Richard Marshal, Earl Bigod, Thomas Grelley, Walter Clifford, Robert Musard, Henry of Erleigh, and Morgan of Caerleon: *ibid.* 320. These are enrolled between August 16 and 25, after the opposition of Richard Marshal and the Bassets.

baronage united, and the threat of another suspension of the law after John's model was laid for ever.

But, reactionary in the weapons they chose to deal with the baronage, Pierre des Roches and his followers conducted their campaign within the court with a very different order of ability, and with results which were to be the model for Henry's personal government in later days. There the problem was to rehabilitate the authority of the king, and through him to gain power over the administration. Symptoms of Henry's emergence from tute*Pierre des* lage may be seen some years before the justiciar's fall. When the *Roches* Breton campaign of 1230 declined towards failure he had wished *and the* *household* to throw the government into the hands of a legate, and Hubert barely succeeded in dissuading him.[1] On his return to England he broke with the custom of the minority, which for fourteen years had conducted all business of state under the personal seals of the Marshal and Hubert, and in November 1230 began to issue letters close under the seal of Geoffrey de Crowcombe, his household steward.[2] In December he first used a private seal of his own. In 1231, when Pierre des Roches, the victim of 1224, was allowed to return, Hubert's late clerk Ralf Brito was displaced from the Wardrobe, and the bishop's son Pierre des Rievaulx became *The* treasurer of the Chamber. By June 1232 the power of the execu*household* tive was sharply divided, the household being controlled by *against the* *great* Hubert's enemies, Geoffrey de Crowcombe as steward, and Peter *offices* des Rievaulx as treasurer, while the justiciarship, the Chancery, and the treasurership of the Exchequer remained to Hubert and his associates of the minority.[3] It now became evident that, in spite of its long abeyance, the king's will was still formidable if he could be brought to assert it, and that the household had been so far developed as to make it a rival to the great offices, in that, even without displacing their holders, it could be used by adroit management to neutralize their functions. In Pierre des Roches,

[1] *Royal Letters of Henry III* (ed. Shirley), i. 379.

[2] T. F. Tout, *Chapters in Administrative History*, i. 210 *et seq.*

[3] The principal magnates who were favourable to Pierre des Roches' coup were probably those of whom a Letter Patent of 3rd September 1232 says that they were retained on urgent business about the king, *i.e.* the earls of Chester, Cornwall, Pembroke, Warenne, and Derby, and the constable of Chester. The marshal soon changed his views, but, according to Matthew Paris, the predominance of the foreigners was not recognized as a grievance until Christmas 1233. Letters Patent, 16 Hen. III, p. 498.

who knew the courts of the Pope and the Emperor, the justiciar of England had an enemy who had little sense of the compromise upon which the minority rested, but who could meet him with a more subtle understanding of the intricacies of power than even his own thirty years of administration had given him. Instead of attacking the apparent sources of his strength, his own justiciarship and the episcopal tenure of the Chancery and Treasury, the Poitevins seemed at first to strengthen them. As late as June 15, 1232, Hubert was made justiciar of Ireland, and at almost the same time the bishop of Chichester was confirmed in the Chancery and the bishop of Carlisle in the Treasury, and all three grants were made by charter and for life. Such charters could be issued upon the eve of revolution only because the charges which they confirmed were already discounted in the plans of the opposition, and they were soon seen to be preliminary to the reduction of the great offices of state under the dictation of the newer offices of the household.

There Pierre des Rievaulx was already supreme. On June 11 he had been made keeper of the king's Wardrobe and Chamber, and treasurer of the household for life, with power to remove any of its officials at will. On June 15 he became keeper of the king's small seal, also for life. Thus, for the first time the various branches of the household were coördinated into a whole under a single minister, while the consolidated ministry was removed from the check of the Chancery by obtaining the freedom of its own seal. Captured and reconstituted by the opposition, the domestic ministry was now to establish points of contact in the offices of state from which to destroy their initiative and secure their conformity with household policy. The creation of a keepership of the small seal had already to a large degree neutralized the influence of the Chancery. The next to be dealt with was the justiciarship of Ireland. On July 28 Pierre des Rievaulx—now Treasurer and Chamberlain of Ireland—was empowered to associate a deputy with the justiciar in the receipt of the Irish Exchequer in the justiciar's special prerogative of exacting the fines of the Irish tenants without royal precept, and in the taking of all assizes. For all these functions Peter's deputy was to keep *contra alios rotulos* a separate roll.[1] Three months later a somewhat similar check was

[1] Letters Patent, 16 Hen. III, p. 493. As was said in another connection, "to keep his roll in witness against" them. Cf. Tout, *op. cit.* i. 248.

placed upon the Treasury of England, still in the hands of Walter of Carlisle, by the intrusion of a clerk of Peter des Rievaulx *residens ad Scaccarium regis loco suo*, who shared with the treasurer and chamberlains a key to, and, presumably, the custody of the main treasure.[1] With the substitution of Stephen Segrave for Hubert de Burgh, the justiciarship was reduced to its function as head of the judiciary, and ceased to be a serious political factor. The design of subordinating the ministries of state to the household is unmistakable. How far the spread of Peter's authority over the provincial administration was part of the same policy of extending domestic government is doubtful. Though it had that effect for the moment, it was not maintained after the Poitevins' position was established, but during the rest of 1232 Peter received almost every provincial custody, all the counties[2]—except the few already granted for life and those held by Stephen Segrave—a number of the castles,[3] the forests throughout England,[4] the custody of all wardships and escheats,[5] of all sees to fall vacant in Ireland,[6] of the vacant see of Canterbury.[7] In January 1233 the Treasury of the English Exchequer was added,[8] and all these were to be held for life. The ministry lasted barely two years, but its effect upon the structure of government was decisive, for on the fall of Pierre des Roches and Pierre des Rievaulx in April 1234, there was no going back upon the advance which their period of power had achieved. Henry's personal rule was to be based upon the household.

Pierre's ministry a turning-point

Thus there ended that transition phase of constitutional growth, during which the powerful, intricate, and potentially tyrannous bureaucracy had sought to tread a middle course between the crown and the baronage, embodying itself in a group of magnate officers devoted to the system rather than to the king, and themselves tenants by barony in lay and ecclesiastical right. Inevitably, it had left unsatisfied every party to the compromise, and it had failed in every major enterprise, but it had gained time for the nation to reflect. The issue between crown and baronage had been confused and delayed for eighteen years, and the new generation

---

[1] Letters Close, 16 Hen. III, p. 118.
[2] Letters Patent, 16 Hen. III, pp. 486–489.
[3] *Ibid.* pp. 487–502.   [4] *Ibid.* p. 489.   [5] *Ibid.* p. 491.
[6] *Ibid.* p. 495.   [7] *Ibid.* p. 486.   [8] *Ibid.* 17 Hen. III, p. 7.

reopened it with more moderation and with a better knowledge of government. The year 1234 marked the reëmergence of the king as head of the executive. We have seen the three great offices of the justiciar, the chancellor, and the treasurer in the main as defences of the minority against disruptive forces, and exposed at times to feudal opposition. Nevertheless, it was evident that Hubert's government never departed from reasonable conformity with its foundation principles, and could always rely upon a sufficient though varying party among the barons. Indeed, as the minority was again and again prolonged, the great offices were beginning to be tinged with that feudal quality which overcame all ministries which were held for a long term of years. The strength of Hubert's position lay partly in his earldom of Kent, his custodies of Gloucester and Gower, and the rest, and Nevill and Mauclerc had been bishops before they received the Chancery and Treasury. The Chancery was a charge from which the routine profits went to the chancellor, and from February 1227 Ralf Nevill had held by charter and for life. In 1232 Hubert received the justiciarship of Ireland, Nevill, by a second grant, the Chancery, and Mauclerc the Treasury for life. Besides their natural resistance to the spirit of change inherent in personal government, it could not but be that such offices, held indefinitely, should form associations and habits of coöperation among the moderate baronage. Their procedure and traditions reflected their fixity of tenure, and responded slowly to innova- *The king* tion. Already John could speak of the "law of the Exchequer". *carries on* Henry III therefore saw in these offices a perpetuation of his *Pierre's* tutelage and an opportunity for undue influence by the magnates. *tradition* It was not in the manner of the thirteenth century to diminish the state of the crown by the suppression of such ministries, but abundant precedent existed for their reduction to a ceremonial function. The hereditary stewardship of England had long become an anachronism, and from 1233 to 1241 the king kept the marshalship in his hand at the cost of a rebellion.[1] In 1238 the Chancery was similarly attacked. Ralf Nevill could claim that he had been granted his office by the council of the realm,[2] and was too strong

[1] Letters Patent, 26 Hen. III, p. 266.

[2] Matthew Paris, *Chronica Major*, sub anno 1223. *Assensu totius regni, itaque non deponeretur ab ejus sigilli custodia nisi totius regni ordinante consensu et consilio.* There may be some exaggeration in this.

to be removed, but the seal was taken from him, lodged in the Wardrobe, and entrusted to keepers from among the Wardrobe clerks. From that year until Nevill's death in 1244 the chancellorship was a profitable title divorced from the power of office, and from 1244 the character of its holders changes in accordance with the policy of governing through the personal servants of the king.

Reduction in rank of the great offices There are no more magnate chancellors for life, but Wardrobe clerks, or knights of legal training, to whom the title of chancellor is at times accorded, but who are often, and perhaps better, characterized as *portitores, custodes sigilli regis.* At least intermittently, the great seal,[1] whose acts had become bound by precedent, was held out of Chancery by its keepers, removed from the knowledge of the Chancery clerks, and its acts recorded in the Wardrobe. At such times the king was relieved of all constraint save such as the more elastic methods of his domestic clerks might impose. As a result, the privy seal[2] almost passes out of record. The king had resumed what he, no doubt, regarded as his natural prerogative of authenticating with the seal of majesty.[3] On going abroad in 1242 he took the great seal with him, and would only accord the Exchequer a specialized form of his small seal to use in his absence, and in 1253 the great seal was laid up in custody under the seals of the regency. No action could more clearly symbolize Henry's refusal to accord any measure of initiative to the great departments, and his intention himself to embody the reign.[4]

Henry resumes custody of the great seal

The two other offices of state did not present the same resistance as the Chancery. Both had yielded to the attack of the Poitevins, and with their fall were in the king's hand. Hugh de Pateshull, one of the most active justices of the minority, was given the custody of the Treasury *quamdiu regi placuerit,* and in 1240 was succeeded from the treasury of the Wardrobe by William de Haverhill. Payments in which the king had a personal interest were transferred from the Exchequer to the Wardrobe according as he was

---

[1] As to the seals and their importance cf. T. F. Tout, *Chapters in Administrative History,* vol. i.   [2] Cf. p. 217 *supra.*

[3] Of writs so authenticated the Chancery clerks knew nothing unless they subsequently received them to enrol. T. F. Tout, *Chapters in Administrative History,* i. 287.

[4] The standing of the untitled custodians who held the great offices must not be underestimated. In 1244 William de Haverhill is described as *non solum de magnatibus sed de majoribus regni.* Letters Patent, 28 Hen. III, 426.

in England or abroad,[1] and in his absence the small seal was used to authenticate the writs of the Exchequer. Against such rivalry in the Exchequer and as the judicial benches took shape the justiciarship was becoming no more than a presidency of the judicature. The appointment of Segrave had in itself been a sign that the office was to be emptied of political importance,[2] as indeed it must be if the king's majority were to be more than a fiction, and with his dismissal it was not revived. In fact, only a strong king, or one so weak as to submit to domination, could afford a strong justiciarship, and of these Henry III was neither.

Although it was much drawn on to staff other offices, Henry's *Henry* Wardrobe remained a household treasury, except in war-time, *III's* when it became more important than the Exchequer of London. *Wardrobe* On the fall of Pierre des Rievaulx, Walter Kirkham occupied the treasury of the Chamber, no doubt somewhat in the spirit of his patron Hubert de Burgh, and was associated with William de Haverhill, whom Professor Tout has called "the first holder of the office afterwards described as the controllership of the Wardrobe".[3] From 1236 to 1240 he was succeeded by an English Templar, Geoffrey, who had served his apprenticeship as almoner to the king, and who brought the financial ability of his order to the service of the state. In these circumstances, like the Chamber before it, the Wardrobe achieved an essential and unobjectionable place in the constitution, in so far as it served a legitimate need as a private exchequer—its receipts and expenses remained level at about £9000 a year—smaller than those of the Chamber of John— and could develop uncriticized. In the process of this growth it became the centre of secondary offices like itself, the queen's Wardrobe, established on the king's marriage in 1236, and the Wardrobe of the prince,[4] which from time to time rendered their accounts either to the king's Wardrobe or the Exchequer, and towards the middle of Henry's reign it became evident that the endless process of subdivision was to be repeated within the king's Wardrobe itself. The purchase of stores for the household, in-

[1] As were the pensions of his brothers of Lusignan. Letters Patent, 26 Hen. III, p. 309.
[2] After his fall Segrave maintained that he had never been in the inner circle of the counsellors as justiciar. Matthew Paris, *Chronica Majora, sub anno* 1234.
[3] T. F. Tout, *Chapters in Administrative History,* i. 244 *et seq.*
[4] Letters Patent, 43 Hen. III, p. 6.

volving knowledge of prices and qualities, storage, and transport which were alien to the accountants' training of the Wardrobe clerks, was beginning to find its appropriate organization and its separate officials. From these outside activities of the Wardrobe, which first became systematized in the late 'thirties, the Great Wardrobe of the fourteenth century arose.

Henry's personal policy

Such, in roughest outline, was Henry's curial machine. It was a product of the time rather than the man, for he had no very strong will, and for long periods undertook no great enterprises of state. The instinct to withdraw the crown within an inner structure of domestic offices was, in him, that of a weak nature which feared the concurrence of the feudatories in open council. Henry's very weakness left the way open to change. Far from sharing the illegalism of his father's reign, his was a time of security of right and of rapid development of process, during which, in the abeyance of the chancellorship, the number of available writs was multiplied many times and the courts took the final shape of their jurisdiction. The writing of Bracton's treatise falls in the years immediately before the upheaval of 1258. The reign was wrecked on personalities. Some recognition of the baronage as the ultimate sanction of government, and a more moderate exercise of the feudal prerogatives of the crown, would have freed Henry to exploit the administrative ability of his Chamber and Wardrobe uncriticized.[1] But, though his positive contempt for his native vassals was less marked, Henry shared his father's respect for foreign capacity. His papal overlord condemned English jealousy of foreigners,[2] and as a catholic and the head of a royal clan which stretched from Poitou to north Italy, he himself never learned to reckon with insular feeling. Disinclined to make his own will decisive, he turned in times of difficulty to a papal legation, which was, perhaps, his ideal of security, to his mother's sons and brothers-in-law of La Marche, and to his wife's Provençal and Savoyard relatives. With this foreign leaning it was easy to make his retreat from the feudal *curia* appear as a dereliction of English

The foreign favourites

[1] With the exception of Pierre des Rievaulx, who was dismissed from the Wardrobe, the barons accepted Henry's existing ministers almost without exception in 1258. T. F. Tout, *Chapters in Administrative History*, i. 296.
[2] *Royal Letters of Henry III* (ed. Shirley), i. 540.

kingship, and to give special bitterness to the hatred which was incurred by any medieval government which taxed and administered great estates of royal demesne. The anti-foreign cry had been raised against William des Longchamps, against John's mercenaries and Pierre des Roches. It was raised again when William, elect of Valence, came to England with the queen, and was found to have mastered the king's confidence at the Northampton council of 1236. Suspicion was maintained by Otto's legation in 1237, though William of Valence withdrew in 1238 in order not to compromise Henry with his subjects. In 1240 the king's Wardrobe fell into the hands of Pierre d'Aigueblanche, William of Valence's treasurer. The period of foreign control of the Wardrobe lasted until 1258,[1] but those who exercised it were able and apparently not unpopular, and the Chancery, Treasury, and Judiciary remained the preserve of Englishmen. The real target of anti-foreign feeling was not the working clerk, but the nobles of Henry's family who came to fill the court and set the tone in counsel, who took their share of the wardships and custodies with the English, and whom the feudal confusion of lordship and wardship set to interfere in the fortunes of the greatest English families. The migration of brothers and uncles began in 1241 with Peter of Savoy, the uncle of the queen, Bernard of Savoy, and, a little later, Peter, son of the count of Geneva. Of the king's half-brothers, sons of Isabella by Hugh of La Marche, Guy de Lusignan was in the king's service in Gascony in 1242, and all four, William, Guy, Geoffrey, and Aymer, settled in England in 1247. The charge of pillaging the wealth of England which was commonly made against the princes of Savoy and Lusignan is hardly confirmed by the records. They were active statesmen, who served the king at court and upon foreign missions, and Thomas of Savoy came to be essential to Henry's continental system. Henry treated them as it was usual to treat important foreigners, and even Englishmen, whose fidelity was desired, and settled yearly sums upon them, nominally secured by promised grants of land, but actually issuing as pensions from the Wardrobe or the Exchequer.[2] Where lands were given

---

[1] Peter Chaceporc, 1241–54; Artaud de Saint Romain, 1255–7; Pierre des Rievaulx, 1257–8.

[2] Thomas of Savoy received 500 marks yearly (Letters Patent, 30 Hen. III, p. 489), William of Valence £500 (ibid. 31 Hen. III, p. 509), Guy de Lusignan

they were usually an endowment from the escheats upon the foreigners' first coming to court, and were not greatly increased in later years. Peter of Savoy, who was given custody of the earldom of Richmond, and William of Valence, whose wardship of the heiress Joan de Monchesni[1] led to his marriage and to the revival of the earldom of Pembroke in his favour, were the principal beneficiaries, and such grants hardly formed more than a suitable lodgment in the feudal hierarchy if Henry's policy of grafting his French relations into the English feudal stock were to be carried through. Whether the anglicized aristocracy of the Normans would submit to a further indraft from the Continent, and that from the doubly alien families of the Languedoc, was another matter.

Feudal diplomacy
It would, however, be unfair to ignore the element of policy in Henry's dealings with his relations; his son did the same with no sense of wrong. Amid the growth of new institutions it is easy to forget that the king had lost none of the rights of a feudal lord. How careful of feudal convention Henry could be we may see in his formal diffidation of Richard Marshal in 1233[2] and of the Montfortians before Lewes,[3] and in this relation, where his action was most personal, he appears, especially in his later years, as a persistent, though, perhaps, too ambitious manipulator of the domestic diplomacy of feudalism. From time to time in his long reign many of the great honours passed into his hands in wardship or escheat. Henry had been taught to study the example of the French crown[4] in the use of the lord's right of marriage to draw the counties of Namur and Ponthieu into dependence. Hubert de Burgh applied the same policy in marrying the earl Marshal to the king's sister, and when Henry grew older he used the marriage of his own children and of the princesses of Poitou and Savoy to extend the family tie over the principal English feudal

300 marks (*ibid.* p. 502), Geoffrey de Lusignan £500 (*ibid.* 41 Hen. III, p. 406). When we consider that the practice of pensioning the Poitevin nobility reaches well back into the period of Hubert de Burgh (William l'Archeveque was given a pension of 100 marks in 1226: *ibid.* 11 Hen. III, p. 102), that a good pension for a king's clerk was 60 marks, and that Simon de Montfort allowed himself to receive a pension of 600 marks, these amounts do not seem excessive for the king's brothers.   [1] Letters Patent, 39 Hen. III, p. 419.

[2] Wendover, ii. 55.   [3] Rishanger, *De Bellis*, p. 28.

[4] *Royal Letters of Henry III* (ed. Shirley), i. 246: *considerante etiam exemplum quondam regis Franciae Philippi.*

houses.[1] In individual cases these marriages were not always suc- *Extinction*
cessful. Gloucester had his Poitevin marriage annulled, and the *of the*
whole policy was arraigned in 1258.[1] Nevertheless effective opposi- *feudal*
tion seems to have been delayed for many years by the friendship *dynasties*
which Henry established with Richard de Clare during the latter's
minority, and by the accumulation of the earldoms of Leicester,
Pembroke, and Richmond in the hands of his relations. These
earls formed a firm royalist group in the 'fifties, and it was only
the quarrel within that group which gave back to the baronage its
natural leaders and made the crisis of 1258 possible. Moreover,
Henry pursued a steady policy of keeping the great escheated
honours in his own hands, which, together with the disaster of
Evesham and the extinction of a number of honours by inter-
marriage or the failure of heirs, helped to bring about a social
revolution. The baronage with which Edward had to deal was
far less formidable in power and ambition than that of Henry's
early days. In 1216 the number of earldoms held by Englishmen
not of the court circle was twenty-three. In 1272 only Warwick,
Hereford-Essex, Gloucester-Hertford, Norfolk, Lincoln, Surrey,
and Huntingdon survived. Edward held Chester; Edmund
Leicester, Derby, Lancaster, Aumale; Henry's son-in-law, Count
of Brittany, held Richmond; and Valence held Pembroke.
The great line of feudal dynasties, Chester, Derby, Leicester,
which had repeated its traditional opposition in 1173, 1215, and
1264, had vanished, and how little weight remained in the surviving earldoms Edward's treatment of the tenure of Bohun,
Clare, and Bigod was to prove. Partly by good fortune, partly by
the policy of a weak but consistent ruler persisting through two
generations, the thirteenth century saw the end of the great

1 *Volens omnes Regni sui nobiles degenerare.* Matthew Paris, *Chronica Majora,*
sub anno 1252. John, earl of Surrey, *m.* Alais de Lusignan; Robert, earl of Derby,
m. Mary de Lusignan; Baldwin, earl of Devon, *m.* Margaret of Savoy; Edmund,
earl of Lincoln, *m.* a daughter of the marquis of Saluzzo; John de Vesci, *m.* Mary
de Lusignan; Gilbert, earl of Gloucester, *m.* Alais de Lusignan; Joan de Monchesni, *m.* William de Valence; Matilda de Lacy, *m.* Peter of Geneva. *Murmur*
et indignatio per Regnum, ibid. sub anno 1247. The barons claimed that marriages
of great feudatories in ward should be arranged in consultation with them.
Ibid. sub anno 1238.
2 A later John de Warenne complained that he had been forced to marry
Joan de Bar when in ward to Edward *vi et metu qui cadere poterant in constantem*
virum. Northern Registers (Rolls Series), p. 229.

territorial units of the Conquest. The fourteenth century nobility was to rise upon the impulse of the Hundred Years War, and was royalist and inspired by the nationalistic ideals of the Round Table and the Garter.

With the exception of the Gascon war of 1253-4, Henry carried through no single enterprise of moment. Upon the surface of events his will played feebly, straying from object to object, and withdrawing nervously before an opposition which became automatic as the belief in his unkingliness hardened. But, though he could never master any crisis or outface any opponent, he had an inner fixity of purpose which conformed to those currents of the time which were setting away from feudalism. To this half-realized drift of events the recurrent opposition of Henry's reign *Baronial* was a reaction, and, as its direction revealed itself, so the policy *opposition* of the barons, at first opportunist and individual, began to draw together and to clothe itself in constitutional form. In the beginning it was an opposition of distrust rather than of grievance, and for many years it exhausted itself in complaints of ill-advised and foreign guidance, and restless schemes for baronial counsel, which, lacking the coöperation of the crown, it had not the vitality to carry through. It was, indeed, the malaise of feudalism under the first king who placed no value upon the tenurial incident of counsel, and who yet offered no positive target of misgovernment. Baronage was being deprived of significance both as a territorial power and in the *curia*, for, as the writer of the *Song of Lewes* complained, *rex vult sibi vivere*.

In weighing the motives of the baronial opposition we must remember to what forces the baron was exposed; the justices, the chancellor and his writs, the king and his rights of wardship and his demands for aid, the incidence of government upon their great franchises, rather than the general plight of the country. A baron of the king is a dangerous man for a sheriff to handle.[1] Provincial maladministration may to some degree pass him by. The common law, the judiciary, the great offices, and the council will be the

---

[1] So the county of Lancaster, having tried to levy a distress upon Montbegon of Hornby, refers the whole matter to the council *cum ipse magnus homo erat et baro domini regis.*

first consideration of the feudatories, for, much more than the shrievalty, each of these has maintained its hold upon that peerage of baronial immunities which is, in the eyes of the magnates, the *communitas Angliae*. But this central mass of the baronage fades into the classes above and below it. The substantial knight tenant, the baron with few fees, may feel his interest to be with the mass of county freeholders. At the other end of the scale there is a tendency for a separate order of the earls to come into being. There is at times a desire to distinguish between the *magnates, proceres,* and the *universitas baronum.* De Montfort, with his stewardship, the residual claim of his sons to the throne, and his Welsh alliances, never worked easily with the *universitas baronum,* and Gloucester and Warenne also were involved from time to time in more exalted ties of policy. Thus there were always rifts in the opposition, which tended to widen as soon as it had achieved success.

Again, we must remember that opposition to personal monarchy *Political* was no longer entirely governed by the near view of practical *theory of* politics. Throughout western Europe these two generations were *opposition* concerning themselves with the problems of law, authority, and counsel, setting the *regale dominium* against the *regimen politicum.* England was poor soil for political definitions, but that sense of the responsibility of kingship which was diffused throughout Christian thought was here and there being intellectualized and brought to a more definite application. Difficult to localize or define, the same thought inspires the most diverse quarters. Alike for Bracton and the anonymous cleric of the Song of Lewes the king has his associates, almost his masters, in his council, and his native counsellors are the barons of his realm.[1] Less specifically, this was the doctrine of the Franciscans and of Grosseteste, and the leaders of revolt in two generations, Richard Marshal and Richard Seward, and again Simon de Montfort may have found inspiration in Grosseteste's friendship and writings.[2] More practically, the

---

[1] Bracton, *De Legibus Angliae,* II. xvj. 3: *Rex autem habet superiorem . . . item curiam suam, videlicet comites, barones, quia comites dicuntur quasi socii regis, et qui habet socium habet magistrum*: Moreover the king has a superior in his court, *i.e.* his earls and barons, for by earls (*comites*) is meant companions of the king and he who has a colleague has a master (probably an interpolation, but an early one).

[2] Simon had read Grosseteste's treatise *De Principatu Regni et Tyrannidis* in common with the third of this group of friends, Adam Marsh. C. L. Kingsford, *The Song of Lewes,* Introduction and Appendix.

king's minority focussed attention upon the ministers and counsellors and upon the crown. The problem of the central will, its
relation to the kingdom, its control by external forces, and the
channels through which it made itself felt, in short the problem of
sovereignty, must inevitably have forced itself upon the political
leaders of England within measurable time, but the reign of a king
whose acts were the reflection of a succession of advisers stronger
than himself shortened the period of consideration and compelled
an unnaturally quick solution, all the more so because from 1240
onwards the counsel which influenced the king was principally
that of foreigners. For this reason the conciliar schemes of 1244
and 1258 have the violence of immaturity and revolution, though
they are inspired by the oldest elements in English political
thought.

The baron's view as to their own constitutional status is a confusion of the ideas of two epochs slowly clearing as the reign goes
on. First is a survival of the older conception of the feudal *curia*,
that the king's natural counsellors are his barons, that his principal
officials should be barons, or at least such as the barons can
associate with their order, and that what affects the generality or is of
great moment—*magna negotia regni*—should be decided in full
curia of the magnates. According to this curial view of the realm
—curial or honorial because all institutions should draw their
strength from the *curia* of the vassals and take their tone from the
chivalrous and domestic ideals of the honour—the political
function of the barons is exhausted in the service and counsel of
the king, and the furthering of his ends, and the *commune consilium*
is the king's *curia* swollen to its full membership. Governed by
this survival of an ideal feudalism[1] which has been unrealizable
for half a century, and inclined to revert to the simplified structure
of the private honour as the norm of the state, the barons reject
Longchamps as of base birth and substitute for him baronial
justiciars in the king's name, grudgingly accept de Burgh as a
magnate of new standing, and find it their first gravamen against
Henry III that he rules without a justiciar, chancellor, and treasurer

---

[1] Henry himself at times appealed to this kind of loyalty: *Ecce Rex . . . ex
abrupto advenit . . . protestans quod eorum honor suus foret et e converso*: he came in
suddenly and protested that their honour and his were inseparable. Matthew
Paris, *Chronica Majora, sub anno* 1244.

of baronial or prelatical rank, and takes counsel with foreigners. Secondly, supervening upon this older notion, and never perfectly extricated from it in Henry's reign, is the more modern notion of the assembly of the barons as an institution of the community rather than of the crown, whose affinities are with the *universitas regni* or body of tenants in chief, for which it acts as representative, approaching the government from without, and "parleying" with the king and his council in meetings which are coming to be called *colloquia* or *parliamenta*. In this phase—the two phases overrun each other—the breach in the *curia* is accepted. It is taken for granted that the baronage can associate themselves with the crown only by mastering it. They begin to claim a constitutional control in order to recall the king to his trust; the more enlightened will say to his trust for the *communitas Angliae*, those less so will think of it as a trust for the *universitas* of tenants in chief. We cannot, of course, interpret the *parlemenz* of the Provisions of Oxford as incorporating a developed estate of the realm. Nevertheless, the assembly of magnates, representative of a nation-wide if not a national constituency, summoned to meet the king and council *pur treter des besoingnes le rei et del reaume*, is a necessary passage in the evolution of parliament, and a profound break with the curial and tenurial outlook of the past.

The barrier to progress along this line was the belief of the *The prob-*
feudal order that counsel was an incident of tenure and that the *lem of*
assembly of the magnates was the king's council par excellence, as, *counsel*
exceptionally, it still was for John.[1] This view was flattered by the fact that Henry never really abandoned the practice of summoning the council of the whole baronage at intervals, nor tried to take aids without its consent. The notion of the *commune consilium* as a body of opposition was thus slow in forming. Conversely the magnates won with difficulty to the conception of a king's council distinct from the *commune consilium* of the feudatories, and which should attend unremittingly to the king's business, and put itself under special vows of secrecy and integrity. Such an idea was

[1] Cf. John's use of *magnates regni nostri* and *concilium nostrum* as equivalent phrases. Letters Patent, 8 John, p. 72. A late instance before 1258 when the term *curia regis* was used of the assembly of magnates acting legislatively with the king is at the council of Merton in 1236, *provisum est in curia domini regis . . . coram majore parti comitum et baronum angliae. Statutes of the Realm,* i. 1.

essentially opposed to the feudal strand of thought in the minds of both king and magnates, for feudatories who were admitted to a special council submitted themselves to a new kind of obligation and were required to bind their consciences to unfamiliar standards,[1] and to show a new kind of discretion. Homage and fealty bred feelings and loyalties of quite a different order. Thus, the barons were reluctant to detach themselves from their equals,[2] and for the same reason the king rarely found suitable counsellors among his magnates, unless, like William Marshal, Montfort, Warenne, or Salisbury, they owed him a family loyalty also. According to the papal view he was free to ignore tenurial qualification as soon as he came of age, and to govern *cum consilio domesticorum*,[3] but Henry was hesitant as a doctrinaire and satisfied to evade the issue by giving his foreign relations a titular footing in English feudalism and using them together with his clerks and sufficient of the more compliant of the English barons to placate moderate opinion. Both sides, therefore, were slow to clear their minds as to what was the actual issue. It took many years for the baronial assembly to exchange the habits of a feudal *curia* for the persistent independence and mutual loyalty of political opposition.

In so far as the barons had a consistent view, they had come to maintain that the *commune consilium* was the primary council of the realm, and to complain if great affairs of state were done without it. The king and his barons should be at one. They were aggrieved that the imperial marriage of 1236 and the Poitevin alliance of 1242 were carried through without their advice, and in 1237, when summoned only to grant an aid, they expressed their surprise that no *magna negotia regni* were put before them.[4] They could not help realizing that the *domestici* and *familiares*, who were always with the king, had to be reckoned with as a secondary council. They knew it bridged the intervals between the meetings

[1] The conflict between the two kinds of counsellor, and the failure of contemporaries to understand it is well illustrated by the quarrel between Richard Percy and Gilbert Basset recorded by Matthew Paris, *Chronica Majora*, *sub anno* 1237.

[2] *Sine paribus suis tunc absentibus nullum voluerunt responsum dare*: they would make no answer without those of their peers who were absent. *Ibid. sub anno* 1255.

[3] *Ibid. sub anno* 1223.

[4] *Ibid. sub anno* 1237. *Imperialia et alia ardua negotia.*

of general councils, but they were jealous and affronted if it showed signs of becoming the primary council. The mind of the king must be fully open to his magnates;[1] there was no more certain occasion of offence than for one of the permanent council to affect secrecy with the king in the presence of the barons; he might be reminded that they were the king's intimates also and were not to be treated as outsiders.[2] Henry, for his part, gave intermittent justification for the belief that he was withdrawing himself from baronial counsel. Coming to London, the magnates often found themselves still without access to the king's person and that familiarity of his court which vassals ought to enjoy. At times when the *colloquium* of barons assembled at Westminster he removed from the Palace to the Tower, and would only address them through one of his clerks[3] as speaker.[4] Frequently they found the real identity of the court was not the king's. They had been brought not to hear their natural lord but the elect of Valence as in 1236, or a Roman legate as in 1237. In reaction, they began to accept the breach in the traditional unity of the *curia*. Since he is not with them as in his council, they counsel with each other rather than with the king, withdraw and debate secretly,[5] and return with a common answer.[6] Their solidarity becomes proof against bargaining. Individuals and groups learn to refuse to answer *sine communi universitate*.[7] In 1244 a committee of twelve drawn from prelates, earls, and barons is empowered to answer for the whole. The constitutional problem is a difficult one. General assemblies cannot be multiplied indefinitely, and individual barons will not easily adapt themselves to the functions of *familiares*. If they do they become suspect themselves.[8] Nevertheless, it is this expedient which is tentatively adopted, and in 1237 a baronial wing is added

---

[1] *Vestrum omnium, quasi fidelium et naturalium hominum, consiliis se subdere*: to be guided by the counsel of you all as of his natural lieges. Matthew Paris, *Chronica Majora, sub anno* 1237.

[2] *Ibid. sub anno* 1237.

[3] As through William of Cailli in 1237.

[4] *Quasi mediator inter Regem et regni magnates. Ibid. sub anno* 1237.

[5] *Secesserunt in locum seorsum secretiorem . . . inirent consilium*: they went aside by themselves and held counsel. *Loc. cit.*

[6] *Ibid. sub anno* 1242: *Magno inter eos tractatu praehabito . . . dederunt consilium*: they offered counsel after preliminary discussion among themselves.

[7] *Loc. cit.*

[8] As did the earls of Lincoln and Leicester in 1237. *Ibid. sub anno.*

to the council. This was perhaps the first explicit recognition of a permanent council as a separate entity, and Henry underlined its distinctive standing by exacting from Warenne, Ferrars, and John fitz Geoffrey, the baronial nominees, an oath that they would refuse bribes and give impartial counsel. It was a declaration of policy. The oath of homage no longer qualified the greatest vassal to share the inner confidence of the king.[1] Henceforth there were two councils recognized as there had long been two in function; the one permanent, advisory, and executive; the other occasional, critical or revisory, increasingly obsessed by political grievance.[2]

On the whole, this dualism in the *curia* seems to have conformed to Henry III's views, and he emphasized it from the 'forties onwards in a way which became increasingly distasteful to the barons. The king continued to summon the magnates, but not at regular intervals, and with the limited purpose of granting aids or debating war-like enterprises for which the military action of the barons would be necessary. Writs have survived summoning the magnates to advise on, or mentioning their agreement to, the Scotch expedition of 1244,[3] the subsequent Welsh campaign,[4] and that of 1258,[5] and to solicit aid, as for Gascony in 1254,[6] when a campaign had already been begun, and there are, of course, other notices of such councils in the chronicles.[7] Henry's rule, indeed, was roughly according to the letter as opposed to the spirit of the Great Charter. He had no chance of getting an aid without the *commune consilium*, and, except for bargaining with individuals, did not try to evade it; and sometimes, though not always, he went further than the Charter demanded and asked the opinion of his magnates on the policy for which the aid was required. But further than this he would not go. Just as he withdrew the administration within the circle of the domestic ministers, so he

---

[1] Apparently the first instance of a sworn council was in 1233.

[2] Cf. the writ of 38 Hen. III when the king was in Gascony: *vobis mandamus quatenus sitis apud Westomonasterium coram regina nostra et Ricardo comiti Cornubiae fratre nostro et aliis de consilio nostro . . . audituri beneplacitum nostrum et voluntatem et cum praefato consilio nostro super predictis negociis tractaturi. Report on the Dignity of a Peer*, iii, p. 12. [3] *Ibid*. p. 9.

[4] *Ibid*. p. 11.   [5] *Ibid*. p. 17.   [6] *Ibid*. p. 12.

[7] *E.g.* to hear the claims of the Scotch king in 1237, to consider the war in Poitou in 1242, and in 1246–7 to find means of meeting the papal demands.

retained the general conduct of government, the allocation of the castles, counties, escheats, and wardships, the judiciary, the itinerant commissions, the sanctioning of writs, as the prerogative of himself and his familiar council.[1] In taking upon itself the discontents of its order, the general *colloquium* had, in Henry's view, disqualified itself for that favourable counsel which a lord might demand from his vassals.[2] Upon the one side and the other, the breach in the feudal *curia*, long a fact, was becoming avowed.

When once the end of the traditional union of crown and baronage in a joint feudal régime was realized a struggle to control the king was inevitable. During the minority the magnates could still regard themselves as constituents of the government in right of their tenure in chief of the honour of England. They felt secure in the new safeguard of a reaffirmation of the Charters. Progressively, as they were forced into the position of spectators and saw clerks and foreigners in the great charges of state, there grew in their minds the possibility of seizing upon the government and dominating it from without. A precedent for baronial control of the executive had already been set. Bishop Nevill could claim to have been given the chancellorship *in communi consilio regni*. By the 'forties the barons were becoming critical of the detail of government. In 1241 they secured the relegation of the customary revenue to trustees from the Temple and the Hospital.[3] In 1242 they refused an aid on the ground of previous grant, and questioned the method by which escheats were kept, emphasized the great exactions of the recent eyres and pleas of the Forest, and doubted

---

[1] The king's claim to supremacy over the executive is very clearly put in *The Song of Lewes*, 11, 492 *et seq.*: "it is no affair of the magnates to whom the king entrusts his counties and castles, or employs as his justiciars. He is determined to have whom he will as chancellor and treasurer, to choose his ministers from any nationality, and to appoint and dismiss his ministers at his discretion. Every earl has this degree of control within his own honour, as, indeed, the king desires him to have it." Cf. also Matthew Paris, *Abbreviatio*, 291.

[2] As late as the Lincoln parliament of 1301 Edward I insisted that the magnates were bound by their oath (of homage) to offer no counsel and put forward no claim which might trench upon the *jura corone: prelati, comites, barones, et ceteri magnates . . . ad observandum et manutenendum jura regni et corone una nobiscum juramenti vinculo sint astricti*: prelates, earls, barons, and other magnates are equally bound by oath with ourselves to observe and maintain the rights of realm and the crown. *Report on the Dignity of a Peer*, iii. p. 121.

[3] Letters Patent, 25, Henry III, p. 249.

Opposition aims whether they had been properly collected and kept. They are sceptical of the king's guarantee of the Charter, and they will not be placated by his offer to redress any grievance that individuals put forward. In short, they are at last disillusioned with the old safeguards. Reaffirmation of the Charters has come to be a form. The *commune concilium* is summoned to reflect the king's intentions. At first they are inclined to resort to old methods. Only obstinate insistence can restore reality to the feudal constitution. In 1244 —again the authority is that of Matthew Paris [1]—they fulfilled the implied threat of 1242, and approached the king, not with individual complaints, but with a programme which was a practical challenge to Henry's whole view of the state. They would go back to the old ways. Four nominees of the barons were to follow the king, of whom two at least were to be in constant attendance. As with the barons who coöperated with Henry II in the work of *Scheme of 1244* government, it is hard to say whether they were regarded as justiciars or counsellors. They were to combine executive and advisory functions, their title, if any, was that of conservators of the Charters, they were to sit with the king to give immediate remedy for legal wrongs, to deal with the king's treasure according to their view and provision, and the chief justiciar and the chancellor were expected to be chosen from among them.

The remedy for the assumed defects of the council, the elected *conservatores*, is, in fact, an idealization of some less specialized constitution of the twelfth century. The rest of the scheme, because it deals with concrete abuses, is of its own day, and shows that the opposition have come to some understanding of Henry's system and of their own disabilities under it, by which the reality of power is escaping them. The target is now the personal government and specifically the lapse of the great offices, particularly that of the chancellor, which is responsible for the impoverishment of the crown by the wasting of escheats and for a threat to the security of landright by the issue of writs against precedent and custom. [2]

---

[1] Historians have neither accepted nor rejected Matthew's account very confidently, but it bears some marks of being a contemporary draft or memorandum, and the confusion of functions suggests inexperience. Strong reasons have been advanced for associating it with the crisis of 1237–38. N. Denholm-Young, *English Historical Review*, vol. lviii. pp. 401 *et seq.*

[2] *Per defectum cancellarii brevia contra justitiam pluries fuerant concessa.* Matthew Paris, *Chronica Majora, sub anno* 1244. Writs with the *non obstante* clause, noticed

With the Great Seal at Henry's discretion, a wide door was open for that legal experiment altering right which the barons most of all feared. Henceforth, therefore, there was to be a justiciar and a chancellor elected by the magnates, not to be changed without *commune consilium*, and to prevent such evasions as the merely titular chancellorship of Nevill, all writs were to be invalid if the king deprived the chancellor of the seal. As a further safeguard, two of the justices of Common Pleas and the justice of the Jews were to be elected, and some action unspecified was to be taken as to the eyre jurisdiction. Aid will be unnecessary if the chancellor conserves the escheats instead of giving them to foreigners and the conservators handle the royal treasure wisely. To that end two elected barons are for the future to serve at the Exchequer.

The interest of this programme is not as a constitutional actuality, which it never was, but as a scheme which, even if it came from the brain of Matthew Paris only, would still reflect the uncertainties of a transitional phase of thought. In it we see the barons in mid-course of their evolution from a curial to a parliamentary status. They are already sound critics of the executive, but they have lost their old standing and their future function in the state is yet to find. The parts of the Angevin machine are already so familiar that each can be effectively padlocked by the check of baronial deputies, but, as reconstituted, that machine is expected to run of its own motion under the conservators. The feudal creed that the first duty of a vassal is to serve his lord in council is set aside as an anachronism; in fact the scheme will release the feudatories from a curial duty which has no longer any meaning. The *universitas* is not to be again summoned until the conservators find good cause; the *conservatores* will be the king's chief councillors. The offices which on the first occasion are filled by election may in future be left to the nomination of the conservators, who, like the Twenty-Five of the Great Charter, are in name and function conservators of feudal liberties. Upon the positive side there is nothing, no sense that the *commune consilium*, having lost its function of afforcing the crown, may find a new one as the voice of the *universitas*, criticizing and opposing where the interests of the crown and the community are at variance, conveying

as a new abuse in 1250 and frowned on by conservative justices, were particularly unpopular, as was the *quo warranto* writ when used of land.

advice and support where they are identical, that it may need to meet regularly, and even to compel the king to meet it, to "hold parliament" with it. If this reflects reality, to be a baron of the king meant in politics less than for some time before or after, for the *commune consilium* has become meaningless or burdensome and the parliament is as yet some years in the future.

This constitution was never put into force. If it had even that degree of authority, it was a party document such as those provisions which the prelates drew up in 1257 "to be given effect at some more favourable conjuncture".[1] At any time during the next fourteen years the occurrence of such an opportunity seems to have waited only for some coincidence of persons and events which should carry the gathering impatience with Henry across the line of action. He himself displayed a genius for bringing the magnates to the verge of an explosion and then dissipating the tension by ingenuously displaying his alarm and his haste to placate them. In a succession of general councils, whenever an aid was asked for, in 1248, 1249, 1255, the same comedy was played, the confirmation of the Charters, which no longer convinced anyone, was demanded and granted—Henry himself liked to take a leading part in the ceremony of pronouncing excommunication against those who should break them—and the more solid scheme for the restoration of the great offices was as regularly presented and refused. Aid was denied the king, and he proceeded to pay his way by papal taxes on the clergy, by begging from individuals, pressing the pleas of the forest, selling his woods, and cutting down his household expenses to a degree which his subjects thought disgraced the nation.[2]

Preliminaries to revolt

There was no apparent reason why this cat-and-dog relation should not have been continued indefinitely. The rank and file of the barons were under a growing sense of responsibility to the feudal classes, but with the magnates the king's position even improved. In 1255 Gloucester, Leicester, Warenne, Lincoln, and Devon were all upon his side. Richard of Cornwall, whose prestige and wealth were enormous at that time, was neutral, and blocked all action. The archbishop of Canterbury was abroad, and was no party man when at home, and the see of York was

[1] Matthew Paris, *Chronica Majora, sub anno* 1257.
[2] Letters Patent, 39 Hen. III, p. 433.

vacant. The Poitevin lords had grown rich, confident, and secure. The *universitas* felt itself leaderless and became resigned to inaction. Henry could not rally the baronage to himself, and when Rostand brought the royal ring of Apulia to Prince Edmund in 1255 even Richard would take no share in its acceptance, but still the group of English and Poitevin magnates who dominated the council[1] were strong enough to discourage opposition, and were working with the king to carry the Sicilian scheme forward,[2] although Norfolk, Hereford, and Oxford held aloof. There still need, perhaps, have been no constitutional crisis, or at least none that could not have been overridden, had not the always precarious peace of the royal family been shattered in the autumn of 1257 and the spring of 1258 with an effect not greatly less than that of the breach which preceded the Wars of the Roses. Henry himself had quarrelled with the earl of Norfolk two years earlier, and had been upon the verge of a quarrel with his son Edward, now lord of Chester, Gascony, and Ireland, which had caused him to reflect upon the family wars of his grandfather. In May the influence of Richard was removed when he sailed for Germany and the lesser members of the family were left to face each other uncontrolled. The Welsh war, falling upon the perennial jealousies of the Welsh March, broke the vital alliance of Leicester and Gloucester with the Poitevins. The former were accused of inspiring Llewellyn's ravaging of William of Valence's earldom of Pembroke.[3] In this confusion of hatred and suspicion the *universitas* at last found its leaders. Leicester denounced the immunity of the king's brothers from legal accountability and made it the pretext for some show of turning for justice from the king to the barons.[4]

This time, also, the crisis might have faded into the usual stalemate had not Henry been compelled to persist in demanding an

[1] Letters Patent, 40 Hen. III, p. 451. Henry announces that privileges concerning the affair of Apulia are being sealed with the counsel of the bishops of Hereford and Winchester, William de Valence, Geoffrey de Lusignan, the earls of Gloucester and Warwick, John Mansel, and others.

[2] Gloucester and Leicester were committed to the manœuvres by which the money for Apulia was borrowed and secured. *Ibid.* pp. 498, 563, Leicester and Richmond were commissioned to Rome in the affair as late as June 1257. *Ibid.* p. 567.   [3] Matthew Paris, *Chronica Majora*, *sub anno* 1257.

[4] Matthew Paris, *Chronica Majora*, *sub anno* 1258: *Non tamen regi sed universitati praecordialiter est conquestus*: he complained warmly not to the king but to the baronage.

aid, since he had gone too far in Apulia to retreat. Thus he kept the barons meeting at intervals during the first half of 1258, and, in the course of what was almost a single prorogued council, they worked themselves into a mixture of fear, mutual loyalty, and anger, which produced a revolutionary impulse such as had not been seen for forty years. It was the mood in which the Londoners locked their doors against the Cahorsins and Jewish assassins, in which sober clerks estimated the crown's current expenditure at 850,000 marks,[1] and country gentlemen dismissed their cooks for fear of Poitevin poison.[2] But it also had the genuine political grievances of two generations to work upon. Not only the magnates, but the church,[3] and, as it proved later, the lesser feudatories, had had time to clarify their discontents and to prepare themselves to seize upon any real break in the stability of the realm.

Outbreak of the revolt of 1258 The beginning of the crisis was the work of a group of the greater magnates. They had made it inevitable by breaking the king's circle, and the ultimatum was presented to him by his personal enemy Roger Bigod. It demanded the expulsion of the foreigners[4] and a reform of the realm impoverished through them by the counsel of English nobles. In return, they would persuade the *communitas regni* to grant an aid for Sicily. This was on April 30, 1258. On May 2 Henry promised to submit to a purge of his government by the provision of a committee of twenty-four, twelve of his own party and twelve chosen from that of the barons. He and the Prince bound themselves to accept its decisions and to meet parliament on June 9 at Oxford to give them effect. Of the grievances which precipitated the crisis, other than the sense of their loss of constitutional function and the hatred of the king's family, we may judge by the so-called Petition of the Barons, which is thought to have been drawn up by the twelve baronial commissioners in the interval before the Oxford parliament.[5] They are of the familiar type, supplementary to and corrective of the

Demands of 1258: petition of the barons

---

[1] Matthew Paris, *Chronica Majora*, *sub anno* 1257: *Quod est horribile cogitatu,* and also, it must be said, entirely untrue.   [2] *Loc. cit.*

[3] Cf. the bishop's Articles of grievance compiled in 1257 but withheld "for a more favourable occasion". Matthew Paris, *Chronica Majora*, *sub anno*; *Additamenta.*

[4] Safe-conduct for the king's brothers to leave England under conduct of the earls of Hereford, Warenne, and Aumâle was issued on July 5, 1258. Letters Patent, 42 Hen. III, p. 640.

[5] R. F. Treharne, *The Baronial Plan of Reform, 1258-1263.*

standing articles of the Charters, and there is a visible reaction against Henry's exploitation of feudal right for the advantage of foreigners.[1] Castles are to be entrusted to native Englishmen, and heiresses are not to be disparaged by marriage to men not of English birth. The reference is evident, and beyond this there is little that is new—minor inconveniences of the use of wardship, abuses of the king's right in the forests, of his use of escheat, of sheriffs' claims to more suit than is their right, of their misuse of the *murdrum* fine and so forth, and of the Wardrobe's buyers' purchases by way of prise.

The crisis was, it seems, no revolt against intolerable wrongs. *Provisions* There was no general threat to the common law as under John, *of Oxford* and there had been no forced levies. Rather, at the end of a long period of maturing political experience, the time was ripe for a readjustment of the status of king, council, and *communitas regni*, which could no longer be expressed in the old formulae of the *curia regis*. It was likely that the occasion would release almost more than was required of the political inventiveness of the barons, which had been stored up during thirty years of enforced inactivity, and though there was, perhaps, no single article of the reforms for which precedent could not be found, the Provisions of Oxford sum up the end of an epoch because they recognize the changes which Henry III's reign have brought about and stereotype them in a constitution. The scheme of 1258 was realistic where that of 1244 was reactionary. It abandoned the past frankly. The confusion of executive and judicature in a committee of baronial justiciars was dropped, and the contemporary division of powers and functions accepted. Specifically, the permanent advisory council was recognized and made the centre of the system, to which end four electors were taken from the two parties and empowered to choose fifteen magnates as king's councillors. The *commune consilium*, on the other hand, was relegated to what had *Parliament* come to be its true function as an assembly roughly representative of the *universitas* and watching conciliar government from a distance, informing the permanent council as to the state of the community, and treating with it *des communs besoignes del reaume et del rei*. It is not a serious anachronism to say that the intermittent assemblies of the barons had been becoming decreasingly obedient

[1] Petition of the Barons, 4 and 6.

to the canons of the feudal *curia* and increasingly independent, or, as we may almost say, parliamentary, for the sense of parliament is a parley of antagonists. From 1246 Paris called such assemblies parliaments; the term is used officially of the Easter parliament of 1255,[1] and the Twenty-Four ordain in the Provisions that there shall be three *parlemenz* every year at Michaelmas, Candlemas, and three weeks before the feast of St. John. This is the end of a prolonged and gradual evolution in public life, which now receives statutory recognition. The problem of the organization, and, indeed, that of the composition of the *universitas* for parliamentary purposes, remains to be solved. For the time being it is content to elect twelve of its body as a convenient channel through which to treat with the council at every parliament, and itself to remain in some obscurity.

The great offices   The provisions dealing with the executive mark the triumph of the long-standing demand for the restoration of the great offices to their former substance and rank—at least to their independence from the king and the household. The justiciar is to be more than a mouthpiece for the issue of judicial commissions. He is to "amend according to the law the wrongs done by all other justices and bailiffs and earls and barons", in short, to be the guardian of common right. This he is to do by the counsel of the king and of the great men of the realm and according to the provision of the Twenty-Four. He is not to take bribes or fees, and therefore he is allotted the great salary of a thousand marks a year. His office is for a year only, and then he must answer for his term before the king's council and his successor. In fact Hugh Bigod's justiciarship produced the great part of what redress the commonalty received from the baronial government. The chancellor equally is responsible to the council for everything but the routine of his office. He may seal writs of course without reference, but the great wardships and escheats, which have played so large a part in the king's personal rule, must be granted only with the consent of council.[2] The general restriction on the seal's use is a clumsy one; nothing is to be sealed which is against the ordinances made by the Twenty-Four, but, no doubt, the assumption is that the chancellor

---

[1] Letters Patent, 39 Hen. III, p. 399.
[2] A revival of the practice of the minority when escheats were disposed of *per commune consilium*. Letters Close, 3 Hen. III, p. 384.

will obey only the precepts of the council. The Treasurer's office is to be annual; "good men" are to be put into the Exchequer by the ordinance of the Twenty-Four. All the issues of the realm are to be paid there, and further order is to be taken as it seems necessary. As in all changes of government in this age, the provincial charges were taken into account. No baronial government felt itself safe unless the principal royal castles were lodged in the hands of its leading members. As in 1216 so in 1258, the leading *Provincial* magnates of the opposition took security in fifteen of the chief *government* castles[1] before the work of reform was begun. For twelve years the king's precept would be insufficient to compel their surrender without warrant of a majority of the council. The sheriffs were to be vavasours of the counties in which they served, salaried, and appointed for a year only.

The fact that the Provisions of Oxford could be pressed through during the few weeks of the Oxford parliament suggests that they embodied changes which had become a familiar prospect to most public men. Indeed they were approved by such royalists as Walter de Kirkham and Peter de Savoy. They were brought in almost without change of ministers, Lovel retaining the Treasury[2] and Wingham the Chancery. Only Pierre des Rievaulx was removed from the Wardrobe. But in the hands of the reformers the constitution of the Provisions of Oxford was unworkable for *Defects* any length of time. It lodged all authority in the council, and pre- *in the* supposed the elimination of the king's will, while requiring the *Provisions* form of his consent to every act of government.[3] Yet without a single dominant will the council was itself ungovernable. The nervous ingenuity with which its original membership was contrived betrays its instability. It represented, or was under pressure from, a dozen interests which were only united by hatred of the Poitevins—the magnates of the king's party, the group of Norfolk and Hereford, the persons and interests of Gloucester and Leicester, the habitual conservatism of the *universitas* of the barons, the more radical bachelors, and the unrepresented mass of freeholders, who

[1] Letters Patent, 42 Hen. III, p. 637. June 22, 1258.

[2] Until November 1258. *Ibid.* 43 Hen. III, p. 1.

[3] *Et nus averun ferm e estable quanque lavant dit conseil ou la greinure partie fera*: and we will hold established whatsoever the said council or the greater part of it shall do. *Ibid.* 42 Hen. III, p. 645.

had the best reasons to press consistently for reform.[1] Only at its peril could the council of the Fifteen put its quality of a reformed government to the test, and commit itself to action. The balance achieved in the summer of 1258 was, indeed, at the mercy of every change of favour or circumstance. The momentary absence of the chancellor in July 1259[2] let slip a writ from Chancery which might have embroiled the council with the pope.[3] The Peace of Paris took the king to France and made necessary a duplicate government, whereof the king's half was rapidly converted to be a replica of his personal rule, and a royal party was re-knit. Simon played his own hand in the negotiations for peace, and quarrelled violently with Gloucester. By the time of his return in April 1260 Henry was able blandly to address the justiciar and the rump of the council with an assumption of common anxiety for the peace of the realm now threatened by the alliance of Montfort and Prince Edward, while at the same time he withheld the writs for a parliament which might have rallied the supporters of the Provisions. The crown was showing itself indispensable, and that *Decline of baronial unity* Henry was able to dismiss the justiciar and chancellor in April 1261, and to absolve himself from his oath to the Provisions, was due less to his personal skill, though he made no mistakes, than to the fallacy essential to a scheme of government which affected to rule a monarchical system without a king. The victory of Simon's party in 1263 was no more than a check to the coming victory of the crown, and the *Forma Regiminis*, which confirmed it by contracting effective power to the voice of three electors or nominators of the council, acknowledged those vices of division of authority and faction which no baronial government could shake off. As with Cromwell after him, only the assumption of the crown could have perpetuated Simon's rule, and the Edict of Kenilworth, which pronounced the sentence upon the baronial régime in 1266, opened with the reassertion of the personal

---

[1] The efforts made to accord such reform are described in a proclamation of October 20, 1258, and their official embodiment is in the Provisions of Westminster. The eyres of the justiciar and the other commissions which sought to redress local wrongs are described by Professor E. F. Jacob in his *Studies in the Period of Baronial Reform*.

[2] Letters Patent, 43 Hen. III, p. 29.

[3] *Ibid.* p. 35: the safe conduct for Valascus, the papal nuncio for the affair of the diocese of Winchester.

authority of the monarch—"that the most serene prince lord Henry shall have and fully hold his lordship, authority, and kingly power".[1]

Between 1258 and 1265 the forces of feudalism and monarchy, which had been fencing with each other for a generation, were brought to measure their strength and to declare their principles. Politically, the victory of the future king at Evesham was decisive. The original nobility of the Conquest, which had been the mainstay of the rebellions of two centuries, was destroyed as a distinctive force, and left the field to the newer, and for the time being weaker, nobilities of the North and the Welsh Border. As clearly as does their fall, the barons' moment of success reveals to what a point the nation had advanced beyond even the more moderate conceptions of feudalism. The Provisions of Oxford, designed *Triumph* to constrain the king, go almost the whole way to accept the *of the* monarchical state. Government of the realm by a feudal king in *monarchi-* and through the *curia* of his vassals is abandoned even in the modi- *cal system* fied form in which it had been entertained fourteen years earlier. The government of the Provisions takes over the division of executive functions, the specialized and powerful bureaucracy, even the members of the king's government. It recognizes the permanent sworn council as the motive force of the state, and relegates the *universitas* of the tenants in chief to a parliamentary status. Faced with the necessity of justifying twenty-five years of opposition, the barons establish control of the king's will, but capitulate to the monarchical régime. It was, perhaps, a natural reaction to a period during which the art of monarchy had been advanced while the king had lost the respect of his nobles, but it was an abandonment of the basic thesis of feudalism. No longer was it even conventionally maintained *quod debet rex omnia . . . facere in regno . . . per judicium procerum regni.*[2]

Yet the effects of Henry's misfortunes and of the baronial movement were very far from being extinguished at Evesham. The story of the first three-quarters of the thirteenth century is superficially one of discord, triviality, and failure. Without great causes and therefore without great men, it is a time of disillusionment with the older ways, while the new growth of the Edwardian

---

1 Dictum de Kenilworth, 1. Stubbs, *Select Charters*, p. 407.
2 Leges Eadwardi Confessoris, xi. 1. A6 (early thirteenth century).

Summary reigns is as yet unattainable. But for that very reason it is one of the great formative periods of English constitutional life. If one formula should be chosen above all others to explain it, it must be that the old coöperation between the crown and the vassals in the feudal state is dissolved. The nature of the vassal's counsel changes, ceases to be a fortification and a willing servant of the will of the supreme lord, and is diverted into independence, criticism, and distrust. *Commune consilium* comes to be something that the king has reason to fear, because it embodies a will which is self-determined and for the most part antagonistic to his own. It becomes parliamentary instead of curial. For its part, the crown goes its own way also, carried by the growing complexity of government to associate itself with advisers and ministers whose standing has been won by efficient service. A new council grows up about the king, skilled in the writs and rolls of Chancery, Treasury, Chamber, and Wardrobe, and engaged by every interest to forward the crown's official policy. In so far as the genius of English political institutions is determined by a permanent principle of opposition between the executive on the one side and the community and those who speak for it on the other, an opposition of court and country, the reigns of John and Henry III were decisive of the temper in which our parliamentary government should be carried on. Without this dualism it would have been impossible. Upon neither part is the process of evolution yet complete. The institutions which will one day arise to embody the national will to opposition are yet undreamed of. That will itself is still hardly more than a persistent instinct to distrust and hamper government in an aristocracy which has lost its traditional part in the régime. Those who have the opportunity to express what is under Henry still a grievance rather than a policy have but a doubtful qualification to do so, for the rule that defined *commune consilium* in the Great Charter was never practicable and has become increasingly untrue to legal and social reality. As a political order their day is over. Of the multitude of tenants who could have claimed to come to the *commune concilium* of 1215, less than a hundred will find a place in the *magnum concilium* of parliament, and the commons representation will depend upon a theory of politics of which feudalism knows nothing. Parliament, with a handful of royal nominees standing for the feudal magnates, and its elected deputies of the *Communitas Angliae* of all free men, is a creation of another world from that of Henry's middle years. But, in spite of this, every move in the slow integration of parliament is an answer to the problems set in these two generations. The crown, which under Henry has narrowed its confidence to a domestic officialdom and turned inward to exploit its demesne right, sets itself under his successor to exploit the realm of England with greater courage, and can afford to rebuild the *commune consilium regni* upon a new basis of parliament, choosing what can best serve it from the remnants of feudal counsel and from the rising political capacity of the communes. But it takes, and cannot but take, into the new régime of the community those forms of political consciousness which have been bred under John and Henry. Parliament will be neither the undifferentiated council, judicature, and executive which was the primitive feudal *curia*, nor the useful servant of prerogative which Edward I perhaps thought to make it. The magnates, even the commons whom he summons before him, will bring with them something of the old judicial function of the *curia* and the form of humble petition which was appropriate to the rule of a king governing by prerogative in council; but in the long run more of the spirit of opposition. From the fissure in the unity of the feudal *curia*, first apparent under John, and hardened into persistent antagonism under Henry, comes that principle of division and balance, statute in the form of redress of grievance, revenue bought by concession, the alternate domination of parliament by court and country, which became the established rhythm of parliamentary government.

IV

1272-1377

i

THE NATIONAL AND LOCAL COMMUNITIES

Franchise brought to rule IT is in the third quarter of the thirteenth century that we first become certain that feudal principles are losing hold. It is not that positive feudal rights are lost; on the contrary, the crown analyses and recognizes them; but by the act of recognition their further growth is stopped. The vagueness in which feudalism flourished begins to clear at the end of the twelfth century. Charters affect a new precision as to what they give, and purport to convey every known incident of privilege, current or obsolete, appropriate or not to the locality of the grant. Neither chancellor nor grantee could say what may or may not be the admissible limits of franchise, and, for that reason, they are determined that no liberty of which they have ever heard shall be omitted. Conversely, the regular entry of the king's justices into the county courts is causing immunities to be examined and referred to the *curia* when doubtful,[1] and what is not in writing is becoming hard to establish on the ground of mere prescription or as inference from general phrases. By the middle of the thirteenth century the *quo warranto* enquiry and the "subtlety" of royal lawyers are established feudal grievances, and if the immunist "exhibits his charter and claims some certain franchise as being implicit in a general clause, it profits him nothing unless the said franchise is mentioned in express terms".[2] The clergy considered that such judgments were

[1] Cf. the instructions to an eyre of 1218 (Letters Close, 3 Hen. III, p. 383): *Omnes autem demandas que coram vobis fuerint quas homines exigunt de libertatibus, videlicet quas dominus Archiepiscopus Cantuariensis, Gilbertus Comes de Clara, vel alii exigunt in respectum ponatis . . . coram consilio nostro apud Westmonasterium.* Where liberties had been exceeded the eyres were already seizing land and franchise into the king's hand. *Ibid.* p. 400.

[2] *Rotuli Parliamentorum*, i. 57. The abbot of St. Mary's, York, complains of the *subtilitas modernorum* in explaining away the *verba generalia* of charters.

violations of the Great Charter: *mirabile est dictu quod longissima* Denial of
possessio non prodesse contra regem.[1] Indeed, the denial of the inde- right by
feasible right of time marks the end of unchallenged feudal *prescription*
privilege, for it is as much as to say that all right comes from the
king. King's proctors claimed that a rule had been made by common council of the realm[2] that any claim to franchise by charter
must be established by definite and unambiguous words in the
grant, and for his great enquiry *quo warranto* Edward I could claim
and in part make good that time establishes no prescription
against the crown—*quod nullum tempus occurit regi.*[3] Finally,
Edward will go beyond even this and assert that when franchise
clashes with the welfare of the community the king may by
prerogative declare it void.[4]

But no reign is less open to the charge of being an age only of The idea
decline than that of Henry III. The great feudatories are losing of com-
their old constitutional place, but new orders are rising to take *munity in the shire*
their share; it is the age of the coming to maturity of provincial
government. The presage of this is a gradual change of life in the
shires and boroughs, which will have to develop many of the
characteristics of true communities before they are qualified to
play a constitutional rôle. The shires never in this age became truly
counties corporate; indeed, their community, even for administrative purposes, was only slowly attained. The shire had been a
unity of law since its creation, and from the time of Cnut was
entrusted with administrative action such as the pursuit of
criminals, but the Norman kings did not summon it as a whole
for other than legal business, or make it corporately responsible for
more than judgment[5] and a very few acts of local government.
For failure in these it could be amerced as a unit; but more than
this it had not entered into the mind of government to do, and
small experience of constitutional unity could come of it. Henry I

[1] Articles of the bishops: it is much to be wondered at that however long
possession (of franchise) is proved it should not be accepted as valid against the
king. Matthew Paris, *Chronica Majora, Additamenta, sub anno* 1257.

[2] *Placita de Quo Warranto,* p. 210: *de communi consilio regni Regis nuper
provisum.*   [3] *Ibid.* p. 4.

[4] *Rotuli Parliamentorum,* i. 71. *Dominus Rex, pro communi utilitate, per prerogativam suam in multis casibus est supra leges et consuetudines in regno suo usitatas:*
by prerogative and for the good of all the lord king is above the laws and
customs of his realm in certain cases.

[5] *Leges Hen.* I, 48, 2.

could conceive of no use for the shire except its judgment between honours, or some exceptional call for judgment or inquest upon the demesne rights of the crown,[1] nor, as we have seen, did he base upon it his occasional experiments in itinerant justice. Moreover, such rudimentary public functions as the shire possessed were gravely trenched upon by feudal immunity, since the view of frankpledge and freedom from amercement and common fine, and even from the sheriff's tourn, were common forms of franchise. Many barons and ecclesiastics could withhold their tenants' suit from shire and hundred and exclude the king's officers from entering their land after strayed cattle or to enforce pledge, while some received and served the king's writs, so that no sheriff or royal bailiff had any power within their franchise.[2] Far from being a single community at the disposal of the king's agents, the county was a patchwork of administrations, some where the king had all, some where a greater or less degree of privileged right prevailed, and much of which it could be said, *ibi domino Regi nihil accrescit*—"here the lord king has nothing". Alike in borough and county, franchise and community were opposing forces.

Royal action in the shire   Until the middle of the twelfth century the tide was with such feudal enclaves, but with Henry II a process of attrition began. At a stroke, the Assize of Clarendon re-created for the justices a community which had been partially lost to the sheriffs, placing the oath of every man of whatever fee at the disposal of the justices' inquest, and giving entry to the royal sheriffs into every bailiffry —"even the Honour of Wallingford"—to arrest under the Assize.[3] This was no isolated measure, for not only were the franchises brought into the machinery of the Inquest of Sheriffs, but the king tried to cancel the commonest of all immunities, that of view of frankpledge.[4] The shires were to experience a first lesson in administrative unity under the session of the justices, for it was the channel through which Angevin government was directed as

[1] Hen. I, Ordinance of the Shires and Hundreds, 1: *Precipio ut amodo comitatus mei et hundreta in illis locis et eisdem terminis sedeant, sicut sederunt in tempore regis Edwardi, et non aliter.* 2: *Ego enim, quando voluero, faciam ea satis summonere propter mea dominica necessaria ad voluntatem meam.*

[2] *Placita de Quo Warranto*, p. 675: *ita quod nullus vicecomes, ballivus, aut minister Regis manerium aut membra predicta ingrediantur ad districciones aliquas facere pro tallagiis sectis aut aliis consuetudinibus.*   [3] Assize of Clarendon, 11.

[4] *Ibid.* 9. Unlike Henry's other assizes, this rule had no visible effect.

it grew. The swearing of allegiance, the presentment of crime, the assizes, the affairs of the king's demesnes, escheats, custodies, the conservation of the peace, the assize of arms, all were under the survey of the justices or passed under the verdict of the hundreds, vills, and boroughs which made up the shire and which collectively soon came to be spoken of as *commune comitatus*.[1] Duties imposed one by one bred a habit of obedience until, within fifty years of the Assize of Clarendon, the shire was summoned to the justiciars' sessions to hear and obey the king's commands at large—*ad audiendum et faciendum*,[2] as in the later writs of parliament.

In community the shire could do much that it could not do in its first judicial function, or could do it more easily. Common obligation created a common outlook, and the counties began to take an effective part in their own government. To some extent the crown encouraged this as an offset against its own bailiffs. Petitions were admitted to claim local liberties,[3] and John, especially, consulted the shire on such matters as forest administration,[4] and the rights of the debtors of the Jews.[5] Almost certainly, by summoning four knights from every shire *de negotiis regni*,[6] he set the precedent that de Montfort and Henry III were to follow forty years afterwards, though it was as yet no more than a measure taken in a crisis, and had no immediate sequel. Beginning with John's reign the shires were to act upon their own initiative and in their own interest, combining to buy privileges and to secure the appointment of officials whom they could trust.[7] As the magnates withdrew into opposition and were confined more and more to their rare appearances in parliamentary meetings with the king and council, the counties fell into the hands of knights or freeholders and the stewards of the magnates, who declined to attend in person and were exempt by privilege from doing so.

Common action in the shire

[1] Assize of Northampton, 1.

[2] Letters Close, 3 Hen. III, p. 380: *audituri et facturi preceptum nostrum*.

[3] Letters Patent, 16 Hen. III, p. 456. Cumberland secures the reduction of the king's sergeants of the county to four.

[4] *Ibid.* 14 John, p. 129.   [5] *Ibid.* p. 132.

[6] Stubbs, *Select Charters*, p. 282.

[7] Pipe Roll, 8 John (Lancs.). Lancashire fines 100 marks to have Richard Vernon as sheriff. Letters Patent, 10 Hen. III, p. 45: Somerset and Dorset receive leave to elect a sheriff. *Ibid.* But when John sells the forest rights of Devon it is not as yet to the county but only to certain persons who subscribe to the fine. *Ibid.* 8 John, p. 70.

*The
change
from
feudal to
national
aids*

The shire must become a taxable community before it can
qualify to take its place beside the magnates as a community in
parliament with a voice in taxation. In the twelfth century the
great tenants-in-chief were intermediaries between the crown and
large sections of land and people, but during the thirteenth group
after group of tax-payers were extricated from their control and
brought into immediate responsibility to the Exchequer. The responsibility of the magnates came to be confined to their own land
in demesne and villeinage, and was finally abolished altogether,
and their knights and free tenants fell away into the body of the
county, which thus became a fiscal unity immediately accountable
to the crown. Setting aside the Danegeld and the Saladin Tithe,
the first of which was obsolete and the second, being upon the
ground of religious obligation, no analogy for secular action,
the taxation of Henry II's reign had been feudal. He tallaged his
demesne—in which royal boroughs, farms, and ministerial tenures
were included—and received aids and scutages from his tenants-in-
chief by military service. Both forms of revenue seem to have
passed through the sheriffs' hands, but the county as such was not
the basis of the tax. The honours bore it, and the non-military freeholders, free socagers, and the like, must have gone untaxed. The
military sub-tenants of the honours seem not to have been bound
by a scutage or aid imposed upon their lords unless the latter were
empowered to recover it by writ.[1] The taxing power of the crown
—it was upon customary occasions and not a true taxing right—
thus originally treated the lordship as a whole under the tenant-in-
chief, and was feudal, in right of tenure; but the earliest Chancery
enrolments show John carrying the crown's action into the stratum
of the mesne tenures. It seems clear that he empowered the sheriffs
to collect scutage directly from the knights of the honours.[2] At
the same time as this departure from feudal correctitude was
hazarded, there came a shifting of the basis of taxation which

[1] Pipe Roll, 15 Hen. II (Yorks.). The abbot of Ramsey made special agreements
with his tenants to recoup him for the *auxilium expedicionis*. The bishop of
Norwich makes an aid to the king, who orders the burgesses of Lynn to recoup
him by an aid from themselves. Letters Patent, 11 Hen. III, p. 114.

[2] Letters Close, 7 John, pp. 43 and 46. The marshal's government returned to
precedent in this matter (*ibid.* 2 Hen. III, p. 371), but the sheriff would distrain
in case of recalcitrancy (*loc. cit.*). The same precedent was followed in 1235
(*ibid.* 19 Hen. III, p. 188).

made established rules difficult of application, and indeed for a time left the crown without any settled principle. In 1198 Richard went beyond the feudal aid on the demesne and the knight's fee, and laid a five-shilling *auxilium* upon the plough; in 1204 John took a seventh of their moveable property from the earls and barons and from the parochial and conventual churches; while in 1207 was set the vital precedent of taxing the whole nation, not upon the fee or the plough, but upon the sum of the year's rent and the chattels of every subject. The levy of 1207[1] was, in fact, the beginning of national taxation, and the change from a feudal to a national basis was expressly realized. The tax, a shilling in the mark, loosely referred to as a Thirteenth, was to be upon every lay-man who had chattels to the value of a mark throughout England *de cujuscunque feodo*. The tax upon moveables was to assert itself as the chief source of revenue in the thirteenth century though not entirely without opposition; as late as 1232 the bishop of Durham, Gilbert de Umfraville,[2] and other northern immunists, claimed that the Fortieth could not be levied within their liberties, and resisted payment for three years. Liability and consent were not, however, all. New tax-forms raised new questions of authority and machinery of collection which must affect the whole structure of the county. The matter of assessment alone was of the first importance, for assessment was at this time akin to assent,[3] since in every appeal for aid the assumption was that the vassal desired to aid his lord and that his gift was only limited by his capacity.[4] *Providere quale auxilium nobis impendere voluerint*—"to ordain how much aid and of what nature they will give us"—is the phrase used in summoning the vassals to debate supply, and the practice of allowing the individual to determine his own capacity was not unknown.[5] Thus assessment and collection were a practical problem hardly different in kind from that of grant. Every levy

[1] Letters Patent, 8 John, p. 72.

[2] On the ground of the regalian status of Redesdale. The bishop, no doubt, stood on his palatine immunity. Letters Close, 19 Hen. III, p. 184. The earl of Chester had even been able to refuse a papal Tenth in 1229. Stubbs, *Select Charters*, p. 323.

[3] Indeed the phrase *assisare auxilium* originally conveyed the idea of assent.

[4] This is particularly clear in the *auxilia* of the boroughs of 1227, assessed by the communities themselves *per se secundum facultates suas*. Letters Close, 11 Hen. III, p. 114. Thus the question of consent arises, but only at the stage of assessment.

[5] Letters Patent, 8 John, p. 72.

brought it to an issue and the expedients adopted were inevitably tests of the unity or disunity of the county. The task was entrusted to commissions under the title of collectors or justiciars, assigned to each county, sometimes from among its own knights and free-holders but with the addition of a king's clerk. These, in coöpera-tion with the sheriff, put in action the current scheme of assessment, received the tax, and conveyed it to the Exchequer or elsewhere as directed.

Growth of fiscal unity in the shire

With each new method of assessment, the crown gradually ad-vanced the disintegration of the fiscal unity of the honours and brought all but their lords' demesne into the body of the shires, which thus became consolidated communities for the levy of aid. So was created that division between baronial and county assess-ment which later extended to the right or duty of the two groups, nobility and communes of the counties, each to tax its own order. The consolidation of the county was, it is true, only arrived at slowly. In 1225 [1] the assessment for the Fifteenth was made under two separate schemes—on the one hand the *feuda*, the demesnes and villeinage of earls, barons, and knights, *i.e.* all the land held in knight service, and, on the other hand, socage, burgage, and other rentals and freeholds—the feudal land being assessed by oath of the reeves of liberties. But a number of spiritual magnates were allowed to extend their immunity of assessment to cover the lands of their burgesses and free tenants, and some to join their bailiffs with one of the justiciars for the assessment of their knights. [2] In 1232 the Fortieth was assessed by the oath of elected men in every vill, but the stewards of baronies and liberties were accorded a roll, and permitted to collect and distrain for the tax throughout their lord's lands, [3] while the earls of Cornwall [4] and Pembroke, [5] the masters of the Temple and the Hospital, and most of the spiritual magnates, were allowed to stand aloof and find their own machinery of assessment and collection. In 1237, however, most of these exemptions had vanished. Gilbert de Umfraville was allowed

[1] Letters Patent, 9 Hen. III, p. 560. The clerical carucage for the siege of Bedford was assessed and collected by the clerical magnates from the lands of their knights, free tenants, and villeins as well as from their demesnes. *Ibid.* 8 Hen. III, p. 465.   [2] *Ibid.* pp. 571–575.

[3] The clergy were apparently allowed special commissioners for their estates, though they were assigned by the king. Letters Close, 16 Hen. III, p. 160. *Ibid.* 17 Hen. III, p. 283. The northern immunists refused this aid outright.

[4] *Ibid.* p. 291.   [5] *Ibid.* p. 295.

to make his own levy in Redesdale,[1] and the clergy were given liberty to collect the aid within their fees when assessed, though few seem to have availed themselves of the privilege;[2] but, apart from these minor exceptions, the collectors of the Thirtieth were able to summon the men of the vills throughout the counties without the intervention of their lords, to whom no more was allowed than to send their stewards to attend the assessment if they saw fit to do so.[3] Thus, though it had been clung to as a valuable safeguard of feudal liberty,[4] the magnates' right of separate assessment had by 1237 been restricted to their personal goods and revenues. Those in mesne tenure, knights, freemen, and villeins, had been progressively detached from their lordships and absorbed into the body of the shire. The sole fiscal immunity in the counties was now that of the crown itself, whose demesnes were to be subject to tallage and exempt from the general tax upon moveables until the sixteenth year of Edward II, when they also were for the first time included in the vote of the counties.[5] For taxation, therefore, the *communitas comitatus* was already a fact in the last two decades of Henry III, and it seems right to associate with this recognition of a consolidated shire unit the innovation that on the next occasion of a general aid, in 1254, knights were summoned to the king *vice omnium et singulorum* in their counties. With the precedent of 1237 as a guide, a single constituency of each and all in the shire was at last available as a basis of representation.

Fiscal constituency a prelude to parliamentary constituency of the shire

The question of whose consent was necessary was hardly capable of solution until the process which has just been outlined had brought into being a unified constituency for taxation. It had remained open for half a century, the Crown using one method and one formula after another to secure aids. John had overridden the tenants-in-chief and collected the scutage from their knights,[6]

[1] Letters Close, 22 Hen. III, p. 45.
[2] The archbishop of Canterbury, the bishop of Winchester, the abbot of Cluny, and a few others. *Ibid.* pp. 8, 9, 15, and 18. In the reign of Edward I the Knights Taxers were ordered *taxer en ceste taxacione les biens as vileins des Ercesvesqes, Evesqes, Religieux, e de toutz autres Clerks, qui quil seint. Rotuli Parliamentorum*, i. App. p. 239. [3] Stubbs, *Select Charters*, p. 358.
[4] *Ad conservationem libertatum vestrarum concessimus* . . . Letters Close, 17 Hen. III, p. 285. [5] *Report on the Dignity of a Peer*, i. p. 283.
[6] For the *auxilium* of two marks on the fee in 1235 the sheriffs distrained for default, but *ad mandatum domini*. Letters Close, 19 Hen. III, pp. 186, 188.

and, since the tax on moveables was invariably granted by *commune consilium*, must have been considered as being taxed in the right of their lords. Nevertheless, the crown began to betray uneasiness as to the authority of its taxes, and to lay claim to a width of consent which it certainly never received. John was content to rest upon the *commune consilium et assensus concilii nostri*, but Henry III claimed the consent of *omnes magnates et fideles totius regni* for the carucage of 1220,[1] and for the Fortieth of 1232 that of the "clergy, earls, barons, knights, freemen, and villeins of the whole realm".[2] It is almost certain that no representatives from the lower tenures were called to London, and unlikely that they were consulted in their counties and hundreds,[3] yet for the Thirtieth of 1237 the same protestation was virtually repeated: the earls, barons, knights, and freemen have granted the aid "for themselves and for their villeins". Thus, Henry III never ventured to assert bluntly that the assent of the magnates to taxation carried with it that of the counties, and, consent and assessment being closely identified, their right to bind anyone but the tenants of their own demesnes became ever more doubtful, especially when the whole business of assessment and collection was taken out of their hands and given to knights elected by the county. The magnates were, indeed, the first to admit this, and it was at their instance that knights were first summoned to consent to an aid in 1254. A generation after this it had become an established principle that the community of each county was the author of the aid, giving its individual consent through its elected attorneys, the knights.[4]

The knights of the shire   In less than a century, therefore, the shire had achieved much of the quality of a fiscal and administrative community. In practice, its voice was that of the knights of the shire. The term *miles comitatus* denoted property, prestige, and tenure within the shire, rather than tenure *per loricam*,[5] and distinguished the independent

[1] Stubbs, *Select Charters*, p. 349.   [2] *Ibid.* p. 356.

[3] A dispute in the county court of Yorkshire as to the authority of the carucage of 1220 seems to have been a protest by the bailiffs of the local magnates that their lords had not been consulted in *commune consilium*. It may have represented an appeal by the lesser landholders to clause 14 of the Great Charter.

[4] *Rotuli Parliamentorum*, i. App. p. 226: *Decima, quam tota communitas comitatus Warwick Regi in subsidium guerre Regis concessit* (22 Edw. I).

[5] Perhaps over £20 yearly rental.

landowner from the bachelor or stipendiary knight of the king's household, such as usually rose to castellanships and custodies of escheats and bailiffries and sheriffdoms. Their activity in the thirteenth century is associated with the withdrawal or ousting of the greater barons from the routine of government. Since the reign of Richard I the recurrent special commissions which supplemented the eyres were no longer drawn from the barons, and, in the latters' stead, the knights were making their appearance upon the fringes of government. The knight of Henry III's reign might at intervals find himself a justiciar, though for a few days only, for much of the justice upon assize was done by inquest upon individual cases. For such causes a day and place were appointed within the county, and three or four local freeholders were assigned as justiciars,[1] with a king's clerk joined with them *ad hanc justiciam*. Similar commissions as justiciars[2] were issued to the knights who assessed the taxes upon moveables, and these again were drawn from the counties within their circuit, except for one or more official members. These knight-justiciars were, of course, in addition to the elected knights who on some occasions did the actual work of assessing the hundreds, and they may be supposed to have learned their work in the subordinate capacity. Other commissions, for the tallaging of the king's demesnes, for inquisitions into assarts or purprestures, breaches of the peace, or for such exceptional enquiries as that which followed the fall of Pierre des Roches in 1234, administrative duties, the assigning of knights to receive the oath to the peace in the Edictum Regium of 1195, with the custody of felons,[3] the enforcement of the Assize of Arms,[4] called for constant service by the knights of the counties, and occasionally they rose into official prominence as sheriffs or escheators, or, *The* as in 1226,[5] came to the council with presentments of county griev- *busones* ances. In the early 'thirties there were in Hampshire about a score of knights who had had experience under one sort of commission

---

[1] Letters Patent, 7 Hen. III, p. 409: *X. Y. et Z. constituti sunt justiciarii ad assisam capiendam quam A. aramiavit . . . versus B. de recognitione utrum.*

[2] *Ibid.* 9 Hen. III, p. 560 (For the Fifteenth of 1225): *Rex X. Y. et Z. salutem. Assignavimus vos justiciarios nostros ad quintamdecimam omnium mobilium assidendam et colligendam in comitatibus A. B. et C.*

[3] Stubbs, *Select Charters*, p. 258.

[4] *Ibid.* p. 362.   [5] *Ibid.* p. 353.

or another as justiciars, who had no official connection with the central administration, but were county landholders of moderate means.[1] Such county notables, knights who were foremost in the judgment of the local courts and in provincial administration, were distinguished by Bracton and others as *busones*, and were a recognized class in the community, the product of a new age. They emerge as a quasi-official administrative class as the shire outgrows its feudal disunity, becomes a fiscal whole, realizes a new kind of identity: they are the fore-runners of those who will take the newly integrated shires as their constituencies and represent them to Parliament.

Early history of the borough

Self-government and the sense of communal unity were even stronger in the boroughs. They possessed a kind of immunity from the beginning; indeed they were older than the shires by half a century. The earliest towns seem to have been centres of provincial government, like Wye, or Bamborough, or Winchcombe: some of them were, of course, national capitals, and others, like the Cinque Ports, began as trading stations, perhaps even for the petty trade of monasteries or lord's halls. During the Danish wars the fortified town or burh became the sole centre of government, and for a period of years at the beginning of the tenth century England was governed by borough reeves, while as yet there were neither shires nor hundreds. The boroughs emerged into the settled régime of the eleventh century with courts and administrations covering the urban area and a greater or smaller portion of the surrounding fields, but they had become subordinate to the shires in which they lay. Even London was not a county, though its sheriffs farmed the county of Middlesex from the reign of Henry I, and the rule that the pleas of the borough courts were those of the hundred probably had no exception before the Conquest. The burgess of the eleventh century was an agriculturist rather than a craftsman if London and some of the larger seaports

[1] A typical instance was Walter de Rumsey, in private life steward of Rumsey Abbey. He was justice to enquire into breaches of the peace in Hampshire in 1218, into assarts of the forest in 1219, upon a case of homicide in 1221, for the assessment of the Fifteenth in 1225, for an assize of darrein presentment and one of novel disseisin in 1226, and for another in 1228, all three at Winchester. He was added to the eyre for his own county in 1227, made escheator of Hampshire in 1232, and was collector for the county for the feudal aid of 1235. Letters Close and Patent, *passim*.

be excepted, and the towns were dominated by privilege and rank. Beginning as places of justice and defence, they were under the control of the ministerial nobility. For the discharge of his service of judgment and administration every king's thegn had his borough residence, and the borough thegns were a synonym for the borough community,[1] as were the shire thegns for that of the shire. They brought their privilege with them, and even London was riddled with the sokes and immunities of the king and queen and the great ecclesiastics, while one of its wards, the Knightengild, perhaps took its name from the franchise of a gild of London thegns. As late as the reign of John the soke and the soke reeve were important factors in London government and found their place in the London Custumal.

Thus, the borough inherited the elements which were universal *Borough* in Saxon politics. As a community it was a folk of freemen em- *constitution* bodied in its court—in London the "folkmoot"—its custom, varying from district to district, but conforming to the broad lines of old English court procedure by oath and ordeal. As an administrative area it was under the government of a royal reeve, port-reeve, or borough reeve, who presided over the court, took its wites for the king, enforced its judgments, and directed its frankpledge. There was, therefore, much in the boroughs which derived from and was governed by inflexible and conservative institutions. All Saxon courts proceeded by rules coming out of a remote past and preserved a nucleus of custom of fabulous antiquity. The burgesses clung to these forms through the Conquest,[2] bargained with the Norman and Angevin crown for exemption from the new law, and became the last stronghold of ancient Teutonic process in an age of legal revolution. In the London of Henry III's reign the old procedure of defence by compurgation[3] remained the palladium of the burgess oligarchy, by which the aldermen and the conservative burgess families defended themselves against the unholy

[1] J. M. Kemble, *Codex Diplomaticus*, 857: *Eadward king gret Willem bisceop, and Leofstan and Ælfsi porterefan, and alle mine burhthegnes on Lundene.*

[2] The Conqueror grants that the Londoners shall "be worthy of all their law as they were in the reign of King Edward". Stubbs, *Select Charters*, p. 97.

[3] Charter of Henry I to London: *per sacramentum quod judicatum fuerit in civitate se disrationet homo Londoniarum. Ibid.* p. 129. *Placita de Quo Warranto* (Edw. II), p. 449: *et quod nullus de misericordia pecunie judicetur nisi secundum legem civitatis quam habuerunt tempore Regis Henrici avi Regis Henrici avi Regis Henrici avi Regis nunc.*

alliance of the crown, a democratic mayor, and the commune. Here and elsewhere the defence of borough liberties took the form of a fanatical clinging to archaic rules of court. Moreover the administrative machinery, similar to that of shire and hundred, shared its inelasticity; the future self-governing corporations of the towns and cities set out equipped with nothing more than courts confined to judgment between parties and even more conservative than the courts of the counties, and governing officials who were stewards of a lord's demesne. Beneath the reeves' government the burgesses were headless, without unity beyond that of their common membership of their court: even their lordship was sometimes divided among several lords, and their primary allegiance might be less to their borough than to some external manor in the shire.[1]

Burgess organization   Within this inexpansive framework there lay and worked the most mutable social material of the age. The free play of money, sale and purchase, credit, interest, and wages, were closely restricted by convention and a public opinion which condemned usury and held by the rule of the just price; much of the industry of the lesser towns was still agrarian, and tenure and lordship preserved a degree of stability even in London. But, in spite of all this, the burgesses of even the smallest boroughs were beginning to look beyond fixed rents to profit, and to see that buyers and sellers could find more useful social forms in the free association of equals and rivals in craft or commerce than in the passive and defensive devotion of man to lord. Slowly, therefore, lordship and tenure began to be undermined by newer and more real loyalties, and the mutual oath of gilds and communes became stronger than the oath of fealty. Had the burgesses found nothing to serve their turn but the public powers of the *firma burgi*—the right to compound for the king's dues by a farm—tradesmen and artisans would have remained within the shell of the Saxon borough without a law merchant, without action for debt or contract, without rules for employment, apprenticeship, or standards of craft, without power to protect their merchants in foreign parts,

---

[1] Thus the burgesses of New Romney were for the most part tenants of the archbishop's honour of Newington, and under that manor they are entered in Domesday, where all mention of the borough is omitted. Domesday Book, i. 4A.

or to govern themselves as the crowded populace of a city. The borough as such was powerless even to levy upon its burgesses for the care of streets and bridges or to keep a common purse.[1] It could judge, collect the king's dues, and keep the king's peace, but for the townsmen themselves it was no better than a negative safeguard, an immunity.

Some of these freedoms they arrived at indirectly by grant of *The gild* the gild merchant, which may have come into the towns by way of English *cnihtengilds*[2]—the earliest is of about A.D. 860[3]—or may have been a spontaneous growth of Norman England. By this they got franchise of tol and team—the right of warranting sale —with the assize of weights and measures which went with it. The gilds were spreading through the towns soon after the Norman Conquest, and must have given an outlet to burgess activity for a generation before the *firma burgi*[4] was commonly enjoyed. The root privilege of the gild was the right of retail trade within the franchise, but it seems also to have conferred a power of positive action. Thurstan granted a *hans hus* or gild hall to Beverley *ut ibi sua statuta pertractent ad totius villatae emendationem,*[5] and most gilds achieved a very full organization under a gild alderman, a group of governing jurats, a treasurer, and a court of morning-speech. Not every town had a gild merchant—London found a substitute in its aldermen and *probi homines*, and later in its commune—but many found in the morning-speech the authority to fix standards of work and wages, enforce contracts, to give sanction to the rules drawn up for themselves by the several crafts, and to apply those conventions of fair trading for which there was as yet no action at common law. Especially where the burgesses did not as yet farm the bailiffry, there was a natural tendency to concentrate upon the gild at the expense of the borough. The rota of those capable of responsibility was small, and the jurats or *judices* of the town

---

1 The lesser towns had to apply to the crown for grants of murage, pontage, and pavage for these purposes. F. Pollock and F. W. Maitland, *History of English Law*, i. 662.

2 F. W. Maitland, *Domesday Book and Beyond*, p. 191: "When, not long after the Conquest, we catch at Canterbury our first glimpse of a merchant-gild, its members are calling themselves knights: knights of the chapman-gild".

3 W. de Gray Birch, *Cartularium Saxonicum*, 515.

4 Cf. *infra*, p. 320.

5 Stubbs, *Select Charters*, p. 131. "With right to make statutes there for the good of the town."

must also be jurats of the gild, and sit both in the public court—the portmanmoot or hustings—and in the morning-speech of the gild also. Thus there was a useful confusion between the spheres of the gild and the borough; where the latter could not act the gild was to be found levying upon its members for the expenses of the town,[1] and the gild merchant might come to regard itself as the real source of borough government.[2]

The gild a solvent of feudalism   Whatever their later history, the gilds merchant of the twelfth century were powerful solvents of the feudalism of the towns. The portmanmoots had been subject to the prevailing aristocratic trend in judicature. The lawmen's office of the Danelah boroughs and the aldermanries of London and Canterbury were originally heritable and could be bought and sold. The gild, on the other hand, was a community of presumed equals; the phrases *communitas gildae*, even *communa gildae*, are not uncommon. The morning-speech, though the predominant merchant families no doubt had their way, was an open aristocracy of wealth and ability, and, while the elective principle was not native to the borough, it was everywhere recognized, at least in name, in the gild. Moreover, the rise of the gilds accompanied a progressive decline in the landed interest, and in the judicial and administrative immunities which had arisen from them to divide the borough structure. Legal change was in any case reducing the soke and manor courts to the rank of a minor justice of trespass and the peace; the suit of burgesses to external courts was cancelled by the almost universal privilege "not to plead outside the walls", and, with the bait of gild privilege,[3] the tenants of the intra-mural franchises were less and less disposed to cling to their immunity from amercement, common fine, and tallage, or to claim the protection of their lord's reeves. Bargains by which such discordant groups as the bishop of Lincoln's fee in Leicester[4] accepted the full obligation of scot and lot in return for the right of gild marked the abandonment of

[1] M. Bateson, *Leicester Borough Records*, II. xlvii.

[2] At Bedford the burgesses claimed to be able to extend the full borough franchise to non-burgesses by making them members of the gild. *Placita de Quo Warranto*, p. 18.

[3] Great landholders found it worth while to seek membership of town gilds as did the earl of Norfolk and the East Anglian religious houses at Norwich and Ipswich.

[4] M. Bateson, *Leicester Borough Records*, i. 192.

franchise for burgess freedom, and brought the boroughs nearer to effective community. It was a minor revolution in English social life, the difficulty of whose achievement we have lost the ability to estimate, when the men of bishops, earls, and barons surrendered their special status, and placed themselves at the king's mercy with their fellow burgesses, accepting the disabilities of tenants on ancient demesne of the crown.[1]

Without the stimulus of the gild, constitutional growth was slower but not impossible. Every English court and the population it served had the potentialities of political self-government, and we have already seen the counties make some advance towards it in the first half of the thirteenth century. Both in their popular composition as folkmoots and in the official groups of doomsmen which had formed within them—lawmen at Lincoln and Cambridge, deman at Chester, aldermen in London, jurats in the Cinque Ports—the boroughs had a root of self-government, though it was hard to bring it past the phase of judgment to counsel and law-making. The greatest borough of all contrived to govern itself until the reign of Richard I without a gild merchant or a commune, using, presumably, its port-reeve and aldermen to pass by-laws by way of assize,[2] and its folkmoot as a general assembly for frankpledge and the hearing of the king's precepts. Nevertheless, it is clear that the habit and expectation of controlling their own affairs bred in the gild merchant counted for much, and were preparing the towns to desire more explicit recognition. They were in fact managing their own affairs roughly upon the basis of equal citizenship, but they were doing so either on sufferance, as *probi homines* called in at discretion to advise the judicial oligarchs as in London, Norwich, or the Cinque Ports, or, more questionably still, by using the machinery of the gild to do that business which the town could not.

The struggle between these two principles, the rigidity of royal or seigneurial administration and the free industrial or commercial coöperation of fellow townsmen, is the main theme of borough history in the Middle Ages. It is that which we have already seen in

[1] *Placita de Quo Warranto*, p. 158 (Derby): *Quicunque in burgo manserit cujuscunque feodi sit, reddere debet cum burgensibus tallagium* (Cf. also Nottingham).
[2] Such as the Building Assize of 1189. *Munimenta Gildhallae*, i. 319; F. Pollock and F. W. Maitland, *History of English Law*, i. 660.

the counties, but fought out with clearer purpose and a more decisive result. In part the deadlock was solved by the reception of the foreign political form of the commune, but the crown would hardly have admitted the commune into its cities had it not already bartered away a great deal of its demesne right. The twelfth century saw a series of bargains to buy out the seigneurial right in the court of burgesses and the burgess tenements, to secure the election of the reeve and his subordinates, and to compound the rents and profits for a fixed *firma burgi*. The rudiments of this process appear in Domesday—Dover has already bought out its sake and soke[1]—but it is one which proceeds irregularly. The majority of the greater towns answer for their own farm by the year 1200 and a number claim to have done so since the reign of Henry II; but there are exceptions, of which Winchester is the chief. Leicester is buying itself free from the lordship of the earl item by item until well into the fourteenth century.[2] London secured its farm in the later years of Henry I. Its charter[3] gave the citizens the right to elect bailiffs, who should also be sheriffs of Middlesex, a shire justiciar, who should also hold and keep the crown pleas of the city, and to render the king's profits, both for city and county at a farm of £300 for all issues. By this charter, except for the difference between farm and fee-farm, *i.e.* farm in perpetuity, the position of the Londoners was that of the de Viponts in their hereditary shrievalty of Westmorland, or of those short-lived sheriffdoms and shire justiciarships which were granted to Geoffrey de Mandeville and Miles of Gloucester a few years later, and the parallel is worth considering. Neither the London liberties nor those of the magnates offered the basis of a new political life. The boroughs got from their farm not a general power, nor authority to advance their political form towards self-government, but immunity. They were no longer at the discretion of a stranger who could make his profit by inventing reasons for amercement or exceeding the dues of custom. But in their courts, their rents, and services, nothing was changed. Some more positive recognition was wanted if the burgesses were to govern themselves in their own right and not as farmers for the crown.

The firma burgi

---

[1] Domesday Book, i. 2.
[2] M. Bateson, *Leicester Borough Records*, passim.
[3] Stubbs, *Select Charters*, p. 129.

This they found in an idea of community, most intensely *The idea* realized in the boroughs, though even there it is rather a general *of com-* concept of the state, varying in intensity according to time and *munity in the* place, than a borrowing of specific foreign institutions. It was, *borough* indeed, an influence that affected all England in the thirteenth century, changing the value of political forms, modifying political action, and breaking down the restrictions and immunities of feudalism. Its governing idea is the recognition of a general political association of which the basic right, status, and duty of all the members are identical, and where obedience and loyalty are owed equally by all to the political form in which the commune is embodied. That form is immaterial to the political concept, and the fact that the term commune suggests first to our minds the self-governing town is a mere accident of modern historical study. We shall treat it in what follows as only one of many types of commune, for in the Middle Ages the word is universally applied, though with varying reality—the commune of the county, the realm, the borough, the commune of parliament, communes of merchants. The capacity to perform a joint legal act seems to be sufficient to gain for its makers the name of commune with contemporaries. Communes were apparently instituted formally only in a few of the great boroughs and over a period of about twenty years. A forgotten pioneer, Thomas de Ultra Usa, tried to set up a commune of York during the anarchy of 1174,[1] there is London's commune of 1191,[2] and of those cities which had mayors under John, Oxford, Winchester,[3] York,[4] Bristol,[5] and Lynn, three soon claimed the status of communes,[6] and were among the first to use a common seal. These city communes certainly stood for something very definite. In 1175 York was punished as for a revolutionary act, and Richard I's chronicler feared them as *tumor plebis*. Winchester thought the commune worth having without a farm of its bailiffry. Indeed, it is likely that at the beginning of its history, while its meaning was still

[1] Pipe Roll, 22 Hen. II (Yorkshire).
[2] J. H. Round, *Commune of London*, passim.
[3] Letters Close, 6 John, p. 2. Northampton also. *Ibid.* 16 John, p. 188.
[4] *Ibid.* 15 John, p. 150.
[5] Letters Patent, 18 John, p. 195.
[6] Letters Close, 5 Hen. III, p. 405 : *Littere majoris et commune Londonie et Majoris et commune Wintonie et proborum hominum Suthhamtonie.*

clear cut and foreign, the *communa* had much to offer to the
theory and even the practice of corporate life. The boroughs had
become partially feudalized, their only bond of unity was the
feudal oath, and the burgesses were the men of this or that soke
or manor if they were not the men of the king by a supposed right
of ancient demesne; the commune offered them an oath to their
city and to their confraternity.[1] It will not do to insist that any
single implication of this oath was realized and applied, but
London under its commune was tallaging itself for civic purposes
consensu omnium, de cujuscunque feudo, while many boroughs still
needed royal license to do so. Associated with the commune is the
mayoralty, though it cannot be said with certainty that it arose
from it. In London the first mayor was in office within two years
of 1191, and the mayoralty soon identified itself with the popular
element in the folkmoot. As an institution it answered to the
political unity promised by the commune, for, unlike any other
civic office, it conferred authority over all the discordant parts of
the borough,[2] the king's bailiffry, the aldermen, and the craft gilds.
It embodied in itself both the elective right of the community
and the royal commission, so that the king appointed a mayor to
Lincoln as *ballivus noster et major vester*,[3] and, being added to
the court of aldermen or jurats, it represented the town to the
outside world.[4] Either as an outcome of the commune, or as an
alternative way of conferring the same benefit, the mayoralty
coördinated the borough into an entirely new unity of authority.
Among the Gildhall memoranda is a draft for a communal oath
with *echevins*, *cent pairs*, and *prudeshommes*.[5] There was no such
formal reception of the commune as this, and no English town

*The
mayoralty*

---

[1] For the same reason the phrases *communa gildae*, *communitas gildae* were
applied to the gild merchant.

[2] The general power of the mayor and the delimited office of the bailiff are
distinguished in the *quo warranto* plea of Nottingham (*Placita de Quo Warranto*,
p. 618): *Major . . . presit ballivis et aliis de eadem villa in omnibus que pertinent ad
. . . ejusdem ville regimen et juvamen. Ballivi . . . ea que pertinent ad officium suum
exequantur*: the mayor is over the bailiffs and others in the town in all things
which pertain to its government and welfare. The bailiffs do that which pertains
to their office.

[3] Letters Patent, 2 Hen. III, p. 160.

[4] F. Pollock and F. W. Maitland, *History of English Law*, i. 681 n.: *Et factum
maioris in hiis que tangunt communitatem est factum ipsius communitatis.*

[5] J. H. Round, *Commune of London.*

altered its constitution to suit a foreign model. No doubt, if its full implications had been realized, the aristocracies of the towns themselves would have been the first to repel it. But the communal doctrine lifted civic patriotism on to a new basis. It was a theory of political association alternative to feudalism, it was allowed to establish itself beside the law of tenure in the towns as alternative to feudal loyalty and to make demands additional to feudal obligations. It gave a colour of constitutional right to the inevitable advance of industrial over agrarian factors in borough government, and in the end it made the civic status of the burgess more important than any status by tenure which might survive.

Communal practice was at its strongest in London, where *communa* became the cry of a violent democracy.[1] Here an almost Italian precision of civic consciousness was achieved, the folkmoot standing for the *parliamento*, while the London magnates followed the aldermanry as the *grandi* clung to the consulate of the Italian cities. Other towns passed through the same conflict, though less consciously and with less disorder, but on the whole the boroughs soon forgot the enthusiasm of the commune and passed under a government of crafts and liveries; community, therefore, did not in the long run mean popular government, but rather a transfer of power from an aristocracy of lords of sokes, manors, and burgess tenements to one of traders. But, though the struggle between the classes was short-lived, the two centuries during which urban franchise was pieced together left their mark on the nation, since they brought the boroughs into being as *Growth of* separate units of administration and converted burgess right from *borough* a variety of tenure to the status of an independent order of the *immunity* state. While the counties had been developing powers of selfgovernment and absorbing the elements of feudalism into their community, a similar but more persistent instinct had been withdrawing the threads of local government and taxation from the sheriffs, and giving the principal boroughs independence within the counties in which they lay. After a period during which the Angevin judiciary had held borough and hundred in a common responsibility to the eyre court of the county, English administration was coming to be split into two distinct elements, standing for the respective interests of the minor landed gentry and free-

[1] *Liber de Antiquis Legibus* (Camden Series), *passim*.

holders and the organized wealth of industry. The order in which
the various immunities were come by varied. On the whole, the
freedom from external lordship was earliest. No burgess could be
involved in villein status, or put into court on any subject's plea
beyond the walls of the city, and this, the right to immunity from
foreign courts, destroyed equally the county's claim to burgess
suit. Londoners were even allowed to set a court at the Tower for
the justices of the king's pleas, and some other towns were privileged to be the place of session of the eyre,[1] and to have their special
session of gaol delivery.[2] Almost all had the trial of civil right in
their hustings and that minor criminal justice which was known
as the *placita vicecomitis*. On the administrative side the election of
bailiffs gave a certain security, but it left the borough at the
obedience of the sheriff. In most large boroughs, therefore, city
coroners were elected[3] and the bailiffs of the town were allowed
to present the farm in person at the Exchequer,[4] and in the
thirteenth century many came to have the return of writs of both
Exchequer and common law courts. It could then be said that "no
sheriff or bailiff of the king or any other person might enter the
borough to perform his office,"[5] except in case of default by the
bailiffs of the franchise. This was the liberty which in another
connection was said to be "a crown in itself"; in simpler terms it
was complete exemption from the government of the county,
and, although the phrase belongs to a later century, it was in this
right that some towns came to be called counties corporate,
and to have the title of sheriff for their reeves. By the reign of
Edward I an important group of boroughs stood outside the *corpus
comitatus* and presented a distinct problem of government.

*Fiscal
unity
of the
borough*

As in the counties so in the towns, the rise of the boroughs
towards a parliamentary status is heralded by the clarification of
their fiscal relation to the crown. Upon what ground the early

---

[1] *Placita de Quo Warranto*, p. 158: *et habere quod comitatus de Derby imperpetuum
teneatur apud Derby.* Lesser towns, such as Dunwich (Stubbs, *Select Charters*, p.
311), had liberty *quod nullam sectam faciant comitatus vel hundredorum nisi coram
justitiis nostris*, and that by suit of twelve representatives.

[2] *Loc. cit.*: *et quod Rex et heredes Regis mittent justiciarios nostros usque burgum
predictum ad gaolam predictam . . . deliberandum.*

[3] Cf. Stubbs, *Select Charters*, p. 306. John's charter to Northampton.

[4] *Ibid.* p. 305. John's charter to Nottingham.

[5] *Placita de Quo Warranto*, p. 158.

boroughs were treated as royal or seigneurial demesne[1] we do not know. As late as the reign of Henry II this is the basis of a curious classification in which cities, boroughs, thegns, drengs, *firmarii,* and demesne vills are grouped together as liable to tallage: lords of franchises might tallage their boroughs when the crown tallaged its demesne.[2] From this base, tenurial status the towns gradually rose during the twelfth and thirteenth centuries. Perhaps the first phase of advance can be found in the assertion by certain of the larger towns of their own fiscal unity. Early in John's reign Derby and Nottingham, and, no doubt, other towns, secured the elimination of tenurial immunities from taxation, and every burgess, of whomever he held, must join with the town in tallage.[3] But not all towns cared to deal with the king's tallagers as communities,[4] and well into the fourteenth century the tallagers were licensed to tallage the burgesses by poll or in common as they thought best.[5] Individual responsibility was the answer to *Transition* persistent abuse of joint levies upon the community, but upon *from* the whole the communal system was gaining ground, and the *tallage to aid* power of bargaining which it gave began to lift the burgess out of the demesne status. Arbitrary assessment had indeed been increasingly difficult to apply as Henry III's reign proceeded. Again and again the sums imposed had to be reduced, and for many towns an agreed amount settled into custom. London came to regard 1000 pounds as the limit of its tallage and in 1255 resisted the king's demand of 3000 marks, and offered 2000. Henry complained that the citizens' conduct was equivalent to a claim to be taxed by voluntary aid instead of by tallage,[6] but, indeed, the time was coming when it would be more profitable for the crown to transfer the towns to the voluntary system. Already the difficulty of estimate had made it necessary to allow the greater towns to tallage themselves through elected burgesses, and the narrow

[1] *Placita de Quo Warranto,* p. 241: *Burgus de Gloucestria qui est de antiquo dominico Corone.*

[2] Letters Patent, 7 Hen. III, pp. 373, 385. Chichester, Exeter, Wilton, tallaged for the queen-mother when the king tallaged his demesne.

[3] *Placita de Quo Warranto,* pp. 158, 618.

[4] In 1243 London was tallaged by an individual canvass.

[5] Letters Patent, 44 Hen. III, p. 76; *Rotuli Parliamentorum,* i. 449 (8 Edw. II), *separatim per capita vel in communi, prout ad commodum nostrum magis videritis expedire.*

[6] Letters Close, 39 Hen. III, p. 160. *Optulerunt domino regi duo milia marcarum nomine auxilii.*

difference between an aid and a tallage imposed arbitrarily and then reduced on the ground of poverty or custom to what the burgesses were willing to pay was further obscured by the fact that custom already extended the tallage to the franchises and would make towns in seigneurial demesne equally liable with their free neighbours. In 1297, therefore, the Eighth granted by the citizens and burgesses, though it is still linked with tallage by the taxing of the crown demesne with the boroughs, is levied not only from those of the king but from the mesne boroughs also— *totes citiez e Burghs, petitz e grantz de Reaume, qui quil seient, e de quinque tenure ou fraunchise*.[1] Under Edward II the rare tallages are made at the same uniform fractions of revenue as the aids,[2] tallage and aid have become almost indistinguishable, and the boroughs contribute regularly to the latter, and, having shaken off their connection with the demesne,[3] stand as a distinct and independent order of the community.

By the end of the thirteenth century the compactness of community in the towns had become such that "a new line had to be drawn between the boroughs and other *communitates*. Bracton saw this, though he saw it dimly."[4] Nevertheless it is true that *communa*, used almost exclusively of the boroughs, and *communitas*, with reference to the county, are latinizations of a single vernacular term *commune* which was modifying the estimate in which institutions were held both in country and town, and was making

The idea of community and the nation

possible a readjustment of national institutions. At points we may believe that the fact that the commune was so clearly exemplified in the boroughs may have influenced the country's rulers consciously. The commune in the boroughs achieved its greatest reality under John, and we cannot dissociate it from his innate antipathy to feudalism and willingness to foster any rival political theory. He gave the commune to London under Richard, and, in his own reign, almost certainly to Winchester [5] and perhaps to York and Bristol. He instituted a sworn commune of England for the defence of the realm and the preservation of the peace

[1] *Rotuli Parliamentorum*, i. 239.

[2] In 1314 a Fifteenth of moveables and a Tenth of revenues. *Ibid.* i. 449.

[3] As from 1319. *Ibid.* i. App. 455.

[4] F. Pollock and F. W. Maitland, *History of English Law*, i. 687.

[5] Which acquired a commune between 1190 and 1220 (Letters Close, 5 Hen. III, p. 445).

in 1205,[1] the thought of which must have been near to that of the contemporary London compilation of the Articuli Willelmi, *ut omnes liberi homines totius regni nostri sint fratres coniurati ad monarchiam nostram.*[2] Two years after his proposed *commune* of the realm, he transferred taxation from a feudal basis to the community at large, and in so doing repeated the phrase by which the boroughs were securing the right to tax the tenants of the intra-mural immunities to their tallage: *quicunque . . . cujuscunque feodi sit reddere debet simul cum burgensibus talliagia*[3]: *quilibet de cujuscunque feudo sit . . . det nobis in auxilium.*[4] Thus the crown was not above using the practice of the *commune* to support its innovations upon feudal custom.

The theory of community, though in a less concrete form, also played its part in the rise of baronial opposition. It applied less aptly to equals in tenure than to association in urban or rural groups, nor does the honour ever seem to have been considered in terms of the *commune*, but it was, perhaps, by some extension of the earlier and more limited use that the body of the tenants-in-chief came to be spoken of as *communa, communitas,* or, quite as often, as *universitas, regni,* the *regnum* being thought of in this connection as the special lordship of the king over his immediate vassals rather than the sovereignty over all subjects.[5] The gradual expansion of loyalty from the ideal of a special fealty of *barones dominici* to the king to one of faith to some imperfectly defined national cause was, no doubt, prompted first by the partial breakdown of the exclusiveness of the baronial circle. Many baronies had fallen into fractions between coheiresses, and the number of tenants *per baroniam* was vastly greater than that of the baronies. The simple knight might often be richer than his "baronial" neighbour.[6] Yet the transition was certainly made easier by

[The tenants-in-chief as communitas]

---

[1] In 1202 John had already tried a temporary, regional commune in the district about Harfleur as a means of rapid and coordinated defence against Philip. Letters Patent, 4 John, p. 14.

[2] *Willelmi articuli Londoniis retractati,* 9.

[3] *Placita de quo Warranto,* p. 158.   [4] Letters Patent, 8 John, p. 72.

[5] In this sense Henry I spoke of the *regnum* as an honour of which his barons were the members, *barones mei honoris.* Hen. I, Ordinance of the Shires and Hundreds, 3.

[6] The *Modus Tenendi Parliamentum* was ready to assert that the tenant *per loricam* should be deemed a baron for parliamentary purposes if he held as much as thirteen and a third fees.

a background of theory, however, imperfectly apprehended. The authority of the *communitas regni* was constantly urged against Henry III, and, on one occasion at least, the magnates asserted their need of a common seal of the *universitas*.[1] This use had, as we shall see, a considerable future in the vocabulary of parliament, but as yet it was not the opposition that exploited the idea of community with the greatest effect, but the crown, which, by using it to effect the awkward transition from the feudal limitations upon its dealings with the counties and boroughs, made the word "commune" a vital one in the terminology of the national assembly. There was never any likelihood of the English estates establishing themselves upon the ground of tenure; the many kinds and degrees of tenure and their lack of clear differentiation made them unsuitable for representation in a national council. Indeed, the general and uniform taxation of moveables, and with it elected representation, were possible only in so far as the immunity which so many tenures carried was overridden and the innumerable interwoven interests of property, tenure, and lordship, which neighboured each other in the shire, were endowed with some fiction of joint personality. It was not tenure-in-chief, nor tenure by barony, nor knight service, nor the forty-shilling freeholder, nor freehold as such, which came to be represented in parliament, but the combination of all these—and through them even of the villeins—into the community of the shire; the constituencies of parliament were to be *les communes de la terre*, the communities of shires and boroughs, the commons. The rise of the shire to a measure of community accompanies and makes for the evolution of its fiscal and administrative unity, and both are expressed in the writ forms of the summons to elected representatives: *ex parte communitatis comitatus*,[2] *vice omnium et singulorum*,[3] *pro comunitatibus eorundem comitatuum habentes plenariam potestatem*.[4]

The parliamentary commune

The implications of a claim to communal status were so im-

[1] The earls and barons seem to assert their representative quality in 1244 in demurring to an aid *quod sine communi universitate nihil facerent*. Stubbs, *Select Charters*, p. 327.

[2] *Report on the Dignity of a Peer*, iii. p. 35 (49 Hen. III).

[3] *Ibid.* p. 13 (38 Hen. III).

[4] *Ibid.* p. 46 (11 Edw. I). The formula occurs as early as 49 Hen. III in the summons to the capitular clergy (*ibid.* p. 36).

perfectly understood [1] in the counties and even in the towns, that it is perhaps surprising that the *commune* should have had so large a share in the transition from feudal *curia* to parliament. This was, indeed, its most important achievement in England, where social relations and the routine of provincial life outside the towns continued to be governed by feudal motives and the custom of tenure, and, as time went on, by the free play of money. It helped, half consciously, to free the crown partially from its commitment to the magnates for aid and counsel, and—by recognizing *communes des comtés*—to weaken their claim to be the *communitas regni*. It brought the crown into direct contact with all grades and kinds of tenure with a new colour of constitutional right, and it provided a ground of principle when parliament was being brought into being empirically and almost entirely at the crown's discretion. For such reasons the period during which the threads of ancient right were summarily cut by giving the qualities of a *commune* to any group which it was inconvenient to deal with as individuals is a phase in the history of the constitution which it is impossible to ignore; a new non-feudal colour spread over the administrative organization of the provinces with an influence upon the growth of parliamentary estates which is difficult to analyse but none the less real. In Scotland the line of growth is clear. As in England, the tenants-in-chief establish themselves as the *communitas regni par excellence*. They are joined in the first half of the fourteenth century by two other *communitates*, those of the clergy and burgesses, and these, by their representatives, take their place as the three "communities", the future three estates, of the Scotch parliament. In England the process is less simple, but the principle is the same. The English baronage asserted during the thirteenth century a *communitas regni* which was understood, with more or less clarity, as an embodiment of the principal tenures-in-chief of the crown; but with the loss of the Barons' Wars there came a break in baronial tradition. Only a minority even of the magnates attended the parliaments of the fourteenth century, and their attendance was so plainly at the will of the crown that, though the *communitas procerum* holds its place in the

---

[1] There are, as has been said, many uses of the term in a vague and general sense. The *communitas bacheleriae Angliae*, and so on.

language of parliament for a time,[1] the fiction of a parliamentary community of nobles was hard to maintain. By the reign of Edward II the representatives of the *communes* of shires and boroughs had attracted the title of *communitas regni* to themselves,[2] and, in default of an equivalent *communitas baronum*, the "three communities of parliament" were never adopted into English constitutional phraseology. The magnates in parliament never, in fact, after Evesham recovered that clear sense of embodying an order which had inspired them as a *curia* of feudal tenants *in capite* and might have justified them in claiming the status of a parliamentary *commune*. In the Edwardian parliaments they represented nothing, the commonalty became the one community in the English parliament, and it was only when the stability and continuity of the magnate element was being established in the patented peerage of the fifteenth and subsequent centuries that they were able to assume a fixed legislative status by the vaguer title of "estate". Even so, community plays a great, perhaps a decisive part, in the first vital century of parliamentary history. The view of the counties and boroughs as *communes*, achieved so laboriously in the face of feudal privilege, and held firmly by the year 1300, not only made it possible for the crown to handle them as units and deal with them through their representatives, but it also blocked the way to direct negotiation with individuals and groups. By the ninth year of Edward II the crown had ceased to approach the royal demesnes directly for the aid on moveables, and the shire faced it as an indivisible whole. Edward I and Edward III were disinclined to complicate their task of ruling and fighting by debating political abstractions, and accepted the community notions which were making headway in provincial organization and used them without question as material for their

---

[1] So of the "Bill" of the prelates and *proceres* in the Lincoln parliament of 1301, *non placuit Regi set communitas procerum approbavit.* Parliamentary Writs, i. 105.

[2] *Ibid.* ii. 157. The grant of service for the Scotch war in 9 Edw. II was made by the *magnates et communitas regni.* This is explained in the writs as referring to the earls, barons, *liberi homines et communitates.* It is probable from the phrase *les Contes, Barons, et la communante de la tere* in the First Statute of Westminster that the transference had taken place by the beginning of the reign of Edward I. An assertion of the community of the barons is made in 1272, when certain magnates wrote in the name of the *communitas procerum* to announce the accession of Edward I. Rymer, *Foedera,* i. 888.

machine of parliament. The *communitas*—in the French vernacular, *commune*—became, indeed, the most versatile political concept of the day, and, with all the exceptions which are to be found in the practice of any inchoate theory, it played something of that directive part in the growth of public institutions that was played by notions of tenure in the preceding age. Indeed, it is mainly because of this change in terms and in the beliefs they stood for that with the accession of Edward I, most of all in his dealings with parliament, we are conscious that a new age is in being. Feudalism, if the episode of the Ordinances be excepted, has ceased to be a general standard to which the validity of institutions and acts of government is automatically referred. It is yielding to monarchical empiricism, community, and economic realism. A parliament embodying the elected representation of shires and boroughs in a Communes'—Commons'—House is as natural an outcome of the age in which community is the basis of political thought as is the witenagemot of that of the law-worthy folk, or the *commune consilium* of tenants-in-chief of that of the feudal honour.

ii

PARLIAMENTARY MONARCHY

The progress of our constitution is so slow, proceeds by such slight advances, and is subject to so many reversals, that it is impossible to divide its history into compact periods. Nevertheless, *Summary of the period* there is something to be gained by surveying that progress at long range and watching the emergence of new principles of the most general kind. Political history imposes the accession of Edward I as the beginning of an age, and it is possible to see in the reign of the three Edwards the consolidation and completion of a new phase of the constitution. Speaking with the widest latitude, the reign of Henry III had seen a weakening of feudalism as the idiom of practice and theory in political life. It was no longer so easy to believe that the *regnum* was no more than a supreme and intricately ordered example of honorial government, and one merit of the reign of Edward I is that he had the courage or the insensitiveness to break with the feudal past, and to found what, at least as a system, was a new régime, upon the basis of prerogative exercised in parliament. But Edward did no more than increase the force of the king's will as prerogative and give the future estates their earliest essays in politics. In prerogative a source of authority was put forward for legislation now that new law was coming to be made, but the state still waited for a reconciliation of its uncoördinated parts. The principle of government was still discord rather than harmony; Chamber and Wardrobe were rivals of Chancery and Treasury, the Great conflicted with the Privy Seal; the king taxed on the right hand by a consent imposed by the ancient rules of tenure, and on the left with the rising strength of prerogative; parliament, as yet no more than the servant of the king, was hardly an effective critic, still less the master of this complexity and disunity. In the reign of Edward II there opens the struggle to impose interdependence and common subordination upon the ministries, to consolidate taxation upon a single authority, and to bring the whole under the survey of the magnates in parliament; but throughout the reign the objects aimed at are never clearly seen. The problem is clarified by victories won in turn by the dying feudal cause, by parliament, and by the domestic officers of the crown, each crisis adding its legacy of experience. Some order is gained after the victory of the middle party and the Despensers, but it is precarious. At any time the king might have defeated opposition politics and established government upon the Chamber, the Wardrobe, and the Privy Seal. The striking of the final balance is, therefore, the work of the long reign of Edward III. Naturally opportunist, ready to be compliant at home in return for the nation's generosity in paying for his crown of France, he came to see that the household offices should be used, not as Henry III had used them, however feebly, as a personal administration threatening at any moment to take power openly, but either as working offices with little influence, or as responsible ministries embodying the will of the king, but of the king as head of the state, leaving the main work of administration to Chancery and Treasury, and coördinating them with each other and both with the crown. When this reconciliation between the offices of the household and the offices of the state had been accomplished, and when parliament had come to be accepted as the controlling influence within which the various powers of the executive performed their functions, the parliamentary monarchy may be said to have been firmly established. It was a new political form, replacing the régime of feudalism, though embodying much that survived from feudal theory.

In spite of Henry's six final years of uncontrolled rule, the *Position at* accession of Edward I had something of the character of a restora- *Edward I's* tion. For the first time since 1258 a clear personal will coördinated *accession* and directed the state. In Edward the country found a leader more single-minded than de Montfort, and one whose instinct in what he felt to be essential for the good of the country chimed more exactly with its own than that of any king since the Conquest. War for the king's right in Poitou, wherein Henry had vainly tried to convince the barons that "his honour was their own", gave way to the more real menace of the Welsh and Scotch borders, "to which, God willing, we mean to put an end, thinking it best and most seemly that we and our people should labour and spend for the common weal at this one time for the utter extirpation of the evil".[1] It is a change of aim which justifies a new language from the king to his people, confidence and leadership, the capacity to accept and use the real distribution of forces within the nation; only when the threat is to Gascony has Edward to descend to persuading. The conjuncture was one where a generation had reached the end of its capacity for effort and events waited for a fresh impulse. Edward was no doctrinaire, certainly no democrat; there was little that was entirely new in his scheme of government, or, if there was, it was in the clearer assertion of prerogative. He ignored theory and made his way straight to action, and his reign carried the country no further than the phase of experiment in what we call parliamentary government; what he did was not final in form and might have been undone by a strong king following him. Nevertheless, much that was settled neither by the baronial rebellion nor by the return of Henry III to power had found by the end of his reign at least a provisional answer, or, more strictly, a choice of answers. The ministries of state, the county and borough communities, the king's council and the *colloquium* of the magnates had come far since the death of John, changing their functions and shedding many of the

[1] Parliamentary Writs, i. 10.

prejudices and pretensions of feudalism. Under the feeble and de-bilitating rule of Henry III the feudal control of the state had lost its vigour, the experiment of replacing it by a nominated council of magnates had failed in 1261, and the field was open to a king who could make the crown the centre of unity. It was, in fact, a point of history when everything turned upon the accession of a king who could ignore the jealousies and prejudices of the last reign and was prepared to take parties and institutions as they stood and to reconcile them in a practical order of government.

Change in the theory of law   The liberal historians of the nineteenth century accepted the entry of the commons into parliament as the outstanding con-stitutional event of this period, and saw in Edward I the creator of English constitutionalism. The growth of representative institu-tions at this time and during the preceding half-century is, indeed, one of the outstanding facts of English history. We shall, however, miss its true significance if we forget that it was accompanied and made possible by a change in public life which determined not who should participate in politics but the very basis of taxation and law-making. Until well into the thirteenth century the primi-tive conception of a society living within the frame of an inherited law had deprived the king of the quality of legislator and restricted the *commune concilium* to recognition of custom and participation in adjustments of right and procedure by way of assize. Vital changes were, no doubt, made, but they were made in such a way as to obscure their real nature as legislative change.[1] The right to legislate, therefore, never came into dispute. If a choice of the crown, or of the *commune concilium*, or of both con-joined, as legislator had been faced, the last would have been chosen without question, but the issue was, in fact, scarcely realized. Thus it was that the country approached a second great period of legislative activity, comparable to that which Henry II had carried through under the colour of assize, unprepared with any clear opinion as to where lay the right to make new law. With the accession of Edward the community was upon the edge of a new phase of making law by statute,[2] that is by enactment consciously

[1] Bracton considered it right *legem in melius converti* but not *legem mutari*. F. Pollock and F. W. Maitland, *History of English Law*, i. 176 n. So the barons at Merton in 1236, *nolumus leges Angliae mutari*.

[2] *Ibid.* i. 178 *et seq.*

changing or adding to the body of unwritten custom and done by a mere act of authority. What this meant is only in process of realization under Edward. The recording of enacted statutes, the corpus of written law as opposed to custom, later to be gathered into the Statute Roll, is an innovation of his reign, and its first-fruits is the Statute of Gloucester. The very force and nature of statute is still doubtful, and will remain so for a generation, and, since the basic conception of law as custom is shaken, it is a time of confusion as to the ultimate authority from which the new law which is not custom comes. Extreme and contradictory views are possible among men who are almost contemporaries, but the drift is towards prerogative. For Bracton and Grosseteste, enacted law is the exception, and is the province of the king in the council of his barons. For the Edwardian Britton, all law is statutory and its initiation lies with the king. Britton would find many to contest his view, but the doubt is there, and, beneath the play of political events, the age is committed to a search for something radically new in its polity, a legislator—the king if the demand at once for change and stability is to bear down the feudal right of the past and the rising activity of the *communes*; some revival of feudal councils, or some new council or councils of the nation, if the older view of the popularism of law is to prevail.

In so far as it is possible to generalize about a problem upon which the Edwardian lawyers and statesmen had themselves no steady mind, doctrines and practices drawn from two separate phases of history contributed to the theory of legislation during the fourteenth century. The older strand of thought, arising out of the feudal past, endowed any assembly of magnates summoned by the king with some of that power to declare custom and to innovate by assize which inhered in the character of the tenants-in-chief and especially in *commune consilium*. This power had been effective only rarely during the reign of Henry III—the Statute of Merton was perhaps the last occasion on which it was unequivocally admitted by the crown[1]—and the failure of the baronial reformers had gone far to discredit it. This full power to provide, to make law, is replaced, and that only intermittently, by that *assensus* of the clergy, magnates, and *communitas* by which the first

The magnates and legislation

[1] The Provisions of Westminster, claiming much the same authority as those of Merton, are a document of the opposition.

Statute of Westminster and Edward's last Statute of Carlisle were issued. Theoretically, it remained as a possible ingredient of any share the barons might be asked to take in a future parliamentary model, and in successful opposition they tended to revert to it. It was recognized at Lincoln in 1301, when that strand of political theory which rested the stability of law upon the Great Charter with the *consilium regni* as its guardian experienced a revival, but taking the general trend of theory rather than any specific enunciation, it would seem that such legislative function as the barons derived from their curial past, at best never clearly defined, was losing in efficacy by the reign of Edward, and that the idea of claiming a similar function for the commons was still not yet entertained.

The reign of Edward was thus a time of slack water between the dying impulse of feudalism and that political life of parliament which was in the future; momentarily it was possible for the crown to emerge in the decline or absence of rivals as legislator *Preroga-* by prerogative. Such prerogative was a newly emergent power, *tive and* but it was held firmly and just so long as to determine the form *legislation* of legislation when parliament came to maturity. The king as legislator was a new factor in the thirteenth century. His was, indeed, a power arising imperceptibly, evading criticism by its intangibility, a principle built up from the gradual transformation throughout a century of the king's relation to privilege, and therefore to law. Franchise, once it was subject to inquest, had come to be no longer regarded as inherent in landright or indefeasible. Even the verdict of the countrysides was not now accepted as final as to its validity. Edward, on the contrary, claimed that custom itself was at the mercy of prerogative when *Preroga-* it conflicted with the public interest,[1] and, though this might *tive and* be an extreme view, as a matter of practice under Henry III, in *petition* the theory of Bracton, and by express order in council under Edward, all franchise had come to be subject to justification by the express words of royal charters. Every liberty not warranted by charter must be sued for to the king, and, in addition, all redress

[1] *Rotuli Parliamentorum*, i. 71: *Dominus Rex pro communi utilitate, per prerogativam suam in multis casibus est supra leges et consuetudines in regno suo usitatas.*

not obtainable in the common course of law[1] could be obtained only by his grace and favour. The result was to inject a new virtue into the crown. It became the target for innumerable petitions from individuals for warrant of privilege,[2] which it withheld or conceded at its will. Petition and grant in the king's Council became one of the busiest functions of the crown. This was in itself a making of law, albeit of minimal law, privilege, and the more numerous the petitioners, the greater the group of the beneficiaries, the nearer shall we be to calling it legislation. Grant of liberties to the *commune* of one county[3] in answer to the petition of that county may leave us doubtful—is it privilege-making or law-making? If the *communes* of all the counties unite to petition, the king's grant of what they ask will make law of general application, will be a change of national custom—legislation—and legislation by the king's sole prerogative moved by the petition of his subjects: *Dominus Rex ad Parliamentum suum . . . de gratia sua speciali et etiam propter affectionem quam habet erga Prelatos, Comites, Barones, et ceteros de regno suo concessit*[4]: "the Lord King at his Parliament has granted". It is not, moreover, the commonalty alone that petitions. The magnates, both prelates and others, make petition at the king's parliament,[5] and, in the guise of petitioners to the king to confirm old law or concede new, seem to occupy the common ground of subjects rather than that from which the barons of Merton declared *nolumus leges Angliae mutari*. Much will depend upon whether they are to take the first or the second, the higher or the lower status in parliament. If they assume at once the rank of a feudal *curia*, they will in some measure inherit its function and control the legislation from the beginning. If they appear as petitioners, there must be a long struggle before their petitions can acquire a coercive power over the initiative of the crown.

By the accession of Edward, however, the possible claimants to

[1] *Tortz et grevances faites a eux, qe ne poent estre redrescees par la commune Ley ne en autre manere santz especial garant. Rotuli Parliamentorum.* i. App. 444.

[2] *Ibid.* i. 50: *Priorissa de Amesbir' . . . petit quod Rex ei concedat fines et redemptiones hominum et tenentium.*

[3] *La commune de Cestresire prient a lour Seigneur le Roy. Ibid.* i. 6. *Communitas ville de Gloucestre conqueritur . . . et supplicat Domino Regi. Ibid.* p. 47.

[4] *Ibid.* i. 36.

[5] *Ibid.* i. 35. So also the Statute Quia Emptores: *Dominus Rex in Parliamento suo . . . ad instantiam Magnatum Regni sui, concessit, providit, et statuit. Ibid.* i. 41.

Council and legislation act as legislator were no longer two but three. Between the king and the feudal Council, and widening the gap between them, there had arisen the permanent sworn council of state, and, since it contained the principal ministers and the king's intimates, and had the almost decisive advantage of knowledge of administration, constant session, and continuity of policy, it was likely to be the strongest claimant of the three. Its claim was especially valid because the developments of the last fifty years or so had placed the council athwart the line of that main stream of future legislation, the subject's right of petition and the king's power to redress grievance. After the courts of King's Bench and Common Pleas and the court of the Exchequer established their several spheres of jurisdiction, the Council retained a function which was more restricted but no less preëminent than that of the undivided *curia*. It remained a court of reference for all causes which came before the Benches, the Exchequer, the eyre, and the courts of justices assigned, and which yet in any way exceeded their competence. It often instructed the justices to transfer cases involving important interests to its own consideration, and it admitted of direct petition from individuals or communities, which might be referred to the appropriate court or answered directly by the king in Council. It was the supreme court for the consideration of franchise. The amount of justice dispatched *coram ipso rege* diminished after the reign of Henry II, but the number of petitions for extra-legal redress and relief from the undue harshness of the law or for new privilege, the germ of prerogative law-making, increased—the emergence of a special jurisdiction of Chancery under the Edwards is proof that this was so—and the permanent Council became more and more a body for the hearing of

The Council as the germ of parliament petitions. By the middle of Henry III's reign[1] it had already adjusted itself to this influx of legal and extra-legal business by concentrating it upon certain seasons of the year, when it sat at

[1] Letters Close, 3 Hen. III, pp. 383, 409, 410. The Michaelmas session of the Exchequer early came to be used for this purpose, the Council conferring with the barons of the Exchequer and sitting in the Exchequer to receive reports of inquests and to hear pleas of right. *Ibid.* 4 Hen. III, p. 437. Sheriffs enquire into the present tenure of King John's lands, especially of the *terrae Normannorum—et inquisicionem illam . . . facias scire nobis et consilio nostro . . . apud Westmonasterium in Crastino Sti. Michaeli*—all those who hold such lands attending with the sheriffs to show cause.

Westminster for readiness of reference to charters and to the rolls
of the Treasury, and ordered the attendance of any justices who
might have been upon eyre or commission, of the barons of the
Exchequer and the justices of the Jews, and also of the benches—a
full quorum of legal and conciliar lore.[1] These special sessions of
council became stereotyped before the end of Henry's reign, and *The*
early in that of Edward they appear as a sharply distinguished *Parliament*
organ of the state of extreme importance under a name which *of Council*
they share with the *colloquia* of the magnates—Parliament, *con-* *in Parlia-*
cilium regis ad parliamenta sua or *in parliamento*.[2] This parliament of *ment*
law and council of Edward was a large body.[3] It consisted of the
sworn counsellors of state, afforced, since the matter before them
was principally legal, by the justices of both benches, and the
barons of the Exchequer.[4] It contained, of course, the great
officers of state, notably the chancellor, and, since it entertained
petitions not only from individuals but from communities, and
since the power of the king to create new privilege, to which it
was hard to set a limit, was habitually exercised with the advice
of his parliaments of council, the latter's jurisdiction constantly
verged upon legislation. Edward, accordingly, associated the
council with himself as the authority of statute.[5] Any lapse of the
impulse of the magnates to act as mouthpiece of the *universitas regni*,
and any failure of the communes to establish regular constitutional
access to the crown by representatives—both possible eventualities
in the generation that followed the battle of Evesham—might at
any time have left the council *ad parliamenta*, since it embodied
the king's prerogative,[6] not only the highest jurisdiction but the

[1] These sessions, sitting most commonly a fortnight after Easter and Michaelmas, were clearing-houses for petitions for favour and examination into
franchise. In the 'fifties meetings of the *colloquium* of the barons were often
summoned to coincide with them, and rolls and chronicles sometimes accorded
the title of *parliamentum* to the occasions of which they formed part. The
material and some of the function of parliament existed in them. Cf. J. E. A.
Jolliffe, *Some Factors in the Beginnings of Parliament*. Transactions of the Royal
Historical Society, vol. xxii.   [2] *Rotuli Parliamentorum*, i. 15.

[3] 70 in 1305. F. W. Maitland, *Memoranda de Parliamento*, p. cvi.

[4] For the composition of the Council in Parliament in 1305 cf. *Ibid.* p. xliii.

[5] *Rotuli Parliamentorum*, i. 78: *per ipsum Dominum Regem et consilium suum
provisum est. De commune consilio statuit (Rex).*

[6] It is curious to notice how closely king and Council are identified in their
official acts. Even the routine questions to petitioners take form of a joint
address from king and Council: *et super hoc, per ipsum Dominum Regem Anglie
et consilium suum quesitum est. Ibid.* i. App. 226.

sole legislative authority of the realm. In this phase of its history, the embryo legislative function of the Council was indeed already detaching itself from the mass of legal business; by 1280 petitions triable by the benches, the Exchequer, or the chancellor were given only a first hearing by Council, and found a *complementum justitiae*, as it was called,[1] in the old-established courts. Reserving its full judgment for a residuum of doubtful causes, such as oftenest called for legislation, the Council might have come eventually to recognize its function as essentially that of a legislature, and the very terms of the Council's resolution of 1280 show that upon this matter it was very near to realizing its new function; "in this manner the king and his Council may be able to attend to the great affairs of his realm (the *magna negotia regni* that had been laid before the barons under Henry), and of his foreign lands without charge of other affairs".[2]

Definition of parliament   It may need an effort of imagination to detach our minds from the subsequent meaning of "parliament" as an assembly of the peerage and the representatives of the people, but the rolls of the early Parliaments leave no doubt that in this phase of their beginning their only essential elements were the king, the sworn Council, and the various justices, and that the "parleying" from which they took their name was primarily legal. *Placita et petitiones*, trial of causes and petitions for legal redress, are the only business upon some of these rolls. The hearing of such *placita* and petitions seems to be the fact which distinguishes a parliament from the various *colloquia, tractatus*, and so on, which the king held from time to time with his magnates, with representatives of shires and boroughs, with the clergy, with merchants; the presence of the king, the Council, and the judges, seems to be the fact which distinguishes a parliament in composition from such other assemblies. Chancery marked parliaments proper by issuing writs of summons *de veniendo ad Parliamentum, de Parliamento tenendo*; writs for other assemblies it endorsed *de veniendo ad tractandum, de subsidio petendo, de tractatu habendo*, and the like. An assembly embodying prelates, magnates, knights, and burgesses, without the Council, and summoned *ad colloquium habendum*, would be no parliament—in the reign of Edward III it would be called a *Magnum Concilium*. A

---

[1] *Memoranda de Parliamento*, ed. F. W. Maitland, p. 131.
[2] Letters Close, 8 Edw. I, p. 56.

meeting only of the king, the Council, and the justices to try *placita* and hear petitions might, on the other hand, be perfectly a parliament.

The future of legislation would turn chiefly upon how far the Council in Parliament was left to realize its potentialities without rivals. A consistent lead by Edward during his thirty-five years reign might have encouraged it to do so. The *colloquium* of the magnates might have been summoned only to grant aid, the shires and boroughs, assize being near to assent, might have been approached through justices *ad auxilium assidendum*, or formal assent to aid might have been got in the courts of the shires,[1] and the cities and towns tallaged as ancient demesne. Alternatively, an estates system, either of the old *universitas* or with deputies of all orders, might have been created, and allowed, like the *états* of France, to vote subsidies and present grievances at a safe distance from contact with the real centre of government in the conciliar *Parlement*. As in France, this would have answered the political ambitions of the nation till the monarchy had reached its full growth, and the end would have been that of the French *états généraux*, a prerogative taxation by tallage and estates convinced of uselessness and falling into desuetude. Thus, the death of Henry left the field open to experiment. The constitutional force of feudalism was partly spent, and the king's prerogative was rising towards the ascendant, and it might be necessary to reconstitute the *commune concilium* about this centre and upon a new system. Given a king of Edward's qualities, one thing alone was certain, that the Council, especially the Council in the Parliament, would be increasingly the motive force of government. The composition of his father's councils was, indeed, retained and accentuated. Knights, justices, clerks, and officials of the household were the mainstay of Edward's Council and filled the great offices. No

Possible alternatives in development

[1] As was done in 1282 when John de Kirkby went the round of the country negotiating supply—*curiale subsidium*—in the shire courts (Stubbs, *Select Charters*, p. 457), and, on a smaller scale, in 1292, when the barons owning land in Wales and the *communitas* of Chester gave a Fifteenth. Stubbs, *Constitutional History*, ii. 129. The recurrent assemblies of merchants to grant exceptional customs are a device of the same kind. The towns granted a Sixth by separate negotiation in 1294.

great ministers of the baronial type served during his reign, but men like Burnell and Hamilton as chancellor, and Kirkby as treasurer. Against such men the cry for baronial ministers could not be raised, for Edward was strong enough to value able servants and ruthless in sacrificing them when it became necessary to save his credit.[1]

The "parliaments" of that collection of *placita* and *petitiones* which we know as the *Rotuli de Parliamento* are primarily such meetings of the Council *ad Parliamenta* as we have been describing.[2] But Edward, and probably in the last decade of his reign, Henry before him, had been in the habit of afforcing them by summoning a selection of the magnates, and even representatives of the communes by a writ *De Veniendo ad Parliamentum*. The *colloquium* or *parliamentum*[3] of Henry's barons was upon occasion conjoined with the Parliament of Council. The purpose of this addition of the magnates to parliament was the holding with them of *colloquium et tractatus* upon great affairs of the kingdom, which the king and Council did not care to dispatch alone, and the nature of which is generally stated in the summons. They are such matters as the affairs of Gascony or Scotland, the demands of the Pope, or the peace of the realm, and, taking the first place upon the agenda of the later parliaments of the estates, they came to be distinguished as "the king's business", "les busoignes le Roy", as opposed to the *placita* and *petitiones* of subjects. It has been held that "this amalgamation of 'estates' and 'parliament' constitutes Edward's claim to be the creator of a model English parliament".[4] Taken together, the evidence of the writs of summons, of the petitions in parliament, of the more representative memoranda of the parliament of 1305, of the preambles to statutes, and of the chroniclers is fatal to the view that Edward was the sole pioneer in this. From the beginning of Edward I's reign the magnates were summoned by writs which the Chancery advisedly classed as brevia *De Veniendo ad Parliamentum*. The

[1] As the treasurer William Marsh was sacrificed in face of the outcry against the taxation of 1295, and Hengham, Weyland, Bray, and Stratton after the king's absence from 1286 to 1289.

[2] *Report on the Dignity of a Peer*, iii. p. 170.

[3] Chroniclers, using the older and more general meaning of the term, sometimes gave the name *parliamenta* to what were only *colloquia* of the magnates.

[4] A. F. Pollard, *Evolution of Parliament*, pp. 47 et seq.

assembly of 1275 included prelates, earls, and barons *et la communaute de la tere*; in the words of its Statute of Westminster, it was *le primer parlement general apres le corounement*.[1] The phrase presupposes earlier "general parliaments"[2]—the Edwardian Close Roll[3] calls the assembly at Winchester after Evesham a parliament—and it might be inferred that the clerks who drafted it were of the opinion that some at least of those sessions of Henry's reign, to which not only the unofficial historians of his day but the king's secretaries gave the name of parliament, were essentially like that of 1275.[4]

1 Stubbs, *Select Charters*, p. 442.
2 It may, however, be suggested with some hesitation that *generale* or *plenum parliamentum* was used rather of the full session of the conciliar parliament, as opposed to the various committees of triers of petitions appointed during its term or to the chancellor's court, than of a full assembly of "estates".
3 Letters Close, 4 Edw. I, p. 274.
4 Letters Patent, 39 Hen. III, p. 399. A parliament three weeks after Easter, 1255. This was Matthew Paris' parliament of *omnes nobiles Angliae tam viri ecclesiastici quam saeculares, ita quod nunquam tam populosa multitudo ibi antea visa fuerat congregata*. It met *in quindena Paschae, quae vulgariter Hokeday appellatur*. There is no doubt that the magnate assembly of Oxford in 1258 was called a parliament in letters patent and the Provisions of Oxford gave the title to their triennial sessions of the Council with the representatives of the *universitas*. Knights were summoned *ad Parliamentum* in 1264, twenty-five earls and barons were called in 1261 *ad instans parliamentum* (*Report on the Dignity of a Peer*, iii. p. 23), and clergy, barons, knights, and citizens were similarly called *ad instans parliamentum quod erit Londoniis in octavis Sti. Hilarii* in 1265. The objection that "there are between 1275 and 1298 nine assemblies summoned by 'parliamentary' writs, and fifteen sessions whose business is recorded in the rolls, and . . . not one of the nine coincide with one of the fifteen" (A. F. Pollard, *Evolution of Parliament*, pp. 47 *et seq.*) is not quite conclusive. All the rolls of Parliament, *i.e.* the collected *placita* and *petitiones*, are wanting for the years 1-6 and 6-18. Chroniclers record "parliaments" attended by magnates and representatives at intervals throughout the reign, and the nature of our record is certainly insufficient as evidence to prove that these were not parliaments in the strict sense. There seems, therefore, no reason to regard parliaments in which the Council are joined by magnates and representatives as an innovation of the last years of Edward's reign, nor, necessarily, of Edward's reign at all. Henry III almost certainly had recourse to them, though Simon de Montfort, though he might summon knights to a *colloquium*, had not the royal power which alone could summon a parliament. During the last two decades of Henry III's reign the use of the term parliament was probably in process of becoming fixed. Many assemblies which seem to merit the description are not officially so called, or at least we have no record of their being so called, and it would not be surprising if further research revealed the fact that the principal difference between the later assemblies of Henry III's reign and the earlier assemblies of Edward I's were one of name. Certainly, the parliamentary business of *placita* and *petitiones* seems to have been carried on actively in Henry's parliaments.

Fluidity of Thus, although it is true that the parliament of the future was to
parlia- consist in the interlocking of the *colloquium* or *parliamentum* of the
mentary magnates with the parliament of Council, and that some precedent
institution for this was certainly set in Edward's third year, and probably
in 1272 under his father, the whole constitution was still fluid at the
beginning of Edward's reign, and remained so in some measure
until its end. Among the dubitabilia, as to which the policy of the
king was likely to be decisive, we may place the choice of magnates to receive the direct writ—the basis of the future House of
Lords—the calling or not of representatives from the *communes*
of the counties and boroughs, and the degree to which assemblies
other than parliament were to be used to dispatch more or less of
the *ardua negotia regni.* As to the powers of parliament and its
several members when summoned, the situation, in the ambiguous
phase of law which then prevailed, was even more obscure. Were
the magnates to be legislators in their traditional feudal character,
or counsellors whose advice might be set aside, or assessors whose
assensus was valuable but not vital to statute, or simply petitioners
awaiting the result of the king's discussion with his Council? Was
statute to be by authority of the king in the inner parliament of
Council, or in the parliament with Council and magnates together? And were the representatives of the *communes* summoned
in any legislative capacity at all? Finally, were magnates, or magnates and *communes*, to be incapable of granting aid except in
parliament, or would local or general non-parliamentary assemblies suffice, and could the magnates act in their old capacity to
grant on behalf of the *communes* as well as for themselves, or must
the latter be consulted through their representatives? None of these
questions was settled when Edward came to the throne nor were
they finally answered during his lifetime, for they only arose in the
light of later experience of the working of parliamentary institutions; but his reign established certain precedents of value.
According to the answer that might be given to them, there was
material for perhaps a dozen constitutions other than that which
ultimately grew into being.

It may be said at once that no statute ever issued except from parliament, that is from an assembly of which the parliament of Council

at least formed a part. The *colloquium* of magnates alone—the *Magnum Concilium* as it came to be called under Edward III—never legislated. In that sense the king in his Council in his parliament was the centre of the state. It is nevertheless true that other forms of assembly, without parliament, were summoned late in Edward I's reign, and long after it, and that they were concerned with deliberative business which we should call parliamentary—but which contemporaries would not[1]—though none of them was summoned by the writ *De Veniendo ad Parliamentum*.[2] Throughout his reign Edward continued indifferent to the exact composition of these occasional assemblies. At his convenience he summoned them in any part of the kingdom, from all classes that he wished to use, and laid upon them any fiscal or executive burden they could be induced to bear. If there is any principle it is that a proportion of magnates should be present in any council that is required to grant a general aid. Such assemblies were more variously constituted than was parliament, were often summoned to deal with some immediate crisis, and had at times so strong a military quality that they are hard to distinguish from simple summons to service in the host. Such is the summons to some two hundred barons and knights to come to Ross on the Nativity of the Virgin in the 25th year *de quibusdam negotiis nos et regnum nostrum specialiter tangenciis . . . locuturi et tractaturi*.[3] It was in an assembly of the host summoned by writ of bodily service for Gascony[4] that the most dangerous crisis of the reign was fought out in July 1297, the confirmation of the Charters being granted, and reconciliation

Non-parliamentary assemblies

[1] Professor Tout's comment upon one of these assemblies summoned to *magnum consilium* in 1338, that it "can fairly be reckoned a parliament" (*Chapters in Administrative History*, iii. 80 n.), ignores the radical character of parliament as containing the Council *ad parliamenta* and entertaining *placita* and petitions.

[2] The distinction between parliament and other assemblies is very clearly marked in the writs of 17 Edw. II, (*a*) for a *tractatus* at Hilarytide to which lay magnates, knights, and burgesses were summoned by writs *De tractatu habendo*, and (*b*) the parliament summoned for the Purification by writs *De veniendo ad Parliamentum*. The difference was, no doubt, that parliament sat to hear all petitions, while the *tractatus* was summoned to discuss some certain matters of general import. *Report on the Dignity of a Peer*, iii. p. 344.

[3] *Ibid.* iii. p. 83.

[4] It is noteworthy that the form of the writ for this meeting was actually challenged by the malcontent nobles, but on the ground that it did not specify the place to which the host was to go and gave insufficient time for preparation. That it was insufficient as a summons upon which aid was granted and great affairs discussed seems to have occurred to no one.

made between archbishop and king. Others are called with the express intention of massing the feeling of the nation behind the king in some dangerous or invidious business, as when the laity, magnates, and representatives of shires and boroughs, are called to Shrewsbury to advise on the fate of David in 1283.[1] They are used as a means of securing sectional aid or administrative coöperation[2] from those who have not been called to parliament, as in 1283 when two provincial assemblies are called *de subsidio petendo* to Northampton and York. Here the magnates were not summoned —being then in personal service with the king in the field—the king himself proposed not to be present, but the clergy and representatives of the *communes*—who did attend—were induced to render some personal contribution to the war of which we do not know the nature. Wykes records assemblies of magnates in 1286 and 1288 which were not parliaments, but in one of which aid was granted, and in the other deferred, for the whole kingdom. In these non-parliamentary assemblies there was far more elasticity than in parliament; Edward maintained Henry's practice of going beyond the circle of the baronage on such occasions, and in those which were summoned to grant an aid there seems to have been no reason to secure a large assembly. Half the full parliamentary list of magnates, acting if they so wished through attorneys, was considered sufficient to commit their order to the aid of 34 Edw. I for knighting the prince of Wales.

The magnates in parliament   Routine business of state Edward did in his Council, since this was the highest court of justice, and because, even more than his father, he treated every administrative order and every change in custom as matter of prerogative, the king in Council in parliament was the essential authority of statute. It was, perhaps, with very little desire of giving greater validity to acts which needed no confirmation that Edward summoned other elements to parliament, but rather to keep himself in touch with national feeling, to maintain that sense of national leadership with which he had begun his reign, and to get independent advice as to the effect in practical working of statutes and judgments. Since, therefore, the

[1] Parliamentary Writs, i. 16.
[2] As with the knights called to York in 1300 *ad faciendum et exequendum pro observacione cartarum. Ibid.* i. 87.

utmost variety prevailed in the composition of assemblies other than parliament, it is not surprising that the structure of the fullest parliaments also reflects the free choice of the king and his needs, rather than feudal right. Baronial franchise had, indeed, become almost useless as a qualification for political power. Tradition and existing realities both demanded some recognition of the community of the tenants-in-chief, and at least the greater of them were accustomed to individual summons. But the application of this principle was vague enough to give scope for almost any plan which might commend itself to the king. During the baronial wars there had been much talk of the *universitas regni*, and again under Edward II a distinctive political right was claimed for the *baronagium*. Under Henry III, at least when the crown was weak, it is probable that this baronage assembled much as it liked, and often in great numbers.[1] But those who put themselves forward upon such vague qualifications in time of unrest were in no position to establish a legal claim to summons to any formally constituted parliament.[2] The same forces that had been favouring the drawing together of the shire community into a suitable constituency for parliament had been working for the disintegration of the baronies: baronage had almost ceased to denote a political order and was now little more than a variant of free tenure, and tenure *per baroniam* had itself developed intricate degrees. Tenants of a whole barony were few, tenants *per baroniam*, holding a fraction in right of partition of coheiresses,[3] were very numerous, and often of little standing. Barony was coming to be blended with the unprivileged tenure of the counties, and was ceasing to be a valid determinant of parliamentary or any other public status. Apart from the decline of the tenure, the right to summons had never received more certain definition than the vague rule of Magna Carta, and recent usage had set no clear precedent.

[1] Matthew Paris, *Chronica Majora*, anno 1255: *Omnes nobiles Angliae . . . ita quod nunquam tam populosa multitudo ibi antea visa fuerat congregata*, attended the Hokeday Parliament.

[2] At an earlier period the lords of Yorkshire denied the validity of an aid because they had not been summoned to the Oxford council which had granted it. *Royal Letters of Henry III* (ed. Shirley), i. 151.

[3] The distinction between those who held a whole barony—*integra baronia*—and those who held only a fraction of one *per baroniam* had certain legal and constitutional consequences in the reign of Edward III. It is doubtful whether they were recognized under Edward I.

It would have been uncharacteristic of Edward I to prejudice the immediate usefulness of his parliaments by leaving the right of attendance to be asserted as a franchise. In so far as the magnates were not indifferent,[1] the result would have been litigation for which even the principle was lacking, and an indefinite period of debate. The author of the *Modus Tenendi Parliamentum* despaired of using tenure as a qualification, and, with a kind of premature Whiggery, asserted it upon the ground of landed wealth, and claimed the direct writ for all those who held thirteen-and-a-third knight's fees or more,[2] whether by barony or not.[3] Edward, less trustful of wealth as a guarantee of loyalty and wisdom, took an even cruder test. The list from which the chancellor's clerks dispatched the writs *De Veniendo ad Parliamentum* to the secular magnates in his last eight years was the list of summons to the host to Carlisle at Pentecost 1299.[4] From this roll of eleven earls and a hundred and four other magnates—not all of them were barons[5] and some not even tenants *per baroniam*—with frequent omissions, and more rarely with the addition of a name or so, parliaments continued to be summoned until the end of the reign.[6] The heads of many baronies and honours were omitted from it, and were thus disfranchised; some who had regular summons can have been no more than knights; but it had the advantage of settling outright

[1] Cf. F. W. Maitland, *Memoranda de Parliamento*, lxxxvii.

[2] Some baronies were mere fractions of such an estate. Cf. that of William Martin, who sat in Edward I's parliaments. It was *integra baronia*, but consisted of the manor of Blagdon (Somerset), of one knight's fee. Public Record Office, *Calendar of Inquisition Post Mortem*, vi. 707.

[3] Stubbs, *Select Charters*, p. 501.

[4] Parliamentary Writs, i. 321. There is no consistent evidence as to practice earlier in the reign, but the roll for the Salisbury parliament of 25 Edw. I is identical with that for the host of Newcastle of the same year, the same order of names being followed throughout, though thirteen magnates who were called to parliament were not called to the host (*ibid.* i. 51, 302). As a result of the change from this list to the one adopted finally in 1299, some thirty magnates were cut out and others substituted. Such men as Ralf Nevill of Raby, Ingelram de Gynes, and Gilbert de Gaunt were not summoned for the rest of the reign.   [5] In the sense of not holding *baroniam integram*.

[6] The summonses for Edward's last large parliament, that for Carlisle, at Hilary 1306, are identical with the military summonses seven years earlier in the order of the names and the men summoned, with the exception that, out of the hundred and four magnates, other than earls, who were called to the host in 1299, thirteen are omitted in the parliament of 1306, and five names are added, Edmond Deyncurt, John de St. John of Lagenham, Geoffrey de Geynville, Amalric de St. Amand, and Henry Tregoz. *Ibid.* i. 181.

a problem which was insoluble by any rule then existing, and it provided Edward with magnate counsel of proved fidelity and wisdom, since it was that of men whom he had chosen to lead the Scotch war. Had Edward I lived longer or had Edward II retained his list of council unchanged, peerage of parliament might have been established in the descendants not of those called to the "model" parliament of 1295, but of those summoned to the first, abortive war of Caerlaverock. As it was, the principle of treating the prelates, the earls, and a minority of the baronage, arbitrarily chosen from time to time, as a parliamentary peerage, dates in fact from Edward I, though it was not admitted as a principle, nor stereotyped as the basis of an hereditary right, until after a long period of maturing prescription which was perhaps hardly completed in the fifteenth century.

With this extremely artificial treatment of the future second *Commons in parliament* estate in mind, we shall not look for Edward to be very strictly bound by precedent in his treatment of the other parts of his parliament, nor to be governed by popular principle for its own sake. The famous dictum *quod omnes tangit ab omnibus approbetur* seems to have been nothing more than an effort to convince the archbishop and his suffragans that further aid for the relief of Gascony, which Edward suspected would be refused on the ground that the clergy were not concerned, was really in their own interest.[1] Nevertheless, the tide already ran in that direction. Omitting royal and seigneurial demesne, the shires had long been taxable unities,[2] sometimes assessed and levied upon by resident knights. Upon these developing constituencies Edward fastened, his originality lying mainly in the fact that, with a few exceptions in the earlier part of his reign and after a certain amount of experiment, he established the practice of summoning the counties and boroughs to parliament, instead of staving them off into occasional *ad hoc* assemblies. The first step towards the association of the

---

[1] *Res vestra maxime sicut ceterorum regni ejusdem concivium agitur in hac parte*: your interests are equally involved with those of the rest of the realm in this affair. Stubbs, *Select Charters*, p. 480. Edward had tried to establish this sense of common interest in a writ to the archbishop of York of the previous year—*quos communiter negocium istud tangit*—but without as yet suggesting the propriety of all concerned lending their consent. Parliamentary Writs, i. 25.

[2] Cf. *ante*, pp. 310 *et seq.*

knights with the clergy and magnates in granting aid may, perhaps, be taken as that occasion in 1254 when the magnates would
not pledge the counties for an aid for Gascony, and knights were
summoned *vice omnium et singulorum* to make a grant.[1] The practice
seems to have had many precedents by 1272. Knights were summoned in 1264 and 1265, and possibly later in Henry's reign, and
with a hardening sense of their representative quality, of their
speaking with the authority of the communities,[2] which were to
hold *ratum et acceptum*—valid and agreed—whatever was done in
their name.[3] Throughout the reign of Edward representatives were
called at intervals to provide aid in special assemblies, and upon a
number of occasions to parliament.

As has already been suggested, much would turn upon what
the magnates and the representatives were required to do when
present at parliament. Edward's parliament was not yet a body of
fixed constitution. Rather, it was a *colloquium* between the Parliament of Council and certain magnates and representatives of
communities, selected, and differently selected, from time to time
according to the king's convenience and his judgment of what was
convenient for the realm. Nevertheless, certain combinations of
these elements were beginning to recur more frequently than
Function others, and the "model" parliaments of 1295 and 1296, containing
of com- prelates and magnates, proctors of the clergy, knights and bur-
munes in gesses, were so nearly an epitome of the nation's life that this
parliament form came in the end, though hardly in Edward's reign, to be
accepted as the proper constitution of a full parliament. Equally,
certain broad principles as to the function of these various elements
when attending parliament were beginning to emerge, though
they were not those which were finally to prevail. Except in
1275,[4] the *communes* were never summoned to parliament with

[1] *Royal Letters of Henry III* (ed. Shirley), ii. 101.

[2] *Vice omnium et singulorum* (1254), *pro toto comitatu* (1264), *pro communitate
comitatus* (1265).

[3] Cf. J. G. Edwards, in *Essays presented to Dr. Salter*, p. 149.

[4] An exception occurs in the October parliament of 1275, but the representatives summoned were not ordered to be elected, and were to be *de dis-
crecioribus in lege*. Unlike the elected knights of later parliaments of the reign
they were commissioned *ad tractandum cum magnatibus*, and shared in the enactment of a statute, that of Westminster I. C. H. Jenkinson, *English Historical
Review*, vol. xxv. This plan was not repeated in any subsequent assembly
summoned by writ *de veniendo ad Parliamentum*.

any fuller commission than to execute what others had decided.[1]
The magnates came to discuss—*tractaturi vestrumque consilium
impensuri*—and the representatives might be asked for advice on
occasion,[2] but they were required to have full power from their
shires and boroughs only to hear and do—*ad faciendum quod tunc
de communi consilio ordinabitur*;[3] it was not until the Lent Parliament of 1313 that their parliamentary writs began to summon
them *ad consentiendum*.[4] The commission *ad faciendum* is the same
power that is required for them when they are called to non-
parliamentary assemblies to hear and carry out some particular
executive enactment, as at York at the Ascension of 1300, when
knights attended *ad faciendum et exequendum pro observacione
cartarum*, or in 1283, when called to York and Northampton to
receive the king's precept, *ad audiendum et faciendum*, for some
unspecified coöperation in the Welsh war, one outcome of which
was the grant of the Thirtieth. Knights who were elected to the
parliament of 1295 *ad audiendum et faciendum* were later nominated
by the king to assess and collect the Eleventh and Seventh in nineteen out of the thirty counties[5]: and this, together with the convenience of receiving petitions during the time of parliament, and by
the hands of accredited representatives, may be the king's principal
motive in summoning the *communes* to parliament.

For knights participating in counsel and decisions made, we
must look for the most part outside parliament to special non-
parliamentary gatherings, especially to such as are called to grant
an aid. To the Shrewsbury meeting which considered David's
fate, knights and burgesses were summoned because "the King
wishes to speak with them upon that and other matters".[6] In 1290
they were called to Westminster after parliament had dispersed to
consider certain requests for privilege put forward by the magnates, and again it was *ad consulendum et consenciendum*.[7] Four years
later they were called at Martinmas, not to parliament but to

*Function of
the com-
munes in
non-parli-
amentary
assemblies*

---

[1] Cf. Parliamentary Writs, *passim*.

[2] As for the Statute of Carlisle which drafted *post deliberationem plenariam et
tractatum cum comitibus, baronibus, proceribus et aliis nobilibus ac communitatibus
regni sui habitum*: after deliberation and consideration with the earls, barons,
notables, other nobles, and communities of the realm. *Rotuli Parliamentorum*,
i. 217.   [3] Parliamentary Writs, i. 183.

[4] *Report on the Dignity of a Peer*, iii. p. 223.

[5] Parliamentary Writs, i. 34, 45.

[6] *Ibid*. i. 16.   [7] *Ibid*. i. 21.

colloquium—the object of which was, apparently, an aid for the
Gascon war ¹—again to offer counsel, but also to consent to what
the earls, barons, and *proceres* should have decided. In 1306 they
were called *ad tractandum et ordinandum de auxilio . . . faciendo et ad
consenciendum hiis que ordinabuntur in hac parte*. This last phrase
defining their powers in 1306 was identical with that in the writ
on the same occasion to the clergy and magnates,² and it is in
such councils, and such only, and not in parliament, that the
communes of the shires and boroughs are seen to share some
measure of deciding power with the magnates.³ There, as readily
as they later will in parliament, they exercise the ancient right of
all feudal lieges to determine the occasion and amount of aid.

*Function
of the
magnates
in
parliament*   The standing and function of the magnates in parliament was
less clearly determined, but it was far short of that which they had
occupied in former reigns. Their writs summoned them *ad
colloquium et tractatum* and with the underlying assumption that
their attendance was justified less by a routine membership of a
supreme governing body of parliament than because some special
circumstances moved the king in parliament to consult them. The
summons, therefore, was to special business, and not to the
whole session of parliament. At times the writ would say what
that business was, as in 1299 about Gascon affairs—*super negociis
nostris transmarinis* ⁴—or in 1304 the better establishment of the
realm of Scotland,⁵ or in 1296 to fulfil the promise of an aid.⁶ Or
the magnates might be informed that the reason of their attendance would be told them when they reached parliament,⁷ or be
summoned simply to give their opinion about certain arduous
matters unspecified, which the king did not wish to dispatch
without their presence.⁸ They were summoned, then, to consider
whatever was put before them by king and Council in parliament, not to the full range of the Council-in-parliament's business.
Much of the work of the session might be dispatched before they
came, much which was done while they were technically at
parliament would never be brought to their notice, and they were

---

¹ Parliamentary Writs, i. 26.   ² *Ibid*. i. 164.
³ The nearest they get to such power in Parliament is when they are admitted
to "deliberate" in 1306. Cf. note 1, p. 351 *supra*.
⁴ *Ibid*. i. 78.   ⁵ *Ibid*. i. 136.
⁶ *Ibid*. i. 47.   ⁷ *Ibid*. i. 81.   ⁸ *Ibid*. i. 28.

often dismissed while parliament had several weeks to run. Their attendance was to limited agenda predetermined by the king. It follows therefore that, though feudal tradition gave to every baron and indeed to every tenant-in-chief the right of counsel, the magnates in parliament did not constitute, nor were even added to, the king's sworn Council for the period of parliament.[1] Their summons invites them only to attend *cum ceteris magnatibus et proceribus regni*, while the councillors' writ summons them *cum ceteris de consilio nostro*.[2] They remain an external body called to intermittent *colloquium* and *tractatum* with the Council during the period of Council's session *ad Parliamenta*. Though it will come in Edward II's reign, there is as yet no merging of the magnates and Council into one body during the session of Parliament either for judgment or legislation.[3] Statute is, indeed, in strict form, not made by the magnates, though their assent may be recorded, and the distinction set up between magnates and councillors is maintained in the rolls of parliament. According to the letter of their preambles it is the king, *rex in consilio*, who makes statutes. Never after the First Statute of Westminster do the lords join in enacting it. They will not do so until the period of the Ordainers under Edward II.

Devised to make prerogative strong, and yet sensitive to the

[1] Cf. the proclamation during the parliament of 1305: "Archbishops, Bishops, and other Prelates, Earls, Barons . . . the King wishes to return for the time being to their countries . . . except for those Bishops, Earls, Barons, Justices, and others who are of the Council of our Lord King. Let them not go without special leave of the King". *Rotuli Parliamentorum*, i. 159.

[2] This form of writ was issued to a few magnates in the very small Parliaments of 1297 and 1305. But it is likely that they were magnates who were also members of the sworn Council.

[3] Mr. Baldwin's view that "the identity of the Council was immediately lost when any larger assembly was brought together", though true of the period of the Ordinances, does not seem to be borne out by the records of Edward I. J. F. Baldwin, *The King's Council*, p. 307. Thus in the Easter Parliament of 1285 *plures de regno tam Prelati . . . quam comites et Barones* petition the king as to the confirmation of charters and he answers them *habito super hoc cum suo consilio tractatu*. Letters Close, 13 Edw. I, p. 331. A clear sense of the distinction between provision and judgment, and of the more restricted function of assent to them or petition for them, is shown in an objection made in 1414 to the judgment upon the earl of Salisbury: *come les ditz declaration et juggement ne furent donez par le Roi, mais soulement par les Seignurs Temporels, et par assent du Roi; quelle juggement doit estre donez par notre Seignur le Roi qi est soverein Juge en toutz cas, et par les Seignurs Espirituels et Temporelx, ove le assent de les communes de la terre ou a lour petition. Rotuli Parliamentorum*, iv. 18.

needs of the nation, and set against a background of unstable and variable survival from past constitutionalism, the Edwardian parliament appears as a new institution, hardly as yet more than an experiment, but marking a radical break with that growth of the constitution which had hitherto proceeded smoothly from the root of the feudal *curia*. It contains elements which are old, but they have been so re-set that their practical effect is new, and they might well carry government away upon fresh lines at a tangent from the past. The magnates retain the function of *tractatus et colloquium* which the baronial *curia* had exercised, though decreasingly, under Henry; but it now takes the weaker form of petition and advice, and the baronage as a whole has lost its standing. The magnates of Edward's parliaments were a minority, arbitrarily chosen by the king, and given a parliamentary status artificially maintained. Much time would be needed to harden their status into parliamentary peerage, leaving many of their peers in tenure to lapse into the body of the unprivileged commons. Nor do those who were summoned seem to have been given the full standing of the Council in parliament. Their rudimentary legislative function, which had been growing in the past, was rarely appealed to by Edward after 1275, if at all.   The most they are called upon to do is to "assent to", to "approve" the action of parliament.[1] Edward's rule was to legislate by prerogative, sometimes upon petition, and though the assent of the magnates was recorded more often than that of the representatives it was clearly not essential to the validity of statute.

By the parliament of 1306 the future commons had come to the verge of securing for themselves an extension of the barons' much attenuated function of council and assent. They did, in fact, enjoy it from time to time in occasional non-parliamentary assemblies, for which their writs of summons were identical with those of the clergy and the secular magnates. They actually established their right to join the *universitas regni* upon questions of supply. But they carried no legislative right into parliament. To parliament they were summoned *ad faciendum*, and their

---

[1] This intermittently recorded *assensus* is to be contrasted with the power of the feudal *curia* to "provide", *i.e.* to decree enactments. Cf. the Statute of Merton: *ita provisum fuit et concessum, tam a predicto Archiepiscopo, Episcopis, Comitibus, Baronibus quam ab ipso Rege et aliis.*

function was that of an executive link with the counties and boroughs. Their share in future legislation will always be that of petitioners. Thus, though a planned constitution was probably no part of Edward's conscious policy, circumstances and his habitual decisiveness in dealing with involved issues conspired to make his reign a time of vital readjustment. The new parliament was not the old *curia*; rather, it was a servant and petitioner of the prerogative. In spite of the fact that he was not bound to work through them, the rapid succession of parliaments afforced by magnates, knights, and burgesses in his last decade sufficed to establish them as the norm of English government, and issues which might have been, and in the earlier years of his reign were, fought out in assemblies gathered *ad hoc negotium*,[1] were gradually drawn into the orbit of parliament, and in time, though not immediately, became matter for parliament alone. It is this, perhaps, as much as the new mechanics of parliament, which makes the reign of Edward crucial—that all the great business of state is coming to pass under prerogative, and prerogative chooses parliament as its vehicle.

The hesitation between feudalism and the political community, *Supply* which distracted all forms of public life in this generation, is well *under* shown in the confusion as to the basis of national finance, which, *Edward I* in spite of bold language in the *Confirmatio Cartarum*, lasted throughout the reign. There has, perhaps, never been a period of greater diversity of principle in taxation. The purely feudal taxes persisted. In 1279 the king took a scutage of forty shillings for Wales, in 1290 an *aide pur fille marier*, and in 1306 one for the knighting of Prince Edward. Only the aid of 1290 was made in parliament, and that in a parliament which seems to have been attended by a minority of magnates only, and those not summoned by parliamentary writ, and to have been vouched for only *quantum in ipsis est*.[2] The tax upon moveables was an established

---

[1] *E.g.* in occasional *colloquia* with a handful of magnates, with clergy alone, and in 1303 even with an assembly of merchants *ad colloquium et tractatum*. Stubbs, *Select Charters*, p. 496. H. S. Deighton, "Clerical Taxation by Consent", *English Historical Review*, vol. lxviii.

[2] *Rotuli Parliamentorum*, i. 25.

Arbitrary levies

principle, but, though he took a Fifteenth in 1275 and again in 1290, and a Thirtieth in 1283—of which only the first was strictly parliamentary[1]—it seemed for a time that Edward intended to evade the unequivocal necessity for consent which attached to the aids, and to find his revenue as far as he might by prerogative, or upon the ground of custom. The magnates of the parliament of Easter 1275 sanctioned the *magna et antiqua custuma* upon exports of wool and leather as permanent revenue, but in 1303 Edward added to it the *nova custuma* by a private bargain with the alien merchants. Between 1288 and 1294 perhaps the largest source of supply was the crusading Tenth imposed by papal authority for two successive periods of six years, and, in addition to such extraneous aids, years of crisis, such as 1294 and 1297, brought unconcealed prerogative taxation into action, in the former year in the seizure of the cathedral treasures and the wool and leather of the merchants and in the forcing of the clergy to yield a moiety of their revenues upon pain of outlawry, and in 1297 the maltolt upon wool, and what was again virtually a forced levy of a Third upon the clergy. Besides these taxes, which contemporaries contested as unconstitutional, the personal lordship of the king admitted as late as 1304 of a tallage of the royal demesne and of the boroughs, of a "gracious aid", *curiale subsidium*, from the towns in 1282, and in 1292 of a Fifteenth from the royal earldom of Chester, both of which, though aids in form, were probably polite substitutes for tallage.

Extra-parliamentary grants

Between 1279 and 1295, and 1297 and 1301, and again from 1301 to the end of the reign, all taxation was in the strict sense extra-parliamentary. That is to say it was either prerogative or derived from custom, or granted in special assemblies not summoned by writs *De Veniendo ad Parliamentum*. There was as yet no clear idea that aid was an inalienable function of the whole parliament; at times official language suggests that the magnates granted for their order, while each of the counties gave individual assent to its own grant;[2] but some kind of assembly of a more or

[1] The grant of 1283 was made by the provincial assemblies at York and Northampton.

[2] *Rotuli Parliamentorum*, i. App. p. 226: *Decima quam tota communitas Warr' Regi in subsidium guerre Regis concessit* (ibid. 22 Edw. I). *Ibid.* p. 242: *Quinta decima . . . Nobis nuper in Parliamento nostro Lincoln' a communitate comitatus predicti, sicut a ceteris communitatibus aliorum comitatuum* (ibid. 29 Edw. I).

less representative nature was usually called to accord it. The principle of consent was never seriously challenged, and even the *curiale subsidium* of Kirby's quest for aid in the counties must have been sued for in the county courts. The Thirtieth of 1283 was granted in provincial assemblies of knights and clergy. Knights granted a Tenth at Westminster in 1294, and knights and barons an Eighth in 1297, though the first was done in a *colloquium*, not a parliament, and the second in the host called by writ of military summons *De Veniendo cum Equis et Armis*, and without representation. The aid to knight the prince was made in an extra-parliamentary assembly of clergy, magnates, and knights at Pentecost 1306. Special meetings of the clergy out of parliament, as at Ely in 1290, were, perhaps, the commonest way of raising clerical subsidies.

In contrast, parliaments of Michaelmas 1275 and 1279, of *Grants in* November 1295, at Bury in 1296, and at Lincoln in 1301, all *parliament* granted taxes on moveables, and in a Council *ad Parliamenta* in 1290 those magnates who were present granted the *aide pur fille marier quantum in ipsis est*. But it is clear that taxation in parliament was no more than the seizing of a convenient occasion. How indifferent the magnates were to the nature of the assemblies as long as they were substantially representative of the order taxed is shown by the protest against the taxation of 1297. An Eighth from barons and knights and a Fifth from the burgesses were granted in July by a section of the magnates in the host; the taxes were quashed by a parliament which met in October after Edward's sailing, but not as unparliamentary, but because they were conceded before the king had made that Confirmation of the Charters for which they were held to be the reward. The financial safeguards in the *Confirmatio Cartarum* itself are subject to the same limitation of outlook. The pressure under which the grants of 1297 had been made gave some ground to fear for the immemorial principle that aid was by the mere grace of the vassal, and Edward was recalled to the promise of the Great Charter. He will not, nor will his heirs, says the *Confirmatio*, "take such aides, mises, and prises *fors qe par commun assent de tut le roiaume*".[1] He is not bound to parliament, for that is not as yet regarded as the sole vehicle of feudal constitutional right. A meeting such as that of Pentecost

[1] Stubbs, *Select Charters*, p. 490.

1306 *ad tractandum super auxilio ad militiam Edwardi* will amply fulfil the sixth clause of the *Confirmatio Cartarum*.

But, though the principal constitutional issues were for the time being in abeyance, Edward's government was too strong and impartial not to arouse opposition. Much of his achievement had lain in the realm of common rather than of constitutional law, and it was here, rather than through parliament, that his rule pressed upon the privileged classes. The Statutes of Westminster, Winchester, and Gloucester, *Quia Emptores*, and *De Religiosis*, the great inquisitions of 1274 and 1279, show him defining, elaborating, and restricting the rules of franchise, legal administration,[1] and public order with a purpose of which the general end is unmistakable. The power of the crown and the rights and convenience of the generality are the supreme tests of the pretensions of groups and individuals. The subject, not the franchise, is the unit of Edward's scheme of state, and common law, partnered by a jealously guarded regalian right, outweighs the validity of all other custom in England. Such a purpose was not to be maintained without a steady assertion of will against the multitude of individual ambitions inspired by the fresh opportunities of the times or by the surviving privilege of the past.

Feudal privilege threatened by Edward's reform

Bureau-cratic tendencies

The long campaigns in Wales and Scotland and the problems of administering those countries as additional provinces of the realm would in themselves have forced Edward to exaggerate the bureaucratic tendencies in his father's government,[2] and from the 'nineties onwards a certain revival of baronial opposition forced him at once to narrow the circle of the ministers and to throw some of the executive routine upon the knights and burgesses of parliament. The domestic ministries, and especially the Wardrobe, became more and more important in government, and the bureaucratic element in the sworn Council increased at the expense of the magnates, some of whom Edward was pur-

---

[1] Among the reforms of legal administration at this time may be placed the *Nisi Prius* circuits of Statute of Westminster, II. 30, the fixing of four circuits of assize for biennial visitation in 1293, the addition of commissions of Gaol Delivery to those of assize in 1299. Stubbs, *Constitutional History*, ii. 284.

[2] T. F. Tout, *Chapters in Administrative History*, ii. 60 *et seq.*

suing in a spirit of personal revenge. As under Henry III, the Wardrobe was the travelling treasury; it received revenue direct from the collectors of taxes, issuing tallies by which they could acquit themselves at the Exchequer, and from 1296 the normal relation of the two offices was reversed and the Exchequer became in practice dependent upon the Wardrobe. The pliability of Wardrobe traditions favoured the more liberal principles of finance to which the king was forced by the clamour of all classes against taxation. Through the Wardrobe he could borrow without check or criticism, and revenue prospects for years ahead were anticipated by loans from foreign bankers secured upon the Exchange and the Customs. By 1289 the king owed £107,000 to the Riccardi, and in his later years borrowed almost as freely from the Frescobaldi. John had been £200,000 in hand in 1213.

Irregular as it was, according to more modern principles of finance, this use of the Wardrobe was nothing new. It was unavoidable with armies out on the remote campaigns in Wales, Gascony, and Scotland. But, governed by no general financial policy, it involved the Crown in serious difficulties by the end of the reign, though they were difficulties which a generous agreement by the subjects to pay for Wales and Scotland by a short period of stiff taxation might easily have met. It would be unfair to justify baronial opposition upon the ground of these financial irregularities, of which the magnates were largely unconscious. Some attempt was made to clear up the arrears of the Wardrobe under the Ordainers, and the attempt was repeated in 1322, but on the whole the nation realized only a few of the symptoms of which the financial problem was the cause. Opposition under Edward I found little new to say and drew its programme from the past. The feudal order had modified its claims and held them for the most part in abeyance, but it had not renounced them, and, beneath the salutary innovations which we are bound to regard as the primary interest of the reign, the grievances and desires of the medieval subject worked as they had in every generation and were not greatly changed. Edward's taxes, his purveyors, customs gatherers, and tallagers, were as much hated as those of John, for government was unpopular in proportion as it was strong, and the system rather than the immediate policy of the reign made for harshness and extortion.

Ineffective   Thus, there was opposition in Edward's reign, though of the
nature   traditional ineffective kind, attacking every incident of taxation
of the   or administration separately when grievance was felt, justifying
opposition   the sense of wrong by the abuse of custom, seeking remedy in the
many times discredited device of a reissue of the Charters. In the
absence of any new constitutional theory the various interests
defended themselves individually, the clergy—the butt of the
crown in the taxation of the years 1294-8—fighting on the special
ground of the traditional exemption of their spiritualities and of
the bull *Clericis Laicos*, and a section of the magnates in 1297 taking
some obscure and unverifiable ground of privilege, the drift of
which has never been clear.[1] In that year the Constable and the
Marshal stumbled into a constitutional quarrel in the course of
urging an individual grievance, and, drawing a certain number of
the magnates after them, broadened their demands to question, as
The year   they had some reason for doing, the future of taxation, and
1297   especially the increased customs duties imposed three years earlier
by prerogative decree. In form, at least, the crown suffered a
defeat, and, though Edward's surrender was caused only by the
coincidence of three essentially separate problems, the French war,
the quarrel with the magnates, and that with the clergy, he
promised to respect the principle of consent for "all such aids,
tasks, and prises" as his recent levies upon the wool, and submitted
to a covering grant from the Pope when he taxed the clergy's
spiritualities, as he continued for the rest of his reign to do. Moreover, once set in motion, the demand for redress was not satisfied
by the general terms of the Confirmation of 1297, and the
grievance was renewed from time to time when the king was least
able to resist it.

The support of the magnates for the Scotch war of 1298 had to
be bought by a further confirmation of the charters and the
promise of a perambulation of the forests, by which the foresters'
encroachments of recent years might be detected. The problem of
the forests, once raised, involved the king in long and intricate
negotiations. He anticipated that the perambulation with its

---

[1] As to the constable and marshal that they were bound only to personal
attendance upon the king in transmarine wars, and for the rest, with a new
straining of the letter, that the clause *affectuose rogamus* in the writ of summons
might be taken as license to abstain from attendance if they so desired.

inquests would invite pleas for redress, warned the country that
the Council could not postpone the urgent concern of papal
affairs to a flood of forest litigation, and stipulated that the returns
should lie with him until they could be released for action with
safety. He would take no steps which might prejudice the *jura
regni et corone*. Even under these restrictions the complaints
widened to include the usual range of grievances. In a parliament
in March 1300, with clergy, magnates, and commons, the Great
Charter and the Charter of the Forest were reënacted, and the
public appetite for their reiteration was gratified by a decree that
they should in future be published four times in every year.
Twenty new articles, *articuli super cartas*, were added, much in the
spirit of those of 1297, but with certain reversions to the stock-in-
trade of past opposition, which show that the spirit of 1258 was *Articuli
not entirely dead.*[1] In the forefront remained the demand for an *super
enquiry into abuses of the Charters and especially of the Forest *cartas*
Charter. It was now satisfied by the grant of an elected commission, a concession destined to force Edward into his most
serious quarrel with his secular lieges. The knights elected in every
county carried through their enquiry in the summer of 1300, and
by September their report was in the king's hands.[2] Edward *Parliament
summoned parliament for Hilary 1301 to Lincoln to consider it, *of
Lincoln*
warning the magnates that they were equally bound with himself
to maintain the *jura corone*. The commissioners attended as knights
of the shire,[3] and all the foresters of every county came with them
to give expert counsel. A rather obscure wrangle between the
king and the magnates ensued at Lincoln, in which either party
sought to throw upon the other the responsibility for any en-
croachment upon the rights of the crown that possible concessions
might cause. An outlet to the deadlock was found in the presentation of a series of articles, introduced by Henry de Keighly, one
of the commissioners for Lincolnshire,[4] but backed by the mag-

[1] Of these the licensing of the election of sheriffs where the counties desired
it is the most striking.   [2] *Report on the Dignity of a Peer*, iii. p. 121.

[3] From the writs (*ibid.*) it is evident that the knights who attended at York
in March 1300 were appointed commissioners to enquire into abuses of the
Charters, and were again summoned to Lincoln at Hilary 1301, to parliament,
as knights of the shires.

[4] He was, of course, a parliamentary representative of the county, but presumably offered his bill of grievances in virtue of his membership of the forest
commission.

nates and formally accepted by the king. The parliament of Lincoln is interesting as much for Edward's attempt to rally the magnates to the interest of the crown and its rights as against a too generous interpretation of the Charters as for its hint of a coming renewal of opposition, but the dismissal of the treasurer was demanded—an avowal of dislike for Edward's government which could hardly have been made at any earlier period of the reign.

Dislike did not, however, gather head to extreme action during the king's lifetime. Edward's reign was for contemporaries, and still remains, one whose balance of good and bad it is difficult to assess. It is a period in which the greatest variety of constitutional form prevails. Survivals and new experiments are so evenly balanced that it is only in the light of later history that we can determine the real direction of the reign. At Edward's death two constitutional principles seem likely to prevail, the primitive principle of consent to taxation, and the new principle of the change or adjustment of law by prerogative. The latter will certainly be exercised in parliament, but there is as yet only a probability that the enacting body in parliament will be wider than the permanent Council. Taxation will continue to be by consent unless the customs and some extension of tallage come to outweigh the taxes on moveables in importance, but on the whole it seems improbable that consent will be given in parliament. Non-parliamentary assemblies, perhaps provincial negotiation, seem more likely here, and if they prevail there will be no true parliament but an estates system upon the model of France. The reign of Edward I, though it propounds a number of alternative answers to the problems raised by the break-up of the feudal régime, and offers at least some experience of the Parliament of Estates as a possible substitute for the *commune concilium* of feudalism, leaves the nation upon a point of doubt. A strong volition, royal, oligarchic, or popular, might deflect the constitution into any one of several paths, and the final choice is yet to be made.

The natural corrective to monarchy had been in abeyance since Evesham. Although the growth of opposition cannot be ignored in any account of Edward I's reign, its real interest lies in its history during that of his son, and then less in its conscious principles than in the effect upon parliament of the mere fact of opposition.

The crown which Edward II inherited was not a popular one. *Accession* His twenty years of incompetent rule gave such a check to the *of Edward* smooth increase of kingly power as to alter the whole history of *II* monarchy and of that parliamentary system which it had built to serve it. Edward I had left the Council supreme in parliament. Under him the magnates were spectators and auditors whose agreement might be sought at the king's discretion, and the commoners petitioners and executants of parliamentary decrees in their constituencies. By the end of his son's reign the magnates had established themselves as the king's primary Council in parliament, absorbing the sworn Council into their larger body, and resuming their primitive function as the enacting authority of legislation. The *communes*, in their turn, had also drawn nearer to the centre of parliament, and now occupied a status distinctly more influential than that held by the barons in 1307. Their advice and assent to policy was called for as that of the barons was by Edward I, but with the added advantage that it had at least once been by statute declared essential.

We cannot attribute this profound change to the intention of the Ordainers. They were moved by the perennial causes of medieval opposition. They disliked paying aids, thought that the king should live of his own and avoid the expenses of war, at least of war in Gascony, and found Gaveston as dangerous as the foreign advisers of Henry III and more offensive. They were less capable of devising a constitutional revolution than the barons of 1258, and, except for a demand that the Wardrobe should cease to anticipate payments to the Exchequer, they put forward no scheme of reconstruction. They accepted the very restricted parliamentary assembly of magnates convoked by Edward I and they gave no fresh encouragement to the *communes*. If anything, they would have narrowed the governing clique still further and proceeded by ordinance *du commun assent del roy e de ses countes*.[1] The movement of the Ordinances was, therefore, no overt attack upon the Edwardian constitution as embodied in parliament, or

[1] T. F. Tout, *Chapters in Administrative History*, ii. 193 n., citing the *Mirror of Justices*.

at least it was not attacked upon what at the present day seems the obvious ground of the monopoly of the parliamentary writ by a handful of magnates and the exclusion of the *communes* from a full share of legislation. The slightness of the change produced in the summonses to the baronage caused by the accession of Edward II is, indeed, remarkable. The first two parliaments of the reign were made up of a selection from those who attended Edward I's last parliament at Carlisle.[1] That of Easter 1309 admitted Cromwell, Tiptoft, Butler of Wem, and Grelley of Manchester[2]; but the success of the opposition caused no influx of barons discontented at past exclusion,[3] and the parliament of March 1310, when the magnates carried their demand for a committee of Ordainers, contained only thirteen names which were strange to the later parliaments of Edward I.[4] Of the six first parliaments of Edward II's reign, only the first and last contained representatives of the *communes*. The attack was not, therefore, upon any lack of popularism in Edward I's parliamentary legacy.

Probably not a tenth of the record which was actually made of the work of parliament during the reign of Edward II has survived, and whole periods of years have left us nothing. In addition, the records were, of course, not intended to assert principles, of which, indeed, contemporaries were largely unconscious. The ambiguous term *consilium* is still used when we should be glad of a precise statement as to the particular manifestation of counsel intended. Nevertheless, it is clear that the beginning of the reign saw not the least decisive of the reversals which have from time to time overtaken English political forms, and the clerks of parliament were compelled in some measure to change their terminology to reflect it. In brief, the change is that the sustained mood of opposition, of which the appointment of the Ordainers in 1310

[1] *Report on the Dignity of a Peer*, iii. pp. 174, 178.

[2] *Ibid*. 189.

[3] It is true that of the thirty-two men who launched the ordinances, five had been neglected in the parliaments of Edward I, William Marshal, Tiptoft, Botetourt, Baddlesmere, and Cromwell.

[4] *Ibid*. 197. The king himself complained that the ordinances were the work of a small caucus. Eleven bishops, eight earls, and thirteen barons took the responsibility for them. *Rotuli Parliamentorum*, i. 443.

and the publication of the ordinances in 1311 are typical, revived the ambition of the baronage to dominate the crown and the government, that it was at least temporarily successful, that it brought about a profound change in the status and functions of the magnates in parliament, and in the end profoundly modified those of the *communes* also. That the baronage fastened upon parliament at this time—and not upon some convocation independent of parliament, like the convocations of the clergy—is, perhaps, the most important single fact in the course of parliament's evolution.

The Council in Parliament of Edward I, that enacting group which was the real core of the constitution, was not the baronage but the sworn permanent Council of the king. It was this which received, considered, and answered petitions, at times seeking the *consilium* and even the *assensus* of those who were summoned by the magnates' writ *ad colloquium et tractatum*. The Council in Parliament of Edward II, at least over that portion of his reign after he came under baronial influence—from which most of our rolls of parliament are derived—was the *commune consilium* of the magnates or an active group of them who were regarded as representative of their order, and who were not sworn of the permanent Council. Departing from the opposition programme of the thirteenth century, the Ordainers rejected the permanent Council[1] as the centre of parliament. Redress of wrongs, they said, should be by the king and his prelates, earls and barons *ad querimoniam vulgi*,[2] and upon this principle, a reversal of the practice of Edward I, but having good medieval theory behind it, they tended to treat the whole body of the magnates in parliament as the primary Council. By them auditors were appointed to try petitions[3]—less than this had been refused them by Edward I[4]—

Magnates become the Council in Parliament

---

[1] One good reason for this may have been a failure of Edward II's Council to carry on the steady application of remedies offered by that of Edward I. In 1310 the knights and burgesses complained that "they found no one to receive their petitions, as was done in parliament in the days of the lord king his father." *Rotuli Parliamentorum*, i. 444.

[2] *Annales Londonienses*, i. 211. Stubbs, *Constitutional History*, ii. 353.

[3] Cf. the account of the Lincoln parliament of 1315. *Ibid.* ii. 350.

[4] At Lincoln in 1301 the magnates begged that complaints against breaches of the charters should be tried by *auditours a ces assignez qe ne soient pas suspecionus des Prelatz Contes e Barons*. Edward replied "*non per tales auditores.*" Parliamentary Writs, i. 104.

and many petitions seem to have been heard by the whole or a preponderance of the magnates under the title of *Magnum Consilium*.

Magnum
Con-
silium

This *Magnum Consilium* as the centre of parliament[1] appears first in 1312, though, since the rolls of the previous years are wanting, it may have come into being earlier. It acted principally when the regalian right or the conduct of royal officials or the requests of great persons were concerned,[2] and, although a *consilium*—presumably the sworn Council—was sitting at the same time, it was as an independent body, and from time to time referred cases to the *Magnum Consilium* as to an overriding authority[3]; on occasion its decision was reversed.[4] During 1315 the heading *Coram Magno Consilio* covers the whole recorded business of parliament.[5] In later years only occasional entries show that the great as well as the ordinary Council has been in action. From the material at hand it is hardly possible to be positive as to its precise constitutional affinities, but it was in all likelihood the general body of the peers. The name was used in later days of meetings of magnates without parliament[6] and usually without the lower grades, and also for the small continual councils of the Lancastrians, but the rolls suggest that in Edward II's reign it was identical with the parliamentary magnates, or at least composed of such a proportion of them as was deemed to stand for all. It may well be that, while the appearance of the *Magnum Consilium* stands for the assumption of control by the lords of parliament, its exact relation to *commune consilium* on one side and the sworn Council on the other remained undefined; upon one occasion the *Magnum Consilium* postpones a decision to the next parliament because "certain great lords, prelates and

---

[1] *Rotuli Parliamentorum*, i. 288: *Placita coram Magno Consilio in Parliamento. . . .*

[2] As with the petition of the Countess of Ulster *coram Rege et Magno Consilio suo* in 1334. *Ibid.* ii. 73.

[3] *Ibid.* i. 419: *remittatur peticio cum transcriptis coram Rege et Magno Consilio. Ibid.* i. 306. *Responsum est per consilium quod . . . Postea recitata fuit ista petitio cum responsione coram Magno Consilio.* Thus John Mowbray petitions the king and Council in 1334, and because he is asking for a revocation of outlawry "nothing can be done *sine Magno Consilio*". *Ibid.* ii. 74.

[4] *Ibid.* i. 296.

[5] *Ibid.* i. 288.

[6] The first instance of this use in the rolls seems to be in 1371. *Ibid.* i. 304.

othcrs, are not at this Parliament, and those that are will not
undertake to give judgment without them",[1] and on another
Mortimer of Chirk's claim to lands resumed under the Ordinances
is postponed "because such lands are not to be restored without
the common assent of the magnates, and the number now in
Parliament is insufficient for the purpose".[2] The *Magnum Consilium* may be referred to simply as the *majores*.[3] Such phrases would
be consonant with a Council which regarded itself as a quorum of
the whole of the lords in parliament, sitting in the place of the
sworn Council in Parliament of Edward I.[4] As a rule the petitions
which come before it seem to involve royal right or the action of
officials, and in such causes the form of the petitioners' address
occasionally varies from the usual *a nostre seigneur le Roi et a son
conseil*, and is made *a nostre Seigneur le Roi et son Conseil, Prelatz,
Countes, et Barons de sa terre*.[5]

The character of the Great Council of the rolls of parliament of
Edward II as a subsuming of the king's Council *ad Parliamenta*—
and so of the parliament in the sense in which it was hitherto
understood—into the whole body of magnates summoned, is
probably identical with the usage of the early fifteenth century.
From the ninth year of Henry V we have the so-called "Book of
the Council", considered by Sir Harris Nicolas[6] to have been compiled by the Council's clerk, and therefore authoritative as to its
view of its own procedure and composition in that and succeeding
reigns. It seems from this book that the sittings of the ordinary
or continual Council were afforced during times of parliament
or after special summons by the lords spiritual and temporal
and the judges. The minutes of such sessions during parliament
continue to be embodied in the book of the permanent Council's
proceedings, the same business is done—though many of the

[1] *Rotuli Parliamentorum*, i. 306.
[2] *Ibid.* i. 305.
[3] *Ibid.* i. 336.
[4] By the middle of Richard II's reign the term Grand Conseil is clearly being used for the permanent council which was set by parliament to control the king. *Ibid.* iii. 258.
[5] As in Hugh of Audley's claim to the earldom of Cornwall, lapsed after Gaveston's forfeiture into the king's hand. *Ibid.* i. app. 453.
[6] H. Nicolas, *Proceedings and Ordinances of the Privy Council*, v. 1 *et seq.*

petitions at that time being promoted in parliament come up for disposal—but the Council is joined by the peers and the justices, who apparently participate upon equal terms, and lend an equal authority to judgment and decision. Thus throughout July 1423 the continual Council of the minority is in session attended by all or the majority of the following sworn councillors —the duke of Gloucester, the archbishop of Canterbury, the bishops of Winchester and Worcester, the duke of Exeter, the earl of Warwick, the lords Fitz Hugh, Cromwell, and Tiptoft, the chancellor, treasurer, and keeper of the Privy Seal. There is then a gap in the proceedings, parliament meets upon the 21st October, and they are resumed on the 23rd October, "present the Duke of Gloucester, the Archbishop of Canterbury, the Bishops of Winchester, Norwich and Worcester, the Earl of March with divers other lords *of the Parliament*,[1] the Lords Cromwell and Tiptoft, the Chancellor, Treasurer, and Keeper of the Privy Seal and all the Justices, serjeants, and attorneys at Law of the King".[2] During the session, meetings of the ordinary Council are taking place, and it would be easy and natural for any particular cause to be reterred from the smaller to the more general meeting as they were under Edward II. On the available evidence it can hardly be said that the name *Magnum Consilium* was given consistently to these councils of the lords in parliament,[3] but that it was occasionally so used until well into the fifteenth century is certain.[4] In general, Great Council seems to be a common description of any body considered to be representative of the magnates, whether nominated in parliament as a continual council, or summoned by writ of Privy Seal to a special Council, or summoned under writ

---

[1] So again in 1425, *et aliis dominis de parliamento*. H. Nicolas, *Proceedings and Ordinances of the Privy Council*, iii. 169.   [2] *Ibid*. iii. 117.

[3] The term *Magnum Consilium* seems at times to be a mere honorific description of the continual council as well as a name for the occasional meetings of magnates which were still summoned. *Ibid*. iii. 95, 113, 222, 271. A specially summoned council of magnates contrasted with the *consilium privatum*—no doubt the permanent council. *Ibid*. iii. 322.

[4] Thus, during the July parliament of 1432, there are meetings described alternatively as being of the *domini magni consilii Regis in camera consilii parliamenti* and of the *domini consilii Parliamenti. Ibid*. iv. 120. So (*ibid*. iv. 287) the king . . . "hath by his greet consail in parlement be advised". On the other hand, in April 1434 a great council was summoned, clearly as a substitute for parliament, and under writ of Privy Seal, and also sat *in camera parliamenti. Ibid*. iv. 210

of the Great Seal to parliament, as was the case with these *Magna Consilia* of Edward II's parliament.

The essential fact of Edward II's reign is, no doubt, this capture *The* of the Council in Parliament by the magnates, since it gave back, *Ordainers* at least to an important section of the feudal order, that power of *and* judgment which the whole *commune consilium* had possessed a *parliament* century ago, and which it had been steadily losing. When normal times return the peers survive as the authority to which, with the king, the commons make their petitions, and, by bringing parliament under the control of the one order of the realm which was capable at that time of claiming it, the episode of the Ordinances was decisive of much of later parliamentary history, perhaps of the survival of that institution at all. The *communes* were, moreover, soon to find a more defined place in parliament, for the magnates, having established the supremacy of parliament and their own control of it, made less than they might have done of their opportunity. Lancaster, at least, though his party was that of the Ordainers, showed no disposition to carry out their constitutional policy. According to the Ordinances, parliament was to have had an overriding voice in peace and war, power to prevent the king from leaving the kingdom, and to appoint a regent when he did so. All the great officers, from the chancellor to the controller of the Wardrobe, were to be named by counsel of the barons in parliament. Government of this kind, which dispensed with the sworn magnate council of the Provisions of Oxford, would have required frequent parliaments, and the Ordainers determined that they should meet once or twice a year; but, no sooner had Lancaster come into power, than they ceased altogether. During the two years and a half from January 1316 to August 1318, when Lancaster lost his influence, only one parliament was summoned, and that was twice prorogued and then dismissed. By this indifference to what was coming to be recognized as the legal course of government, the baronage put an invaluable weapon into the hands of their enemies, and, by a curious reversal, first the middle party of Pembroke[1] and later the king and the Despensers became for the time being the champions of parliament in all its branches and especially of the commons. Indeed, like several of our more

[1] The York parliament of October 1318 took up the Ordainers' abandoned policy of enforcing the Ordinances in parliament.

incompetent kings, Edward II was inclined to advance popular principles. It can hardly be a coincidence that the change in the parliamentary writ of the *communes* to a form summoning them to consent as well as to obey dates from the Lent parliament of 1313, when the earls, still in disgrace for Gaveston's death, were ignoring the king's writs and avoiding parliament. The moment was opportune, for the *communes* themselves were beginning to

Increased influence of the commons

recognize the value of parliament. A petition in 1310 urges that properly constituted authority shall be present to receive petitions needing redress other than that by common law,[1] and in 1315 this petitioning power was for the first time turned against the magnates, and the king promised to withhold the exceptional legal commissions which they were beginning to use against their poorer neighbours.[2] In 1316 the *Communitas Angliae* asked that those who sought the office of sheriff should be obliged to forgo all private agreements with great neighbours and *faire office de vicomte pur le Roi et pur le Poeple*.[3] Thus, the interest of both crown and people combined with the incapacity of baronial leadership and the first warnings of the over-mighty subject to thrust the commons forward. The knights were beginning to see their function in a clearer light, they attend *pur eux et pur le poeple*,[4] and, if the *Modus Tenendi Parliamentum* is really a product of this reign, we must recognize that some surprisingly ambitious claims as to the status of the commons were current. To the author of the *Modus* they were the one essential element of parliament, without which no parliament was valid, "because they stand for the community"— *quia representant totam communitatem Angliae*—while of the magnates the best that can be said is that each stands for himself.[5] That such theories were in the air we may well believe, since the parliament

Commons' petitions

after Boroughbridge declared that all matters concerning the king and the realm were in future to be accorded and established by the commons as well as by the prelates and magnates. This is less likely to refer to legislation by statute, in which the commons' place was to be that of petitioners, than to that congeries of questions of policy, *les busoignes le Roi*—Scotland, Gascony, or the peace of the realm—which confronted most parliaments before they

---

[1] *Rotuli Parliamentorum*, i. 444.   [2] *Ibid.* i. 290.
[3] *Ibid.* i. 343.   [4] *Ibid.* i. 444.
[5] *Est pro sua propria persona ad Parliamentum et nulla alia.*

could come to their own concerns[1] of grievance and petition, but even petitions by the commons are beginning to have a new authority. Petitions of the *Communitas Angliae*, petitions *pur tote la commune*, have become more frequent, though they are not always formally urged by the knights[2] nor will it be for many years that the common petition will emanate only from the commons and become the initiating force of parliamentary legislation.

The accession of Edward III thus followed upon a period of rapid parliamentary growth. It would be natural to expect that it would be still further advanced by the overthrow of the throne and the forced abdication of the king. It is true that the revolution of 1327 was carried through in as strict a parliamentary form as Edward himself had observed after Boroughbridge, but, like revolutions of later days, it could not solve the contradiction that the prerogative was itself the maker of parliaments. Though the prince sent out the writs they went out in the king's name. So, when parliament met, though it came near to the point of deposition, setting its charges against Edward in six articles of incompetence, evil counsel, loss of provinces, oppression of the church, default of justice, and incorrigible misrule, and adopting them by almost general acclamation, though an oath to maintain the cause of the queen and the prince was taken by the prelates and magnates, and the prince was brought to Westminster to be acclaimed by the people as the future king, the vacancy of the throne was the act of Edward II himself. Deputies of the prelates, earls, barons, and judges went to Kenilworth, the king yielded the throne freely to his son, and only then, not in the act of a sovereign assembly, but by the withdrawal by procuration of all the several

Revolution of 1327

---

1 The assent of the commons to statute was not assumed to be necessary until the reign of Henry V. The substance of the declaration of 1322 was in fact observed for the future, and in 1369 Edward III was able to tell parliament with justice that "he had at all times during his reign acted with the advice by the counsel of the magnates and commons *en touz les grosses busoignes qe toucherent lui ou son Roiaume* and that he had at all times found them faithful and loyal". *Rotuli Parliamentorum*, ii. 299.

2 In 1325 certain persons who hold the forfeited lands of rebels proffer a petition *pur tote la commune. Ibid.* i. 430. In 1315 there is a petition *quorundam de Regno, petentium pro se et communitate. Ibid.* i. 295. A transition form which is almost that of the common petition occurs in 1314: *Prie la Comunalte de la terre, nomement ceux de l'eist de Londres. Ibid.* i. 308. Cf. G. L. Haskins, *Speculum*, xii. 315.

fealties of the lieges,[1] was the allegiance to the king broken. In so far as precedent was followed, it was that of the diffidation of John, in so far as parliament set the course of events, the prelates, magnates, and high officials assumed that they themselves were parliament, and no intelligible precedent was set for the future. The facts were, indeed, unprecedented; an abdication, and a diffidation which had lost its authentic feudal quality yet was not claimed as the act of a community embodied in parliament;[2] and they were so little reconcilable with contemporary or former experience that the theory of parliament could gain little from them.

State of parliament at Edward III's accession But, setting aside the palace revolution of 1327 and the national discontent which it brought to a focus, it is a very much changed parliament which emerges from Edward II's reign. In form at least, the magnates are now its centre and the *communes* are being admitted to a greater share of business. Parliament, it may be said, has come in a rough and unsystematic way to be shared between the king and the nation. The future, however, is even yet unsure. The particular adjustment of forces to which Edward III succeeded might have proved to be nothing more than a momentary balance struck by the weight of political parties as the last twenty years had left them. The grip of the nobles on the *Magnum Consilium* might have been relaxed again, the *communes* might have fallen back into their original impotence. As it happened, the general balance of 1327 was preserved without essential modification for the next two centuries; but, even so, almost the whole of the constitutional history of parliament remained to be written.

In fact, it was the outward form of parliament which, in broad outline, had been settled by 1327. Though it was still to meet without one or other of its components upon occasion, and though the non-parliamentary assembly of magnates[3] persisted at increasingly

---

[1] Stubbs, *Constitutional History*, ii. 380 n.: *les homages et fealtez a vous Edward roy d'Engleterre . . . rend et rebaylle sus.*

[2] *Ibid.* The renunciation, made by William Trussell, was that of *prelatz, contez et barons et altrez gentz en ma procurage nomes*, and thus preserved a convenient vagueness as between a possible authority of parliament and that of the individuals named. Legally the act is not better defined than that of the twenty-five barons whom the Great Charter empowered to make diffidation for the "whole commune of the realm".

[3] The meeting of estates out of parliament, sometimes including prelates, clerical proctors, magnates, knights, and burgesses (*e.g.* in July 1338 at Northampton), was an occasional feature of Edward III's reign.

rare intervals until the age of the Stuarts, it had become essential to great affairs of state.[1] For the time being, the weightiest business of all was likely to engage those magnates who were coming to call themselves the Peers of the Realm, though they were as yet no more than counsellors summoned at the king's discretion. They undertook the great treason trials with which Edward III's reign began, the quashing of Lancaster's process, the condemnation of Mortimer and his accomplices, the retrial of the case against Edmund, earl of Kent. It is clear that they were acting again, as their feudal ancestors had acted, as the highest court of the realm, the greatest council of the king—*come juges de Parlement*.[2] Though they would not admit that their jurisdiction extended to each and every trial in first instance, they habitually heard petitions from all conditions of men, which were "read and heard" "before our Lord the King, Prelates, Earls, Barons, and other magnates of the said Parliament",[3] and answered "by their request and assent". As common petition by the knights and burgesses became the rule, their assent began to have the force of legislation. The term *Magnum Consilium* was still used,[4] and it was an apt description of the number, dignity, and high function of the peers acting as the king's primary council in parliament. The opening of the Hundred Years War gave a strong stimulus to the growth of the internal order of parliament and especially to the rise of the commons. The political matters put before it became more and more absorbing. From point to point Edward consulted it upon the critical phases of war and truce, and left the organization of support from England in the hands of Council and parliament working together. Successive sessions record little but national business, in which the commons are treated almost upon an equal footing with the magnates, while their separate identity is preserved and accentuated. The parliament which emerges from this process of internal evolution is seen to preserve the dualism of

Growth in the structure of parliament

---

[1] *Rotuli Parliamentorum*, ii. 69: *le Roi . . . fist assembler un Conseil a Everwitz des Grantz et autres tielx come poet illocques avoir. A quel conseil feu avis, que les busoignes estoient si chargeantes q'il busoigneroit a somondre Parlement.* The statute of 1340, decreeing that all aids shall be granted in parliament, is a landmark in this matter. *Statutes of the Realm*, i. 289.

[2] *Rotuli Parliamentorum*, ii. 54.

[3] *Ibid.* ii. 123: *par les Prelatz, Countes, Barons, et autres du Parlement.*

[4] *E.g.* in 1334. *Ibid.* ii. 73.

its origin in the bringing together of the *colloquium* of magnates and the parliament of the Council. Sprung from these two roots of *colloquium* and supreme court for redress, the session proceeded by two stages.[1] In the first, *colloquium*, the business of the king, aid, and counsel of state, which formed the matter of the chancellor's charge to the lieges, and for which the writs were avowedly issued, divided parliament according to its grades, and a series of sectional meetings in the White or Painted Chambers, or in the Chapter House of the Abbey, broken by occasional visits from grade to grade for consultation, prepared the magnates and the representatives to face the king with a considered view of his difficulties and of the means to be taken to meet them. With this they returned, reconstituted the full parliament, and made their answers. In the second, we are back in the ancient judicial parliament of Edward I, the magnates sitting with the king in their capacity of Great Council, or acting under individual commissions as triers of petitions.[2] Before this session the commons appear in their original status as petitioners: "if they have any petitions of grievances done to the common people or for amendment in the law, let them put them in to the parliament".[3] The king, together with the Council of magnates,[4] accedes to or refuses their petitions,[5] refers them to some other form of redress, or promises to consider the matter further.

Relation
of the
order
of the
session
to the
structure of
parliament

These two phases of the parliamentary session, and the procedure made necessary by them, determined the later division of parliament into two houses and three estates. The upper and lower houses come, of course, from the primitive division between the king's Council and its petitioners. In presenting themselves before the official Council of Edward I, or before the *Magnum Consilium* of Edward II and Edward III, the commons appear as an external

---

[1] The first record of some such division appears in 1315. It may well have been derived from the primitive dualism of *colloquium et tractatus magnatum* and council *ad parliamenta*. *Rotuli Parliamentorum*, i. 350.

[2] In such apartments of the Palace as the Chamberlain's Room and the chamber of Marcolf. *Ibid.* ii. 309.   [3] *Ibid.* ii. 237.

[4] *Ibid.* ii. 237: *si vindrent les dites Communes devant nostre Seigneur le Roi et touz les Grantz en Parlement et monstrent.* . . . *Ibid.* ii. 238: *il plest a nostre Seigneur le Roi et a les grantz de la terre.* Upon occasion petitions are endorsed *les Seigneurs se aviserout. Ibid.* ii. 318.

[5] *Ibid.* ii. 319: *le Roi et lez Seigneurs ne sont pas en volunte a ceste foitz de change la commune ley.* The magnates have recovered the status of the barons of Merton.

subordinate body, and, though they find unity for themselves in joining to present common petitions, there is never any tendency for them to become merged in the magnate Council. The idea that the knights could ever have joined the lords of the Council in a joint house rests upon nothing tangible and ignores a fundamental division in the structure of parliament. On the other hand, if the two houses arise from the second, petitioning, phase of the session, the three estates are formed in the sectional consults of the first phase, the debate and advice upon "the king's business", the consideration of aid and the *magna negotia regni*. The division into two houses is foreshadowed in Edward I's writs, which calling magnates *ad colloquium et tractatum de quibusdam arduis negotiis que regnum Anglie tangunt"*, and knights and burgesses *ad audiendum et faciendum quod tunc de communi consilio ordinabitur*, though, since the change made in the commons writ in 1313 and the declaration of 1322, the commons have entered into a share of deliberation upon the king's business.

In proportion as the full parliament came to be the principal forum in which policy was debated, the three estates began to take their form. It was during the reign of Edward II that the proctors of the parochial and capitular clergy began to hold back from parliament. They felt safer in their convocations[1] in a reign when any parliament might be required to condone a *coup d'état* or to proclaim judgment of death upon a defeated party. The prelates and magnates, on the other hand, began to claim the right to private consultation within parliament, and so confirmed the principle of separate orders. Behind this grouping we can see vaguely defined a conception of estates of the realm, since the earls and barons in parliament claim to stand for "their peers of the land", *Beginning* those who hold *par baronie*, and to grant aid for their demesnes *of division* as well as for their own.[2] Much of the business of the early years *into* of Edward III's reign could only be done by the secular peers— *houses* the removal of Edward of Carnarvon to Kenilworth, the trial of the Mortimers—and even upon general matters they and the prelates were inclined to debate separately.[3] At the Salisbury

[1] It was even difficult to enforce their attendance at Convocation when the king's business required it. *Rotuli Parliamentorum*, ii. 146.   [2] *Ibid*. ii. 107.
[3] *Ibid*. ii. 52. In 1315 the prelates and magnates still debated together in the chapter-house of Lincoln. *Ibid*. i. 351.

parliament of 1330 the prelates *estoient assemblez au dit Parlement en une meson pur conseiller sur les busoignes nostre Seigneur le Roi,* and in this they were copied, in the parliament of the Nativity of the Virgin in 1332, by the other two orders.[1] At the ensuing parliament all three grades made their replies separately to the crown. During the king's absence in 1339 and 1340 parliament undertook the burden of supply and internal peace, and the commons took an active part.[2] At Easter 1343 the identity and independence of the future two houses was further emphasized by the dispatch of the prelates and magnates to the White Chamber, and the knights and burgesses to the Painted Chamber to discuss the king's business separately,[3] and their replies, together with the bills of grievance which the knights and burgesses attached to them, mark an advance in parliamentary procedure. In this parliament we hear for the first time the name of the reporter of the commons' advice, Sir William Trussell, who has been taken as the first in the line of the commons' speakers.[4]

Commons'   In time, also, the habit of separate debate began to reflect back
petitions   upon the form of petitioning and to bring the petition of the commons into being as an unique parliamentary function, exercised without the magnates, though sometimes after consultation with them. Independent discussion made the older joint petitions "by Prelates, Earls, Barons, and the commonalty of the realm" an anachronism, and in 1343, although there was still only one clerk of parliament,[5] the commons' deliberations found record

    [1] *Rotuli Parliamentorum,* ii. 66: *euent trete e deliberation, c'est assaver les ditz Prelatz par eux mesmes, et autres Grantz par eux mesmes, et auxint les chivalers des countes par eux mesmes.*
    [2] At Hilary 1332 the twelve magnates of the duke of Cornwall's council, the other prelates and magnates, and the knights and burgesses treated of the king's business as three orders. Their conclusions were reported to the king by the chancellor. *Ibid.* ii. 69. The presentation of a formally digested common opinion will certainly be made by a single person in the name of the rest. In 1343 the knights and burgesses "replied by Master William Trussel". *Ibid.* ii. 136. *Ibid.* ii. 117: *apres grant trete et parlance entre les Grantz et les dites Chivalers et autres des Communes.*
    [3] *Ibid.* ii. 136. By 1376 the chapter-house was "the ancient place" of the commons. *Ibid.* ii. 322. The allocation of the chapter-house of Westminster to the commons dates from Hilary 1352. *Ibid.* ii. 237.
    [4] *Ibid.* ii. 136: *Vindrent les Chivalers des counteez et les Communes et responderent par Monsieur William Trussell.* In 1377 *Monsieur Thomas de Hungerford, Chivaler . . . avoit les paroles pur les communes d'Engleterre. Ibid.* ii. 374.
    [5] *Ibid.* ii. 147.

in a special section of the roll under the heading "Petitions of the Commons and the Responses to them".[1] In 1348 the commons' petitions were still more clearly marked by being delivered to the clerk of parliament, while the petitions of individuals continued to be handed to the chancellor. The former were answered seriatim *par nostre Seigneur le Roi, et par les Grantz en dit Parlement*, and in 1344[2] the commons asked that the answers should be circulated to the shires and boroughs in the form of letters patent "for the comfort of the people". At this time the "grievances of the Commons" become an accepted feature of parliamentary procedure; they are invited in the opening address of the chancellor or chief justice; the commons themselves become jealous that their bills shall contain nothing that is not genuinely national in scope,[3] and thus the rule of legislation by petition of the commons and assent of the king and peers is roughly foreshadowed. In 1376 a petition was rejected on the ground that it had not been sponsored by the commons.[4]

It will be seen, also, that a radical change has overtaken the normal course of legislation. It has been by provision of the *commune consilium* of tenants-in-chief, then by the more or less absolute prerogative of king in Council in parliament, and lately, under Edward II, by the king and magnates in parliament, and the last form of authority has never been in form dispensed with. But in the past its inception has lain with the king and his men learned in the law, more rarely with the *proceres*. Now it is coming to lie with the commons. From 1327[5] the petition of the commons is mentioned as the initiating force in the preamble of statutes, while the authority of enactment remains that of the king and magnates. Common petitions, which, since they have adopted them and sponsored them to parliament, have come to be the commons' petitions, are a normal, though not the only,[6] prelude to statute, *Commons initiative in legislation*

---

1 *Rotuli Parliamentorum*, ii. 139. In 1344 there was similar schedule for petitions sent to the king by the prelates and other clergy.　　2 *Ibid*. ii. 150.

3 In 1372 they complained that personal grievances were being clothed in the form of common petitions. *Ibid*. ii. 310.

4 *Ibid*. ii. 333: *Pur ce qe ceste Bille ne fust mye advouez en Parlement.*

5 *Statutes of the Realm*, i. 255.

6 In the last parliament of the reign the commons declared that "we will not be bound by any Statute or Ordinance of yours made without our assent , but the dying king put the demand aside; "let this matter be more explicitly declared". *Ibid*. ii. 368.

and prompt the majority of ordinances. To say this is, of course, not to say that the commons' petitions always, or even frequently, issued in statute. They were often not intended to do so, for the greater number demanded only the putting into effect of existing law, the redress of partial grievances, or some change in administrative routine, which could best be effected by ordinance in council[1] or letters patent. In 1351 the commons sponsored thirty-nine petitions. To three of these the king, in giving favourable answers, added in *Statute*   effect *accorde est qe le respons de ceste petition soit mis en Estatut*, and they were adopted in parliament as the Statutes of Labourers, Provisors, and Servants. To others the answer was that "it pleases the King well that the said law should be enforced as heretofore", "that the said statute should be held and kept". Of some the petitioners were invited to appeal for redress to the Council. Others the king considered unreasonable and refused. Of a few, *le Roi s'avisera*. Statute, therefore, is a comparatively rare necessity, adding to the corpus of standing law of which the Charters are the heart,[2] and seems to be prompted less by the comparative importance of the object aimed at[3] than by the desire to give the king's concession that permanence which was attributed to the Great Charter and to place it beyond alteration or revocation; for it is already an old belief that statute is the province of parliament and can be annulled by parliament alone.[4] The latter years of the reign

[1] Thus in 1362 the commons ask that the king in Council shall make an ordinance increasing the currency, *ordeiner plente d'or et d'argent*, *Rotuli Parliamentorum*, ii. 271. In 1363 the commons were asked "whether they wished to have the matters accorded embodied in statute or ordinance". They chose the latter so that any necessary amendments might be made in the next parliament. As between ordinance in parliament and ordinance in council the commons seem to have been influenced chiefly by the fact that the council was not a court of record and they preferred certain matters to be entered on the parliament roll. *Ibid.* ii. 253. There is little appearance of jealousy as to authority. Mr. H. L. Gray observes that the legislation of only six of the ten parliaments following on 1343 directly answered commons' petitions (*Commons' Influence on Early Legislation*, p. 225), but, as is pointed out above, statute is not the only acceptable answer to petition.

[2] Cf. the archbishop's charge to parliament in 1422: "their liberties and franchises by them rightfully enjoyed and never repealed, nor by the common law repealable." *Ibid.* iv. 423.

[3] In 1363 a special statute was devoted to the return of strayed falcons to their owners. *Ibid.* ii. 282.

[4] In his last parliament Edward III acknowledged *qe les Estatutz faitz e a fairs en Parlement . . . ne purroient estre repellez sanz assent du Parlement*. *Ibid.* ii.

showed a certain hardening and definition of the nature of statute.[1] Judges were refusing to exercise their past laxity of interpretation and protesting the sacredness of its letter, to the profit of Chancery, whose market for equitable redress was strengthened by the timidity of the common lawyers, but also to the advantage of the authority and fixity of statute. Ordinance of king and Council began to be subordinate to statute. The Ordinance of the Staple of 1353 was not thought to have sufficient force till the ensuing parliament adopted and reënacted it.[2] From this period dates the first statute roll, into which the Chancery clerks incorporated the legislation of previous years from the accession of Edward I.

Parliament is, nevertheless, to some degree at the mercy of the king, the chancellor, and the triers of petitions, for the form that statute or any other answer to their petition may take. Commons do not yet put their grievance in a draft which itself contains the literal form of the required redress.[3] Statutes and ordinances are cast in such form as the Council considers will secure the substance of the commons' demands in so far as the king is advised to grant them,[4] and they may not be seen by the actual parliament which has moved them. Some bills may be suppressed by the triers, and it is suspected that the king has this done to petitions he does not like.[5] The aggressive parliament of 1340 was allowed to assent to the king's assignment of triers for their petitions and to associate certain commoners with them, but this was an exceptional concession.[6] In the last years of Edward III's reign the commons are, it is true, beginning to assert that the main purpose of parliament is

Treatment of commons' petitions

368. In 1351 the commons had asked that no statute should be altered on the petition of individuals nor its application modified. The king, however, asked for more explicit petition before he gave an answer, and this the commons do not seem to have been able to provide. *Ibid.* ii. 230.

[1] Plucknett, *Statutes and their Interpretation*, pp. 121-122.

[2] Professor Tout thinks that the petition of the commons in April 1354, that all the ordinances made in the late council should be "affirmed in this parliament and held for statute for ever", "suggests the exact date of the final differentiation of statute and ordinance". (*Chapters in Administrative History*, iii. 182 n.) This is, perhaps, too rigid a judgment.

[3] On the part taken by the commons in composing the form of statute cf. H. L. Gray, *Commons' Influence on Early Legislation*, pp. 201 *et seq.*

[4] "The king will ordain what it seems to him should be done with the advice of his Great Council." *Rotuli Parliamentorum*, ii. 320.

[5] *Ibid.* ii. 272: *Lesquex Seigneurs et autres assignez, si rien touche le Roi, font endocer (endorse) les billes Coram Rege: et issins riens est fait.*

[6] *Ibid.* ii. 113.

to redress their grievances,[1] and to insist that their petitions shall be fairly dealt with within the period of the session.[2] Common petitions are coming to be dealt with as a whole before parliament passes to those of individuals.[3] In 1363 the petitions with their answers were read by the chancellor in the White Chamber before the king, prelates, magnates, and commons. There were, moreover, intermittent efforts to associate redress with supply, either, as in 1352, by inscribing the promise of the aid upon the same roll with the petitions,[4] or, as was done for a while in the sixties, by postponing the grant until the petitions had been heard and answered.[5] On the whole, however, the form of legislation grew throughout Edward III's reign without serious conflict, and, therefore, without adding much to the theory of its nature. Edward's subjects would have been satisfied with some such generalization as that statute was law promulgated in parliament by the king's grace at the petition of the commons, and with the counsel and consent of the lords. Of these elements, the king's grant was still the chief essential, at least its supremacy was not overtly challenged, and he had not yet promised that he would make statute on none but common petition.

Indeed, there were few signs of conscious innovation. Exceptionally in 1340 parliament granted a Ninth "on the condition that the king would grant their petitions",[6] but such methods were not consistently applied, and were rather devices to make effective the petitions of the current parliament than considered contributions to parliamentary practice. They were used and dropped according to circumstances.[7] The Peers had lost the mood of consistent opposition and had been caught up into the king's cause and the ideals of the Round Table. They were a nominated group

---

[1] H. L. Gray, *Commons' Influence on Early Legislation*, 113. "Since this Parliament was summoned to redress the divers grievances and mischiefs done to the Commons."

[2] "Please the king of his good grace to ordain that the said bills should be seen, answered, and endorsed before the departure of the said Parliament." *Rotuli Parliamentorum*, ii. 272.

[3] *Ibid*. ii. 243. "After the petitions of the commons were answered, a petition was entered by Sir John Maltravers, etc., etc." (1352).

[4] *Ibid*. ii. 237.　　　　　　　　　　　　　　[5] *Ibid*. ii. 273.

[6] *Rotuli Parliamentorum*, ii. 113.

[7] From 1365 to 1376 the grant of aid was again allowed to come before the consideration of petitions.

of about fifty earls, barons, and even bannerets, most of whom had made their names in France. Nor, till the very end of the reign, had the commons that sense of rising power that we are apt to attribute to them. The burgesses made little showing, except, perhaps, the Londoners, and they preferred to urge their petitions as an independent force in parliament. The knights showed nothing of the conscious authority which inspired the feudal barons of the early thirteenth century. We should be wrong to discount altogether the forms of ceremony and address which accompanied the growth of respect for the king's person and formal deference to the crown. It was fact as well as form that redress was now obtained by petitions to the king's grace. The victory of Edward I's prerogative had not yet lost its substance, nor was the modest address of the commons, "*a lour tres-doute et graciouse Seigneur le Roi supplient ses povres liges Communes*", entirely without meaning. It is the unnoticed pressure of reality, rather than any conscious assertion of principle, that is bringing parliament to express a national will and make it respected.

Any account of the fourteenth century would be incomplete it *The* it were treated as a story of new growth only. Before parliament *opposition* could find its full strength it was forced to destroy much which *to the* had had its value in the past. There is a story of opposition— *crown* principally that of feudalism against the rapid retrenchment of its influence by the crown—which recurs intermittently through the reigns of the three Edwards, and under Edward II has a success of far-reaching consequence.

The evolution of parliament is that side of the reigns of the three Edwards which has most apparent relevance to later history. There is, however, another side to the constitution which seemed more important to contemporaries—perhaps, indeed, at that time was more important. Parliament met to secure redress of grievances which common law could not deal with. It was still a meeting of petitioners at law, and it was occasional only. Largely beyond its understanding, and almost wholly beyond its control, lay all those factors of government which we call executive, and they constituted perhaps the most pressing problem of the fourteenth century, for they had become numerous, powerful, jealous of their tradition and of each other, Chancery, Treasury, Chamber, Wardrobe, and their several officers pursuing a constant struggle to consolidate and extend each its particular sphere of power, and to fend off external criticism. Of this rivalry the most aggravated and dangerous form was the cleavage between the two offices—the Chamber and the Wardrobe—which had had their origin in the Household, and the Chancery and the Treasury, which they had from time to time almost superseded, the former working through the warrant of the Privy Seal, and affording the readiest weapons for a king who wished to develop his own personal policy. These executive offices were the target of most of the opposition of the early fourteenth century, the baronage seeking to depress the Wardrobe and the Chamber, to strengthen the Chancery and Treasury, and to keep the latter under baronial control, while the king preferred to withdraw his initiative within the offices of the Household.

Had the barons succeeded in their policy, the result might well have been disastrous. It would have meant the guidance of the executive routine not by the single will of the king, but by that of an external body of magnates. Its best chance of success—indeed, its only one—would have been the maintenance of a strong permanent Council of magnates, such as was called a continual Council in the fifteenth century, and it is to be doubted whether the barons of the fourteenth century had the application or level-headedness to keep such a Council in effective action. If, on the other hand, the king had succeeded in directing the main functions of government away from the Chancery and the Treasury, that might well have been the prelude to despotism. There would have been little check upon the expenditure of revenue, and provincial and central government would have been freed from the rules imposed by the need to secure the Great Seal for the king's precepts. We have become familiar with this conflict under Henry III. It is largely in abeyance during the reign of Edward I, breaks out violently in that of Edward II, and receives its final quietus under Edward III by the recognition of the king and his ministers that the king's government must be carried on, not by encouraging and exploiting the differences between the various offices, but by finding the most useful function of each in the state, and establishing a recognized subordination of parts to the whole.

To this Edward III contributed by his willingness to abstain from undue interference with the minutiae of government, and, as long as support for his French enterprise was forthcoming, to allow the various ministries to find their own levels within a balanced constitution. Turning from parliament, therefore, we must give some attention to this gradual process of adjustment within the executive and to the various phases of opposition which arose during its accomplishment.

At the accession of Edward II it seemed possible that the strong, *Adminis-* but latterly inefficient, administration of Edward I would be carried *tration* on with better acceptance. The household of the Prince of Wales *policy of Edward II* was drawn upon to dilute the officialdom of the last reign, but only Walter Langton, the treasurer, and the old king's weapon against the earls, was sacrificed. The barons who had been in opposition under his father rallied to Edward, and the abandonment of the Scotch war may, perhaps, be taken as the first-fruits of an alliance of king and magnates in a policy of peace. The break up of this first season of fair weather is to be attributed in part to the despair of the more zealous of the ministers of bringing order into the financial chaos bequeathed from the past—Benstead, and then Droxford, succeeded to the Wardrobe, and, failing to achieve reform, drifted into opposition—but still more to the folly of Gaveston and the irascibility of the earls. Gaveston was exiled—for a second time— in 1308, and in 1309 the Stamford Articles revealed what political *Opposition* programme, other than hatred of the favourite, the magnates had *of 1309* to offer. It was of the most conservative character, and, except for the cardinal fact that it was chosen as the governing body of the state, little use was, in fact, made of parliament. There was hardly a phrase in the Ordinances which might not have been taken from the Articles of 1300, or, indeed, from the earlier programmes of opposition under Henry III. The subordination of the Wardrobe to the Exchequer in finance, of the Exchequer to the Chancery in the framing of writs, the appointment in parliament of the great officers—to whom were added the keeper and controller of the Wardrobe—together with the principal members of the king's Household, exhausted the political inventiveness of the Ordainers, and established a baronial control of the government without effective reform in administration. To this conservative revolution the king reacted as his predecessors had done to earlier challenges of the same kind, suppressing the chancellorship and treasurership, since he might no longer make his own appointments, and ignoring the promise of that purge of the Household which was the real desire of the baronage. Then followed a struggle between the barons and the king for the control of the Chancery and the Treasury, in which the former drove the king's representative from his presidency of the Easter exchequer, and the latter frightened the Chancery clerks into sealing proclamations of Gaveston's loyalty which had been drafted in the Wardrobe. In 1312 constitutional manœuvres were driven out of the minds of both parties by the tragedy of Gaveston, and by Edward's attempt to cover up his shortcomings by a renewal of the war with Scotland, but Bannockburn, throwing him upon the mercy of the country, and shutting up the nation with its own domestic rancours, brought him to humble himself to the Ordainers. For the first time, the Ordinances would be executed without fear of defiance or evasion by the king. At the York parliament of 1314 the great offices and the ministries of the Household were filled with baronial nominees. "The opposition had become the government." [1] It was not, however, until 1316, that that "government" passed the phase of administrative interference, and attempted to establish an adequate conciliar control. Lancaster was set at the head of the Council established at Lincoln in that year, *de consilio Regis capitalis*, but his idle interventions and his still more troublesome lapses into indifference had already discredited him with his own party, and, at the outset of their enterprise of governing England, the cause of the barons went to pieces. Warenne took the field against Lancaster, Lancaster's supporters fell into disorder for lack of leadership, and those who were of neither faction, Roger d'Amory and Bartholomew de Badelesmere, under the guidance of Edward's cousin Pembroke, came to the fore as a middle party, not hating or favouring either extreme, but looking to the rehabilitation of the king and the reconstruction of a government which, in its three elements of crown, council, and ministries, was losing all cohesion and exhausting itself in a crossfire of mutually conflicting writs and precepts. In April 1318 the

Triumph of the opposition

[1] T. F. Tout, *Chapters in Administrative History*, ii. 202.

process of reconciliation was complete. The king and the earl gave *The*
sureties for their future conduct to each other in the Treaty of *middle*
Leake, and Lancaster, by forfeiting all hold upon the Council except *party*
a single representative, passed out of effective influence. The power
that he had lost, or failed to make good, went to a Council like
that of 1258, and from this Council, in which Pembroke predominated, and by which Badelesmere was made steward of the
Household and Hugh Despenser chamberlain, the first great
administrative reforms proceeded in the Household Ordinance of
York.

The way to reform had been to some degree prepared by the *Household*
work of the Ordainers. The trend was, of course, towards im- *Ordinance*
personal government and the exaltation of the office above the *of York*
caprice of the king, and it was undertaken with some measure of
skill. Like his predecessors, Edward had made his personal policy
effective by writs under a Privy Seal kept in the Wardrobe and
unchecked by external authority. It was the special weapon of
prerogative. The baronial answer to its arbitrary use was twofold,
to restrict the occasions on which it could be used to the detriment
of the Great Seal, and to bring the Privy Seal under the guardianship of a nominee of their own.[1] In the first year of Edward II,
as under his father, the controller of the Wardrobe united with
that office the personal secretariate of the king and the custody of
the Privy Seal. Its use to withhold redress at common law was *The*
petitioned against in 1309, and prohibited in the Ordinances of *Privy*
1311,[2] by which the commissioning of sheriffs by writ of Privy *Seal*
Seal was also forbidden. But these were mere elaborations of
Edward I's concessions of 1300—perennially ineffective—and the
vital contribution made to the future of the seal in 1311 was the
ordinance that in future "a suitable clerk be appointed to keep the
Privy Seal". This was the beginning of the keepership as a distinctive charge, intended to acquire those standards of office which
put the established ministries beyond the personal caprice of the
king, and guaranteed of independence by its inclusion among those
offices the holders of which should be elected in parliament.

Under the guidance of Roger Northburgh and his successors the
Privy Seal developed along the lines of a separate office, accumu-

---

[1] T. F. Tout, *Chapters in Administrative History*, ii. 282.
[2] Clause 32.

lated a staff of subordinate clerks, and, as might have been expected from the auspices under which it was created, began to pass out of the circle of the Wardrobe and to be drawn into the Council where the baronial reformers predominated. Writs *per assensum concilii* testify that the seal is being affixed in council and has ceased to be private to the king. Indeed the keeper remained in London, employed by the Council, while Edward was residing in the North and conducting his correspondence with the still more personal warrant of the Secret Seal. Thus the Privy Seal was following the course of the Great Seal at the end of the twelfth century, and the Ordainers, like the barons of 1258, were seeking to bring its use under constitutional control. It is a feature of the revolutions of this time that most of the constitutional changes enforced by successful opposition are adopted by the crown when its power is restored, and the enhanced status of the keepership under the Ordainers survived the victory of the middle party and the king's victory of Boroughbridge without much diminution. It has been said that "if the Keepership of Northburgh represented the triumph of the Ordainers and that of Charlton became an emblem of the Pembrokian compromise, the next keeper"—Baldock, who held the seal from 1320 to 1323—"stood once more for curialistic policy",[1] but, although the controllership of the Wardrobe came again for a time to be held by the keeper, the functions of the two offices were not confused, and the office of the Seal remained distinct and important. We shall see that it had a part of real value to play in the reign of Edward III. Baldock was, in fact, the most important official of his day. After he had been raised to the Chancery his intelligence inspired the government of Edward and the Despensers, and Baldock's successors, justices and clerks of Chancery, with no experience of the Wardrobe, carried the Privy Seal yet further from dependence upon the Household and developed its identity as a second Chancery.

The Wardrobe   The history of the domestic offices under Edward II follows closely the course of development of the Privy Seal, their special warrant. Upon the whole, the characteristic of the period is the reduction of the disorderly independence of the Household offices and the reconstitution of the authority of the older and greater offices of state. The Wardrobe, being the principal source of the

[1] T. F. Tout, *Chapters in Administrative History*, ii. 299.

private finance of the king, and the open sluice through which the revenues of the crown had been poured out for his uncontrolled expenditure, presented itself to the Ordainers as an office whose activities must be curtailed, and figures only negatively in the Ordinances. Its keeper and controller are to be appointed in parliament, and all the issues of the kingdom are to be paid directly into the treasury of the Exchequer. In so far as this rule was made effective, the Wardrobe would be deprived of its power to order the payment of revenue to itself upon writs of Privy Seal, and would become dependent upon the Exchequer, where the king's private expenditure could be controlled and limited. The abolition of the financial independence of the Wardrobe was, in fact, the sole means by which the king could be made to live of his own, and it is conjectured that the cutting off of the Wardrobe's separate access to revenue at a time when the Exchequer was at the mercy of the earls had much to do with the fall of Gaveston and the king's submission to the Ordainers.[1]

Equally restrictive are the ordinances made by the middle party at York in 1318 and at Cowick in 1323, for, while accepting the organization of the Wardrobe as it then stands, the first deals with it—together with the rest of the Household—as a staff of officials whose status and duties are to be defined and thus deprived of the indefiniteness of function upon which their importance thrives, while the second puts into effective working that Exchequer control which had been broadly asserted by the original Ordinances. In this, as in so much else, the reign of Edward II was a decisive one, for the Wardrobe, perhaps that one of the domestic offices which was most dangerous to the proper authority of Chancery and Treasury, then reached and passed its maximum of importance. The policy of the Ordainers was in part ineffective, but it was inherited by Pembroke in 1318, and, in a less aggressive but no less salutary form, by the royalist government of the Despensers. Under such governments many factors conspired to constrain and reduce the old undirected growth of Wardrobe influence. The detachment of the Privy Seal deprived it of its character as a domestic chancery, the York ordinance confined its several

[1] *Chapters in Administrative History*, ii. 235 n. The Wardrobe receipts of 1307–8 were some £78,000, and, in addition, it received five-sevenths of the income of the Exchequer. In 1312–13 they had fallen to £8400.

officials within the restrictions of recognized function, and the ordinance of 1323 systematized the restored primacy of the Exchequer and reduced it to routine and rule. Regular Wardrobe accounts were to be made the personal business of every executive officer through whose hands its moneys passed, the keeper of the Wardrobe was allotted a personal responsibility for the whole, the general account of the Wardrobe was to be rendered to the Exchequer, and the treasurer was given power to punish all defaults in account by the arrest of the offender and the seizure of his lands and goods. A third ordinance of 1324 prohibited the keeper from receiving any moneys except from the Exchequer, and the Great Wardrobe, the external purchasing staff of the Wardrobe, was now detached from its parent office, and its clerk directed to make his account to the Exchequer alone. There was some return by Edward III to the older independence of the Wardrobe when war conditions made a revival convenient, but upon the whole its great days were over. An office among others, and with its subordinate nature now recognized and confirmed by a succession of ordinances, the Wardrobe of Edward II's later years is well characterized by the phrase which then came into use, "the Wardrobe of the Household". Its place in history would henceforth be a minor one as a domestic office of the king.

The Chamber   In contrast with the slow decline of the Wardrobe under Edward II is the meteoric revival of the still older office of the Chamber, which flourished for a few years, carried the weight of the king's personal policy when the Wardrobe and the Privy Seal were under the jealous eyes of the baronage, and bid fair to establish itself as a permanent bulwark of prerogative in the heart of a constitutionalized state. Its progress was that of all its forerunners in the monarch's private service. As the Wardrobe once diverted money from the Chamber in the early days of its own growth, so the Chamber began to avenge the past by receiving the direct payment of Edward's foreign borrowings *pro quibusdam secretis faciendis*,[1] as to the nature of which the king "refused to inform his Wardrobe". In 1309 the Chamber came by a capital of land from which a permanent revenue might be expected. The custodians of the estates of the disgraced treasurer, Walter de Langton, and of

[1] T. F. Tout, *Chapters in Administrative History*, ii. 315 n.

part of the vastly greater lands of the Templars, were ordered to *The* make their account to the Chamber. In 1310 all the Templars' *Chamber* lands were under the single custody of Wingfield, "clerk of the *lands* King's Chamber". In 1311 the partial execution of the Ordinances diverted revenues of the Chamber lands to their proper account at the Exchequer, but a few weeks later the king succeeded in imposing a compromise by which the Wardrobe was made responsible. In 1312 much of the estate of Edmund of Cornwall's widow was added to the same fund of estate, and before the end of the year the Chamber had again replaced the Wardrobe as the office of receipt for its revenues.

The Chamber seems to have come under little criticism from the Ordainers. In 1313 it is found in possession of its own, the Secret Seal, and by 1318 the office of chamberlain is of sufficient importance to be added to those whose holders need the confirmation of parliament and to be taken by the younger Hugh Despenser. From 1322 to 1326 it was the chief weapon of that régime which passed for personal government and was in fact the rule of the Despensers. Great estates, the forfeit of successive treasons, were added to the Chamber's account, the lands of Badelesmere in 1321, in 1322 those of Mowbray together with the castles, lands, and moveables of ninety-three principal rebels, and, again, the forfeitures after Boroughbridge. It would seem that Edward had in the immense resources accumulated under the Chamber a promising source of revenue by which the crown might maintain itself without parliamentary grant, and it is characteristic of his lack of persistence that it was never reasonably exploited,[1] and that the temporary emergency of the Scotch campaign of 1322 induced him to abandon it. In July the issues of the Chamber lands were diverted to the Exchequer, then at York for the conclusion of the war, and when the truce was resumed the Exchequer continued to receive them. While they were the property of the Chamber these revenues were expended on the furthering of Edward's personal aims, upon the expenses of the messengers of

---

[1] The sum that reached the crown was about £2000 a year. The real revenue must have been vastly greater. T. F. Tout, *Chapters in Administrative History*, ii. 355. It is too much to say that the curial officers and the private seal were equal rivals to parliament and the great offices under so negligent a king as Edward II, but their failure under him closed an obvious line of alternative growth.

his secret seal, the maintenance of his ships, and upon the wages and equipment of men-at-arms in his special service. Intelligently used they might have saved the king in 1326. It has been well said that the Chamber lands might have been made into a state within the state, and the reversal of the policy which brought them together is a rare instance of the crown voluntarily foregoing one of the most promising aids to its own absolutism. Without the resources which its lands had given it, the office lost its influence at Edward's fall, and under his successor it returned to the comparative obscurity whence his personal needs had drawn it.

The Household under Edward III

Under Edward II the development of the domestic seals and offices is either curialistic in an unfavourable sense, that is to say, it is designed to obscure the responsibility of officials and to free the king to follow his own course, or dictated by the malcontents. Under Edward III the situation is changed; the king, the nobility, and the commons are substantially at one to support the war, and the king is trusted, and in the main rightly trusted, to exploit what adaptability and specialized capacity in the national business exists in his household, even though it should trench upon the independence of the older ministries. The day is gone when the Chancery and Treasury are supported against the crown by a jealous nobility. The king, as we have seen, works in harmony with the orders in parliament, and in administration he is given and deserves a freer initiative than ever before. The first manifestation of this new spirit is in the Walton ordinances issued in July 1338, when Edward was upon the point of sailing for

Walton ordinances

Flanders.[1] The principal effect of these is the bringing of Treasury and Chancery for certain purposes under the control of the Privy Seal; their most striking feature—in the light of the struggle for the seal in the last generation—is the unconscious confidence with which Edward applies what has once been the weapon of an unprincipled prerogative, and is still largely under the king's own hand, to discipline the great offices which till now have been regarded as the strongholds of administrative independence and probity. By the Walton ordinances every payment made by Treasury—except routine and fixed fees—was henceforth to be

[1] T. F. Tout, *Chapters in Administrative History*, iii. 69 *et seq.*

warranted by a writ of Privy Seal. Chancery writs of *liberate* where they were still employed were to be accompanied by such writs; in time, indeed, they came to be largely supplanted by them. That such a use of the Privy Seal could be accepted as a reform is *Supremacy* explained by the regularizing of the keepership which the opposi- *of the* tion of the last reign had effected, and its use for warrant of *Privy* *Seal* *liberate* is proof that the traditions of the office had already formed along sound lines. Warrants were to be issued "with the assent of the king and of a sufficient person appointed for the purpose", they were to be enrolled by a permanent clerk, with a counter-roll kept by a clerk of the Chamber, and all Exchequer issues upon order of the Privy Seal were to be audited annually by a clerk using the counter-roll, together with an independent com-mission of a bishop and a banneret. As a final and vital safeguard, the writ was to avoid vagueness of statement as to the ground upon which the issue was warranted—such as "for the King's secret needs"—and to embody its precise purpose. Such a use of the Privy Seal, in the best traditions of public service, constitutes a revolution in its conduct, and no less a revolution is marked by the curbing of Chancery and Treasury initiative. Most significant of all, the crown, using the most characteristic weapon of its prerogative, has replaced the magnates as the motive power of reform and control. "Chancery and Treasury were henceforth in leading strings",[1] the hand which held them was that of the king, and the change was very far from being the former indis-criminate extension of royal influence, for the Wardrobe was included under the extended authority of the Privy Seal. How far it corresponded to a new and more popular orientation of the crown may be seen by the association of the clauses bringing the great offices under the seal with a further curtailment of their power in the interests of the provincial communities. The sheriffs and all other "great officers of the shires", and the customers of the ports, were in future to be elected annually "by the good men of the shire", and to be such as they could answer for at their peril. It was a reform long petitioned for in previous crises, and now made doubly necessary by that decline in the integrity of the provincial officialdom which had followed upon the death of Edward I, and it was made, not under pressure, but as a spon-

[1] T. F. Tout, *Chapters in Administrative History*, iii. 71.

taneous act of crown.[1] The great offices were coming to be ground between the upper and nether millstones of popular initiative and a crown which trusted and was accepted by it. The Walton ordinance deserves to be understood for the light which it throws upon the changed and happier adjustment of the constitution which prevailed under Edward III. Professor Tout, perhaps with some exaggeration, has said that the committee of audit of the ordinance "was clearly intended to be the keystone of the monarchical arch, with the office of the privy seal, the chamber, the king's council, and the local courts on the one side, and the chancery, exchequer, and wardrobe on the other".[2] Whatever the ordinance's original intention, the need to give freedom of action to the Exchequer during the Flemish campaign made it impossible to maintain the more stringent restrictions upon it, but the former jealousy no longer attached to the domestic offices, and the Privy Seal and the Wardrobe provided a secondary government for the king in Flanders and were accepted and supported by parliament as such.

The year 1341

With the force of this unanimity behind it, the general settlement of the government under Edward III was strong enough to survive the storm of the king's quarrel with Archbishop Stratford and the malcontent parliament of 1341. Arising from the inadequacy of medieval administration to maintain adequate supply for an expedition and a mercenary alliance on the scale of that of the Low Countries, the dispute developed into a wholesale attack by the king and his curialist barons and officials upon the Chancery and the Exchequer, for which the archbishop and the clerical ministers stood. Behind the latter the secular magnates of the Lancastrian tradition ranged themselves, and the stage was set for a repetition of the events of 1311, with Stratford playing the rôle of Winchelsea and appealing to memories of Becket. The demands of the parliament of 1341 brought out again the time-worn counters of opposition, election of the great officers, oath to the Charters, judgment of lords by their peers in parliament. But in all this fury—the controversy was waged in speech and

[1] It was somewhat sparely acted upon.

[2] T. F. Tout, *Chapters in Administrative History*, iii. 76: "The specific task of the committee was to secure the harmonious working together of the various elements of the administration in the execution of the royal will".

writing more violent and more explicit than upon any previous occasion—the significant fact is that there was no real victory for either party. The very fact that the issues were now realized with a new and complete clarity guaranteed that the struggle should not be urged to a conclusive issue. Forcibly as king or prelate might urge the claims of their contrasting views of the state, the experience of fifteen years had told them that it was upon the Edwardian compromise between prerogative and parliament that the government must finally be rested. There were formal, indeed, in some matters, admittedly feigned, concessions by the king, and an equally formal submission to the king by the primate. When all was over the anger died away, and for a quarter of a century king and parliament worked in general harmony.

But, more striking than this temporary tolerance of household *Reduction* activity, more lasting than the quarrel of the king and the ministries *of the* in 1341, and more typical of the growing consolidation of the whole *influence* state as a uniform machine of public government, is the gradual *Household* reduction of the scope of the domestic offices. This was brought *offices* about voluntarily, though the increasing influence of parliament may have been its ultimate cause. The king, or the ministries acting for him, gradually extinguish the independence of those departments which were outlets for the king's personal will, and return the full control of business to the great impersonal offices of the crown. We have seen how the Privy Seal was officialized and claimed for the public service. During the same period the private seal or Griffin ceased to be applied to precepts of importance. The king's seals were thus all in the hands of public servants, who were bound to consider the rules of their office as well as the king's wishes.[1] The campaign of 1338–40 was the last upon which the Great Wardrobe followed the king abroad as a travelling treasury, and the year 1359–60 the last in which, from its now stationary office at Westminster, the main Wardrobe handled the bulk of the finances of a campaign. It was returning to its primitive function of disbursing and accounting for the king's Household. The same declension came upon the subordinate offices of the Great and Privy Wardrobes, though the latter's importance had never been great. In 1356 the practice of entrusting the Chamber with the custody of part of the royal estates was discontinued, and

[1] T. F. Tout, *Chapters in Administrative History*, iii. ch. 9, and v. ch. 17.

the voluntary action of the crown put an end to what might have been an important source of personal revenue. In 1360 the accountability of the Great Wardrobe was incorporated in that of the Exchequer. A feature of the time which is a practical expression of the increasing unity of government is the massing of the lesser offices under the shadow of the old great offices at or near Westminster. In 1361 the Great Wardrobe settled at St. Andrews in the south-west of the city. In 1365 the commons petitioned that the king's bench should be settled at Westminster, or, when necessary, at York. Such quiet adjustments of ministerial relations were among the best fruits of a reign whose share in the settlement of constitutional form has received scant justice. If Edward III makes a greater showing in the now unpopular rôle of the conqueror of France, much credit is also due to the spirit of compromise and accommodation which made him accept administrative change without resistance and almost without comment. The unification of the administration under the crown, the rough conformity of the king's will to parliament, and a willing response by lords and commons to the unending demands of the French war, were the outcome of the administrative planning of his earlier years, and of the new understanding that had been won from the very violence of the brief storm of 1341. Until the king's physical decline and the Good Parliament, England enjoyed more ordered government than it had known since the days of Edward I, and our constitution made a full generation of progress towards maturity.

Revenue   The problem of revenue followed much the same course of alternate clash and compromise as did that of administration. The attempt to build up a new and personal revenue for the crown, to give the king a landed estate which should be beyond the reach of treasurer and chancellor and therefore immune from parliament, was in part a reaction to the decline of the prerogative power of taxing by the crown. The issue was still seen only obscurely. No parliament of Edward II's reign would claim that all supply must be parliamentary. Such new fiscal principles as gained acceptance in the fourteenth century did so because the facts that underlay them were changing, not because the age had a new theory to propound. The governing rule is that of the past: aid is by the free will of the subject; the king should live of his own. If the scope of the king's right to tax is narrower than it has been in the past, it is in part because scutage and the obligatory aids bear a small proportion to the vastly swollen mass of revenue, and in part because "the king's own" has come to mean less as his feudal status loses reality and his sovereign hold upon the nation hardens. On the other hand, the limitation of prerogative taxation was not achieved without a struggle. Neither parliament nor any-one else had any power over the king's demesne right. Edward I had defended the sanctity of the *jura regalia* wherever they seemed to be threatened, and, in the absence of any clear distinction between the sovereign and feudal qualities of the king,[1] his right to exploit the latter was limited by no existing principles as long as he kept within the rules of common law.

The fiscal history of the fourteenth century is that of a desultory *Pre-* duel between the king and the commons, in which the former *rogative* sought to supplement the aids by exploiting the profits, allowable *revenue* according to feudal theory, of his demesne lordship of the *Regnum Angliae*. Of these profits the oldest and the most easily come by was the tallage. The common right of feudalism left not only the royal lands but the royal cities and boroughs at the king's discretion as demesne,[2] for in their beginnings the townsmen were tallageable with tenants on ancient demesne. But by the fourteenth century the burgesses had risen in public estimation; "our cities and boroughs are nobly enfranchised, such franchises being heritable and approved, as of lordship, for the maintenance of lawful merchandise, wherein the greater part of the riches and common profit of all realms consists".[3] Tallage, therefore, was becoming an anomaly, *Tallage* the more so when the burgesses, taken into parliament with their

[1] The Ordainers maintained some such distinction in their doctrine of an impersonal crown, but it was not expressed with any clarity.

[2] As late as 1315, when trying to enlist the special favour of the king, the burgesses of Lostwithiel address him as from *ses demeigne gentz de sa Ville de Lostwithiel. Rotuli Parliamentorum*, i. 296.

[3] *Ibid.* ii. 332. The schedule for the Poll Tax of 1379 contains an interesting comparison of various civic classes with other ranks to whom they were to be reckoned as equivalent in wealth: "the Mayor of London pays like an Earl, £4; the Aldermen of London, each like a Baron, £2; the Mayors of the great towns of England, each like a Baron, £2; all the Jurats of the good towns and the great Merchants of the Realm pay as Bachelors, £1." *Ibid.* iii. 58.

fellow *communes* of the shires, shared with them the common aid upon moveables and even paid it at a higher rate. As early as the reign of Henry III there were signs that arbitrary tallage as demesne no longer accorded with burgess ambitions, at least in the greater towns, and the estimates of the tallagers were constantly subject to revision in favour of communities who claimed to have established a customary limit to their liability. Towards the end of the reign, London asserted that its tallage must not exceed two thousand marks, and its pleading was so directed that the king accused the citizens of claiming the right to contribute by way of gracious aid rather than by tallage, or, in other words, of denying their demesne status. In so far as the citizens were seeking to shake off the king's demesne right, their case was strengthened by the financial policy of Edward I, though it was not such as to put an end to doubt. Under Henry the royal demesnes and the boroughs had been granted exemption from the general aids in acknowledgment of their tallage,[1] but in 1283 Edward prejudiced his right in some measure by begging a "courteous aid" from towns and counties alike, and by including the burgesses in the aid of a Thirtieth which was granted in the same year. In 1294, while the special position of the boroughs was recognized by their exclusion from the Fifteenth, and by the fact that they were not summoned to the parliament which granted it, they were allowed to negotiate separately with the king's commissioners, and their grant of a Sixth must have been capable of explanation either as a tallage or an aid. Their final inclusion within the aid-paying community may, perhaps, be dated from the burgess grants of a Seventh in 1295 and an Eighth in 1296, but to be invited to join in the gracious aid of the community was not necessarily to be freed from the bondage of the demesne, and for many years the towns continued to suffer the rigour of both conditions. In spite of appearing regularly in parliament, and contributing a larger aid than the counties, they were tallaged in 1304, in 1312, and again in 1332, though on the last occasion the levy was not collected. On none of these occasions was there any

---

[1] The statement (Parliamentary Writs, i. 12) in the schedule for the assessment of the Thirtieth of 1283 that the burgesses had been taxed to the aid in the "days of the King's ancestors" is contradicted by the records of Henry III's reign.

general criticism of the crown's claim, nor does that claim ever seem to have been explicitly abandoned.[1] Rather, it fell naturally into desuetude with the changed status of the burgesses, the absorption of the demesne into the fiscal community of the shire, and the rise of other ways of taxing the towns, but its history is, for that reason, the more significant as showing the slow change of constitutional practice without crisis and even without conscious innovation. The most purely arbitrary of our taxes dies slowly with the decline of feudalism and not by any conscious effort towards the freedom of the subject.

The customs arose from the demesne right of the king, as did *The* the tallage, but from a different aspect of it and upon a different *customs* principle. They were increasingly important in the fourteenth century, and, from the ease and rapidity with which the wool subsidy could be collected, it became the mainstay of supply during the Hundred Years War. If prerogative taxation was not to become the rule, the control of the customs was therefore of the utmost importance to parliament, and it presented a problem of the greatest complexity, since it was one for which the traditional rules of gracious aid had no formula. Custom, the levy of dues upon the movement or sale of merchandise, is a right of feudal lordship which we may, perhaps, derive remotely from the franchise of toll and team, and as such, of course, as much part of the right of the crown as of that of many of the magnates; in its lowest form it was made up of various minor tolls and dues, varying with the custom of each district, and in its highest it extended

[1] The term tallage is a general one, the tallage of the demesne, and of the towns in right of demesne, being no more than a particular application of it. It is commonly used, especially by chroniclers, as a synonym for *auxilium*, *carucagium*, and the like, and for that reason it is unsafe to give it a special meaning when it is not applied explicitly to the prerogative taxation of boroughs. Hemingburgh's Latin version of the *Confirmatio Cartarum* purports to place tallage with aid upon a voluntary basis, and it was taken into the body of the Statutes of the Realm and appealed to in the Petition of Right. But the authentic French text has no mention of tallage, and Hemingburgh probably used the term in the general sense of "levy", with no special reference to the towns. The concessions made in 1348, 1352, and 1377 seem far too vague to be attached to the tallage of boroughs in virtue of demesne. *Rotuli Parliamentorum*, ii. 201, 238, and 365. But cf. Stubbs, *Constitutional History*, ii. 402. Cf. the use of "subsidy or tallage" as a general phrase for all kinds of taxation in 1376: *Rotuli Parliamentorum*, ii. 323. As late as 1450, Cade's followers complained of the excessive "taxes and tallages" which were inflicted on the country.

to the right of the king to license, direct, or arrest traffic throughout the honour of England, and of other lords to do the same in
the palatinate of Durham, the lordships of the Welsh March, the
lordships of the Irish Pale, and so forth.[1] By the crown it had
already been used under Henry III to regulate shipping during the
recurrent war with France, and, by a very ruthless interpretation
of the right of arrest, to seize the goods of the merchant and
to hold them until he had made his peace with authority by
fine.[2]

Magna et
Antiqua
Custuma

One of the first acts of Edward I was to put the customs upon
a regular instead of a variable basis and to treat with the merchants of England as a whole in order to secure their acceptance
of a national tax. This was in 1275, when, "at the instance and
request of the merchants" in parliament, he accepted from them
a grant of half a mark from every woolsack exported, and a mark
from every last of hides to him and his heirs, which became
established as the *Magna et Antiqua Custuma*. The concession was
said to have been made in parliament and by consent, but it was
not only or principally the consent of the magnates acting in
parliament as *commune consilium*, as would have been the case with
an aid. The act of assent was composed of two elements, the
"request" of the *communes de Marchaunz de tot Engleterre*[3]—which
was given, in all probability, in consideration of some remissions
of custom which are not recorded[4]—and of the individual consents of a number of great men confirmed by their letters patent
severally issued, *unusquisque pro se*.[5] The reason for this procedure
is clear, and explains much of the subsequent constitutional history
of the customs. The *Magna Custuma*, being in its nature a commutation of certain customary rights enjoyed by the king in the
royal ports and demesnes but also by the majority of the magnates
within their franchises, was not an aid, did not affect the *com-*

[1] Thus Abbot Sampson claimed that Richard I had no right to regulate the
tolls in the town of Bury, where he had no demesne right, and where that right
belonged wholly to the Saint.
[2] In 1218 the marshal arrested the wool of the merchants at Bristol, and
exacted six marks upon the sack for its release. Stubbs, *Constitutional History*,
ii. 200.   [3] Parliamentary Writs, i. 1.
[4] Possibly, also, in recognition of the fact that a three years' embargo on the
export of goods to Flanders had recently been lifted.
[5] *Ibid.* i. 2.

munitas regni directly, and so was not strictly subject to the consent of *commune consilium*. The consents legally necessary were first that of the "community of merchants", since they were submitting to a new composition for a variety of dues, and, second, that of those magnates—the letters patent of twelve secular lords are recorded —who gave their consent as individuals because they were foregoing their tenurial right, and allowing the new customs to be collected by the king's officers within their franchises.[1]

How far the bargain between king, magnates, and merchants could be construed to involve the *communitas regni* and to need the added sanction of its consent, came in the future to be a constitutional issue. In 1275 it existed only as a possible complication of the position created by the *instancia et rogatus mercatorum* and the consequent letters patent of the magnates, but it cast a doubt over the transaction and confused the formulae in which the king announced the grant to the appropriate officials. The authority of the individual letters patent, rightly described in one writ as that of *quidam magnates terre nostre*,[2] is in others given more loosely as that of *touz les granz de Realme*,[3] and in one as that of *Archiepiscopi, Episcopi, Abbates, Priores, Comites, Barones, Majores, et tota communitas regni nostri*.[4] On this, the first occasion when the customs appeared as an issue of importance, they were treated principally as the demesne concern of the king and a number of holders of franchise. The national interest in them was not consistently affirmed, and was certainly not fully realized, and a precedent was unconsciously set for the king to bargain in the future with the merchants and with any other parties who might be thought to be concerned. But still the shadow of future parliamentary claims to assent already lay over the king's right. The customs were to share neither the clear prerogative justification of the tallage nor

[1] So William de Valence: *nos (Willelmus) ad instantiam predictorum mercatorum concedimus pro nobis et heredibus nostris quod idem Dominus Rex et heredes sui in singulis portubus nostris in Hibernia tam infra libertates quam extra habeant dimidiam marcam de quolibet sacco lane etc. etc. . . . percipiendam per manus custodum et ballivorum ipsius Regis.* Parliamentary Writs, i. 2.

[2] *Ibid.* i. 1, no. 4.   [3] *Ibid.* i. 1, no. 2.

[4] *Ibid.* i. 1, no. 3. This is, perhaps, an inaccurate expansion of the formula used in the king's letters patent ordering the arrest of wool until Holy Trinity 1275: *prelati et Magnates ac tota Communitas Mercatorum Regni . . . concesserint* (*ibid.* i. 3, no. 11), but it shows that the constitutional nature of a consent given by private parties but within parliament was not clear to Chancery.

the equally clear parliamentary authority of the aids, but would occupy a debatable ground between the two, the centre of converging rights and interests which had yet to be clarified and reconciled with each other.

The taxation of 1294 and 1297 was governed by national crises and hardly represented Edward's considered policy. In both years he ignored any possible right of common consent and proceeded upon the assumption that the customs were at the discretion of the king and the merchants, and in 1294 the tolts upon wool and leather were raised to the enormous sums of three and five marks respectively.[1] In 1297, by a procedure which could have no constitutional justification, except the theory that the foreign merchants, like the Jews, were collectively within the king's demesne right, the wool of the greater traders was seized, the king giving security for future payment, while the lesser merchants were allowed to purchase exemption for a maletolt of forty shillings and to proceed with their trade. The violence of this action brought a protest from those who claimed to represent the nation, and in August 1297 the marshal and the constable included the prise, or seizure, of wool in their grievances. Edward abandoned a policy which in any case could hardly be repeated, and the Confirmation of the Charters granted that the recent prises should not create a precedent, revoked the maletolt of forty shillings, and promised that in future no such tax should be taken without consent of the commonalty of the realm. Three years later the constitutional position was set in a much clearer light by the admissions made in the *Articuli super Cartas*. For the first time the crown recognized a national concern in its handling of the merchants—"the most part of the community of the realm feels itself heavily burdened by the maletolt upon wool"[2]—and a line was drawn between the great and ancient custom of 1275, recognized as a fixed due, and any new levies to which, if they should become necessary, the common consent and goodwill of the community of the realm would have to be obtained. In addition to this, the events of 1275 were referred to in terms which threw upon them a retrospective recognition of parliamentary authority: even the *Magna et Antiqua Custuma* appears as "the custom upon wool,

1 Stubbs, *Constitutional History*, ii. 551.
2 *Confirmatio Cartarum*, cap. 6.

wood-fells, and leather granted to us aforetime by the said community of the realm ".

An acknowledgment extorted from the king in August 1297 could hardly be maintained when his authority was restored. It is, rather, remarkable that the assertion of the community's control of the customs should have been made at so early a date, for it went beyond the strict letter of constitutional right and prejudiced the *jura regalia* to a degree which Edward could certainly never have admitted. In consequence, we find him six years later turning again to the customs for revenue, and, though restricting his demands to very moderate proportions, acting with complete indifference to the constitutional principles he had been forced to admit in 1297. In 1303, his mind having been, perhaps, clarified by opposition, he proceeded towards both English and foreign merchants upon the ground of demesne right only, summoned first the Italian companies and then the English burgesses to York,[1] and, dealing with them not in parliament but in the Exchequer, offered them a bargain to which there should be no other parties, and in which no national interest was recognized. He promised a "quittance of our prises together with divers liberties".[2] The Italians agreed to add 50 per cent to the *Antiqua Custuma* in return for these concessions: the representatives of the English cities and boroughs, being offered the same bargain, refused to increase "the customs anciently due and accustomed". Edward did not press the matter—the profits of the duty would come mainly from the foreigners, in whose hands the export trade mainly lay[3]—and the *Parva et Nova Custuma* remained as an acknowledgment of the right of the crown to burden the foreign merchant by agreement, and without recognition of any parliamentary interest in the transaction. In spite of one striking victory for the principle of common consent in 1297, Edward I's dealings with the customs left him in possession of the main point of prerogative right, but with the warning that it could not be pressed too far without rousing the general resistance of the nation.

Under Edward II the customs were only occasionally a con-

Parva et Nova Custuma

---

[1] *Parliamentary Writs*, i. 134.

[2] *Ibid.* i. 406.

[3] In 1273 English merchants conducted 35 per cent of the export of wool.

stitutional issue. In 1309 [1] the Community of the Realm petitioned
upon the ground of hardship against the "little customs on wine,
cloth, and goods sold by weight", which formed part of the *Nova
Custuma*—they were said to raise prices 50 per cent against the
consumer—and the king, taking the same ground of expediency,
promised to suspend the custom for a year to see where the
burden really fell. In 1311 the Ordinances abolished all customs
and maletolts which had been imposed since the accession of
Edward I and denounced the treaty of 1303 which had brought
into being the *Nova Custuma.* The prerogative use of the customs
was thus definitely ranged amongst those practices which were
against the Great Charter. New customs, it was said, must be by
consent of the magnates. The *Magna et Antiqua Custuma* upon wool
and leather was expressly saved to the crown, and, though the
economic effect of uncertain and arbitrary charges seems to have
been more fully understood than it had been in the past, the basing
of the restriction of the king's action upon the text of the Great
Charter and his promise to secure the consent of the "baronage",[2]
carried the case of the opposition little further. In this it shared
the vice of almost all the work of the Ordainers and would hardly
be a sufficient safeguard in the future. Accordingly, in 1317 we
find Edward borrowing from the merchants by way of a duty of
ten shillings on the woolsack, five shillings on the tun of wine,
and so forth, and turning his victory of 1322 to account by reviving
the *Nova Custuma,* and placing a heavy subsidy upon the wool of
both native and foreign merchants. Under Edward III the farming
of the subsidy and the customs in anticipation, with a formal act of
grant by parliament *ex post facto*, avoided a constitutional deadlock
and assured the king of an easily accessible revenue.

*Wool
subsidy*
Crown and opposition thus avoided serious disputes over the
customs as such. As soon as they secured parliamentary tolerance,
if not recognition, the main question of authority was at an end,
and much the same compromise between the ancient rights of the
crown and the claims of parliament was followed in the treatment
of the wool subsidy. This had been resisted under Edward I and
Edward II, but the initial popularity of the French war, and the
idea that trade would benefit from the conquest of France, re-

[1] *Rotuli Parliamentorum,* i. 444. Cf. Stubbs, *Constitutional History,* ii. 553, for
what follows.   [2] *Rotuli Parliamentorum,* i. 282.

moved some of the objections to a commercial tax. When the
king was in Flanders the merchants could be required to pay at
least a proportion of the levy in cash to the Wardrobe in Bruges.[1]
King and parliament, therefore, collaborated to make it profitable.
In 1332 the magnates advised Edward to have recourse to the
merchants, and he imposed a half-mark on the woolsack and a
pound upon the last of hides, and followed this impost by a slightly
larger one in 1333. Between 1336 and 1340 the parallel authorities
of king and parliament were curiously illustrated. In the former
year the king arrested the wool at the ports and parliament imposed the heavy tax of two pounds on the sack from natives and
three pounds from aliens. In 1337 the arrest on the wool was, on
the contrary, made by statute, and the king in Council set the
subsidy at two and four pounds upon natives and aliens. In 1339
the magnates attached to their grant the request that the maletolt
should be abandoned, and themselves substituted for it a tax of
forty shillings.[2] In 1340 parliament in a changed mood, resolved
itself into a series of committees to negotiate with the several
groups and individuals of the English, Italian, and Flemish merchants[3] to secure the arrested wool and the payment of maletolt
of forty shillings. Throughout the period parliament showed no
reluctance to recognize the need to finance the war, though it would
not assent to the king's view that the burden of indirect taxation
falls solely upon the exporter. By 1343 it had brought itself to
insist that it ought in reason—perhaps it was not sure of the point
of law—to have the assent of the commons.[4] The king in reply
evaded the constitutional issue and pointed out that, since the
price of wool was fixed by statute, it could no longer be lowered
to the disadvantage of the English producer. From this time onward, however, Edward took the precaution of anticipating any
question in parliament by pledging the whole of the customs to
a group of English merchants, the magnates rejected the commons'
protest in 1346 because of the emergency of the war,[5] and in spite
of resistance, which was based upon the statute of 1340, the practice

---

[1] Rotuli Parliamentorum, ii. 120.   [2] Ibid. ii. 104.
[3] Ibid. ii. 122: dont, Seigneur . . . nous ferroms de jour en autre a traiter ove
Marchandz et totes maneres de Gentz ove queux nous purroms.
[4] Ibid. ii. 140: qar ce est encontre reson, qe la Commune de lour biens soient par
Marchandz chargez.   [5] Ibid. ii. 161.

Parlia-
mentary
control of
subsidy

was continued until 1362,[1] when the king promised that no subsidy or other charge should be placed on wool or leather without assent of parliament. In 1371 he repeated the assurance and apparently recognized his previous promise as constituting a statute.[2]

The technicalities of revenue, though the indirect taxes might rise to fifty thousand pounds in a single year, would not be of great interest were they not part of the process by which the various elements, public, private, feudal, and sovereign, of the king's power were being brought into a single concept of royal authority exercised under the eye of parliament. Under Edward III prerogative revenue might well have become a fatal issue between king and people. By 1377 that risk had been averted by good sense on either side, while at no single moment was the conflict of prerogative and parliamentary taxation such as to cause real anxiety to the crown. It is an immense result to have been achieved without serious constitutional discord, and it is typical of the process by which the country was moving from a feudal to a parliamentary régime. Feudalism looked in general to a fundamental custom as the security for its right, and to feudal war, more or less violent, as the law's safeguard. The Great and the Forest Charter and the host of armed vassals in *commune consilium*, or, in the last recourse, in rebellion, were the two bases upon which the thirteenth century rested. We may see the progress towards a less archaic view of the state in the appearance of the first additions to the body of fundamental law, the *Confirmatio Cartarum*, the *Articuli super Cartas*;[3] perhaps, also in the ordinances of 1311. By the broad fact that they took parliament as the executant of their policy, the Ordainers were leading the country away from the feudal habit of amendment or redress by royal prerogative under threat of diffidation. But the victory of parliament, a real one over the ensuing period of fifty years, was not won in any spectacular defence of liberties, was made possible, indeed, by a

Summary
of the
progress
under the
Edwards

---

[1] *Rotuli Parliamentorum*, ii. 271.   [2] *Ibid.* ii. 308.

[3] In the first century of its history statute in parliament gained its peculiar authority as much from its association with the Charters as from any notion of the preëminent right of parliament. *Qe la Grande Chartre, la Chartre de la Foreste, et les Estatutz faitz avant ces heures . . . soient fermement tenuz et gardez*, is the first petition of parliament.

process of slow and piecemeal reform which destroyed the usefulness of the great feudal leagues of the past. Common and frequent petition, without the threat of force, took the place of prolonged discontent and the abrupt presentation of a confused cahier or grievances at the point of the sword. Changes no longer came by violent crises divided by long periods of sulking, but by the milder pressure of successive parliaments. There was much that was imperfect and inconclusive in the petitions and statutes of the fourteenth century. The commons' requests were often ill-conceived and badly presented, so that the power of the king and Council to reject, to distinguish, and to recast petitions was as vital to the country as the right of petition itself. But the great fact that the crown and nation were kept steadily informed of each other's needs, and that what was common ground between them could be embodied in the new expedient of statute and so be added to the permanent body of law, was a revolutionary change from the rigidity of feudalism. In so far as it had the imagination to do so, the nation obtained the power to determine its own future and to shake off the dead hand of the past. In statute, indeed, and in the less permanent ordinances in parliament and letters patent, was found a new power to change not by rebellion nor by the unchecked initiative of officials. It hardly detracts from the greatness of the change that few of the constitutional principles of parliament were yet established, or even recognized for what they would come to be. That maladministration, or law which had outgrown its usefulness, or innovation that created hardship, were already habitually petitioned upon by the representatives of all the shires in common, that the king habitually accepted such parts of common petitions as were unobjectionable, and gave them permanence as statutes, that statute in parliament had come to be established as the highest kind of law, overriding all prescription, all these things as the settled practice of parliament make up a far more significant phase of the constitution than the period of crystallization which succeeds it. It is to the reigns of the three Edwards that we owe the creation of parliament, and the peaceful and almost unnoticed growth of its most essential principles.

Nevertheless, Edward's reign was not to be lived out in com-

plete unanimity. The peace of 1360 created a financial crisis, since
the motive for the granting of extraordinary aids vanished. The
Exchequer tried to bring revenue and expenditure together by
systematic finance, and even produced between 1359 and 1364
the first national budgets, though they were inaccurate and incomplete; but the attempt to carry on a peace government without
the revenue which a fourteenth-century parliament would only
grant for war had little prospect of success. When the sums
allocated for various unavoidable charges were written off, the
king had barely £3000 a year to spend, and the deficit for 1362-3
was £55,000, and that for 1364-5 £65,000. As against this, the
French ransoms had brought in some £200,000 by 1364. In the
face of this it is remarkable that a parliament was found in 1369
to advise Edward to resume the crown of France, and to grant a
three years' subsidy upon wool and a clerical tenth to promote his
claim. Indeed, the opposition which clouded the last years of the
reign first showed itself in excessive loyalty to the crown, when,
after the unhappy experience of the campaign of 1370, the court
party in the parliament of 1371 attacked the ministry of William
of Wykeham and Bishop Brantingham, and in general the prelate
in office, much as Edward had attacked Stratford thirty years
earlier. Disillusion was coming upon the country, but it did not yet
involve the king or the princes. Nevertheless, from this time
onwards opposition grew. The lay ministry—Scrope of Bolton
and Thorpe as treasurer and chancellor—blundered in finance, the
prince returned ill from Gascony, and the king was compelled to
emerge from retirement and take the relief of La Rochelle upon
himself. One by one the great figures of the court were discredited:
Pembroke was captured in 1372, Edward's expedition failed, John
of Gaunt ruined his reputation by the *chevauchée* of 1373. After
1373 the king's age kept him inactive and, though he came to
parliaments, most of his time was spent at Windsor, Sheen, or
Eltham. Councils were held at Westminster without him, and his
influence upon the detail of government declined. The prince,
also, was ill, and John of Gaunt was absorbed in foreign schemes,
and often abroad. The influence of Alice Perrers began to dis-
solve the court party, which had already suffered from the loss
of its leader Pembroke. In April 1376 the first parliament for
three years, which was to gain the name of the Good Parlia-

ment,[1] met under the influence of the Prince of Wales and William of Wykeham, convinced that the virtue had gone out of the old king's reign, and prepared to attack the whole conduct of its recent years.

As the exponent of the accumulated discontent of the years since 1373, the Good Parliament is proof of the extent to which the general frame of government, and the relation of its parts to each other and to the whole, had found stability and acceptance. The leaders of the opposition, and its temper, were utterly different from those of the reformers under Edward II. The demand was now not for revolution, but for the right use of the constitution as it then stood, for the punishment of those who had worked the system corruptly and for an enquiry into the misdirection of the king's finances. The impulse of what had been the Lancastrian party of feudal constitutionalists was now almost entirely spent. The attack was a parliamentary one, directed, more than by any other influence, by the commons, and, in so far as they were strengthened by support from outside their order, it was by the encouragement of the prince, and of William of Wykeham, who had lost his chancellorship in 1371 to the party whose successors were now themselves under impeachment. The commons called, as they had sometimes done in the past, for the advice of twelve of the lords, but those whom they helped to choose for the task were not of the temper of the Ordainers, and stood rather for the sound military and administrative loyalty of the middle years of the reign. The gravamina of the opposition were presented as commons' petitions through a prolocutor, Peter de la Mare, and their first requirement was for an audit of accounts. The Staple had been manipulated to enable individuals to rob the crown, the king had incurred debts to his favourites at exorbitant interest, and they had been allowed to buy up his bad debts from his creditors and secure their payment by court pressure. The courtiers and merchants specially indicted were the chamberlain, Lord Latimer; Richard Lyons, who had acted as broker for the wool subsidy; William Ellis of Yarmouth, his deputy; and John Peach, who had

The Good Parliament

---

[1] The best contemporary account of the Good Parliament is found in the *Anonimalle Chronicle* (ed. V. H. Galbraith), and in the *Chronicon Angliae*, 1327–1383 (Rolls Series). The former is of exceptional value as a record of the detail of procedure.

bought the monopoly of sweet wines for London. At a later phase in the crisis Alice Perrers was accused of securing unjust sentences by maintenance, and banished upon the curious ground of the statute prohibiting women from practising in the courts of law.

All this is significant of a new though, perhaps, transitory strength in the commons, and of the decline of the leading power of the magnates, and it has the constitutional interest of being the first great occasion when impeachment by the commons was directed against ministers who were not also in the enmity of the king. Still greater interest is to be found in the fact that no minister, except the chamberlain, nor any part of the constitution was attacked, that all the commons' indignation was reserved for *les privez le Roi*, and that their demands for change sought for the strengthening of the constitution in the form into which it had already settled. To almost all the commons' petitions Edward could answer that they were already provided for by statute, and, in granting the afforcement of the Council by certain lords named in parliament,[1] he was able to insist that the chancellor, treasurer, keeper of the Privy Seal, and other officers should not be subject to their censure. "The king and his sons" were actually made the judges of any councillor who might be accused of taking bribes. So far had matters come from the days when the main purpose of every opposition was to secure control of the great ministries,[2] and to fetter the king with baronial councils. Edward III's reign at its weakest produces not a constitutional crisis but an attack upon ministers and financial incompetence. It is clear, also, that the knights are confident of their power to serve the country and express its grievances adequately, for annual parliaments and the election of representatives[3] "by the best men of the counties" are the only constitutional demands of permanent importance made in 1376. The Parliamentary Crown may be said to have achieved its settled embodiment and to have been accepted by the nation.

[1] Apparently not as a measure of distrust, because the number of "officers the king has had about him are insufficient for such great government as the wars at the same time in France, Spain, Ireland, Guienne, and Brittany call for". *Rotuli Parliamentorum*, ii. 322.

[2] Richard Lyons' handling of the impositions on wool "without any controller, record, or responsibility to the Treasurer", is reminiscent of the former tendency of the household offices to become irresponsible, but the attitude of the commons is entirely different from that of their predecessors. *Ibid.* ii. 323.

[3] *Ibid.* ii. 355.

V

1377-1485

i

THE DECLINE OF THE MEDIEVAL COMMUNITY

"BEHOLD, Lords, whether there was ever Christian King or Lord *Introduction* that had so noble and gracious a lady to wife and such sons as our Lord the King has had, both Princes, Dukes, and others. For of the King and his sons all Christian peoples have had fear, and by them the Realm of England has been most nobly amended, honoured, and enriched, more than in the time of any other King. And our Lord the King may here, by the grace of God, see the son of his son, and has sent him as his Lieutenant to this Parliament to give you comfort and joy of him, as it is said in the Scriptures, 'This is my beloved son, this is the desired of all nations'. But if we his subjects desire and will to prosper in his grace in this year of Jubilee, and to take comfort from him who is the Vessel of Grace or chosen Vassal of God, needs must that we set ourselves in all virtue to receive that grace and to flee all wrongdoing."[1] These were the words of Adam Houghton, the chancellor, in his charge to parliament in the Jubilee year of Edward III, in what was to be the last parliament of his reign. As a forecast of the immediate future it went beyond any natural good fortune that a realm under a minority could expect, but not beyond the reasonable hope of one who looked back upon the long stability of England under the Plantagenet kings. In spite of intervals of factious rebellion, the English state had grown steadily in strength and unity in the past two hundred years, till it was to all appearances the most firmly based in Europe, and the commons acknowledged that Edward had "set them beyond the servitude of other lands".[2] The chancellor's words, however, contained a warning. If the crown was at once stronger, more national, and set more equably

[1] *Rotuli Parliamentorum*, ii. 361. [2] *Ibid*. ii. 276.

towards every member of the state, than it had ever been, that virtue which he posited as the condition of future prosperity was a fact no longer to be assumed without question. If we may take it to be that peculiar virtue upon which Angevin, Norman, and Saxon government had in fact rested, the virtue of the lawful man, whose oath was unquestioned, and whose integrity was the safeguard in turn of Saxon judgment and Norman inquest, the fourteenth century had degenerated from the past. Part of the appearance of decline in public virtue is due, no doubt, to changes in the nature of records, and to the new power of the commons to present fraud and violence before the parliament in general terms. Common petitions tell us more and more explicitly what are the prevailing social vices. But even so, the parliament rolls show that the honesty of provincial courts was declining, that the law itself was coming to be a weapon in the hands of the unscrupulous, and that open violence was on the increase.

The beginning of decline in justice

The period of the Ordinances either gave the opportunity for misconduct or encouraged the counties to appeal against it. In the Hilary parliament of 1315 the commons turned the weapon of petition for the first time against the lords, and showed how county influence could be used to pervert the forms of justice into oppression. The matter of the petitions[1] is to be familiar in time to come, but in that year it was new. Lords invent trespasses on the part of their enemies and secure commissions of oyer and terminer for justices who are favourable to them. They influence the sheriffs to appoint days of trial without warning the defendants, and so they lose their case by non-appearance. They appoint places for trial in remote districts where their victims dare not come, and have juries empanelled who know nothing of the cause. In suits of land great lords maintain each other, so that the opposing parties dare not proceed. Much of the technique of the legal tyranny of the fifteenth century seems already to be familiar. It can hardly have been entirely new in 1315, but at least it has never been so clearly and so generally exposed. Already the principal vices which were to bring the medieval order to ruin are present, lordship unlawfully exercised,[2] the corruption of juries, sheriffs who use the letter

Period of the Ordinances

---

[1] *Rotuli Parliamentorum*, i. 290.

[2] Matthew Furness could not be sued in the county court of Somerset *pur sa seignurie*. *Ibid.* i. 289.

of the law to deny fair trial, justices whose decision is prearranged. Innocent men, it is said, may be put falsely upon their defence for charges involving a few shillings, and led from process to process till their amercements amount to hundreds of pounds and their estates are sold to pay them. Two stock figures of the coming anarchy, the lord who "maintains" his friends at law by the un-avowed threat of his wealth and influence, and the conspirator, are already a threat to the commons at large. Conspiracy, indeed, has come to be a profession, and holds whole counties in its power. "They boast that the King and his Council can never touch them".[1] It is noteworthy that the very explicit complaints of the commons got little sympathy in this time of baronial government. The Council refused to be alarmed: "Let those who so suffer seek their remedy at Common Law".[2] Nor were they more than occasionally referred to in the next generation.

The reign of Edward III seems to have taken means to restore *Recovery* order to a fairer level. Besides such devices as the annual nomina- *under* tion of sheriffs, which was imperfectly observed, the Conservators *Edward* *III* of the Peace were, by statutes of 18 and 34 Edward III, empowered to hear and determine charges of felony, and now, as Justices of the Peace, acted in the intervals between the itinerant commissions. Nevertheless, the declining strength of the reign weakened the local peace also, and the petitions of the Good Parliament de-nounce much the same state of affairs as did those of 1314 and 1315. It is to be noticed, however, that the intervening half century has brought about a change. In 1315 much of the blame was laid upon the sheriffs. Not only the community, but several counties individually, then complained that their people were being undone by "false juries" chosen by the sheriffs.[3] In 1376, though the *Com-* commons do not trust the shrievalty entirely—they repeat the *plaints at* *the end of* demand for annual appointment—they attribute the dishonesty *Edward* of juries rather to the "little ministers", bailiffs, sergeants, and *III's* others, and seek a remedy in laying a responsibility for checking *reign*

1 *Rotuli Parliamentorum*, i. 299. "The community of England complains of conspirators who are in every City, Borough, Hundred, and Wapentake in England bound by oath to maintain and procure false parties against law and right, and have allied to themselves many of the jurors of assizes and inquests".

2 *Ibid.* i. 290.

3 *Ibid.* i. 291. Lincoln.

all juries upon the sheriffs themselves.[1] A period of steady administration had clearly led to a better control of the shrievalty, and the
Good Parliament no longer wished it or the Justiceship to be
elective offices. On the other hand—and the symptom was a
dangerous one for the future peace of the realm—the illness of
Edward, which had made possible the financial scandal of Latimer
and Lyons, was also encouraging the court to extend its influence
into the counties, and to use the power of the crown to pervert
local government; sheriffs were being nominated *par brocage en la
Courte du Roi*,[2] justices of Assize and Gaol Delivery were being
sent out into counties where they had their lords and friends,[3]
justices of the Peace were being appointed by maintainers, and
commonly practised maintenance themselves,[4] and even the
officers of the Exchequer were using their hold over the sheriffs
to coerce them into dishonesty.[5] The remedies suggested show
an equal disillusionment with provincial election and with the
crown in its weakness as the source of commissions. The commons asked that the justices of the Peace should be nominated in
parliament.

But, although the corruption of the court in Edward's last years
gave a foretaste of the future disintegration of society from above,
the full danger was not yet evident. At the beginning of Richard's
reign, though the Chancellor warned parliament that "the rule of
force was coming to be divorced from the rule of law",[6] the
problem was still seen as a local one. The lords were confining
themselves to the less blatant form of indirect pressure known as
maintenance, livery was only realised as a danger when it was
adopted by associations for conspiracy, violence seems to have
been confined to bands of robbers and to the disorderliness of
vagrants and unemployed labourers, and parliament still hoped to
deal with it by the local machinery of the peace. In general, the
middle rank of country gentry, in alliance with the sheriffs, were

    [1] *Rotuli Parliamentorum*, ii. 331.
    [2] *Ibid.* ii. 331. In the middle years of Edward III's reign there had been a
marked tendency to return to the feudal practice of appointing earls to life
shrievalty of counties. T. F. Tout, *Chapters in Administrative History*, iii. 188.
    [3] *Rotuli Parliamentorum*, ii. 334.   [4] *Ibid.* ii. 333.
    [5] In the next parliament the officers of the Exchequer were accused of
intimidating the sheriffs to procure maintenance, *Ibid.* ii. 368.
    [6] *Ibid.* iii. 33.

looked to as sufficient to restrain the active crime of the provinces. The commission of the justices of the Peace had, indeed, wholly exceptional powers at this time, and was even coming under suspicion as a danger to feudal privilege.[1] Subordinate to the sheriffs, *The justices of the Peace* in the sense that they rendered the records of their sessions to them, they yet had a far higher justice than the old *placita vicecomitis pro pace servanda*. The ordinance of 1380[2] gave them the jurisdiction of the Statutes of Winchester, Northampton, and Westminster for the conservation of the peace, power to bind any person to keep the peace, power to search out by inquest, hear, and determine a list of offences typical of the day, robbery, maiming, homicide, the bearing of livery for purposes of maintenance or conspiracy, breaches of the Statutes of Labourers; in short, to exercise in their quarterly session far greater power than the sheriffs had held within the last century and a half, and virtually to replace the criminal jurisdiction of the eyre and gaol delivery. After the Peasants' Revolt the commons asked and obtained that the justices might hold session upon emergency when and where they thought fit,[3] and in 1392 they were given the extraordinary power of raising the counties against those who invaded their neighbours with bands of men-at-arms and archers, and the sheriffs were to place themselves under their orders.[4] Unlike that of the sheriffs, but like that of the eyre, their commission ran through every franchise. The whole jurisdiction was an extraordinary experiment in justice which was at once anti-feudal and a reversal of the hitherto universal trend towards centralization. It was typical of the day, in that it conformed to the rise of the county community and to the growth of a county interest neither feudal nor royal. Whether that interest would prove strong enough to master the problem of order within its own communities would depend at least upon the tolerance of the magnates. Significantly, the commons wished the commission of the Peace withheld from the lords,[5] and preferred provincial landowners, not necessarily

[1] In 1380 the prelates protested against the justices' commission to try charges of extorsion as likely to impinge upon the rights of the Ordinaries. *Rotuli Parliamentorum*, iii. 83.
[2] *Ibid.* iii. 84.
[3] *Ibid.* iii. 118.
[4] *Ibid.* iii. 290.
[5] *Ibid.* iii. 44.

learned in the law,[1] but independent,[2] to visitations from Westminster.[3]

Deteriora-   It is apparent that the position deteriorated fast under Richard II.
tion under The nation was coming to be sick both in head and members.
Richard II Most fatally, the central judicature was losing its independence,
and the judges of every class, forgetting that they should be as lions
beneath the throne, were seeking lordship. By 1384 "the justices
of both Benches and the Barons of the Exchequer were retained
and salaried by lords and others",[4] and habitually took great
bribes. Justices of Assize were commonly sent into their own
countrysides, where they had formed ties of lordship "and had
great alliances and affinities".[5] Judgments, when rightly rendered,
were made valueless by falsification, perversions of the verdicts
really returned, or erasure from the rolls,[6] and in the provincial
courts it was often impossible to obtain any sort of record by
which a case might be carried in appeal. Ordinances were made to
stop these abuses, but, whatever betterment may have resulted in
the central courts, the commons came to lose all faith in the
itinerant commissions, and to regard the eyre, trailbaston, and oyer
and terminer as disastrous to the counties they visited and devoid
of all judicial value. They would welcome commissions of oyer
and terminer if assigned to men of standing in the district to be
visited and chosen in parliament,[7] though the hold of Chancery
had been so far loosened that numbers of such commissions never
reached the persons to whom they were assigned,[8] but almost
yearly after 1382 they petitioned against the itinerant judge from
Westminster under whatever commission he came.

Clearly, the decay of the integrity of royal justice brought the

[1] They held that two justices with legal knowledge among the six or seven
in the county would be sufficient. *Rotuli Parliamentorum*, iii. 65.

[2] In 1439 the commission had to be withheld from all who had less than £20
in yearly rent, since the poorer justices had proved open to bribery and intimidation. *Ibid.* v. 28.

[3] *Ibid.* iii. 90. The commons pray that during the war justice of eyre and
trailbaston may not run among the poor commons, but that the justices of the
Peace shall hold their courts according to the tenor of their commission. Commissions of oyer and terminer were especially hated, and commons petitioned that
they should only be issued if the plaintiff could get three substantial men to
back his application. *Ibid.* iii. 94.

[4] *Ibid.* iii. 200: *sont de retenue et as fees des Seignurs et autres.*

[5] *Ibid.* iii. 139 and 200.   [6] *Ibid.* iii. 201.

[7] *Ibid.* iii. 140.   [8] *Ibid.* iii. 498.

nation to the edge of incalculable possibilities. The high royalist principles of Richard II, the foreign and English titles of the princes, his French alliance, and the luxury of his court, were worthless substitutes for the primitive legal virtue of past generations [1] and the iron administration by which the stronger of his predecessors had kept the realm in check. Social and political life was passing into a dissolution, and the forms in which it would reconstitute itself were still not to be conjectured. Richard II's commons seem to have diagnosed the danger rightly, and to have seen it as one in which the provinces must find their own salvation with little help from a corrupt or powerless judiciary. To raise the justice of the Peace to a judicial monopoly in his county, to make his authority as far as possible ubiquitous and immediately applicable when disorder broke out, and to give him the military support of the shire, was the general purpose of their petitions. The policy, sound enough in the circumstances, though it involved the admission that the Angevin judicial bureaucracy was no longer trustworthy, was vitiated by one unavoidable weakness—the commons had not the support of any sufficient body of the magnates, who, indeed, were themselves learning to profit by anarchy, and they neither dared to employ them as justices nor to attack them in their petitions. They could not venture to go above the substantial shire-knight for their justices, and, beyond a general accusation of maintenance, they never dared to force their charges against the nobles home; the small man who took a lord's livery or sought his favour against the king's law was petitioned against; the great man who shared his guilt equally went unquestioned, or it was left to the crown to draw the inference of his implication and to turn the edge of the statute against him.[2]

It is not entirely safe to assume that disorder and conspiracy is accurately reflected by commons' petitions, but if we take them as a rough guide we shall be inclined to conclude that the reign *Recovery under the first Lancastrians*

---

[1] Though the complaint that the justices of the Benches were in the fee of the nobility may partly explain that habit of putting aside their opinion in favour of his own when causes were on trial before Council which was the practical expression of Richard's principle that the "law is in the king's mouth".

[2] Thus in 1393 the commons' petition for a penalty of £20 for those who obtain writs from nobles to hinder their adversaries from proceeding against them at Common Law. The crown includes in the penalty the lords who issue such writs. *Rotuli Parliamentorum*, iii. 305.

of Richard II saw the first serious deterioration of public order, that the accession of Henry IV was marked by some attempt to grapple with the problem, that this was not entirely unsuccessful, that the reign of Henry V was one of good peace,[1] and that a really acute phase of the disease set in again in the thirties after a generation of comparative improvement. The accession of Henry Bolingbroke was at least marked by the first attack upon livery as a crime of lords rather than of their retainers and by the restriction of it to its legitimate use as part of the decencies of a great *Statutes* man's household. By a statute of 1399 livery of company, *i.e.* the *against* military livery of the squires, men-at-arms, and valets, was done *livery* away with in England in time of peace, except for the servants of the king, and even the king's men were to wear it in the presence only.[2] In 1401 the livery of peace, the badge and livery of cloth, was restricted to the counsellors, ministers, and menials of the magnates, though the king's livery and the prince's livery of the Swan might be worn throughout the realm by the noble families and by gentlemen of lesser rank about the court.[3] The penalty for disobedience to this new sumptuary law was fine at the king's mercy, and it was not till twenty years later that its abuse became again a subject of complaint in parliament.[4]

Disorder, conspiracy, and forcible disseizin did not cease during the reigns of Henry IV and Henry V, but they would seem to have been in part warded off to the frontiers[5] and to have been less a chronic condition than an outcome of the periodic rebellions. The violence of the nobles is specially mentioned in the autumn parliament of 1402,[6] and in 1417 the general unrest, which the authorities associated with the Lollard movement, showed itself

[1] An assize which the parties proposed to attend "with strong party on bothe sides" was in 1420 sufficient to provoke a letter to the Council from Sir Thomas Erpingham then an "agid man evermore willyng and desiryng good pees". The Council admonished the parties to present themselves attended by none but men of law. H. Nicolas, *Proceedings and Ordinances of the Privy Council*, ii. 272.   [2] *Rotuli Parliamentorum*, iii. 428.

[3] *Ibid.* iii. 477.   [4] *Ibid.* iv. 329 (1427).

[5] Henry V's first parliament presented a series of articles for the restoration of the Peace which they considered to have been indifferently guarded in the last reign. "Due obedience to the laws within the realm" came last in a list calling for good governance in Ireland, the Marches of Wales, Scotland, and Calais, the Duchy of Guienne, and the safety of the sea. *Ibid.* iv. 4.

[6] *Ibid.* iii. 497.

in "assemblies in manner of insurrection armed and arrayed to make war".[1] But, as in the matter of livery, the handling of the danger was more decisive than it had been under Richard, or than it came to be under Henry VI. The powers of the justices of the Peace were extended; after the rising of Kent and Salisbury Council decided to allot them armed retinues salaried by the crown[2] and the commission was sometimes used as a summary, quasi-military jurisdiction over wide areas of country, as when in 1406 Prince John and Ralf Nevill held it jointly "for the parts of the North";[3] but there is also renewed confidence in the central judicature. The chancellor was enjoined to accord special assizes without suit at common law in the case of violent disseizin, to punish the aggressors with imprisonment,[4] and to associate with each such commission a justice from one or other of the Benches. The justices of the Benches had, moreover, regained the country's confidence as justices in oyer and terminer, and in the dangerous year 1417 it was to such commissions, nominated by the chancellor, that the government of Bedford had recourse.[5]

If the first two Lancastrian reigns gave the country some small *Decline of* measure of that "abundant governance" that the commons *justice* demanded of Henry IV, five years of minority would seem to *under* have brought all the old evils to the surface. Council was making *Henry VI* a creditable fight against the growth of faction upon a national scale, but corruption and conspiracy were regaining their hold on the provinces. 1427 was a great year of grievance. The justices of the Benches were retained in private interests,[6] the justices of the Peace were being made helpless by maintenance, the livery statutes were not kept, the election of the shire knights was corruptly managed, assize jurors were bought, the sheriffs were the tools of greater men, and, through their power over juries, the law of the country was at their mercy.[7] In 1430 the dangers of maintenance

---

[1] *Rotuli Parliamentorum,* iv. 117.

[2] H. Nicolas, *Proceedings and Ordinances of the Privy Council,* i. 109.

[3] *Rotuli Parliamentorum,* iii. 604.

[4] *Ibid.* iii. 497.   [5] *Ibid.* iv. 114.

[6] William Paston of the Common Bench was said to have had retainers of fifty shillings yearly from the town of Yarmouth, of the abbot of Ramsey two marks, of the town of Lynn forty shillings, and so on, "against the king for to be of their council for to destroy the right of the king". *Paston Letters* (ed. Gairdner), no. 19.

[7] *Rotuli Parliamentorum,* iv. 329-331.

figure in the chancellor's charge as one of the principal reasons for the summoning of parliament.[1] Council also was induced in this year to pass a self-denying ordinance renouncing livery and maintenance for its own members.[2] The virtue of the lawful man and the sanctity of oath, upon which the English *Attempt to* system had rested for a thousand years, had been replaced by *reform the* their characteristic perversions, maintenance, false verdict, and *jury system* fraud. The parliament of 1432, believing that integrity might still be found in the substantial landholders, wished drastically to narrow the field from which the most vital juries—those of attaint, which pronounced upon verdicts challenged as false—were chosen, and would have excluded all who had less than five pounds of annual rent of freehold from such panels.[3] To this the Council refused its consent, though it had accepted a parallel petition for the limitation of parliamentary franchise to the forty-shilling free-holder, and it is, indeed, likely that the decay of political morality had spread to all classes. Without the restoration of a strong crown and some sharp restriction of liberty there could be no reform. Neither Henry IV nor Henry V had had the qualities needed for such a lead from the crown, the lords were indifferent or guilty; the knights of the commons, still holding to the tradition that shire government was the prerogative of their class, could see no solution but the fortification of the commissions of the Peace and an occasional resort to oyer and terminer in times of crisis. By the thirties things had gone so far that neither of these jurisdictions could surmount the strength of local interest and the prevalence of conspiracy, and both were sharers in the very abuses they were set to repress.[4] Fifty years earlier the chancellor had warned parliament that "law and might were divorced in England"; the

1 *Rotuli Parliamentorum*, iv. 367.

2 H. Nicolas, *Proceedings and Ordinances of the Privy Council*, iv. 64.

3 *Rotuli Parliamentorum*, iv. 408. Raised to £20 a year in 1436. *Ibid.* iv. 502.

4 H. Nicolas, *Proceedings and Ordinances of the Privy Council*, v. 39. A curious instance of the clash of these two jurisdictions occupied the Council in 1437. Two commissioners, Peke and Ludshope, had been sent to enquire into felonies and insurrections in the Midlands. They set up their sessions at Silshoe, where-upon Lord Grey, a justice and of the quorum of Bedfordshire, came with sixty armed men, complained that it was his town, that the intention was to "vex his tenants", and threatened that if the court was continued he would set up his own sessions and take the enquiry into his own hand. The king's commissioners were forced to withdraw.

commons of 1436[1] confessed the truth of his warning in the bitter experience of its fulfilment: "Please oure said Soveraigne Lord to consider, that the Triall of the Life and Deth, Landes and Tenementz, Goodes and Catalles, of every Persone of his Lieges remayneth and stondeth, and dailly is like to be hade and made, by the othes of enquestes of xii men, and to considre also ye grete dredeles and unshamefast Perjurie that orriblely contynueth and dailly encresseth in the commune Jurrours of ye said Roialme".[2] In 1442 the chancellor's charge to parliament turned mainly upon the "horrible crime of perjury more prevalent in these days than ever before",[3] and a few years later a justice of Common Pleas, whose honesty had won him the name of the "Good Judge", felt it necessary to urge a friend, who had been wrongfully ejected from his tenement, not to have recourse to law, "for, if you do, you will have the worse, be your case never so true. For he is feed with my Lord of Norfolk, and is much of his counsel, and also you will get no man of law in Norfolk nor in Suffolk to be against him, and, forsooth, no more might I, when I had a plea against him. Therefore my counsel is that you make an end, whatsoever the pay, for he will else undo you and bring you to nought."[4] England had fallen into that most irreparable form of tyranny in which centuries of effort have built up the safeguards of individual right upon the guarantee of popular verdict, and fear and favour have made honest verdict unobtainable.

Generations probably do not vary greatly in their inherent capacity for virtue. A decadent age is one in which energy, devotion, and altruism have been diverted from their conventional channels into others which are either indifferent or inimical to established institutions. At such times traditional social and political practice is upon the defensive, and, finding it without a creed, the idealist is apt to be driven to extremes of impracticable theory, and the unimaginative mass finds secondary and often unworthy objects for its loyalty and ambitions. It would be difficult, though

Underlying causes of the failure of order

---

1 *Rotuli Parliamentorum*, iv. 501. So again in 1439, false indictments, perjury, conspiracy by sheriffs, etc. *Ibid*. v. 28, 29.
2 *Paston Letters* (ed. Gairdner), no. 42.   3 *Rotuli Parliamentorum*, v. 35.
4 *Paston Letters*, no. 28. *Rotuli Parliamentorum*, v. 181.

of extreme interest, to determine the underlying causes of the
disillusionment which came upon the end of the fourteenth and
the first half of the fifteenth centuries. There had been a succession
of party revolutions, beginning with the reign of Edward II, in
which one group of the ruling caste after another had convicted
its rivals of treason, and from the Good Parliament onward the
royal house allowed itself to be involved. There was, no doubt,
weariness and some despair with the war, and the insecurity of the
sea was bringing ruin to the ports of the Channel. But the causes
of disillusionment went deeper and had troubled men of thought
and religion while the reign of Edward III retained something of
its glory and while social disorder was still kept within bounds.
A significant change had long been growing upon the temper of
scholastic thought. In the thirteenth century, in so far as the theory
of the state went beyond legal and moral generalizations as to the
duty of the ruler, it was catholic in the sense that it sought to
reconcile the existing orders of men and institutions within a
universal whole, and so leaned towards a constitutionalism which
found a political function for every estate. As the work of men of
learning and religion, it lacked urgency of feeling and was neither
very deeply reasoned nor the fruit of much experience. In England
this mild constitutionalism had shown itself in the clerical support
which the barons had enjoyed in 1258, but it did not survive the test
of political strife, and already in the papal and imperial quarrel of the
early fourteenth century controversy was stirring deeper levels of
thought; the left wing of the Franciscans was attacking the material
Break-up basis of the church, and Marsiglio and John of Jandun were fore-
of the shadowing a secular justification of the empire. Such radical
catholic questionings were unlikely to form a unified system, nor did the
unity various critics of the catholic world-order necessarily draw upon
each other, although authority, challenged for the first time,
tended to confuse them in a general condemnation. Wycliff's
doctrine of dominion by grace, in fact a very specialized application of the accepted doctrine of the divine trust of all rule, was
consistently denounced by Rome as "the heresy of John of Jandun
of cursed memory", and in this there was at least the truth that
it was a rationalizing of political pessimism, reflecting no reality
Political save that inner unrest which its creator shared with his generation
infidelity throughout Europe. Such theory had indeed no value for the

times, as Wycliff himself confessed, and, though the two movements can hardly have had any close relation to each other, the
vague and exalted Christian democracy of the Peasants' Revolt
more nearly expressed the political creed of Lollardry than did
the principles of any movement or party of the day.

Wycliff himself feared so modest a threat to the stability of
property as the confiscation of the lands of the alien priories, withdrew before the consequences of his own doctrines, and left them
to trouble the country for fifty years, during which Lollardry and
social rebellion became firmly identified in the mind of the
orthodox.[1] The wide spread of Lollardry among the poor was a
symptom of a general refusal to accept the old fixities of social
order, and especially those burdens and duties which had no warrant
but custom or ancient agreement. The rising of 1381 was in the
main one of free peasants, copyholders, gavelkinders, sokemen,
small burgesses, who, if they were under any shadow of villeinage
at all, had ceased to regard it as anything but an invidious and
unreal survival. Asserting the human dignity of the individual, the
natural man in his right in the Christian community, they saw its
chief enemy in a conventional rule of law, and vented their anger
upon monastic and borough archives and upon the lawyers. The
suppression of the rising and the hanging of its leaders could not
restore that essential of civil life, belief in the validity of the law's
right over the subject. Scepticism of its claim, and readiness to
deny legal rights upon general grounds of humanity and public
interest, often associated with religious libertinism, continued to
show themselves, occasionally in the form of serious risings as in
1417 and 1431, more constantly in resistance to particular obligations by individuals which yet reveals the rebellious mind of the
objectors.[2] By the second quarter of the century any heat of

[1] Cf. the commons' petition of 1414 against Lollardry: "forasmuch as great
insurrections have been lately made in England . . . by those who are of the
sect of heresy called Lollardry with the intent to annul and subvert the Christian
faith and the law of God within the said Realm, and also to destroy our right
sovereign Lord the King and all manner of estates of the said Realm, as well
spiritual as temporal, and all political order (*toute manere pollicie*), and the very
laws of the land". *Rotuli Parliamentorum*, iv. 24.

[2] Like that friar John Bredon, who, in supporting certain recalcitrant
parishioners of Coventry against the priory of St. Mary there, called the Prior's
rule the "Thralldom of Pharaoh", and committed himself to the dictum that
"eny custom howe long so ever hit be, thowe hit be of a hundred yeres, if hit

feeling and thought in such matters seems to have come to be confined to the masses, or to an occasional eccentric among the clergy or the learned; after the one effort of 1381 the social discontents did not gather head in rebellion. But the dead-weight of indifference and disillusionment paralysed those who had the task of maintaining law and order upon the established principles. Men continued to act wrongly in practice because they had no guiding principles of thinking.

If the strength of the age was renouncing the old habits of loyalty, belief, and obedience, it must needs find others by which to live. While the schoolmen had nothing or, rather, worse than nothing to offer for their guidance, the times were alive with new sources of power and the community set itself instinctively to exploit them unguided by the traditional sanctions of authority and with leaders who had no altruism and little political sense. It would be wrong entirely to eliminate the original structure of feudalism from the living forces of the fifteenth century. Some of the Conquest honours survived more or less intact, though the first Norman nobility had passed away. But that feudalism which had been so mastered and confined by the Plantagenets as to be a safeguard of provincial stability rather than an excuse for disorder had lost much of its force. That trend in legislation of which *Decline of* Edward I's statute *Quia Emptores* was the type, whatever its in-*feudal* tention, had made for the dissolution of great honorial estates, *authority* and the number of small tenures which were immediate to the crown had increased largely, while at the same time the decline of feudal values had been emptying the tenurial tie of its implications of loyalty and strengthening its meaning as a business contract. Commutation of services had begun to undermine the solid villeinage of the midlands—though the midland peasantry were still politically inert beside the turbulent gavelkinders and free

be in prejudice of commone wele it is unlawfull". The Council scented civil as well as ecclesiastical sedition—"against God's law and oures"—and the friar had to recant in the parish church. H. Nicolas, *Proceedings and Ordinances of the Privy Council*, vi. 43 (1446). So in 1440 the abbot of St. Edmunds complains that "daring misdoers daily make resistance and interrupt the franchise against all good rule of the law of your realm, and will suffer no law to be executed therein". *Ibid.* v. 125.

sokemen of the east—and tenure by copy of court roll was giving a new stability even to villein right. The peasantry were not alone in their impatience with the older, tenurial lordship. A commons' petition of 1379,[1] though it is true that it was directed to the one point of contribution to the payment of members of parliament, objected to lords taking the phrase *lour Hommes* so widely as to include those who hold freely or by court roll. It might indeed have been well for the peace of the country if the oaths of homage and fealty had retained more of their force, for the common law had made its terms with them and brought them within sufficient safeguards. The feudal oaths required man and lord to maintain each other at law, but not to the point of perjury or intimidation, and their right to use force in each other's defence had since the twelfth century meant almost nothing. But, as the exploitation of land for living had given rise to feudalism in the past, so now the coming of capitalism and wealth for profit was working towards a new integration of society, which was to reproduce the worst features of feudalism without its stability and almost without restraining rules. Edward III's battles were fought chiefly with *Rise of* English mercenaries, and, as the war dragged on into the second *extra-legal lordship* generation, the fortunes and reputations made in France brought to the fore men who had neither tradition nor property in land. Of these military notables the bannerets were the type. They were men who had served the king with at least ten lances, and who had been ennobled for their service upon the field of battle, and among them were such men as Sir John Chandos, the Fleming Walter Manny, Cobham, Dagworth, and Calverley. Many of them sat among the magnates in parliament, where the bannerets are recorded as the lowest estate of secular nobles, and, of course, in the Council, and his Gascon birth did not prevent Guichard d'Angle from being made an English earl of Huntingdon. The *The new* influence and popularity of the bannerets was not without its *chivalry* effect upon the prestige of the titular nobility, as an incident recorded by Froissart shows. The earl of Oxford, sitting at the prince's table, protested at the cup being presented to Chandos before himself. Chandos told him, "for all who liked to hear", that he himself served the king with sixty lances, Oxford with only four, and that he had waited to be ordered by the king before he

[1] *Rotuli Parliamentorum*, iii. 64.

came abroad: "So I may of right be served and walk before you, since my dread Lord the King of England and my Lord the Prince will have it so". In fact thirty years of war were bringing into being a new chivalry, more exacting than the old and calling forth loyalties which cut across the remaining feudal ties, and the Order of the Garter, which was its focus, has been called "a new nobility by livery". Like feudalism before it, this new social relation had its material nexus, not usually of land, as was that of the former, but of pensions and wages. From the king, who made his newly created dukes and earls pensionable upon the Exchequer, downwards, the propertied classes were reviving the old voluntary associations of lord and man which had prevailed in the tenth century, divorced, as they always were, from land, and contracted by indentures for a term of years or for life, but, unlike them, unfettered by legal restrictions, and as time went on increasingly indifferent to right and wrong. The origin of the revival was *The new* military, and it never wholly lost its military character. Edward I *lordship* had gradually replaced the *servitium debitum* of feudalism by the more adaptable and efficient system of salarying barons, bannerets, and knights to raise their own contingents for his wars, and they in their turn began to retain knights and troopers in permanency. A transitional form between the old enfeoffment and the new salaried indenture may be seen in those grants of lands by great nobles in Edward I's reign, of which the earl of Norfolk's cession of the manor of Lidden in Norfolk to John, Lord Segrave, is typical. Segrave was to bear the earl's livery "in as rich a guise as any banneret may", to serve him for life within England, Wales, and Scotland against any man but the king with six knights and ten men-at-arms, and beyond the sea with twenty knights at hire. Such treaties, accompanied sometimes by leases of land, but more often at wages, soon spread beyond the circle of the mag- *Indenture* nates and formed associations of liveried and salaried retainers *and livery* under men of standing which were invaluable to the campaigns in France but which gradually crept into civil life and began to constitute a new and dangerous kind of seigneurial influence. For a long time these "affinities", as they were sometimes called, escaped the criticism of parliament, to which only covins and conspiracies which used livery for confessed robbery were suspect. As late as 1389 livery was permitted by statute for those who had bound themselves as retainers by sealed indenture for life.[1] Until the middle of the fifteenth century it is, perhaps, true that the life indenture was the least dangerous form of the new salaried association, but with the reign of Richard II indenture for the period of a specific undertaking was being encouraged upon such a scale as to offer the opportunity of rebellion to any noble who could put his hand upon a supply of ready money. Neither king nor parliament saw the danger but rather encouraged it. In 1382 six hundred men-at-arms and nine thousand archers went to the Scotch war under the banner of John of Gaunt. Lancaster himself, Buckingham, and Bishop Despenser, were encouraged to lead armies out of England upon their own concerns but with public sanction and support, and, by these licensed arrays of thousands of the king's lieges in the pay and livery of a subject, the growth of the abuse proceeded logically until in 1403 the Welsh Border and the North could be raised "by gathering of power and giving of liveries",[2] and brought to battle with the king at Shrewsbury. Nor was it possible to go to extremes with the rebels even when Hotspur was dead and Northumberland a prisoner. The lords, "having heard and understood as well the Statute of Treasons of 25 Edward III as the Statutes made against Livery", adjudged the earl, who, though he had marched towards Shrewsbury, had not reached it, not guilty of treason "but guilty of trespass only",[3] and he "humbly thanked them for their righteous judgment".[4]

The reign of Henry VI saw an intensification of all those relations *Revival of* which honest men feared under such names as covins, affinities, *seigneural* indentures, and the like, and which now flourished so in peace as *justice* to place standing armies at the disposal of the more powerful lords, and so to fill the courts of the shires and the hundreds, the shrievalties, the benches of the justices, and the jury lists with men sworn "of their affinity", that the king's writ was of no

[1] *Rotuli Parliamentorum*, iii. 265.

[2] *Ibid.* iii. 524. "Secretly assembled and marching to join him (the earl) with the crescent badge on their arms". H. Nicolas, *Proceedings and Ordinances of the Privy Council*, i. 210.

[3] *Rotuli Parliamentorum*, iii. 524. Hotspur and Worcester were taken as the principals and condemned of treason, but their lands in fee tail were allowed to descend to their heirs. *Ibid.* v. 12.

[4] The commons had maintained that the lords must of necessity know much of the rebellion which the king could not know, and demanded that they should conduct the trial *sanz curtoisie faire entre eux en ascun manere*. Ibid. iii. 524.

effect except for the men of the predominant party. One curious
result of this hardening of local power in the hands of provincial
partisans was a sinister parody of those franchise jurisdictions
which had long ago lost their vigour to the Benches, the Eyre, and
the itinerant commissions. Some lords were great enough to set
up conciliar tribunals of their own, trying causes [1] and issuing
writs of summons counter to those of the king, and forcing
plaintiffs to show cause why they had had recourse to the royal
courts against the lord's retainers.[2] Others, less sure of their
immunity, used the hundred and wapentake courts, where "the
little ministers" were most easily intimidated, and brought actions
there for trespass against those who defied them. For their own
persons, the lords resisted or evaded the king's jurisdiction and
ignored writs of the Great and Privy Seal summoning them to
Chancery or Council.[3] In these ways, and by every device by
which an intricate and supposedly popular court procedure could
be turned to the advantage of a predominant clique, the centralization of three centuries was undone, and the country came to be
parcelled out into spheres of influence, where no will prevailed
but that of the great man and his affinity. The commons could
say against one who is generally held to have had the county's
welfare at heart, Henry VI's earl and duke of Suffolk, that he "had
made Shirreves to be appliable to his entent and commandement
. . . whereof ensued that they that would not be of his affinitie in
their Countreys were oversette, and every mater true or fals that
he favoured was furthered and spedde".[4] So, the lord Percy of

[1] *Rotuli Parliamentorum*, iii. 285: "The king's lieges are made to come before
the Councils of divers lords and answer there for their free tenements which
ought to be proceeded on according to common law".

[2] *Ibid*. iii. 305: "So that the said plaintiffs dared not proceed".

[3] One Northerner, Percy of Egremont, "withdrew him from his dwelling
place accustomed, and kept him apart in secret places" when summoned to
answer to Council and parliament for his disorders in the North. *Ibid*. v. 395.

[4] *Ibid*. v. 181. It is worth recalling that five years before parliament had
represented to the king that Suffolk "hath been to labour all his days for
conservation of the peace in the King's laws within this Realm in repressing
and expelling all manner riots and extortions within the same". *Ibid*. v. 73.
But the *Paston Letters* amply illustrate the prevalence of his influence in East
Anglia, cf. *Paston Letters* (ed. J. Gairdner), nos. 53, 56. "There xal no man
ben so hardy to don nether seyn azens my lord of Southfolk, nere non that
longeth to hym; and all that have don and seyd azens hym, they xal sore repent
hem", no. 66.

Egremont from his Cumbrian stronghold terrorized the neigh-bouring parts of Yorkshire, Cumberland, Westmorland, and Northumberland: "whereof your people of the same shires have been and yet be, sore hurt, vexed, and troubled, and dare make no entry, nor action attempt upon nor against them at the law, for fear of death, to their likely destruction".[1]

The power which was displayed in successful opposition to the normal course of the law was a tremendous incentive to lesser persons to seek lordship, and the strength of the greater families grew by its own momentum. The crown itself, forgetful of the carefully sustained policy of attrition, by which the older feudalism had been reduced to manageable scope in the twelfth and thirteenth centuries, lent itself to the building up of local supremacies for the great families of the Welsh Border and the North. It was held that "March should suffice against March", and to realise this economy of force Edward III and his successors deliberately put lands, custodies, and offices into the hands of the Nevills and Percies, until only the accident of their mutual hatred saved the north of England from being at their mercy. The Percies' achievement of an *The* exceptional standing was in part the work of Edward III, by whom *Nevills* Henry Percy IV was made earl of Northumberland and earl marshal. *and Percies* By this earl's marriage with Maude de Lucy, widow of Gilbert de Umfraville, the de Luci honours of Cockermouth, Copeland, and Wigton were gained in 1385, together with the Umfraville's castle of Prudhoe. Richard II made him warden of the Northern Marches, and, for his support of Henry IV, he received the Isle of Man in inheritance, the custody of the lands of Mortimer, and the constableship of England. In 1403 the district of southern Scotland —Roxburgh, Selkirk, with much of Berwick, Peebles, Dumfries, and Lanark—were made over to him, though his power there was not made good before his rebellion and fall. The Nevills had always been barons of importance in the North. They rose to an equality with the Percies under the first earl of Westmorland, Ralf Nevill of Raby, who made his career under Edward III and Henry IV, the latter giving him the castle and honour of Richmond, the custody of the Dacre heir and lands, and part of those of the earl of Wiltshire in minority. Lord Furnevall, Ralf's brother, was given Annandale and Lochmaben Castle. In the fifteenth century a

[1] *Rotuli Parliamentorum*, v. 395.

persistent marriage policy made the Nevills more powerful than their rivals. Ralf's second son acquired the earldom of Salisbury by marriage with the heiress of the Montacutes, his fourth son became Lord Latimer, and the fifth married Elizabeth Beauchamp and became Lord Abergavenny. His sons-in-law were Lord Dacre of Gilsland, Lord Scrope of Bolton, Richard, duke of York, Henry Percy, earl of Northumberland, and Humphrey Stafford, duke of Buckingham. In 1459 parliament reminded the king of the earl of Salisbury that "he and his had in rule all your castelles and honourable offices fro Trent northward".[1] It was the North that first became entirely unmanageable by the crown at the approach of the Wars of the Roses in 1453 and 1454, when the feud of the younger Nevills with the Percies called out large armies and caused the pitched battle of Stamford. For this the crown was in some measure to blame, for since the beginning of the fourteenth century it had neglected that careful diplomacy of marriage by which Henry III and Edward I undid the domestic league of their nobles, and drew them generation after generation into the royal circle. A far-reaching marriage policy such as Ralf of Raby's would have met with decisive opposition from either of these kings.

Affinities   Besides the titles and the lands properly annexed to them that these great lords held, and which the crown could in some measure have controlled, there was the ever growing accretion of influence which flowed in to such centres of "good lordship" during the fifteenth century, and which neither Council, parliament, nor king seemed able to check. The crown was content to bribe the principal magnates into loyalty by grants of land and custodies, and there were a countless number of subjects who were willing to buy protection on the same terms. When Henry IV's earl of Northumberland fell, a special section in the act of forfeiture was needed to deal with "the lands with which persons have enfeoffed the Lords Northumberland and Bardolf for the great confidence they had in them for the furthering of their desires".[2] Thus landed wealth accumulated more by the mere attraction of its influence. There was, moreover, a vast system of affiance with-

---

[1] *Rotuli Parliamentorum*, v. 347.

[2] *Ibid.* v. 11: *pur la graunde affiance que gentz que eux enfefferont avoient a eux, de fair ou perfournere lour voluntee.*

out land, in which an exchange of pledges by way of indenture—"saving the faith due to the King"—bound lord and client to support each other, so that by 1450 whole countrysides stood in the same patron's obedience, as did northern Yorkshire to the Nevills, Cumberland to Henry Percy, Lord Egremont, and Suffolk to the duke of Suffolk. There the duke in the days of his ascendancy was a better patron than the crown and the king admitted that it was so.[1] All this had its effect in the sphere of law before it came to be openly decisive in politics. From soon after the accession of Henry VI the local courts became inaccessible to any but the predominant party, traps for the man who had not lordship, where he might be ruined by false indictments, bought juries, and partial judges. Even the great ecclesiastics were at the mercy of oppressors "coveryng theym under lordship".[2] In the middle of Henry's reign "affinities" and livery began to tell in politics also. Parliament could be overawed by them, men came "armed and arrayed in manner of war" to the elections,[3] and, if held in one of the great spheres of lordship, they were helpless like the parliament of Bury St. Edmunds in 1447, or the Lancastrian parliament of Reading in 1453.[4] At last the Yorkist influence in London became so strong that the king could not with safety hold parliament there. The government itself was in part to blame for bringing force into parliament. In 1449 Suffolk urged the lords "to come in their best array and with strength";[5] for the parliament of February 1454 the great lords engaged whole quarters of the city—Somerset bought up the lodgings about the Tower, St. Katherine's, Mark Lane, and Thames Street—and sent the weapons and harness of their retinues before them, riding up themselves with armies of "every man that is likely and will go with them" raised by public proclamation in the shire towns.[6] In

1 H. Nicolas, *Proceedings and Ordinances of the Privy Council*, v. 125. The abbot of St. Edmund's to the king, 1440: "the earl of Suffolk is a grete lord in the cuntre and goodly to your said monastery. Like it unto your hieghnesse and good grace to geve him in comaundement undir your grete seal to support and maynteyne and defende youre seide monasterye and correct suyche personys as be there mysdoerys and opresseres." (The king issued letters patent to that effect.)
2 *Loc. cit.*   3 *Rotuli Parliamentorum*, v. 8.
4 Stubbs, *Constitutional History*, iii. 167.
5 *English Chronicle* (Camden Society), p. 62.
6 *Paston Letters* (ed. Gairdner), no. 195.

February 1458 the Lancastrian lords came "with great power", and it was left to the Londoners to proclaim that they came against the peace and to refuse them lodging.[1] The royal family itself is carried away inevitably in the current towards militarism and begins to build up vast liveried associations throughout the country.[2] Such was the end of the long chain of decline through the petty dishonesties of juries, the weakness of bailiffs and justices, and all that decay of strength and integrity in local government which at last brought it about that dependence and lordship were necessary for survival both for the great man and the small. It is the end of an age if, as we well may do, we take the supremacy of the law as the cardinal principle of the medieval world; and the attempt of the weakened monarchy to master disorder and conspiracy by the traditional expedients of continual council and parliament, and its substantial failure, is the main theme of the constitutional history of the fifteenth century.

ii

PARLIAMENT, COUNCIL, AND THE NEW FEUDALISM

Intro-
duction

The history of the constitution in the fifteenth century sees much advance in practice without the formation of adequate constitutional theory to direct and maintain it. There is no doubt that parliament is already esteemed the highest embodiment of the government of the realm. But historically this is so because in the past parliament was the highest court of the king, that in which he himself sat and with the fullest pomp and power of his regality. The estates have come to be conjoined with the parliament, the Great Council sits in parliament, and brings with it what survives of the virtue of the ancient *commune consilium* of magnates, and the commons have risen to a new status, in which their assent is necessary to the full and common consent of the realm. But when we come to examine this in practice, its effect is seen to be partial, imperfectly applied, and intermittent. The feudal authority of the

---

[1] *English Chronicle* (Camden Society), p. 77.
[2] In 1459 Queen Margaret "made her son called the Prince give a livery of swans to all the gentlemen of the county (Chester) and to many others throughout the land". *Ibid.* p. 80.

commune consilium is in process of being forgotten, that of the commons is new and unconsolidated. It is true that when the fullest approval and confirmation of the community of the realm is sought it is to parliament that the king goes, but as yet there is no rule of constitutional law to determine what must be done with such approval and what can be done otherwise. Aid is, and has for long been, increasingly matter for parliament, but the limits of what the king can exact by ways other than commons' grant are barely fixed. Change in the fundamental common law can only be made in parliament, but the restriction is one hard to define when concrete cases arise. War, peace, treaties, matters of state, the descent of the crown, are all matters which will be most fully established if they have been passed upon by lords and commons, but there is no rule that every man would accept, and in times of emergency the king and the Council will act without apology and ask no indemnity afterwards. The value of parliamentary authority is still less that of establishing acts and laws as against the will of the king, or against that of groups or orders of the community, than of giving to any enactment the permanence which was attributed to statute, together with the full publicity and acceptance of national assent. The older feudal dissension between crown and magnates has been fought out and finished; the final clash between crown and commons will not come until the seventeenth century. It is a time when there are few fundamental differences as to the constitution, when king and commons, and the lords also in some measure, proceed upon the assumption of common interest, and can meet without friction in parliament, accepting each other's advice and consent as useful elements in a common decision, without deeply questioning the right from which they proceed. One effect of the absence of constitutional controversy—the reign of Richard II is, of course, a partial exception—is the absence of any historical sense as to the growth and institution of parliament. The commons make statements as to what is the "ancient use and custom of Parliaments" which could be contradicted by the memory of a normal lifetime, and no one cares to correct them.[1] Another is that king or commons make or

[1] Thus in 1388 they claimed that impeachment was among the "ancient ordinances and liberties of Parliament". *Rotuli Parliamentorum*, iii. 232. As early as 1376 they believed that the county representation in parliament was *de*

admit from time to time claims which seem to us, from our more experienced view, to presuppose wide principles of autocracy or parliamentary right, but pass them almost without comment. Things are done in one parliament which ought to set the precedent for a radical diversion of the line of constitutional progress, but are done without emphasis or debate and forgotten in the next. It is a time of apparent clashes of principles which produce no explosion and pass without effect, only to be denied the character of an age of constitutional experiment because the variety of practice is the result of indifference to rules which we think essential but which are then made and broken lightly as advantage serves.

In spite of a kind of shared inertia as to fundamentals, there are, of course, repeated dissensions upon minor issues, mainly upon the spending of the revenue and especially that part of it which goes for the royal household. For that reason, the commons of Richard II and Henry IV are constantly trying to control the size, personnel, and expense of the king and queen's households, and, partly from the same motive, they concern themselves in the membership of the Council, though both these interests begin to flag with the reign of Henry V and the renewal of the war upon a great scale. Because of these recurrent disputes, the rule of the house of Lancaster, with its prelude in the unsuccessful attempt of Richard II to rule by prerogative, has acquired the reputation of being a time of constitutional experiment. It would be wrong to deny that habits of parliamentary initiative—especially that of the commons—and a great deal of compliance on the part of Henry IV and Henry V, do give the appearance of a new character to the period. Henry IV is the first king to whom it has happened to say in the face of opposition that he "well understands that that which the Lords and Commons do or ordain is for the welfare of himself and his realm",[1] though he himself can see no reason for their actions. The generalization is, however, a dangerous one if it prepossesses us to interpret every act of parliament and crown in the light of modern constitutionalism. There is a real increase in parliamentary experience, a real improvement in procedure, and at times, as in 1401, 1404, and 1406, a display of new energy in

---

commune droit du Roialme: *ibid.* ii. 368. The clergy also are ready to assert that their aids never were and ought not to be granted in parliament: *ibid.* iii. 90.

[1] *Rotuli Parliamentorum*, iii. 525.

parliament. On the other hand, a great deal of this was by allowance of the crown, a great deal of initiative remained to king and Council and had not been conceived of as a possible function of parliament, we find little consistent theory, and certainly no general principle of constitutionalism entertained by the crown or urged consistently by the commons. Above all, as we approach the middle of the century, the decay of order begins to affect every aspect of life, and the progress which has been made towards parliamentary government becomes more and more a mere screen for dynastic and party intrigue. As these forces assert themselves there is a decline not only in the independence, but in the energy of parliaments. Those of the late 'thirties and 'forties do little but petition upon commerce and trade, and the requests of individuals. They have almost ceased to grapple with the prevailing lawlessness, and the charges made at the opening of sessions become lifeless and perfunctory. In 1437 they are content to leave a body of unfinished business to the Council, who are asked to dispatch the outstanding petitions and have them inserted in the Parliament Roll;[1] Richard II's requirement of a parliamentary commission to continue such business after the day of dismissal at Shrewsbury had been a principal charge against him, but it was a less serious derogation than this to the competence of parliament. The weakness of the commons is confirmed under the Yorkists, when they seldom moot business of real national importance and when parliamentary legislation is beginning to be made at the initiative of the crown. To sum up the balance of loss and gain in constitutional progress under the Lancastrians is, and must remain, an attempt at generalization which can produce no exhaustive formula, for to do so assumes principles which were only slowly being built up out of the experience of contemporaries. Parliament is strong by allowance when government is strong, weak—and with little courage to assert its rights upon principle—when faction is dividing the nobility and the country is in disorder. From much parliamentary activity little change in the theory of the state emerges and certainly no clear doctrine of a parliamentary crown.

It was inevitable that a further century of practice should

[1] *Rotuli Parliamentorum*, iv. 506.

Structure develop and stereotype the procedure and the nominal rights of
of parliament; apart from a period of success and some formal
parliament advances in the first Lancastrian generation, it probably lost
rather than gained in power during the fifteenth century,
and suffered the same decay as was coming upon all the
institutions of a degenerate community. Nevertheless, however
unreal the development may have been in apparent parliamentary
right, it was capitalized in the later ages of the real power of
parliament, and must be studied for its own sake and for our
understanding of the future. The most difficult problems still
centre upon the structure of parliament, its houses and estates.
Already the substance of these divisions had been achieved. They
were the product of the formative reign of Edward III working
upon an original dualism in function and personnel; but a minority
was still sufficient to revive the function of the magnates as a
commune consilium, the original trustees of the self-government of
the nation and in a more ancient right than that of the commons,[1]
and official language had not yet been brought into accord with

The modern developments. The term "estate" was already in use before
estates the end of the fourteenth century, but the commons of 1381 still
applied it to denote all the various components of parliament.
"The said commons pray, that the Prelates by themselves, the
great temporal Lords by themselves, the Knights by themselves,
the Justices by themselves, and all the other Estates separately, be
charged to treat and consider of their charge".[2] The idea of three
estates against the crown has not yet mastered the forms of
parliamentary language. The king's judicial officers are still
involved among the estates,[3] and in this, if in no other feature,
common speech is still determined by the tradition that the

[1] Thus in 1427 Council decided that the king's authority was complete in
spite of his nonage "but the execution of the king's said authority . . . belongeth
unto the lords spiritual and temporal of this land at such time as they be
assembled in parliament, or in great council". H. Nicolas, *Proceedings and Ordinances of the Privy Council*, iii. 233, 238. In 1377 the prelates and commons were
addressed together by Richard Scrope without the temporal lords, who had
clearly been in council on the minority as the constituent authority of the new
reign. *Rotuli Parliamentorum*, iii. 5.

[2] *Ibid.* iii. 100.

[3] This still seems to be so in 1406, when the justices are commanded to make
observations upon the ill-government of the country along with the peers and
commons. *Ibid.* iii. 579.

Council *ad Parliamenta* is the core of the institution. The parliamentary estates are not yet reduced to three, and are therefore not yet fully accepted as standing for the future three estates of the realm. Indeed, if we replace the term "estate" by the older *gradus* the classification is that of the author of the *Modus Tenendi Parliamentum*. Half a century of change has not yet been assimilated. If the commons of 1382 put too low a value upon the growth of coöperation within the various orders of parliament, those of 1401 carried their acknowledgment of the consolidation of the estates of the realm too far. Blending the clerical and temporal orders into one, they spoke of a realm of king, lords, and commons, "showing how the Estates of the Realm may well be likened to a Trinity, that is to say the person of the King, the Lords Spiritual and Temporal, and the Commons". Clearly language is wavering between several interpretations and reflects a variable parliamentary habit, but it is moving towards its final choice, and in 1421[1] there swore to the Treaty of Tours the *tres status Regni*—the "Prelates and Clergy, the Nobles and Magnates, and the Communities of the said Realm". This also is a mixed conception in which the estates of the realm and the estates of parliament are not clearly differentiated,[2] but it marks the virtual realization of parliament's final form. The completed formula comes with the reign of Henry VI, when "the King and the Three Estates of the Realm" are recorded as the components of parliament.[3] The components of the estates—lords spiritual and temporal on the one hand, and commons on the other—had, of course, long been accomplished fact,[4] but we have to wait until late in Henry VI's reign for the convenient phrase the "two Houses of

[1] *Rotuli Parliamentorum*, iv. 135.

[2] The "Prelates and Clergy" make up the first estate of the *Realm*, while the assent to the treaty can only have been that of the estates of parliament.

[3] *Ibid.* v. 213: *Domino Rege et Tribus Regni Statibus in pleno Parliamento comparentibus.* This quotation shows that the estates of the parliament were still regarded as the estates of the realm in parliament, since by representation they bore their persons. *Report on the Dignity of a Peer*, App. v. p. 213; 11 Hen. VI: *in trium statuum ejusdem Parliamenti presencia*; *Rotuli Parliamentorum*, v. 213: *Domino Rege et Tribus Regni Statibus in pleno Parliamento comparentibus*, 1450.

[4] The last occasion on which the burgesses were treated as a separate order was in 1372, when they were kept back after the knights had gone home, and, "in a room near the White Chamber", made a grant of sixpence on the tun of wine. *Ibid.* ii. 310.

*The
Houses*

Parliament" to denote it. In 1450 "the Speker of the Parlement opened and declared (the charges against the Duke of Suffolk) in the Commen Hous", and "there were sent unto the seid Chanceller certeyn of the seid Hous" to convey the commons' further indictment of the duke.[1] Finally, a gradual realization that the Council and the executive form no part of the parliamentary estates is marked by the admission of the judicial officers themselves, who, consulted by the lords as to the privilege of freedom from arrest in the case of the speaker, Thomas Thorpe, answered in 1454, "that it hath not be used afore tyme that the Justicez should in eny weye determine the Privilegge of this high Court of Parlement".[2]

Membership of parliament: the peers

The personnel of parliament, and the right by which its members attended, is clearer than in the fourteenth century. The quality of peerage is at last being clarified. Bishops, dukes, and earls, and the holders of the new honours of marquess and viscount, presumably sat without question. Their creation had always been by letters patent; for this reason there was no doubt of their title, and peerage of parliament seems to have been assumed to inhere in it.[3] But with the baronage a new procedure has to be recognized. In his eleventh year Richard II made the innovation of creating a baron, John Beauchamp of Holt, by patent,[4] and, though he was only summoned once, in the year of his creation, and nearly half a century elapsed before the next patented barony was made, Henry VI created nine between his eleventh and twenty-seventh years. There is little doubt that the reduction in the number of those who were called to parliament by no higher title than baron was one of the reasons for this departure, and that part of its motive at least was to strengthen parliament[5]; the vital point for the history of peerage is that these patents include among the privileges of the new title a seat and precedence there. This is

---

[1] *Rotuli Parliamentorum*, v. 177.   [2] *Ibid.* v. 239.

[3] Nevertheless the justices determined that, although the name of earl descended by common law, the right to a seat in parliament was cognizable only by the king and the peers. H. Nicolas, *Proceedings and Ordinances of the Privy Council*, iii. 325 (1429).

[4] *Report on the Dignity of a Peer*, App. v, p. 81.

[5] Among the motives given for the creation of the barony of Lisle in 1436 is "to add to the number of those by whose counsel our realm may be guided". *Ibid.* 466, p. 245.

expressly stated by Richard II of the Beauchamp honour of Kidderminster—*locum . . . in futurum in nostris consiliis et parliamentis*—and in all the patents of Henry VI,[1] and it compels us to enquire whether the fifteenth-century peerage had not already reached its modern basis of a determinate list of honours beyond which the king did not extend the direct writ without formal creation by patent, and all of whose holders might rightly expect a summons to parliament? Had not all the ambiguities of the tenure of baronage and its relation to parliament become things of the past, and were not the peers of parliament a group of the greatest of the tenants by barony who had established a monopoly of the direct writ by prescription or letters patent?

If we go by the text of the letters patent, we shall probably *Basis of* answer "yes" to all these questions. In creating the barony of *parliamentary* Sudeley Henry VI granted Ralf Butler "the estate of a baron of *baronage:* our realm of England as well in session in Parliaments and Councils *patented* as in other matters",[2] and in this, albeit obliquely, he seems to re- *right* cognize a parliamentary quality in barony, and a writ *De Veniendo ad Parliamentum* of 27 Henry VI (which, it is true, stands alone) recognizes the modern principle that summons to parliament in itself creates peerage, for to the routine clauses summoning Henry Bromfleet it adds "for we desire that you and your legitimate male heirs shall take rank as barons de Vessy".[3] Prescriptive right by the mere fact of summons and patented creation seem, therefore, to alternate in practice, nor can we doubt that the fact that about a quarter of the barons who sat in the parliaments of Henry's middle years were secured in their parliamentary right by letters patent must have reflected favourably upon the older and more substantial baronial honours, whose titles were by ancient inheritance. If these were beginning to regard their seats as prescriptive and of right, they would be confirmed in their claim when new baronies were being accorded seats in parliament as part of their baronial privilege, and it would become increasingly hard to deny them what was secured to lesser men by royal grant. Certainly

[1] *Report on the Dignity of a Peer*, App. v. 239: *status baronis regni nostri Angliae tam in sessione in parliamentis et consiliis nostris quam alias.*

[2] *Loc. cit.*

[3] *Ibid.* App. i. p. 919: *volumos enim vos et heredes vestros masculos de corpore vestro legitime exeuntes barones de Vessy existere.*

prescription was appealed to with increasing acceptance in other
aspects of parliamentary right.

Precedence and prescription

Lords, patented and unpatented, knew their order of precedence
and seating in parliament, and guarded it jealously. As early as
1405 the king decided that the earl of Warwick should be "preferred in his seat" in parliament and Council above the earl of
Norfolk, and Lord Grey above Lord Beaumont,[1] and in 1425[2]
the earls of Norfolk and Warwick again disputed each other's
precedency, and the blood royal of Warwick was set against an
alleged prescriptive precedence, going back, it was said, to the
reign of Henry III, by which the earls of Norfolk sat above those
of Warwick. Parliament evaded a decision by making Norfolk a
duke, but during the pleadings an "inheritance of place in Parliament" was acknowledged. Thus prescription was a recognized
element in the status of peer; that it should be coming to be so, if
only by custom and courtesy, would have been consonant with
what was happening even earlier with the order of abbots, and
with the boroughs. By the end of Edward III's reign at latest the

Analogy of the abbacies and boroughs

townsmen considered that the list of parliamentary boroughs
had been fixed by custom and that any addition to it was to be
petitioned against by the borough affected as a result of the
"malice of the sheriff",[3] while as early as 1341 it was asserted that
not every abbot or prior who held by barony owed attendance in
parliament, but only those whose duty to do so had been established by custom.[4] Prescription, therefore, was becoming a ruling
principle in peerage, though the de Vesci writ, which was not
used as a precedent, may have been thought to express it too
absolutely.

Practice in issuing writs

In spite, however, of the language of the letters patent with their
apparent recognition of a fixed and known body of baronial peers,
the practice of Chancery was such as to make us doubt whether
the crown yet felt obliged to adhere to an unvarying rule in the
issue of writs.[5] Even peers by patent were sometimes not summoned; John Beauchamp sat only once, in the year of his creation,

[1] H. Nicolas, *Proceedings and Ordinances of the Privy Council*, ii. 104.
[2] *Rotuli Parliamentorum*, iv. 267.
[3] Cf. the case of Torrington. *Ibid.* ii. 459.
[4] *Report on the Dignity of a Peer*, i. p. 342.
[5] For the facts as to the issue of writs which follow see *Parliamentary Writs*
under the years named.

for his patented barony of Kidderminster. John Cornwall, baron of Fanhope by patent of 11 Henry VI, was omitted from the parliaments of the twelfth and twenty-third years; Thomas Percy of Egremont and Thomas Grey were not summoned until two years after their creation. The barons by ancient descent were subject to about the same degree of discrimination in the issue of their writs. Lord Scales sat in the last three parliaments of Richard II and in the first two of Henry IV and in that of Henry's fourth year. He was omitted from those of the third and fifth. Lord Seymour was not called in the third and eleventh years of Henry IV. Thus the parliaments of Richard II and the Henries, except when they were depleted by foreign expedition, continued to give seats to a group of barons which did not alter substantially, but which yet varied from session to session sufficiently to make it likely that the king retained and used a certain discretion with individuals. Richard's parliaments contained about forty temporal peers of baronial rank or below it, Henry IV's thirty-four or thirty-five, Henry VI's barely half this number at first, though they were added to as the reign went on.[1] The solid block of great men whose names come in the first two-thirds of the list of writs vary little, the names which commonly stand in the last third of it vary rather more. It does not seem that party had much effect upon the membership of the upper house. Richard II made no significant changes in the summonses for the parliament of September 1397, which was to try Gloucester, and for which the writs were issued three days after his arrest.[2] Henry VI called almost exactly the same lords to the Lancastrian parliament of Reading in January 1453, as had sat in that of 1450-1451, in which there had been a strong Yorkist interest. Whether all those who were summoned attended these or any other parliaments is, of course, another matter. Thirty-seven lords below the rank of earl were invited to that of 1397, but only twenty-four took the oath

[1] The drop in the number of writs under Henry V and Henry VI is no doubt due to attendance upon the king and Bedford in France. It shows, however, that Chancery does not yet summon a full list of peers as a matter of course.

[2] Of those who had attended the last parliament, the lords Montacute and Zouche of Harringworth were omitted from that of 1397, while the lord Fitz Walter was added. 1395, when eleven names were suddenly dropped, is the only year when Richard II's parliaments showed a sudden change in personnel. But this is probably to be accounted for by the Irish expedition.

to hold its proceedings irrevocable. It must have been almost impossible for those who were present to avoid doing so, and it is likely that the other thirteen had absented themselves. If we are to assume that these thirteen or some of them were summoned with the clear knowledge that they would not venture to appear, there is the more reason to think that the king was beginning to feel constitutionally bound to accord the direct writ to the forty-odd lords who made up the active parliamentary nobility, and that the peerage was upon the point of becoming a closed body. Whether that obligation was actually binding during our period there must still be room for doubt, but it was coming to be so.

The personnel of the commons had reached what was to be its final form until the reign of Henry VIII, and such progress as there was took the form of definition of privilege and procedure. The commons have forgotten that their summons once depended upon the pleasure of the king, and assert that "by common right of the Realm there are and ought to be two persons elected from every county of England to be in Parliament for the commune of the said counties".[1] They claim favourable points of procedure as "the ancient custom and form of Parliament", though they may be barely a generation old.[2] Especially, since the late fourteenth and the fifteenth centuries saw the first attempts to influence parliamentary election by wrongful means, the forms of election and the right to the franchise were the subject of statute. Throughout the reign of Edward III efforts had been made, by commons' petition and by orders incorporated in the writs, to secure that only good, discreet, or sufficient knights were returned, but in 1376 it still had to be requested that the sheriffs should accord open *Freedom of* election, and the request was shelved by the crown. In 1387 *election* Richard inserted in the writs the requirement that the knights returned should be "indifferent to the present dissensions", and in 1404 Henry forbade the election of lawyers. The commons, however, continued to prefer unfettered election, and in 1406, having protested that sheriffs were used to nominate members without submitting them to the county, obtained a statute by which forthcoming elections were to be proclaimed in every market

---

[1] *Rotuli Parliamentorum*, ii. 368 (Hilary, 1377).
[2] As that the commons should make their petitions before considering supply. Stubbs, *Constitutional History*, ii. 600.

town fifteen days before the poll,[1] and the elections themselves made in full county court. The *plenus comitatus* was, perhaps, as ambiguous in application to contemporaries as it is to us, but the intention was to secure choice by the most substantial elements in the shires, for the act of 1406 required that the names of the representatives should be written in an indenture and sealed with the seals of those who chose them, which indenture should, with the writ, be returned into Chancery. The effect of this, as far as the indentures are a guide, was to reduce the effective voices to a number which rarely exceeded forty, and might fall beneath twelve,[2] but it can hardly be doubted that those who appended their seals did so in the names of many others who had none. The statute of 1430 limiting the right to vote in parliamentary elections to those who held freehold of the annual value of forty shillings, settled the point of right, and became the rule of the constitution until the nineteenth century, but it seems to have done little to secure independence in election.

The estates were approaching their final form, but there can *Function* be no more fruitful sources of misunderstanding as to the nature *of the* of the fifteenth-century parliament than to seize upon each antici- *estates in parliament* pation of modern parliamentary practice as it appears as a permanent victory for popular government. To do so is to read into the second century of parliamentary history the common will and purpose, the reasoned jealousy for its rights and powers, the fuller sense of its place in the constitution, which only came to parliament after it had fought its way to predominance against the Stuarts. The parliaments of Lancaster and York were still ancillary to the Council, which remained the permanent governing power of the realm, and the commons of the parliament which established the Lancastrian monarchy asked for and received a delimitation of their parliamentary function: "they are petitioners and demanders ... saving that in making statutes, or for grants and subsidies, or in like matters for the common profit of the realm, the King wishes to have especially their advice and consent".[3] Their sessions were seldom for more than a few weeks, and not in every year, the only function that they discharged with any willingness was that of petition, and, as we shall see, commons' petitions continued

---

[1] *Rotuli Parliamentorum*, iii. 588.   [2] Stubbs, *Constitutional History*, iii. 422.
[3] *Rotuli Parliamentorum*, iii. 427.

to be a force which was only spasmodically effective in legislation. For the commons at least, the ideal was "plentiful governance" by King in Council, smooth working of the courts of common law, a crown which lived of its own and needed little subsidy from its "poor lieges". They were never conscious of being radical reformers; two years after the Merciless Parliament they "pray our Lord King in full Parliament that the royal right and prerogative of our Lord the King and of his Crown be guarded and maintained in all things . . . and that our said Lord King be as free in his time as his noble progenitors Kings of England were in theirs".[1] Parliaments were to secure redress for exceptional hardships and supplement the knowledge of a benevolent government. For the king, the "four points which belong to every Christian king to do in his Parliament were first that holy church be governed in full peace and liberty, second that all his subjects be governed in justice and peace without oppression, and evil-doers punished according to their deserts, third to maintain the good laws of the Realm, and to amend or make new law where the old is lacking, and lastly to defend the people of his Realm from their enemies without".[2] The commons' role is a passive one compared with that of the great legislating parliaments of later days, but the realities of this age, still essentially medieval in its limitations, have been obscured, partly by the busy search of the historian for constitutional precedents, and still more by the series of political and dynastic crises in which parliament was dragged more or less unwillingly into the train of the victorious party and used to give a colour of popular initiative to what was essentially the legalizing of successful faction, and this is hardly less true of the lords than of the knights and burgesses. Except for a few great individuals, the prelates dissociated themselves from politics and confined their real activities to the convocations, and the secular lords were a much depleted body. When, as in 3 Henry V or 2 Henry VI, the number of the lords was no more than nineteen and twenty-two respectively, some of whom were also members of the Council, it is idle to think of the peers in parliament in terms of the great feudal assemblies of the early thirteenth century. Powerful as single nobles may have been, the house of lords was too weak not to have been the prey of the predominant party in the court and

---

[1] *Rotuli Parliamentorum* iii. 279, 256.   [2] *Ibid.* iii. 337.

the Council, and it was, in fact, in Council that ambitious individuals looked for the political leverage to make good their schemes.

Almost without exception, therefore, parliament appears as the *Parliament* tool rather than the maker of revolutions. The Merciless Parlia- *in times of* ment of 1388 met under the influence of the Appellants.[1] It sat *crisis* under the menace of the armed companies of Gloucester, Warwick, and Arundel, and the cause of the Appellants in the country was buttressed by the imposition of oaths of confederacy with the five lords taken in the counties and towns. All subjects were enjoined by sheriff's proclamation to lend no credence to reports or opinions against the tenor of the appeal.[2] It is not surprising that many men of standing in the retinue of certain of the magnates were not to be found when the oath was exacted. The Appellants averred that for some time past the lords of Parliament had been prevented from speaking honestly for fear of their lives. The accusation may well have been true, but the Merciless Parliament was clearly no more independent of Gloucester than earlier parliaments had been of the king. The Shrewsbury parliament of 1397, again, met under the threat of Richard's Cheshire bowmen. Intimidation had, indeed, come to be notorious as the excuse of the peers for their subservience to the predominant faction. The commons of Henry IV's first parliament[3]—who had seen many of the same lords who had judged Vere and the archbishop of York condemn Gloucester, sanction the prerogative rule of Richard, and then depose him and put Henry on his throne—asked that the lords spiritual and temporal and the justices should never again be excused from their past acts by plea of mortal fear, "for they are more bound to stand by their oaths than to fear death or forfeiture".[4]

That the commons should be disillusioned is natural enough, since in most crises, as in 1397,[5] they were driven through a show of initiative which was little more than a cover for the revenge of

[1] *Rotuli Parliamentorum*, iii. 228.   [2] *Ibid.* p. 400.

[3] *Ibid.* iii. 433.

[4] Norfolk's fears of treachery, which he confided to Hereford and thereby secured his own and Hereford's exile, show the atmosphere of suspicion and hatred which prevailed in Richard's court and paralysed all independent action. *Ibid.* iii. 360.

[5] Richard conducted his revenge on Gloucester in the form of a commons' impeachment.

the king or the ambition of a prevailing clique of magnates, for
every revolution was staged in parliament, and the law of parliament was explored desperately to give perpetuity to the statutes
by which it was sought to embody the proscriptions and dis-
herisons of the *coup d'état* in fundamental law.[1] To challenge the
statutes of a crucial parliament was made treason, as in 1397,[2] or,
as in 1387, all and singular were required to swear that they would
never consent to their repeal.[3] But parliament remained variable
as ever. In September 1397 eighteen spiritual and forty temporal
peers swore upon the shrine of the Confessor that they would
"never suffer the judgments, statutes, and ordinances of that year
to be revoked or annulled", and heard the bishops of the two
provinces pronounce excommunication from the high altar of
Westminster upon all who violated the oath;[4] at Michaelmas 1399
the same lords spiritual and temporal, "examined severally in full
Parliament", advised that the said statutes and ordinances and the
whole acts of the parliament that made them, "be altogether
repealed and annulled for ever".[5] It was natural, therefore, that
the commons, who regarded parliament as a means of sober
government, should shrink from the periodic proscriptions of
which it was made the scene. The impeachment of Suffolk in 1450
was, perhaps, the only occasion when they were clearly eager to
press an indictment against the will of a majority of the lords and
the king. In contrast, in 1399 they were careful to put it upon
record that the responsibility for the judgment of great offenders
was with the lords,[6] and in the worst crises the commons feared
to fulfil the duty of knight of the shire.[7]

[1] *Rotuli Parliamentorum*, iii. 359 (1397). "The Justices and Sergeants of the
King were questioned by the King whether they knew any other sure way to
confirm and keep perpetually the said judgments, establishments, statutes, and
ordinances; and they said that the very greatest surety that could be is that
which is ordained and affirmed by Parliament". On hearing this Richard had
the peers sworn a second time and meditated writing to the Pope to get papal
confirmation of the statutes.   [2] *Ibid*. iii. 372.
[3] "Then all the said prelates, lords temporal, and commons made publicly the
oath as follows. You shall swear that you will never suffer or consent as far as
in you lies, that any judgment, statute, or ordinance made in the present
parliament, shall be in any way annulled, reversed, or repealed for all time to
come." *Ibid*. iii. 252 (1387).
[4] *Ibid*. iii. 355.   [5] *Ibid*. iii. 425.   [6] *Ibid*. iii. 427.
[7] *Paston Letters* (ed. Gairdner), no. 249: "Sum men holde it right straunge to
be in this Parlement and me thenketh they be wyse men that soo doo" (1455).

No doubt a great deal of the illusion of spontaneity in commons' action was due to packing and intimidation in the counties. This is a common accusation by an angry parliament against its predecessors, and indeed it is hard to see how the interrelation of party connections about the countrysides could have left room for independent elections. A parliament which met within the sphere of influence of one of the great lords might be hardly more than a party convention.[1] In an electioneering letter of 1455 the duchess of Norfolk tells John Paston that "it is right necessary that my Lord have at this tyme in the Parlement suche persones as longe unto him, and be of his menyall servaunts".[2] Richard II is said to have issued his writs to the sheriffs, naming the knights to be returned in 1387 and 1397.[3] Northumberland's rising of 1405 denounced the unlearned parliament of Coventry as a packed one[4] and the parliament of 1460 reflected upon that of 1459 that its members were returned "some of theym without dieu and free election, and some of them withoute any election".[5]

Years like 1387, 1397, 1399, 1450, and 1460, when parliament *Parliament* was called upon to commit itself to the reversal of a régime, were *and the* exceptional. At such times lords and commons acted automatically *crown* in response to external force, and the prelates retired into politic obscurity till the storm was past.[6] On such occasions constitutional theory is not deeply involved, and even the vacating of Richard's throne—in which, indeed, the forms of resignation and the renouncing of homage were carefully preserved—followed by the act of 1404 regulating the succession by statute, left no new or deep mark upon the constitution. The so-called "statutory right" of the Lancastrian throne had so little imaginative hold that in the

[1] Thus, Suffolk held the parliament which was to undo Gloucester at Bury St. Edmunds, where his influence was unassailable, "and alle the weyez aboute the said town off Bury, be commaundement of the said duke of Suffolk, were kept with gret multitude of peple of the cuntre, wakyng day and nyghte". *An English Chronicle* (Camden Society), p. 62.

[2] *Paston Letters* (ed. Gairdner), no. 244.

[3] *Rotuli Parliamentorum*, iii. 235 and 420.   [4] Walsingham, ii. 265.

[5] *Rotuli Parliamentorum*, v. 374.

[6] The failure of the prelates to give any political direction is one of the cardinal weaknesses of the parliaments of this age. They made no effort to protect the archbishop of York in 1388, or the archbishop of Canterbury in 1397.

elaborate justification of the Yorkish claim by "Godds Lawe, Mannys Lawe, and Lawe of Nature", put forward by the commons of 1461,[1] it was not mentioned even to be refuted.[2] That a bad or incapable reign broke the bond between the king and the lieges, and that the throne could be claimed and filled with their assent, was immemorial belief, hardly a formal departure from constitutional precedent, and certainly not the creation of a new monarchy. It is true that Richard had offended the constitutionalism of the day, not only in his affront to common law and his vaunt that "the law was in the King's mouth, and often in the King's breast", but also by attacking what had come to be accepted as parliamentary custom, asserting that it was for him to lay down the order of parliament's business and dismiss it when he would, and by dictating the personnel of the commons and continuing full parliament after most of its members had been dismissed.[3] But, in so far as this motive of opposition was genuine, the remedy sought was to change the person of the king and not to restrict the monarchy: "At the request of Richard lately King of England . . . the Commons of Parliament granted that he should be in as good liberty as his progenitors before him; by which grant the said king said that he might turn the laws to his good pleasure, and turned them against his oath (of coronation). Now in this present Parliament the Commons, of their own free and good will, trusting in the nobility, high discretion, and gracious governance of the King our Lord, have granted him that they desire that he shall be in as full Royal Liberty as his noble progenitors before him."[4]

Judgment of treason upon the defeated, and statutes revoking previous judgments against the members of the predominant party, decreeing the resumption of the former's lands, and in general comprising the results of the *coup d'état*, were the means by which revolutions strove after permanence and security, and these things they could obtain only from the highest court of the realm, and from the assembly whose assent to statute had become

1 *Rotuli Parliamentorum*, v. 463.

2 In dealing with Gloucester's demand for a definition of his powers as Protector in 1427 the lords carefully avoid any positive definition, and content themselves with saying that Henry V could not dispose of the realm beyond his own lifetime without the assent of the estates. *Ibid.* iv. 326.

3 *Ibid.* iii. 417 *et seq.*   4 *Ibid.* iii. 434.

essential. Thus revolution must pass through parliament before it becomes legitimate, and it was connivance in a legal process, and the permanence and publicity of parliamentary act, rather than the spontaneous judgment of the estates or the nation, that was sought for.

Thus it would be a mistake to think of the fifteenth-century *Parliament* parliament as a power embodying a true national will, controlling *and* the destinies of the nation and changing them by a conscious right *legislation* to revolutionize law. There was, however, greater reality and value in the routine work of parliament, and especially in that of the commons, in normal years of peace, when no revolutionary force was breaking in upon the session from without.[1] Indeed, the best warrant for the reputation of the house of Lancaster for constitutionalism in the modern use of the term lies in the larger share which the commons came to take under them in law-making. There is less difference between statute and ordinance in the fifteenth century than in the past, the terms being used almost indifferently for acts of parliament, but both have come to be referred to lords and commons before they become valid. The commons of 1376 had failed to establish the necessity of their assent to statute, but during and after the reign of Richard II bills which are put forward by the lords are minuted *soit baillés aux communes* as an almost invariable practice. In 1414 the commons are able to assert that "hit hath evere more be thair liberte and fredom that thar sholde no Statute ne Lawe be made oslasse that they yaf therto their assent".[2] At no time is it true, even in the Lancastrian reigns, that all or almost all the petitions of the commons are made good in legislation, but under Henry IV and Henry V more of them are accepted as the basis of statute than at any other time in the Middle Ages. There seems, indeed, to be a fairly consistent relation between the rise and fall of prerogative pretensions in the crown and the commons' parliamentary influence. Beginning with the last four parliaments of Edward III, we find that of 255 articles of petitions presented by the commons only five left any trace on the statute rolls, while in the reign of Richard II the periods during which most petitions were made acts in parliament were those when the king was most closely

[1] For what follows see H. L. Gray, *Commons' Influence on Early Legislation.*
[2] *Rotuli Parliamentorum*, iv. 22.

under control, 1381-83 and 1388-94. The great days of commons'
influence began, however, with the accession of Henry IV.
"Throughout his reign and that of his son practically all legislation
arose from commons petitions",[1] and what is, perhaps, even more
striking than the fact that the response by statute to petition was
continued and accentuated, is the almost complete absence at this
time of legislation by the initiative of the crown. In all Henry IV's
reign only seven statutes originated apart from the commons, and
only one of them, made in favour of foreign merchants, can be
thought to have offended popular feeling, while in that of Henry V
only a single statute was officially inspired. Moreover, in 1414,
perhaps stimulated by certain changes made in their petitions of
1413 before they were put into statute, the commons were able
to secure that in future commons' demands and statute should
correspond textually. In the course of their protest the commons
had asserted that they were "as wel assenters as peticioners",[2] and,
probably in recognition of this, the king's responses of 1414 began
with the new introduction, "the King, with the assent of the
Lords Spiritual and Temporal and of the Commons, wills. . . ."
From this it seems that amendments made in the petitions were
referred back to the commons, and that their assent was now
obtained to the final draft of statute, and at least between 1414 and
1421 this correspondence of petition and statute seems to have
remained the rule.

Up to the outbreak of the Wars of the Roses—specifically until
the parliament of 1453—the predominance of the commons in
legislation was maintained, though not so completely as before
Henry VI's accession, since their bills were more often subject to
amendment. Such amendments, however, seldom affected the
spirit of the enactments. These facts, which are the result of
Mr. H. L. Gray's examination of commons' bills and rolls of
parliament published in 1932, go some way to restoring the
view that the régime of the Lancastrian monarchy was more
"constitutional" than those which preceded and followed it.

True as such a conclusion seems to be of the means by which
statute was made, it still remains the fact that the influence of the
commons was at any period of the Middle Ages strictly limited,

[1] H. L. Gray, *Commons' Influence on Early Legislation.*
[2] *Rotuli Parliamentorum*, iv. 22.

and that the real power lay in the king and Council while government was strong, and in the local influence of magnates when it was weak. Even in legislation the commons' power may be flattered by dwelling too exclusively upon what they actually achieved, for the king retained his veto which was from time to time expressly recognized,[1] hardly half of the commons' petitions reached the statute rolls, and those which did dealt on the whole with matters which—as between king and commons at least—were not controversial. The regulation of commerce and trade, and the whole machinery of the Peace in all its aspects, were constantly legislated upon, but there were few great issues such as the religious problems of the following century. In legislation king and commons may be said to have been acting in an alliance under cover of which the real strength or weakness of the latter was not put to the test. When great political factions intruded personal issues into parliament the resistance of both lords and commons was, as we have seen, very easily overcome.

Moreover, in the matter of legislation proper the commons came towards the middle of the fifteenth century to find a serious rival in the crown itself, and in the last quarter of the century their initiative was largely eclipsed. The commons' bill was the principal source of statute until 1453, but the crown was already producing bills which it presented to the two houses and passed into statute.[2] These official bills were, presumably, originated in Council, and there is no sign of challenge or amendment by lords or commons. In form public bills, since they preserved the procedure of consent by both houses, they were in fact legislation by the king in parliament and without petition addressed to him, and, as might be expected, they reflect the personal interest of the crown. Typical of them are an act of 1455 appropriating £3000 to the "expenses of the King's honourable household"[3]—which may be set in

---

[1] As in 1414, when the commons themselves asserted it. *Rotuli Parliamentorum*, iv. 22.

[2] H. L. Gray, *Commons' Influence on Early Legislation*, p. 58.

[3] *Rotuli Parliamentorum*, v. 320. The change in initiative from commons to crown is marked in this case by the changed formula of the introduction—"it pleaseth the Kyng oure Soverayne Lord, by the aide and assent of the Lordes Spirituell and Temporell, and Commyns"—as against the older form of commons' petition, "prayed the Communes in this present Parlement assembled".

contrast to the contrary action of parliament in restricting the king's domestic expenditure by commons' bills under Henry IV— grants made to various great persons such as the king's mother and the duchess of Exeter, bills of attainder against the king's rebels, such as that upon the duke of York in 1459, and revocation of patents of privilege and protection exacted from the king by his enemies, as after St. Albans, Blore Heath, and Ludford.[1] After 1465 the acts of resumption of alienated royal lands, which had become largely punitive in intention, were also introduced by official bills. It is clear that the violent nature of the times, and the need for ruthless action upon the moment, is reviving the need for executive action clothed in parliamentary form, and the laborious pretence of popular initiative which concealed the real nature of the acts of 1388 and 1397 is no longer maintained. It was to be expected that parliament would not retain in the period of the Wars of the Roses that initiative which it had obtained in the more peaceful Lancastrian reigns. The commons seem, however, to have lost not only the coercive, emergency legislation which carried on the war in parliament, but much of their constitutional function as law-makers at large. After 1450 their influence upon general legislation began to decline. Important commons' bills were rejected in 1453 and 1455, under Edward IV few acts of any kind were made, and under Richard III, and still more under Henry VII, the crown became increasingly active at the expense of the commons. Thus the end of the Wars of the Roses sees a change as important as that with which the Lancastrian reigns began. In Richard III's parliament of 1484 the old preponderance of commons' over official bills was reversed. Nine statutes of that year were introduced by the crown as against only four by the commons.[2]

Parliamentary privilege   The reality of parliamentary power in its rise and decline centres upon the history of legislation. Less fundamental, but still issues of importance, are those acknowledgments of the privilege and special standing of parliament and of its members which mark its growing prestige even if they are not always observed by contem-

[1] H. L. Gray, *Commons' Influence on Early Legislation*, p. 102.
[2] *Ibid.* p. 137.

poraries or given that importance in the constitutional order which is attributed to parliamentary privilege to-day.

" The acceptance of the Speaker completed the constitution of the house of commons".[1] From Thomas Hungerford in 1377 the Speaker of every subsequent parliament is known. He asked at the opening of every session that if he misrepresented the words of the commons unintentionally he might be held guiltless, but this, of course, conferred no general liberty of speech upon the house, and though, in general, the topics chosen for debate and petition by the "poor Commons" were not at this time likely to be resented, a sensitive king might regard any especially hostile attack as seditious and proceed against those who made it. In January 1397 Richard II denounced the attempt of the commons to control his household as against the regality,[2] and ordered the Speaker to reveal the name of the person who had prompted a bill to this end. The commons gave up the name of Sir Thomas Haxey, came before the king "in all humility and obeisance, in great grief, as appeared by their demeanour", "well knowing and acknowledging that such matters at no time pertained to themselves", and submitting themselves to the king's grace and favour right humbly. Parliament then proceeded to adjudge Haxey to death as a traitor, but on the petition of the prelates he was granted his life and committed to their custody "solely by the special grace *Liberty of* and will of the King".[3] In the same parliament [4] the commons had *speech* to make an equally humble disclaimer of any intention to criticize the king's projected voyage into Lombardy, but the events of this session were, of course, quite exceptional, and the interpretation which Richard chose to put upon Haxey's bill was extravagantly harsh. The commons explained that they had meant no more than to commend the state of the king's household for consideration to the lords in the way of humble advice, and upon many occasions the Lancastrian parliaments discussed similar matters, and made their recommendations upon them without rebuke. In fact, though, when the issue was raised formally, the commons did not

[1] Stubbs, *Constitutional History*, iii. 473.
[2] *Rotuli Parliamentorum*, iii. 339.
[3] *Ibid.* iii. 341.
[4] *Ibid.* iii. 338. The general charge against the commons of this parliament was that of presenting articles which would infringe "the Royal Right, Estate, and Liberty". *Ibid.* iii. 339.

venture to claim complete freedom as to the matter of their petitions,[1] or as to the terms in which they discussed them. Henry IV began his reign by a promise not to enquire too closely into the commons' debates among themselves,[2] and in 1404 the Speaker asked and received leave to report criticism of the king's own governance without offence,[3] and a very considerable latitude was accorded in practice. The abstract question of liberty of speech was hardly one which presented itself to contemporaries as of any urgency. Upon the only occasion in the Lancastrian period when the claim was made explicitly, it was by an individual, and, though the commons presented the complainant's petition, the king remitted the matter to his Council, and, as far as record goes, the grievance was not pressed further.[4]

Liberty of person   The more tangible matter of the immunity of members from violence to their persons, or from certain kinds of legal process, during the session of parliament, and while going to and coming from it, was pressed more confidently. Since the right of the magnates to judgment by their peers was of long standing, the matter was mainly one for the commons, but certain minor privileges were shared by both houses. Barony excused the lords from service upon juries and assizes, and from 8 Edward II at latest this immunity was shared by the representatives during session.[5] In 1404 the commons raised the question of violence to members of parliament, both lords and others, together with that of their immunity from arrest, in both cases claiming to extend the privilege of the member to his servants, and to those who travelled or resided with him.[6] As to their safety from assault they

1 Haxey's condemnation was reversed on the accession of Henry IV, but only on the ground of erroneous judgment. The issue of privilege was not raised. *Rotuli Parliamentorum*, iii. 430.   2 *Ibid.* iii. 456.   3 *Ibid.* iii. 523.

4 The case was that of Thomas Young, member for Bristol, who proposed in the parliament of 1451 that the duke of York should be declared heir to the throne, and was subsequently imprisoned in the Tower for his presumption. In 1455 he petitioned for damages alleging "the olde liberte and fredom of the Comyns of this lande . . . for the time that no mynde is, [that] alle suche persones, as for the tyme been assembled in eny Parlement for the same comyn, ought to have theire fredom to speke and sey in the Hous of their assemble, as to theym is thought convenyent or resonable, withoute eny maner chalange, charge or punycion therefore to be leyde to theym in eny wyse". *Ibid.* v. 337.

5 *Ibid.* i. 450.

6 *Ibid.* iii. 542. The case was that of Richard Cheddar, who was in the company of Thomas Brook, member for Somerset.

appealed to the special protection of the king over those obeying a royal letter of summons, and the basis of their claim was, for that reason, hardly a special privilege of parliament,[1] but they proceeded to beg that such special privilege should be established; the murder of members and their attendants was in future to be ranked as treason, and lesser assaults were to be punished by a year's imprisonment and fine at the king's mercy. The king refused to make a new crime of violence against members of parliament, and reduced the commons' demands to a stricter process to secure the surrender of the party charged, who, if he failed to present himself for trial, might be attainted in absence, condemned to double damages and amercement at the king's discretion, and this modified security was made statute and governed the law until 1433, when the commons secured the substance of their demands of 1404 while the doubling of the damages and arbitrary amercement was made the penalty, whether the defendant presented himself for judgment or no. The safeguard was, however, restricted to members and was not extended to their servants or companions.[2]

Freedom of arrest for members and their servants seems to have rested upon older principles. In 1314 Edward II issued writs to restrain all action by assize against members of either house during the session,[3] and in 1315 stigmatized the arrest of the prior of Malton on his way from parliament as against the king's peace, and as giving him a claim to damages. In 1393 occurred a curious incident, the bearing of which is doubtful from lack of evidence as to the charges involved, but which at least shows that the commons were at that time more jealous of their status than were the king and the peers. Philip Courtney, a knight of the shire for Devon, "came before the King in full Parliament saying that he had been accused and slandered to the King and the Lords both verbally and by bill of certain heinous matters", and that pending trial he wished to be discharged of his membership of Parliament. The King and the Peers thought this reasonable and "discharged

Freedom from arrest

---

[1] The later statute of 1433, also, did not confine the protection to members of parliament, for the king extended it to lords attending his Council. H. L. Gray, *Commons' Influence on Early Legislation*, p. 300.

[2] *Rotuli Parliamentorum*, iv. 453. The case was that of an assault upon Richard Quartermain, one of the knights for the county of Oxford.

[3] Stubbs, *Constitutional History*, iii. 514.

him in full Parliament". Five days later, however, the commons asked that he should be returned to his place to take part in business, and "because he had shown himself reasonable, and had lent himself to a compromise with the complainants" their request was granted, "and he was restored to his good fame in full Parliament"[1]. In 1404 the commons claimed by ancient custom freedom from arrest for debt, trespass, or contract,[2] that the freedom should extend to their servants, and that those who infringed it should be fined at mercy and pay treble damages. The king admitted the principle, but said that sufficient remedy was already available. In 1429 the privilege was defined as covering arrest for all offences short of treason, felony, or the peace, and commons asked for it to be put into statute, which was refused, and by the reign of Edward IV it had become customary when occasion arose to execute an act of parliament authorizing the chancellor to issue a writ of release for those imprisoned on process of the crown, and for those arrested on the suit of subjects to obtain a writ of privilege and so stay the action till after parliament was over. The most famous case of this kind, since it arose from party enmities and left no doubt as to the necessity of parliamentary immunity, was that of Thomas Thorpe, who was Speaker in the parliament of 1453.[3] Thorpe had attacked the interest of the duke of York during the first session of this parliament, and, upon reassembling after a prorogation, the commons learned that he was in the Fleet pending payment of a thousand marks damages for trespass and theft, which the court of the Exchequer had awarded against him in favour of the duke of York. The case is notable for the failure of the commons to establish their principle—the only occasion upon which it was rejected—for, after a protest by the justices that it was not for them to meddle with privilege of parliament, and a colourless statement of custom as we have already seen it applied, the Lords declared without further justification for the duke, and the commons were ordered to elect a new Speaker. This they did, apparently without protest, and Thorpe remained in prison. The declaration of the judges may be taken to prove that parliamentary privilege in this matter was now firmly established, while the issue of the case shows how helpless the

---

[1] *Rotuli Parliamentorum*, iii. 301.

[2] *Ibid*. iii. 541.   [3] *Ibid*. v. 239.

commons still were in the face of the lords' prerogative as judges of parliament, and the material power of the predominant Yorkist clique.[1] It is weakness in the face of faction, rather than privilege—unquestioned as that may be in theory—which is the truest character of the fifteenth-century commons, and, in a less degree, of the lords also.

In spite of their subservience to outside influence, the parliaments of the fifteenth century had a secure place in the constitution, and their form did not vary as the power of the king increased or diminished. Parliament met with the same fullness under a strong king as under a weak, and was allowed a greater share in legislation under the powerful Henry V than in the later days of his imbecile *A new* son. Matters were very different with the king's Council. Here, *form of* where the secrets of the king were known, where he was in daily *Council* contact with his counsellors, not as the crowned figure in parliament speaking in formal phrases to the estates, but as a man with weaknesses and prejudices or policies which he pursued behind a screen of deference to opinion, the problem of counsel was as acute as it had been under Henry III, the Council was no less certainly the real centre of government, and its form was no nearer to definition. Thus, while the structure of parliament grew to completion without controversy and almost unnoticed, the Council remained, under Richard II as under Henry III, the target of converging ambitions, the subject of conflicting schemes for its constitution, variable, responsive to the changing fortunes of king, lords, commons, and parties. Through all the controversies and struggles of the fourteenth and fifteenth centuries it was the first stronghold to be attacked by opposition and the last to be surrendered by the king.

There is, therefore, no one formula which will characterize Council of the later Middle Ages either in form or function, for both reflected faithfully the temperament, policy, and immediate purposes of the reigning monarch, or, in the times of his weakness, the views of the opposition party of the day. Among other

[1] The privilege of the lords was recognized in the case of a servant of Lord Scales arrested in time of parliament in 1450. H. Nicolas, *Proceedings and Ordinances of the Privy Council,* vi. 103.

generalizations that which sees the Lancastrian councils as parliamentary, controlled by statute, and intended to reproduce the composition and temper of the estates, is misleading, for, though such views were occasionally and imperfectly expressed by opposition under Richard II, the development of the Lancastrian reigns is towards a small but powerful Council of magnates, more strong in relation to both crown and parliament than any which had gone before it. There is, of course, no question that the king's Council was of the utmost concern to the nation and therefore to parliament, and, since the latter expressed popular grievances very freely, Council was often the subject of petition. But, looking back from the modern standpoint, it is easy to misinterpret the desire for an effective Council as a demand for constitutional control—to attribute to the fifteenth-century commons our preoccupation with the form of the constitution, and to believe that when they petitioned for "abundant governance", "wise and sufficient council", and the like, they were asserting a right to dictate the exact form of the king's Council and to control its membership. That this was not so we shall realize if we remember that commons never once presumed to suggest the name of a councillor, and only once went so near to making requirements as to its composition as to ask that it should be made up "of divers estates," that only in two years, 1376 and 1386, were wholesale changes in Council made against the king's will in compliance with parliamentary demands, and that occasional compliance with the request that the name of the councillors should be announced in parliament, and their oath taken there, in no way bound the king not to make subsequent changes as he wished. Indeed, the particular form taken by the Lancastrian Council, that of a small body of great nobles, was promoted as much by the personal policy of Henry IV and Henry V as by external pressure, and after 1423 no statute dealing with Council was passed, nor was Council sworn in parliament, nor, except occasionally, was parliament informed of the names of the councillors.

Two views of Council

But, though we cannot speak of a parliamentary régime in Council, the late fourteenth and early fifteenth centuries were faced with a conciliar problem upon which the commons held very strong views, upon which they constantly petitioned, and as to which they were, if not of the better opinion, at least of that to which Henry IV and his successors finally rallied. We shall probably come nearest to the way of thinking of contemporaries if we say that from the end of Edward III's reign two views held the field, that which desired a "continual" Council—the term appears first in 1376, and carries the implication "unofficial", since councillors who were of the household were without saying continually about the court—one in which certain notables, usually men of standing from the several estates, should be sworn to attend continually upon the king's person and occupy themselves with the national business, and, as against this, the view which accepted the king's sense of what was convenient as final in the selection of councillors, which required no defined or permanent composition for Council, and which was probably indifferent not only to the existence of a formal Council but even to the acknowledgment by individual councillors of the special obligations which were undertaken in the councillor's oath. Usually, though not always, a "continual council" was the constitutional programme of Richard's parliaments, and especially of the commons, while the king preferred to retain freedom of choice and that power to give or withhold his full confidence of which any settled rule would deprive him. In the past, Councils had usually been of the latter sort. Inevitably, the great officers, the chancellor, treasurer, keeper of the Privy Seal, and usually the chamberlain and steward, were in the king's secrets and of his Council. Beyond that official nucleus the range of the Council varied with the personality of the king. Edward I, whose preoccupation with government for its own sake imposed the same impersonal quality upon his relations with every competent minister, worked without friction or discrimination with a large council which included, with the great officers, the justices of both Benches, the chamberlains and barons of the Exchequer, a selection of knights and clerks of the Council of less specialized function, and a sufficient number of prelates and temporal lords. His Council might on occasion rise to seventy. With rather more friction, notably in the year 1341, Edward III continued to exercise his free choice of councillors, and with Richard II it was a point of principle that the king should be "free and unfettered to remove his Officers and Councillors when and as he pleased".[1]

[1] *Rotuli Parliamentorum*, iii. 258.

Under an able king the habit of distributing confidence and responsibility as the various exigencies of government and counsel required worked-satisfactorily. The country submitted to thirty years of this sort of government contentedly enough under Edward III. But, because this arbitrary choice of advisers could not create a sense of joint and equal responsibility in the Council, it was essentially the method appropriate to prerogative rule, and could be nothing else. Indeed, the royal Plantagenet Council was devised less to formulate and control policy than to maintain contact with the chief ministries of war and peace, and to bring their holders into personal contact with the king and each other when consultation was necessary. Under Edward III, and, indeed, much later, large meetings of the Council were rare, the members were summoned *ad hoc*, and, if the business were of great moment, were likely to be merged in a *Magnum Consilium* of magnates, while the daily Council about the king might be no more than a handful. Many of the Council—Exchequer officials, justices, an occasional foreigner, provincials, could not give constant attendance; to them the king's confidence could be only at times and partially extended. From such a council there was absent all that sense of equal participation and responsibility which is sought in cabinet government, and for that reason, if for no other, it could never be used to embody the politics of the nation or of a predominant party and to enforce them upon the king; inevitably, it was upon these defects—the need for "continuous" attendance, and equal participation—that parliamentary criticism centred when the crown fell out of favour with the nation. There were, however, defects of a more permanent kind. It is apparent that a Council so informally conducted could not be representative of parliamentary interests, and equally it provided no safeguard against the intrusion of unpopular persons into the king's confidence, or against the monopolizing of it by self-interested groups. It is probable that the councillor's oath was not always exacted, especially from the nobles, and that men were retained of the Council as a mark of honour whom the king no longer employed actively, or whom he only consulted upon the ground of some special qualification and at intervals. Within this large and heterogeneous body the group actively coöperating in the principal concerns of government at any given moment might be kept together by the king's

Defects of Council

favour, and might represent its best or worst elements according as his sympathies lay. The worst effects of this indefiniteness were seen in the last years of Edward III, when the membership of the Council blended imperceptibly into a group of *privez autour le Roi*, some of them, like Nevill and Latimer, councillors, and some, using their influence with Council to forward their own schemes, as did Richard Lyons, who, as the commons complained, "made himself busy about the Palace and the King's Council", and got authority to act "by covin made between him and certain of the King's Privy Councillors". Thus the sovereign authority came to be accessible to private persons, and the commons marked the danger accurately in accusing Lyons of "accroaching to himself royal power",[1] since, not being a councillor himself, he presumed to act by Council's authority, as, indeed, in his defence he claimed to do.[2] Thus the Council's monopoly of counsel was insecure. Walsingham tells us that Richard II was influenced more by the clerks of his chapel than by his nobles,[3] and in 1406 parliament had the king's confessor removed, probably from the same motive.[4] All this was especially dangerous at a time when bribery, maintenance, undue influence, and all kinds of conspiracy were coming to have a strangling hold upon the community, and it was the defects of Council as giving opportunity for financial corruption which most, indeed almost solely at first, engaged the commons. As with Latimer and Nevill, so with Richard's earl of Suffolk, the clearest charges were those of misuse of office to make private profit, and in the first seven years of Henry IV the principal requirement of parliament, that gifts and grants should be made openly in Council, showed that the king's confidence was being abused by his intimates much as that of Richard had been.

The current remedy for this was a reform of Council, sometimes the appointment of a defined and influential body of councillors, sometimes the lodging in Council of the warrants by which all grants must be initiated. The theory behind parliament's petitions was a restricted one, of the infancy of parliamentary control, not of its maturity. Parliament professed, and probably felt, a

---

[1] *Rotuli Parliamentorum*, ii. 323.

[2] *Ibid.* ii. 324: "By the commandment of the King himself and of his Council".

[3] Walsingham, ii. 113.   [4] *Rotuli Parliamentorum*, iii. 525.

very real reverence for the office and prerogative of the king. Four times between 1377 and 1413 it asserted its wish that Richard, or Henry, should "enjoy the right, power, and prerogative of his progenitors undiminished". Its action against corrupt councillors was in theory *plus royaliste que le Roi*. The commons' impeachments assumed a kind of ideal monarchy, from which it was treason to divert the king, and to which, as soon as he returned to his senses, parliament would accord all its accustomed prerogative.

Efforts at reform

The purpose of the agitation was, therefore, to establish conditions under which reputable men could act effectively, and the publishing of names in parliament was mainly, as was so often the case at this time, to bind all the parties to their obligations; such a precaution made clear who were not councillors, and gave those who were a better warrant for insisting on being heard, and did not bind the king not to change them without consent of parliament.[1] It was sometimes required by the councillors themselves as a condition of taking office, and in fact the pressure towards defining and improving the rules of Council did not always come from the commons. Henry IV himself, perhaps in part because he felt criticism of recent alienations could not be staved off any longer, accorded a "bill" of rules for Council in 1406[2] which shows how closely the councillors' difficulties in existing circumstances had been appreciated, and promised them the undivided confidence without which their office would be useless. From 1376 to 1410 parliament continued to approach the problem of the Council in this spirit. It did not claim power to create Councils; but intermittently it presented the crown with the necessity of confining the king's confidence to men of representative standing, and put forward rules by which the ideal of "sufficient counsel" could be realized in face of his desire for free hands and of the nobles' reluctance to serve. It did so with a decent assumption that the king was equally anxious for integrity of Council, and on one occasion, in his bill of 1406, Henry IV lived up to the assumption. Commons' petitions show a very creditable understanding of the difficulties of official councillors to a king who has no great

[1] Thus the list of councillors announced in the parliament of May 1406, had been considerably changed before parliament met again in the autumn. H. Nicolas, *Proceedings and Ordinances of the Privy Council*, i. 295.

[2] *Rotuli Parliamentorum*, iii. 572.

enthusiasm for their advice, and under a constitution which has not yet incorporated the rules of secrecy, loyalty, and mutual responsibility into its canons of Council. Taken as a whole, they might be consolidated into a treatise in which almost every aspect of the councillor's craft would be illustrated.

Indeed, if the history of the fifteenth century shows no conscious attempt to set up a new constitutional theory by which parliament might assert a general control of government through parliamentary Councils, it is, nevertheless, concerned with something of fundamental importance. Ideal or practice, as they worked their way through the phases of feudalism and monarchical bureaucracy, had lodged government first in the *concilium* of the feudal *curia* and later in the royalist Council of Henry III and his successors, and each of these had demanded a different technique of counsel, different loyalties, a different kind of faith, different skill. With the continual Councils we come to still a third type, whose purpose is to be not a servant of the crown, nor of the feudal magnates, nor a clearing house for the work of the crown offices, but a neutral guardian of the interests of both king and nation. The demands made upon such councillors were in their kind new. The change in function called less for a change in form than for a new political type, almost for a new political morality. If the continual Council was to be what the commons at times desired it to be, an epitome of the estates,[1] it must contain nobles who would lay aside the commitments and interests and jealousies of their rank and devote themselves to conciliar routine for long periods without favour or self-interest, and with them men of the third estate capable of putting aside their commoners' prejudices and understanding and supporting the legitimate needs of the crown. Even when all parties had resigned themselves to government by a group of nobles, Council could not be true to its enhanced authority without a break with the bad tradition which made the individual councillor the head of a party connection and brought the ambitions and dissensions of factions into its meetings. There were lacking even those elementary conventions of conduct which would preserve judicial fairness and the rudiments of loyalty between one councillor and another. Council, or at least the continual Council as it was then understood, had, in fact, still to find

Problems of the continual Council

---

[1] *Rotuli Parliamentorum*, iii. 5: *De divers estatz.*

itself. More than for a new political institution, the commons were petitioning for councillors who should understand the elements of their own function, loyalty to the crown, to the parliament, and to each other, disinterestedness, diligence, freedom from factions, secrecy, and discretion. In short solidarity in the interest of the king, the nation, and their own—a new technique of counsel.

Various recommendations   The Good Parliament and the Appellants, self-interested as the latter were, did something to define current abuses and their remedy in a continual Council. The admission of external interests to collaborate in Council business was the substance of the charge against Nevill, Latimer, and Lyons. In 1386 the grievance was discrimination in the degree of confidence accorded to individual councillors, even to the point of the binding of the king by oath to be guided only by Suffolk, Oxford, and Bishop Nevill. By their influence the king had "departed from the Council of the realm".[1] The remedies proposed in 1376 were that the lords of the continual Council should always be about the king, that no great matter should be dispatched without the consent of all, that no report of Council's deliberations should be made save by its members authorized to do so, and that all officials of state should act on its warrants without demur.[2] In 1386, when the grant was made conditional upon a definition of the rights of the continual Council, it was required that it should remain in London to have access to records and to be in touch with the Justices, and that no one not a Councillor should offer advice to the king.[3] In 1390 Council itself adopted a fixed hour of assembly, asserted the principle of payment of wages, and made certain orders as to the conduct of business.[4] In December 1406 a number of commons' articles renewed the recommendations of former years,[5] repeated *Articles of 1406* the request that no one should share the secrets of the Council, and made the suggestion that its unity should be preserved by those

[1] *Rotuli Parliamentorum*, iii. 230.
[2] *Ibid.* ii. 322. At some time unascertained during the minority of Richard, Council drew up similar but more stringent rules for the king's conduct towards itself. H. Nicolas, *Proceedings and Ordinances of the Privy Council*, i. 84.
[3] *Rotuli Parliamentorum*, iii. 220 and 221.
[4] H. Nicolas, *Proceedings and Ordinances of the Privy Council*, i. 18a.
[5] *Rotuli Parliamentorum*, iii. 585. The Council made some reservations on grounds of expediency. H. Nicolas, *Proceedings and Ordinances of the Privy Council*, i. 296.

who remained in attendance keeping those who were absent informed of Council business. The king was asked to put equal trust in all the councillors, and to wait for proof by appeal before he let himself be prejudiced against any of them by charges of misconduct. He was required to receive no promptings other than from the Council in any plea, and to refer any who ventured on them to Council to be dealt with. All petitions for offices in the king's gift were to be made and granted in the presence of Council, and no councillor was to give special advocacy to the request of any petitioner, and finally every matter before the Council must be fully considered by each of its members, and absent members were to receive minutes of decisions with the reasons for them, and to signify their assent or dissent by letter.[1] In the previous parliament of this year, in May 1406, the king had, for his part, already insisted on a substantial Council[2]— apparently in part because of his illness, and in part to carry off the routine business of finance and justice and leave him free to attend to affairs of state[3]—and in December he also made his contribution to the right practice of counsel in a series of articles. He will name the councillors in parliament that they may be the more ready to act, he will support them in all things, place all his confidence in them, will suffer no impediment to hinder their task, will make no difficulties for them nor suffer others to do so. He will have all letters touching the matters assigned, whether letters of the chamberlain or under the Signet, and all other mandates addressed to the chancellor, treasurer or keeper of the Privy Seal, endorsed by the advice of the Council. The sphere of the latter's actions is limited by previous usage, excluding charters of pardon and collations to benefices and offices; but the king's rules are a model for the relations of king and Council. Finally, if he found that he was obstructed in carrying out his office, any councillor might resign "without the King's indignation", and Lord Lovell, who had a cause pending before the Council, was careful to

1 *Rotuli Parliamentorum*, iii. 623. The parliament of 1410 summed up their demands from the councillors in an oath to give counsel "loyally . . . without favour, fear, affection, or affinity".

2 *Rotuli Parliamentorum*, iii. 572. The names were considered in Council. H. Nicolas, *Proceedings and Ordinances of the Privy Council*, i. 288.

3 "Because he cannot devote himself (to affairs) as much as he would like." *Ibid.* p. 291.

abstain from taking his place until it was settled. The king's "bill" was entered upon the roll of parliament at his own command, and thirty years later it was still thought sufficiently to embody the obligations of Council, and was rehearsed before the then councillors at the assumption of his regal authority by Henry VI.[1]

Council freed from parliamentary criticism Thus the rules of a new institution of state were elicited from the experience of Henry IV's reign. The Council which was commissioned to govern the minority in 1422 had for the most part served throughout the reign of Henry V, and gave proof that the duties and obligations of their status had come to be much more fully realized. From this time onwards the Council does not receive direction from without as to how to conduct its business. It puts its own procedure in order by articles issued from time to time,[2] and brings them to parliament only for the sake of the permanent record of the parliament roll.

In part these articles were directed to securing the authority of Council against the Protector—offices, benefices, farms, and wardships and escheats were to be at their disposal—but they also show a clearer sense of the unity and stability of Council. Council alone was to know the state of the king's treasure, four or six were always to be present for the conduct of business, and decisions were to be made by the vote of the majority present; in 1423[3] Council had a further schedule of articles placed upon the roll of parliament forbidding the usurpation by single councillors of the right to answer petitions and make grants, announcing its intention of *Articles* calling the judges into consultation where the king's prerogative *of 1423* or freehold were concerned, requiring the ministers present to be *and 1426* unanimous before the Council decided upon suits "touching the weal of the king and of his Realm", and even foreshadowing later doctrines of joint political responsibility by requiring an outward show of unanimity from all councillors in matters of foreign relations: "for as miche as it is to greet a shame, that in to strange Countrees oure soverein Lord shal write his Letters by th' advyce

---

[1] J. F. Baldwin, *The King's Council*, p. 186.
[2] A contrast with the conduct of the councillors of Henry IV, who refused to swear to the articles of 1406 without an express order from the king. *Rotuli Parliamentorum*, iii. 585.
[3] *Ibid.* iv. 201, H. Nicolas, *Proceedings and Ordinances of the Privy Council*, iii. 148, and J. F. Baldwin, *The King's Council*, p. 174, attribute this to 1424, but it is upon the parliament roll of October of the second year.

of his Counsail . . . and singular persons of the Counsail to write the contrarie". In 1426[1] thirty-nine articles record and guard against the friction inevitable when a body so small as the Council has to deal with matters of great interest to its members individually. No councillor is to make himself party to any cause moved before Council,[2] every member is to have full right of speech, due reverence being given to order and estate, and none is to admit grievance against another for words used in Council. Proceedings are to be confidential, for the disclosure of what has been said has caused jealousy between councillors and has put some of them in danger. For this reason no one is to be admitted during the sessions unless upon special summons. No bill is to be passed upon except in the Council chamber, in formal session, and after formal reading. Finally, an important article tries to secure independence from the characteristic danger of the time by enacting that no lord of the king's Council shall be sworn of the Council of any other person. Neglect of this provision was to play a part in the fall of Suffolk twenty years later.

That these precepts were not always carried out in practice *Import-* is a commonplace of Lancastrian history, but their conception *ance of* is a constitutional fact of the greatest importance, for they mark *Council* the emergency of Council from that phase of its history when it was a chaos of conflicting wills with no common policy or loyalty to itself. As a body of conventional procedure the self-imposed rules of Council are of the same importance to itself and to the nation as the procedure of parliament. They enable Council to function as an organic institution, and to rise to the task of government with an impersonal, corporate purpose, and it is not to be forgotten that Council did succeed in the very formidable task of stifling the quarrel of Beaufort and Gloucester and kept the realm in outward unity for over twenty years under a helpless king. Hitherto, the country had always gone to pieces when the leadership of the crown was withheld, and the compromise and firmness shown by the nobles who served on the Lancastrian Council—many of them for long terms of years—is

[1] *Rotuli Parliamentorum*, v. 407. H. Nicolas, *Proceedings and Ordinances of the Privy Council*, iii. 214.

[2] "But oonly to answere that the bill shal be seen by all the counsail and the partie suyng to have resonable answere." *Rotuli Parliamentorum*, v. 407.

proof of the effectiveness of what was in all essentials a new branch
of the constitution.

Function
of
Council

It is impossible to bring the work of the Council under a single
formula. Its authority as stated in the 8th year of Henry IV[1] and
reasserted in the 16th of Henry VI was to "hear, treat . . . and
determine" all matters brought before it except "charters of
pardon, appointments to benefices and offices and other matters of
grace", "matters of great weight and importance" being referred
to the king that his advice and pleasure might be taken therein.
Being at the centre of the state, it did all that work of government
which had not become appropriated to any of the courts or
ministries. The more any function had been specialized and reduced to routine, the more likely it was to have its acknowledged
official channel and to proceed automatically under its appropriate
seal without Council's intervention. This is clearest in justice.
Council still represents that ultimate fountain of judgment which
comes from the king, but it has become a rule of the constitution—
broken, no doubt, upon occasion by Richard II, and, very in-
frequently, under his Lancastrian successors—that it cannot judge
In justice in common law. It cannot, that is to say, hear any cause which
already has redress by writ and action in either of the Benches.
From time to time it is suspected of doing so (parliament petitions against the abuse),[2] but precedent is against it.[3] Again,
the chancellor, who has been the presiding officer of Council
justice since the thirteenth century,[4] is beginning, though he has
not completed, a formularized jurisdiction of his own. By the
beginning of the fourteenth century he has been presiding over

---

[1] *Rotuli Parliamentorum*, iii. 572.

[2] The conclusion of a long controversy is best summarized in the Council's
own articles of 1426: "that all the bills that comprehend matters terminable
at the common law be remitted there to be determined, but if it so be that the
discretion of the Council feel too great might on that one side and unmight on
that other, or else other cause reasonable that shall move them". H. Nicolas,
Proceedings and Ordinances of the Privy Council, iii. 214.

[3] *Rotuli Parliamentorum*, iii. 44, 587.

[4] For a phase of the earlier history of Chancery cf. F. M. Powicke, "Chancery
during the minority of Henry III", *English Historical Review*, vol. xxiii.

special sessions of the Council, or of part of it, to redress those wrongs for which there is no common law remedy, or for which that remedy has proved for some reason ineffective. In 1319 we hear of the "Council of the Chancery,"[1] though the "Council in Chancery" would be a more appropriate phrase. The rise of a chancellor's jurisdiction in such matters was, no doubt, as inevitable as that of the older jurisdiction of the court of the Exchequer.[2] It arose from the discrepancy of a stereotyped system of writs with many of the grievances it was devised to remedy. When the Chancery could not offer an appropriate writ the plaintiff expected informal justice, the king allowed it to be provided, and the Council, deferring to the legal knowledge of the chancellor, acted under his presidency, and, as time went on, was glad that he should choose his own collaborators, who were more and more likely to be taken from the ranks of the justices, serjeants, and others learned in the law. Precedent, moreover, tended to establish procedure, and, like the common law justices before him, the chancellor began to act by rule, to follow set stages *in consimili casu*, and to develop a characteristic procedure of Chancery. Thus, long before the theory that the chancellor's jurisdiction was the jurisdiction of Council in Chancery died, its so-called "common law" or "Latin" side had hardened into routine; appeals against letters patent, petitions of right, claims for recovery of property against the crown, and similar claims, for which no suit at common law lay, might be sued for directly to the chancellor, and carried through by his procedure in a court which came to look less and less like the Council and more and more like one of the Benches in action. In Henry VI's reign we have an account of a session of chancery in which the Chancellor sits with the Master of the Rolls, two other justices, and four Masters in Chancery.[3] On the whole, both parliament and Council seem to have been glad to encourage the passage of Council justice into Chancery. Especially in those cases where the simple fact of violence—fraud, violent maintenance, intimidation, refusal of access to courts, or of remedy by the courts themselves—entered into the grievance, petitioners

Jurisdiction of Chancery

---

[1] J. F. Baldwin, *The King's Council*, p. 238.
[2] Indeed, it seemed for a time that the Treasurer might become the principal judge in equity. *Ibid.* p. 237.
[3] *Ibid.* p. 253.

were referred to the chancellor, and statutes appointed him as the authority to whom grievance must be presented. Where a choice of remedy seemed open, petitioners themselves felt their best choice of address to be the chancellor rather than the king, the Council, or the commons, and towards the end of the fourteenth century—the process is rapid under Richard II—the flood of petitions to Chancery grows and they come to exceed all others in number. We cannot say that a defined, recognized and invariable body of chancery law, nor an unmistakably separate court of Chancery, has been acknowledged within our period, but the jurisdiction is being practised, the Council has been relieved in practice of the greater portion of its judicial preoccupation, and has become free to devote itself to business of state. In Henry IV's reign Council was able to reduce its judicial sessions to two days of the week, and in that of Henry VI to one.[1] Without such a development, the small, continual Council of the nobility would hardly have established its tradition and found leisure to govern England.

Executive functions   Thus, more exclusively than any Council before it, that of the Lancastrian kings was a Council of State, and little is gained by trying to analyse and classify what is in effect the whole domestic and external business of English government. Under Henry IV perhaps its most pressing preoccupation was with the inextinguishable unrest of Wales and the threat from the Scotch. The safety of the Welsh and Northern Marches, the pay and provisioning of garrisons, the commissioning of officers, the answering of the perennial complaints of ill-supported captains, take up much of Council's sessions. With the reign of Henry VI the interest shifts to Guienne and Calais. The agenda for November 2, 1401, provide for taking the king's pleasure concerning the terms to be offered to Owen Glendower, and the orders to be sent to the Prince of Wales, then on campaign against the rebels; for considering letters from the English and Scotch Wardens of the March of Scotland, and providing for the security of Roxburgh Castle; for debating the possibilities of action in the event of the French denouncing the truce. It is thought useful, in view of the scarcity

---

[1] H. Nicolas, *Proceedings and Ordinances of the Privy Council*, iii. 214. Even so, judicial sessions were to be postponed to "great and notable causes touching the King's realm and his lordships".

of corn, to consider removing the custom duty for a period of six months. Letters patent of friendship with the Frisian merchants are suggested, and consideration is given to an embassy into Picardy and to the commission of Admirals for an enterprise in the Channel. Finally, it is intended to ask the king to inform Council of the contents of a recent letter from Bayonne, and to ascertain whether he wishes to make public the recent news from Ireland.[1] Such matters, the routine of war and peace, regulations of commerce, were, of course, the constant charge of the Council, and, especially under the minority, they were added to by many considerations of domestic diplomacy which might normally be thought to fall to the king. From 1425 onwards the burden of the dissensions of Gloucester and Beaufort fell upon their shoulders, and, though they invoked the help of Bedford and the parliament, the prolonged crisis necessitated a series of placatory letters, the engineering of conferences, and the devising of conditions of agreement. Besides these high matters of state, there is a daily routine of executive and of the prompting of executive acts by others. New acts of Parliament are rehearsed before the Council by the clerk of parliaments for their necessary action,[2] and upon one occasion the commons actually ask that Council shall deal with all petitions not dispatched at the rising of the session, and have them engrossed upon the roll of parliament.[3] During Henry VI's minority Council appoints the great officers, justices, and barons of the Exchequer,[4] and has all power except alienation of the king's inheritance and annulment of his letters patent. It summons the great duke of Bedford to its presence, and he is "ruled by the lordes of the counsail, and obeyes unto the King and to theim as for the King, as lowely as the leest and poverest subgit that the King has in his land".[5]

The continual Council, embodying such rules of counsel and exercising such powers, established itself slowly over a period of *Parliament and Council*

1 H. Nicolas, *Proceedings and Ordinances of the Privy Council*, i. 173. The decisions arrived at in most of these matters are to be found at p. 177.

2 *Ibid.* iii. 22.

3 *Rotuli Parliamentorum*, iv. 506.

4 H. Nicolas, *Proceedings and Ordinances of the Privy Council*, iii. 70, 121.

5 *Ibid.* iii. 235 (Bedford to the Council).

some thirty years. The demand for it came intermittently from the commons, who, just as they appealed for a commission of peers to advise them at the beginning of every parliament, still believed that the nobility were the natural counsellors of the crown and leaders of the community, but their demands came at such long intervals, and were so far from being informed by any clear design, that it is impossible to attribute to them any constant policy of making council a parliamentary institution, and towards the end of Henry IV's reign such petitions ceased. The commons of the Good Parliament demanded only the strengthening of the ordinary Council by additional lords,[1] the continual Council of 1377 was in fact, though not in name, a regency, and in 1380 the commons, having found its three years of office expensive, petitioned that it should be discharged and that the king should govern with no Council but his five great officers. Between 1380 and 1386 parliament was brought to realize the constitutional problem with which it was faced, and the great and continual Council of nine notables, with the great officers, which was forced upon the king in the latter year, was the first occasion upon which the new constitutional remedy was clearly formulated. It is no discredit to Richard and his supporters that the restriction upon his right of choice of advisers seemed a dangerous and intolerable innovation. It was in effect to reimpose the tutelage of his minority, and the answer which he made, that of appointing additional councillors, withdrawing himself beyond reach of his official Council, and finding an alternative in the advice of Suffolk, Vere, and Alexander Nevill, can only be condemned on grounds of expediency. Nor did the opposition theory justify itself when *Continual* the Merciless Parliament put the policy of the Appellants into *Council* action with a free hand. The continual Council of 1388 claimed *under* *Richard II* £20,000 for the salaries of its members. In January 1389 the councillors themselves pleaded for their discharge on the ground of their "great labour and cost", and Richard, in assenting to their reappointment in parliament for a further term, announced that for the future he intended to be free to choose his ministers and councillors and to dismiss them as and when he thought fit,[2] and,

[1] The commons petitioned in 1377, not very precisely, for a Council *de diverses estatz. Rotuli Parliamentorum*, iii. 5.
[2] *Ibid.* iii. 258.

having freed his hands without arousing protest, set himself to restore the normal system of a large Council of diverse elements. By the end of 1390, though its original members were retained, the identity of the continual Council was lost in a body of councillors, of whom thirty-four have been noted from the records of proceedings,[1] and many of whom were knights and clerks of no parliamentary standing. Thus the continual Council was pressed for no more than intermittently by the opposition under Richard, and had very indifferent success in practice. When it was resorted to in the later years of Henry IV it was largely at the proposal of the king.

It is clear, indeed, from his own words in 1399, that Henry *Under* was in a position to use his discretion in the matter of Council: *Henry IV* "it is the King's pleasure to be advised by the wise men of his Council in matters touching his own estate and that of the Realm, saving his liberty".[2] The same politic evasion was repeated in substance to petitions made in 1401 and 1402.[3] Parliament, for its part, contented itself until 1404[4] with asking that alienations of royal lands and revenues should be made with the advice of Council, without seeking to determine its form, and, though the first rising of the Percies revived the old cry that the king should have better advisers about him, it was not until Henry's health began to fail[5] that the continual Council again became essential, and then the initiative was shared by the king; the chancellor made his charge to the parliament of 1406 from the text "in the multitude of counsellors there is wisdom",[6] and Henry himself put forward a bill of conciliar reform. In a sense the history of the continual Council as a permanent institution begins with this action of Henry IV's. At this time it changes its nature, ceasing to be an occasional concession to criticism, becoming a permanent institution fostered by the crown, and drawing the few members

[1] J. F. Baldwin, *The King's Council*, p. 132.
[2] *Rotuli Parliamentorum*, iii. 433.   [3] *Ibid*. iii. 473 and 495.
[4] In this year Henry appointed twenty-two councillors, seven of them commoners, and reported their names to parliament. This was in response to "great instances and special requests made to him on several occasions in this Parliament by the Commons". *Ibid*. iii. 530.
[5] Henry fell ill, and was unable to travel, before April 28, 1406 (H. Nicolas, *Proceedings and Ordinances of the Privy Council*, i. 290). The Council was appointed on May 22.
[6] *Rotuli Parliamentorum*, iii. 567.

who are not also peers from knights who hold office in or are attached to the court.[1] Under Henry V and Henry VI the continual Council is a royalist institution. There are independent elements—Savage is one—in the Council of 1406, but it is the first of an unbroken succession. The archbishop of Canterbury, the bishops of Winchester and Exeter, the duke of York, the earl of Somerset, the lords Roos, Burnell, Lovell, and Willoughby, the chancellor, treasurer, keeper of the Privy Seal, chamberlain, and steward, with Hugh Waterton, John Cheyne, and Arnold Savage, were named in the bill. They were allotted substantial salaries, and, though they did not all survive till the next parliament and those who did resigned at the parliament of Gloucester in 1407, a similarly composed Council carried on their work and was succeeded by others, in which the parties of the king and the prince were alternately predominant,[2] until the end of the reign. The commoners were eliminated in 1407, and the nomination of councillors in parliament was only resorted to on one other occasion, in 1410,[3] but it may be said that the crown finally adopted the principle of the continual Council between 1406 and 1413, resigning itself to governing through a small group of magnates who were given a great measure of confidence and authority. No doubt the continual Council was riveted upon the constitution in part by the rivalry between the king and his son, which made it dangerous for either's supporters to relax their attendance, and which, with the payment of salaries, overcame the great men's reluctance. By 1415 the principle had justified itself sufficiently for Henry V to rest his government upon a small but extremely influential Council, which for much of the reign acted under Bedford as custos of the realm with commission to do all things with the consent of the Council,[4] and such a Council governed the country until the rise of Suffolk in 1445 or 1446.

There is, then, a specific constitutional form which may be

[1] Thomas Chaucer (1423) had been four times Speaker, but he was also the king's butler. William Alington was a member of Henry V's Council and Treasurer of Normandy. J. F. Baldwin, *The King's Council*, p. 173 n.

[2] *Rotuli Parliamentorum*, iii. 632.   [3] *Ibid.* iii. 623.

[4] The archbishop of Canterbury, the bishops of Winchester and Durham, the earl of Westmorland, the prior of the Hospital, the lords Grey de Ruthin, Berkeley, Powys, and Morley. The councillors of 1410 were the prince, three bishops, two earls, and lord Burnell. H. Nicolas, *Proceedings and Ordinances of the Privy Council*, ii. 157.

called the Lancastrian Council. It is not wholly the creation of *The Lan-* either king or parliament, and, though the rise of parliament had *castrian* made either a wholly feudal or a wholly ministerial council almost *Council* impossible to maintain, it is not the outcome of a consistent parliamentary scheme to control the state. More immediately, it comes into being in response to certain defects which characterize the age, of which the greatest is the prolonged weakness of the monarchy, which from 1370 to 1461 never gave the country a strong king resident in England for more than a few years together. The degrees in which these defects were realized by king and parliament varied almost year by year, but every crisis brought the problem nearer to its solution, and if we recognize, in the parliamentary view at least, an intermittent desire that the Council should be drawn from all the estates, we may admit that when the institution reached its normal shape under Henry V it represented a compromise, in which the element of strength and continuity required by parliament was compensated for by the exclusion of elements of possible opposition and the restriction of membership to nobles who were the relations or close friends of the king.[1] A council like that of 1415,[2] which consisted of the duke of Bedford, the archbishop of Canterbury, the bishops of Winchester and Durham, the prior of the Hospital, the earl of Westmorland, and the lords Grey of Ruthin, Berkeley, Powys, and Morley, and which served till a new commission was issued in 1417, satisfied the commons' requirements for a continual Council of great men, but it had no immediate relation to parliament, either in the nature of its authority, which was by letters patent, or in its membership.[3] The crises of 1376 and 1377 had fallen upon a crown which lacked any conciliar system capable of carrying on the king's government without the decisive leadership of the king. The death of Henry V showed that this defect had been to a large degree remedied, and that fifty years of canvassing of the ethics of

[1] Commoners were again admitted under Henry VI—the archbishop's charge to the first parliament of the reign called for "honorable and discreet persons and from every estate of the realm"—but they were usually men holding office of the crown. *Rotuli Parliamentorum*, iv. 169.

[2] J. F. Baldwin, *The King's Council*, p. 165. The fact that the magnates attend only irregularly during these years is an additional failure to carry out the full conciliar ideal of parliament.

[3] The last occasion on which the commons asked to be informed of the names of councillors seems to have been in 1423. *Rotuli Parliamentorum*, iv. 201.

the councillor's office, and the habit of action in council formed
in the nobility under Henry IV and Henry V, had provided the
nation with a Council which could master the offices of state,
reduce faction to manageable proportions, and conduct what was,
in effect, if not in name, a regency of the peers and great officers.

Minority   This Council sat from 1422-1437. According to the views then
of   held, it was ultimately the creation of the authority of the king
Henry VI   exercised by the lords spiritual and temporal in virtue of his
minority. Acting with this warrant, the lords initiated the new
reign by ordering a parliament by the king's letters patent *de
avisamento consilii*,[1] and appointing the duke of Gloucester to act
in it *vice Rege*. There the infant king appointed Gloucester
Protector and Defender of the Realm and Church and Principal
Councillor in the absence of John of Bedford, and, by "the request
of the commons" and "the advice and assent of all the Lords",
seventeen persons were named *pur Conseillers assistentz a la
governanz*.[2] Council, once created, became not assistants to government but the government itself, and its own arbiter. At no time
after 1422 does it seem to have been dismissed as a whole, and it
had, therefore, a continuous existence, usually filling vacancies by
coöption. The only case of the naming of a new councillor in
parliament, that of the bishop of Durham in 1426, was "by
election by the Council in Parliament", and in 1433 parliament
acknowledged the principle that the Council should appoint its
own members. In 1430 Council decided that no councillor should
be added or removed without Council's consent,[3] and in 1433
Bedford secured parliamentary recognition of the rule as a condition of taking office.[4] It was a somewhat larger Council than that
of Henry V, usually something over twenty. By the beginning of
the minority it had won itself clear of commons' criticism, become
an accepted institution, and had sufficient jealousy for its charge
of the king's government to make rules for itself in the common
interest and to insist upon a standard of attendance and conduct
which was markedly higher than that of any continual Council

---

1 *Rotuli Parliamentorum*, iv. 169.   2 *Ibid.* iv. 175.
3 H. Nicolas, *Proceedings and Ordinances of the Privy Council*, iv. 38.
4 *Rotuli Parliamentorum*, iv. 424.

up to the death of Henry IV. The chances of Council holding together were, no doubt, greatly enhanced by the payment of salaries, which the councillors secured for themselves by their own ordinance in 1424 upon a graded scale according to rank from 8000 marks for the duke of Gloucester to 40 marks for the simple esquire. Every day of absence was to be paid for by a fine. But it is probable that the indirect opportunities for influence and patronage were even more attractive, for precisely at the point which the commons of recent reigns had considered the most valuable function of the continual Council—the conservation of the crown's resources and the prevention of too lavish alienations— Henry VI's Council had little conscience, and parliament soon ceased to be an effective critic. "The patent rolls are filled with grants to Lords Cromwell, Hungerford, Tiptoft and others",[1] and the balance of power in the Council came, at least towards the end of the reign, to be watched eagerly by the many clients who were ranked behind each of the lords[2] and sought a point of vantage for preferring their petitions. In Council, as elsewhere, maintenance came to be a danger to justice.[3] Councillors promised to abstain from it, and denounced it in their articles, but with what success we cannot say.

These abuses were inevitable in the England of Henry VI. It is *Success* more remarkable that for twenty years of such a reign the Council *of the* kept together as a governing body. In this the strength of the *minority* institution was seen to rise above that of individuals,[4] and it was *Council*

[1] J. F. Baldwin, *The King's Council*, p. 179.

[2] So Margaret Paston, writing to her husband in 1448, concludes that "Daniel is out of the King's good grace, and he shall down with all his men, and all that be their well-willers". *Paston Letters* (ed. Gairdner), no. 56.

[3] An early and fairly unobjectionable instance of maintenance is a letter by the Black Prince to the justices of the Common Bench in which he asks them to be "as favourable and lenient (*cedauntes*) to the poor tenants of ancient demesne at Merton" against the prior of Merton "as they are reasonably able to be". *Stonor Letters* (Camden Society, ed. C. L. Kingsford), no. 4. From 1440 we have the story of a piece of legal chicanery by Suffolk which, since it involved the connivance of the treasurer, and did not need to use violence, is an even better example of a councillor's power to manipulate the law to maintain his men. *Paston Letters* (ed. Gairdner), no. 27. The contrast between the two methods may be taken as a rough measure of the decline in political morality in the first men of the land between 1351 and 1440.

[4] In 1427 they claimed to be "one whole (united) council for the king as they ought to be". H. Nicolas, *Proceedings and Ordinances of the Privy Council*, iii. 232.

not until the king became a rallying point for faction in the late
'forties that Council began to lose its unity, though before that
time it was preserved with a difficulty which shows the magnitude
of its task, and survived several dangerous crises. An united loyalty
was preserved against a threat of treason from the earl of March
and his supporter John Mortimer in 1423, and again in 1425, when
the quarrel between Warwick and Norfolk threatened to divide
the nobility, a number of notables, among whom were most of
the councillors, put themselves upon oath to remain impartial and
maintain the peace and had their act recorded upon the roll of
parliament,[1] and this oath seems to have been first planned in
Council.[2] From the outset of the reign there had been growing
a still more dangerous force of disunion, the jealousy between
Gloucester and the Beauforts, fanned by Gloucester's disappoint-
ment with the terms of his Protectorship and by the general dislike for his personal adventure into foreign affairs.[3] By the begin-

Crisis of
1426
ning of 1426 Gloucester was accusing Bishop Beaufort of plotting
his own murder and the seizure of the king's person, and it was
not until 1427, after Bedford had spent fifteen months in England
to secure the peace, that the quarrel was got under control.
Throughout this long period of uncertainty, when the formation
of parties behind the Beauforts or the duke would have meant
civil war, the Council acted with a due sense of their responsibility,
and probably with as much firmness as the circumstances would
allow. No faction emerged to support Gloucester's Flemish
ambitions; in April 1425 power was taken from parliament to
invite the arbitration of the queens of France and England, of the
duke of Bedford and of the Councils of France and England[4]; in
January 1426 Council, by Bedford's advice, urged Gloucester to
meet Beaufort at Northampton and promised safe-conduct and
mediation,[5] persuaded the bishop to keep his men in hand,[6] and

1 *Rotuli Parliamentorum*, iv. 262.
2 H. Nicolas, *Proceedings and Ordinances of the Privy Council*, iii. 177.
3 He married Jacqueline of Hainault in March 1423.
4 *Rotuli Parliamentorum*, iv. 277.
5 H. Nicolas, *Proceedings and Ordinances of the Privy Council*, iii. 181; Stubbs
Constitutional History, iii. 105.
6 "At the stirring of my said lord of Bedford and my said lords of the consail
he is agreed to send from him notable part of his meyne that he is now accompanied with and to content him of such number as shall be thought... reasonable
for his estate". H. Nicolas, *Proceedings and Ordinances of the Privy Council*, iii. 184.

in the Leicester parliament of February 1426, together with the lords, forced a settlement. Thenceforward they maintained a strict neutrality as far as Gloucester would permit them to do so, constantly put before him the need of unity in the Council and the realm, and, while they insisted that Bishop Beaufort should offer legal proof of his innocence, constantly resisted Gloucester's claim that he was accountable to no subject for his actions while the king remained a minor and that the powers of the crown, so long as Bedford remained in France, were vested in his hands by right of descent. The final settlement, coming after Beaufort's resignation of the Chancery and followed by his voluntary exile upon pilgrimage—Gloucester withdrawing his charges, and swallowing his failure to make the Protectorship absolute—was a triumph for the Council backed by Bedford and the parliament. That it was made less galling for Gloucester by large loans of money on the security of the Council was probably inevitable. The Council's survival of the prolonged test of its loyalty and firmness which these two perilous years imposed is more striking than any concessions made to the great contestants for power, and the successful proof of its quality may be said to have secured another twenty years of comparative peace for the realm. In 1427 Bedford was able to say that "it was unto him one of the greatest gladnesses that ever fell to his heart to see the King in this tenderness of age to have so sad, so substantial, and so true a council".[1]

As a result of this victory the Council was able to repress a further attempt by Gloucester to convert the Protectorate into a regency in 1427. It was now asserting its capacity to govern without the coöperation either of the princes or of the leader of the Beauforts, and with a neutral lord, the earl of Warwick, as tutor to the king, and basing its authority, as always, upon the undiminished authority of the crown,[2] carried through his coronation in November 1429, when the lords of parliament

[1] H. Nicolas, *Proceedings and Ordinances of the Privy Council*, iii. 235.

[2] In 1427 they had told Gloucester that he had no more power in Parliament than he would have had "the King being in Parliament, at yeres of most discretion", and that Henry was "like with the grace of God to occupy his own royal power within few years". *Rotuli Parliamentorum*, iv. 327. "Not in our names, but in our said sovereign lord's name, whose authority we have". H. Nicolas, *Proceedings and Ordinances of the Privy Council*, iii. 239.

declared the Protectorate at an end. Gloucester himself, helped no doubt by the unpopularity which Bishop Beaufort's cardinalate had brought upon him, seems to have extricated himself from his isolated position, and assured the parliament of 1432 that he had no intention of claiming more than an equal voice in Council and parliament,[1] and that "the Lords Spiritual and Temporal were in unanimous and cordial agreement with each other".

Parties in that year seemed ready to subordinate themselves to Council's leadership, and, with the return of Bedford and the king's approach to years of discretion, it might have been expected that the dangerous years were passing and that the Council had brought the nation precariously but without disaster to the safety of active kingly rule again. The year 1433 was, indeed, a turning-point in the history of the nation, for which the cause *Return of* of unity and order was not yet lost. Bedford returned to England, *Bedford* and a few months were enough to show how the mere presence of a great and wise, and, above all, a good prince, was enough to shame and frighten the violence and corruption of all classes into a show of amendment. While he had as yet taken no powers other than those his birth gave him, "the restful rule and governail of this land" had "greatly grown and been increased by his pre-sence by the noble mirror and ensample that he hath given to others".[2] In the parliament of 1433 the king and all the estates petitioned Bedford to regard his work in France as finished, and to devote himself to the saving of peace and law in England, and this he agreed to do "as far as it may goodly be with the weal of the King's lands and lordships beyond the sea" and "unto the time that it shall like my Lord to take the exercize of the govern-ance of this his Realm in his own person". The principles upon which the duke intended to rule are expressed in the articles which he put before parliament[3] "for the good of his Lord", and they are governed by his sense of his own commanding qualities, not questioning that he would receive the loyal coöperation of all those "who will take upon them to be my Lords Councillors", nor asking for the compulsion of law to confirm his leadership. The articles vest the government of the realm, as any statesman

---

[1] *Rotuli Parliamentorum*, iv. 389.
[2] Commons' address in the parliament of 1433. *Ibid.* iv. 423.
[3] *Ibid.* iv. 424.

of the day would have been compelled to do, in Council, whether in the filling of the great offices and bishop's sees and of vacancies in the Council, or in the calling of parliaments, and they ask no more for Bedford as chief of the Council than that he shall be informed of all its intentions and give his "advice and opinion wherever I am in my lord's service". It can hardly be doubted that, had he lived to the normal term of life, the prestige and wisdom that he brought to Council's action would have carried government securely during his lifetime, and, perhaps, transferred it peacefully to York or to a wiser Gloucester at his death. More than this, his example in life, "restfully governing himself and all his keeping, and obeying the King's peace and his laws",[1] might have turned the disordered forces of society into safer channels, and checked that disintegration of order which made the Wars of the Roses inevitable.

The fine and rather pathetic address in which the commons pleaded for the services of Bedford for England reveals at once their mistrust of such assurances of the unanimity and disinterestedness of the nobility as Gloucester had offered in 1432, their sense of lack of guidance, and their instinctive turning to the leadership of the single person who, as nearly as might be, stood for the accustomed preëminence of the crown.[2] It is, indeed, certain that the diversion of Bedford a second time to France by the worsening of Burgundian relations, and his death at Rouen in 1435, sealed the fate of the Lancastrian dynasty and of the political order of the Middle Ages in so far as it still survived. Gloucester was now heir presumptive, the Beauforts had to face the possibility of a succession which would mean their irreparable ruin, and York was brought within two degrees of the throne. The rise of French nationalism, marked in 1436 by the fall of Paris, committed the government to a losing war with France which swallowed the revenues of the kingdom and the reputation of almost every noble whose rank might have qualified him as Bedford's successor. In so far as any lieutenant of France came out of the test undiscredited, it was York, whose prestige was beyond all others that which it least profited the crown of Lancaster to enhance.

[1] *Rotuli Parliamentorum*, iv. 424.
[2] "The greatest surety that could be thought to the welfare of the King's noble person . . . and of this land". *Ibid.* iv. 423.

*Beginning
of the
Council's
decline*

The record of Council had been good up to this time—at least
its standard of political morality was higher than that of the
generality. But for some years there had been signs that this
higher standard had needed an effort to maintain it. As early as
1426[1] the articles of the Council bind its members not to harbour
wrongdoers or maintain parties to suits by intimidating their
adversaries or the justices or officers concerned. The articles of
1430 make the prohibition more explicit and add maintenance by
giving of livery and the intimidation of justices by letter.[2] It is
true that this was by way of "example of restful rule and good
governail to all subjects", but it can hardly have been without
reference to the growth of the Beaufort and Gloucester connections and to the sense of instability which prompted the recall
of Bedford to England. The disruptive forces gained against the

*The king
enters
politics*

state. Moreover, the king was ceasing to be a negligible factor. He
had been crowned in 1429, and in 1434 the Council was already
finding it necessary to warn him against being influenced "by
stirrings or motions made to him apart in things of great weight
and substance" and especially any directed against their joint
authority.[3] By 1438 Henry was granting pardons on his own
initiative "to his own great disavail" and in despite of Council's
authority,[4] and had given away the constableship of Chirk Castle
without its advice.[5] In 1437, being then about fifteen years old, he
began himself to sit in Council, and in 1440 Gloucester was attri-
buting his eclipse to Beaufort's hold upon his confidence. The
disorderly state of the country was forcing itself upon the Council
in these years, as far as their records go, for the first time, if the
Lollard rising of 1431 be treated as exceptional. In 1437 a commission at Silsoe in Bedfordshire to repress riots and felonies was
openly defied by Lord Grey and Lord Fanhope, who prevented
their business with armed bands and threatened to hold the king's
sessions themselves. Council apparently swallowed the insult and
did not summon the offenders.[6] At the end of the same year a
general proclamation against riot and breaches of the peace was

[1] H. Nicolas, *Proceedings and Ordinances of the Privy Council*, iii. 217.
[2] *Ibid.* iv. 59: "Maintenance as by word, by deed, or by message, or by
writing to judge, jury, or party, or by gift of his clothing or livery or taking
into his service the party".   [3] *Ibid.* iv. 288.
[4] *Ibid.* v. 88.   [5] *Ibid.* v. 90.   [6] *Ibid.* v. 35, 57.

necessary. Henry's approach to his majority may, perhaps, have played some part in the gradual reëstablishment of Cardinal Beaufort's influence, which was marked by the growth of a peace *Rise of* party in 1439 and introduced into the Council its first serious *the peace* cleavage upon a fundamental matter of policy. Against Glouces- *party* ter's opposition an embassy left England in May 1439 with orders to make large concessions in the cause of peace, even, as the later phases of the negotiations revealed, to the point of relinquishing Henry's title to France. Of the terms of this commission Gloucester later professed ignorance, not only on his own behalf but on that of the Council. Against the release of Orleans, which was carried through by the peace party in 1440, he appealed from Council in a protest to the king that "I never was, am, nor never shall be consenting, counselling, nor agreeing".[1] His protest was followed by a letter of general indictment of Cardinal Beaufort and the archbishop of York, Kemp, whom he charged with gaining an illicit ascendancy over the king and shutting out himself and the duke of York from their proper share of Council. Whether the embassy and the release was the work of a minority of councillors or of Beaufort's influence with the king, it marks the end of that "unity of council" for which Bedford had pleaded, and which had been maintained, however precariously, for seventeen years, and *Council* from about that time the character of Council changes. Clearly *loses its* Gloucester, once he had realized that his antagonism to the treaty *unity* had committed him to permanent opposition, and that his follow- ing in the Council was insufficient to make his word of any weight, began to absent himself. From attending assiduously, as he did in the days of his power, he becomes a rare visitor, showing himself only sufficiently to avoid the appearance of a complete abdication. Cardinal Beaufort's influence is said to have predominated from this time until his death in 1447, but as far as Council attendance goes the party of peace for which he stood was represented more often by his supporters, the archbishop of York and the earl of Suffolk. In the early 'forties the most frequent attendants are the chancellor, the cardinal of York, and Suffolk, who may be taken as the working body of the peace faction, Adam Moleyns of the same party, the earl of Huntingdon, who Gloucester said had been

[1] H. Nicolas, *Proceedings and Ordinances of the Privy Council*, v. lxxxiv.; Rymer, *Foedera*, x. 764.

offended at Beaufort's supremacy, and, less regularly, the earls of Stafford and Northumberland. The attendance of the cardinal of York and the earl of Suffolk throughout 1442 and 1443 is almost unbroken, and this must have been the time when the latter was building up his hold upon the king. Thus, with the less regular appearances of the cardinal of England, his party had a steady supremacy.

Supremacy of Suffolk   It may be said, therefore, that, after 1440, the government was in the hands of that one of two bitterly antagonistic parties which had secured the ear of the king. To this extent Gloucester's accusations were justified, and the situation was made even more dangerous as Suffolk's power began to rise above that of the two cardinals. In 1444, apparently with real reluctance, Suffolk undertook the great embassy which ended with the cession of Maine and Anjou and the Angevin marriage. The result of this revolution in foreign and domestic politics was to establish Suffolk in unquestioned control by his influence with the king and queen, and to commit the court and the court party to bringing the French treaty to a conclusion which would satisfy national pride, silence Gloucester, and prevent the war party from making capital out of the awkward fact that Suffolk was admittedly close friends with the king of France and the duke of Orleans. In 1447 Suffolk was left in a still more dangerous eminence by the death of Cardinal Beaufort and of Humphrey, Duke of Gloucester.

We have very few council records for the period of Suffolk's unchallenged supremacy, and it has been considered [1] that this in itself is a proof that its power was failing, and that the favourite withdrew all but the least important business from its control. The attendance fell away, leaving such business as was done in the hands of the archbishop of York, Moleyns, and the state ministers; Suffolk himself ignored the Council and acted as sole counsellor with the king and queen. Such, setting aside the childish accusations of the commons—that he "had sold the realm of England to the King's adversaries of France" and was fortifying the castle of Wallingford to receive a French invasion [2]—was the main gravamen against him in 1450. He had monopolized the confidence of the king and used it to carry through an extremely

---

[1] J. F. Baldwin, *The King's Council*, pp. 191 *et seq.*
[2] *Rotuli Parliamentorum*, v. 176 *et seq.*

hazardous foreign policy which was ending in a resounding disaster. If the accepted opinion of conciliar history between 1445 and 1450 be the right one, Suffolk is deeply responsible for the collapse of the Lancastrian régime, for it depended upon the unity of the Council, and to a less degree on the support of parliament, and here again the holding of parliament in his own countryside at Bury to put Gloucester at his mercy is a breach with the more decent conventions of the past thirty years. The ruthlessness of the commons' attack in 1450 may have been in some measure a revenge for his intimidation of the parliament of 1447.

The impeachment of Suffolk in March 1450 may be taken as a *Fall of* necessary political move if the crown were to be saved, though it *Suffolk* included grotesque charges, and was prompted to a large degree by the mistaken hope that the French possessions might yet be saved. Had the sentence of temporary exile not been darkened by his murder it would have been accepted as a wise and not unduly severe measure to remove a too powerful counsellor. But the events which followed the minister's fall showed that Henry and his remaining councillors could not govern England. Somerset was in France, York in Ireland, Suffolk and Moleyns dead, the latter murdered in January in a riot in the camp at Portsmouth, and in the interval before the need of reconstituting the Council was realised the great revolt of Cade broke out in May 1450. Its political programme was not without wisdom, since *York and* it attacked the exclusion of the great lords from the Council and *Somerset* demanded the return of the duke of York, but it did his cause no good, for it confirmed the court in its belief that he intended treason. Henry, moreover, had been persuaded that the murderers of Moleyns were acting in York's interest. Accordingly, though the leaders of the two parties—Somerset the heir to the connection of the cardinal and Suffolk and to their favour with the court, and York the exponent of a restored conciliar régime—returned to England, they came laden with the hatreds and suspicions bred of recent happenings. Both York and Henry saw the essential need to be "sad and substantial Council",[1] but York was at first denied landing by the king's officers and had to force his way into the king's presence. Angered at this reception, he coupled his demand for a Council and a parliament with one for justice upon those

[1] *Paston Letters* (ed. Gairdner), xcvii.

reputed to be traitors, and the parliament of January 1451—
strongly Yorkist in favour—accordingly petitioned for Somerset's
removal from court. From parliament, also, came the first fatal
reference to the question of the succession. A number of the
commons petitioned for the recognition of York as heir to the
throne in the event, which now seemed likely, of Henry dying
without issue.

The circumstances of this petition show that the Lancastrian
crown—as distinct from the persons and factions who claimed to
be its principal supporters—still had a substantial party behind it.
As the lords of parliament had refused to try Suffolk for treason,
so now they rejected York's claim to recognition as heir, and on
this cleavage between lords and commons the long session of
parliament was dismissed. It is clear that the majority of the
magnates were still independent of party, and that Henry's influence was not exhausted.[1] The year 1451 ended in a dead-lock,
Somerset retaining his place at court, and York remaining in the
country, and for the time being holding his hand. It may be
guessed that at this stage a decisive victory by either party would
have produced a sufficiently compliant parliament and a general
response from the nobility, but the long tension between York
and Somerset, which lasted throughout the rest of the year 1451
and was made the more dangerous by the fall of Bordeaux and
Bayonne in the summer, discredited the cause of compromise.
York's In February 1452 York made his initial act of avowed war,
first rising raised the West Country, and, with the earl of Devon and Lord
Cobham, marched on London. Again the magnates remained
neutral, the rebels were obliged to accept a formal promise of
redress by way of common law—they did not think it worth while
to pursue it—Somerset remained, and York disbanded his forces.
This was the position when, in September 1453, the king first
showed signs of derangement, and by the time of the October
parliament he was clearly incapable of rule. The situation had been
made more difficult by the birth of Prince Edward, but, faced
with a choice between a regency of the queen or the duke of York,
the nobles began to rally to the latter, and he was able to come to

[1] Even as late as February 1458 there was a neutral party of bishops—one of
their rare acts of self-assertion in this age—and nobles, who persuaded the
parties to a brief peace. *English Chronicle* (Camden Society), p. 77.

the parliament of February 1454 supported by the earls of Warwick, Richmond, and Pembroke.[1] It was a parliament in arms;
even Cardinal Kemp armed his retainers for his protection, the
duke of Buckingham had badges for two thousand men preparing,
and the duke of Somerset "had spies in every lord's house, some *Protec-*
as friars, some as shipmen taken on the sea, and some in other *torate*
wise";[2] but it produced a tolerable settlement. Many of the *York*
Council favoured York,[3] the lords chose him as Protector, offices
and benefices were shared fairly evenly between the two parties,
Somerset was put in ward but no motion was made to try him.

At this point, when the country became committed to a civil
war which could only end in the extinction of one or other of
the two parties, it may be well to take stock of those three Lancastrian reigns which have been given the credit of being an
experiment in constitutional rule, and to see how far their own
utterances or the estimate of contemporaries establish their claim
to a distinctive political theory. How far was the constitutional
position of the crown altered by them, and a new and more liberal
view of the constitution evolved? Difference of practice there
certainly was, for the continual Council is a new feature in the *Theory of*
constitution, but it arose less from a new theory than from the *the crown*
necessity created by Henry IV's illness, Henry V's absences abroad,
and Henry VI's long minority and subsequent ineffectiveness. It is
true that the Lancastrian Justice Sir John Fortescue thought of
England as *dominium politicum et regale* as opposed to the autocratic
dominium regale of France, but he wrote his "Governance of England" at the height of Edward IV's power—in 1473—and he did
not claim that his "mixed polity" was a Lancastrian innovation.
Indeed he thought it was the original form of the English state,
the work of Brutus, its first known king.[4] Nor did any parliamentary right of Lancaster figure largely in controversy in the
revolutions which founded the dynasty or brought it to its end.
In so far as the house of Lancaster was committed to a constitutional theory of the crown, it might be expected to be embodied

---

[1] *Paston Letters* (ed. Gairdner), no. 195.   [2] *Loc. cit.*
[3] Stubbs, *Constitutional History*, iii. 171.
[4] *The Government of England* (ed. C. Plummer), p. 112.

in the indictment of Richard II's reign presented by the parliament
which deposed him. This indictment [1] consisted of thirty-three
articles—*objectus contra Regem*—and seems to have aimed at stating
every grievance against the late king from his claim to pronounce
law by his own mouth to his taking the crown jewels out of
England. But it is devoid of logical plan, hardly rises to general-
ities, and presents no doctrine of constitutional monarchy which
Richard might be supposed to have violated and from which he
As ex- was to be deposed. The objections are, indeed, typical of that ill-
pressed in directed age, in which the catholic-feudal treatises of the scholastics
the deposi- are out of favour and no fresh review of monarchy has yet been
tion of
Richard II made, and they reflect the confused, though still highly practical,
mentality of their makers. To this extent they are of value as
showing the minds of those peers, knights, burgesses, and justices
who had been driven through the reign of Richard, hectored by
both parties in turn, till one order of the realm after another
confessed that "they feared for their lives to speak honestly". If
we look for theory in them, they show a clinging to the familiar
safeguards, rather than any hope for a new régime. The centre of
the case for Richard's unfitness is the time-worn doctrine of the
king's trust for the law and of its sacrosanctity. Sitting in Council
to hear the pleas of subjects and instructed by his justices as to the
law appropriate to each, he had used to answer "austerely and
with anger" that "the law was in the king's mouth, and often in
his breast"—"that he could make and change the laws of his
kingdom"—and thus many subjects were deterred from seeking
their legal remedy. He had so brow-beat his justices in Council
that they did not dare speak the truth. Specifically in the Shrewsbury parliament, he had forced them to rule according to his
own view of the case against Gloucester and Arundel. He had said
that the lives and goods of his subjects were at his mercy—thus
intending to "enervate" the primary civil rights—had had men
appealed for *lèse majesté* in the military court of the marshal and
constable and forced to defend themselves by the duel, and had
banished Bolingbroke and archbishop Arundel without trial. He
had stayed process in the courts Christian by letters under his signet
when the chancellor had refused to issue them under the Great
Seal. All this is unquestionably sound defence of the proper

[1] *Rotuli Parliamentorum*, iii. 417.

standing of the king in relation to common law right, and had been written constitutional law since the Great Charter. It is the weightiest part of the indictment. With this traditional matter go certain complaints which reflect the special status which had come to attach to statute law, and this is the most modern element in the articles. Whereas statutes are binding till revoked by statute, Richard induced the commons to petition him to "be as free as any of his progenitors", and on this excuse did many things which were against statutes, ignoring those which prescribed the election of sheriffs and their vacation of office after a year. He had procured the Shrewsbury parliament to commit its authority to certain of its members for the hearing of unanswered petitions only, but upon this pretence had proceeded to certain matters touching the whole parliament. At any time within the past two hundred years similar offences would have called forth, and in many instances had called forth, similar complaints, and the whole of this defence of the law falls within the accepted limits of medieval kingship without new remedy, and, except for the prominence given to statute—itself not new—without any extended views of a constitutional crown.

The same medievalism of outlook is betrayed in the handling of Richard's great political offences by which the Appellants and Bolingbroke and Norfolk had suffered. Even the cancelling of the commission or Council of 1386, which involved the setting aside of parliament's favourite constitutional expedient of a continual Council, was condemned not on constitutional grounds, but on that of unjust proceedings against its individual members and of royal coercion of the justices. Apart from those legal irregularities which we have already mentioned, the king's dealings with Gloucester, Bolingbroke, and the archbishop were handled not so as to bring out any proof of violation of constitutional practice, but to fasten upon him those sins of cruelty, duplicity, and, above all, of perjury, which canonically unfitted a man from legitimate wearing of the crown. In article after article the climax is reached with *et ideo est perjurus*, and the conclusion sums up for deposition upon grounds of moral guilt *attentis perjuribus multiplicibus ac crudelitate aliisque quampluribus criminibus dicti Ricardi*. The sum of all this should make us slow to believe that those who made the revolution of 1399 had any wide constitutional scheme to put forward, still less one that was new. What was out of the accustomed order in the past reign had been upon the side of Richard, who from time to time used words which might have come from a Renaissance prince. Parliament asserted the accustomed rule and little more. Yet such was the change in the times that things were said and done in 1399 that did not suggest themselves in 1327. There was a fuller recognition of parliament and statute, and a complaint against the packing of the commons. The vacating of the throne involved a process which had not been attempted in 1327, judgment upon the king by parliament in the person of a commission of its members, and a formal act of deposition. Richard's own confession of insufficiency for his office was indeed taken into account, but it was not like that of Edward II an abdication, and the commission deposed him "by definitive sentence", and only after this had been pronounced did the members of the estates, interrogated one by one, appoint proctors to renounce their homage. In 1327 the diffidation, though it had followed upon the king's renunciation, had itself been the effective act which broke the reign.

The Lancastrian right

If the deposition had been carried through without the formularization of a constitutional creed, the Lancastrian accession was made with none also. Henry advanced to the throne in parliament and made his claim by virtue of the right blood of Henry III, and as such was accepted, the right of Clarence's heir being neither put forward nor denied and parliament making no other motion than that of the customary acceptance and swearing of allegiance. On his death-bed Henry IV is said to have repented this act of assumption, "only God knows by what right I took the crown".

It is true that in 1404 [1] the estates made an "affirmation" of their loyalty to Henry's reign and reaffirmed their oaths to him and to the succession of the prince, and that this was accepted as a statute, but their intention was clearly to put their own allegiance beyond doubt and to declare the order of the succession rather than to assert the parliamentary basis of Henry's right. It is also true that in Henry IV's first parliament the archbishop announced that the king intended to be "counselled and governed by the honourable, wise, and discreet persons of his Realm",[2] but this is a voluntary statement of policy, though one which, as we have seen, Henry and his successors conformed to in the main. There is no

[1] *Rotuli Parliamentorum*, iii. 525.   [2] *Ibid.* iii. 415.

act or occasion which can be pointed to as explicitly giving to the Lancastrian dynasty a statutory right or as binding them to any specific form of government. In 1460 the defence of the Lancastrian crown was, of course, a forlorn hope, no doubt half-heartedly undertaken. The appeal to Henry himself to "search the chronicles"[1] for a justification of his own case shows that the lords had little hope that much could be got from the rolls of parliament, and the justices, in claiming that the matter of the crown was above all cognisance but that of the "Princes of the King's blood", indirectly admitted the same.[2] There was some tendency upon the part of the lords to assert that a statutory right had been built up in the course of the Lancastrian reigns by "the great and notable Acts of Parliaments . . . of much more authority than any chronicle",[2] but this was not pressed against York's retort that such statutes were neither many nor great but no more than the one statute of 1404 regularising the succession as between Henry IV's sons, and that this would not have been needed had his descent been good. The statute could, indeed, hardly bear the interpretation which it was sought to put upon it, and against the patently superior lineage of the dukes of York the descendants of John of Gaunt, once they were challenged, had nothing better to urge than that their rivals had borne the arms of Edmund of Langley and not of Lionel of Clarence. In 1460 the throne was saved to Henry for his life, not by any constitutional principles admitted, or even asserted, but by the newness of the oaths sworn to him by the nobles at Coventry, and perhaps by some lingering conscience that the oaths of homage ought not to be broken without diffidation, and diffidation not made with more cause of offence than the unfortunate Henry VI had it in his power to give. Thus neither in 1399 nor in 1459 when the Lancastrians had most need to make the dynastic right good, nor in 1460 when Edmund of York assumed the throne by hereditary right almost unopposed, did either party—if we except a faint-hearted offer to plead a statutory claim for Lancaster—formulate a distinctive political theory of its crown.[3] The Yorkists came nearest to doing so when, the way for

---

[1] *Rotuli Parliamentorum*, v. 376.   [2] *Loc. cit.*
[3] A Lancastrian tract of Edward IV's reign put forward the Salic Law as a bar to his claim through Clarence. J. Fortescue, *Government of England* (ed. C. Plummer), p. 354.

The
Yorkist
crown

Richard III's accession having been cleared by the denunciation of
Edward IV's marriage as invalid, Richard's claim was rehearsed
in parliament.[1] His title, it was then said, was perfect by the laws
of God, of Nature, and of the realm; but in view of the ignorance
of the people, and because of their willingness to put "faith and
certainty" in what was rehearsed by the three estates in parliament,
it was now declared by statute. It may be suspected that Henry
IV's statute of 1404 on the succession was scarcely intended to do
more than this.

Edward IV, therefore, took the throne with no new theory of
kingly right, but with the same right as that of Henry, though by
a better lineage. Nor did he announce any new theory of kingship.
The tradition of his house, in so far as his father had had an opportunity to display it, had been the normal, constitutional government of the day, a council of notables, a right course of common
law, the king to live of his own. It was the policy of Suffolk's
opponents continued against the personal rule of the queen. That
Edward IV did not follow it, and, indeed, allowed both parliament and Council to take a far less prominent part than they had
done in the early years of Henry VI, is due less to any settled theory
of government than to the general failure of confidence in these
institutions which had overcome the nation. The change is, however, a marked one, and becomes even more so as the reign goes

Decline
of the
Continual
Council

on. The form of the Council changes entirely, reverting back to
those large bodies of officials whose joint responsibility was very
slightly emphasized, and whose members the king took counsel
with or neglected according to his conscience and to the business
in hand. No continual Council was appointed in 1461, nor at any
subsequent date. The Yorkist lords were careless in attendance—
Warwick especially—and even the king made no rule of presiding,
and the mass of the council were of the secondary rank of the
court, knights of the Household, justices, serjeants, and attorneys
predominating, the legal members being so numerous that it has
been questioned whether the term King's Counsel had not already
acquired its modern, restrictive, legal meaning. In spite of this
influx of lawyers, Council was far less active in justice than it had
been in the past, and in the first seven years of the reign its judicial
function was almost in abeyance, with the result that it largely lost

[1] Stubbs, *Constitutional History*, iii. 235.

its preëminence as the principal authority for redress of grievance. Not only did the chancellor's jurisdiction thrive rapidly upon this change of practice in petition, but petitions to the king in person became common, and Edward, whose intention of strong government was apparently genuine, took the initiative in many cases when the peace was broken, and summoned the culprits to appear before himself or the Council. The drift of events, accentuated after the alienation of the Nevills by the great reduction in the number of the peers who were willing to serve in Council, was thus in the direction of personal government in the literal sense of the term. More frequently than any of his predecessors, it was Edward himself who was responsible for acts of government, and the eclipse of the Council is reflected in the fact that warrants commanding action *per consilium* fell in his reign to something like a twentieth of their accustomed proportion to the whole.

The decline of parliament was hardly less marked. Not only were there many years in which no parliament met, but Edward, having tested and approved the temper of any one assembly, tended to retain it in being by prorogation over a series of years. Thus, the parliament of April 1463 sat until 1465, and that of 1472, the first after Edward's restoration, was not dismissed until the spring of 1475. Between January 1478 and January 1483 no parliament was summoned. In this it does not seem that the king was going counter to any strong popular demand, for parliaments did little when summoned, and the stream of commons' petition had run almost dry. To all appearances this tendency was, as has already been said, less a characteristic feature of Yorkist rule than the accentuation of a decline of parliament which had already set in in the later years of Henry VI. From about 1450 the initiative of the commons had become less frequent, fewer commons' petitions were presented, they dealt with less important matters, and the crown was far less ready to accept them;[1] indeed, in the first four years of Edward IV's reign there was even a slight revival of commons' activity and of the king's complaisance towards it. But from 1465 to 1483 only twenty-six such bills were approved in four parliaments, and of these the majority were of little general importance and dealt with the redress of local grievances or gave remedy to groups or individuals at the instance of the commons.

Decline of parliament

[1] H. L. Gray, *Commons' Influence on Early Legislation*, pp. 98 and 118 *et seq.*

In the last parliament of Edward's reign only four commons' petitions became statutes, and they dealt with minor matters of sumptuary law and trading practice.

Parliament as the king's servant   The crown did not cease to use parliament. Rather, it drew the lesson of recent years as to its value as an obedient servant of any power which happened to be predominant, called it when convenient, and, keeping it in being over two and three years together, used the publicity and special authority of statute to give effect to its own enactments. The official bill, prompted by the crown, introduced in the lords, but passing through the form of commons' assent, which was a not infrequent device of the last decade of Henry VI's reign, became common in that of Edward IV, and in Richard III's one parliament took in importance the first place in legislation. Richard III's estimate of the value of parliamentary enactment may perhaps be taken to be that of the Yorkist crown at large: its value for the monarch is declaratory as giving "faith and certainty" to the matter enacted.

The same willingness to accord to parliament a part in the task of government, together with much initiative in which the rôle of parliament is not considered, characterizes the haphazard but not unsuccessful conduct of Edward IV's finance. In part Edward relied upon the normal course of parliamentary grant. He took no tax until 1463, but received a Tenth and Fifteenth in that year, tonnage and poundage for life in 1465, two Tenths and Fifteenths in 1468 on the promise of an expedition to France, and single Tenths and Fifteenths in 1473, 1474, 1475, and 1483. But by 1473 he was coercing individual subjects in numbers into "voluntary" gifts of money—benevolences—and this device, together with sharp fines imposed for breaches of the peace, either in his own reign or in that of Henry, together with the use of the crown's shipping upon private trading ventures of the king, made him to an increasing degree self-supporting, and enabled him to go for periods of years without the help of subsidy. There was little tendency to systematize these occasional, though large, sources of revenue into a prerogative taxation like that of France, nor, perhaps, was the revenue vastly augmented in Edward's reign, but the financial policy of the reign is another proof of the comparative independence of the crown and of a new power to ignore the criticism of parliament and the country. It is the lack of apparent system in Edward IV's rule—Richard III's was too brief to have revealed its real trend, but it began with a denunciation of Edward's despotism—which makes it difficult to speak of a new monarchy, or to regard its effects as lasting. Edward acts with great spontaneity and far more effect than Henry, but it is the self-assertion of a powerful individual who governs empirically and does not care to build up institutions for the future. The usurpation of Richard is itself a proof of this, for it was made in the face of what was at best indifference on the part of the people, and a strong Council might well have made it impossible. It was the dwindling of all those forces which habitually surrounded the throne which, as in the earlier tragedy of Margaret and Henry, left the royal family alone to work out their own fate undefended and unimpeded.

Thus time, as it discredited one remedy after another, bringing *Con-* with it no new inspiration, confirmed the nation in its belief that *clusion* salvation must come from the crown, and bred even a sort of indifference. At the end of the fifteenth century the demand was still for "plentiful governance", a king who "gave good lordship", a strong Council. But the ancient means to these ends were almost discredited. It is not a mere seeking to introduce a pattern into history which sees in these last reigns of the fifteenth century the end of the Middle Ages, for the institutions which the medieval community had built, and in which it had flourished, had reached what was probably their fullest expression at a time when the society they had grown up to serve was losing its old beliefs and its original integrity. If there is a single predominant theme in the institutions of the first thousand years of English history it is the supremacy of law and the function of the community to declare, and, if necessary, change it. Given a community of lawful men, these fundamentals were secured century after century, according to the method of each generation, by popular assembly, or by councils really or fictitiously representative of that part of the nation which was politically recognized. Whether, as in the full age of feudalism, through the *commune consilium*, or, as later, by continual council and parliament, this idea did not fail, nor was its realisation entirely frustrated, until the mass of individuals began to lose their vision of the community and to grasp at immediate material interest, until wealth and private power ceased to stand in any organized relation to the state. When this had come to pass medieval constitutionalism in county and parliament could no longer be maintained. Parliaments became rarer than in the past, and more perfunctory when they met. Fortescue, the only articulate theorist in a declining age, no longer believed in the continual Council of the nobles, but looked forward to some such strong, royalist Council as the Tudors made. The problem of order had, indeed, outrun the resources of the medieval state, and the expedients of government in 1485 were as yet medieval. However much our knowledge of the uses to which it was to be put in later days may blind us to the fact, its presumptions were still feudal. Even after two hundred years of parliament, the view—no longer true to facts, but still determining action—was held that the ultimate governing right lay between the king and some body of magnates standing in the place and inheriting the virtue of the *commune consilium regni*. In the final recourse the constituent core of parliament even in the fifteenth century was the king sitting in the Great Council of the peers. It was to these that the royal power lapsed in minority, and, though the commons had secured a more or less firm acceptance of the necessity of their assent to statute, their habits, traditions, and outlook were still those of petitioners. They had no real defence against the packing of their house, they did not react against dictation with any confidence, and they reflected slavishly the political colour of the moment. According as opportunity presented itself, they were either petitioners or critics, never equal and confident participators in the task of government with the king and the lords; they never mastered its difficulties or associated themselves with the crown in its responsibilities. Therefore they wanted the executive power to be strong and successful, and at the same time cheap to the point of carrying on war in France and maintaining peace in England upon those revenues which were derived from the royal demesne and barely sufficed for the upkeep of the king's household. Fortescue is the first writer to recognize clearly that, beyond the ordinary revenue for his person, he needed an extraordinary revenue of state. Not until the restricted medieval view of kingship was enlarged, and the belief in the limitation of the subjects' obligation—derived from the fixed custom of the feudal tenant—was relaxed in a sense of common interest and identity of purpose with the crown, could parliament be more than a place of redress of grievance. No medieval king or parliament could rise to the full implication of an impersonal crown responding to and putting into action the will of parliament, nor, for its part, could parliament accept frankly the directing power of the crown, as it was to do more fully in Tudor times. It was an age when that system of checks and balances, which was to be read into the English constitution of the eighteenth century, was still a reality. Such a system was, indeed, the natural expression of the feudal relation, but in the lawless, faithless, and over-wealthy society of the later Middle Ages it made steadily for the paralysis of all government. In that contraction of the force of all legitimate institutions, and in the freeing of lawless power from its ancient legal restraints, the long history of feudal England was drawing to its close.

BIBLIOGRAPHICAL NOTE

THE following list of books, though not exhaustive, will be found useful in following up the various topics dealt with in this volume.

In spite of the amount of research which has been carried out since the last edition of Bishop Stubbs's *Constitutional History of England*, it still remains incomparably the best study of English medieval history, and there is little probability of its being replaced. In one field only has a wholesale addition been made to the corpus of constitutional history, the investigation by Professor T. F. Tout of all that side of government which was carried on through the domestic offices which is contained in his *Chapters in Administrative History*. With these two general works it is, however, necessary to read such studies of constitutional law and economic history as may be found in F. Pollock and F. W. Maitland's *History of English Law before Edward I*, Professor W. S. Holdsworth's *History of English Law*, and E. Lipson's *An Introduction to the Economic History of England*. Other general works of constitutional history which may be read with profit are R. Gneist's *Englische Verfassungsgeschichte* (translated by P. A. Ashworth), F. W. Maitland's *Constitutional History of England*, and that of Professor G. B. Adams. C. Petit-Dutaillis' *Studies Supplementary to Stubbs's Constitutional History* discusses a number of the more debatable passages in Bishop Stubbs's work in the light of more recent knowledge.

(i) The nature of Teutonic society in general may best be studied in the works of the German scholars of the last century. Of these the most comprehensive is G. Waitz's *Deutsche Verfassungsgeschichte*, while the structure of the kindred may be studied in K. von Amira's *Erbenfolge und Verwandschaftsgliederung nach den altniederdeutschen Rechten* and H. Brunner's *Sippe und Wergeld*. The particular form of such institutions among the Anglo-Saxons is best shown in H. M. Chadwick's *Studies in Anglo-Saxon Institutions*, K. Maurer's *Angelsächsische Rechtsverhältnisse*, *Essays in Anglo-Saxon Law* (Boston, 1876), and F. Seebohm's *Tribal Custom in Anglo-Saxon Law*.

The economic structure of Saxon England may best be studied in K. Rhamm's *Die Grosshufen der Nordgermanen*, P. Hatschek's *Angelsächsische Verfassungsgeschichte*, Professor P. Vinogradoff's *The Growth of the Manor*, F. W. Maitland's *The Domesday Book and Beyond*, F. Seebohm's *The English Village Community*, and *Customary Acres and their Historical Significance*.

A work of a special general scope, but still bearing upon constitutional history, is H. M. Chadwick's *Origins of the English Nation*.

(ii) The following works bear upon one or other aspect of constitutional or social history in the later centuries of the Saxon era. J. C. H. R. Steenstrup's *Normannerne*, Professor P. Vinogradoff's *English Society in the Eleventh Century*, L. M. Larson's *The King's Household before the Norman Conquest*, H. M. Cam's *Local Government in Francia and England*, W. A. Morris's *The Frankpledge System*, P. Guilhiermoz's *Essai sur l'origine de la noblesse en France au moyen âge*. J. M. Kemble's *The Saxons in England* is still of value. The notes of the Rev. C. Plummer to his *Historia Ecclesiastica* of Bede and to the *Two Saxon Chronicles Parallel*, which he edited together with J. Earle, contain a very great deal of learning, and R. H. Hodgkin's *A History of the Anglo-Saxons*, now re-issued, bring together the results of the studies of the last thirty years and are invaluable surveys of every aspect of Anglo-Saxon life. Professor J. Goebel's *Felony and Misdemeanour* is important for its examination of the growth of Frankish law in relation to that of England and of the development of the Frankish and Norman franchise.

(iii) For the Norman and Angevin reigns the first essential is an understanding of feudal custom, and for this the best general survey is that of Professor F. M. Stenton in *English Feudalism*. Sir Henry Spelman's *Of Feuds and Tenures by Knight Service* is still valuable, as are T. Madox's *Baronia Anglica* and W. Dugdale's *The Baronage of England*. The custom of the Norman Duchy is best studied in C. H. Haskins's *Norman Institutions*, and various incidents of feudal tenure and administration are examined and illustrated in the works of J. H. Round, *Geoffrey de Mandeville*, *Feudal England*, and *The Commune of London*, in Sir Maurice Powicke's *Loss of Normandy*, J. F. Baldwin's *The Scutage and Knight Service of England*, H. Denholm Young's *Seignorial Administration in England*, and Miss H. M. Chew's *English Ecclesiastical Tenants in Chief*. For the history of law, besides the works already cited, there should be read M. M. Bigelow's *History of Procedure in England*, H. Brunner's *Die Entstehung der Schwurgerichte*, E. Jenks's *Law and Politics in the Middle Ages*, J. B. Thayer's *A Preliminary Treatise on the Common Law*, J. W. Jeudwine's *Tort, Crime, and Police in Medieval England*, F. W. Maitland's *Equity*, and *Roman Canon Law in the Church of England*, and Professor P. Vinogradoff's *Roman Law in Medieval Europe*. Legal administration is described in W. A. Morris's *The Frankpledge System*, W. C. Bolland's *The General Eyre*, and in *Self-Government at the King's Command*, by A. B. White. Miss H. M. Cam has made the medieval hundred her special study, and her *Studies in the Hundred Rolls* and *The Hundred and the Hundred Rolls* should be read. The higher branches of the administration are best described in S. B. Chrimes's *Introduction to the Administrative History of Medieval England*, in *The Medieval English Sheriff to 1300* by W. A. Morris, W. Parow's *Compotus Vicecomitis*, and C. A. Beard's *The Office of the Justice of the Peace in England in its Origin and Development*. Much has been written about the boroughs, studies of particular aspects of which may be found in T. Madox's *Firma Burgi*, C. Gross's *The Gild Merchant*, M. Bateson's *Borough Customs*, M. de W. Hemmeon's *Burgess Tenure in Mediaeval England*, F. W. Maitland's *Township and Borough*, A. Ballard's *The Domesday Boroughs*. Professor J. Tait has brought together the existing materials into a volume, *The Medieval English Borough*, which is the only authoritative work upon the subject as a whole.

Of the central government of the Norman and Angevin reigns, the Exchequer has been the subject of studies by T. Madox, *The History and Antiquities of the Exchequer of England*, R. L. Poole, *The Exchequer in the Twelfth Century*, H. Hall, *Antiquities and Curiosities of the Exchequer* and *An Introduction to the Pipe Rolls*, and *Dialogus de Scaccario*, edited by Charles Johnson, and receives constant illustration from the essays of J. H. Round. For the court and household, besides Professor Tout's first volume, there should be read Professor G. B. Adams' *Council and Courts in Anglo-Norman England*, R. W. Eyton's *Court, Household, and Itinerary of Henry II,* together with J. E. A. Jolliffe's *Angevin Kingship*. The working of government in practice is also shown in Bishop Stubb's collected *Historical Introduction to the Rolls Series*.

Professor E. A. Freeman's *History of the Norman Conquest* and *History of the Reign of William Rufus* can still be read with profit if taken with some caution. C. Petit-Dutaillis has recently published a comparison of the growth of the English and French monarchies during the period, *La Monarchie féodale en France et en Angleterre, x^e-xiiie siècle*.

(iv) The constitutional activity of the thirteenth century naturally takes its rise from the Charter. For this there should be read W. S. M'Kechnie's *Magna Carta*, *Magna Carta Commemoration Essays*, ed. H. E. Maldon, Professor F. M. Powicke's *Stephen Langton*, the introductory matter in C. Bémont's *Chartes de libertés anglaises 1100–1305*, and *The First Century of Magna Carta*, by F. Thompson. The later phases of the conflict are covered by C. Bémont's *Simon de Montfort* (ed. E. F. Jacob), by Professor E. F. Jacob's *Studies in the Period of Baronial Reform and Rebellion (1258–1267)*, Professor R. F. Treharne's The *Baronial Plan of Reform (1258–1263)*, and G. W. Prothero's *The Life of Simon de Montfort*. S. K. Mitchell's *Studies in Taxation under John and Henry III* should also be used, and the history of the revenue may be followed in J. H. Ramsey's *Revenues of the Kings of England*, S. Dowell's *A History of Taxation and Taxes in England*, and H. Hall's *History of the Customs Revenues in England*. Social relations which have their reaction upon political life are dealt with in Professor P. Vinogradoff's *Villainage in England* and *Custom and Right*, H. L. Gray's *English Field Systems*, and F. Mugnier's *Les Savoyards en Angleterre au xiiie siècle*. The political thought of the age is best studied in R. L. Poole's *Illustrations of the History of Medieval Thought and Learning*, C. H. M'Ilwain's *The Growth of Political Thought in the West*, A. J. Carlyle's *A History of Medieval*

Political Thought in the West, and O. Gierke's *Political Theories of the Middle Ages,* translated by F. W. Maitland.

(v) Perhaps the best treatments of the latest phase of constitutional theory and growth is to be found in S. B. Chrimes's *English Constitutional Ideas in the XVth Century.* Various aspects of the origin and development of Parliament are to be studied in the introduction to F. W. Maitland's *Memoranda de Parliamento,* in Professor C. H. M'Ilwain's *High Court of Parliament,* Professor A. F. Pollard's *Evolution of Parliament,* in the Report of the House of Lords' Committee *On the Dignity of a Peer,* L. W. Vernon Harcourt's *His Grace the Steward* and *Trial by Peers,* D. Pasquet's *The Origin of the House of Commons* (translated by R. G. D. Laffan), in H. L. Gray's *Commons Influence on Early Legislation,* L. O. Pike's *A Constitutional History of the House of Lords,* M. V. Clarke's *Medieval Representation and Consent,* M. M'Kisack's *The Parliamentary Representation of the English Boroughs during the Middle Ages,* and in essays by Mr Richardson and Professor Sayles in the *English Historical Review* (vols. xlvi., xlvii.), the *Transactions of the Royal Historical Society,* 4th Series, vol. xi., and the *Bulletin of the Institute of Historical Research,* vols. v., vi., and xi. For the development of legislation T. F. T. Plucknett's *Statutes and their Interpretation in the First Half of the Fourteenth Century* should be read, and for taxation J. F. Willard's *Parliamentary Taxes on Personal Property, 1290–1334.* For the history of the Privy Council the principal authority is J. F. Baldwin's *The King's Council,* and there is a short study of the medieval council in A. V. Dicey's *Privy Council.* The Chancery is dealt with by E. H. Goodwin in *The Equity of the King's Court before the Reign of Edward I* and D. M. Kerly's *An Historical Sketch of the Court of Chancery.* J. E. Morris' *The Welsh Wars of Edward I* is of great value for its account of the decline of feudal obligations in the host. Studies of constitutional movements in individual reigns are Professor T. F. Tout's *The Place of Edward II in English History,* H. Wallon's *Richard II,* and J. H. Wylie's *The History of England under Henry IV.*

A full bibliography of English history, including periodical sources, will be found in C. Gross's *Sources and Literature of English History to 1485.* This was re-edited and revised in 1915, and for the years 1915–1929 the *Short Bibliography of English Constitutional History,* by H. M. Cam and A. S. Turberville, will be found of value. To the dates of their publication the bibliographies of the Cambridge Medieval History, arranged according to the several subjects of its chapters, are full, reliable, and extremely convenient for reference. An article, "Some Recent Advances in English Constitutional History (before 1485)", by Gaillard Lapsley in the *Cambridge Historical Journal,* vol. v., no. 2, discusses recent historical production under the heads of Parliament, Law, and Constitutional Theory.

INDEX